# THE VANCOUVER ISLAND TREATIES AND THE EVOLVING PRINCIPLES OF INDIGENOUS TITLE

*The Vancouver Island Treaties and the Evolving Principles of Indigenous Title* illuminates the history of the enigmatic Vancouver Island treaties of the 1850s, offering new interpretations based on a fresh, exhaustive, and multidisciplinary critical analysis of relevant evidence.

To understand as fully as possible the motivations, intentions, and understandings of the Indigenous and non-Indigenous signatories to the treaties, Ted Binnema places the treaties within the context of thousands of years of Vancouver Island history and hundreds of years of land-purchase agreements involving Indigenous peoples. The book explores the evolving concepts and principles of Indigenous title from the first Dutch and English treaties with Indigenous North Americans in the 1620s to the increasingly detailed articulations fuelled by debates and crises in Australia and New Zealand in the 1830s and 1840s.

Binnema explains that Indigenous people themselves played important roles in the formation and elaboration of the principles of Indigenous title in the British World. Drawing on previously neglected archival documents and multidisciplinary evidence in linguistics, archaeology, anthropology, fisheries biology and biological sciences, and oral historiography, the book provides a new model for the study of the idea of Indigenous title and Indigenous land-purchase treaties worldwide.

TED BINNEMA is an emeritus professor of history at the University of Northern British Columbia.

# The Vancouver Island Treaties and the Evolving Principles of Indigenous Title

TED BINNEMA

UNIVERSITY OF TORONTO PRESS
Toronto Buffalo London

© University of Toronto Press 2025
Toronto Buffalo London
utorontopress.com

ISBN 978-1-4875-5407-1 (cloth)     ISBN 978-1-4875-5411-8 (EPUB)
ISBN 978-1-4875-5409-5 (paper)     ISBN 978-1-4875-5410-1 (PDF)

Library and Archives Canada Cataloguing in Publication

Title: The Vancouver Island treaties and the evolving principles of Indigenous title / Ted Binnema.
Names: Binnema, Ted, 1963– author
Description: Includes bibliographical references and index.
Identifiers: Canadiana (print) 20240491092 | Canadiana (ebook) 20240490398 | ISBN 9781487554071 (cloth) | ISBN 9781487554095 (paper) | ISBN 9781487554118 (EPUB) | ISBN 9781487554101 (PDF)
Subjects: LCSH: Land titles – British Columbia – Vancouver Island – History – 19th century. | LCSH: Hudson's Bay Company – History – 19th century. | LCSH: Vancouver Island (B.C.) – History – 19th century. | CSH: First Nations – Land tenure – British Columbia – Vancouver Island – History – 19th century. | CSH: First Nations – British Columbia – Vancouver Island – Treaties – History – 19th century.
Classification: LCC E78.B9 B56 2025 | DDC 971.1/00497 – dc23

Cover design: John Beadle
Cover image: Paul Kane. *Fishing Lodges of the Clallams, Vancouver Island* (detail), c. 1851–1856. Oil on canvas, 45.7 × 74.3 cm. Transfer from the Parliament of Canada, 1955. National Gallery of Canada, Ottawa.

We wish to acknowledge the land on which the University of Toronto Press operates. This land is the traditional territory of the Wendat, the Anishnaabeg, the Haudenosaunee, the Métis, and the Mississaugas of the Credit First Nation.

This book has been published with the help of a grant from the Federation for the Humanities and Social Sciences, through the Awards to Scholarly Publications Program, using funds provided by the Social Sciences and Humanities Research Council of Canada.

University of Toronto Press acknowledges the financial support of the Government of Canada, the Canada Council for the Arts, and the Ontario Arts Council, an agency of the Government of Ontario, for its publishing activities.

 Canada Council for the Arts    Conseil des Arts du Canada

*For Helen*

# Contents

*Preface* ix

*Acknowledgments* xi

Introduction 3

1 The Hudson's Bay Company and Vancouver Island Land Policy to 1849  15

2 The Hudson's Bay Company and Indigenous Title, 1668–1849  29

3 The History of the Northwest Coast to 1774  50

4 Indigenous and Exogenous Peoples on Vancouver Island, 1774–1821  64

5 Indigenous Peoples of Vancouver Island and the Hudson's Bay Company, 1821–1849  83

6 Articulating Principles of Indigenous Title, 1835–1846  115

7 The Colonial Office, Local Authorities, and Indigenous Title, 1846–1849  138

8 Land Acquisition Policies in New Zealand and Vancouver Island, 1846–1850  154

9 The Treaty of Akaroa and Fort Victoria Treaties, 1848–1850  178

10 The Fort Rupert Treaties of 1850 and 1851  201

11 Governor James Douglas and the Saanich and Nanaimo Treaties, 1851–1854  218

12 Indigenous Title on Vancouver Island and British Columbia, 1854–1875  239

13 The Evolving Memories of the Vancouver Island Treaties to 1934    266

Conclusion    289

*Appendix A: "Original Indian Population Vancouver Island"*    297

*Appendix B: A 1934 Account of a Fort Victoria Treaty Attributed to David Latasse*    301

Notes    309

Bibliography    393

Index    431

*Illustrations follow page    180.*

# Preface

Historians should be humble. Their collective goal is akin to assembling a jigsaw puzzle without the picture, pieces scattered about, many of them missing. The puzzle can never be completed. I first got interested in the Vancouver Island treaties when I started lecturing on them in introductory Canadian history courses. Relying on secondary literature and general texts, I became confused by apparently contradictory basic "facts" about the treaties. Subsequently, I taught (poorly, I now realize) several courses that compared the Indigenous histories of Canada, the United States, Australia, and New Zealand. As I became more familiar with the history of treaties throughout North America and elsewhere, the scholarly literature on the Vancouver Island treaties became increasingly implausible. Either the picture that emerged from the fragmentary evidence was deeply flawed – in which case the treaties deserved another look – or the Vancouver Island treaties were profound outliers in the history of land-purchase treaties in the English-speaking world – in which case they definitely deserved a book-length treatment.

During years of research on other topics, particularly during my research for *Enlightened Zeal*, I became aware that historians of the Vancouver Island treaties had overlooked most of the rich documentary evidence related to the Vancouver Island treaties, and HBC-Indigenous relations in the region generally, at the Hudson's Bay Company Archives, in Winnipeg, Manitoba. I also found that even scholars who stated that the Vancouver Island treaties ought to be understood in the context of the history of the British Empire more generally, had contextualized them only superficially. No one had yet attempted to understand the Vancouver Island treaties in the context of the history of other HBC treaties. Finally, historians of the treaties had undertaken only cursory research into the long history of the Indigenous signatories to the Vancouver Island treaties. In short, although the puzzle will always be incomplete, scholars were attempting to discern a historical picture without gathering some of the most valuable pieces.

As the scholarship on land-purchase agreements elsewhere in the English-speaking world advanced over the last decade, it became increasingly clear that the scholarly literature on the Vancouver Island treaties appeared to suggest that the treaties were even more unusual than scholars believed, or that a history of the Vancouver Island treaties might contribute crucial pieces to a bigger puzzle – a history of the logic and patterns that explain treaty-making policy in the English-speaking world over the course of hundreds of years of land-purchase agreements in North America, Australia, and New Zealand. As it turns out, both of those possibilities are true. Unfortunately, we can be sure that some of the most important pieces of the puzzle are missing. We will never complete the puzzle. Moreover, a contextual global history such as this one is so complex that any contribution now will inevitably have lacunae and errors. So, the present study is not intended to be the last word. I hope that my contribution to the ongoing task of finding and fitting as many pieces as possible into this fascinating incomplete puzzle will inspire others to do likewise.

# Acknowledgments

It bears mentioning upfront that I bear responsibility for the contents of this book, particularly for the inevitable errors, gaps, and misinterpretations. However, the deficiencies are fewer than they would have been had it not been for the several people who generously agreed to read all or part of this study in its manuscript stage. First and foremost, I acknowledge my colleague Jacqueline Holler, who read the manuscript very thoroughly more than once and made many detailed suggestions for improvement, and Jon Swainger, who scrutinized the proofs. Others who read the entire manuscript and made suggestions included Tolly Bradford, Adrian Clark, Gerhard Ens, Brian Gobbett, Robin Fisher, Bob Irwin, and Ian MacLaren. I benefited much from the suggestions, critique, and encouragement I received from each of these people. I am fortunate to have friends and colleagues who do not hesitate to call out what they consider to be nonsense and misinterpretation. Bill Angelbeck and Alan McMillan were kind enough to provide detailed commentary of an earlier version of chapter 3, and their suggestions contributed significantly to the version of that chapter published here.

During my research, I was supported by the efficient staff in the UNBC library who responded to my many interlibrary loan requests with alacrity and good humour. The staff at the Hudson's Bay Company Archives, City of Victoria Archives, British Columbia Legislative Library, and Nanaimo Community Archives were also generous and accommodating. During the pandemic, archivists and librarians in New Zealand and Australia were kind enough to scan documents for me. This book reaches completion as I contemplate my impending retirement from the University of Northern British Columbia. I am indebted to UNBC for paying me for twenty-four years to pursue my passions in research and teaching in the part of the world in which I graduated from high school. I hope that UNBC and other research universities in relatively remote parts of the world are increasingly able in the coming years to serve the oft-neglected communities in which they are located. I particularly thank my colleagues in the History Department and in the faculty union at UNBC with whom I have worked over the years.

# THE VANCOUVER ISLAND TREATIES AND THE EVOLVING PRINCIPLES OF INDIGENOUS TITLE

# Introduction

Although the weather was "uncommonly fine" when the Hudson's Bay Company (HBC) SS *Beaver* steamed from Fort Rupert, Vancouver Island on Tuesday, 9 April 1850, George Blenkinsop (1822–1904) could be forgiven for feeling overwhelmed. Sure, his superiors regarded him as a promising clerk, but at a mere twenty-seven years old, Blenkinsop was too young and untested to oversee any HBC post, certainly too inexperienced to supervise the "Lunatic asylum of the Coast."[1] The Cornishman had joined the HBC less than ten years earlier and had been promoted to clerk only in 1846. Moreover, he had just returned to Fort Rupert on 21 March from sick leave.[2] Nevertheless, when Chief Trader William Henry McNeill (1801–1875) (Blenkinsop's father-in-law) departed aboard the *Beaver* on 9 April, the young Blenkinsop was left in charge of one of the most unsettled HBC posts.[3]

The HBC's Fort Rupert post journals report that only six days after Blenkinsop assumed oversight of Fort Rupert, the people at the post "were stopped by all the Chiefs from working in the Garden on the lower part of the Fort." For several days previous, Kwakiutl labourers and HBC servants had been planting peas, beans, and potatoes in the post's kitchen garden, but the chiefs "told us we should inclose no more of their lands as we had not paid them for it and that it blocked up their roads to the forest for wood &c."[4]

Blenkinsop did not need another crisis. Fort Rupert's buildings and defences were still incomplete. Only two days earlier, men at the fort had detected eight canoes of Bella Coola (Nuxalk) warriors watching the fort for an opportunity to avenge a deadly Kwakiutl raid of the previous September. Meanwhile, dissatisfied Scottish coal miners whom the HBC had brought to Fort Rupert the previous year were on the verge of striking – they would down their tools the next day. Over the previous weeks, conflicts between those miners and the neighbouring

## 4 The Vancouver Island Treaties

Kwakiutl villagers had also flared up. The crisis over the garden was comparatively easy to resolve. Blenkinsop dealt with it promptly: "Knowing it to be had in contemplation by the authorities that the land was to be purchased of them I thought it advisable to make each of them payment for the land necessary for garden purposes &c. They willingly sold me all right to the land in the neighbourhood of the Fort for a Blanket and shirt each. I made them all put their marks to an agreement drawn out to that effect so we may now consider ourselves the sole owners of the land."[5] Thus, it was in response to the demands of Kwakiutl chiefs on 15 April 1850 that George Blenkinsop negotiated the first of fifteen treaties concluded between agents of the HBC and Indigenous villagers on Vancouver Island.

The little-known Garden Treaty of 1850 underscores the fact that the history of the Vancouver Island treaties remains poorly understood, although they have been the subject of considerable research (and litigation) since the 1960s. In fact, so confused and contradictory is the scholarly literature on the treaties, that today's non-specialists will find it difficult to answer basic questions about the treaties. How does one reconcile the account of the Fort Rupert Garden Treaty with scholarly accounts of the Vancouver Island treaties that state that the first purchases occurred near Fort Victoria? Where do the origins of the treaties lie? Should we look to Fort Rupert's garden, the beginnings of agricultural settlement near Fort Victoria, or to the development of coal resources on northern Vancouver Island? Who were "the authorities" Blenkinsop was thinking about? Richard Blanshard (1817–1894), the inaugural Governor of the newly formed colony of Vancouver Island – freshly arrived from London – had visited Fort Rupert from 27 to 29 March, less than three weeks before Blenkinsop made his purchase. Did he convey instructions from the British Colonial Office? James Douglas (1803–1877), Chief Factor in charge of the HBC's operations on Vancouver Island, had visited Fort Rupert in January, and Blenkinsop had accompanied Douglas to Fort Victoria for his sick leave. Were Blenkinsop's "authorities" James Douglas and the Board of Management of the HBC's Columbia District or the London Governor and Committee of the HBC? What did he mean by "they willingly sold me all right to the land"? How important to the history of the Vancouver Island treaties were the demands of Indigenous people? What did the Indigenous chiefs who put their marks to the Vancouver Island treaties think of the agreements into which they entered? Where did the wording of the treaties originate? Did the treaties represent the British Crown's acknowledgment of Indigenous title to Vancouver Island? If so, how did the agents of the Crown define Indigenous title? The scholarship makes it difficult to answer these questions.

The Vancouver Island treaties attracted little scholarly attention until the 1960s. In 1969, anthropologist Wilson Duff, who had served as an expert witness in the first litigation relating to the treaties, published what may still be the best study of the Fort Victoria treaties.[6] Because Duff used treaty documents to address anthropological questions about the villagers of the Victoria district, he had no reason to discuss the other treaties. Scholars interested in the origins of the Vancouver Island treaties should have studied all of the treaties, but have inevitably focused on the Fort Victoria treaties, discussed most other treaties only tangentially if at all, and never mentioned the Kwakiutl Garden Treaty.[7] The scholarship has been impressively multidisciplinary, with geographers, political scientists, archivists, historians, and legal scholars making notable contributions.[8] However, since Duff's 1969 article, most scholars – regardless of discipline – have evinced juridical preoccupations (geared towards how the courts should or might interpret the treaties in the present) or other presentist concerns. These two characteristics of the scholarly literature – multidisciplinary approaches and presentist orientation – are evident in the most recent contribution, an edited volume of conference proceedings.[9] Because of its presentism the scholarly literature on the Vancouver Island treaties is badly flawed.

The textbooks and general histories that many non-specialists, lecturers, and the public rely on illustrate the deficiencies of the peer-reviewed literature. Based on the scholarship, when J.R. Miller summarized the Vancouver Island treaties in the third edition of his history of Indigenous–state relations in Canada, he wrote that "when [James Douglas] asked the Colonial Office for advice and models as Europeans began to encroach on Aboriginal lands in British Columbia, London referred him not to the Royal Proclamation of 1763, but to New Zealand's Treaty of Waitangi."[10] A widely used university text presents a different but equally mistaken interpretation: "under pressure from the British government, the HBC sent instructions to James Douglas to purchase Aboriginal land on Vancouver Island. Douglas took it upon himself to negotiate treaties. Following the dictates of the Royal Proclamation of 1763, he recognized 'Indian Title' and believed that it was necessary to purchase the land before new settlement occurred."[11] In 2008, John Lutz, also apparently relying on other scholars, wrote that "to acquire formal title to the lands that he had occupied and to open up settlement for the newly established colony, Governor James Douglas, at the behest of the British Colonial Office, signed individual treaties in 1850 with six family groupings."[12] Hamar Foster in 1989, and Paul Tennant in 1990, already dubbed the Vancouver Island treaties the "Douglas treaties," and the continued use of that name perpetuates the mistaken belief that the treaties were the brainchild of James Douglas.[13]

A disciplinarily historical perspective – one oriented towards understanding how the Indigenous and non-Indigenous parties to each of the treaties understood the treaties at the time they were negotiated – is now sorely needed. Until now, scholars have betrayed their presentist bias by focusing overwhelmingly on the post-treaty period, dealing only superficially with the time before 1850. My study addresses this gap. Doing so demands extensive use of previously neglected documents. This is the first study of the treaties based on exhaustive research in the Hudson's Bay Company Archives. It is also the first to use linguistic, archaeological, environmental, historical, and ethnographic evidence, and Indigenous accounts, to try to understand how the Indigenous peoples of Vancouver Island might have understood the treaties in the 1850s. Moreover, rather than focus myopically on the Fort Victoria treaties, I explore the history of all of the Vancouver Island treaties.

Although the scholarship on the Vancouver Island treaties is flawed, the Australian historian Bain Attwood has made an extraordinary recent contribution to the broader field of the history of Indigenous title in the British Empire. Based on thorough research into the history of the British colonies in New Zealand and Australia between 1835 and 1848, and rooted in a historical rather than juridical approach, his book convincingly argues "that sovereignty and rights of property in land were made – or not made – *historically*, in that they came into being only as the result of deeply historical processes, which were rarely linear in nature but halting, contingent and ultimately reliant on a large degree of chance."[14] Attwood argued that "we need to set aside any notion that the treatment of sovereignty and native rights in land was *determined* by particular norms, whether they be intellectual, legal, political or moral in nature, though there can be no doubt that norms of this kind played an important role in the making of claims."[15] By revealing the historical contingencies that determined whether or how questions regarding Indigenous title emerged or did not emerge in particular colonies, Attwood also explained that the approaches to Indigenous title in Britain's colonies in New Zealand and Australia were less divergent than many scholars have assumed.

Attwood has already shown for the 1830s and 1840s that the nature of debates and non-debates over the issue of Indigenous title in Australia and New Zealand was a function of local circumstances. Local conditions help explain why there was much debate and discussion relating to Indigenous sovereignty and Indigenous title in New Zealand from the mid-1830s to the end of the 1840s. Ironically, although New South Wales had been one of the primary sites of the debate over the nature of Indigenous title in New Zealand, there had been little discussion about the question of Indigenous title in New South Wales itself, except in relation to an attempt by private interests to buy land in the Port Phillip area.[16]

The Vancouver Island treaties cover only a tiny area of Vancouver Island, and, apart from the eleven treaties in the southeastern corner of Vancouver Island, treaties cover only a two-mile-deep strip of land along the coast between Hardy Bay and Port McNeill on the northern part of the island, and a rectangular area of about 200 square miles (520 square kilometres) at Nanaimo (see figure 1). Only about 1,000 square kilometres of Vancouver Island – about 3 per cent of its area – are covered by treaties.[17] The juxtaposition of treaty and non-treaty areas on Vancouver Island is so interesting because it mirrors patterns of treaty and non-treaty areas in Australasia and elsewhere in the English-speaking world.

Our understanding of the Vancouver Island treaties requires a fresh, thorough, and multidisciplinary critical analysis of the evidence. I aim here to reconstruct to the extent possible the motivations, intentions, and understandings of the signatories to the treaties at the time the treaties were concluded. To that end, I place the treaties within the context of thousands of years of Vancouver Island history, the history of the HBC's approach to Indigenous title, and the history of the policy and practice of agents of the British Crown in regard to Indigenous title, particularly in the 1830s and 1840s. The signatories to the Vancouver Island treaties (and other treaties) may not have regarded them as important when they were concluded, but their significance has grown considerably since. A contextualist history of the Vancouver Island treaties sheds more light on the history of treaties in the British world than scholars have acknowledged.[18] The treaties reveal much about the history of British approaches to Indigenous title, treaty policy, and Indigenous land purchases in the British Empire, particularly in those colonies in which exogenous[19] peoples came to dominate the Indigenous peoples politically, demographically, and economically. They also reveal tantalizing evidence about Indigenous people's perspectives on those same issues. And while they shed particular light on the pivotal period between the late 1830s and the early 1860s, they reveal what may be *the* most important and consistent driving force behind treaty policies in the British world from the 1620s to the 1870s: expediency. The word *expedient* crops up repeatedly over centuries in reference to Indigenous title. The importance of expediency helps explain why few, if any, proponents of land-transfer treaties in Australia, New Zealand, and Vancouver Island in the period under study were thought of as humanitarians. Few people discussed in this study who had any bona fides as abolitionists or as advocates for the interests of Indigenous people in the British Empire appear to have believed that land-transfer treaties were a key ingredient of a just and fair Indigenous policy (and some of those who advocated for treaties did so for cynical reasons). In short, those in the British Empire who advocated for land-transfer treaties in the 1830s, 1840s, and 1850s were not more likely to have any plausible credentials as humanitarians than those who did not.[20]

Until now, researchers have focused on explaining why treaties were *not* negotiated in some English-speaking colonies (in Australia and British Columbia, for example), implying that the fact that treaties *were* negotiated in others (New Zealand and most of Canada and the United States) requires little explanation. Regarding Vancouver Island, they have been perplexed that James Douglas stopped negotiating treaties after 1854, but not that he started doing so in 1850.[21] Chapter 1 examines the period between 1835 and 1849 to argue that it is as important to ask where and why treaties were negotiated, as to ask when and why they were not. It shows that, as the perceived importance of coal deposits of northern Vancouver Island grew, agents of the British Crown and the HBC grew increasingly anxious to secure their possession of the coalfields. In 1848, British Navy officers performed a rite of possession at the coalfields that ignored Indigenous title, and the Governor and Committee of the HBC explicitly denied Indigenous title. Chapter 1 should convince readers that concluding land-purchase treaties might not have been a default option in 1848.

Chapter 2 shows that the HBC's December 1848 denial of Indigenous title was not out of character with its policies and practices in the previous 180 years. It argues that the HBC rarely negotiated land-purchase treaties between 1668 and 1850, but that it did so when its officers or directors considered it expedient to do so. Throughout its history, the HBC defended its land claims by reference to right of discovery, rites of possession, Crown charter, prior occupation, and the naming of geographical features by its officers, but beginning in 1683 governors of the HBC also defended HBC claims against French claims by asserting that their agents had negotiated land-purchase treaties as early as 1668. During the 1680s the directors also instructed its officers to conclude treaties until it became obvious that such treaties carried no weight against the company's rivals. This earliest history of land purchase can be attributed to Zachariah Gillam (1636–1682), a New Englander who worked for the HBC in 1668–69. Because Gillam must have been inspired by precedents set in the New Netherlands and New England starting in the 1620s, the origins of treaty making along the North American eastern seaboard are also explained. Treaty making appears to have originated in the unique circumstances of the eastern seaboard in the 1620s: Dutch and English colonists with authority to negotiate treaties with Indigenous people, but no authority to conquer each other, resorted to treaty making to bolster otherwise disputable claims based on discovery, government charter, or prior occupation. The only other land-purchase treaty with which the HBC was connected was Lord Selkirk's treaty with Saulteaux and Cree bands at Red River in July 1817. The Selkirk Treaty, like the other HBC treaties and like the Dutch and English treaties on the eastern seaboard, was intended to bolster land claims against rivals. Notwithstanding these treaties, agents of the HBC – including James Douglas in 1847 – often relied on the company's charter and on rites of possession to support claims to land. Still, the practice of negotiating treaties became part of a long process that led to the development of the legal principles of Indigenous title (not vice versa). Chapter 2 having explained the HBC's treaty history to December 1848, and the Kwakiutl role in the Garden Treaty of 1850 already described, the focus turns to a deep history of the Indigenous people of Vancouver Island.

A recent trend has seen historians of Indigenous people neglect the time before contact with Europeans.[22] But given that only one long lifetime separated the arrival of Europeans to Vancouver Island and the completion of the Vancouver Island treaties, the previous 125 to 200 human lifetimes of human history on Vancouver Island must have profoundly influenced the relationships that formed between Indigenous villagers and exogenous peoples after 1774, and must have influenced the Indigenous villagers' conduct and understanding of the negotiations and the treaties. Uniquely salmon-reliant, semi-sedentary, hierarchical societies inhabited the Northwest Coast for thousands of years before Europeans arrived. Chapter 3 turns to archaeological, linguistic, environmental, and ethnological literature to explain how social, economic, political, environmental, and military realities may have influenced leaders of those societies when they interacted with newcomers after 1774, and when they negotiated the Vancouver Island treaties in the 1850s. It argues that for thousands of years environmental circumstances placed villagers along the rim of the Salish Sea at a significant disadvantage vis-à-vis many of their neighbours.

Probably because scholars of the Vancouver Island treaties have been driven more by juridical than historical questions, they have paid scant attention to the history of Vancouver Island between 1774 and 1850 or the abundant historical records produced by the Hudson's Bay Company.²³ Chapters 4 and 5 explore this important period. Chapter 4 argues that, between the arrival of Europeans in 1774 and the establishment of the HBC on the Northwest Coast in 1821, two generations of Indigenous islanders experienced tremendous demographic, social, economic, political, and geopolitical change. The economic and military position of villagers along the shores of the Salish Sea and along the east coast of Vancouver Island generally, deteriorated further as communities with better access to furs (particularly sea otter furs) gained privileged access to European wares, including weaponry. Cruelly, those same people suffered the effects of epidemics more severely than others. Chapter 4 also shows that the history of little-known land purchases concluded (or purportedly concluded) by British and American traders on western Vancouver Island between 1788 and 1791 is reminiscent of those discussed in chapter 2. Rival village leaders appear to have entered those agreements to gain privileged access to Europeans and their wares.

The establishment of the permanent trading posts on the Northwest Coast after 1821 marks a turning point in the history of the region. Chapter 5 explores the complex and tumultuous period between 1821 and 1849. In the span of only one generation, the fortunes of the communities along the Salish Sea changed dramatically. Warfare escalated, forcing communities to fortify their defences. Indigenous leaders wanted to have trading posts near them. Villagers who could, consolidated their settlements near HBC posts to seize upon new economic opportunities and military security that came with their proximity to trading posts. Such villagers had to accept certain trading principles upon which HBC officers insisted. Moreover, such opportunities exacerbated internal tensions within those societies, as both established elites and their rivals sought to bolster their own social and political positions. The context helps explain why no Indigenous leaders on the Northwest Coast demanded compensation from the HBC before 1850 even though the company's trading facilities, farms, and grazing lands occupied thousands of acres adjacent to Indigenous villages and surrounding some of its forts.

To fully explain why no one in the British government called for treaties on Vancouver Island, chapters 6 and 7 examine British policies and practice in the antipodes. Lured by ambiguous and inconsistent British policies and interventions towards New Zealand, the New Zealand Company and many private individuals negotiated purchases from Māori iwi (tribes) between 1835 and 1846. Then, between 1840 and 1846, the many competing claims to land in New Zealand forced rival private purchasers, government officials, politicians, lawyers, and judges to draw upon history in North America and Australasia to formulate consistent, systematic, and legalistic principles of "Native title." Several influential people defined it quite narrowly. Chapter 6 explains that on 9 July 1840 in Sydney, the capital of the Australian colony of New South Wales, Sir George Gipps (1791–1847) delivered one of the most influential articulations of principles of Indigenous title in the British world – one that found its way into the HBC's instructions to James Douglas. Gipps and his opponents drew upon history as far back as the 1620s in New England to support their contrasting arguments. The HBC directors' understanding of Indigenous title was also influenced by the narrow interpretation of Indigenous title put forward in the report of the 1844 British Select Committee on New Zealand, written by Viscount Howick (1802–1894), who would go on, as Henry Grey, 3rd Earl Grey, to be British Colonial Secretary during the years when all but the last of the Vancouver Island treaties were concluded.

Chapter 7 examines Earl Grey's policies and colonial practice in New Zealand between 1846 and 1849. It argues that Earl Grey's views on Indigenous title during his time as Colonial Secretary were consistent with those he had articulated earlier. It also argues that the oft-cited ruling in *R. v. Symonds* (1847) was significant for upholding the Crown's exclusive right to pre-empt Indigenous title without challenging the narrow interpretation of Indigenous title that prevailed among British authorities at the time. In sum, the first seven chapters of this book explain why when the British government established the colony of Vancouver Island in January 1849 no one assumed that it was necessary to extinguish Indigenous title by land-purchase treaties, although they describe historical contingencies in which such treaties were nonetheless negotiated. Chapters 8 to 11 describe how and why treaties were negotiated in New Zealand and Vancouver Island between 1846 and 1854.

Chapter 8 argues that local circumstances explain how and why policy and practice towards Indigenous title in New Zealand and Vancouver Island between 1846 and 1850 diverged from Earl Grey's and George Gipps's principles. In New Zealand, Governor George Grey (1812–1898) – with access to money to fund treaties – found it expedient to negotiate purchases that departed from the principles that guided the Colonial Office. The Vancouver Island treaties would later reflect the same deviations. Treaty policy for Vancouver Island originated at the top of the HBC, not at the Colonial Office, and not with James Douglas. The Vancouver Island treaties were the brainchild of Andrew

Colvile (1779–1856), the Deputy Governor of the HBC since 1839, and the brother-in-law of Thomas Douglas, 5th Earl of Selkirk, who had previously completed the so-called Selkirk Treaty. Colvile persuaded John H. Pelly (1777–1852), the London Governor of the Company, and George Simpson (1792–1860), the HBC's North American Governor, to arrange land purchases on the island. Simpson explicitly doubted the existence of Indigenous title, but, worried about potential competing claims for the coalfields of northern Vancouver Island, he agreed that it would be expedient to secure land-purchase agreements from Indigenous communities to bolster the company's possessory claims to the coal. Accordingly, the Governor and Committee instructed James Douglas to negotiate purchases with the villagers at Fort Rupert in the first place; Fort Victoria did not factor into the earliest discussions. James Douglas wrote a letter recommending land-purchase agreements on 3 September 1849, but his letter arrived in London too late to influence the decisions that his superiors had already made.

Chapter 8 argues that the HBC's instructions to Douglas were influenced by the principles laid out by George Gipps in 1840 and in the report of the 1844 Select Committee on New Zealand in 1844, and held by the Colonial Secretary of the time, Earl Grey. It also shows that James Douglas was able to negotiate treaties between 1850 and 1854 because he had access to funds for the purpose that British colonial governors did not always have. It might be expected that the HBC and James Douglas, both unaccustomed to negotiating land purchases with Indigenous people, would go about the process in an idiosyncratic manner, but this chapter shows that Douglas negotiated strikingly anomalous agreements. The Fort Victoria treaties of April and May 1850 were oral agreements; to signify their agreement, Indigenous chiefs put their marks at the bottom of blank pages! Douglas committed the terms and conditions of the oral agreements to paper only in a brief letter to the London Governor and Committee, in which he also asked for the directors to supply him with a written treaty document. George Simpson may have envisioned land purchases based upon the model of the Selkirk Treaty, but the Governor and Committee turned to New Zealand.

Chapter 9 explains that the directors of the HBC responded to Douglas's request for a written treaty document by using the Treaty of Akaroa (Kemp Deed) – a choice that they should have known was injudicious – as their template.[24] The Treaty of Akaroa was concluded on the South Island (then usually referred to as the Middle Island) of New Zealand on 12 June 1848. After Henry Tacy Kemp (1818–1901) reported on the treaty negotiations, lieutenant-governor Edward John Eyre (1815–1901) judged that Kemp had deviated so badly from his instructions that Eyre doubted that the agreement was legally valid. This chapter shows that the HBC's reliance on the Treaty of Akaroa accounts for some of the idiosyncrasies of the Vancouver Island treaties, although James Douglas's offhand approach to treaty making explains other anomalies. The Fort Victoria treaties must rank as some of the oddest Indigenous treaties in the British world.

Scholars have focused on the Fort Victoria treaties, but each Vancouver Island treaty is unique. The Governor and Committee of the HBC were particularly anxious that Douglas purchase the coalfields of northern Vancouver Island. Chapter 10 places the Fort Rupert treaties in historical context. It argues that the very unsettled circumstances at Fort Rupert explain why Kwakiutl chiefs put forward the demands that resulted in the Garden Treaty. It also explains why Douglas concluded two treaties with identical boundaries but with two different communities (the "Quakeolths," and the "Queackars") on 8 February 1851. Chapter 11 examines the histories of the Saanich treaties of February 1852 and the Nanaimo Treaty of 1854. The Saanich treaties were the first Douglas negotiated while Governor of Vancouver Island (although he did not sign any of the treaties concluded before 1854). He claimed to have concluded them at the insistence of the Saanich villagers, although he did not inform the Colonial Office about them. Only seven months after negotiating the Saanich treaties, Douglas hurriedly had one of his junior officers perform a rite of possession and establish HBC occupation at Nanaimo when the value of the coal there became apparent. Two more years passed before Douglas finally carried out the HBC directors' instructions to purchase those coal lands from the Nanaimo, and he apparently failed to produce a written treaty at Nanaimo even then. These two chapters argue that Douglas's enthusiasm for treaties waned significantly by the time he belatedly negotiated with the Nanaimo. They also explain the role of relations between Indigenous communities and the HBC, inter-ethnic relations among Indigenous communities, and tensions and rivalries within them, in the history of the Vancouver Island treaties.

While students of the Vancouver Island treaties have underemphasized the history of Vancouver Island before 1850, several have tried to explain why Douglas stopped negotiating treaties in 1854. Chapter 12 argues that Douglas probably did not experience a momentous change of mind. Earlier chapters show that Douglas was less influential in the development of treaty policy than scholars have assumed, that he did not conduct treaty making with the formality that most treaty commissioners did, his enthusiasm for treaty making had diminished before 1854, and few people in the mid-nineteenth century regarded treaty making as an essential component of a just and fair Indigenous policy. Chapter 12 argues that after 1854, when Douglas enthusiastically supported British agrarian settlement, his commitment to protecting Indigenous communities from settlers remained undiminished. The slow pace of settlement in the Cowichan Valley (which certainly would have been next in line for a treaty) influenced his decision making before 1858, and his overwhelming workload was a factor after 1858, but Douglas probably saw little distinction between his Indigenous policies of pre- and post-1854. At no time between when negotiating treaties was started in 1850 and when he was asked explicitly about his Indian land policies in 1874 did Douglas place much importance on the Vancouver Island treaties. In place of treaties, Douglas adopted a policy of establishing Indian reserves according to the wishes of the Indigenous peoples themselves, and establishing anticipatory reserves in advance of exogenous settlement. Perhaps ironically, Douglas was briefly impelled to advocate for treaties on Vancouver Island in 1863–64 when the colony's Legislative Assembly petitioned the British government, unsuccessfully, to pay for treaties. Apart from that, he failed on several occasions between 1856 and 1874 to seize the opportunity to recommend treaties, or even to mention that he had concluded treaties.

Chapter 13 examines accounts of the Vancouver Island treaty negotiations dating after James Douglas's death in 1877 by people who were present, or claimed to be present, at the negotiations. It argues that eyewitness and participant accounts by Indigenous and non-Indigenous people presented many years after the actual events offer useful evidence not available elsewhere, but that they are inevitably influenced by the frailties of human memory, and by the context in which the events are later recalled. Accounts preserved many years after the events they purport to describe pose special interpretive challenges, but they reveal much about how memories of the Vancouver Island treaties changed.

The interpretations presented here are revisionist. I hope that the contextualist historical approach employed contributes significantly to our understanding of the Vancouver Island treaties and the history of Indigenous title, and that it stimulates and encourages further inquiry.

# 1 The Hudson's Bay Company and Vancouver Island Land Policy to 1849

On a showery 5 August 1835, Dr. William F. Tolmie (1812–1886), the twenty-three-year-old surgeon at the HBC post of Fort McLoughlin, on Milbanke Sound, north of Vancouver Island, noted the arrival of "three canoes of Quaghcuills" (Kwakiutl).[1] Those visitors must have told him about coal "in their country."[2] John Dunn, the interpreter at the fort, later recalled that the Kwakiutl teased the traders for importing coal from Great Britain when it could be obtained in their territories "of the richest quality close to the surface, rising in hillocks, and requiring very little labour to dig it out." According to Dunn they mockingly announced that "they had changed, in a great measure, their opinion of the white men, whom they thought endowed by the Great Spirit with the power of effecting great and useful objects."[3]

Tolmie convinced these Kwakiutl visitors to bring him a sample of the coal. Traders at Fort Vancouver (located on the lower Columbia River at today's Vancouver, Washington) (for the location of trading posts mentioned in this text, see figure 9) had found coal along the Cowlitz River in about 1833, but rapids along that river made it impossible to transport that coal to any of its posts economically.[4] To fire their forges, the blacksmiths at the company's posts along the Northwest Coast therefore depended on costly locally manufactured charcoal, or coal imported from Great Britain. Given that the HBC was also about to introduce a steamship, the *Beaver*, to the Northwest Coast, Tolmie was wise to seize upon the possibility that a local supply of accessible coal might replace coal imported from Britain. It must have been the "large band of Quaghcuils" that arrived at Fort McLoughlin on 14 August that brought Tolmie the sample of coal he requested.[5] Tolmie sent it to the man in charge of the HBC's Columbia District, Chief Factor John McLoughlin (1784–1857), at Fort Vancouver.[6] McLoughlin in turn wrote Donald Manson (1796–1880), then in charge at Fort McLoughlin, about the coal, speculating that "from the specimen sent here by Dr. Tolmie I suppose it would answer for the Steam Boat," and directing him, "please get all the information you can about it."

Most of a year elapsed before HBC traders at Fort McLoughlin visited the coalfield. When they did, the job fell to Chief Factor Duncan Finlayson (1796–1862), then briefly in charge of the HBC's coastal trade and a talented and respected trader. He had attracted positive attention soon after joining the company as an apprentice clerk in 1815, and his rapid promotions to Chief Trader in 1828 and Chief Factor in 1831, reflect the excellent reputation he enjoyed within the HBC. In 1835, George Simpson described him as a "man of good Education and superior abilities to most of his colleagues."[7] John Dunn joined the party led by Finlayson that confirmed the report of coal at the mouth of Suquash Creek (about halfway between Hardy Bay and Port McNeill). In a book published in 1844, Dunn wrote that "the natives were anxious that we should employ them to work the coal; to this we consented, and agreed to give them a certain sum for each large box. The natives being so numerous and labour so cheap, for us to attempt to work the coal would have been madness."[8]

Before dismissing the notion, Finlayson became the first person to propose purchasing the coalfields from the Kwakiutl. He pointed out that the coalfield was located within 2.5 miles (about 4 kilometres) of "a very populous village of Quaquill Indians, consisting of from 50 to 60 houses." The villagers at Cluxewe insisted that "they would not permit us to work the coals as they were valuable to them, but that they would labour in the mine themselves and sell to us the produce of their exertions." Finlayson judged that option unappealing because "from the indolent habits of Indians, even if the materials for working it, were in their hands that in six months they would not furnish a sufficient quantity for the consumption of a day." But he considered buying the coalfield from the villagers even less promising, because he thought the company could not safely mine the coal without the protection of a fort, as its miners would be "exposed to the attacks of other tribes who frequent this spot."[9] Although much of his experience in the HBC territories had been east of the Rocky Mountains, Finlayson's suggestion that the coalfield might be purchased implies that he believed that the Kwakiutl might consent to let the HBC mine the coal if the HBC purchased it, but that he also keenly understood the tumultuous geopolitical situation that prevailed among the Indigenous people in the region in the 1830s. On the other hand, he underestimated the willingness of the Kwakiutl to mine the coal.

Given that the HBC posts on the Northwest Coast were all dependent on Great Britain for their coal, and given that the *Beaver* had just been added to the HBC's fleet of ships, the HBC officers' initial interest in the coal is unsurprising. In early 1837 Finlayson and McLoughlin, the two men then in charge of the HBC's Columbia District, agreed "to remove Fort McLoughlin to the Coal mine when it can conveniently be done."[10]

The HBC did not follow up the notion of purchasing the mine or establishing a post at the "coal mine" until 1849, at least in part because the company's interest in the coal quickly waned. For several years, the HBC was satisfied with an occasional trade in coal. In 1838, when John Work (c. 1792–1861) was stationed at Fort Simpson, he visited the coalfield. Work, an experienced HBC trader who had joined the company in 1814 and had first been assigned to the Columbia District (which included Vancouver Island) in 1823,[11] would later play an important role in the development of the coalfield. In his report of 1838, Work mentioned that William McNeill had acquired 16 tons of coal for Fort Simpson earlier that year, before he described his own purchase of coal at Port McNeill, about 4 miles (6 kilometres) southeast of Suquash. He concluded that the Kwakiutl mined the surface coal without difficulty. He also found that, although the coal worked well for both blacksmiths' work and the company's steamer, the *Beaver* would probably rely more on the abundant wood of the coast than on coal. He also echoed Finlayson's concerns about the dangers of the HBC's trying to mine the coal itself: "It would be unsafe for white men to go ashore during the greater part of the season when the Indians resort in great numbers to that quarter, even were it found practicable to work the coals to advantage. Early in the spring the natives are off at their fishing ground on the main, and few to be met with in the neighbourhood of the Coals."[12]

Finlayson and Work had identified several large villages in the vicinity of the coalfields (for locations in northern Vancouver Island mentioned here, see figure 2). The "very populous village" referred to in Finlayson's letter is certainly a reference to the Kweeha and Kwakiutl summer villages at the mouth of Cluxewe [Klickseewy] River.[13] The Spanish explorers Dionisio Alcalá Galiano and Cayetano Valdés y Flores had visited those villages, which they identified as Majoa and Quacos, in August 1792.[14] Work also mentioned "Cheslakees Village [Whulk] of Vancouver," at the mouth of the Nimpkish River, one of the most abundant salmon rivers on Vancouver Island. George Vancouver had visited this village at the mouth of the Nimpkish River in July 1792.[15]

Work hinted at reasons for the HBC's loss of interest in the coalfields: that the *Beaver* could be fuelled more conveniently with wood than coal, and that the place was unsafe on account of the many "Indians" in the area. Work's account, however, suggests that HBC personnel in 1838 still thought the coal there was of high quality. Officers in the HBC soon concluded otherwise.

On 14 October 1839, James Douglas wrote from Fort Vancouver to the HBC's London Governor and Committee that the HBC's *Nereide* had brought about 100 tons of coal to Fort Vancouver, but that it had "not given satisfaction, as our Blacksmiths cannot use them."[16] For that reason he argued that Fort Vancouver would have to continue importing coal from England. In the same letter, he reported that the *Nereide* was carrying a load of Vancouver Island coal to England as ballast.[17]

The London Governor and Committee hoped that the coal on Vancouver Island and the Cowlitz River would save the company the inconvenience and expense of transporting British coal to the Northwest Coast.[18] In 1841, after noting that John McLoughlin had ordered 60 tons of coal in 1840, the London Committee responded that there was "little probability" of its being able to meet that order, because of lack of room in the ships. They told McLoughlin that he would "have to provide the establishments from Coal mines on the Coast or on the Cowlitz river, or provide Charcoal for the forges; under those circumstances it will not be necessary to include the article of Coal in your future indent."[19] They also asked him "to forward us specimens both of the coal on Vancouvers Island and on the Cowlitz, in order that we may know their qualities respectively."[20] McLoughlin protested that neither the Cowlitz nor Vancouver Island coal were suitable before he warned of "the ruinous consequences which will result if we are deprived of Coals to manufacture &c. the Iron Works for the Trade."[21]

By 1842, the HBC officers in North America appear to have all but forgotten about the Vancouver Island coal. In that year George Simpson raised the possibility of establishing a post in the area around Johnstone Strait, because he believed that it had great potential as a source of salmon.[22] He did not mention the coal. It is not that Simpson was not interested in finding a replacement for imported British coal; Simpson was always interested in finding ways to cut costs. But by 1842, he pinned his hopes on better methods of manufacturing charcoal from wood. In the long letter in which he proposed establishing a trading post at Johnstone Straits, he acknowledged the news that "about 40 tons of coal have been sent by the *Vancouver*, and that a further quantity will be forward by the *Prince Albert*." He continued by noting that during his visit to Sitka, he had arranged with the Russian American Company to hire for one year two of their men with expertise in making charcoal. He hoped that "we shall thus be enabled to dispense with coal in future from England, the freight on which alone renders it a very costly article."[23]

The plan failed. In October 1842, John McLoughlin reported that "the Russian has tried to make coals but finds the wood at this place, does not answer to make Coals so well as that at Sitka, it will be well to send as great a part of the sea coal in our Requisition as possible, it will cost as much to make Coals here as to import them, and those made here will not answer so well as the imported."[24] By then the London Governor and Committee conceded that Vancouver Island coal was not a viable alternative. They responded to the bad news, not by reference to the coal, but by expressing their hopes that locally manufactured charcoal might yet replace imported coal at Fort Vancouver.[25] So, despite short-lived optimism, people within the HBC showed little interest in the Vancouver Island coal between 1842 and 1846.

Thanks to the publication of John Dunn's account of coal in *History of the Oregon Territory and British North-American Fur Trade* (1844, quoted above), knowledge of the coalfields spread beyond the HBC. Dunn published his book just as the British and American navies were adopting steam power, quickly increasing the strategic importance of coal supplies.[26] Apparently intrigued by Dunn's account, Robert C. Wyllie, the British Proconsul in Hawaii,[27] wrote to McLoughlin in September 1844 to ask about the coal. McLoughlin responded that "some of the crew of the steamer who are here [Fort Vancouver] tell me the coal on Vancouver's Island will not answer for Steam – I will make further enquiry when our steamer returns from the North West Coast and let you know."[28]

The perceived importance of the coal on the Northwest Coast of North America increased further during the Oregon Crisis in 1846. With tensions high as a result of the Oregon Dispute, the British Royal Navy dispatched no fewer than five of its ships to the region, including the *Cormorant*, the first Royal Navy steamship to visit the Northwest Coast, which arrived at Victoria in June 1846.[29] A second Navy steamship, the *Driver*, delivered Richard Blanshard (1817–1894) to Victoria, from Panama, on 9 March 1850.[30] The fact that Blanshard visited Fort Rupert aboard the *Driver* only seventeen days later suggests the importance that he placed upon the coal resources there.

The Admiralty had been surprisingly slow to adopt steam-powered ships – the United States Navy had embraced steam power more quickly – but by 1846, the officials in the British Navy understood the importance of ensuring secure supplies of coal. Thus, although coal had been economically significant for decades, the British Navy's turn to steamships in these years was rapidly making coal a resource of great military and strategic value, and coal on Vancouver Island was the only known readily accessible source along the entire west coast of the Americas at the time. It is not surprising, then, that the Admiralty showed interest. In January 1846, Sir George F. Seymour (1787–1870), Commander-in-Chief in the Pacific, based at Valparaiso, Chile, dispatched Captain John Alexander Duntze (1806–1882) of the *Fisgard* to the Northwest Coast. As part of his instructions, Seymour told Duntze to try "to preserve a friendly state of feeling on the part of the Natives, Canadians, and all others who frequent the Shores; and you are to obtain every information in your power as soon as possible after your arrival, whether the Coals which are represented to abound on the Northern part of Vancouver's Island can be collected in sufficient quantity to afford a Supply for Steam Fuel."[31]

Duntze began his investigations of the coal on Vancouver Island by asking HBC officers at Victoria to provide whatever information they had. On 7 September 1846, Peter Skene Ogden and James Douglas responded with a long letter, indicating that "it appears very probable that this mineral abounds over all the north-eastern part of Vancouver's Island; that is to say, from Choslakers [Cheslakees], latitude 50°36′, to Cape Scott," although the location known to the HBC as the "coal mine" was around Port McNeill.[32] Ogden and Douglas explained that the HBC had only ever acquired the coal by trade, but that "a large quantity of coal may at any time be got there by employing the Indians, who are numerous and active, to dig and transport them to the ship. They are by no means averse to such employment, and ask a very moderate remuneration for their labour."[33]

Realizing that the Royal Navy might not be satisfied with a desultory trade, but that the Admiralty might insist on a regular and reliable supply, Ogden and Douglas explained the possibilities and challenges:

> If the British Government has any intention of making this coal available for the use of their steam navy, it will be necessary, in order to keep a constant supply on hand, to form an establishment on the spot of sufficient force to protect it against the natives, who are numerous, bold and treacherous; and also to carry on the mining operations. We would, in such case, recommend that an application on the subject be made to the Directors of the Hudson's Bay Company in London, who could in a short time take measures to get the necessary means collected, under the management of experienced persons acquainted with Indian character, and capable of drawing the greatest possible advantage from their presence.
>
> We shall be most happy to do anything in our power to forward this object, but it will in the first place be necessary to enter into arrangements

with the Directors of the Company in London, as we have not the means in the country, and we do not feel at liberty to undertake a measure of such importance without their sanction.

We take the liberty of making this suggestion as to the proper mode of proceeding, in order that no time may be lost hereafter in carrying out the ulterior arrangements, should Government deem it an object of importance to form an establishment at M'Neil's Harbour, or at some other point, for the purpose of collecting coals for the regular supply of the steam navy in the Pacific.[34]

Although Douglas and Ogden implied that the HBC could organize the mining of the coal, at the time this was written – shortly after the conclusion of the Oregon Treaty but before the colony of Vancouver Island was created – the HBC's rights to the coal of Vancouver Island were uncertain at best. At the time of the merger of the HBC and NWC in 1821, the British government had granted the amalgamated company a twenty-one-year exclusive licence to the fur trade of the region, a licence that had been renewed for a further twenty-one years on 13 May 1838, but that licence did not include mineral rights. Under British law, the British Crown possessed the rights to the coal, and had full discretion to allocate the rights to mine it. For that reason, it was prudent for Ogden and Douglas to downplay the importance of expertise and experience in mining (which the HBC did not possess), and emphasize the dangers posed by the Indians, and the importance of the company's having "experienced persons acquainted with Indian character."

Douglas and Ogden's report prompted Duntze to investigate further. On 15 September 1846, while at Fort Nisqually, Duntze ordered Captain George Thomas Gordon of the *Cormorant* to visit the site.[35] It made good sense to send a steamship to test the coal. So, at Duntze's request, the HBC instructed James Sangster, of its own naval service, to guide the *Cormorant* to the coal mine where, according to Douglas and Work, the coal was "found to steam remarkably well, and the Engineers of the Cormorant had no difficulty in welding and doing their other forge work with them, in fact they were used in preference to the English Coal on board the Cormorant."[36] Gordon's official report to Duntze indicated that when he arrived at Port McNeill, Gordon had Sangster inform the Kwakiutl that he wanted coal,

and the next day several canoes came laden with coal, and they continued to increase in number until our departure. At the advice of Mr. Sangster, I slung a tub, holding about 6 cwt., from the fore-yard, which was lowered into a canoe and quickly filled; in this manner we received 62 tons from the 24th to the 26th, paying for each tub as it came up, by articles of trifling value, which I procured at your suggestion from the officer in charge of Fort Victoria. The whole of the expenses incurred, including a few presents necessarily made to the chiefs, will make the coals average not more than 4s. per ton.

...

It is my belief that the field does not extend further to the westward than the eastern shore of Beaver Harbour, and to the eastward than the Minkish [Nimpkish] River, marked in the accompanying plan [not located] by a dotted line; indeed the feature of the country from Beaver Harbour to Shucharte [Shushartie] is quite different, being covered with hard blue whin rock, without any appearance of freestone whatever.

It is impossible to form any opinion of the extent of the field in an inland direction; but, from the appearance of the country, I am of opinion that it is very considerable. On first going on shore, the natives appeared tenacious of our examining the coals, and accused us of coming to steal them; but, having made a few presents to some of the chiefs, they entered into our views and became very active, and I am only surprised that, with the rude implements they have for digging, viz., hatchets and wooden wedges, they were able to procure so large a quantity in so short a time; and I am persuaded that, with the means we have, assisted by the natives, we could fill our coal bunkers in from 10 to 14 days.

The natives are a fine race of men, and appear industrious and friendly, but much addicted to thieving.

In conclusion, I beg leave to remark that the coal district is, in my opinion, admirably situated, possessing, as it does, excellent anchorage in its neighbourhood, and being so far north that vessels of almost any burthen can approach it by way of Cape Scott, thus avoiding the difficult and dangerous navigation of Sir George Seymour's Narrows and Johnston's Straits.[37]

Gordon's visit in September 1846 was an important milestone in the British Navy's growing interest in the coal resources of Vancouver Island.

Sensing from the Admiralty's queries that the British government might be interested in the coal for the Royal Navy, James Douglas and John Work addressed a letter to the London Governor and Committee about it in December 1846. Douglas and Work were not optimistic that the HBC could mine the coal at the site profitably, but suggested that, even if the company did not make a profit of the mine, the Governor and Committee might want to develop the resource to prevent "other parties" from making a claim to the location:

> In case your Honors should wish to enter into any arrangement with Government for supplying Coals, we beg to state that it will be necessary to form an establishment, on the spot, and employ Indians to work the Coal beds, These being on or near the surface can at present be worked at very little cost, but when the surface beds are exhausted, and it becomes necessary to mine, the expenses will be increased tenfold, and with our imperfect implements, and total ignorance of mining operations the project may perhaps terminate in failure and disappointment.
>
> We can now purchase Coals from the Indians at about ten shillings a ton, but when larger quantities than we now purchase are wanted, the price may be expected to rise, and will be further increased by the expenses of the establishment, and they will probably cost more in the end than they do at Valparaiso [Chile], where English Coals can often be purchased at twenty shillings, and are considered high at Forty shillings a ton.
>
> Taking the expense of the Establishment at £800 a year, and supposing that Government would contract to receive 1400 or 1600 tons annually deliverable on the spot, at forty shillings a ton, we might clear expenses for a few years, until the beds become difficult to work; and we would further derive some benefit from the fur trade, and fisheries and eventually secure the Coal district for the Company, which may otherwise prove an attraction to other parties.[38]

Douglas and Work did not identify what "other parties" might be attracted to the coal district, but they clearly feared that other British entities with experience and expertise in coal mining might acquire rights to the coal. They cannot have relished the prospect of dealing with a settlement on Vancouver Island populated by people not employed by or under the control of the company.

The *Cormorant* was next back in England in December 1847, having brought with it samples of Vancouver Island coal.[39] Soon thereafter British newspapers featured stories of the coal "which is put on board by the Indians at a mere nominal price."[40] The travels of the *Cormorant* and the newspaper coverage outdid Dunn's book in capturing the attention of many people in Britain and North America, including Samuel Cunard (1787–1865), the Halifax-born merchant and owner of a steamship company (eventually to be known as the Cunard Steamship Company) that held the British government's contract to carry mail between Great Britain and the United States. As an early adopter of steamships and a person who had previously operated coal mines on Cape Breton Island, Cunard took interest in news of coal. In early 1848 he wrote a letter to Henry George Ward (MP), First Secretary to the Admiralty, that was to have significant influence among those in the Admiralty. He warned that:

> Individuals in the Oregon Territory will be alive to the advantages resulting from the possession of this valuable article, and will endeavour to obtain the best situations or acquire any right the natives may have, or suppose they may have.
>
> It may therefore be well in granting lands on this island, to reserve the mines for the use of the Crown, and to take such measures as may prevent the natives or others from acquiring or ceding rights to these mines.
>
> This subject will not long escape the vigilance of the Americans in that neighbourhood.[41]

While Cunard emphasized the threat posed by potential American interlopers, the HBC officers correctly anticipated that British subjects would soon seek to develop the coalfields. In early 1848, John Shillinglaw published a "A Proposal to Form a Company for the Purpose of Working the Coal, and Establishing a Colony in Vancouver's Island," and in February 1848, James Edward Fitzgerald inquired with the Colonial Office "whether they are about to give the right of working the Coal to the Hudsons Bay Company, or whether they are prepared to listen to the proposals of any other Company formed for the purpose Specified in the Enclosed Circular; and if so upon what terms the grant will be made, or lastly whether it be contemplated to keep the mines in the property of the Crown."[42] In light of the fact that American forces were occupying Mexico City when Cunard wrote his letter, Cunard may not have seen the notion that Americans might seek to seize Vancouver Island as far-fetched, although the officers in the HBC considered British subjects a far more realistic threat.

Cunard was right. By the time the *Times* published its articles in early 1848, Americans had already shown interest. Perhaps word of the coal had spread from the *Cormorant* itself as it steamed back to Great Britain from Vancouver Island. In any case, on 22 December 1847, Captain Joseph L. Folsom of the United States Army, stationed at San Francisco, wrote to James Douglas inquiring about the possibility of obtaining coal either for military service or for two steamers being constructed to carry mail between Panama and the Columbia River.[43] Douglas may have been more eager to court American customers for Vancouver Island coal than he was to encourage British entities. An HBC contract with American customers would help secure the company's rights to the coal.

Douglas responded to Folsom with a misleadingly positive assessment of the coal: "there is no question that an excellent quality of bituminous coal is to be found in the greatest abundance on the north eastern coast of Vancouver's Island."[44] He continued by stating that the HBC "might be induced by the prospect of a large contract to commence mining operations on Vancouver's Island, but it would require two or perhaps three years preparation before large supplies of Coal could be depended on."[45] He immediately reported Folsom's inquiry to George Simpson.[46]

Encouraged, the owners of the Pacific Mail Steamship Company (PMSC), to which Folsom alluded in his letter, contacted the HBC's directors. In November 1847, the United States government had awarded William Henry Aspinwall, a New York merchant, the contract to transport mail between Panama and Oregon, a service that was to be inaugurated by 1 October 1848.[47] Hoping that the Vancouver Island coal would prove to be a cheap supply of the fuel, Aspinwall began discussions with George Simpson in March 1848.[48] Even before the negotiations were complete, Simpson wrote to the officers in charge of the Columbia District to state that the prospect of a contract:

> has brought to view a very important branch of trade, which promises to be attended with great advantage to the concern and I am of opinion no time should be lost in opening up the Mine, to which end I have to beg you will, without delay, establish a post, upon as moderate a scale of expenditures as possible, at the mine, & it is to be hoped that the profits on the fur trade and fishery, even if the coal trade should prove abortive, may go far towards covering the outlay; and it will also have the advantage of securing to the Company the right of possession of the Mine, which may hereafter be of great Value.[49]

It is significant that Simpson immediately raised the "right of possession" of the coalfields when he considered the possibility that domestic rivals might wish to mine the coal. Simpson followed up that correspondence with another letter in June which betrayed his preoccupation with establishing a post at the location as soon as possible to assert the company's right. He informed the Columbia District Board of Management that the HBC's Northern Council had decided that "it is very desirable to form a post as early as possible at the most favorable spot for a coal depot, with a view not only to immediate results, but by prior occupation to secure the coal fields against any persons who might seat themselves down upon them."[50]

British naval officials also showed growing interest in, and concern about, the coal of Vancouver Island, and in issues of possession. In July

1848, George W.C. Courtenay, in command of the British frigate *Constance*, announced his arrival at Esquimalt Harbour by penning a letter to James Douglas and stating that Rear Admiral Phipps Hornby, Commander in Chief of the Royal Navy's forces in the Pacific, "is particularly desirous of being informed of the present state of the Coal formation in Vancouver's island, if a supply should hereafter be required for Her Majesty's Service at what rate per Ton it could be furnished on the spot, and at what rate, if freight could be procured for its conveyance, it might be delivered at any of the principal Forts in Chile and Peru, or other places."[51] Over the next few days Courtenay sent several letters to Fort Victoria, one stating that "upon the subject of the coal formation in Vancouver's Island, ... I strongly recommend the Officers of the Honorable Company of Hudsons Bay to keep a vigilant look out thereon, and in the event of any persons settling near the Coal mines or attempting to work them, either to cause their removal or serve them with notice to depart,"[52] and another, sent with a copy of Samuel Cunard's letter of 3 January 1848, asking Douglas "to remark how important it is to keep all intruders from the neighbourhood of the coal formation."[53]

On 17 August 1848, Courtenay, clearly influenced by Cunard's letter, wrote to James Douglas to inform him that he had decided that:

> it would be desirable to take possession of that district for Her Majesty. I am informed that the practice in these parts on taking possession of Land is to build a Hut thereon. I have therefore to request that you will as soon as convenient cause the same to be erected, and in addition to have a board with the enclosed inscription, which I have prepared and sent to Fort Victoria, placed in some conspicuous position. I have caused this transaction to be inserted in the Constance's Log Book and beg to suggest that the same be registered in the Honorable Company's Archives so as to give the transaction due weight and authority in the event of a question being raised hereafter.[54]

Courtney's inscription read as follows:

### – Notice –

These and the adjacent Lands together with the Coal and Minerals contained therein, are taken possession of through the agency of the Honb[le] Hudsons Bay Company, by me George Courtenay, Esq. Captain of Her Britannia Majesty's Ship Constance, acting on behalf of Rear Admiral Hornby, C.B. Commander in Chief of Her Majesty's Squadron in the Pacific, For Her Majesty Victoria Queen of Great Britain and Ireland, Her Heirs and Successors.

All persons are therefore warned not to settle, thereon, or to visit these the said lands for the purpose of working the coal or other Mines.
Good save the Queen
Given on board the Constance in Port Esquimalt the 17th August 1848.
The Twelfth year of Her Majesty's Reign.
'signed' G.W.C. Courtenay[55]

Douglas and Work were unimpressed by Courtenay's effort. They wrote dismissively to the London Governor and Committee on 5 December 1848 to inform them that Courtenay had:

> taken possession of the Coal mines of Vancouver's Island, in behalf of the Crown, a measure recommended in a letter, bearing the signature of "S. Cunard," to the Lords Commissioners of the Admiralty, to prevent the encroachments of American Citizens, an alarm which appears groundless, as since the late Treaty no American Citizen can, by settlement, acquire any legal rights to lands within the limits of British Oregon.[56]

However, given that by the Treaty of Guadalupe Hidalgo that ended the Mexican-American War in February 1848, the United States had acquired much of northern Mexico, Cunard and Courtenay probably thought there were more grounds to fear American encroachment than Douglas and Work did.

It is unclear whether the members of the Admiralty knew about the HBC's negotiations with the PMSC, but those negotiations progressed quickly, even as Courtenay worried about American interest in the coalfields. During the summer of 1848, Captain William C. Stout, general agent for the PMSC, sought to arrange the purchase of coal from Vancouver Island, and by the end of September the HBC had inked a contract with Aspinwall to supply 1,000 tons of coal at a cost of 20 shillings per ton, to be picked up by the purchasers at the mines.[57] Then, in October, the HBC hurriedly dispatched Scottish miners hired in Edinburgh for the long voyage around Cape Horn. In the meantime, George Simpson, concerned that the PSMC would need coal before the miners arrived, instructed the Board of Management of the Columbia District to "use your utmost endeavours, by the formation of a post, the employment of Indians or otherwise to provide with the least possible delay and have placed in the most convenient spot for shipment from 500. [to] 1000 Tons of Coals, or as much more as can be collected." He recommended that if the board could not spare enough men to establish a post at the location "the next best mode I can suggest would be to station the steamer [*Beaver*] as near the mine as possible with a view to affording protection to the people there employed, and in that case you would have to depend more on Indian labor than on the work of your own people."[58]

Even as late as 1 December 1848 – shortly after the contract with the PMSC was concluded and the HBC Committee decided to establish a post at the coalfield, and shortly before the HBC was given jurisdiction over the colony of Vancouver Island – the officials in the HBC had no plans to conclude formal land purchases with Indigenous communities in the colony. Their perspective, like that of George Courtenay, was that the rights to the land might be contested among non-Indigenous people, but that the Indigenous people did not have rights to any land not cultivated or permanently occupied. Archibald Barclay, Secretary to the London Governor and Committee of the HBC, made this clear to Peter Skene Ogden and James Douglas in December 1848. Barclay wrote that:

> With respect to the settlement to be made in the coal district, you will of course treat the Natives with kindness and discretion, holding out to them the advantages which they will derive from being regularly employed in working the coal or otherwise from the establishment of a permanent post among them. But you must at the same time make them understand firmly and decidedly that the Company will work this or any other mines at their own discretion, and will not admit any outward claims of the wandering natives to lands which were not cultivated or permanently occupied: and by kindness and judicious presents to the influential men the Board have no doubt of your making your arrangement without difficulty or collision with the Natives.[59]

As of December 1848, British Royal Navy officers and directors of the HBC assumed that Indigenous people had no right to lands that were not by nineteenth-century British standards cultivated or permanently occupied. No one intended to negotiate land-purchase treaties on Vancouver Island. People within the government and the HBC were worried that non-Indigenous interests, whether other British subjects (perhaps even the British government itself) or foreigners, would assert a right to the coalfields. The history of the period between 1835 and 1849 reveals that it is as important to ask how and why treaties *were* concluded in certain times and places as it is to inquire as to why they were not. That history also shows that it would be prudent to ask whether the HBC's denial of Indigenous title in December 1848 was inconsistent with previous HBC policy and practice. It is to that question we now turn.

## 2 The Hudson's Bay Company and Indigenous Title, 1668–1849

Several scholars have simplistically argued that the HBC recognized Indigenous title.[1] In connection with the Vancouver Island treaties, the political scientist Paul Tennant wrote that "they stand as unequivocal recognition of Indigenous title."[2] The historical record paints a much more ambiguous picture. Documents show that the HBC Governor and Committee's 1848 flat rejection of "any outward claims of the wandering natives to lands which were not cultivated or permanently occupied" was consistent with HBC policy over the company's previous 180 years. It is not that the company had not concluded land-purchase agreements with Indigenous peoples before 1850, but the company's superficially inconsistent policies permit us to understand better the context of its actions on Vancouver Island. During the first period in which the HBC adopted a land-purchase policy, one of its personnel appears to have been inspired by the first such treaties concluded by Dutch and English companies that, like the HBC, negotiated independent of their national governments and without reference to any legal principles, to bolster their land claims against foreign and domestic rivals. During this first period, the HBC's treaty policy was driven by expediency. The Cree signatories to any purchases that might have been made were sparsely populated nomadic peoples, certainly not people who practised cultivation or built any permanent structures. Neither did the company intend to make extensive use of the land surrounding the forts it was establishing there. No principles of Indigenous title except expediency can explain why the HBC Governor and Committee sought treaties in the Hudson Bay lowlands for a few years in the late seventeenth century, but not during the subsequent 130 years in the interior where the Indigenous communities were more populous and powerful and the company used the land more intensively.

Thirteen decades after abandoning all pretence of purchasing Indigenous land, the HBC had established trading posts across a vast swathe of northern North America. While some posts were in territories not much more densely populated than the Hudson Bay lowlands, those in and along the margins of the northern plains were among populous and powerful Indigenous communities. Moreover, some of them, including Edmonton and Carlton, were surrounded by cultivated fields and livestock. Yet, the HBC made only one land purchase in the interior of North America in its entire history. The so-called Selkirk Treaty of 18 July 1817 is relevant to the history of the Vancouver Island treaties because HBC officials considered using it as a template for the Vancouver Island treaties. Understanding that treaty helps us better understand the Vancouver Island treaties. In short, the few occasions upon which the HBC concluded land-purchase treaties with Indigenous peoples before 1850 are exceptions that prove the rule that the HBC denied Indigenous title to lands not actually cultivated or permanently occupied by Indigenous people.

During the 1680s, the Governor and Committee of the HBC directed some of its officers to conclude land purchases with Cree bands when they established new posts along the coast of Hudson Bay. The first land-purchase agreement made – or purported to have been made – by any agent of the HBC occurred in late 1668. If the purchase was made, it represents the first Indigenous land purchase concluded within the present-day boundaries of Canada, and probably among the earliest in the British world. In 1683, James Hayes, the Deputy Governor of the HBC, claimed that Zachariah Gillam, captain of the HBC's *Nonsuch*, had made the agreement during the company's inaugural trading mission to Hudson Bay. According to Hayes, in September 1668, even before "The Governor and Company of Adventurers of England, trading into Hudson's Bay" had received its charter, Gillam arrived at the mouth of a river near the bottom of James Bay "where he met with the Native Indians & haveing made a league of Friendship wth. the Capt. of the said River & firmely purchased both the river it selfe & the Lands there aboute, he gave it the Name of Rupert River."[3] Given the fact that Gillam's instructions from the Governor and Committee of the HBC did not mention purchasing land from the Indigenous inhabitants of the territory, and given that the unchartered company may not have had the authority to do so, Gillam probably did so – or claimed to have done so – on his own initiative, inspired by purchases made in New England.[4]

The thirty-year-old Gillam had been born and raised in Massachusetts, the son of a prominent Boston merchant and shipbuilder, Benjamin Gillam.[5] The Gillams lived in Massachusetts during pivotal years when land-purchase agreements with Indigenous communities emerged as a common way for rivals to buttress their claims to land. The origins of those treaties along the northeastern seaboard of North America after 1625 are crucial for an understanding of land-purchase agreements throughout the English-speaking world.[6] Land-transfer treaties in the 1600s were negotiated by and at the initiative of officials connected with various English colonies and companies without any evidence that the English Crown considered land-transfer treaties as necessary or legally significant.

The first land-transfer treaties signed within the British world were signed in the 1620s between representatives of New England colonies and neighbouring Indigenous groups, emulating prior transactions negotiated by officials of the Dutch West India Company (WIC) with Indigenous neighbours of the New Netherlands.[7] These land-transfer treaties are historically significant in that they set a precedent of a type: they demonstrated that such treaties with Indigenous peoples were inexpensive political expedients worth using in other contexts when the situation recommended it. They are important for our understanding of land purchases in the HBC, because the origin of treaties in the HBC is in the treaties of New England and New Netherlands in the 1620s, not in the Royal Proclamation of 1763.

During the period of dramatic European expansion beginning in the late 1400s, all European powers asserted the justice and legality of their acquisition of land outside of Europe, but during the years of early exploration and settlement they did not agree about what made such appropriations valid. Depending on their own interests and national cultures, Portugal, Spain, and France typically invoked papal grants, the right of discovery, the performance of ceremonies of possession, and/or the conversion (and otherwise conquest) of non-Christian peoples to support their claims to territories outside Europe.[8] The English and the Dutch were latecomers to exploration and colonization, so those arguments did not work well for them. To support their claims, those countries therefore tended to add to claims of discovery arguments related to Crown grants, patents, and charters, and/or prior occupation. However, during the early seventeenth century, Dutch and English colonists began using land-transfer agreements with Indigenous peoples to further bolster their claims against those of colonists from other countries, and even against colonists from the same country. The English and Dutch colonial systems gave the leaders of their colonies and companies the latitude to make treaties with Indigenous people; officials in the more centralized French and Spanish empires did not have such authority.

The conduct of the English/British Crown before 1763 implies that the Crown did not acknowledge Indigenous land rights, even if its own subjects had already initiated the process by which Indigenous title was being made and defined. In 1606, King James I, in the charter of the Virginia Company, gave licence to the company:

> to make Habitation, Plantation, and to deduce a colony of sundry of our People into that part of America commonly called VIRGINIA, and other parts and Territories in America, either appertaining unto us, or which are not now actually possessed by any Christian Prince or People, situate, lying, and being all along the Sea Coasts, between four and thirty Degrees of Northerly Latitude from the Equinoctial Line, and five and forty Degrees of the same Latitude, and in the main Land between the same four and thirty and five and forty Degrees, and the Islands hereunto adjacent, or within one hundred Miles of the Coast thereof.[9]

The only obligation to Indigenous people placed upon officials of the company was to propagate "the Christian religion to such people, as yet live in darkness and miserable ignorance of the true knowledge and worship of God, and may yet bring the infidels and savages, living in those parts, to human civility, and to a settled and quiet government."[10] Likewise, in his royal patent for Massachusetts (1628), King Charles I instructed the colonists to "wynn and incite the Natives of [the] Country, to the Knowledg and Obedience of the onlie true God and Savior of Mankinde, and the Christian Fayth."[11] The Charter of the HBC, granted by King Charles II on 2 May 1670, followed precedent by granting lands to the company without any stipulation regarding Indigenous title:

> We have given, granted and confirmed, and by these Presents, for Us, Our Heirs and Successors, DO give, grant, and confirm, unto the said Governor and Company, and their Successors, the sole Trade and Commerce of all those Seas, Streights, Bays, Rivers, Lakes, Creeks, and Sounds, in whatsoever Latitude they shall be, that lie within the Entrance of the Streights commonly called Hudson's Streights, together with all the Lands and Territories upon the Countries, Coasts and Confines of the Seas, Bays, Lakes, Rivers, Creeks, and Sounds aforesaid, that are not already actually possessed by or granted to any of our Subjects or possessed by the Subjects of any other Christian Prince or State.[12]

The charter furthermore declared the HBC "the true and absolute Lords and Proprietors, of the same Territory, Limits and Places aforesaid." The Crown undoubtedly felt empowered to make such a grant by the fact that earlier English expeditions led by Thomas Button, Luke Foxe, and Thomas James had explored the region, had erected crosses at various places along the coast of Hudson Bay, and had given names to rivers, points of land, and territories, to stake England's claim to the territories bordering the inland sea.[13] There is no evidence from English charters or patents, or from the practice of the English Crown, that the Crown recognized Indigenous title before 1763.

Rival land claims of the Dutch in New Netherlands and English colonists at Plymouth and Massachusetts Bay between 1620 and 1650 explain the origins of land-transfer treaties. These competing claims were complex, but because of them no European claimant could easily appeal to any doctrine – right of discovery, oldest government charter, or earliest effective occupation – to establish an irrefutable right to the lands which they claimed.[14] However, the English government did rely on such arguments to bolster claims to the North American eastern seaboard. For example, in December 1621, the English ambassador to the Netherlands, Sir Dudley Carleton, was directed to complain on behalf of the English government of the unlawfulness of the Dutch colony at the mouth of the Hudson River. The letter from the English government to Carleton read:

> Whereas his Majesty's subjects have, many years since, taken possession of the whole precinct, and inhabited some parts of the north of Virginia, (by us called New England,) of all which countries, his Majesty hath, in like manner, some years since, by Patent, granted the quiet and full possession unto particular persons; nevertheless we understand, that the year past, the Hollanders have entered upon some part thereof, and have left a Colony, and given new names to the several ports appertaining to that part of the country, and are now in readiness to send for their supply six or eight ships, – whereof His Majesty being advertised, we have received his Royal Commandment to signify his pleasure that you should represent these things to the States General, in his Majesty's name, (who, *jure primæ occupationis*, hath good and sufficient title to those parts) and require of them that, as well those ships, as their further prosecution of that Plantation may be presently stayed.[15]

Clearly, the English government based its land claim on first occupation and royal patent. It did not mention Indigenous rights. The situation became only more complex in 1624 when the WIC took control of the New Netherlands after receiving a patent from the Dutch States

General.[16] Unlike the HBC's charter (and other English charters), the WIC's charter included no grant of land but did give the WIC a twenty-four-year monopoly on trade and the authority to make treaties.[17] Until then, the Dutch claimed Manhattan Island only by right of discovery and occupation. In April 1625, the company's Amsterdam directors, having concluded that they needed more grounds upon which to defend their claims against English complaints, instructed its first local Director General, Willem Verhulst, to make land-purchase agreements with Indigenous people, although Verhulst's directorship ended before the task was completed.[18] Thus it was Peter Minuit, Verhulst's successor, who, as the nineteenth-century historian John Romeyn Brodhead famously wrote, completed the agreement "by which the entire island of Manhattan, ... was ceded by the native proprietors, to the Dutch West India Company, 'for the value of sixty guilders,' or about twenty four dollars of our present currency."[19] A century and a half later, historian Mark Meuwese less famously wrote that to bolster the weight of purchases from Indigenous people, Verhulst should "conclude written agreements with the Indians, 'signed according to their customs,' when purchasing land. According to the Amsterdam directors, these 'contracts could be very useful to the Company in other situations,' meaning situations where the English challenged the Dutch."[20]

Thus, the first land-transfer treaty in North America originated in the efforts of WIC officials to bolster land claims against rival English claims in the knowledge that their right to occupy the Hudson River region based on any other arguments – right of discovery, first actual occupation, or charter – was vulnerable. Since the Dutch and English were at peace, English colonists at this time could not consider conquering New Netherlands.[21] The WIC produced at least forty written land-transfer deeds in New Netherlands, typically adopting both Dutch and Indigenous protocols and traditions to ensure that the Indigenous signatories respected and understood the terms of the treaties.[22] The WIC also used these land purchases to assert its rights against the Dutch States General.[23]

Some English colonists realized the potential value of the Dutch innovation. If WIC officials insisted that purchases added weight to their claims, they would have to respect similar purchases made by the English. On 19 March 1628, King Charles I granted a charter to the Massachusetts Bay Company. The charter granted the company land between the Charles and Merrimack Rivers. During the same year, John Endicott led the company's preliminary voyage to North America. On 19 April 1629 the company's directors wrote their first general letter of instruction to Endicott and its Council, stipulating that "if any of the salvages pretend right of inheritance to all or any part of the lands granted in our patent, we pray you endeavour to purchase their title, that we may avoid the least scruple of intrusion."[24] In their second general letter of instructions, dated 28 May 1629, the Company referred to their first letter before ordering Endicott and his Council:

> to discover and find out all such pretenders, and by advice of the Council there to make such reasonable composition with them as may free us and yourselves from any scruple of intrusion; and to this purpose, if it might be conveniently done, to compound and conclude with them all, or as many as you can, at one time, not doubting but by your discreet ordering of this business, the natives will be willing to treat and compound with you upon very easy conditions.[25]

Endicott's instructions came from the directors of the company, not from the Crown, and these instructions were clearly based on the belief that signing treaties could be an inexpensive expedient.[26] These purchases, now pursued and respected by colonists from two different countries, played an early part in a process by which the notion of Indigenous title would become weightier over time.

With the arrival of the Massachusetts Bay colonists and the expansion of the older nearby Plymouth colony, which did not occupy land granted it by charter, rival claims among English and Dutch colonists in the region became complicated and pressing. Matters came to a head in the spring of 1632 after bad weather forced a Dutch ship, the *Eendracht*, to take refuge at Plymouth during a voyage from New Amsterdam. The ship was arrested on the charge of illegal trade.[27] In the ensuing dispute, the Dutch mustered the usual evidence for their right to occupy New Netherlands – discovery, prior occupation, government charter – but also disputed England's right in Brodhead's words, "to claim sovereignty over territories of which the Dutch had obtained the title, by treaty and honest purchase from the native owners."[28]

The English government respected claims based on discovery, occupation, and charter, but it rejected this last claim. It replied that the Indians were not "bona fide possessors" of the land, and that the Dutch had furthermore been unable to prove "that all the savages had contracted to the Dutch title by purchase."[29] Nevertheless, Charles I, unwilling to risk conflict with his Dutch allies, released the *Eendracht*. Thereafter the Dutch continued to make purchase agreements with Indigenous communities.[30] In 1632, disputes over the Connecticut Valley loomed. Brodhead explained that "it was, therefore, thought expedient that, to their [Dutch WIC] existing rights by discovery, and exclusive visitation, should be added the more definite title, by purchase from the aborigines. In the course of the following summer, the Dutch traders on the Connecticut were accordingly directed to arrange with the native Indians for the purchase of 'most all the lands on both sides of the river.'"[31]

In addition to their attempt to establish a right by making a purchase, the Dutch claimed the moral high ground by purchasing Indigenous land. Wouter Van Twiller, Minuit's successor as Director of New Netherlands, wrote in the fall of 1633 that "it is not the intent of the States to take the land from the poor natives, as the King of Spain hath done by the Pope's donation, but rather to take it from the said natives at some reasonable and convenient price, which, God be praised, we had done hitherto. In this part of the world are divers heathen lands that are empty of inhabitants, so that a little part or portion thereof, there needs not [be] any question."[32] Van Twiller's rhetoric cleverly avoided criticizing the English by condemning the behaviour of the common enemy of the Dutch and English.[33]

In the face of Dutch purchases of land in the Connecticut Valley, it was strategic for the Plymouth colonists to follow suit, since the Plymouth colonists could appeal to no charter to support their expansion into the Connecticut valley. So, in 1633 the Plymouth Colony purchased land from Natawanute – evidently their first land purchase. Natawanute told the Plymouth colonists that the Pequot had driven him from the land, and then sold that land to the Dutch.[34] Once the Dutch and the Plymouth colonists had signed treaties, their officials had to respect the right of rivals to conclude treaties, inevitably contributing to the making of Indigenous title. Given that these treaties were inexpensive, there was little reason to refuse to sign them. Soon towns in Massachusetts Bay were signing land-transfer treaties even for land upon which they had already built.[35] These treaties, Neal Salisbury has argued, were not based upon any legal principle, but "were pragmatic adaptations of those principles to a situation in which justice was not a consideration. They were employed, as the Company's directors had anticipated in 1629, when 'any of the salvages *pretend* right of inheritance to all or any part of the lands granted by our patent.'"[36]

Not only colonial officials, but also private individuals seized on the possibility of buying land from Indigenous people. Before long, however, the General Court of Massachusetts Bay stipulated that individuals needed the General Court's approval of all land purchases from Indians.[37] In this way, the General Court participated in the process that established the principle that agents of the Crown had the exclusive right to extinguish Indigenous title. Private individuals could not purchase land directly from Indigenous people.

In 1630, John Winthrop (1588–1649) became first Governor of the Massachusetts Bay Colony. He argued that the Indigenous communities, not possessing sovereignty, did not have legal rights to the land. In 1629 Winthrop wrote that "the first right was naturall when men held the earth in common, every man sowing and feeding where he pleased: Then as men and cattel [sic] increased, they appropriated some parcells of ground by enclosing and peculiar manurance, and this in tyme got them a civil right."[38] The Indians, argued Winthrop, did not acquire this right because they did not use the land intensively enough and did not settle in permanent towns. Winthrop's statement resembles the idea behind *terra nullius*, but no one used that term at the time.[39]

Despite Winthrop's argument, by 1633 – three years before Zachariah Gillam was born in Boston – the Massachusetts Bay Company began signing treaties without acknowledging that they had any obligation to do so, and without any orders from the English Crown. The behaviour of the Massachusetts Bay Colony, at least after 1633, does not always seem consistent with this belief, but the colony never officially conceded the existence of Indigenous title. Subsequently, other officials connected with colonies, most famously William Penn and Pennsylvania, signed land-transfer treaties, but without instructions from the English Crown, and often to bolster their claims against other English claimants.[40] So, governments, and even private individuals, had been basing their claims to land against foreign and domestic rivals during Gillam's entire life in Massachusetts. Gillam simply adopted – or later claimed to have adopted – the same practice at the mouth of the Rupert River in 1668. It was the first land-purchase agreement with Indigenous people made within the present-day boundaries of Canada.

Notwithstanding that some officials in British colonies began negotiating land-transfer treaties, the historical documents show that the English Crown did not follow suit. The work of legal theorists of the eighteenth century summarizes the belief among European nations in the eighteenth century that they were not obligated to negotiate land-transfer treaties with Indigenous communities, particularly with those who did not practise agriculture.[41] The Crown in London appears to have been reluctant to acknowledge, ratify, or endorse any of the land-purchase agreements made by its subjects until it issued the Royal Proclamation of 1763, at which time it promised to purchase land from Indigenous people only in lands specifically reserved for Indians. It explicitly excluded Rupert's Land from these guarantees. For its part, the government of the United States, having repudiated the Royal Proclamation of 1763 upon declaring independence, did not commit to purchasing Indian title until it passed the Northwest Ordinance in 1787.

Although treaties throughout the British world and the United States of America have their origins in colonial New Netherlands and New England, the history of treaties in the HBC, Canada, and the United States took divergent paths.

The practice of Dutch and English colonists and the Indigenous peoples with whom they treated in the 1620s, set in motion the slow process that made and defined Indigenous title. The English Crown appears to have avoided commenting on such treaties in the early 1600s, but when forced to, as it was in the case of a purchase by William Claiborne in 1635, it denied their legitimacy.[42] Or as in the case of the Charter for the Colony of Providence (1643), the Crown acknowledged that English inhabitants at Narraganset Bay "have also purchased, and are purchasing of and amongst the said Natives, some other Places, which may be convenient both for Plantations, and also for building of Ships, Supply of Pipe Staves and other Merchandize," but it did not instruct colonists to purchase land, nor did it comment on the significance of these purchases.[43] The process was slow enough that courts did not recognize or define Indigenous title for many decades thereafter, but it was in the crucible of the 1620s on the Atlantic seaboard of North America, that the process, unbeknown to the historical actors, began.

If Zachariah Gillam did negotiate a land purchase at the mouth of Rupert River in 1668, he undoubtedly did so to bolster HBC claims against any claims the French might make or had already made to the same territory.[44] The French did later claim that Guillaume Couture, having been invited by Cree visitors from Hudson Bay to do so, made a "Voyage in the year 1663 and Caused a New Crosse to bee affixed on the Lands at the Bottom of the Bay, and the Kings Armes Ingraven upon Copper fixed between two peeces of Lead at the Bottom of a Greate Tree."[45] If Guillaume Couture did as the French claimed he had, it is likley that the Cree people Gillam met in 1668 apprised him of Couture's ceremony of possession.[46]

Whether or not Couture's expedition was fiction, the French took notice of the HBC's activities on Hudson Bay almost as soon as they began. To counter Gillam's post (Fort Charles) at Rupert River, a French party led by Father Charles Albanel travelled overland in 1671–72 from Quebec to investigate English activities there and to trade with the local peoples. While there, Albanel baptized some Cree and "planted a Crosse and left the Kings Armes upon a Tree by Consent of Capt. Kias Kow chiefe of all the Savages which Inhabite the North Sea & Hudson's Bay."[47] However, the French did not assert their claims to Hudson Bay aggressively during the 1670s.

In the late 1670s, as the relationship between the English and French Crowns deteriorated and French activity increased, the HBC's Governor and Committee became alarmed.[48] For their part, realizing that the HBC was drawing off furs that would otherwise go to New France, the French responded more assertively to the HBC in 1680s. In 1680, the Quebec merchant Charles Aubert de la Chesnay travelled to France to seek the support of King Louis XIV of France for his efforts to trade into Hudson Bay, and in 1682, he established a partnership, the Compagnie de la Baie d'Hudson (CBH).[49] Since the French and English Crowns were then at peace, the Governor of New France, Joseph-Antoine Le Febvre de La Barre, a supporter of the CBH, also undertook diplomatic rather than military efforts to press French claims to Hudson Bay. In early January 1683, the French ambassador submitted a letter to the English government, claiming that the French king had taken possession of the coast of Hudson Bay a full twenty years earlier.[50]

It was in response to the French ambassador's 1683 letter that James Hayes first mentioned Gillam's purported purchase. Writing to King Charles II, Hayes emphasized the rights gained by discovery, Crown charter, actual occupation, and the naming of geographical features, but he also mentioned land purchases from the Cree. In the first place, he appealed to past English explorers, such as Martin Frobisher, Henry Hudson, and Thomas Button, who had "for above 100 yeares last past Discovered and frequented the said Bay & the Rivers Islands & Territorys thereabouts and from time to time in the reignes of severall of your Royall Predecessors have taken possession of severall places there."[51] He also noted that Zachariah Gillam had discovered and named Rupert River, "and built [Charles] Fort, & tooke possession of the said River & all the Land & Territory there aboute in the name of your Majesty."[52] Hayes also cited the company's charter. But he also relied upon the purchase and agreement of the Indians.[53] After mentioning Gillam's 1668 purchase (already quoted) Hayes claimed that "the above mentioned agreemt. made by Zachary Gillam with the Indians was afterwards repeated and confirmed wth. one Charles Baily [Bayly] who was sent as Governour [sic] of the affaires of the Company with in the said Bay," and that the company had made additional forts "still making solemne compacts and Agreements with the Natives for their Rivers & Territories."[54] The wording of all of the claims except the one relating to 1668, however, makes it uncertain whether Hayes purported that the agreements with the Cree were commercial agreements or land purchases. E.E. Rich has indicated that in 1673, at Moose Fort, Charles Bayly made a treaty with local Indians "giving the English trading rights and possession of the soil."[55] Then, in 1674, at the

Albany River, Bayly "treated with the King, and his Son made them a promise to come with a Ship and trade with them the next Year."[56] It is unclear whether Bayly's treaty included a land purchase. The English government responded to the French ambassador, in part, by including a French translation of most of Hayes's letter, including the references to purchases made from the Indians.[57] There is no indication that anyone in the English government knew about the purchases before that time, and there is no indication that the English government placed any weight upon the purchases.

Alert to the growing danger of French claims and activities in the early 1680s, company officials intensified their efforts to bolster their claim to the lands surrounding Hudson Bay. They did so by beginning to instruct the HBC's North American traders to purchase land from the Cree. Their instructions state that the company's orders were rooted in securing its claims against foreign powers, not in notions of Indigenous title. For example, in May 1680, the London Committee cited the fact that "wee are informed there are designs already on foot of interloping," and the "designs of our enemies," when they ordered John Nixon to establish posts in advantageous locations, and to "contrive to make compact wth. the Captns. or chiefs of the respective Rivers & places, whereby it might be understood by them that you had purchased both the lands & rivers of them, or at least the only freedome of trade."[58] Nixon was also told to "cause them to do some act wch. by the Religion or Custome of their Country should be thought most sacred & obliging to them for the confirmation of such Agreements."[59] The directors' instructions to use the "Religion or Custome of their Country" indicates that they (like the directors of the WIC) thought it was important that the Indigenous people understood that they were parties to a solemn agreement. The lack of instructions to produce documents might be explained by the fact that the English rarely produced written deeds of Indigenous land purchases before the mid-seventeenth century.[60]

After being confronted with the French diplomatic letter, the Governor and Committee continued instructing the company's traders to secure land purchases. In a letter of instructions of 15 May 1682 (see figure 4) the directors ordered John Bridgar when establishing a post at Port Nelson to "Endeavor to make such Contracts with the Natives for the River in & about Port Nelson as may in future times ascertain to us a right & property therein and the Sole Liberty of trade & Comerce [sic] there, and to make Leagues of friendship & peaceable Cohabitation with such Ceremonies as you shall finde to bee most Sacred and Obligatory amongst them."[61]

During the summer of 1682, the CBH, led by HBC defectors Radisson and Groseilliers, established a trading post at the mouth of the Hayes and Nelson rivers, shortly before Bridgar's HBC ship, the *Prince Rupert*, arrived to establish a fort at Port Nelson (although shortly after interlopers from Boston, led by Benjamin Gillam, Zachariah Gillam's son, had also done so). The HBC competed alongside the French all winter, but the French seized the HBC traders and destroyed their post in the spring of 1683.[62] Unfortunately for the CBH, in 1684, after the diplomats had argued the relative merits of the French and English claims to Port Nelson, the French government ordered that Port Nelson be returned to the HBC.[63]

On 27 April 1683, sensing the growing French threat to its operations in Hudson Bay, the Governor and Committee warned Henry Sergeant, the company's top bayside officer, that "you must look upon them [the French of Canada] as a standing Enemy from whom you are never to expect any Friendship or faire Dealeing."[64] Sergeant was instructed to seize French interlopers if they were "within the limits of our Charter."[65] This certainly suggests that the company was relying, in the first case, upon its charter to defend its claims against all foreigners. The Committee also urged Sargeant to use all appropriate measures "to conciliate the good will and Friendship of the Natives thereabouts by wch. means you will have early notice & Intelligence from them of any Designe the French may have upon us."[66] They later continued with the following order:

> There is another thing we have alwaies given in our Instructions to your Predecessors & now repeate it to you as a thing of very great Importance to the Comp$^a$. and that is that in the severall places where we are already settled or shall hereafter make new Discoveries you contrive to make such compacts and Agreements with the Capts. and chiefs of the Rivers & Territories that our right & propriety therein may be alwaies understood & owned by them and the sole freedome of Trade there and let such Leagues of Friendship as they are capable of makeing be made wth. them by such Ceremonies as you shall finde to be most sacred and obligatorey to them.[67]

The urgent tone of the letter to Sargeant was clearly influenced by renewed French activity in the bay. Nevertheless, it is not certain that Sergeant or any other trader actually made land purchases – no written deed or treaty has been preserved. Moreover, after a French expedition captured Rupert House (at the mouth of the Rupert River), Moose Factory, and Fort Albany in 1686, the HBC continued to defend its claims based on right of discovery, its charter, its naming of geographical features, and its occupation, but no longer based on any purported land purchases.[68] Indeed, in 1687, the HBC mentioned Gillam's 1668 expedition, but revised its account to claim only that Gillam "mett with Native Indians, with whom haveing made a League of Freindshipp, hee gave it the name of Rupert River, ... and built a Forte there, which hee called Charles Fort."[69] Even as the French appear never to have bothered refuting the legitimacy of purchases from the Cree, the HBC appears to have concluded by 1687 that its claims to have made such purchases carried little or no weight.[70] Basing claims on purchase became even more futile in 1689 when war broke out between France and England. Thereafter, conquest and actual occupation of locations were all that mattered between French and English rivals. More than 160 years would pass before the HBC was next connected with a purchase of land from Indigenous people.

The HBC always defended its claims to land primarily upon its charter, discoveries, rites of possession, and actual occupation of land. For example, in 1687, when the HBC gathered evidence to defend its rights to the Port Nelson area against French claims, it acquired a sworn statement by Nehemiah Walker that stated that Governor Bayly, with his party, "arrived in port nelson River in September 1670 and the said Governor Baily and this Deponent and Severall of the Shipps crew, went on Shoare on the North Side of the Said River, and lay in an Indian Tent, they found there, one night, and the next day the said Governor Baily in the presence of this Deponent and the rest with him, Declared he tooke possession of Port Nelson and all the Lands and Territoryes thereof, for his Matie. and in tocken thereof nayld up the King's Armes in Brasse on a Small Tree there."[71] On that occasion, Bayly was precluded from making any agreement with Indigenous people by the fact that he encountered none. After the mid-1680s, the Governor and Committee of the HBC ceased instructing its traders to arrange land purchases. Had the Governor and Committee continued to believe that it was either just or expedient to make land purchases, they would have instructed Henry Kelsey, one of the first HBC men to travel a substantial distance inland, to purchase lands. However, in 1690 Kelsey noted in his awkward verse-journal that "I took possession on th$^e$ tenth Instant July/And for my masters I speaking for th$^m$, all/This neck of land I deerings point did call."[72] The behaviour of the HBC between 1668 and 1690 suggests that the Governor and Committee (may have) sought to purchase Indigenous lands, or at least claimed to have purchased Indigenous lands when they believed that such purchases might support their claims against the French, but abandoned all pretence of making such purchases in the second half of the 1680s when the French simply ignored them.

HBC "explorers" normally followed long-standing English/British practice, as did Kelsey in 1690, in taking possession of newly "discovered" land by performing rituals or ceremonies of possession – building structures, naming geographical features, and making maps – that did not require the approval, or even the knowledge, of Indigenous people, as Kelsey did in 1690. For example, when Moses Norton sent Samuel Hearne inland to search for the "Coppermine" River, about which HBC personnel had heard since about 1716, he instructed Hearne that if the Coppermine proved navigable "you are to take possession of the same in behalf of the Hon.^ble Hudsons Bay Company as first processors by Cutting out on some Remarkable place or places on the Rocks with a Superscription of your Name the Date of the Month Year, &c. you are also to take the same method with any other River that you think Can Conduce to the Benefit of the Company."[73] The first edition of Hearne's journals, published in 1795, indicates that in July 1771 when Hearne was near the mouth of the Coppermine River, "For the sake of form, ... after having had some consultation with the Indians, I erected a mark and took possession of the coast, on behalf of the Hudson's Bay Company."[74]

Agents of the HBC continued performing acts of possession into the years immediately preceding the Vancouver Island treaties. For example, in August 1837, at Point Barrow, when the HBC expedition led by Peter Warren Dease and Thomas Simpson turned back at Point Barrow during their explorations of the Arctic coast, they "hoisted their flag, and with three cheers took possession of their discoveries in his Majesty's name."[75] Simpson later wrote James Hargrave that "Two large villages of the natives witnessed our ceremony of taking possession at Cape Barrow, and joined their shouts with ours."[76] During the following year's explorations, Thomas Simpson reported that at Kent Peninsula "I took possession of the country, with the usual ceremonial, in the name of the Honourable Company, and for the Queen of Great Britain."[77] And on 19 April 1847 – three years before the Vancouver Island treaties were concluded – John Rae, exploring in the Arctic on behalf of the HBC, near Boothia Peninsula, reported that "having taken possession of our discoveries with the usual formalities, we traced the inlet eastward."[78] Similarly, when he reached the end point of his survey of the Melville Peninsula, he wrote "we took possession of our discoveries with the usual formalities, and retraced our steps."[79] And, most relevant to the history of the Vancouver Island treaties, on 3 August 1847, when the ambiguous wording of the Oregon Treaty of 1846 made the possession of some of the Gulf Islands in the Salish Sea uncertain, Roderick Finlayson (1818–1892) wrote in the Fort Victoria post journal

that "Early this morning I started out in Canoe with [Thomas] Ouamtany and [François Xavier] Cote & 5 Indians for Belle view Island to
take possession of it, pursuant to orders from Mr. C.F. Douglas, travelled
nearly from one end of it to the other & erected poles at a few places
showing my having taken possession of it in H. Britic M's name."[80]

Unless the Governor and Committee of the HBC had an extraordinary corporate memory in 1848, they knew nothing of the HBC's treaty
policy of the 1680s, but they did know that Thomas Douglas, the Fifth
Earl of Selkirk, had concluded a "deed" of purchase with the Saulteaux
and Cree of the Red River Valley on 18 July 1817, and aspects of that
agreement are relevant to the Vancouver Island treaties (see figure 5).[81]

On 12 June 1811, the Governor and Committee of the HBC granted
more than 300,000 square kilometres (116,000 square miles) – an area
larger than Great Britain – to Lord Selkirk to establish an agricultural
colony in the Red River Valley.[82] The HBC's grant stipulated that the
HBC had the authority to grant the land on the basis that they "are
seized to them and their successors in fee simple, as absolute lords and
proprietors of all the lands and territories ... called Rupert's Land."[83]
The HBC directors obviously believed that they could grant land to
Lord Selkirk without the consent of Indians, and without compensating the Indians. The first settlers arrived at Red River in the autumn of
1812.

The timing of the Selkirk Treaty is significant. In 1811, Selkirk instructed Miles Macdonell, slated to be the colony's first governor, that
"if the jealousy of the Indians appears to be roused, the proposal of
purchasing the land must be brought forward. The purchase ought to
be, in part at least, and as much as possible by way of annuity, rather
than a price to be paid at once. An annuity ... will form a permanent
hold over their peaceable behaviour, as they must be made to understand that if any individual or the tribe violates the treaty, the payment
will be withheld."[84] But no treaty was negotiated at the time. Instead,
Lord Selkirk hurriedly concluded a treaty for only a small portion of
the granted land on 18 July 1817, almost six years after he received his
grant, and almost five years after colonists arrived.[85] Why?

Between 1812 and 1817, the Red River Colony became one of the
main theatres of a virtual private war between the North West Company (NWC) and the HBC. During those years, in its attempt to destroy
the Red River Colony, the NWC attempted with some success to incite
the Saulteaux and Cree bands and the Métis against the colony. On 18
October 1814, the HBC surveyor and trader at Red River, Peter Fidler,
wrote that "Captn [Cuthbert] Grant an Indian tells bad stories when he
is drunk about their Lands being taken from them – this is put into his

head by the Canadians – all others seem very glad to see white people Come to Cultivate their Lands & they imagine that for the future they will want nothing."[86] Reports of the violent conflicts between the NWC and HBC at Red River and elsewhere spurred Canadian and British officials to act. In response to news of the Battle of Seven Oaks (June 1816), the Governor General of British North America, Sir John C. Sherbrooke, commissioned William B. Coltman, a respected member of the Executive Council of Lower Canada, and John Fletcher, a Quebec lawyer, to investigate. Sherbrooke also gave Coltman an appointment as lieutenant-colonel in the Indian Department.[87] Not surprisingly, Lord Selkirk, whose interests were those of the HBC, understood that a commission of Canadians appointed by a Governor of Canada to investigate a dispute between the HBC and an influential Canadian company (the NWC) would – at least initially – probably be sympathetic to NWC. He shrewdly acted accordingly.

William Coltman arrived at Red River in late spring 1817 to begin his investigation (Fletcher did not travel beyond Fort William). On 17 July, Selkirk informed Coltman that "some weeks ago," Selkirk or his representatives had negotiated the terms of a land purchase with Saulteaux and Cree bands at Red River.[88] He then invited Coltman to attend the signing of the agreement. Selkirk was upfront about his motives. Even as Coltman was meeting with the Saulteaux and Cree leaders, he received a letter from Selkirk that frankly stated that Selkirk sought the agreement to refute the NWC's argument that the local Saulteaux and Cree resented the Red River colonists:

> You are aware that one of the allegations which have been made in vindication of the NW.Cº is that the outrages committed here, have arisen from the jealousy of the native Indians against agricultural settlements, & their resentment against my Settlers for having taken possession of their lands without their consent or any purchase from them. – I believe you have already heard enough to satisfy you how little foundation there is for any such idea. But it would be still more satisfactory if the sentiments of the Indians on that point were explicitly & formaly declared in your presence, & still more so, if they would consent to a specific cession of a portion of their lands to be set aside for the express purpose of agricultural settlements.
>
> With a view to obviate misrepresentation & to show in a more decided manner their sense of the benefits likely to arise from agricultural Settlements, I would propose to them not a sale, but a Gift. If a large quantity of goods were offered for the purchase it might be said that the temptation of immediate advantage had induced them to sacrifice their permanent interests. I would therefore purpose to them merely a small annual present,

in the nature of a quitrent, or acknowledgment of their right: – & having specified what I intend to give in this way, I would leave it to themselves to specify the boundaries of the lands which they agree to give up on that consideration, & to appropriate to me for the exclusive use of the Settlers.[89]

Selkirk added that the treaty would serve to validate the HBC's interpretation of its 1670 Charter: "I am aware that such a cession from the Indians can be of no avail unless the grant of K. Charles 2$^{nd}$ to the H.B.C°. be found to include this country. But at all events the transaction would serve to facilitate the Settlement of the Country under Crown grants, in the event of my title being found defective."[90] Selkirk was eager to have Coltman, as a government agent, participate in the process, actually inviting Coltman to amend the draft agreement: "If you approve of the suggestions I will transmit without delay for your revisal, a draft of such a Deed as may answer the purpose."[91] On the same day, Coltman responded by writing that:

Nothing could be more satisfactory than all that I have heard of the sentiments expressed throughout this conference by the Indians in general even by some among them who are considered as the most attached to the NWCo. & it is particularly pleasing to observe that they consent to make the proposed cession of land for a direct & nominal consideration of trifling value, it is because they form a just estimate of the collateral advantages which they will obtain from a progress in the arts of civilized life.[92]

Then, perhaps before his meeting with the Cree and Saulteaux had ended, Coltman wrote another letter to say that:

It appears to me as far as I can yet see that the Indians wish the Settlement for their own advantage & would scarcely require any consideration for allowing to the Settlers an exclusive possession of a reasonable portion of land something will however perhaps be expected as the subject has been so much talked of & certainly an annual present seems best, as it is evident that the interests of the colony would require the Indians friendship to be ensured in this manner even if they gave their lands voluntarily.[93]

The impression gained by Coltman was substantiated years later by Peguis (c. 1774–1864), a Saulteaux signatory to the Selkirk Treaty. In about 1857, he sent a letter to the Aborigines Protection Society stating that:

We are not only willing, but very anxious after being paid for our lands, that the whites would come and settle among us, for we have already derived great benefits from their having done so, that is, not the traders, but the farmers. The traders have never done anything but rob and keep us poor, but the farmers have taught us how to farm and raise cattle. To the missionaries especially we are indebted, for they tell us every praying day (Sabbath) to be sober, honest, industrious, and truthful. They have told us the good news that Jesus Christ so loved the world that he gave himself for it, and that this was one of the first messages to us, "Peace on earth and good will to man." We wish to practise these good rules of the whites, and hope the Great Mother will do the same to us, and not only protect us from oppression and injustice, but grant us all the privileges of the whites.[94]

Understandably, although Coltman had as much authority as Selkirk to conclude a treaty on behalf of the British Crown, he wanted to maintain distance from Selkirk's plan. He responded by writing that "I shall take care & get the sentiments of the Indians on this & other subjects faithfully recorded, but have some doubts of the propriety of my taking part in any deed of Sale; on this point I will reflect and will at all events send to your Lordship before the Indians leave me & communicate to any Agent you may send what they say & my own ideas."[95] Selkirk had anticipated Coltman's reluctance and had previously assured him that "I am perfectly aware, that you do not give any pledge on the part of the Gov$^t$. on the subject of the sale by the Ind$^s$ & that it is only as a witness of the fairness of the transaction between us that you attend. But considering the misrepresentations to which I am continually exposed, I consider your testimony on that point as of the greatest consequence."[96]

Whether or not Coltman attended the transaction, he did not sign as an official witness. When the deed was signed the next day, Selkirk signed on behalf of the colony (although the treaty text stipulated that the land was ceded to "our Sovereign Lord the King," not to Selkirk, the Red River Colony, or the HBC) and all of the witnesses were associated with the Colony or the HBC.[97] The Indigenous signatories signed with pictographs representing their dodems.[98] According to Peter Fidler, representatives of the NWC "used every persuasion to prevent the Indians from signing it."[99] In May 1818, when he submitted his report to Sherbrooke, Coltman explained the treaty to his superior:

At the period of my leaving Red River, in September last, the number of settlers, chiefly Europeans, remaining there, might be from 100 to 150 men, of whom many had families. It was principally on account of these people, that I thought it right to give some encouragement to the inclination existing on the part of the Saulteaux Indians, to convey a portion of their lands to the Earl of Selkirk for an annual quit-rent; the particulars of this transaction, and of the precautions I took to avoid the possibilities of my committing Government.[100]

The HBC Governor and Committee's rejection of "outward claims" of the Indians on Vancouver Island in 1848 was consistent with its policies of the previous 180 years. On those few occasions upon which the Governor and Committee instructed its traders to execute land purchases, and the occasion upon which Lord Selkirk arranged a purchase from the Saulteaux and Cree of Red River, they did so for the sake of bolstering their own claims to land against foreign and domestic rivals, not because the company acknowledged Indigenous title.

Following the example set by the WIC and New Englanders in the 1620s, Zachariah Gillam – a New Englander employed by the HBC – claimed to have negotiated land purchases at Hudson Bay, and the HBC subsequently briefly adopted a land-purchase policy for reasons of expediency. However, it abandoned the policy by the 1690s. Selkirk similarly secured his 1817 treaty to bolster the HBC's land claims.

It is impossible to know whether the HBC's 1848 acknowledgment of Indigenous title to lands that were "cultivated or permanently occupied" was a change in policy or a new policy, because it was the first time the HBC Governor and Committee ever articulated a principle of Indigenous title. Indeed, it would be challenging to devise any principle – beyond expediency – to explain the fact that the Governor and Committee instructed the company's traders to conclude purchases along the coast of Hudson Bay (one of the most sparsely populated parts of Rupert's Land where the company itself carried out only minimal cultivation) but never sought to purchase land in other locations (especially along the margins of the plains where the company engaged in substantial cultivation and stock raising and where Indigenous communities were much more populous and formidable). In keeping with the words of the company's charter, the HBC always considered themselves "in fee simple, as absolute lords and proprietors of all the lands and territories" in Rupert's Land.[101] The company did not make that claim to any of the land in the Columbia District or Vancouver Island, but it could not take its position regarding Rupert's Land unless it also claimed that the British Crown enjoyed the unencumbered right to grant such title in all of its territories.

The HBC's explicit denial of Indigenous title in December 1848 was entirely in character for the company, but the circumstances on Vancouver Island in 1848 were similar enough to those along Hudson Bay between 1668 and 1683 and at Red River 1817 that it is possible to imagine why the HBC might have judged it expedient to conclude treaties. The evidence that Cree and Saulteaux signatories to the Selkirk Treaty welcomed the "collateral advantages" that they hoped the treaty would bring them, and the evidence that the Kwakiutl chiefs insisted on the Garden Treaty in 1850, suggests that a contextualist history of treaties should always inquire into the perspectives of Indigenous people. In a comparative study of Indigenous treaties in the Pacific Northwest, Daniel Boxberger correctly argued that "it can never be said with any degree of certainty how the words of the treaties were understood by the natives at the time of negotiation."[102] Even if we can achieve only a fragmentary and tentative understanding of the Indigenous perceptions of the Vancouver Island treaties, a full consideration of the treaties must include a deep history of Vancouver Island.

# 3 The History of the Northwest Coast to 1774

Intending at first to buy a small plot of land at Cordova Bay for the Vancouver Island Steam Saw Mill Company in February 1852, James Douglas decided instead to purchase the whole Saanich Peninsula because he found it "impossible to discover among the numerous claimants the real owners of the land in question."[1] A decade later, Richard C. Mayne (1835–1892), a Royal Navy officer who had conducted a nautical survey of Vancouver Island between 1857 and 1861, explained that, while it would be desirable to purchase land from Indigenous people on Vancouver Island, if "one chief or tribe were paid for a piece of land without the acknowledgement on the part of adjacent tribes of the vendor's right to the land sold, five or six other claimants would in all probability come forward asserting the land to be theirs, and founding their title to it upon some intermarriage of its former possessors."[2] These comments, and abundant evidence from other treaty negotiations for which there is more documentation, reveal that Indigenous treaty negotiators could be profoundly influenced by their social, economic, political, and geopolitical circumstances. Documents relating to the Vancouver Island treaty negotiations say little about the motivations and understandings of the chiefs who negotiated those treaties, but a survey of the deep history of Vancouver Island is crucial for understanding the relationships that formed between Indigenous villagers and exogenous peoples after 1774, and permits us to better understand the treaties.

Linguistic and archaeological evidence suggests that people lived on the Northwest Coast for many thousands of years. The extraordinary language diversity (forty-five distinct languages) along the Northwest Coast of North America, shows that the people lived there long enough for their languages to diverge significantly.[3] The linguistic history of the Northwest Coast is further complicated by the fact that some languages – even unrelated languages – converged over time. Such linguistic convergence suggests that many people moved permanently between and among communities (through intermarriage, adoption, and enslavement) for centuries.[4] Multilingualism must have been common. The discontinuous distribution of related languages along the Northwest Coast shows that communities displaced others before Europeans arrived (see figure 6).[5]

Representatives from two language families – Wakashan and Salishan – became signatories to the Vancouver Island treaties. Salishan languages probably developed originally in the resource-rich delta of the Fraser River.[6] The environmental uniformity and protected waterways of the Fraser delta and the rim of the Salish Sea facilitated the spread of Salishan speakers to the southern and eastern coasts of Vancouver Island and northward and southward along the mainland coasts.[7] Ease of travel along the rim of the Salish Sea permitted frequent interaction (peaceful and hostile) among the Salish speakers, explaining the many affinities among Halkomelem Salish dialects of those who had fisheries along the Fraser River, and among Northern Straits Salish dialects of those who used reef nets to harvest salmon in the Salish Sea.

The Wakashan languages probably originated on northwestern Vancouver Island, perhaps in the vicinity of Brooks Peninsula.[8] Differences between northern (Kwakiutlan) and southern (Nootkan) Wakashan languages suggest that those two branches of Wakashan diverged about 2,900 years ago.[9] Perhaps attracted by the salmon of the Nimpkish River – one of the few rivers on Vancouver Island with abundant sockeye salmon (*Oncorhynchus nerka*) runs – and the eulachon (*Thaleichthys pacificus*) of the Knight and Kingcome inlets, ancestors of the Kwaikiutl expanded eastward to northeastern Vancouver Island around 500 BC from western Vancouver Island, displacing or absorbing Salishan peoples.[10]

People may have inhabited the Northwest Coast of North America for fifteen thousand years or longer, but until about 6,000 years ago, it was an austere subarctic coast cooled by the effects of interior glaciers, much like today's coastal Greenland.[11] Sparse nomadic human communities employed broad subsistence strategies that included hunting large game, gathering shellfish, fishing for a variety of species, and gathering berries and roots. Around 5,000 years ago the larger rivers flowing from the interior stabilized sufficiently to support large salmon runs.[12] Shorter rivers, such as those on Vancouver Island, stabilized earlier. As the salmon and other marine resources proliferated, the people were drawn to depend more heavily upon them.[13] Over time, the Northwest Coast became an extraordinarily abundant region, but its resources did not fall onto the laps of Northwest Coast peoples.[14]

The salmon-dependent societies of the Northwest Coast emerged between 6,500 and 5,000 years ago and developed the social, political, and economic characteristics of the early contact era between 4,000 and 2,500 years ago.[15] The Northwest Coast was an ideal location for societies gradually to increase their reliance on fish and other marine resources. They did not initially need complex technology to catch fish and collect shellfish, but invented more sophisticated technologies to capture salmon, including hooks, spears, harpoons, weirs, traps, and nets, as their reliance on salmon intensified.[16] But full-time reliance on salmon required more than technological innovation. Because mature salmon were available for only part of the year, and because salmon spoil quickly after being harvested, nomadic communities employing broad subsistence strategies had to make comprehensive economic, social, political, and cultural adjustments to transition to year-round reliance on the resource. Scholars have assumed that if successful salmon dependence in the region required these changes, historical documents that described Northwest Coast lifeways in the late 1700s and early 1800s can be used cautiously to describe ways of life that had prevailed for at least two thousand years.

Thousands of years ago, salmon dependence also induced Northwest Coast peoples to develop semi-sedentary ways of life atypical of non-agricultural peoples. Northwest Coast winter villages normally comprised between 100 and 600 people consisting of households of between eighteen and twenty-five people (four to six families) (see figure 3).[17] These villages were stratified, comprising nobility, commoners, and slaves. Villages of under 100 people were uncommon and may not have been stratified, but may have been dominated by leaders of larger villages who could demand anything from them in exchange for protection.[18] Archaeological evidence is not amenable to proving the existence of slavery in the pre-contact era, but it offers clear evidence of inequality, including unequal access to wealth and nutrition.[19] The nobility (sometimes referred to as titleholders) wielded far more authority and influence than anyone could in most hunting-fishing-gathering societies. Considering the degree of social and economic inequality, Northwest Coast societies had remarkably weak and informal political systems. Although rank had a hereditary dimension (from both the mother's and father's side among Vancouver Island societies), it could also be achieved.[20] The most prominent nobles (chiefs) of households controlled resource-gathering sites (at least seasonally), but could not command the labour of their free kin; commoners were induced to work by persuasion and the knowledge that the destiny of their households (and their leaders) depended on collective effort.[21] Few leaders exerted influence beyond their households, and all leaders faced rivals from relatives, both within their own households and in other households in the village and elsewhere.[22] At least during the period for which there is documentary evidence, and probably before that, leaders of villages (particularly those with lesser access to salmon) sometimes formed affiliations that shared food through feasting, although perhaps not by sharing access to resource-procurement sites.[23] In such contexts leaders may have believed that they were not obliged to obtain the consent of commoners, or the even of leaders of other households, when they negotiated with outsiders. But in the context in which rivalry was continuous, negotiating agreements with outsiders could be a way to gain prestige and status.

Chiefs orchestrated the work required during the busy time of the year when salmon were harvested and processed simultaneously. The amount of salmon meat that could be processed and preserved (the work of women), not the number that could be captured (the work of men), determined how much food was available once the salmon runs ended. That is why there could never be enough women, and why polygamy and slavery were so important to Northwest Coast societies. Chiefs could persuade wives and female commoners to work, but could force slaves, regardless of biological sex, to do the work of either gender. Slaves were crucial to the processing of salmon. Slavery was not incidental to Northwest Coast societies; Northwest Coast societies were slave societies.[24] Slaves did not have equal access to the necessities of life (food or clothing).[25] Indeed, slave owners exerted over their slaves the power of life and death.[26] After visits to Fort Vancouver and Fort Victoria in 1847, Paul Kane wrote that:

> Slavery in its most cruel form exists among the Indians of the whole coast, from California to Behring's Straites, the stronger tribes making slaves of all the others they can conquer. In the interior, where there is but little warfare, slavery does not exist. On the coast a custom prevails which authorises the seizure and enslavement, unless ransomed by his friends, of every Indian met with at a distance from his tribe, although they may not be at war with each other. The master exercises the power of life and death over his slaves, whom he sacrifices at pleasure in gratification of any superstitious or other whim of the moment.[27]

Slaves had no rights during deliberations over the affairs of a household or village. Commoners must have had less, and chiefs more, influence than typical members of hunting and gathering societies during treaty negotiations. Indeed, the nobility may have conducted external relations without consulting commoners.

Each community had its seasonal round, which, notwithstanding the anthropological models that imply uniformity and continuity, could vary from year to year and village to village. In general, households dispersed from winter villages in early spring to eulachon, herring, or other fish-spawning locations or camas (*Camassia quamash*) grounds, before congregating at salmon fishing sites during the summer months (see figure 7). For many communities the seasonal round included locations on and off Vancouver Island. For example, the Nanaimo and Cowichan had large summer fisheries along the lower Fraser River and winter villages on the island. The Songhees and Saanich conducted reef fisheries at San Juan Island, Boundary Bay, and Point Roberts.[28] The Kwakiutl and Kweeha had winter villages in the Broughton Archipelago and spring eulachon fisheries at Knight and Kingcome Inlets, but most resorted to summer villages at the mouth of the Cluxewe River on Vancouver Island in the summer. James Douglas understood this reality well before negotiating the treaties. In May 1840, when just north of Cheslakees, he noted trading with thirty members of the "Quakeeolth Tribes," before explaining that the rest of the populous people were then at Knight Canal fishing for eulachon, but "they will return early in June to Cheslakees, for the Salmon season which extends from July to November and reside there until the following January, when they again repair to the Canals. Such is the general outline of Quakeeolth life, the cause and object of their migrations."[29] Thus, many villagers, including the signatories to the Vancouver Island treaties, resided only part of the year on Vancouver Island. That meant that the territories of several communities extended beyond the limits of the colony of Vancouver Island, created in 1849, and were bisected by boundaries between British and American territories after 1846.

The patterns of seasonal movements of Northwest Coast peoples produced an unusual phenomenon: the winter villages where these peoples spent the largest portion of the year did not need to be, and typically were not, adjacent to their most important resource-gathering sites. The most important attributes of winter villages were the shelter that they could provide from inclement winter weather, their defensibility, their proximity to firewood, and probably their proximity to emergency food sources (including shellfish) that might be accessible even in winter. Only a small portion of the resources of a community was acquired on the lands surrounding a winter village, although in innovative examples of mariculture, villagers in many locations modified foreshores near their villages to enhance their shellfish productivity, particularly in butter clams (*Saxidomus gigantea*) which are amenable to preservation.[30] Some Vancouver Island peoples, particularly the

Salish of southeastern Vancouver Island may also have managed terrestrial lands to increase their productivity in camas, berries, and other resources.[31] In 1849, Walter Colquhoun Grant noted that the Songhees set fires between August and October "to clear away the thick fir and underwood in order that the roots and fruits on which they in a great measure subsist may grow the more freely and be the more easily dug up."[32]

In 1857, Walter Colquhoun Grant described the winter villages on Vancouver Island as the main villages.[33] He also described summer villages:

> Most tribes [on Vancouver Island], besides the main village, which is placed in some sheltered spot, have a fishing village, in a more exposed situation, to which they resort during summer, and the fishing grounds of some tribes extend to a distance of several miles from their fixed habitation. The Tsomass [Songhees], for instance, have fisheries on Belle-Vue [San Juan] Island, some 15 miles distant from their winter village. And the Cowitchins [Cowichan] and Sanetch [Saanich] both have fishing grounds at the mouth of Frazer River, on the opposite side of the Gulf of Georgia. To these fishing stations they emigrate in the salmon season, with their wives and families and all their goods and chattels.[34]

Gilbert Malcolm Sproat described the seasonal villages in similar terms:

> Following the salmon as they swim up the rivers and inlets, the natives place their summer encampments at some distance from the seaboard, towards which they return for the winter season about the end of October, with a stock of dried salmon – their principal food at all times. By this arrangement, being near the seashore, they can get shell-fish, if their stock of salmon runs short, and can also catch the first fish that approach the shore in the early spring ... If the natives did not thus often move their quarters, their health would suffer from the putrid fish and other nastinesses that surround their camps, which the elements and the birds clear away during the time of non-occupation.[35]

Sproat indicated that the timing and pattern of movements of any village could differ significantly.[36] In fact, Sproat appears to state that some Vancouver Island people did not usually fish for salmon, opting instead to harvest other resources, and to trade them for salmon.

Villagers typically took house boards from their winter villages with them to seasonal resource-gathering sites, leaving only posts behind. While at Nootka Sound on 10 June 1788, John Meares witnessed a "general commotion" in a Nootka village when "as if by enchantment, the greater part of the houses disappeared. – When we went on shore, Maquilla informed us that his people were preparing to remove to a bay which was at the distance of about two miles from the Sound, on account of the great quantities of fish which resorted thither, not only to procure a present stock of whale and other fish, but to take the earliest opportunity to prepare for their winter's subsistence."[37] Abundant evidence from before and after the Vancouver Island treaties were concluded shows that HBC traders and others understood the nature of Northwest Coast villages.[38] In 1856, James Douglas explained to the British Colonial Secretary that the "domestic habits" of the Northwest Coast peoples were remarkably uniform: "they have each a fixed place of residence, marked by large dwelling houses, rudely though strongly constructed, of rough plank, where they reside for the greater part of the year, and only leave for the purpose of paying temporary visits to other parts of the coast, where fish, game, and wild fruits are at particular seasons found in greater abundance than at their usual places of abode."[39] Those familiar with the villagers' practices recognized winter villages, even when they were uninhabited. James Cook's journals noted that "the logs or framings of the houses were standing; but the boards that had composed their sides and roofs did not exist."[40] In the 1860s, Gilbert Malcolm Sproat similarly noted that the framework of houses was permanent, and only the planking was removed.[41]

Aspects of Indigenous life on Vancouver Island remained constant over thousands of years, but these were not people without history. As the peoples of the Northwest Coast came to rely year-round on salmon and other marine resources, the population of the region also grew significantly. As coastal communities became more populous, they exerted significant pressure on terrestrial animals sought after for both food and fur. Fish and shellfish could provide abundant calories and shells could be used for tools, but they could not provide clothing, bone tools, or red meat.[42] Hunters from these villages permanently suppressed the population of game and fur-bearing animals. Moose (*Alces alces*), poorly adapted to evade human and ursine hunters, were entirely absent from the Northwest Coast, even on the mainland, and other species, including elk (*Cervus canadensis*) and deer, were relatively uncommon except in war zones.[43] Bears also probably became less abundant on the Northwest Coast after villagers excluded them from the best salmon fishing locations, evicted them from some caves, and hunted them for food and clothing.[44] Indeed, so large was the environmental shadow cast by the large coastal populations that Vancouver Island could not support nomadic hunting and gathering peoples in its interior. In 1849 Walter

Colquhoun Grant believed that the villagers of the Victoria area held "that the whole interior is infected, with huge giants who punish with instant death any rash mortals, who may attempt to invade their domains."[45] Communities deprived of access to salmon and marine resources were doomed.

The dearth of large game and fur-bearing animals explains the value that northwest societies placed on red meat, furs, hides, and blankets. In the 1790s, Alexander Mackenzie noticed that Indigenous traders conveyed moose hides to the coast from as far away as the Peace River.[46] Blankets were also woven from the wool of mountain goats (*Oreamnos americanus*), or, among some of the Salish with particularly poor access to alternatives, the hair of specially bred dogs.[47] That explains why only the nobility wore furs, and why slaves wore woven cedar bark, or nothing at all. It also explains why blankets of European manufacture became so valuable – even becoming the unit of currency used as payment in the Vancouver Island treaties.

The gradient of resource availability was extraordinarily steep between the Northwest Coast and the Interior. Many resources abundant on the coast (shellfish, salmon, eulachon, and sea mammals) were absent or rare in the Interior, but other resources found in the Interior (furs, hides, and meat of land mammals) were scarce along the coast. This juxtaposition of abundance and scarcity provided the impetus for lively trade between the populous coastal villagers and sparse populations in the Interior.[48] Because trade in perishables is normally invisible in the archaeological record, we can only guess at the volume of such trade in the era before the 1790s, but the conditions existed for a robust trade in food.

For thousands of years, population densities along the Northwest Coast exceeded those in most other regions in North America, including many regions in which people practised horticulture.[49] The population of the Northwest Coast was as likely to approach the carrying capacity of the environment as it did in any other region on Earth, but whether or not it did, communities of the Northwest Coast were as likely to confront occasional shortages, and even great hardship and famine, as people anywhere else.[50] Because slaves with inferior access to food and clothing formed a substantial portion of Northwest Coast societies, commoners, and especially the elite, may rarely have suffered famine or destitution. However, losing access to procurement sites or failing communal labour efforts plunged entire communities into crisis.

Resource availability on the Northwest Coast varied significantly locally, seasonally, and annually in many ways that people could predict and in other ways that they could not.[51] The differences in resource availability between coastal and interior regions – already discussed – were obvious. So were differences along the Northwest Coast itself.[52] Many resources, ranging from Pacific herring (*Clupea pallasii*), rockfish (*Sebastes* spp.), sea otters (*Enhydra lutris*), Steller sea lions (*Eumetopias jubatus*), whales, eulachon, camas, and mountain goats were readily acquired by some communities, but not others.[53] Even salmon were unevenly distributed. Salmon availability varied dramatically from season to season, year to year, and place to place.[54] The salmon runs of the Fraser River illustrate how markedly salmon availability could vary from year to year. Pink salmon (*O. gorbuscha*) ran abundantly only every other year – in odd-numbered years in the Fraser River, but even-numbered years in most northern rivers.[55] The Fraser River's four-year cycle of sockeye salmon was even more important. This remarkable quadrennial cycle was in place when the Vancouver Island treaties were negotiated, and probably for centuries before. Abundant years (known by fisheries biologists as dominant years) were followed by subdominant years in which the sockeye runs were typically between 10 and 25 per cent the size of the dominant year. During the other two "offcycle" years, sockeye runs were as small as 1 per cent of the runs of the dominant year.[56] The sockeye cycle must have been very consequential for the people who fished the Fraser River sockeye, and for other communities beyond.

In February 1843, just before he set off to establish Fort Victoria, James Douglas described the southeastern corner of Vancouver Island as "a perfect 'Eden,' in the midst of the dreary wilderness of the North west coast, and so different in its general aspect, from the wooded rugged regions around, that one might be pardoned for supposing it had dropped from the clouds into its present position."[57] Although southeastern Vancouver Island appealed to Douglas, comparatively few salmon – and virtually no pink or sockeye salmon – spawned in the few and short rivers of the relatively arid part of the island (for a map of locations in southeastern Vancouver Island mentioned in this text, see figure 20). Its villages were therefore smaller, and the more populous and powerful Cowichan, Nanaimo, and mainland villagers could exclude villagers from that region from prime locations along the lower Fraser River.[58]

To compensate for their poor access to the most convenient procurement sites, several Salish communities used ingenious open-water reef nets to capture salmon in the Salish Sea on their way to the rivers. Reef nets, the most complex and sophisticated technology used to capture salmon, were used only by Straits Salish peoples with little access to the

Fraser River to harvest sockeye and pink salmon at strategic locations in the Straits of Juan de Fuca, Haro, and Rosario, at Point Roberts, and in Boundary Bay.[59]

Villagers in southeastern corner of Vancouver Island were also partially compensated for the relatively poorer access to salmon by the distinct climate and ecosystems of their territories. It was drier and more open than neighbouring regions. Accordingly, people there had better access to certain plant resources, particularly the nutritious camas, which was, like salmon, amenable to preservation. Camas was also convenient because the brief camas gathering season in May did not interfere with salmon fishing. Camas was abundant on the drier Gulf Islands, especially San Juan Island, to which these people also resorted for the subsequent fishing season.[60] Because carbohydrate-rich camas could be preserved, it may also have long been a trade item.[61] The open forests may also have supported a relatively large population of elk,[62] perhaps permitting the people there to trade surplus elk hides. In general, however, villagers on western and northern Vancouver Island had better access to abundant marine resources than the villagers on southeastern Vancouver Island. Because they had more abundant resources, they had more populous villages, larger social units, and military advantages.[63]

Internal social tensions and rivalries must have been significant in Northwest Coast societies long before Europeans arrived.[64] But internal social tensions flared in times of rapid change, particularly if changes opened opportunities for social mobility. The arrival of bow-and-arrow technology about 1,600 years ago, for instance, permitted hunters acting alone or with only one or two partners to procure large land mammals, especially deer and elk, and evidence suggests that hunting of land mammals increased at about that time. Archaeologists have argued that the new technology likely enabled non-elite hunters to challenge established elites.[65] However, evidence of internal social tensions is difficult to discern in archaeological records. Evidence of warfare is more obvious.

Northwest Coast peoples were not inherently warlike, but the distinctive features of the environment – and the lifeways that developed in response to that environment – explain why warfare had been pervasive along the coast for thousands of years. Maritime fishing and hunting peoples around the world experienced greater endemic warfare than most hunting and gathering peoples.[66] People who faced scarcity might fight for survival, but affluent communities who had greater resources with which to fight typically struggled to control surplus resources to achieve broader social, political, and economic goals.[67]

The nature of the marine resources, especially the salmon resource – the abundance and predictability of salmon migrations, the concentrated nature of those migrations, and the site-specific nature of crucial resource procurement locations – deeply affected people on the Northwest Coast. Salmon were abundant in many waters, but villagers had the technology to procure them easily in a relatively few prime procurement locations during the specific times of the year when adult salmon passed those locations. People with access to specific locations – rapids, waterfalls, narrows, river mouths, surfs, reefs, or other excellent fishing locations at crucial times each year – could obtain food with remarkably little effort, less than was typically required in early agricultural societies.[68] Competition for the best fishing locations, in abundance or need, was intense, and defending access to those locations – especially since those locations were valuable only during the salmon runs – was difficult but essential.[69] It was catastrophic to lose access to those locations when the resource was abundant, or to fail in other ways to process and preserve enough salmon to feed the community during the period of the year in which salmon were absent. Those exigencies explain why certain lineages in each community came to control those prime resource-procurement sites, why the elite exerted so much control over the labour of their communities, why they and their communities jealously guarded ownership or control of such sites, and why communities valorized the warriors who defended their communities.[70]

Archaeological finds, including evidence of decapitation, wounds, scars, and violent trauma in dental and skeletal remains, of defensive fortifications and hidden camps, and of tools of war (including armour and war clubs), show that warfare was pervasive among Northwest Coast societies for at least two thousand years before Europeans arrived.[71] Communities that experience chronic warfare and continual threats to their security typically become militaristic.[72] Naturally then, Northwest Coast societies honoured the taking of trophies in war, rewarded success in warfare with status and prestige, and valorized those who died in battle.[73] One practice, apparently ubiquitous along the Northwest Coast, was the taking of severed heads as trophies to achieve prestige. The archaeological evidence shows that the practice began thousands of years ago, and documents show that it persisted well into the nineteenth century.[74]

Warfare intensified after bow-and-arrow technology arrived on the Northwest Coast about 1,600 years ago.[75] The escalation of warfare had far-reaching consequences. It induced villagers to consolidate multiple lineages in larger settlements near defensive sites.[76] Communities on the Northwest Coast, including those on both northern and southern

Vancouver Island, also began building fortifications and other defensive structures (including lookouts, refuges, subterranean houses, trench embankments, and palisades) around 1,600 years ago, and those structures proliferated between around 1,100 and 600 years ago, showing that people were responding to intensified warfare.[77] Although defensive sites were found throughout the Northwest Coast, they were particularly common on southern Vancouver Island (see figure 8). One scholar identified eighteen defensive sites in Songhees territory alone.[78]

Early historical documents are replete with references to warfare. When the Spaniard Manuel Quimper met Klallam people on the south side of the Strait of Juan de Fuca, he noted they "carry on continual warfare with those on the north side, thus accounting for the fact that the beaches are strewn with the harpooned heads of their enemies."[79] Quimper also noted that the Klallam had armour made of double-thickness hides.[80] English explorer James Cook noted that the "Nootka" had armour made of "thick leathern mantle, doubled, which, from its size, appears to be the skin of an elk or buffalo, tanned" that was "not only sufficiently strong to resist arrows, but as they informed us by signs, even spears cannot pierce it; so that it may be considered as their coat of mail, or most complete defensive armour."[81]

Archaeological materials cannot be linked decisively to specific linguistic or cultural communities, but the archaeological evidence is consistent with a theory that Wakashan speakers expanded from western Vancouver Island into the northeastern parts of Vancouver Island sometime between 500 BC and AD 300, displacing or absorbing Coast Salish peoples there.[82]

Warfare became more frequent, intense, and deadly among the villagers of the Northwest Coast after Europeans arrived. Although the population of the Northwest Coast might have been falling for several hundred years before 1780, it fell dramatically with the arrival of epidemics of acute infectious diseases (and other causes, including warfare). So, warfare in the nineteenth century may have been less driven by competition over resource procurement sites than it previously had been. However, there were new sources of conflict. Communities and leaders competed for access to European wares, including weaponry, and to the furs with which they could obtain European goods.[83] Before Europeans arrived, each community on the Northwest Coast employed similar weaponry. Any military superiority enjoyed by one group was more a function of numbers than technology. However, the unequal distribution of European weaponry and ammunition and the uneven effects of the first known epidemic magnified pre-existing disparities. The mighty became mightier. In highly militarized contexts such as the Northwest Coast, where success in warfare had been an important route to prestige since ancient times, individual members of a community that enjoyed marked military superiority over their neighbours may have pursued warfare at least as much to achieve status and prestige as for any benefits that the community might enjoy. This is not to imply that communities did not continue to employ intermarriage and redistribution systems as an alternative to warfare, but high-casualty warfare appears to have become markedly more common after 1780.

But warfare and trade were not mutually exclusive. In fact, trade and gift giving were crucial alliance-building and attack-deterring strategies in war-rife regions.[84] Redistributive mechanisms could also serve to suppress internal tensions. Among the hierarchical Northwest Coast societies, the nobility managed the labour of their communities during the salmon procurement seasons, accumulated more food than they could consume, and accordingly redistributed resources to the people upon whose labour and adherence they depended.[85] Methods of redistribution ranged along a spectrum, but even where goods were given away, the giver anticipated reciprocation, and even where goods were traded, exchanges were clothed in rituals of reciprocal gift giving. In feasts and other giveaway systems, the nobility distributed food and goods to their communities, essentially to repay them for their labour or other contributions.

The best-known redistributive mechanisms were feasts and giveaway ceremonies commonly known as potlatches. The fact that such ceremonies were ubiquitous throughout the Northwest Coast, despite the linguistic and cultural diversity, shows that they had been important for managing relationships within and among communities throughout the region for centuries.[86] Leland Donald explained that "at major feasts large amounts of food were consumed and given away and the scale of property dispersal could exhaust most of the material wealth of the host. Gifts included such major wealth items as canoes and slaves, but the mainstay of the property dispersed was furs, which were gradually replaced by blankets after trade with Europeans began."[87] Villagers who hoarded food while neighbours starved courted war. Opting instead to host feasts and giveaway ceremonies mollified less affluent neighbours, built prestige and status, and engrossed social capital that might be repaid when fortunes were reversed. In fact, generosity could turn enemies into potential allies.[88]

Given the ubiquity of evidence of treaties among human societies and evidence for such agreements on Vancouver Island in the 1790s, we can assume that the people of the Northwest Coast engaged in various forms of diplomacy before Europeans arrived, and that the practice of diplomacy required, but also reified, elite status. However, the only way that we might conclude that communities engaged in land-transfer transactions in the period before 1774 would be to extrapolate from evidence from the period between 1774 and 1850 that such practices were already established. However, there is no documentary evidence that the peoples of the Northwest Coast ever conducted land purchases among themselves that were analogous to the Vancouver Island treaties.

Trade networks must have existed since ancient times, although much of the trade was archaeologically invisible.[89] Trade in perishables such as camas, eulachon oil, herring, halibut, reeds, red meat, and furs may have been robust without any archaeological evidence surviving. The variation in abundance of salmon, particularly from year to year, may also have encouraged people reliant on the Fraser River salmon stocks to exchange preserved salmon with neighbours during the more abundant years, the lean years, or both. The people of Vancouver Island were familiar with trade well before Europeans arrived.[90] Evidence for such trade is better for the period after Europeans arrived, however. In the 1840s, HBC Governor George Simpson explained that eulachon "is a great article of trade with the Indians of the interior, and also of such parts of the coast as do not furnish the luxury in question."[91]

The 125 to 200 human lifetimes that had elapsed on Vancouver Island in 1774 dwarf the one long human lifetime between the arrival of Europeans and the Vancouver Island treaties. Octogenarians at the time of the Vancouver Island treaties might have witnessed as children the first visit of Europeans to their villages. The perspectives of the roughly 30,000 Indigenous denizens of Vancouver Island in 1774 were certainly shaped by the dynamic and fluid history of their communities, including by the ancient and complex patterns of subsistence, diplomacy and politics, warfare and militarism, trade, redistributive mechanisms, and kinship. The history of continuity and change in the deep history of the Northwest Coast before 1774 provides important context for understanding the history of relations in the period after 1774, and, as subsequent chapters will show, permits us to better understand how the adherents to the Vancouver Island treaties may have understood the negotiations and terms of those treaties.

# 4 Indigenous and Exogenous Peoples on Vancouver Island, 1774–1821

In the seventy-six years between the 1774 visit of Juan José Pérez Hernández to Vancouver Island, and the first of the HBC's treaties on Vancouver Island, the Indigenous people of Vancouver Island experienced tremendous change. The evidence of cultural continuity, economic and artistic florescence, enduring military power, and political autonomy should not cause us to overlook the fact that the Vancouver Island treaties were concluded at a time of significant demographic, economic, social, political, and geopolitical upheaval.[1] Indigenous peoples knew before 1774 of people from lands unknown to them. Disabled Japanese ships occasionally wrecked on the Northwest Coast during the nineteenth century, sometimes with Japanese crew members still alive in them. Northwest Coast people encountered wrecks, and perhaps survivors, before they ever encountered European ships and people.[2] However, the metal and other items salvaged from Japanese wrecks and the few Japanese people that found their way into Northwest Coast societies, probably as slaves, can have made only a small impact on the people of the Pacific Northwest. But, while Europeans could not dominate Indigenous communities militarily on Vancouver Island before the 1850s, the presence of Europeans and their goods unleashed forces that remade relations among and within Indigenous communities.

Initially, European wares may have had a greater impact than the newcomers themselves. Woollen blankets came to communities that were chronically short of warm clothing. Metal tools and implements of great utility eased everything from preparing food, cutting firewood, and making canoes to carving works of art. European weaponry, especially arms and ammunition, was useful in both hunting and warfare.[3] The arrival of European traders and their goods ushered in economic prosperity and cultural and artistic flourishing.

But these goods had a chequered legacy. Many effects of European goods were not intended, welcomed, or, probably, avoidable. The escalation of warfare occasioned by the proliferation of European weaponry, the repeated visitations of acute infectious diseases, and the introduction of alcohol and new sexually transmitted diseases brought about a dramatic reduction – perhaps 80 per cent – of the Indigenous population of the Northwest Coast. Intensifying warfare was particularly disruptive. Entire villages were destroyed, and the role of warfare changed entire communities. Villagers adjusted to the combined effects of warfare, depopulation, opportunities and challenges brought on by trade with Europeans, and deepened social tensions and political rivalries within and between communities. In response to depopulation, warfare, and trade, formerly separate and autonomous households and villages merged and consolidated, forming new identities and realigning their structures.

Almost imponderable factors influenced Indigenous perceptions of Europeans and may have significantly affected their demeanour towards them. Although it is impossible today to reconstruct Indigenous peoples' understandings of what one scholar has described as the "invisible reality," the behaviour of Indigenous people was influenced by their understandings of the supernatural realm. What a Blackfoot scholar has argued in regards to the Blackfoot-speaking peoples probably holds true for most Indigenous communities in North America: that "the visible dimension was only a small part of their total reality," while "the invisible dimension *was* the real world."[4] It is uncertain whether evidence gathered in 1935 sheds any light on the 1850s or earlier, but Diamond Jenness's Coast Salish informants told him about guardian spirits, including *Hwani'tum* (White Man), whose spirit was said to have been on the west coast before Europeans arrived in the flesh, about spirits that could cause illness and disease, and about sorcerers who could inflict illness and disease on others.[5] Any person or thing might be imbued with some kind of mysterious powers; the purveyors of many useful and unfamiliar wares must have been among them.

While it is impossible to gauge the degree to which Indigenous people feared or respected any invisible powers they might attribute to the newcomers, Europeans were certainly dangerous sources of power. The fact that Northwest Coast peoples often attacked shipboard traders even in the earliest years of contact shows that they were not intimidated by Europeans. Still, European metal goods and weaponry, their writing, their medicine and vaccines,[6] and, in the 1830s and 1840s their steamboats and military skills, made a strong impression on Indigenous people. Indigenous leaders who could exploit on behalf of their communities the benefits of relations with the exogenous traders gained status and prestige.

Northwest Coast villagers likely initially assumed, especially given the coercive nature of leadership on ships and in trading posts, that many people on those ships and in those posts were slaves.[7] Among the many communities that practised head binding of free infants, the fact that exogenous people had "round" heads like their slaves, must also have initially influenced perceptions of the newcomers.

A view that Indigenous people were passive victims of traders has long since been replaced by an acknowledgment that they were eager and sophisticated trading partners. In the case of the Northwest Coast of North America, Robin Fisher has been the foremost historian to have argued that, despite the chequered legacy of the fur trade, Indigenous peoples "exercised a great deal of control over the trading relationship" and experienced enhanced material prosperity and thriving cultural and artistic lives during the fur trade era.[8] Nevertheless, the presence and activities of exogenous peoples on and near Vancouver Island between 1774 and 1850 brought tremendous changes to the island's Indigenous people – changes that in many cases were outside the control of either Indigenous or exogenous peoples. As a result, the military, diplomatic, and trading relations among Indigenous communities and the social, economic, and political relations within Indigenous societies were transformed.[9] Those profound and complex dynamics undoubtedly influenced the understandings and intentions of the Indigenous people who entered treaties with the HBC. While no documents of the period explicitly state why Indigenous leaders willingly consented to land-cession treaties between 1850 and 1854, an understanding of the turbulent relations between village communities and heightened social tensions within them alerts us to the fact that the bilateral treaties made with the HBC were made in the context of fluid and unstable multilateral and internal relations.

The fact that well-established trade networks among Indigenous societies long predated the arrival of exogenous traders to the Northwest Coast helps explain why the trade between Northwest Coast peoples and exogenous people developed so quickly. The lively networks of trade that brought furs from the interior to the Northwest Coast only grew with the European demand for fur. Early ship-borne traders also acted as intermediaries in already established trade along the coast, buying elk hides at the Columbia River and trading them at a profit with northern peoples, and buying and selling slaves for a profit.[10]

Between 1774 and the 1820s, villagers who had long dominated the Northwest Coast militarily and demographically came also to dominate the trade with exogenous people. During the late 1770s British, Spanish, and American ship-borne traders began arriving each year to acquire sea otter pelts. Since the Indigenous villagers on the outer coast had the best access to sea otters, those people also had the best access to European goods, including weaponry. Moreover, those people jealously guarded their economic and military advantages.[11] The competition for access to European goods included competition within communities. Rival west coast leaders vied for control of the trade, and for connections with Europeans. Part of gaining prestige among their own people was being perceived as having influence with Europeans. Such relationship building meant including Europeans in gift giving, rather than in purely commercial trade.[12]

Europeans noted that chiefs and communities jealously guarded their trade with the ship-based traders. James Cook wrote that on 4 April 1778, he and his crew "had a ferious [sic] alarm," when they witnessed Nuu-chah-nulth warriors arming themselves, but they were relieved to learn that the warriors were not preparing to attack them but to defend themselves against about twelve large canoes "of their own countrymen, who were coming to fight them." However, Cook explained that after some negotiations, the parties concluded a "treaty." Thus, the disagreement was settled,

> but the strangers were not allowed to come alongside the ships, nor to have any trade or intercourse with us. Probably we were the cause of the quarrel; the strangers, perhaps, being desirous to share in the advantages of a trade with us; and our first friends, the inhabitants of the Sound, being determined to engross us entirely to themselves. We had proofs of this on several other occasions; nay, it appeared, that even those who lived in the Sound were not united in the same cause; for the weaker were frequently obliged to give way to the stronger party, and plundered of every thing, without attempting to make the least resistance.[13]

Cook's account shows that chiefs and communities sought to monopolize trade with Europeans. His experience was not unique. When John Meares traded with Wikinanish in June 1788, "strangers" tried to trade with Meares's ship without Wikinanish's permission. Wikinanish had one of the interlopers seized, and "this unfortunate man was immediately hurried into the woods, where we have every reason to apprehend that he was quickly murdered."[14] Clearly, leading men jealously guarded their access to Europeans and to European goods for economic, social, political, and perhaps spiritual reasons.

Europeans wanted more than furs from the Indigenous people; they also sought food, especially fish.[15] Indeed, while chiefs appear to have controlled all or most of the trade in furs, especially in sea otter pelts, commoners appear to have been freer to trade fish.[16] Trade in fish between Indigenous people and exogenous peoples was desultory and small-scale before the 1820s, but it began at first contact, and continued thereafter.[17] The journals of George Vancouver make it clear that by 1792 villagers routinely traded salmon and other fish with European visitors.

Social tensions and political rivalries within Indigenous communities cannot have been new to Northwest Coast societies in the early years of contact. They must have intensified simultaneously with the emergence of social stratification itself in ancient times. However, there were many new sources of social tension and political rivalry in the late eighteenth and early nineteenth centuries. Two anthropologists have remarked that "the fur trade provided new forms of wealth and enabled some individuals to gain more power than they might have previously been able to acquire. Certainly, the trade with the British caused some social disruption in the class system of the Puget Sound Indians."[18] Another prominent anthropologist, Wayne Suttles, likewise argued that "the fur trade, while not accompanied by much external pressure, may have led to some internal causes of social disruption. It permitted hunters and trappers to accumulate wealth more rapidly than before and enabled them to rise socially at the expense of the hereditary owners of fishing locations and other productive sites. This increase in social mobility may have stimulated others to seek out sources of prestige and authority."[19]

The first major epidemic of smallpox may have struck portions of the Northwest Coast in the late 1770s or early 1780s, even before most (perhaps all) of its victims had encountered Europeans. Indigenous communities along the rim of the Salish Sea were particularly hard hit. In May 1792, Vancouver observed the "indelible marks" of smallpox on many people along the shores of the Salish Sea south of Cape Mudge.[20] We might conservatively estimate that this epidemic killed 30 per cent of its victims, although the mortality among some communities may well have been twice that. The mortality rate, as horrid as it must have been, however, should not blind us to the psychological, emotional, spiritual, and social effects on the survivors who were forced to carry on after watching helplessly as a third or more of their loved ones died of a mysterious, painful, and disfiguring disease.[21]

Scholars have explored some of the destabilizing effects of epidemics, which often decimated the ranks of the nobility.[22] Keith Carlson has argued that class tensions flared after the smallpox epidemic.[23] He suggested that some lower-class persons and slaves probably took advantage of the first smallpox epidemic of the late eighteenth century to elevate their own status.[24] The epidemic, he wrote, "created a situation rife with the possibility of social change, for the upper-class leadership was undoubtedly less organized than at any time before, and it was faced with the daunting task of re-establishing a degree of societal stability and normalcy."[25] The same could be said for the 1848 measles epidemic that struck the island just two years before the first of the Vancouver Island treaties was concluded.

The smallpox epidemic of the early 1780s also had important geopolitical ramifications. This first epidemic appears not to have struck the Wakashan people of the northern and western parts of Vancouver Island. Thus, the Salish villagers – already at a military disadvantage vis-à-vis their northern and western neighbours because of their poor access to European goods, including weaponry – became even more vulnerable because of the smallpox epidemic.

In some ways, the patterns of warfare in the period between 1774 and 1850 appear to reflect the patterns that had existed for thousands of years on the coast. Northern and western groups, including the Tlingit, Haida, Tsimshian, Heiltsuk (Bella Bella), Nuxalk (Bella Coola), Nuu-chah-nulth, and Kwakwaka'wakw were typically aggressors against groups to the south, especially along the coasts of the Salish Sea, even before Europeans arrived.[26] In fact, during the late eighteenth and early nineteenth centuries, that pattern probably intensified.

Whether or not the population of the Northwest Coast declined after 1300 as some scholars have argued, the population fell appallingly (perhaps as much as 80 per cent between 1774 and the 1870) in the late eighteenth and early nineteenth centuries because of introduced acute infectious diseases and intensifying high-casualty warfare. Competition over access to European weapons and goods injected a new motivation for warfare. That competition could include access (before the 1820s) to the locations to which ships tended to resort, access (during and after the 1820s) to the trading posts, and access (throughout the period) to interior groups with furs to trade. The documents show that such competition occurred between and within communities.

Although warfare had been pervasive on the Northwest Coast for thousands of years, it became markedly more deadly and frequent during the decades after Europeans began trading firearms in the region in the 1780s.[27] As Wilson Duff argued, "warfare suddenly became much more deadly. On the coast some villages were practically wiped out."[28] Bill Angelbeck has summarized that "Coast Salish oral histories are replete with accounts of warfare."²⁹ The fact that this same pattern – a dramatic escalation of warfare after the diffusion of European weaponry – was repeated in countless places around the world, even in places such as the Northwest Coast where Europeans themselves regretted it, shows that it was a development extraordinarily difficult to control.

The journals of George Vancouver indicate that European weaponry was already unevenly distributed along the Northwest Coast in 1792. Groups on the west coast of Vancouver Island and the outer Pacific coast to the north of the island had superior access to European goods, although those on the northern part of Vancouver Island had better access than those in Georgia Strait. In July 1792, while travelling northward from Georgia Strait through Johnstone Strait, George Vancouver noted that he did not see firearms south of Cheslakees, but villagers at Cheslakees (at the mouth of the Nimpkish River), were well armed.³⁰ He believed that the muskets he saw there "were procured immediately from Nootka, as, on pointing to many of them, they gave us to understand they had come from thence."³¹

Some historians may have exaggerated the violence of the ship-based trade and failed to acknowledge the degree to which villagers' attacks on traders may have been retaliation for violence perpetrated by traders. Still, villagers attacked ship-based traders in the late eighteenth and early nineteenth centuries far more often than they attacked HBC traders in the several decades before the Vancouver Island treaties were concluded. The attack on the *Boston* at Nootka Sound in 1803, which resulted in the death of most of the crew, and the attack on the *Tonquin* in 1811 at Clayoquot Sound, which resulted in the death and decapitation of twenty-five crew members and the enslavement of John Jewitt, are two of the most famous examples.³² A less famous attack occurred at Milbanke Sound, which would later become the location of the HBC's Fort McLoughlin. In June 1805, a large party let by a chief named Kiete killed Captain Oliver Porter and ten other men of the *Atahualpa* before they were repulsed.³³ Europeans in this period viewed the trade of the Pacific Northwest as lucrative but dangerous.³⁴ The Governor and Committee of the HBC and their officers in the Columbia District must have been aware when they established their trading posts on the Northwest Coast of the history of attacks on ship-based traders.

The peoples of the Northwest Coast, especially Salish speakers, lived in well-defended villages in the 1790s. When George Vancouver visited a village about three kilometres north of Cape Mudge in July 1792, he perceived that the location had been chosen for defence: "the steep loose sandy precipice secured it in front and its rear was defended by a deep chasm in the rocks; beyond these was as thick and nearly impenetrable forest; so that the only means of access was by the narrow path we had ascended, which could easily be maintained against very superior numbers."[35] Beleaguered Coast Salish villagers of the southeastern part of the island appear to have responded to escalating attacks of the late 1700s and early 1800s with increasingly robust and innovative defensive structures and practices that included palisades and large fortified plank-houses sheltering multiple households.[36] Bill Angelbeck has argued that the distinctly new defensive structures and practices of the period after 1790 represent a response to the qualitatively different context of warfare of the period, one in which the effects of firearms, epidemics, and the fur trade, in the absence of peace-making protocols, made warfare more dangerous and pervasive.[37]

Northwest Coast warriors also continued to collect and display trophies of war. In May 1792, while at Port Discovery on the Olympic Peninsula, George Vancouver observed

> Two upright poles set in the ground, about fifteen feet high, and rudely carved. On the top of each was stuck a human head; recently placed there. The hair and flesh were nearly perfect; and the heads appeared to carry the evidence of fury or revenge, as, in driving the stakes through the throat to the cranium, the sagittal, with part of the scalp, was borne on the points some inches above the rest of the skull.[38]

Earlier, also on the Olympic Peninsula, Vancouver had observed a deserted village, with "several human sculls, and other bones, promiscuously scattered about."[39]

Several late eighteenth-century land purchases along the west coast of Vancouver Island illustrate many of the features of British, American, and Spanish approaches to such transactions over the centuries. One of these purchases is reminiscent of Gillam's purported purchase on Hudson Bay. Others reflect the countless private purchases for which British and American purchasers sought government sanction.

On 8 July 1776, before James Cook departed upon his voyage towards the Northwest Coast of North America, the Admiralty gave him secret instructions that included orders "with the consent of the natives, to take possession, in the name of the King of Great Britain, of convenient Situations in such countries as you may discover."[40] Cook was not instructed to arrange purchases of land in the places he visited. When he arrived at the Northwest Coast, Cook was surprised to find that the Vancouver Islanders had clear notions of ownership of resources. In April 1778, after "Nootka" (Nuu-chah-nulth) villagers on the west coast of Vancouver Island forced James Cook to pay for grass that his men were cutting for the sheep and goats aboard Cook's ship, Cook wrote "Here I must observe, that I have no where, in my several voyages, met with any uncivilized nation, or tribe, who had such strict notions of their having a right to the exclusive property of everything that their country produces, as the inhabitants of this Sound."[41] Shortly after, he added that "they considered the place as entirely their property, without fearing any superiority."[42]

During the late 1780s and early1790s, competition between European powers, particularly between Spain and Britain, for control of Nootka Sound became so sharp that it almost led to war before being settled in the Nootka Convention of 28 October 1790. There was more at stake than the lucrative sea otter trade.[43] Until their surveys of the early 1790s revealed to Europeans that Nootka Sound was on an island, the British and Spanish sought possession of the sound believing that the western terminus of a convenient route across the continent might be found in or near the sound. After several centuries of searching for the Northwest Passage, the British would not easily concede to the Spanish the western entrance to the best route across the continent.

However, in early 1790 the British learned that in May 1789, the Spaniard Estéban José Martínez had seized two British ships at Nootka Sound associated with John Meares and James Colnett and their crews. The British were aware that, by the arguments they had long depended on (as they had against the French claims to Hudson Bay in the 1680s), they appeared to have a weaker claim to the location than the Spanish. As far as they knew at the time, James Cook's "discovery" of Nootka Sound had not been followed up by any British occupation at the site. The Spanish based their claims to the Northwest Coast on the Papal Bull of Alexander VI of 1493, the Treaty of Tordesillas (1494), the discoveries of Juan Pérez and Martínez in 1774 and Arteaga and Quadra in 1779 (with ceremonies of possession), a further elaborate ceremony of possession at Nootka Sound on 24 June 1789 by Martínez, and an actual, albeit temporary, occupation at Nootka Sound.[44]

The British resolved to send William Cornwallis with two ships and a small party of settlers from New South Wales to establish a permanent settlement at Nootka Sound, or any other place "which shall, on examination, be found best adapted for opening an inland communication."[45] The Permanent Under-Secretary of State for the Home Department, Evan Nepean, on behalf of the king, included curiously worded instructions: "if you find any person or number of persons among them who appear to have any rights or sovereignty over the Territory which you shall fix upon for the settlement, You are to endeavour to purchase their consent to the formation of the settlement, and a Grant of Land for that purpose, by the presents with which you are furnished."[46] Nepean wrote these instructions two years after the British established the Australian colony of New South Wales without contemplating purchasing Indigenous title there. Unfortunately, because the Cornwallis expedition never took place, no additional evidence sheds light on how to interpret the instructions given to Cornwallis. Had the expedition been completed, Cornwallis may have explained whether he believed that he found people who had "rights or sovereignty" at Nootka Sound. A formal treaty document would have enabled us better to understand what it meant "to purchase their consent to the formation of the settlement." It would be presumptuous to assume that Nepean's instructions were equivalent to directions to extinguish Indigenous title to a substantial tract of land. Nepean appears to have contemplated an agreement more akin to commercial treaties made with governments to establish British trading facilities within a foreign state. The circumstances, however, are redolent of the situation on the eastern seaboard of North America in the 1620s and Hudson Bay in the 1680s, in that the impetus behind the strategy was to bolster against European rivals British rights to trade and claims to land, not to acknowledge Indigenous title. Inevitably, however, practice contributed to the formation of principles.

The Cornwallis expedition was first delayed because of an outbreak of typhus aboard the ships, and then cancelled when John Meares arrived in London in April 1790 with new information. In a memorial presented to the British House of Commons on 13 May 1790, Meares reported that he had built a settlement at Nootka Sound in May 1788, before the Spanish had, and that he "immediately on his arrival in Nootka Sound, purchased from Maquilla, the chief of the district contiguous to, and surrounding that place, a spot of ground, whereon he built a house for his occasional residence."[47] Meares furthermore added that he had obtained from Wickaninnish "the chief of the district surrounding Port Cox [Clayoquot Sound] and Port Effingham [Barkley Sound], ... in consideration of considerable presents, the promise of a *free and exclusive trade with the natives of the district,* and also his permission to build any storehouses, or other edifices, which he might judge necessary; that he also acquired the same privilege of exclusive trade from Tatootche, the chief of the country bordering on the Straits of John De Fuca, and purchased from him a trade of land within the said strait, which one of your Memorialist's officers took possession of in the King's name, calling the same Tatootche, in honour of the chief."[48]

Meares's journals, hurriedly published in 1790, cast some doubt upon the truth of his memorial. He did arrive at Nootka Sound in May 1788. The fact that he brought with him Maquinna's brother, Comekela, who had been in China, probably added to the warmth of the welcome his ships received. On 16 May, "King" Maquinna and his younger brother, Callicum, led an elaborate welcome ceremony for Meares and his crew.[49] Meares's entry for 25 May, the date of his purported land purchase, indicates that:

> Maquilla had not only most readily consented to grant us a spot of ground in his territory, whereon an house might be built for the accommodation of the people we intended to leave there, but had promised us also his assistance in forwarding our works, and his protection of the party who were destined to remain at Nootka during our absence. In return for this kindness, and to ensure a continuance of it, the chief was presented with a pair of pistols, which he had regarded with an eye of solicitation ever since our arrival. Callicum, who seemed to have formed a most affectionate attachment to us, was also gratified, as well as the ladies of his family, with suitable presents: it indeed became our more immediate attention to confirm his regard, as he had been appointed by Maquilla to be our particular guardian and protector, and had the most peremptory injunctions to prevent the natives from making any depredations on us.[50]

Meares's description of events when his party left for the winter indicates that Maquinna used the occasion to place himself as subject to the British traders:

> Whatever opinion ... we had formed of the capacity of these chiefs for the sentiments of friendship, we thought it prudent, with a view to our future interests, as presents had first obtained it, to secure the continuance of it, if possible, by the same prevailing influence. – We accordingly presented Maquilla, with a musket, a small quantity of ammunition, and a few blankets. Nor did Callicum leave us without receiving equal tokens of our regard.
>
> We made these chiefs sensible in how many moons we should return to them; and that we should then be accompanied by others of our countrymen, and build more houses, and endeavour to introduce our manners and mode of living to the practice of our Nootka friends. – This information seemed to delight them beyond measure; and they not only promised us great plenty of furs on our return, but Maquilla thought proper, on the

instant, to do obedience to us as his lords and sovereigns. He took off his tiara of feathers, and placed it on my head; he then dressed me in his robe of otter skins; and, thus arrayed, he made me sit down on one of his chests filled with human bones, and then placed himself on the ground.[51]

Meares's journal shows that his party went on to visit Wickaninnish's village in June 1788. Meares noted that chiefs were negotiating a treaty among themselves:

We were now formally made acquainted by Wicananish, that a treaty was negotiating between the chiefs Hanna and Detootche and himself, in which we were to be included; the substance of which was, – that all the furs then in their possession should be sold to Wicananish; – that they should live in peace and friendship with us; – that all the otter skins procured after the completion of the treaty, by either of the contracting chiefs, or their people, should be disposed of by themselves, and that they were all to have common access to the ship, where a fair and equitable market was to be opened for them without distinction.

From the jealousy which we already knew to subsist between these chiefs, we were perfectly satisfied, as we since had convincing proofs, that, on our entering the territories of Wicananish, neither Hanna or Detootche would be permitted to trade with, or even pay us a visit without having obtained a previous permission for that purpose. We had not therefore urged or encouraged an intercourse, which, though it would have been very advantageous to us, might, and most probably would have brought on a war between the respective sovereigns. This treaty, therefore, gave us that extension of commerce which we so much wished, in the regular course of friendly negotiation, and we were not backward in forwarding the completion of it.[52]

The description in Meares's journal offers ambiguous evidence at best that Meares himself (to say nothing of Maquinna) understood the agreement of 25 May 1788 to be a land-purchase agreement; Meares may have later reimagined the apparent grant of land, later reciprocated with gifts, as a land purchase. But the journal also makes it clear that the negotiations and agreement took place in the context of complex rivalries among Maquinna, Wickaninnish, and other leaders on the west coast of Vancouver Island. Each man, aiming to capture as much of the commerce as possible, jockeyed for privileged access to European goods. Most historians agree that Wickaninnish was the pre-eminent leader on the west coast of Vancouver Island at the time, and Wickaninnish's ability to have Meares witness and acquiesce to a treaty that placed his rivals in a subordinate position must have been a coup. Maquinna, also subservient to Wickaninnish but superior to other chiefs, granted Meares a plot of land at Nootka Sound. In a context in which sea otter numbers were already dwindling in the region, and ships were beginning to bypass Nootka Sound, Maquinna, Wickaninnish, and others along the west coast of the island sought to protect their advantageous position in trade networks. Maquinna and his people would have benefited economically and militarily if a permanent trading post had been established near their villages.

Even if Meares did understand his May 1788 agreement with Maquinna as a land purchase or grant, he did not consider the transaction as sufficient to claim possession for the British Crown. Aside from claiming to have made purchases from Indigenous leaders, Meares also claimed to have taken possession of lands by using the more traditional ceremonies of possession. His journals note that in July 1788, Meares "took possession of the straits of John de Fuca, in the name of the King of Britain, with the forms that had been adopted by preceding navigators on similar occasions."[53]

The British government seized upon Meares's information to assert that, before Martínez had arrived at Nootka Sound, "the Soil at Nootka, and in some other Parts of the Coast, ... had, been purchased of the Natives, by a British Subject, and the British Flag hoisted thereon."[54] The British government concluded that the planned Cornwallis expedition was redundant, since the British Crown already had "an unquestionable Right to a free and undisturbed Enjoyment of the Benefits of Commerce, Navigation and Fishery, and also to the Possession of such Establishments, as they may form, with the Consent of the Natives, in Places unoccupied by other European nations."[55]

Meares did not even mention a treaty document, suggesting that none was made. Meares may have fabricated the entire account of the purchases, perhaps with the encouragement of British officials. But even if Meares is taken at his word (and some of the details of his journals of May 1788 have the ring of truth), it is doubtful that he himself believed in May 1788 that he was acquiring, on behalf of the British Crown, Maquinna's cession of Indigenous title to the land at Nootka Sound. It seems more likely that he was paying, on his own behalf, for Maquinna's consent to Meares's establishment of a post at the location, that Meares was doing so to convince Maquinna (and the other leaders) to trade exclusively with him, and that he may have been agreeing to acknowledge those leaders' role as intermediaries between Meares and other villages. It is even more doubtful that Maquinna would have understood it that way. In 1804, when applying to the Spanish king for a pension as a reward for meritorious service, the Spanish botanist Martín de Sessé (1751–1808), who had accompanied Quadra's expedition in 1792, wrote that "I went on the expedition in the capacity of naturalist, and having arrived at Nutca [Nootka] I learned the language of those islanders, instructed in which, I not only studied their customs but moreover discovered the falsity with which Captain Meares claimed to have purchased the land, the propriety of which one questioned, and in the presence of impartial strangers I drew this confession from the Chief of those inhabitants."[56]

When Americans entered the sea otter trade of the Northwest Coast, they knew that their opportunities to claim rights to land based on discovery and naming were limited because of prior Russian, British, and Spanish activity there. Their more tenuous claims, however, might be bolstered by acquiring carefully prepared land-purchase deeds from Indigenous people. When a group of Boston merchants led by Joseph Barrell decided to enter the sea otter trade in 1787 (the year of the Northwest Ordinance), they instructed the leader of their expedition, John Kendrick, "if you make any fort or improvement of land upon the coast, be sure you purchase the soil of the natives; and it would not be amiss if you purchased some advantageous tract of land in the name of the owners; if you should, let the instrument of conveyance bear every authentic mark the circumstances will admit of."[57] Complying with those instructions, Kendrick obtained deeds from several leaders, including "Macquinnah" of Nootka Sound on 20 July 1791, "Tarassom" of "New Chatleck" [Nutchatlaht] ("Hootsee-ess") on 2 August 1791, "Norry Youk" of "Ahasset" [Ahousaht] on 5 August 1791, "Caarshucornook" of "Tashees" [Tahsis] on 6 August 1791, and "Wickananish" of "Clyoquot" on 11 August 1791.[58] The deed signed by Maquinna, five of his subordinates, and nine witnesses (although not signed by Kendrick himself) was typical:

> To all persons to whom these presents shall come: I, Macquinnah, the chief, and with my other chiefs, do send greeting: Know ye that I, Macquinnah, of Nootka sound, on the north-west coast of America, for and in consideration of ten muskets, do grant and sell unto John Kendrick, of Boston, commonwealth of Massachusetts, in North America, a certain harbor in said Nootka sound, called Chastacktoos, in which the brigantine Lady Washington lay at anchor on the twentieth day of July, 1791, with all the land, rivers, creeks, harbors, islands, &c., within nine miles north, east, west and south of said harbor, with all the produce of both sea and land appertaining thereto; only the said John Kendrick does grant and allow the said Maquinnah to live and fish on the said territory as usual. And

by these presents does grant and sell to the said John Kendrick, his heirs, executors and administrators, all the abovementioned territory, known by the Indian name Chastacktoos, but now by the name of the Safe Retreat harbor; and also do grant and sell to the said John Kendrick, his heirs, executors and administrators, a free passage through all the rivers and passages, with all the outlets which lead to and from the said Nootka sound, of which, by the signing these presents, I have delivered unto the said John Kendrick. Signed with my own hand and the other chiefs', and bearing even date, to have and to hold the said premises, &c., to him, the said John Kendrick, his heirs, executors, and administrators, from henceforth and forever, as his property absolutely, without any other consideration whatever.

In witness whereof I have hereunto set my hand and the hands of my other chiefs, this twentieth day of July, one thousand seven hundred and ninety-one.[59]

Maquinna had purportedly sold a little more than 650 square kilometres (250 square miles) of territory for ten muskets. In other agreements Kendrick claimed to have purchased more than 2,600 square kilometres (1,000 square miles) (see figure 1 and figure 10).[60]

The transaction is among many by private interests in the English-speaking world purporting to purchase Indigenous land. Such purchases by Americans had long since been banned within the boundaries of the American colonies (and within the United States after independence), although the Supreme Court of the United States would not issue its famous ruling regarding such purchases for several decades. However, the legal weight of such purchases by Americans outside the boundaries of the United States was not settled. Obviously, Kendrick and his superiors hoped that the agreements might be accorded some legal weight.

Fragmentary evidence of what Maquinna and the other chiefs might have thought of those agreements is provided in subsequent letters. Kendrick's party apparently learned of John Meares's claim to have purchased land from Maquinna before Kendrick had. Captains Joseph Ingraham (under Kendrick's command) and Robert Gray claimed to have investigated the claim. On 3 August 1792, they wrote that "as to the land Mr. Meares said he purchased of Maquinnah or any other chief, we cannot say further than that we never heard of any, although we remained among these people nine months and could converse with them perfectly well; besides this, we have asked Maquinnah and other chiefs, since our arrival, if Captain Meares ever purchased any land in Nootka Sound; they answered: 'No, that Captain Kendrick was the only man to whom they had ever sold any land.'"⁶¹ More significant is a September 1792 entry in Joseph Ingraham's journal which indicated that "Maquinnhas executed to the Spaniards a deed of gift, accompanied by a declaration that he never sold any land whatever to Mr. Meares or any other person except Captain Kendrick, whom he acknowledges to be the proprietor of lands round Mahwinna; Captain Magie and Mr. Howard witnessed this deed and declaration."⁶² The Spanish, like the French, did not acknowledge Indigenous title as something that Indigenous people could sell, so the "gift," which was almost certainly reciprocated, appears to have been Quadra's strategy to respond to Kendrick's purchases. When Kendrick learned of the transaction while he was at Hong Kong, he saw great significance in the account that, although Maquinna made the grant to Quadra, Maquinna excluded from his grant the land he previously sold to Kendrick. Kendrick interpreted Quadra's acceptance of the grant as Spanish acknowledgment of the legitimacy of his own purchase. That apparently prompted him to register the deeds with the United States consulate, and send a letter to Thomas Jefferson, then Secretary of State, enclosing copies of the deeds, indicating to Jefferson that the purchases represented Maquinna's acceptance of the right of the United States to govern him.⁶³

Another hint at Indigenous understandings of Kendrick's treaties might be gained from a comment written by George Simpson in the 1840s: "a savage stands nearly as much in awe of paper, pen, and ink, as of steam [power] itself; and, if he once puts his cross to any writing, he has rarely been known to violate the engagement which such writing is supposed to embody or to sanction. To him the very look of black and white is a powerful 'medicine.'"⁶⁴ Simpson's words show that the Indigenous people of the Northwest Coast were familiar with, and attached great significance to, agreements committed to paper well before the HBC concluded treaties with them in the 1850s. Paul Kane also reported that Indigenous people revered writing. When he visited Fort Victoria in 1847, a chief from Nisqually told him that he carried with him an "old piece of newspaper, which he said he held up whenever he met with strange Indians, and that they, supposing it to be a letter for Fort Victoria, had allowed him to pass without molestation."⁶⁵

The signatories to the Vancouver Island treaties made sixty years later may not have known of Kendrick's purchases, but the evidence surrounding the transactions of the 1790s suggests that Maquinna believed that the agreement he made with Kendrick prevented him from granting the same land to the Spanish even as it guaranteed unhindered access to that land for his own people. His agreement for a small payment was made under no duress, but occurred when Maquinna sought to ensure that Kendrick and his successors would continue to make Maquinna's territory the base of their trade – a consideration more valuable than immediate compensation. Maquinna may well have understood the provision that the land would be Kendrick's property "from henceforth and forever," but, given the power relations prevailing at the time, both parties had to understand that Kendrick would be hard-pressed to occupy the land should it no longer be in Maquinna's interest to allow it. As it turned out, for as long as the memory of Kendrick's deeds survived among the Indigenous communities on Vancouver Island, the signatories knew that they had made the agreements at no cost at all. Neither Kendrick nor his successors ever returned to claim the rights Maquinna was purported to have conceded in them.

Notwithstanding any purported land purchases, British explorers continued to take possession and name lands along the coast of North America to bolster their claims. On 2 June 1792, Menzies reported that on the king's birthday, while in Puget Sound, "Cap$^t$ Vancouver landed about noon with some of the officers on the South point of the small Bay where he took possession of the country with the usual forms in his Majesty's name & named it New Georgia & on hoisting the English colours on the spot each Vessel proclaimed it aloud with a Royal Salute in honor of the day."[66]

Between 1800 and 1830, as the sea otter populations of the outer coast diminished, ship-based traders turned away from the west coast of Vancouver Island, especially Nootka Sound, towards the inner coasts between the Queen Charlotte Islands (Haida Gwaii) and northern Vancouver Island.[67] The shift had important repercussions for the villagers of the Northwest Coast, because the economic and military benefits shifted to the villagers along the mainland who controlled trading networks with Interior peoples. The Northwest Coast itself was not rich in furs, but the Interior was. As the journals of Alexander Mackenzie show, ship-based traders probably unwittingly plugged into pre-existing trading networks that channelled furs to the Pacific coast from as far away as the Peace River watershed. Villagers, particularly those who controlled trading centres on the lower Stikine, Nass, Skeena, and Bella Coola rivers, flourished from the increased trade.[68] Villagers occupying the two sides of the straits and gulfs between Vancouver Island and the mainland benefited less from that trade in the first two decades of the nineteenth century, because ships entered the Salish Sea less often. Thus, the military disadvantages under which the villagers of the Salish Sea suffered persisted in the early nineteenth century.

The villagers of southeastern Vancouver Island first encountered Europeans in the late 1780s or in 1790. British trader Charles Barkley may have entered the Strait of Juan de Fuca in 1787, but his journal is lost.[69] Spanish officer Manuel Quimper visited Esquimalt Harbour on 19 July 1790 (naming it Puerto de Córdova). The journals of his expedition state that the bay "was inhabited by Indians who called to him, manifesting their joy," suggesting that the villagers there had already had positive trading experiences with Europeans.[70] In 1792, Galiano's expedition also spent 9–10 June at Esquimalt Bay.[71] Quimper's party was there too early in the year to trade salmon, and Galiano's journals do not mention trading with the inhabitants of Esquimalt Bay, but it is clear from Spanish explorers' journals that the Spanish were, like the British, eager to trade salmon and furs.[72] However, the villagers of the district could not count on more than sporadic and desultory trading encounters.

Northwest Coast societies appear to have responded in various ways to the depopulation and escalating violence of the late nineteenth and early twentieth centuries. It was urgent for those along the rim of the Salish Sea, who became particularly vulnerable, to make the necessary adjustments. Whole communities that failed to adjust may have been destroyed, extirpated, or scattered during these years. Northwest Coast people abandoned, relocated, and consolidated their winter villages for various reasons. The dramatic depopulation and escalating warfare undermined the economic sustainability and military defensibility of some villages. Those forces led to the relocation and consolidation of winter villages. Winter village sites were chosen more for their shelter from winter storms, accessibility to firewood, and military defensibility than their proximity to resource-gathering sites. So, it was much less consequential for a community to abandon winter villages, which might be occupied for more than half a year, than it was to abandon fishing sites, even though the fishing sites might have been occupied for only a few weeks a year. However, as escalating warfare heightened the importance of the defensibility of winter villages, villagers abandoned village sites vulnerable to attacks. Various forces caused the disappearance of some communities and the consolidation of others, but also, probably, the emergence of entirely new communities and identities.[73]

Villagers also appear to have forged broader political affiliations and alliances during the nineteenth century. Ethnographers typically identify the household-extended families or groups of closely related families that shared ancestry or history as the primary units of Northwest Coast societies, although the level of tribal unity may always have varied across the region. However, in a process that occurred so often to be regarded as prevalent, "tribalization" was a common response to the emergence of major military threats.[74] Archaeologist Bill Angelbeck has argued that, even when household groups were at odds with each other, they could still ally against common threats. While it might be more difficult for larger groups (villages and entire tribes) to ally this way, there is evidence that they did so in the face of dire threats.[75] At any rate, the challenges posed by depopulation and warfare led communities that were previously only loosely affiliated to form closer alignments.[76]

The villagers of the Northwest Coast were no strangers to change before 1774, but the arrival of Europeans thereafter injected entirely new forces of demographic, social, economic, political, and geopolitical upheaval. Because the maritime fur trade enhanced the economic and military position of villagers along western Vancouver Island, their chiefs used various measures – including treaties – to protect their privileged position in that trade. By contrast, villagers along the Salish Sea and along the east coast of Vancouver Island had very limited access to European goods, including weaponry, although they apparently suffered at least one epidemic before 1821. The history of the period between 1774 and 1821 provides crucial context for the thirty years examined in chapter 5. Scholars have described that period as stable, but the evidence of cultural continuity should not obscure the dramatic changes of those tumultuous years.[77]

# 5 Indigenous Peoples of Vancouver Island and the Hudson's Bay Company, 1821–1849

The establishment of Hudson's Bay Company trading posts brought economic opportunities and military security to the people along the rim of the Salish Sea, including the lower Fraser River. Villagers on the southeastern corner of Vancouver Island had suffered disadvantages compared with their neighbours for thousands of years. Because salmon were more difficult to acquire there, villages there were comparatively small and vulnerable. Between 1774 and 1821, their relative position deteriorated further. Smallpox devastated the communities in the Salish Sea but spared most of their neighbours. But then those neighbours gained privileged access to European firearms and ammunition, thanks to insatiable demand for sea otters.

In the late 1820s, the fortunes of those along the east coast of Vancouver Island improved. Even though the region was not rich in furs, it became between 1827 and 1850 the site of several HBC trading posts. None became a major fur trading centre, but became instead fish-processing, agricultural, sawmilling, mining, and administrative centres.[1] Villagers seized the economic and military opportunities these posts presented. Those who could position themselves adjacent to the posts benefited most. They greatly outnumbered the HBC traders, and their interactions with the traders were sufficiently mutually beneficial that relations were normally friendly. Like the agreements of 1788 and 1791, the treaties of the 1850s must be understood in the context of the complex relations of the signatory communities with the HBC, their historically vulnerable position vis-à-vis their neighbours, and the internal tensions within those communities.

The HBC had many decades of experience as a trading company, but it was a newcomer to the Pacific slope of North America. Until its merger with the NWC in 1821, the HBC traded almost exclusively with nomadic hunting and gathering peoples. In the subarctic, populations were sparse, and most HBC posts were small and undefended. But the company could draw upon the experience it had gained since the late 1770s at strongly fortified posts in and on the margins of the northern plains where warfare was pervasive. Although HBC traders along the North Saskatchewan River suffered direct and deadly attacks during the 1780s and 1790s, by the 1820s, they had learned to deal successfully with encampments of equestrian, well-armed Blackfoot, Sarcee, Gros Ventre, and Assiniboine bands that outnumbered the personnel in the forts.[2]

Still, when the HBC expanded its operations into the Pacific watershed in the 1820s, it had little experience dealing with semi-sedentary villagers. It drew after 1821 upon the experience of former NWC traders who had prior experience in the Pacific slope, but few were familiar with the Northwest Coast. That explains why Chief Factor John McLoughlin recruited the experienced American ship-based trader William H. McNeill into the HBC's service in 1832.[3] People like McNeill bridged the eras of maritime and land-based trade.

Until 1827, villagers on or near Vancouver Island conducted their trade with Europeans exclusively from ships that visited the region primarily in the summers. Russian posts such as Novo-Arkhangelsk among the Tlingit and American and British posts on the lower Columbia were out of reach of Vancouver Island peoples. When the HBC and NWC amalgamated in 1821, the NWC's operations in the interior west of the Rocky Mountains and the lower Columbia River became part of the transcontinental merged company. It took a few years for the HBC's directors to understand fully their western operations, but by 1827, the company was ready to vie for the lucrative trade of the Northwest Coast.[4] To compete with ship-based traders who arrived on the coast every spring, and Russians, who appeared intent on expanding their claims southward from their posts in Tlingit territories, the HBC initially adopted a strategy of establishing permanent trading posts at strategic locations along the coast.[5] It established Fort Langley on the lower Fraser River in 1827, Fort Nass/Simpson near the mouth of the Nass River in 1831 (relocated to a location near the mouth of the Skeena River in 1834), Fort Nisqually in Puget Sound in 1832, Fort McLoughlin in Milbanke Sound in 1833, Fort Durham (Taku) near the mouth of the Taku River in 1834, Fort Stikine in 1840, Fort Victoria in 1843, and Fort Rupert at Beaver Harbour in 1849 (see figure 9).[6]

Maquinna and Wickaninnish had apparently made their 1788 and 1791 agreements to convince traders to establish posts in their territories, apparently sensing that they and their people would benefit more from permanent posts adjacent to their villages than from even the most regular and reliable visits of ships. People in the Interior also wanted the trading posts in their territories.[7] The Northwest Coast was no different. Villagers sought HBC trading posts in their territories and often resented the establishment of such posts in the territories of their rivals.[8] As the locus of the trade moved from shipboard trade on the outer coasts to land-based posts, methods may have evolved, but villagers and traders alike welcomed the trade, and both parties exerted considerable control over their participation in the relationships.[9]

HBC posts presented villagers with new opportunities for wealth accumulation that far exceeded the trade of furs. Villagers exchanged provisions (especially fish and potatoes), labour (from day labour to six-month engagements), coal, domestic work, and sexual services for a variety of European goods from weaponry (firearms, powder, and ammunition), to tools (including axes, knives, and adzes), utensils (including pots and kettles), cloth (including woollen blankets and baize), and luxury items (including beads). For example, after 1849, HBC wool blankets quickly displaced cedar-bark blankets and those made of sea otter, bear, or other animal skins.[10] HBC posts altered multilateral relations in favour of those with privileged access to the forts, but also changed the dynamics within those societies. Historically, the nobility had controlled important resource procurement sites and had an exclusive right to sea otter furs. Prominent leaders also jealously guarded their privileged access to ship-based traders. Permanent posts had the potential to further enrich the elite but also destabilized the hierarchy by reducing the potential for men to gain status and prestige in warfare, and giving commoners, and even slaves, new opportunities to accumulate and share wealth. HBC woollen blankets were not merely practical items; they became the single most important prestige item. Historical documents do not describe the dynamics in detail, but the realities at villages adjacent to Northwest Coast trading posts were starkly different than they had been during the era of the ship-based trade.

Commoners and slaves must have produced many of the provisions and furs and provided much of the labour at trading posts. It would have been impolitic, given the explicit orders of the HBC's Governor and Committee to suppress slavery, for traders to highlight the importance of slave labour in Vancouver Island societies. The company's directors, and most of the officers in the Columbia District, objected to slavery and attempted to keep it out of HBC posts. But they also understood the difficulties and unintended consequences that might result from attempting to end slavery within the Indigenous communities; slavery persisted in Northwest Coast societies even into the 1870s. Moreover, HBC officers understood slavery well enough, and could differentiate between slaves and commoners, so that they, unlike some other newcomers who inadvertently hired slaves, probably tried to avoid paying owners the wages for the labour of their slaves.[11] But whether they succeeded or not, new economic opportunities inevitably reverberated throughout communities. To the extent that owners did hire out their slaves (and it must have happened to some extent), their ability to accumulate wealth was enhanced. To the extent that they used slave labour to process the furs, salmon, and potatoes that they traded to the HBC, the elite must have been enriched by the company's demand for those products. Still, commoners probably benefited more than the elite because of the new economic opportunities. The company's policy and the inclination of men such as James Douglas to use moral suasion to undermine slavery must have led traders to hire free commoners as much as possible. That trend would only have accelerated after missionaries and clergy arrived. The new economic realities must have produced – especially in a context in which formerly separate villages had consolidated – very dynamic social relations and significant social tension that placed substantial pressures on the leaders of the communities.

Given their circumstances, the villagers of the Salish Sea and Johnstone Strait must have been delighted to see trading posts established in or near their territories. The ship-based traders had largely bypassed them, so until 1827 they had only poor access to European goods. But by 1849 they had exceptionally secure access to those goods. Forts Langley, Nisqually, Victoria, and Rupert became permanent even after the HBC abandoned Forts McLoughlin and Durham in 1843, and Fort Stikine in 1849.

John McLoughlin, the influential Chief Factor in charge of the Columbia District, believed that permanent coastal posts were essential to compete against ship-based traders. By 1832, however, his superior, George Simpson, the North American Governor of the HBC, preferred abandoning some of the permanent posts and acquiring a steamer, which he understood would be much more manoeuvrable than sailing ships were. The historian E.E. Rich credited Simpson with prescience in turning to steam: "the age of steamship predominance lay at least a generation ahead, and it required imagination to make such a suggestion for the Pacific Coast in 1832. But the advantages of steamers were thought to lie chiefly in the navigation of coastal waters, inland waterways, and short ferry-boat trips. On such lines the Pacific Coast certainly seemed a proper ground for a steamer."[12] But Simpson claimed to have additional reasons to adopt a steam vessel. He explained that the HBC's introduction of the *Beaver* in 1836 significantly changed the demeanour of Indigenous people towards the traders.[13] Elaborating, he wrote that "independently of physical advantages, steam ... may be said to exert an almost superstitious influence over the savages; besides acting without intermission on their fears, it has, in a great measure, subdued their very love of robbery and violence. In a word, it has inspired the red man with a new opinion – new not in degree but in kind – of the superiority of his white brother."[14] In the mid-1840s, before Fort Rupert was established, he noted that the Kwakiutl and Nahwitti "had long been anxious that we should form a permanent establishment among them. But the mysterious steamer, against which neither calms nor contrary winds were any security, possessed, in our estimation, this advantage over stationary forts, that, besides being as convenient for the purposes of trade, she was the terror, whether present or absent, of every tribe on the coast."[15] Although Simpson, who was writing for a popular audience, might have been embellishing the effects of steamships upon Indigenous people of the Northwest Coast, his account reflects others that state that steamships impressed Indigenous peoples.[16] The Fort Rupert post journals indicate that when the British Navy's steamship *Driver* visited Fort Rupert in March 1850, "the appearance of a vessel of war has a good effect on the Indians."[17]

And so it was that in March 1836, the HBC's steamer, SS *Beaver*, arrived on the Northwest Coast to increase the HBC's competitive advantage over its rivals, and, apparently, to impress the Indigenous customers of the company. It was so successful at capturing the trade of the Northwest Coast, and – through Indigenous intermediaries the trade of the Interior – that the HBC closed Forts McLoughlin and Durham in 1843, and Fort Stikine in 1849, retaining Forts Vancouver, Nisqually, Victoria, Langley, Rupert, and Simpson as bases, and using smaller vessels, including the *Beaver*, to cruise the coastline.[18] In 1852, the company established Nanaimo. Thus, the villagers of Johnstone Strait and the Salish Sea who had been the most vulnerable before 1827, gained privileged access to European goods, including weaponry.

The HBC learned before it arrived on the Northwest Coast to attempt to convince all Indigenous communities, both those who lived near the posts and those who travelled to the posts from afar, to respect trading posts as neutral grounds.[19] It took some effort to establish the rule, but the HBC attempted to do so by building well-defended forts, strenuously asserting this policy to all who traded at the posts, maintaining strict neutrality when their trading partners were at odds, seeking to broker peace agreements among warring groups when possible, and excluding from the trade those distant bands – and punishing the adjacent ones – who did not respect the neutrality principle. For example, when parties of Haida and Tlingit were on the verge of fighting over a slave boy at Fort Simpson in 1837, "they were told if they had quarrels to settle and must fight, to fight elsewhere for that we would not allow them to fight at our fort."[20] Historians have noticed that HBC posts along the Northwest Coast served as neutral grounds despite chronic regional warfare. Robin Fisher noted that HBC traders on the Northwest Coast tried "to settle intertribal conflicts by negotiation. ... Traders did sometimes try to act as mediators between warring parties of Indians. They wanted Indians to recognize that the forts were neutral grounds where all were free to trade; the Indians were told that their disputes should be settled elsewhere."[21]

The HBC's neutrality policy had consequences for the Northwest Coast elite and their communities. They could not aspire to control trade networks as Maquinna and Wickaninnish had done in the 1780s and 1790s. The HBC – "emporalists" rather than imperialists – even as it enjoyed charters and licences that excluded other British competitors – insisted upon free trade among the peoples of the Northwest Coast.[22] The opportunities for wealth accumulation grew dramatically and were shared more broadly. But the opportunities to gain renown by success in warfare diminished. In short, disruptions altered the fortunes of the elite, commoners, and slaves.

As emporalists, HBC traders rarely initiated violence. They attempted to cultivate friendly relations with all. However, if they could not always be loved, they did always wish to be feared. They considered it essential to deter aggression by avenging all attacks on them.[23] They sought revenge against the individuals responsible for killings, but that was sometimes impossible. In November 1823, a party of Dunne-za attacked and killed five HBC traders at Fort St. John. Finding it impossible to locate the killers, George Simpson informed the Governor and Committee that "it is found necessary to make an example of them by convincing them of their dependence upon us and shewing how easy it is for us if so disposed to punish and make the whole Tribe accountable for the improper conduct of an individual by withdrawing from their Lands altogether and thereby reducing them to absolute starvation."[24] It was not until 1828, when Simpson was convinced that the Dunne-za had attempted to find and punish the killers and were treating them as outcasts, that he responded to their pleas to re-establish posts in the upper Peace River region. James Douglas had himself retaliated against villagers early in his career. In August 1828, Douglas boldly and summarily avenged the 1823 killing of two HBC men at Fort George (New Caledonia) by executing one of the suspected killers in the Nak'azdli village adjacent to Fort St. James.[25] That act helps explain why Douglas ended up on the coast. After Douglas's actions, William Connolly and Douglas feared that Nak'azdli leaders would kill Douglas, so Douglas was transferred to Fort Vancouver in 1830. In short, by 1827, the HBC knew how to establish trading posts as free trade neutral zones, and believed that even threatening to abandon posts often made Indigenous groups more cooperative.

An incident that occurred soon after the HBC established Fort Langley in 1827, illustrates several of the HBC's principles of vengeance. In December 1827, Alexander McKenzie, an HBC clerk from Fort Vancouver, delivered letters to Fort Langley. He then left Fort Langley on 3 January 1828 with four other men and a woman. Some Klallam intercepted the party in Puget Sound, killed the men, and enslaved the woman. Convinced that the attack was unprovoked and mounted merely for the sake of plunder, John McLoughlin considered it essential that the company respond swiftly with an expedition sufficiently punitive to deter any future attacks.

He explained to the London Governor and Committee that he declined the offers of other Indigenous people to take revenge on the Klallam, because he believed that would incite intertribal warfare, put the HBC in the debt of those peoples, and "lower us in their opinion, as they would consider by our employing them that we were unable without their assistance to protect ourselves."[26] Instead, he organized a punitive expedition of about seventy men, employing the *Beaver*, which avenged the killings during the summer by killing twenty-two Klallam, burning their village on the Olympic Peninsula (about 50 kilometres from the eventual location of Fort Victoria), and recovering the enslaved woman unharmed.[27] In defending his actions to the HBC's London Committee, McLoughlin claimed that "we were forced by necessity" to mount a punitive expedition.[28] His superior agreed. After claiming that "treaties or compacts of peace with the nations of the N.W. Coast are attended with no good end, as they are not respected for one moment if a favorable opportunity of breaking them presents itself," Simpson argued that "unless very severe punishment is inflicted, forbearance is ascribed to the want of means or of courage to resent the Outrages they commit upon us, lowering us in the estimation of every Tribe with which we have dealings, and encouraging them to make attempts on our lives and property whenever it can be done with success."[29]

Even if HBC traders were feared, they might also still be loved. The HBC provided medicine, vaccines, and emergency relief and care to its Indigenous clients throughout its territories, although the loss of most of the journals from the Northwest Coast prevents us from knowing the extent of such services there. In 1837, when the HBC was defending its charter to Rupert's Land and applying for an early renewal of its twenty-one-year licence to its territories outside Rupert's Land, including the Columbia District, its London Governor, J.H. Pelly, referred to the "peace, order and tranquillity which have so successfully been maintained by the Hudson's Bay Company, during the last 15 years."[30] George Simpson supported Pelly in a letter stating that HBC posts were "the resort or refuge of many of the natives who, from age, infirmity, or other causes, are unable to follow the chase; they have the benefit of the care and attention, free of expense, of our medical men, of whom about 12 are usually employed in the service; every trading establishment being in fact an Indian hospital."[31] After the American Presbyterian missionary Samuel Parker visited the HBC's Fort Vancouver in 1835-36, he wrote that "here is a well-regulated medical department, and a hospital for the accommodation of the sick laborers, in which Indians who are laboring under any difficult and dangerous diseases are received, and in most cases have gratuitous attendance."[32] Because the peoples of the Northwest Coast were villagers, the HBC dealt with them differently than they did with nomadic peoples (the company was less likely to have to house the infirm, but better placed to provide medicine, vaccines, and minor surgery).

Historian Edward Cavanagh has argued that "by exercising jurisdiction over nearby First Nations, the HBC took steps toward ensuring that its own sovereignty was more formidable than Indigenous forms of sovereignty."[33] Cavanagh also argued that the HBC's "welfare regime" helped it maintain a population of loyal subjects around its forts.[34] Cavanagh probably took the evidence too far, but David Chan Smith was right when he argued that the HBC did not act simply as "slavish economic agents of the state nor straightforwardly sovereign actors."[35] The fact is that other fur trading companies without government charters, including the NWC and the American Fur Company (AFC), provided similar services to sick and infirm Indigenous people.[36]

Northwest Coast peoples continued fortifying villages into the mid-nineteenth century. Many villages were either fortified themselves or had fortifications nearby.[37] If anything, the villagers along the rim of the Salish Sea intensified their use of fortifications in the first half of the nineteenth century. Exogenous observers, even naval officers, were impressed by them.[38] In 1853, William Ebrington Gordon noted "a stockade built in imitation of Fort Victoria" at a village at Porlier Pass, between Galiano and Valdes Islands.[39]

Not all villages were fortified. Communities that had the option of relocating to the immediate vicinity of HBC posts appear not to have fortified their settlements. Although the HBC typically established forts at some distance from the nearest winter village, residents of nearby villages invariably moved and consolidated their settlements at HBC posts. Robin Fisher emphasized the economic motives of the villagers, arguing that these villagers attempted to control the trade of the posts, concluding that "they set themselves up as middlemen between other Indians and the company traders ... [T]hese Indians were keenly aware of the benefits of controlling a fort. They were often pleased when they learned that a fort was to be built in their midst and became angry and hostile when they heard that a fort was to be relocated or abandoned."[40]

Village consolidation had social and political ramifications. The leaders of formerly separate villages tended to jostle for pre-eminence in the consolidated villages, but also formed larger political entities. For example, according to Philip Drucker, when the Tsimshian consolidated nine winter villages near Fort Simpson, they also formed a "loose confederacy" that had not existed before.[41]

HBC journals also show that at least some villages adjacent to HBC posts became permanently occupied. The security offered by proximity to the forts and the many economic opportunities available at the posts explain why some, probably especially those too young, old, or infirm to assist at the fisheries, stayed at the villages near trading posts where they could tend gardens and be paid to work at the posts. However, HBC journals show that even some able-bodied men stayed at the villages adjacent to HBC posts, even during the main fishing season. So secure were the villages near HBC posts, that they were lightly defended compared with other villages in the region.

Fort Langley was the first permanent post accessible to the villagers around the Salish Sea, and it was there that these villagers encountered the HBC's trading practices. Although the fort was not on the island, between 1827 and 1843 it was the primary trading post for many of the communities that entered treaty in 1850, 1852, and 1854, including the Songhees, Saanich, and Nanaimo. The HBC established Fort Langley in 1827, with the dual aim of wresting the coastal trade from American ship-based traders and replacing Fort Vancouver as the headquarters and depot of the Columbia District, should the HBC be forced by a boundary settlement between the British and American governments to withdraw from the Columbia River.[42] However, when an 1828 expedition that included George Simpson confirmed that the Fraser River was impractical as a transportation route between the coast and the interior, it became obvious that it could not serve as a headquarters.[43] Originally established along the lower Fraser River across from the mouth of Kanaka Creek, Fort Langley was relocated in 1839 four kilometres upriver (to the site of the present-day Fort

Langley National Historic Site), where it remained until it was closed in 1889 (see figure 9).[44]

The Kwantlen were the primary beneficiaries of the establishment of Fort Langley. Soon after the fort was built, they moved their main village upstream to the shadow of the fort. But the post became important to Coast Salish of the entire region, including those who had winter villages on Vancouver Island but had fishing sites on the lower Fraser River (Nanaimo and Cowichan) or in the bays and straits near the mouth of the Fraser River (Songhees and Saanich). From 1827 to 1843, Fort Langley was their nearest trading post.[45] Within three years of establishing Fort Langley, the traders at Fort Langley had gathered a great deal of information about the Indigenous groups located around the rim of the Salish Sea, and had received visits from a remarkable number of those groups.[46]

The Fort Langley post journals shed some light on the process by which traders convinced their customers to regard HBC forts as neutral zones. Traders at Fort Langley were initially cautious because of the 2,000 Kwantlen who gathered at the construction site.[47] The Kwantlen wished to exchange their furs for blankets, arms, and ammunition, but James McMillan wrote, while the post was still being constructed, that he judged "it expedient at present to refuse them" any weaponry.[48] In the first years after the post was established, the Cowichan and Lekwiltok attacked the Coast Salish communities of the lower Fraser River in a pattern that predated the establishment of the post. Between 1827 and 1830 the Kwantlen feared leaving the vicinity of Fort Langley to hunt.[49] However, they appear to have assumed that the presence of the lightly manned Fort Langley would offer them protection. On 13 March 1829, Archibald McDonald, in charge at Fort Langley, indicated of the Kwantlen that "although those here abouts are themselves pretty numerous and ought to be able to make a good Stand before Strangers Coming upon them, yet on this occasion they Seem to put their greatest faith in the protection of the Six White men in the Fort – However in Case Something may be pending over us, we keep them all alike at a distance."[50]

The HBC traders believed that the Kwantlen, who benefited most from the HBC's protection, had the greatest obligation to keep peace with people arriving at or departing the fort. After a Snohomish man and his wife arrived at Fort Langley on 30 September 1835 to trade, the man began imprudently "boasting that he either had or would kill some of the people here [at Fort Langley] with Medicine or conjuring." According to John Work, when the couple left Fort Langley on 4 October, a Kwantlen party followed them, "shot the man and cut off his head and brought back the wife with them as a prisoner or slave."[51] John Work noted that when James Murray Yale heard of this, he went "accompanied by a party of men armed, and released the woman and beat one or two of the Indians, for behaving so to any strangers that come here, when at the same time they are depending for their own safety in a great measure on the protection of the fort."[52] Yale would not have been able to punish a Lekwiltok party the same way had it committed the same deed against a Kwantlen couple or against a Cowichan couple, but neither did the Lekwiltok or Cowichan enjoy the protection of any HBC posts.

Presumably to protect themselves and the nearby Kwantlen villagers, the traders at Fort Langley initially refused to arm the Vancouver Island people.[53] However, the policy proved ineffective because they could easily acquire weapons from ship-based traders.[54] And so, McDonald adopted a new strategy in 1829 after learning that the "Yewkultas" (Lekwiltok) were terrorizing the villagers throughout the Puget Sound, even south of the Fraser River, including the formidable Cowichan. On 24 April 1829 McDonald noted that two Vancouver Island chiefs, Scheenuck, a "Sandish" (Songhees) leader, and a Cowichan chief that he called Joe, had arrived at Langley. Joe wanted "to buy for himself a gun and 300 rounds of ammunition for distribution among his followers that are already armed." He wanted the gun and ammunition to enable his community to defend themselves against the Lekwiltok. McDonald remarked that although arming the Cowichan might seem injudicious, "from the general horror at present of the Yewkaltas by all the Indians we have to do with, I think the more we promote the ruin of that detestable tribe, the more effectually we secure the good faith of those nearer home, & convince them of the acquisition they have gained by the Establishment."[55]

McDonald's strategy reflected HBC policy to trade freely, even in arms and ammunition, with all visitors as part of a policy of being impartial in all disputes. Refusing to trade arms with any visitors dangerously violated neutrality. The Kwantlen greatly outnumbered the personnel at Fort Langley, but the traders fortified and armed the fort to make it formidable. The HBC established friendly relations with their immediate neighbours, establishing kin relations and a measure of reciprocity.[56] Rather than refusing trade with others, they preferred making those communities reliant on them for all their trade goods, including weaponry. That gave them the leverage to convince visiting groups not to wage war against other communities near the posts.

The Lekwiltok threat persisted into the 1850s. Between 1841 and the mid-1850s, the Lekwiltok supplanted Coast Salish communities on the east coast of Vancouver Island between Salmon River and Cape Mudge, and terrorized others farther south.[57] Most Salish villagers along eastern Vancouver Island south of Cape Mudge and in the Alberni Valley including the Pentlatch, Qualicum, Sliammon, Nanoose, Opetchesaht, and Comox were decimated, exterminated, forced to abandon their locations, or absorbed by Wakashan-speakers.[58] Scholars have attributed this aggressive expansion to their superior access to firearms.[59] Beleaguered Coast Salish villagers may have allied in the mid-nineteenth century to arrest the aggression and territorial expansion of the Lekwiltok, although they continued to fear their raids and those of other northern peoples well into the 1860s.[60] At the same time, James Douglas, by then the Governor of the colony of Vancouver Island, began to signal to the Lekwiltok that he would no longer tolerate their raids. Reporting on a visit made in August 1853, Douglas informed the Colonial Secretary that he had confronted them and "endeavoured to impress upon their minds, that they must in future, live honestly and dwell in peace with their neighbours, as the time was at hand, when every act of rapine or violence, would be restrained or punished."[61]

At the same time, the Cowichan continued to raid villages along the lower Fraser River. In a paper based on his experiences before 1855, Alexander C. Anderson wrote:

> The Haitlins [Kwantlen], ... inhabiting the lower parts of Frazer's River, rarely venture to its mouth; where, as on the opposite shore of Vancouvers Island, the, Ca-witchans, a bolder tribe, hold sway. Death, or slavery even worse than death, are the alternatives presented to the weaker among these tribes, when they are so hapless as to fall into the power of a more puissant neighbor. Palisaded villages and other precautions against surprise, show that even at home a ceaseless dread prevails. This state of the insecurity I may here mention, pervades the north west coast, more or less, according to the strength of each tribe relatively with that of the neighbors around.[62]

Anderson appears to have described the geopolitical circumstances among the Indigenous villagers accurately. In Puget Sound, the Suquamish nearly exterminated the Chemakum of the Port Townsend region in 1847, only three years before the first of the Vancouver Island treaties was concluded.[63] The Northwest Coast was a turbulent and dangerous place in the first half of the nineteenth century. The dangers Douglas and Anderson described deterred villagers from the Salish Sea from unnecessary travel. According to John Work, after the HBC established Fort Nisqually in 1832, fewer Puget Sound villagers traded at Fort Langley.[64]

Fort Langley became neither a major depot nor a major fur trading centre; it emerged instead as a salmon-trading fort and farm. Although some consideration was given to abandoning Fort Langley when its unsuitability as a headquarters for the Columbia Department became obvious, HBC Chief Factor John McLoughlin realized its economic potential. In 1835, he wrote that "there is no place on the coast where Salmon is so abundant and got so cheap as at Fort Langley; and if we find a sale for Salmon, it would alone more than pay the expence [sic] of keeping up that place."[65] He was right. The traders at Fort Langley bought salmon for consumption by HBC personnel and to be sold on the export market. In 1838, James Douglas, then HBC Chief Trader in charge at Fort Vancouver, wrote that the salmon fishery of Fort Langley was "an object of much importance and merits the utmost attention, if you think its produce could be greatly increased, the means will be furnished of doing it ample justice. The Farm is also of great service and should be carefully attended."[66] Fort Langley remained into the 1850s the HBC's most important salmon procurement and processing centre.[67]

The Fort Langley journals state that several Indigenous communities with winter villages on Vancouver Island, including the Nanaimo, Saanich, and Cowichan, participated in the trade in salmon, and that, although the HBC traders considered them to live mostly on Vancouver Island, the company also understood that these groups had summer fisheries on the Fraser River. For example, the journals noted of the Nanaimo that "during the Salmon Season they occupy a large Village they have about 3 miles below this [Fort Langley across from the mouth of Kanaka Creek] on Same Side the river."[68]

The four-year cycle of the sockeye salmon encouraged traders to depend on the Indigenous fishery. HBC personnel at Langley experimented with procuring fish on their own,[69] but they found that in years when the salmon were scarce the catch was so small, and that in abundant years the price that the Kwantlen demanded was so low, that staffing their own fisheries did not pay the cost of salaries and equipment of their fishermen.[70] On 25 February 1830, Archibald McDonald informed the Governor and Committee that "in years of Scarcity the best regulated fishery of our own would miscarry while in years of plenty such as last [1829 having been a dominant year in the sockeye cycle] the expense in trade would hardly exceed the very cost of Lines and Twine."[71] The HBC also employed Indigenous women to process the salmon, again, because hiring experienced and skilled Indigenous seasonal labourers was more economical than maintaining a cadre of employees to do the work. Documents do not explain how much of the labour was slave labour, or whether owners seized the pay of any slaves, but by the early 1830s, the fishery at Fort Langley provided a significant economic opportunity for the Kwantlen and other villagers.

Trade in salmon for export grew over the years as demand and prices in Honolulu rose. HBC salmon production grew from a then-unprecedented 540 barrels in 1841, to 600 barrels in 1845, and over 3,000 barrels in 1849 (each of these were dominant years in the sockeye cycle), as prices in Honolulu rose from between ten and eleven dollars per barrel to fifteen dollars per barrel.[72] As James Douglas and John Work pointed out, given that the total cost of producing a barrel was about four dollars, the trade was yielding "a considerable profit."[73] Little wonder that the traders urged villagers to bring in as much salmon as they could. By the time the Vancouver Island treaties were concluded, the villagers were engaged in a substantial commercial trade in salmon processed by the HBC for export.

The HBC also cultivated a substantial acreage at Fort Langley. As early as 1835, John Work indicated that there were about 30 acres cultivated in the immediate vicinity of the fort and another 40 to 45 acres at the Langley plain, about 7 miles away. The post personnel grew potatoes, wheat, peas, barley, oats, and Indian corn. They also had about 60 pigs, 20 head of cattle, and 6 oxen.[74] By 1845, the HBC cultivated about 245 acres at Fort Langley, and the wheat, potatoes, peas, and barley were grown for local consumption, to supply other HBC posts, and for export to Russian America.[75]

The HBC were not the only agriculturalists along the Northwest Coast. Indigenous people adopted potato (*Solanum tuberosum*) cultivation quickly.[76] Potato cultivation was already well established on Haida Gwaii by the mid-1820s.[77] The Haida may have acquired potatoes from any number of places. By the 1820s, fur traders had already begun cultivating potatoes in New Caledonia, and Russian traders had apparently brought potatoes to Russian America.

The villagers of Vancouver Island and the adjacent mainland probably adopted potato cultivation somewhat later than the Haida did, but did so well before 1835. In 1835, John Work noted that at Fort Langley, "each of the principal men" among the Kwantlen had a garden, explaining that J.M. Yale, "by encouraging them to till the ground and raise potatoes, has conferred a great benefit, for which he tells me they appear grateful, and indeed well they may, for it is the most effecient [sic] step that could be taken to promote their civilization, and in some measure to secure themselves against the occasional scarcity of food which people dependant on the precarious produce of the chase so often experience."[78] Likewise, in 1839, James Douglas reported that Indigenous people around Fort Langley, and to a lesser extent throughout the region, had begun to cultivate potatoes on their own initiative:

> as a matter likely to interest the friends of our native population, and all who desire to trace the first dawn and early progress of civilization, that the Cowegins around Fort Langley, influenced by the Council and example of the Fort, are beginning to cultivate the soil, many of them having with great perseverance and industry cleared patches of forest Land of sufficient extent to plant each 10 bus$^h$ of Potatoes, the same spirit of enterprise extends, though less generally to the Gulf of Georgia & De Fuca's Straits, where the very novel sight of flourishing fields of potatoes satisfied our Missionary Visitors, that the Hon$^{ble}$. Company neither oppose, nor feel indifferent to the march of improvement.[79]

The wording of this passage suggests that Douglas did not in 1839 understand the Indigenous people to have engaged in cultivation before they began growing potatoes.

Potato cultivation fit with Northwest Coast lifeways. Potato leaves are toxic to herbivores, and potatoes compete well with other plants, even if they are not tended during the busy salmon processing season, so once planted in the spring, the plants could produce a crop, even with minimal care during the growing season. However, the fact that villages adjacent to trading posts appear to have been inhabited year-round suggests that some potato crops were carefully tended for the entire growing season. Moreover, in the mild autumns and winters of the Northwest Coast, harvests could be delayed until less busy times of the year. Given the ubiquity of potato cultivation among villagers in the region well before 1850, those villagers valued the supplements to their food supply. At various posts along the Northwest Coast, the villagers also marketed potatoes to the HBC. Wayne Suttles argued that villagers took up potato cultivation so enthusiastically because the traders bought them so eagerly.[80]

It is impossible to know how potato cultivation affected social and economic relations within villages. Potato cultivation appears to have been the task of women (and probably slaves).[81] John Work's statement that gardens were the possessions of the principal men among the Kwantlen suggests that the actual cultivation was undertaken at least in part by slave labour. It is not clear, however, how potato cultivation affected opportunities for women or non-noble families to accrue food supplies and wealth independent of the nobility. Because documents do not tell us whether individuals or families enjoyed sole rights to the potato harvests, or whether the chiefs had rights as well, it is difficult to assess how the internal dynamics of Northwest Coast communities might have been affected by incipient cultivation.[82] It is obvious, however, that Indigenous potato cultivation, absent on the Northwest Coast before the early nineteenth century, was an endeavour of some economic and social significance by the 1850s. It is also likely that the importance of camas declined as potato cultivation grew.

Even after Fort Langley was established, some people around the Salish Sea could acquire European goods more cheaply by dealing with Kwakiutl intermediaries (who traded with American ship-based traders off northern Vancouver Island) than by trading at Fort Langley.[83] American ships in Milbanke Sound also plugged into trading networks that drew off furs from the HBC's posts in New Caledonia. The HBC established Fort McLoughlin on Campbell Island in Milbanke Sound in 1833 to thwart that competition. However, because the HBC employed predatory pricing until Americans were driven from the region, during the 1830s the Kwakiutl could acquire goods either at Fort McLoughlin or from the ships and trade those goods to the people of the Salish Sea, on better terms than those people could get at Fort Langley.[84] Fort McLoughlin, established as it was on a rugged island, did not occupy much land. Aside from the post, there was a small garden of only three acres in which the traders cultivated cabbages, potatoes, turnips, carrots, and other vegetables.[85]

The Bella Coola (Nuxalk) of Milbanke Sound, vulnerable to Haida and Tsimshian raids, welcomed the establishment of the fort, which significantly improved their security. In 1834, Alexander Caulfield Anderson wrote that, before the HBC established Fort McLoughlin, Sebassa (Ts'ibassa), a powerful chief of the Kitkatla division of Tsimshian, frequently raided Milbanke Sound for slaves, and that the Nuxalk, "not being then able to cope with them, were under the necessity of submitting passively to his tyranny, but since our building there, in consequence of the countenance of the fort, they have become more independent of their ci-devant oppressor, who is not now quite so ready to disturb them."[86] However, the Nuxalk were also initially aggressive towards the HBC traders, as they had been with ship-based traders. "At first," explained George Simpson, the Nuxalk

> were exceedingly turbulent; and one of our people, of the name of François Richard, having disappeared, the chief was seized as a hostage for the restitution of the white man. In a skirmish, which the retaliatory step occasioned, one of the garrison was taken prisoner, and two were wounded, while of the Indians several were wounded and two killed. After much negociation, the chief, who was detained by the whites, was exchanged for

the man who had been captured by the natives. The fate of Richard, however, remained a mystery, till some women gradually blabbed the secret, that he had been murdered by a certain individual. The murderer having been pointed out to me, as he walked openly and boldly about the fort, I took measures for sending the fellow to a distance, as an example to his friends.[87]

In 1841, George Simpson summarized the history of relations at Fort McLoughlin by stating that "the natives who were at one time troublesome are now comparatively peaceable towards the establishment, more from a feeling that they are to a certain extent in our power, than from any good disposition towards us."[88]

Fort McLoughlin was also important to villagers from northern Vancouver Island. During the entire period of the ship-borne trade, the Kwakiutl had more tenuous access to European goods, including weaponry, than their neighbours on the outer coast, but had superior access compared with groups around the Salish Sea. So, although they were on the defensive against some of their neighbours, they were typically aggressors against those to the southeast.[89]

The establishment of Fort McLoughlin may have had the unintended consequence of causing Ts'ibassa to bypass the villages of Milbanke Sound and extend his slave-raiding expeditions farther south. Fort Simpson post journals from 1837 mention that the "Sabassa people" having raided the Nahwitti, "carried off 28 of their women slaves and killed some of their men in consequence of which the Naweitie people were keeping guard lest a repetition of it were take place, and afraid to go to hunt."[90] These slave women appear to have included the wife and daughter of a Nahwitti chief who were subsequently traded to the Tlingit.[91] These raids appear to have induced the consolidation of Nahwitti villages.[92]

Notwithstanding Simpson's 1841 statements, relations at Fort McLoughlin remained strained. The HBC took careful precautions against attack. In 1843, the Northern Council decided to abandon Fort Durham and Fort McLoughlin to free up personnel to establish Fort Victoria. In November 1843, Douglas reported that the plan had been carried out with "imminent risk of bloodshed" because the villagers had been "thrown into a state of extreme excitement" when they caught wind of the HBC's plans.[93] Charles Ross, the person in charge at Fort McLoughlin, had his men plant potatoes and clear new land in the spring of 1843 to convince the villagers that the HBC was staying, then hurriedly abandoned the fort when most of the villagers were absent.[94] In the meantime, American traders having abandoned the competition, the HBC reduced the prices they were willing to pay for furs in that region.

In the late 1830s, the HBC directors intensified their search for a suitable site for a new headquarters for the Columbia District. HBC officials anticipated that any new headquarters would, like Fort Vancouver, occupy an extensive territory. In December 1836, John McLoughlin ordered that William McNeill reconnoitre southern Vancouver Island in the summer of 1837 to find the best location "for an Establishment on a large scale, possessing all the requisites for farming, rearing of Cattle together with a good harbour and abundance of timber, in short containing every advantage which is desirable such a situation should furnish."[95] McNeill did report finding "an excellent harbour and a fine open country along the sea shore apparently well adapted for both tillage and pasturage, but saw no river sufficiently extensive for Mills."[96]

The HBC did not pursue the matter again until 1842, when James Douglas was sent to inspect the southern portion of the island to find the best location for a fort. In July 1842, he reported that "after a careful Survey ... I made Choice of a Site for the proposed new Establishment in the Port of Camosack." He explained that its harbour was safe and accessible, and that timber was abundant, and that rushing tidal waters in nearby narrows could be used to power mills. But the "advantage and distinguishing Feature of Camosack," was "a Range of Plains nearly Six Miles Square, containing a great Extent of valuable Tillage and Pasture Land equally well adapted for the Plough or for feeding Stock."[97]

Douglas did not mention conversations he may have had in 1842 with the villagers about establishing a fort – he did mention that they did not molest him – but he was well aware of the importance of avoiding conflict. On 5 February 1843, as he was preparing to establish Fort Victoria, he wrote that the villagers were "numerous and daring having as yet lost no trait of their natural barbarity so that we will have both trouble and anxiety in the first course of training."[98] Despite his prediction and the HBC's intention to occupy a substantial acreage, no one then raised the possibility of arranging purchases of land.

When Douglas arrived in March 1843 to establish the fort, he invited the young Quebec-born Jesuit missionary, Jean-Baptiste-Zacharie Bolduc, to accompany the HBC party. Bolduc wrote that when the party arrived at about 4 p.m. on 14 March, they initially saw only two canoes, but after they fired the ship's cannon, "we saw the natives issuing from their haunts and surrounding the steamboat. Next morning, the pirogues (Indian boats) came from every side. I went on shore with the commander of the expedition and the captain of the vessel; having received unequivocal proofs of the good-will of the Indians, I visited their village situated six miles from the port, at the extremity of the bay."[99] The arriving party must have been aware of the vulnerable military position of the Indigenous people of southeastern Vancouver Island. Bolduc indicated that the villagers in the southeastern corner of Vancouver Island lived as much in dread of the Cowichan as the Kwantlen at Fort Langley had:

> Like the surrounding tribes, this one possessed a little fortress, formed by stakes enclosing about 150 square feet. The inhabitants endeavor to secure themselves in this manner from the incursions of the Toungletats [Cowichan], a powerful and warlike tribe, one part of which encamps on Vancouver's Island, the other on the continent, north of Frazer's River. These ferocious enemies enter the villages by night, massacre all the men, and carry off the women and children whom they reduce to slavery. On my arrival, all the tribe, men, women and children assembled to shake hands with me; a ceremony which these savages never omit.[100]

On Sunday 19 March, Bolduc celebrated mass in an improvised chapel, probably at the largest village at Cadboro Bay, with more than 1,200 "Kawitskins, Klalams, and Isanisks [Saanich]," and baptized over a hundred people.[101] Proselytizers had made efforts in the region before this date. Indeed, Bolduc claimed that somewhere north of the Columbia River "a certain tribe has possessed for ages a brazen crucifix, bearing the appearance of great antiquity, when, how, and by whom it was brought thither, none can tell."[102] According to anthropologist, Wayne Suttles, the Songhees may have been motivated in part by religious or spiritual reasons to relocate their villages to Fort Victoria soon thereafter.[103]

Douglas had the fort established by fall, with Roderick Finlayson in charge, but did not reside there permanently until 1849.[104] George Simpson reported in June 1844 that Indigenous people in Fort Victoria's surroundings were "not so numerous or formidable as we were led to believe, and seem peaceably and well-disposed; but as yet, judging from the Quantity of Furs brought in, it does not appear that they are very active, either as Traders or Hunters, or that their Country is rich in that Way."[105] Unfortunately, the only surviving Fort Victoria post journals run from May 1846 to May 1850, but several other documents shed light on the first years of Fort Victoria. Letters by Charles Ross, who oversaw the fort until his death on 27 June 1844, indicated in January 1844 that "numerous hordes of the natives (except for a short time while absent at their fisheries) have been about us up to the present moment. So far, however, they have not *particularly* annoyed us, beyond now & then shewing their dexterity at light fingered work. The unreflecting imprudence of our people was, more than once, on the eve of involving us in serious quarrels with them, but all this was in the end amicably adjusted."[106]

When the HBC started building the fort, there were no villages in the immediate vicinity, but mirroring a process that occurred elsewhere, residents of several villages relocated to villages adjacent to Fort Victoria almost immediately (see figure 11).[107] In his autobiography written in 1891, HBC officer Roderick Finlayson explained that "the natives for some time after our arrival kept aloof and would not come near. ... The natives however soon got rid of their shyness began to remove from their village on Cadboro Bay and erect houses for themselves along the bank of the harbor as far as the present site of Johnson Street."[108] Archaeological evidence suggests that some of the village sites abandoned in 1843 may have been occupied for thousands of years. For example, the multiple lineages that occupied a large ancient winter village at Sungayka (Cadboro Bay) – perhaps occupied consistently for thousands of years – appear to have relocated to Fort Victoria within months of the establishment of Fort Victoria.[109]

The HBC quickly came to occupy a considerable area of land around Fort Victoria without any evidence of opposition from the local villagers, probably because of the abundant economic opportunities that came with the HBC's occupation. New land was brought into cultivation each year. Five acres were cultivated, and five more cleared by the beginning of 1844.[110] In 1845, the farming operations produced a surplus of about a thousand bushels of wheat.[111] There were more than a hundred acres in winter wheat at Fort Victoria by the fall of 1846, and at least 27 acres in potatoes in the spring of 1847.[112] That did not include an unknown acreage in spring wheat, barley, oats, peas, hay, and pasture. Two sizable kitchen gardens included cabbages, carrots, beets, turnips, radishes, onions, Indian corn, melons, and cress, the surplus of which was also sometimes sold to visiting ships.[113] A six-acre orchard promised apples, pears, and peaches in season.[114] Hay was also harvested from sources up to eight miles away, and some of it was sold to passing ships.[115]

The HBC also kept abundant livestock. During the first winter of Fort Victoria's operations, the company brought in about a hundred head of cattle and horses from Nisqually.[116] Because cattle were occasionally slaughtered and sold to ships, more were subsequently brought in from the same place.[117] There were at least 200 head of horned cattle at Fort Victoria by November 1847, and probably well over a thousand sheep by the time the Vancouver Island treaties were concluded.[118] There were also over forty milch cows at two dairies, several teams of oxen, and an unknown number of horses.[119] In the very spring that the treaties at Victoria were concluded, the HBC had cultivated fields of wheat, and livestock, including a recent delivery of 800 sheep and 84 head of cattle.[120] April 1850 witnessed the discharging from the *Norman Morison* of a grist mill, the construction of new buildings, the clearing of land, and the planting of wheat, peas, and potatoes.[121]

Despite the activities of the HBC at Fort Victoria between 1843 and 1850, there is no evidence that the Indigenous people on southeastern Vancouver Island and HBC officials ever discussed the possibility of the HBC's renting or purchasing the land that they were occupying. Moreover, no surge of settlement in 1850 can explain why treaties were concluded then. A few settlers brought out by Walter Colquhoun Grant had arrived on Vancouver Island in 1849, but that event does not appear to have influenced decisions to negotiate purchases. Thanks to the fact that the HBC had already claimed much of the land surrounding the fort, Grant and his men settled about 40 kilometres west of the fort, at Sooke.[122]

The fact that the local chiefs advanced no claims for land at Victoria more than seven years after the HBC established the fort may explain why, when Douglas offered to pay them for their lands in 1850, the chiefs agreed for what seems to us to be a trifling compensation. Having apparently demanded or expected no compensation, the chiefs were asked to agree to surrender land rights in exchange for some immediate payments and guarantees of future rights.

Actions on the part of HBC personnel betray some of their perceptions of the rights of possession. On 3 August 1847, Roderick Finlayson wrote in the Fort Victoria post journal that he had departed the fort that morning with a party that included Thomas Ouamtany, the fort's interpreter, and five Indians "for Belle view [San Juan] Island to take possession of it, pursuant to orders from Mr. C.F. Douglas, travelled nearly from one end of it to the other & erected poles at a few places showing my having taken possession of it in H. Britic M's name."[123] Douglas's orders were probably rooted in his understanding that the 1846 Oregon Treaty (Anglo-American Treaty of Washington) was ambiguous about where the boundary line ran through the Salish Sea. Obviously, as of late 1847, Douglas thought it appropriate for the HBC to claim the island on behalf of the British Crown without compensating the Songhees, who harvested camas on that island each spring and stayed at fishing camps there in the summer. Indeed, conforming to practice elsewhere, Douglas and Finlayson appear to have regarded it as important to have Indigenous witnesses to the HBC's taking of possession. To further bolster its claim to the San Juan Island, the HBC subsequently established the Belle Vue sheep farm, which employed Indigenous people (see figure 20).[124]

After Fort Victoria was established, the villagers on southern Vancouver Island continued trading occasionally at Fort Langley, especially since some of their fisheries were closer to Fort Langley, and they may have been able to get better trade terms there than at Fort Victoria, but those villagers experienced many new economic benefits by having a fort nearby. John Lutz, like Robin Fisher before him, argued that villagers could serve as intermediaries between HBC traders and more distant Indigenous groups, either by demanding payment for access to the HBC traders or asking for considerably more from their trading partners than the HBC traders had charged them.[125] That was probably a minor consideration. If local villagers and their leaders wanted to control the trade as Maquinna and Wickaninnish had sought to do in the 1780s and 1790s, they were unsuccessful. The HBC insisted that their posts be accessible to all who came to them. Other economic and military factors were more important than monopolizing trade.

HBC officials understood, even before Fort Victoria was established, that the post would not have a large trade in furs.[126] The HBC's demand for furs was insatiable, but fur-bearing animals were not abundant there. Still, the Fort Victoria journals show that the villagers bartered a wide variety of furs, skins, and hides including those of sea otters, river otters, beavers, muskrats, raccoons, bears, seals, deer, and the occasional lynx, mink, marten, wolf, and wolverine.[127] However, furs must have constituted only a small portion of the income these villagers derived from the HBC.

The Songhees, Saanich, and Klallam traded salmon at Fort Langley before 1843, but the establishment of Fort Victoria greatly improved opportunities to trade fish, especially salmon. Villagers in the vicinity of Fort Victoria began trading salmon there shortly after the post was established in 1843 (an off-cycle year in the Fraser River sockeye cycle). In November of that year, James Douglas informed George Simpson that "the resources of the country in fish, are only known as yet through the supply procured in trade from the Natives, which was abundant after the arrival of the salmon in July, other kinds of fish were not regularly brought in; a proof of their being, either, less sought after or not so easily caught."[128]

The Fort Victoria journals for the years 1846–50 (the only years for which journals exist) suggest that, except in the dominant years of the sockeye cycle when the HBC could not accept all of the salmon the villagers were willing to sell, the company's traders sought as much supply as the villagers could provide. For example, in 1846, a subdominant year in the sockeye cycle, the journal indicated that salmon were "not so abundant this year as the last, consequently we must depend on other sources for the ensuing year's supply."[129] The journals suggest that the Songhees traded few salmon in the off-cycle years of 1847 and 1848. In those two years, other groups (Cowichan, Klallam, and Skagit) are mentioned more often than the Songhees, and when the Songhees traded salmon, they were "not the proper kind for salting."[130] In April 1849, slightly more than a year before he concluded treaties on southeastern Vancouver Island, James Douglas instructed Roderick Finlayson to encourage "the neighbouring tribes of Indians say Clallams, Songies, Sonitch, Sooks, Cowegins, and Skatchats, to extend their cultivation as widely as possible and to bring in every thing in the shape of fish or flesh which you will purchase from them, and salt for future use."[131] That year being a dominant year in the sockeye cycle, the "neighbouring tribes" did not need the encouragement. Various groups, including the Songhees, traded so many salmon that the supply exceeded the ability of the personnel at the fort to handle it. The journal noted that "salmon are now brought in in considerable numbers but we cannot trade more of them for want of casks."[132] Villagers also traded herring and herring spawn, cod, and other unidentified fish.[133]

The scale of the Fort Victoria salmon trade is difficult to gauge, but the documents show that the Songhees traded up to three thousand salmon a day in 1849.[134] Although the HBC personnel consumed much of the salmon traded at Victoria, they preserved more than 500 barrels at Fort Victoria in 1849, and Douglas wrote that "I firmly believe from the quantity of fish taken, that 2,000 Barrels might have been cured."[135] The HBC shipped more than 200 barrels of salmon to Hawaii aboard the *Harpooner* in late September 1849, and 468 barrels aboard the *Columbia* on 10 October 1849.[136] Clearly, by 1850, Indigenous people on southern Vancouver Island enjoyed a ready market for salmon and other fish at Fort Victoria for the local consumption of HBC personnel at Fort Victoria, and for export.

The Fort Victoria journals indicate that the villagers also traded a range of provisions and other goods. For example, they traded deer (meat and hides), ducks, geese, eggs, and strawberries.[137] Whale oil and whale bone were acquired primarily from the Makah from Cape Flattery, but also from Cowichan, Saanich, Klallam, and Songhees.[138] The Songhees also traded rush mats, dentalium shells, and "trifles."[139]

In 1842, even before Fort Victoria was established, James Douglas noted that the villagers in the vicinity were cultivating potatoes, for he mentioned "many small Fields in cultivation which appear to repay the Labour bestowed upon them."[140] The HBC's demand for potatoes also outstripped what Indigenous people were able or willing to supply. In April 1849, Douglas estimated that the villagers might provide at least four thousand bushels of potatoes each year "with manifest advantage to themselves and to the Colony."[141] Although villagers on southeastern Vancouver Island adopted potato cultivation before Fort Victoria was established, and although Douglas indicated in September 1849 that they grew "large quantities of potatoes,"[142] they never traded anywhere near the amount Douglas thought they could. Although the journals frequently mention trade in potatoes, they rarely mention specific amounts. The fact that the journals mention that the Songhees brought in 130 bushels on 2 September 1846 suggests that that was an unusually large trade. On 23 August 1849, the journals note that "a few fresh potatoes are daily brought in by the natives who place an exorbitant price upon them." In 1849, drought devastated the HBC's potato crop at Fort Victoria, so the villagers likely were happy to keep their own small supply unless the HBC was willing to pay a premium. Douglas wrote that he regretted the shortage of potatoes "as we could have sold, almost any quantity, to Vessels calling at this port."[143]

The villagers near Fort Victoria also seized the opportunities to provide wage labour almost immediately upon the arrival of HBC traders. When Douglas informed the "Samose" on 16 March 1843 that the HBC intended to build a trading post among them, it "appeared to please them very much and they immediately offered their services in procuring pickets for the establishment, an offer which I gladly accepted and promised to pay them a blanket (2½) for every forty pickets of 22 feet by 36 inches which they bring."[144] In subsequent years, they contributed most forms of paid labour that might have been conceivably offered them around Fort Victoria, from digging wells and constructing buildings, to stevedoring and drying and dusting furs and hides.[145] They were often hired in agricultural pursuits, including clearing land for cultivation,[146] driving oxen and plowing,[147] and labouring at the company's dairies.[148] Men, women, and children also were engaged in haying, and in cultivating, harvesting, and thrashing the crops.[149] For example, the journals of 1846 indicate that the traders "had all our engaged Indians with some Ind$^n$ women & children clearing & hoeing potatoes."[150] The journals convey the impression that at least some of the villagers preferred paid work in the HBC's potato fields over growing and selling their own potatoes. According to Finlayson, villagers found other ways to profit from the HBC's potatoes: "the Indians are now beginning to steal our potatoes & Sell them to the ships."[151]

The Fort Victoria journals show that most of the Songhees continued to maintain a seasonal round that resembled those that had existed for millennia. The journals mention when they were fishing for herring in April,[152] harvesting camas in May,[153] moving to other fishing locations in spring or summer,[154] returning in the fall,[155] and when they were so busy with their winter "Medicine ceremonies" that it was difficult to get the hired hands to do their work.[156]

Despite the evidence of continuity, some members of the community did not join the community on these rounds. Some villagers worked for the HBC on six-month contracts, evidently with terminal dates normally in January and July.[157] An entry from 18 January 1847 indicated the probable normal terms of such contracts: "12 Indians were hired this evening for six months at the rate of 5 blankets each for that period."[158] Roderick Finlayson probably wrote up contracts for each of these engagements. Recall that George Simpson noted in the 1840s that he believed of "a savage" that "if he once puts his cross to any writing, he has rarely been known to violate the engagement which such writing is supposed to embody or to sanction. To him the very look of black and white is a powerful 'medicine.'"[159] The fact that multiple able-bodied men were engaged to the HBC during the entire year (and sometimes had their wives and children working alongside them) is significant, for it shows that as early as the 1840s, some villagers did not participate in their communities' annual salmon fisheries, and that some people inhabited the village adjacent to Fort Victoria all year. Villagers were also often paid to courier letters between Fort Victoria and Fort Langley and Nisqually – another task that kept them familiar with written documents.[160] Songhees men were also hired as guides and tripmen.[161] Why did villagers take up wage labour so quickly? Were commoners seeking to assert their economic independence from the elite? Were elite hiring out their slaves to add to their own wealth and status? It is impossible to say, although it is remarkable that local Indigenous men were taking on such contracts within a decade after the HBC established a post among them.

The villagers also participated in the HBC's exploitation of the forests of the region. They helped harvest and transport cedar logs and oak wood to the fort.[162] Indeed, in August 1847, they showed the HBC the location of a stream at Esquimalt suitable for a mill. In subsequent months they help build the mill, assisted the company in surveying a suitable route for a road between Fort Victoria and the mill stream, and helped cut the road and build the bridge to the mill.[163] The sawmill was a timely addition when the California gold rush created a robust demand for lumber. By 6 November 1847, Douglas and Work reported

108   The Vancouver Island Treaties

that the villagers were "at all times willing to assist in the labours of the Establishment, and in protecting the farm and running stock against the distant and barbarous tribes inhabiting the Country to the Northward and Westward."[164]

Douglas and the villagers likely expected that economic opportunities for the villagers at Victoria would expand when settlers independent of the HBC arrived in the region. In September 1849, after Walter C. Grant's small party of independent colonists arrived, Douglas wrote that the small group of settlers

> have commenced their bold enterprise, under the most favourable auspices, they have no enemies to dread, and no obstacles to encounter, beyond those which the hand of nature has interposed through the force of a teeming sail. Instead of thirsting for their blood, the Natives are not only kind and friendly, but willing to share their labours and assist in all of their toils, and they regularly bring in large quantities of the finist [sic] Salmon and potatoes, which they part with at a low rate in barter for such articles as suit their fancy or necessities. It has been a work of time and labour, to bring the Indians to that state of friendly intercourse and I have endeavoured strongly to impress on the minds of Captain Grant and his followers, the incalculable importance, both as regards the future well being of the Colony, and their own individual interests, of cultivating the friendship of these children of the forest.[165]

As Douglas implied, the villagers at Fort Victoria had developed between 1843 and 1850 many habits and skills that they could anticipate would be important when settlers arrived. Indeed, there is good reason to believe that they used many of these skills and products in their own communities.[166] In sum, Fort Victoria offered an almost insatiable market for furs, fish, potatoes and other provisions and products, goods, and labour. The new opportunities for wealth accumulation were tremendous.

Consistent with its practice elsewhere, the HBC signalled early that it would not tolerate any plundering or attacks on its people or property at Fort Victoria. In fact, Roderick Finlayson recalled that after Fort Victoria was established, he found himself demanding payment from a Songhees chief whose followers had killed some of the fort's oxen. According to Finlayson, the chief "went away in a rage, assembled some Cowichan Indians to his village, and the next move I found on their part was a shower of bullets fired at the fort, with a great noise and demonstration on the part of the crowd assembled, threatening death and devastation to all the whites."[167] Finlayson decided to make his point. According to his account, after ensuring that the chief's lodge was empty, Finlayson "fired a nine-pounder, with grape in, and pointed the gun to the lodge, which flew into the air in splinters like a bombshell. After this there was such howling that I thought a number were killed, and was quite relieved when the interpreter came 'round and told me none were killed, but much frightened, not knowing we had such destructive arms."[168] Finlayson described another occasion when he attempted to convince the villagers to adhere to principles of "British justice." In the spring of 1845, some Songhees pillaged a party of villagers from Bellingham Bay who had just left the fort after trading "a large quantity of furs." When these people returned shortly after to Fort Victoria to complain, Finlayson judged that

> this was a clear case in which I was bound to interfere to protect friendly Indians coming to trade with us. I then sent the interpreter to get them to restore the goods they took from these friendly Indians, as otherwise I would have to take action on their behalf, as they came to trade with us. After considering the matter for a time these robbers came to the fort and delivered up the goods. The Bellingham bay Indians then left with their property, contented, and to prevent further trouble, I sent a party of our men, armed, to Trial island, to see them safely homeward. Thus these wild savages were taught to respect British justice.[169]

If Finlayson implied that this one incident was enough to "teach" the Songhees, the Fort Victoria journals show otherwise. In June 1846, "a large party of Sinahomish [Snohomish] & Skatchets [Skagit] arrived here by way of Clover point, one of whom put a Bdle furs into the Shop for security until to morrow. In consequence of some old quarrel between them & the Songes the latter began to fire upon them from the opposite side, some of the balls falling amongst our people in front of the Ft. We had therefore to interfere & put a stop to such bold proceedings."[170] In October 1848, a man was given three dozen lashes for killing HBC cattle.[171] And in March 1850, the journals note that "The heads of the Songes families, who were implicated in killing our cattle came across from the village yesterday to make restitution for the damage they had done & promised not to do the same for the future."[172]

Without appearing to be allies of the villagers adjacent to the forts, the HBC officers also needed to convince more distant groups that the HBC would not tolerate attacks on the local villagers. The way that HBC officers attempted to manage the acrimonious relations between the Makah of Cape Flattery and the local villagers illustrates how difficult it could be to avoid becoming embroiled in conflicts among the company's local and distant trading partners. In July 1846, Finlayson noted regretfully that "George the Cape Flattery Chief that left this last Friday was murdered by a party of Tlalums about Rocky point & his property taken by them, which will of course lead to an interruption of our trade with the Natives of C Flattery."[173] Apparently to avoid a similar incident, when a Makah party arrived in September, the HBC lodged the chief and his family in the fort.[174] The Makah, however, were a powerful people accustomed to being aggressors. The HBC had to accept that sometimes the Makah might come to Fort Victoria, as they did in June 1847, without anything to trade, "their object in coming being apparently to see whether there are any hostile tribes at present encamped here."[175] Matters were even more complicated when in July 1847, the HBC caught a Makah man breaking into one of Fort Victoria's storehouses. He was taken into the fort for punishment, when other Makah men prepared their arms for a fight. Finlayson then "called some of the Chiefs aside & represented the case to them & upbraided them for countenancing a thief as being beneath the dignity of Chiefs & told them to walk outside or abide by the consequences which they did very reluctantly. the thief was then flogged having received 18 lashes on the back & kept in prison until the evening when he was set at liberty."[176] Finlayson did not mention the involvement of the Songhees on that day, but Douglas was obviously referring to the same incident when he later wrote that the Songhees "whose lands we occupy consider themselves as specially attached to the Establishment, and lately gave a convincing and useful proof of their attachment by taking up arms against a body of Cape Flattery Indians, who threated to attack the Post in retaliation for a whipping inflicted on one of their number, who was caught in the Act of breaking into one of the Stores."[177]

The Fort Victoria journals suggest that each Makah visit to Fort Victoria thereafter passed without incident until August 1848, when Finlayson noted that Snitlum, at the head of a war party of "Skatchets and Tlalums," had arrived at Fort Victoria with hostile intentions against a Makah party that happened then to be at Fort Victoria. Fortunately for the HBC, Captain Courtenay of the British Navy was nearby. As a warning to the warriors, Courtenay ordered a seven-gun salute from his boats and the HBC replied with a similar salute from its bastions. Finlayson noted that "The quarrel between the Cape Flatteries and Tlalums is not as yet settled, but we must endeavour to do so before they leave."[178] Whatever settlement Finlayson may have negotiated was fragile, for an armed boat escorted the Makah out of the Fort Victoria harbour the next morning.[179]

Four days later, with the "Skatchets" still at Fort Victoria, Courtenay and his forces performed military exercises apparently intended to impress all who witnessed them (see figure 12). On the morning of 29 August 1848, Captain Courtenay and "250 Sailors & Marines came on shore for the purpose of exercising them & were all day performing various evolutions in the Ft. y.$^d$ and in the fields behind. The ship's band were at their head & the march through the Ft. to the field behind was truly grand. Little or no work was performed our people having solicited & obtained permission to enjoy the novel spectacle."[180] Historian John Lutz has argued that this event had a significant impact upon the local Salish people, and that grave markers erected at Laurel Point shortly after this pageant were inspired by the exercises of that day. Lutz speculated that these grave markers are evidence that Salish people sought and incorporated European spirit power into their own.[181] Even if the Songhees understood the significance of the exercises in only the physical realm, they may have erected the markers to remind all Indigenous visitors to the fort of the exercises of 29 August 1848, and of the partnership that existed between the British and the Songhees. The fact that a young Makah chief from Cape Flattery married a Songhees "lady of rank" in September 1849 might have signalled a desire on the part of the Makah to solidify their access to Fort Victoria, and on the part of the Songhees to make peace with their powerful neighbours.[182] The HBC also tried to induce the Cowichan to halt attacks in the Fort Victoria environs by refusing to trade with them until violations were settled.[183]

As at Fort Langley, the HBC could not pacify a territory much beyond Fort Victoria's immediate vicinity before 1850. The Songhees continued to be subject to raids when they were away from the village at the fort. For example, the HBC's Fort Victoria post journal notes on 21 September 1848 that "intelligence was received to day by the Sanges that one of their men was shot, and 6 Women & Children taken prisoners or Captives by Tsoughelum, the celebrated Kewetchin freebooter."[184]

When the Songhees abandoned their fortified village at Cadboro Bay to be near the fort, they moved to a much safer location.[185] Villages along the east coast of Vancouver Island were particularly vulnerable to the incursions of northern warriors, but the village at Fort Victoria was among the securest locations along the Northwest Coast. In October 1849, the Anglican clergyman Robert J. Staines wrote from Victoria that "we are on very good terms with the Indians here, & the proprietors of this part of the Island, the Songass, are a weak tribe, (once powerful, but of late years much thinned by disease) & they are glad of the protection afforded them against their stronger neighbours by the presence of the white man. The tribe numbers from 150 to 200 men & perhaps 500 or 600 in all. Their village is just opposite to the Fort, across an arm of the Harbour."[186] Despite the pervasive warfare in the region, enemy warriors never directly attacked the Songhees village on the inner harbour.

The villagers adjacent to Fort Victoria benefited tremendously from residing in a neutral zone, although the constraints that came with those benefits had broad implications. Because those villagers had probably been on the defensive for hundreds of years, they were probably less militaristic than villagers up island, but even in societies on the defensive, villagers reward successful warriors with renown, prestige, and status. As opportunities as warriors declined for young men, opportunities in economic spheres expanded.

HBC officers were cautious about travelling to locations where they had not yet established a rapport with the villagers. The Cowichan had traded with the HBC since the 1820s, but even in October 1849, when Eden Colvile wrote from Fort Victoria that he had been eager to visit the Cowichan River valley "about 30 Miles to the Northward," he explained that "Mr. Douglas is of opinion that it would not be prudent to attempt it without a larger party than can be collected here at present; as the country is thickly inhabited by a very uncivilised & treacherous tribe of Indians."[187]

In sum, it would be simplistic and misleading to suggest that the HBC officers at Fort Victoria either dominated or were dominated by the villagers adjacent to the fort. Even before they were official colonialists, they viewed their application of force as a legitimate policing function intended to bring the villagers to conform to the conduct expected of British subjects. In that way they exerted a powerful influence on life in the district. But as emporialists, not imperialists, they did not seek "dominance" so much as predictable, peaceful commercial relations. Neither did the villagers seek to dominate the traders. They could have driven the HBC away by harassing traders when they were away from the fort, slaughtering their stock, destroying their crops, and otherwise preventing the company from carrying out its extensive operations outside the walls of the fort. But the last thing that the villagers wanted was for the HBC to abandon Fort Victoria the way they had left Forts McLoughlin and Durham in 1843 and Fort Stikine in 1849. The relationship between the villagers and the company should instead be understood as one in which each party valued the benefits of the relationship and wished it to continue. Village leaders furthermore acquiesced during the 1840s to the HBC's exertion of a certain level of coercion over villagers, even to the point of imposing physical punishment and detention on offenders. The prospect that the HBC might abandon Fort

Victoria would have been far more daunting than that it might expand its operations. Indeed, based on what they had experienced to 1850, the villagers may have welcomed settlers who would offer new markets for their goods and their labour – that the demand for the wage labour and the goods that they provided for the HBC would grow with the coming of new settlers. The timing of the negotiations for the Vancouver Island treaties was good for the HBC. The villagers had adjusted to their mutually beneficial relationship with the HBC, and developed many skills and habits that would be demanded by settlers. However, they had not yet learned much about the monetary value of land, and may not have anticipated that many of the settlers who would come to Vancouver Island would scorn them.

In what Robert Galois described as the first "modern" epidemic in the region, measles spread to the Northwest Coast from the interior, apparently via the Columbia and Fraser River valleys, beginning in 1846. Measles appears to have been transmitted from the east by equestrian Indigenous people and exogenous migrants travelling along the Oregon Trail, and along the coast by the HBC's *Beaver*.[188] It arrived at Fort Victoria later than most places on the Northwest Coast. Word that the epidemic had struck Fort Vancouver and Nisqually reached Victoria on 5 February 1848 at the same time as the news of the 29 November 1847 killing of Dr. Marcus and Narcissa Whitman at Walla Walla.[189] The *Beaver* appears to have transmitted the disease from Fort Vancouver to Fort Simpson, where it caused many deaths in January 1848.[190] It had already struck interior posts as far north as Fort Alexandria in January and February, and appears to have spread inland from Fort Simpson thereafter.[191] Measles broke out at Fort Victoria on 13 March 1848 and soon spread throughout the district, where it, and dysentery, hit the Indigenous people and the Hawaiians the hardest, but also made J.W. McKay very ill.[192] However, Finlayson expressed his belief that it was of a "mild type."[193] HBC personnel appear to have done little to attempt to slow its spread. During the epidemic, the *Beaver*, with sick passengers, travelled north from Fort Vancouver, and on several occasions, parties, including engaged Indians, were sent from Victoria to Nisqually with mail packets.[194] In early April a "woeful account" arrived of the disease's effects among the "Sinahomish."[195] And on 7 April the Fort Victoria journals noted that "the measles are now spreading fast at this place."[196] Dr. Tolmie prescribed medicine to assist the sufferers, and the mortality at Victoria may have been less than it was in other locations.[197] However, as it did elsewhere, influenza arrived shortly after measles ebbed, and it struck Fort Victoria again in January 1849.[198] Because the measles epidemic struck before the HBC was established on northern Vancouver Island, the effects of measles among the Kwakiutl is unknown. However, the traders at Fort Rupert in 1849 remarked that the population of the Kwakiutl had "greatly decreased" since 1841.[199] James Douglas's estimate that the epidemic killed about 10 per cent of the Indigenous population between Fort Hall and Nisqually may reflect the mortality in the entire region, but those numbers only hint at the impact of the epidemic.[200] The deaths may have been a factor in the consolidation of villages (especially at Fort Rupert, which was established shortly after the epidemic). In some cases, survivors may have been incapable of continuing to construct, maintain, and operate complex systems of salmon procurement, leading to the abandonment of some sites.[201] It is impossible to gauge how grief may have contributed to social tensions, and how the events surrounding the epidemic may have influenced the villagers who concluded treaties only a few years after the epidemic passed.

Life on Vancouver Island changed dramatically between 1821 and 1850 when the HBC became established in the region. Even as warfare and social tensions escalated, villagers along the rim of the Salish Sea seized upon the economic and military opportunities that their proximity to HBC posts offered them. Doing so required villagers and their leaders to adjust to principles that HBC officers insisted upon. Furthermore, the land-based fur trade changed the way communities and individuals gained wealth, status, and prestige, heightening social tensions and increasing status mobility even as it enriched entire communities, including the elite. The context suggests why we ought not to be surprised that there is no evidence that any Indigenous community or leader on the Northwest Coast demanded that the HBC pay for the land it occupied before the Kwakiutl chiefs did on 15 April 1850. Because some scholars have argued that the Vancouver Island treaties were concluded at the behest of the British Colonial Office, the Colonial Office's perspective on Indigenous title also demands our attention.

# 6 Articulating Principles of Indigenous Title, 1835–1846

When Sir George Gipps (1791–1847)(see figure 13), the forty-nine-year-old Governor of New South Wales, took the floor of the Australian colony's Legislative Council in Sydney on Thursday, 9 July 1840, he knew that he was about to deliver one of the more consequential speeches of his life, although he could not have anticipated that the HBC's London Governor and Committee would quote that speech on 17 December 1849 when they drafted their instructions to James Douglas at Fort Victoria on the subject of Indigenous title.

Gipps was an experienced and skilled administrator, highly respected in the British Colonial Office. He had been appointed Governor of New South Wales – regarded as a difficult but prestigious appointment – in 1838 after distinguishing himself during a two-year stint in Lower Canada, serving the Gosford Commission, which, from 1835 to 1837, investigated the grievances of the French Canadians in Lower Canada.[1] It was fortunate for Gipps – the eldest son of the Anglican Rector of Ringwould in Kent – that he was also a gifted orator, for on this day he had to defend his bill to empower himself to appoint a commission to investigate and rule on land claims in New Zealand.[2] Although the debate over that bill has generated little scholarly attention until recently, it was, and remains, significant, because in it adversaries were forced to articulate competing principles related to sovereignty and the nature of Indigenous title.[3] The legal, constitutional, moral, and political arguments they put forward reveal much about perceptions of Indigenous title in the years leading up to the formation of the colony of Vancouver Island.

When Gipps presented his principles on 9 July, his opponents had already explained theirs. On 30 June and 1 July, four influential men had condemned Gipps's bill before the colony's Legislative Council.[4] James Busby (1802–1871), who had only recently vacated his position as official British Resident in New Zealand, spoke first (a map showing locations in New Zealand mentioned in this text can be found at figure 14). Claiming to speak at least in part "on behalf of the Chiefs and people of New Zealand," for at least two hours Busby urged the councillors to defeat Gipps's bill.[5] They should do so, he said, based on "the fact of New Zealand having been acknowledged an independent state; the native chiefs having met several times and declared the independence of their country, which declaration was solemnly ratified by the British government."[6] Obviously, Gipps would have to address Busby's argument that his bill was unconstitutional because it claimed the right to rule on land rights in New Zealand at a time when New Zealand was purportedly independent.

Busby obviously remained in the Legislative Council's chambers to listen to William Charles Wentworth (1790–1872) state his case. Wentworth detained the councillors even longer than Busby. Interrupted by falling darkness at about 5 p.m. on 30 June, his presentation spanned two days.[7] Wentworth, described by former governor Ralph Darling as a "vulgar, ill-bred fellow," was an Australian exemplar of the rags-to-riches story, celebrated by many even today.[8] He had been born out of wedlock to Catherine Crowley, a teenager transported to Sydney as a convict in 1789–90, and an impecunious father who had escaped conviction on three charges of highway robbery, and finally, on the fourth charge appears to have avoided prosecution only by agreeing to go to New South Wales as colonial surgeon.[9] Despite these inauspicious origins, which always undermined William's social position, his father's aristocratic connections with the prominent Fitzwilliam family enabled William to acquire a good education in England, including a degree in law, and allowed him to return to New South Wales permanently in 1824 as an ambitious young man with elite pretensions.[10] Indeed, thanks in part to his ability to gain access to networks of patronage, he had, by 1840, risen to become a wealthy and influential explorer, author, barrister, and landowner in Sydney.[11]

Although sometimes repetitive and rambling, Wentworth revealed his oratorical skill. Rhetorically deriding Gipps's "bill of confiscation" and "bill of spoliation," he even mockingly paraphrased Gipps's preamble to the bill with his own "plain English" version: "whereas it is expedient to increase the patronage of the Crown and make a large revenue from the lands of New Zealand, and therefore to dispossess various British inhabitants of that country of their rights, be it enacted by her Majesty that all lands in that country at present owned by Her Majesty's subjects shall be confiscated."[12] But he was dead serious, quoting and citing at length legal commentaries by William Blackstone and Emmerich de Vattel, adverting to case law in Great Britain, and referring to British policy and practice in colonial North America from the early 1600s in New England, to the 1830s in Upper Canada. His conclusion? Every one of Gipps's proclamations regarding New Zealand, and the bill then before the Legislative Council, had been invalid; that the law of nations gave Māori of New Zealand – as independent people – the right to decide to whom they might sell their lands, and that British subjects had the right to own land in New Zealand just as they had the right to own land in France or the United States. Wentworth scornfully summarized the history of British policies towards Indigenous title: "The British government had done wrong in dispossessing the aborigines of America and other countries of their lands, but it was not to be expected that the same practices were to be revived in this enlightened era, especially when the cry of moderation and even-handed justice was in the mouth of every government."[13] He pointed to what he considered an obvious injustice: Gipps's government claimed land in New South Wales – which had never been purchased from Indigenous people – by right of discovery and occupation, while denying sovereign Māori of New Zealand the right to sell their lands.

As to the declaration of independence on the part of some Māori rangatira (chiefs) of the northern part of the North Island of New Zealand in 1835, Wentworth disagreed with Busby. According to Wentworth, not only the northern part of the North Island of New Zealand was independent; every part of New Zealand had been so before any declaration of independence.[14]

Thus, Gipps's speech would have to refute Wentworth's spirited condemnation of the bill.

After sparring for a time with Gipps and the members of the Legislative Council, Wentworth made room for William à Beckett (1806–1869), the legal counsel for the New Zealand Association, of which Wentworth was a leading member. A British barrister who had recently arrived in Sydney, à Beckett was destined for a distinguished career in Australia as lawyer, solicitor general, and chief justice.[15] Although à Beckett said that Busby and Wentworth had nearly "exhausted the subject," he justified his own half-hour presentation by arguing "that the question was one of such immense interest to the welfare of society, and to the natural rights of man, as well as so connected with the law of nations."[16] Another English barrister who had recently arrived in Sydney, John Bayley Darvall (1809–1883), made only a short presentation, but added to previous arguments the point that if Māori were competent to convey the land of New Zealand to the British government through the Treaty of Waitangi on 6 February 1840, they must also have been competent previously to convey land to purchasers of their choice.[17] Gipps had to rebut Darvall's argument too, for it seemed to validate private purchases of Indigenous land wherever the British Crown recognized Indigenous title.

Gipps would have the last word on 9 July, but he could not take that advantage lightly, for Sydney's newspapers had taken positions against him, and he had to assume that Wentworth and his associates would not give up the fight even if the Legislative Council passed his bill. And so George Gipps apparently made the most of his time during the soggy early-winter days of early July 1840, preparing a two-hour speech to be delivered at the second reading of his bill.[18] If the newspaper reports are any indication, many of Sydney's 30,000 inhabitants were captivated by what the Sydney *Colonist* dubbed "this momentous debate."[19] Sydney newspapers immediately published Gipps's speech.[20] Many people elsewhere in the British world were also interested in the debate. The speech – or at least a version of it that Gipps sent to London – was published in the *British Parliamentary Papers* in May 1841 and often quoted in subsequent years.[21] Evidence of its influence can be found in the fact that the HBC Governor and Committee quoted it on 17 December 1849 in their instructions to James Douglas.

On the morning of 9 July, after summarizing the arguments of his opponents, Gipps defended his bill essentially by arguing that no individual had been able to acquire valid title to land in New Zealand from Indigenous people *before* Britain had acquired sovereignty because the land had no legal owner before that date, and no one could acquire valid title from Indigenous people *after* Britain had acquired sovereignty because the British Crown was the owner. Moreover, no British subjects were permitted to form colonies without the permission of the British Crown. As Gipps explained it, the bill was:

> founded upon two or three principles, which, until I hear them here controverted, I thought were fully admitted, and indeed received, as political axioms. The first is, that the uncivilized inhabitants of any country have but a qualified dominion over it, or a right of occupancy only; and that until they establish amongst themselves a settled form of government, and subjugate the ground to their own uses, by the cultivation of it, they cannot grant to individuals, not of their own tribe, any portion of it, for the simple reason that they have not themselves any individual property in it.
>
> Secondly, that if a settlement be made in any such country by a civilized power, the right of pre-emption of the soil, or in other words, the right of extinguishing the native title, is exclusively in the government of that power, and cannot be enjoyed by individuals without the consent of their government.

The third principle is, that neither individuals, nor bodies of men belonging to any nation, can form colonies, except with the consent, and under the direction and control, of their own government; and that from any settlement which they may form without the consent of their government they may be ousted. This is simply to say, as far as Englishmen are concerned, that colonies cannot be formed without the consent of the Crown.[22]

If Gipps had been able to express his argument in twenty-first-century terms, he might have said that people in non-state societies could not sell land to outsiders because they did not have legal title to it. Indigenous communities might *inhabit* the lands, but they did not *possess* or *occupy* them as property in a legal sense. Thus, unless and until they formed state governments capable of granting individual land titles, they had land rights as communities only to the lands that they occupied permanently (in villages) or that they cultivated, as nineteenth-century British people understood cultivation. So, when the British government acquired sovereignty, the Crown at that moment also thereby assumed ownership of the land. Indigenous title did not pre-date that moment; it was only when the British assumed sovereignty that Indigenous title sprang into being. That is because, Gipps argued, "Native title" was not ownership, but was a burden upon the owner – the Crown – created when the Crown acquired sovereignty.

The genius of Gipps's argument rested in the fact that it provided a way for him to refuse to grant title to lands that private individuals "purchased" from Māori chiefs in New Zealand either before or after the British acquired sovereignty. The Crown had the exclusive right and obligation to "extinguish" Indigenous title in the most appropriate way, given the circumstances. Because his was among the clearest and most systematic articulations of British views of Indigenous title at the time, and because it so ably defended the interests of the British Crown, and – many believed – of Indigenous people, commentators quoted and cited it often.

Aware that he was vulnerable to accusations that he was using points of law to defend the unjust dispossession of Indigenous people, Gipps did not concede the cause of justice and humanity. He made it clear that his principles encapsulated the obligation of the British Crown to protect naive and vulnerable Indigenous peoples from dishonest and immoral schemes of its own subjects:

> the adoption of these principles is tantamount to the recognition of an immense responsibility. In declaring our rights, we admit our duties. When a civilised government proclaims itself lord of a soil in the partial

occupation of savages, it thereby to some extent deposes their chiefs, abrogates their laws, and takes them under its own special protection. But such is its responsibility to begin with. The wild man is sure to fare ill in contact with the civilised. He cannot help himself. The civilised state must interfere to help him, and treat him as under disability. Who would put edged tools into the hands of a child or madman? Why then give unintelligible rights to a savage? Protect him, watch over his real interests and comforts continually, respect what he already feels to be property, help him to enlarge his tastes and his store, step by step raise him to an equality with the stranger as far as can be done – treat him as the helpless client of a powerful patron – and, above all, stand between him and the unprincipled speculators always found to infest an infant Colony. This is the only justice the case admits of – the justice due, not from equal to equal, but from a superior to an inferior. This is the only humanity. But to declare him, as the lord of the soil, above your head, while he has not one circumstance in this condition, or one idea in his mind, suited to that title and necessary to its maintenance, is but mockery of justice, and only hastens his fall.[23]

Gipps then responded to his challengers' legal arguments with his own. He quoted and cited Chief Justice John Marshall of the United States Supreme Court, James Kent (1763–1847), Chancellor of the State of New York,[24] Joseph Story (1779–1845) of the United States Supreme Court, and Emmerich de Vattel's *Law of Nations*.[25] He also dealt at length with the Batman Treaty, a land purchase negotiated by a number of British subjects with Indigenous leaders near Port Phillip (then within the colony of New South Wales) only five years earlier, which his predecessor, Governor Richard Bourke (1777–1855), had repudiated, and with which he was familiar.[26]

Gipps scoffed at Wentworth's appeals to justice:

To this I answer, that whatever may be the changes (and thank Heaven they are many) which the progress of religion and enlightenment have produced amongst us, they are all in favour of the savage, and not against him. It would be indeed the very height of hypocrisy in Her Majesty's Government to abstain, or pretend to abstain, for religion's sake, from despoiling these poor savages of their lands, and yet to allow them to be despoiled by individuals, being subjects of Her Majesty. It is in the spirit of that enlightenment which characterizes the present age, that the British Government is now about to interfere in the affairs of New Zealand. That it interferes against its will, and only under the force of circumstances, is evident from Lord Normanby's despatch; the objects for which we go to New Zealand are clearly set forth in it, and amongst the foremost is the noble one of rescuing a most interesting race of men from that fate, which contact with the nations of Christendom has hitherto invariably and unhappily brought upon the uncivilized tribes of the earth.[27]

Then, in his dramatic conclusion, Gipps urged the members of the Legislative Council to summon the courage to take the side of justice, right, and humanity:

> To your hands, therefore, I commit this bill. You will, I am sure, deal with it according to your consciences, and with that independence which you ought to exercise; having a due regard for the honour of the Crown, and the interests of the subject; whilst, for myself, in respect to this occupation of New Zealand by Her Majesty, I may, I trust, be permitted to exclaim, as did the standard bearer of the Tenth Legion, when Caesar first took possession of Great Britain, "*Et ego certe officium meum, Reipublicæ, atque Imperatori præstitero;*"[28] fearlessly alike of what people may say or think of me, I will perform my duty to the Queen and to the Public.[29]

The passage of Gipps's bill was not a certainty; one of the Councillors, Hannibal Macarthur, Lord Bishop of Australia, expressed his doubts about its legality.[30] Nevertheless, as the Sydney *Colonist* tersely noted, on 4 August 1840 "The New Zealand Claims to Grants of Land Bill was read a third time and passed."[31]

Gipps was offended by his opponents' efforts to claim the moral high ground on this issue. Just shy of completing his second year in Sydney, Gipps had already risked much to defend Indigenous people of New South Wales, even when public opinion was against him.[32] According to one of Gipps's biographers, "Gipps's policy towards the Aborigines was humane, practical, and courageous."[33] On 9 June 1838, only a few months after Gipps arrived in the colony, eleven stockmen had massacred about thirty-five Wirrayaraay people in what has become known in Australia as the Myall Creek Massacre. Gipps and the Attorney General, John Plunkett (1802–1869), doggedly sought to bring the murderers – who were defended by William à Beckett – to justice, even to the point of ordering a second trial after the first ended in a blanket acquittal of all the accused. And when the second trial resulted in a guilty verdict against seven of the accused, Gipps had defied public outcry and ordered the seven convicted men hanged.[34] Gipps's defence of Indigenous people earned him the enmity of many in New South Wales.

At the conclusion of Gipps's speech, Plunkett, still the Attorney General of New South Wales, recommended that it be published on the grounds that "it contained more law and information upon principles applicable to colonisation than any account extant." Accordingly, Gipps sent an edited version of the speech to London, where James Stephen (1789–1859), the Permanent Under-Secretary in the Colonial Office, endorsed it.[35] And Lord John Russell (1792–1878), the Colonial Secretary, congratulated Gipps, writing that he read "with much pleasure the very able exposition of your views."[36] The speech was published in the *British Parliamentary Papers* in 1841.[37]

Legal arguments such as those put forward by Gipps, Busby, Wentworth, à Beckett, and Darvall were intended to transcend time and place, of course. That is why they marshalled evidence from as early as the 1600s, and as far away as eastern North America. But these were not the esoteric proceedings of a debating club formed to provide winter amusement and edification for Sydney's population. Gipps was responding to a crisis – or at least a perceived crisis – in New Zealand, that had been years in the making. Context mattered. The debate in Sydney in 1840 is so significant both because the arguments were intended to be normative, and because of similarities between New Zealand in 1840 and Vancouver Island in the late 1840s.

Few in the 1840s would have described British policy towards New Zealand over the previous decades as having been coherent, clear, or consistent. The ambiguities and inconsistencies of British policies – which a Select Committee in 1844 would famously describe as "a series of injudicious proceedings" – formed the crucible in which Busby, Wentworth, à Beckett, Darvall, and Gipps were forced in 1840 to articulate explicitly before the New South Wales Legislative Council the grounds upon which they based their positions.

In his speech, Gipps countered the arguments of Busby and Wentworth by stating that "New Zealand never has been, in point of fact, independent."[38] Gipps rightly pointed out that the commission of Captain Arthur Phillip (1738–1814) in 1787, when he was appointed the first Governor of New South Wales, included the entire continent of Australia east of 135°E and the islands to the east of the continent, plausibly including much of New Zealand.[39] Subsequently, read literally, the commissions of most governors of New South Wales, also included at least part of New Zealand. However, as historian Peter Adams noted, since the boundaries of Phillip's commission bisected the South Island of New Zealand arbitrarily, and since subsequent boundaries also bisected the North Island arbitrarily, British officials probably did not intend the pre-1825 commissions to embrace New Zealand.[40] Moreover, when Van Diemen's Land (Tasmania) was separated from New South Wales in 1825, New Zealand was excluded from New South Wales's new boundaries, whether by oversight or intent.[41]

The status of New Zealand – whether independent or not – before 6 February 1840 (the date of the Treaty of Waitangi), 21 May 1840 (the date when William Hobson proclaimed New Zealand to be a British colony), or 2 October 1840 (the date upon which the proclamations were gazetted) was critical, because Gipps's bill appeared to legislate on the validity of land purchases made before that time. The declaration of independence of "the Northern parts of New Zealand" by "The United Tribes of New Zealand" on 28 October 1835 supported Busby's argument and undermined Gipps's. Busby, who had been the British Resident – an emissary of the British government – on the North Island since 1833, urged Māori chiefs to issue the declaration after learning that Charles, Baron de Thierry intended to establish a French colony in New Zealand.[42]

Gipps correctly argued that the British government's response to the declaration of independence fell well short of Busby's assertion on 30 June 1840 that the British government had "solemnly ratified" it. After receiving the declaration, the dithering Colonial Secretary, Lord Glenelg, warily wrote Richard Bourke, the Governor of New South Wales, addressing only the fourth paragraph of the declaration, which requested that "the King of England ... will continue to be the parent of their infant State, and that he will become its Protector from all attempts upon its independence." Glenelg informed Bourke that he had received the declaration, but wrote only that "with reference to the desire which the chiefs have expressed on this occasion to maintain a good understanding with His Majesty's subjects, it will be proper that they should be assured, in His Majesty's name, that He will not fail to avail himself of every opportunity of showing His goodwill, and of affording to those chiefs such support and protection as may be consistent with a due regard to the just right of others, and to the interests of His Majesty's subjects."[43] Glenelg's letter was published in the *British Parliamentary Papers*, but the guardedly written letter from the Colonial Secretary to a colonial governor hardly represented the British government's official recognition of New Zealand's independence.

But Gipps's argument was hardly unassailable. Much evidence supported Wentworth's assertion that New Zealand had been independent before the 1835 declaration. As early as 1817, a British law had specifically listed New Zealand as a place "not within His Majesty's dominions."[44] Two other British statutes passed in the 1820s appear to have acknowledged the independence of New Zealand.[45] Various other actions, including the appointment of James Busby as British Resident in New Zealand, seemed to signal a British acknowledgment of New Zealand's independence. In that context, someone like Wentworth might attribute the lack of any official British government response to the 1835 declaration of independence to the fact that it had already acknowledged New Zealand as independent. More problematic for Gipps, as recently as 14 August 1839 – less than a year before Gipps denied it – the British Secretary of State for the Colonies, Lord Normanby, had written, in his official instructions to Hobson, that "we acknowledge New Zealand as a sovereign and independent state."[46] Finally, the fact that Normanby then instructed Hobson to secure a treaty in which Māori rangatira were to cede sovereignty to the British Crown, seemed to suggest that the British acknowledged Māori sovereignty – why secure a cession of something that Māori rangatira did not possess?[47] In essence, as Bain Attwood has argued, the British government treated New Zealand as both "sovereign and not sovereign" at the same time.[48]

The events of 1840 had arisen because of the haphazard, indecisive, and ambiguous responses of the British government to the activities of British subjects in New Zealand over the previous decades. Thanks to an influx of European weaponry brought to New Zealand by British traders, by 1806 intertribal warfare was leading to population decline, displacement, and the redrawing of tribal boundaries in New Zealand.[49] In response, British Anglican and Wesleyan missionaries began working among Māori communities in 1814, and soon developed a written form of te reo Māori (the Māori language).[50] And, on 24 February 1815, Samuel Marsden, on behalf of the Church Missionary Society, purchased 80 acres from Māori in the Bay of Islands district.[51] Missionaries made many more purchases between 1815 and 1840. They were usually carefully documented in English and te reo Māori, often sought to keep land out of the hands of speculators, and sometimes placed the land in Māori trusts, but they were purported to be legitimate land transfers.[52]

By the 1830s, missionaries and others were reporting increasing numbers of "atrocities" perpetrated against Māori by British subjects. The most infamous was the *Elizabeth* affair of 1830, in which John Stewart, captain of the brig *Elizabeth*, approached the Ngāi Tahu village of Takapūneke, in Akaroa Harbour, in Banks Peninsula, under the guise of trade (see figure 14). Unbeknown to the villagers, Stewart had permitted a hundred Ngāti Toa warriors to hide aboard the ship and ambush the unsuspecting Ngāi Tahu, killing several hundred, including their chief, Tama-i-hara-nui. It was in 1833, after learning of such outrages, and for the safety of the "well-disposed settlers and traders" in New Zealand, that the British government appointed James Busby as British Resident on the North Island.[53] Following the example of missionaries, Busby purchased land for himself and his family. When he spoke before the Legislative Council in 1840 he was no disinterested observer; he claimed 50,000 acres of land by right of purchase from Māori chiefs.

The appointment of a British Resident – usually considered a diplomatic rank – in New Zealand unleashed a process that continued throughout the decade: each time the British government increased its involvement in New Zealand affairs in response to the growing population of British subjects there, the stream of British migration to the islands quickened.[54] It was not a flood; by the late 1830s, unofficial enclaves of British subjects, totalling perhaps 2,000 people, dotted New Zealand, primarily on the North Island. As might be expected, the British settlements on the North Island comprised the full range of types: respectable and affluent traders who dealt primarily in timber and flax; Protestant missionaries who worked among Māori communities and considered themselves to be protectors of Māori; tradesmen of various kinds; purveyors of grog; "ships' deserters, and escaped convicts, beachcombers and drifters."[55] There were also a number of pākehā-Māori: Europeans (pākehā) who had been integrated into Māori communities.[56] The much smaller European population on the South Island (then usually called Middle Island) and Stewart Island (then called South Island) resided primarily at whaling stations usually in close association with Māori.[57]

By the late 1830s, those populations obliged the British government to pay more attention to the islands because British officials assumed that the British government had dual duties to control and protect British subjects there, and to protect Māori from exploitation by British subjects. Concerns were heightened by the reports of frequent battles among Māori communities. While British subjects had thus far managed to avoid becoming embroiled in those wars, observers believed that they would inevitably be drawn into them.[58] Self-styled humanitarians, at their height of influence in the Colonial Office and in London generally in the latter half of the 1830s, emphasized this second duty, but were influenced by both, just as British politicians, although most attentive to the first consideration, were also motivated by both.[59] By the late 1830s both humanitarians and imperialists urged the British government, already entangled, to intervene directly in New Zealand. For example, on 29 December 1837, Lord Glenelg wrote of New Zealand that "It is an *indispensable duty* in reference both to the natives and to British interests, to interpose by some effective authority to put a stop to the evils and dangers to which all those interests are exposed, in consequence of the manner in which the intercourse of foreigners with those islands are now carried on."[60]

Ironically, public knowledge that British officials were considering direct government intervention in New Zealand made that intervention inevitable and urgent, for once British subjects learned of those discussions, a number of them bought land from Māori rangatira.[61] Then, in 1839 and early 1840, when it became all but certain that the British would make New Zealand a colony, speculators – William Wentworth among them – rushed to buy land.[62] Thus, a distinction might be made between the land purchases made before the British contemplated colonizing the islands, and those concluded afterwards.[63]

Best known among the speculators in New Zealand lands in 1839–40 were the representatives of the New Zealand Company (NZC). Confident that the British government had decided to colonize New Zealand, the NZC hastily arranged for the *Tory* to go to New Zealand to buy land. With the government of Lord Melbourne in disarray, and with the Colonial Office staffed with too many indecisive and pusillanimous bureaucrats, no one prevented the *Tory* from sailing on 12 May. Instead, officials in the Colonial Office hurried their own plans to annex New Zealand, and concluded that all of New Zealand, not just the North Island, should be brought under British control.[64] They sent William Hobson to New Zealand as lieutenant governor, and instructed him "to treat with the Natives for cession of Sovereignty to England."[65] In the interim, in June 1839, the Governor of New South Wales was given jurisdiction over New Zealand.[66]

As well known as the mischiefs of the NZC were in the history of New Zealand, they were not the driving force behind Gipps's bill of 1840.[67] Gipps's bill was intended to address the speculators from New South Wales who rushed to purchase land from Māori in late 1839 and early 1840. When William Hobson arrived in Sydney on 24 December 1839, the land rush became a frenzy. Gipps tried immediately to stem it. He succeeded in preventing a public auction of New Zealand lands in Sydney on 6 January 1840 by sending an officer to announce at the auction hall that "it would be very questionable whether the Home Government would allow titles to land granted by New Zealand chiefs."[68]

On 14 January 1840, Gipps publicly announced that the British government had expanded his authority to include New Zealand.[69] On the same day, he issued his Land Titles Validity Proclamation which stipulated that all pre-1840 land purchases in New Zealand would be subject to scrutiny by a land commission, and that "all purchases of land in any part of new Zealand which may be made by any of her Majesty's subjects from any of the native chiefs or tribes of these islands after the date hereof, will be considered as absolutely null and void, and neither confirmed nor in any way recognised by her Majesty."[70]

To deal with purchases already made, Gipps promised to establish a commission to review them.⁷¹ On 19 January 1840, Gipps appointed William Hobson, Lieutenant Governor of New Zealand, and sent him to New Zealand.⁷² William Hobson, upon arrival in New Zealand on 30 January 1840, issued essentially the same proclamation that Gipps had issued in Sydney.⁷³

As early as 31 January 1840, Gipps, when meeting with several Ngāi Tahu rangatira from the South Island of New Zealand who had sold land to purchasers from New South Wales, informed them that "British subjects had no right to purchase land of savages, in precedence of their own Government."⁷⁴ Gipps later wrote to Lord John Russell, the Colonial Secretary, to inform him that on 14 February, seven rangatira from the Middle (South) Island had been in Sydney, at which time the chiefs met Gipps at Government House, where they were told that "only such purchases of land as should be approved by Her Majesty would ultimately be confirmed."⁷⁵ Gipps tried to convince the rangatira to sign a treaty granting the British "absolute Sovereignty in and over the said Native Chiefs, their Tribes and country," in light of "the evil consequences which are likely to arise to the welfare of the Native Chiefs and Tribes from the settlement among them of Her Majesty's subjects, unless some settled form of civil Government be established to protect the Native Chiefs and Tribes in their just rights, and to repress and punish crimes and offences which may be committed by any of Her Majesty's subjects."⁷⁶ The draft treaty also stipulated that:

> Her said Majesty does hereby engage to accept the said Native Chiefs and Tribes as Her Majesty's subjects, and to grant Her Royal protection to the said Native Chiefs, their tribes and country, in as full and ample a manner as Her Majesty is bound to afford protection to other of Her Majesty's subjects and Dominions. And the said Native Chiefs do hereby on behalf of themselves and tribes engage, not to sell or otherwise alienate any lands occupied by or belonging to them, to any person whatsoever except to Her said Majesty upon such consideration as may be hereafter fixed, and upon the express understanding that the said Chiefs and Tribes shall retain for their own exclusive use and benefit such part of their said lands as may be requisite and necessary for their comfortable maintenance and residence. And that out of the proceeds of the land which may be purchased from them adequate provision shall be made for their future education and instruction in the truths of Christianity.⁷⁷

Gipps reported that the chiefs agreed to come back the following day to sign the treaty; "on the day appointed, however, none of them appeared."[78] Gipps learned that William C. Wentworth and his partner, John Jones, had warned the chiefs "to sign no treaty which did not contain full security for the possession by the purchasers of all lands acquired from the natives." Gipps also noted that Wentworth had "after the issue of my proclamation [of 14 January], in conjunction with four or five persons, purchased the whole of the Middle Island (or all the unsold portions of it) from these very natives, paying them for it 200*l*. in ready money, with a promise of a like sum per annum as long as they should live."[79] "Such was the origin," Gipps explained, "of Mr. Wentworth's claim to 20 millions of acres in the Middle Island."[80] To place this in context, 20 million acres (approximately 81,000 square kilometres) is more than 2.5 times the area of Vancouver Island.

In March and April 1840, a group of over forty men describing themselves as "Landowners of New Zealand" formed The New Zealand Association, chaired by Wentworth, to defend their land claims.[81] They hired à Beckett and Darvall to represent their interests. In response Gipps introduced his bill on 28 May 1840.[82] Much was at stake. By that time, thanks to overlapping claims, the acreage of land in New Zealand claimed by British subjects exceeded the total acreage of the islands.[83] If all of William Wentworth's purchases had been ruled valid, he would have been the largest landowner in the world. He would have owned about a third of New Zealand.

While trying to deal with matters in New South Wales, Gipps learned on 18 February that Hobson had succeeded in negotiating a treaty with Māori rangatira on the North Island of New Zealand.[84] The 6 February 1840 Treaty of Waitangi was not a land-surrender treaty. Although no one then mentioned the similarities, in several respects the Treaty of Waitangi resembled the portions of the Royal Proclamation of 1763 having to do with "the several Nations or Tribes of Indians with whom We are connected." The Crown issued the Royal Proclamation to explain how the Crown intended to rule its subjects (Indigenous and exogenous) in the vast territories it had acquired by the Treaty of Paris of 10 February 1763.[85] Two-thirds of the Proclamation explained the Crown's intentions regarding its new subjects in the established colonies of Quebec, East Florida, and West Florida. The other third explained the Crown's intentions regarding the Indigenous "subjects" in the large part of the newly acquired territory outside the established colonies, and outside the territories granted to the HBC. That portion of the proclamation represents the king's olive branch, designed to avoid a brutal war with Indians west of the Appalachian Mountains. The Proclamation created a vast reserve in that region to ensure that "the several Nations or Tribes of Indians" there "should not be molested or disturbed in the Possession of such Parts of Our Dominions and Territories ... not having been ceded to or purchased by Us." The Royal Proclamation then guaranteed the Indians within those reserved territories the possession of their lands, until they were willing to sell their lands, at which time the Crown enjoyed the exclusive right to purchase such lands. As has been noted, Dutch and English (including the HBC) had concluded purchases as early as the 1620s, but the Royal Proclamation represents the first time that the British Crown promised to negotiate land purchases.

The Royal Proclamation did not refer to legal principles; it explained its provisions regarding Indigenous people on the grounds of expediency: they were "just and reasonable, and essential to our Interest." Neither did the proclamation distinguish between villagers and nomadic peoples, or between occupied and "waste" lands. Fewer Indigenous communities cultivated land or occupied villages in the reserved lands than in the lands east of the Appalachian Mountains. Moreover, when the Crown negotiated land-cession treaties arising out of the promises made in the Royal Proclamation (many concluded before 1840), it always secured the surrender of all territories inhabited by signatory peoples, all of whom, within the borders of present-day Canada, were nomadic hunting and gathering peoples. So, while the Royal Proclamation did not explicitly recognize Indigenous title, it represented a significant step in the development of the principles of Indigenous title, especially since it emanated from the Crown.

The Treaty of Waitangi was originally written in English and translated into te reo Māori. Māori chiefs signed the Māori version, but in the late 1840s officials in the Colonial Office understood only the English version. According to that version of the treaty, the Māori ceded "to Her Majesty the Queen of England absolutely and without reservation all the rights and powers of Sovereignty which the said Confederation or Individual Chiefs respectively exercise or possess." In exchange, the British offered Māori signatories promises resembling those the Crown offered to Indians in the "Indian Territory" of British North America in 1763. The Royal Proclamation assumed that Indians were new subjects of the Crown, while the Treaty of Waitangi included a cession of sovereignty. The treaty promised Māori "the full exclusive and undisturbed possession of their Lands and Estates Forests Fisheries and other properties which they may collectively or individually possess so long as it is their wish and desire to retain the same in their possession," but stipulated that, should Māori wish to sell lands, the Crown would have the exclusive right to purchase them, "at such prices as may be agreed upon between the respective Proprietors and persons appointed by Her

Majesty to treat with them in that behalf."[86] By using the verb "to treat," the Treaty of Waitangi here explicitly anticipated that these purchases could be considered treaties.

Thus, the Treaty of Waitangi, like the Royal Proclamation, assumed that the British Crown enjoyed sovereignty over a territory, and that the Indigenous people of the territory were British subjects. The British Crown promised the Indigenous people of both territories the continued possession of the territory, until those Indigenous people voluntarily sold land to the British Crown by treaty, after negotiating with agents of the Crown. The Royal Proclamation cannot have been intended to protect only lands cultivated or occupied by villages, since the territory was inhabited by nomadic hunting and gathering peoples. The Treaty of Waitangi, at the very least, was also open to the interpretation that the British Crown promised to purchase each community's entire territory, not just the lands that had been cultivated or built upon.[87] Complicating the situation in New Zealand, Hobson, who had thought that the Māori of the South Island were "too savage" to comprehend a treaty, declared British sovereignty over the South Island on 21 May 1840, without reference to the treaty he had concluded on the North Island in February.[88]

Under the confused circumstances, it may have been inevitable that conflict over land ownership was soon to develop. Exogenous land buyers, including missionaries, the NZC, and speculators from Sydney, immediately pressed claims. On 17 June 1843, conflict erupted between pākehā and Māori, when Ngāti Toa chiefs repulsed settlers connected with the NZC who tried to take possession of lands near Nelson that the NZC claimed to have purchased (see figure 14). The Wairau incident, in which twenty-two settlers and between two and six Māori were killed, led 700 settlers in Wellington and the northern South Island to petition the British government for military assistance.[89] After news of the Wairau incident arrived in London, the London public, the NZC, and parliamentarians, took notice. With circumstances in New Zealand deteriorating, and the NZC teetering on the brink of bankruptcy, on 26 April 1844, Henry Aglionby, one of the directors of the NZC, and a Member of the House of Commons, proposed the establishment of a Select Parliamentary Committee on New Zealand. That committee, like Gipps's 1840 speech, was destined to influence developments in New Zealand and Vancouver Island.

Faced with a confusing and potentially dangerous and expensive situation in New Zealand, the members of the House of Commons, on 26 April 1844 approved Aglionby's Select Committee "to inquire into the State of the Colony of New Zealand, and into the Proceedings of the New Zealand Company."⁹⁰ The Select Committee was chaired by the Whig and Liberal politician Viscount Howick (1802–1894). Howick was first elected to the British House of Commons in 1826. From 1830 to 1834, during the Whig ministry of his father, Charles Grey, 2nd Earl Grey, he served as Under-Secretary of State for War and the Colonies, but resigned that posting in 1834 to protest the gradual (rather than immediate) emancipation of slaves. During his time in the Colonial Office, he earned a reputation for his thorough knowledge of colonial affairs. The Select Committee sat from early May to 23 July, and presented its resolutions (endorsed by only seven of the thirteen members of the committee) to the House of Commons on 29 July 1844.⁹¹ The committee's report, written by Howick, quoted directly and endorsed the three principles Gipps articulated in his speech of 9 July 1840, and concluded that "the difficulties now experienced in New Zealand are mainly to be attributed to the fact, that in the measures which have been taken for establishing a British Colony in these islands, those rules as to the mode in which colonization ought to be conducted, which have been drawn from reason and from experience, have not been sufficiently attended to."⁹² The committee found that the British government had erroneously recognized the independence of New Zealand in the 1830s. That error had made it impossible for the government to check or regulate the emigration of British subjects to New Zealand or to police their behaviour once they had settled there. Then, confronted with reports of poor behaviour of British subjects in New Zealand in the late 1830s, the government decided that it was necessary for the government to establish its dominion over the islands.

The Select Committee then noted that the British government again departed from basic principles when an "attempt was made by the New Zealand Company to establish a colony, not only without the sanction, but in direct defiance of the authority of the Crown."⁹³ The committee stated that "it is to be regretted that more decisive measures were not adopted for preventing the sailing of the expedition under these circumstances, since it appears important, with reference to the future, to observe, that such unauthorized attempts at colonization cannot be permitted without leading to the most serious inconvenience."⁹⁴

According to the committee, in trying to repair the damage caused by its previous blunders, the government only compounded its errors in 1839 when officials in the Colonial Office resolved to deal with the situation in New Zealand by sending an emissary to negotiate an agreement with Māori leaders on the North Island to cede their sovereignty to the British Crown in exchange for certain guarantees and rights. The result was the Treaty of Waitangi of 6 February 1840. The Select

Committee of 1844 concluded that the Treaty of Waitangi "though a natural consequence of previous errors of policy, was a wrong one," an error that "amounted to little more than a legal fiction, though it has already in practice proved to be a very inconvenient one, and is likely to be still more so hereafter." The committee argued that British sovereignty could have been declared "on the ground of prior discovery, and on that of the absolute necessity of establishing the authority of the British Crown for the protection of the natives themselves."[95]

More famously, the committee resolved that "the conclusion of the Treaty of Waitangi by Captain Hobson with certain Natives of New Zealand, was a part of a series of injudicious proceedings, which had commenced several years previous to his assumption of the local Government."[96] Not only had the treaty been an error, so had the government's interpretation of it. The committee resolved that "the acknowledgement by the local authorities of a right of property on the part of the Natives of New Zealand, in all wild lands in those Islands, after the sovereignty had been assumed by Her Majesty, was not essential to the true construction of the Treaty of Waitangi, and was an error which has been productive of very injurious consequences."[97] They stated that Hobson's instructions "were not sufficiently precise" in laying out that, when the British assumed sovereignty, unoccupied land would immediately be vested in the Crown.[98] The Select Committee of 1844 furthermore argued that "the evidence before your Committee, both oral and documentary, leads to the conclusion that the natives of New Zealand, till they learnt to do so from Europeans, attached no idea of value to unoccupied land, and that though they had some vague notions of certain circumstances ... giving preferable claims to particular districts, yet, practically, the right by which territory was held, was that of the strongest."[99] Notwithstanding their conclusions, the committee acknowledged that the Treaty of Waitangi having been concluded, they were "sensible of the great difficulty which may now be experienced in changing it."[100]

Lord Stanley, the Colonial Secretary, understood that the Select Committee's recommendations, if adopted, would be a significant departure from the approach of the Colonial Office under his leadership (since September 1841), would "add to the difficulties" of Robert FitzRoy (the Governor of New Zealand), and "would, I fear, lead to most unhappy consequences." So, he snubbed Parliament, ignored the report's recommendations, and directed FitzRoy to do so as well. In an August 1844 letter to FitzRoy, Stanley noted that the Select Committee had accepted George Gipps's assertion that "the uncivilized inhabitants of any country" enjoyed but a "qualified dominion" as its fundamental assumption, but Stanley demurred, arguing that "there are many gradations of 'uncivilized inhabitants,' and practically, according to their state of civilization, must be the extent of the rights which they can be allowed to claim, whenever the territory on which they reside is occupied by civilized communities."[101]

Stanley's elaboration clarifies positions within Lord Stanley's Colonial Office concerning the nature and principles of Indigenous title. Stanley did not reject the principles put forward by the Select Committee so much as dispute the way the committee applied them to New Zealand. Drawing upon stadial history, Stanley attributed any people's land rights to their level of "civilization" and the intensity with which they used the land. It was on that basis that he argued that nomadic hunters had few land rights:

> The aborigines of New Holland [Australia], generally, are broken into feeble and perfectly savage migratory tribes, roaming over boundless extents of country, subsisting from day to day on the precarious produce of the chase, wholly ignorant of, or averse to, the cultivation of the soil, with no principles of civil government or recognition of private property, and little if any knowledge of the various forms of religion, or even of the existence of a Supreme Being. It is impossible to admit, on the part of a population thus situated, any rights in the soil which should be permitted to interfere with the subjugation, by Europeans, of the vast wilderness over which they are scattered.[102]

Stanley did not argue that the colonizer had no obligations to such nomadic peoples, but that justice, policy, and humanity only required colonizers "to embrace the aborigines within their pale, to diffuse religious knowledge among them, to induce them, if possible, to adopt more settled modes of providing for their subsistence, and to afford them the means of doing so, if so disposed, by an adequate reservation of lands within the limits of cultivation."[103] After justifying the lack of any treaties in the Australian colonies, Stanley argued that Māori enjoyed far greater rights on the grounds that

> Their main, though not their sole subsistence, was derived from agriculture, rude indeed, but continuous: rights of property, as between tribe and tribe, and of individuals of each tribe *inter se*, were recognised and well understood; they had been for many years in intercourse with English traders and with Christian missionaries; many of them had adopted Christianity; many were acquainted with the English language and with letters, and, at this moment, a Maori Gazette is published in New Zealand, and widely circulated among them.[104]

Lord Stanley's comparison of the rights of Indigenous people to land is useful to historians of the British Empire, for his commentary articulates general principles upon which he believed Indigenous people could claim rights to land. For historians of Australia and Canada, these remarks are relevant because, although most observers at the time placed the Indigenous peoples of most of British North America on a higher level of "civilization" than the "aborigines" of Australia, most of British North America at the time was inhabited by nomadic hunting and gathering peoples. That assessment would suggest that, had King George III not issued the Royal Proclamation of 1763, the British government may not have negotiated land-transfer treaties in Upper Canada.[105] In fact, by the time of Stanley's tenure in the Colonial Office, much of the land in Upper Canada had been subject to such treaties with nomadic hunting and gathering peoples. Meanwhile, although the villagers of Vancouver Island and the Pacific coast did not fit Stanley's description of Māori of the North Island, they did occupy sizable villages, and many had, by the 1840s, begun to cultivate potatoes.

The resolutions of the Select Committee's report had been published unofficially, even in New Zealand, before the entire lengthy report was published in the *Parliamentary Papers*.[106] However, it became obvious over the course of early 1845 that Lord Stanley had decided to defy the report's resolutions, that discussions to resolve differences between the NZC and the government were at an impasse, that FitzRoy was not reporting adequately to London, and that FitzRoy had exceeded the bounds of his authority in New Zealand. So, Charles Buller, a reformist member of Parliament with links to the NZC, upped pressure on Stanley and the government by moving that the House of Commons approve the resolutions of the Select Committee of 1844.[107] The three-day debate that followed, like the debate in Sydney in June and July 1840, is important because, as Bain Attwood has noted, "many of the speeches – and certainly those of the most important speakers – were highly erudite."[108] It came after years of controversy, during which the principles of sovereignty and native title had been the subject of much discussion. Furthermore, the three days of debate over the motion came as news from New Zealand made it seem that warfare between Māori and the British was almost inevitable.[109] The fact that "the Colonial Minister and a parliamentary committee, composed of his own friends, are at *direct variance*" made the whole affair embarrassing for the government of Robert Peel.[110]

During the debates, Lord Howick, the Whig politician who had chaired the Select Committee, spoke at length, late into the evening of 18 June 1845,[111] clarifying that, although he could not support the actions of the NZC, "the real question for consideration was, whether the policy which had been adopted towards New Zealand had been calculated to promote the welfare either of England, or the settlers, or of the natives," and that "the substantial effect ... of the vote they were called upon to give, was simply this – that the policy pursued towards New Zealand had been faulty, and required to be amended."[112] Howick repeated his assertion that the initial recognition of New Zealand independence in 1831 or 1832 (while his own father, had been Prime Minister) had been, in hindsight, a mistake, and that successive governments had made further mistakes, culminating with the Treaty of Waitangi. He also maintained that between 1832 and 1840, thanks to the activities of missionaries and others, the circumstances in New Zealand had improved, but that in 1840, "from that very moment, instead of things improving, they became far worse than they had been before, and the evils of anarchy were greater than at any former period."[113] "The real interest of the natives," he continued, "was not that they should be permitted themselves to sell the land, for money or goods, which they were sure improvidently to waste, but to have it sold by the constituted authorities in such a manner as to ensure its regular occupation, and to have the price obtained for it so applied as to encourage the investment of capital and settlement."[114] He concluded with words that help explain the Colonial Office's later approach to the colony of Vancouver Island: "when he looked at ... the results of attempting to govern from Downing Street a settlement at the antipodes, he must say experience was decidedly in favour of allowing a Colony to govern itself. ... From some experience of the Colonial Office, he was persuaded that it was utterly impossible for any man, be his talents and industry what they might, adequately to administer such complicated affairs as those of the British Colonies. ... For a Colony, he believed self-government was the best."[115]

Two Members of Parliament at the time had deep connections to the HBC. The influential Edward Ellice (1783–1863) also spoke to Buller's motion. He was Member of Parliament from Coventry, founder of the Reform Club, former member of the HBC's London Committee (1824–37), and father to Edward Ellice, Jr. (1810–1880), a member of the London Committee of the HBC (1837–58). Speaking in favour of the motion on 19 June, he said that "the natives can only retain what is required for their use and enjoyment, and that should be the most liberally conceded and secured to them. The remainder must be brought under the dominion of civilized man. Why not declare this openly, as the course equally dictated by justice and by policy, and for the quiet and advantage of both parties?[116] Ellice added that, after the HBC had been allowed the "self-government of their own affairs" in 1821, the British government had "had no appeal since, either for legislative measures, or money, or military assistance to control the native tribes, and secure the lives and properties of your subjects in the country." He continued by arguing that "I can have no doubt that if you had acted on the same principle, and intrusted them [the NZC] with the management of the affairs of the infant Colony, you would have avoided the difficulties in which we are now placed."[117]

After three days of debate, the House of Commons defeated Buller's motion to endorse the recommendations of the Select Committee by a vote of 223 against, and 173 in favour.[118] But Buller and the opposition had succeeded in embarrassing the government and undermining the Colonial Secretary. Moreover, the defeat of the motion did not put the controversy to rest.

Shortly after the three-day debate on New Zealand ended on 20 June 1845, the news arrived in London of the Battle of Kororāreka by Māori forces led by Hōne Heke, the first Māori signatory on the Treaty of Waitangi. This news ensured that New Zealand again occupied space in the newspapers and time in Parliament. Viscount Ebrington demanded to know how the government intended to deal with the "waste lands" in New Zealand, for he argued that "unless Government made up their minds to grapple firmly with this question, all hopes of a satisfactory settlement would be illusory." Oddly, after averring that "all the great writers on international law were agreed on the subject," rather than quoting one of those "great writers," Ebrington quoted an article published in 1831 by Thomas Arnold during the debates over the Reform Bill. While Arnold drew upon the arguments of eminent theorists of international law (and the Bible), he was derivative and ill-informed, rather than original or correct:

> It is said the land belongs to everybody – nothing belongs to everybody; it either belongs to somebody or to nobody at all. The air belongs to nobody, the open sea belongs to nobody, and for this reason, because man has done nothing and can do nothing to make them better for his use than God made them from the beginning. They are not his property at all; but with the earth or land, and all things on it, is quite different. Men were to subdue the earth, that is, to make it by their labour what it would not have been by itself; and with the labour so bestowed upon it, came the right of property in it. Thus every land which is inhabited at all belongs to somebody.[119] But so much does the right of property go along with labour, that civilized nations have never scrupled to take possession of countries inhabited only by tribes of savages – countries which have been hunted over, but never subdued or cultivated. ... It is true, they have often gone

further and settled themselves in countries which were cultivated, and then it becomes robbery; but when our fathers went to America and took possession of the mere hunting-grounds of the Indians of lands on which man had hitherto bestowed no labour, they only exercised a right which God has inseparably united with industry and knowledge.[120]

Embarrassments over New Zealand would never be enough to bring down a British government, but they did cost FitzRoy his job. In June 1845, Stanley appointed George Grey to replace him. To the new governor, opined the Radical MP Joseph Hume, would fall the "the arduous duty to perform of correcting the calamitous mistakes into which the Colonial Office had been betrayed."[121] Meanwhile, as the debates over the affairs of New Zealand raged, *Phytophthora infestans* was silently destroying the potato crop in Ireland. Controversies stemming from the responses to the ensuing famine on the part of the Conservative government of Robert Peel led Lord Stanley to resign from Cabinet in January 1846, and Peel to resign as Prime Minister in late June 1846 after his opponents, including members of his own party, defeated Peel's Coercion Bill, aimed at suppressing disturbances in Ireland. The collapse of Peel's government permitted Lord John Russell to put together a Whig government that would rule until 1852. During that time the Colonial Office adopted unequivocally those principles articulated by Gipps on 9 July 1840, and the positions taken by Lord Howick in the Select Committee Report of 1844 and in Parliament on 18 June 1845.

The period between 1835 and 1846 was important in the history of Indigenous title. On one hand, the Colonial Office promised in the Treaty of Waitangi to negotiate land-purchase treaties in New Zealand during these years. On the other hand, in response to private entities that also claimed the right to purchase land directly from Indigenous communities, the British government was forced to clarify its position on Indigenous title, sovereignty, and land purchase. The narrow interpretations of Indigenous title put forward by Sir George Gipps and Viscount Howick are crucial to an understanding of the Vancouver Island treaties because the HBC Governor and Committee's position on the question would be directly influenced by those interpretations. But it remained to be seen in 1846, whether those interpretations would hold the day. For that reason, it is important to pay close attention the period between 1846 and 1849.

# 7 The Colonial Office, Local Authorities, and Indigenous Title, 1846–1849

It would be a mistake for historians of Vancouver Island to place too much weight on the fact that the Members of Parliament in 1845 defeated the motion to endorse the recommendations of the 1844 Select Committee Report on New Zealand.[1] Those most closely associated with the government of Robert Peel voted against the motion, but during the debates of June and July 1845, Peel's government, including Peel himself, had distanced themselves from the positions that Stanley had doggedly defended. More importantly for those interested in the Vancouver Island treaties, the authors and supporters of the 1844 resolutions and report were in power in Britain from 30 June 1846 to 21 February 1852, crucial formative years in the history of the colony of Vancouver Island. They included Lord John Russell (1792–1878), who had served as Colonial Secretary between 30 August 1839 and 30 August 1841, would be Prime Minister of Great Britain from 1846 to 1852, and would serve briefly again as Colonial Secretary from 23 February to 21 July 1855. Russell appointed as Colonial Secretary (6 July 1846) Henry Grey, 3rd Earl Grey (formerly Lord Howick), the author and most important proponent of the report of the 1844 Select Committee (see figure 15).[2] Others who had endorsed the 1844 report included Henry Labouchère (who had been Under-Secretary of State in 1839, and would be Colonial Secretary from 21 November 1855 to 21 February 1858), Benjamin Hawes (Under-Secretary in the Colonial Office from 1846 to 1851), Sir George Grey (1799–1882)[3] (Under-Secretary of State in the Colonial Office between 1835 and 1839), Charles Buller (a spirited advocate of the NZC who, though not appointed to the Colonial Office, would play a major role in colonial affairs),[4] and Viscount Ebrington, who had quoted Thomas Arnold in the House of Commons on 30 July 1845 during the debates over New Zealand.[5] Furthermore, Edward Ellice Sr., and Edward Ellice Jr., both of whom voted in favour of the motion to approve the 1844 report, were influential in the HBC in the years that the HBC oversaw the colony of Vancouver Island.[6] In short, the general principles set forth in the report of the 1844 Select Committee on New Zealand were the principles of those in the Colonial Office during the early years of the colony of Vancouver Island.

Russell's ministry moved quickly to grant greater self-government to British colonies, including New Zealand, and to make peace with the NZC. His government soon passed the New Zealand Constitution Act, 1846, and approved the New Zealand Charter, which divided the colony into two provinces, New Ulster (comprising the North Island north of the mouth of the Patea River) and New Munster (all of New Zealand south of the mouth of the Petea River) (see figure 14), a division intended to place the territory in which the NZC was most active, in New Munster.[7] In May 1847, having judged as legitimate NZC demands for compensation for losses caused by government policies, Earl Grey and the NZC arrived at an agreement that included a provision by which, for three years "the Government shall give up to the Company the entire and exclusive disposal of all Crown lands, and the exercise of the Crown's right of pre-emption of lands belonging to the natives in the Southern Government of New Zealand," an agreement codified in law in July.[8] In August, Parliament also authorized a loan to the NZC of up to £67,000, which could be used "toward the Purchase of land in New Zealand, and for satisfying the Claims of the native Inhabitants thereto."[9]

Having been the Chair of the 1844 Select Committee on New Zealand, and already having much experience in the Colonial Office, Henry George Grey, 3rd Earl Grey (formerly Lord Howick), the new Colonial Secretary, moved quickly regarding New Zealand. Before the end of the year, Earl Grey sent Governor George Grey[10] the new Charter for the Colony of New Zealand, with a new set of instructions, which claimed for the Crown the right of all "waste lands" in the Colony, and the right of the governor to alienate those lands.[11] His long covering letter of 23 December 1846 showed that his position on Indigenous title remained consistent with that of George Gipps in 1840, and with the resolutions of the 1844 Select Committee he had chaired.[12] Earl Grey appears immediately to have released the letter to the press, for it was published in the *London Times* six days later.[13] It set forth Earl Grey's perspective on the doctrine of Indigenous title. He began by referring, not to Lord Stanley's interpretation of Indigenous land rights, but to a caricature advocated by few people:

> The opinion assumed, rather than advocated, by a large class of writers on this and kindred subjects is, that the aboriginal inhabitants of any country are the proprietors of every part of its soil of which they have been

accustomed to making use, or to which they have been accustomed to assert any title. This claim is represented as sacred, however ignorant such natives may be of the arts or of the habits of civilized life, however small the number of their tribes, however unsettled their abodes, and however imperfect or occasional the uses they make of the land. Whether they are nomadic tribes depasturing cattle, or hunters living by the chase, or fishermen frequenting the sea-coasts or the banks of rivers, the proprietary title in question is alike ascribed to them all.[14]

He continued by tearing down this straw man, telling Grey that "from this doctrine, whether it be maintained on the grounds of religion or of morality, or of expediency, I entirely dissent."[15] He then set forth his view – much more similar to that of Lord Stanley than he was willing to admit. He quoted the passage by Thomas Arnold that Viscount Ebrington had read in the House of Commons in July 1845 during the debates over New Zealand, oddly describing the passage as authoritative on the topic "not only on account of his high character, but also because it was written not with reference to passing events, or to any controversy which was at that time going on, but as stating a principle which he conceived to be of general application."[16] He then penned what were probably the best articulations of the views of Lord Grey, the Colonial Office, and the British Government at the time the colony of Vancouver Island was formed:

It is true the New Zealanders, when European settlement commenced among them, were not a people of hunters; they lived, in a great measure at least, upon the produce of the soil (chiefly perhaps its spontaneous produce), and practised to a certain extent a rude sort of agriculture. But the extent of land so occupied by them was absolutely insignificant, when compared with that of the country they inhabited; the most trustworthy accounts agree in representing the cultivated grounds as forming far less than one-hundredth part of the available land, and in stating that millions of acres were to be found where the naturally fertile soil was covered by primeval forests or wastes of fern, in the midst of which a few patches planted with potatoes were the only signs of human habitation and industry.

The Islands of New Zealand are not much less extensive than the British Isles, and capable probably of supporting as large a population, while that which they actually supported has been variously estimated, but never I believe so high as 200,000 souls. To contend that under such circumstances civilized men had not a right to step in and to take possession of the vacant territory, but were bound to respect the supposed proprietary title of the savage tribes who dwelt in but were utterly unable to occupy the land, is to mistake the grounds upon which the right of property in land is founded.

To that portion of the soil, whatever it might be, which they really occupied the aboriginal inhabitants, barbarous as they were, had a clear and undoubted claim; to have attempted to deprive them of their patches of potato-ground, even so to have occupied the territory as not to leave them ample space for shifting, as was their habit, their cultivation from one spot to another, would have been in the highest degree unjust; but so long as this injustice was avoided, I must regard it a vain and unfounded scruple which would have acknowledged their right of property in land which remained unsubdued to the uses of man. But if the savage inhabitants of New Zealand had themselves no right of property in land which they did not occupy, it is obvious that they could not convey to others what they did not themselves possess, and that claims to vast tracts of waste land, founded on pretended sales from them, are altogether untenable.

From the moment that British dominion was proclaimed in New Zealand, all lands not actually occupied in the sense in which alone occupation can give a right of possession, ought to have been considered as the property of the Crown in its capacity of trustee, for the whole community; and it should thenceforward have been regarded as the right and at the same time the duty of those duly authorized by the Crown, to determine in what manner and according to what rules the land hitherto waste should be assigned and appropriated to particular individuals.

There is another consideration which leads to the same conclusion. It has never been pretended that the wide extent of unoccupied land, to which an exclusive right of property has been asserted on behalf of the native inhabitants of New Zealand, belonged to them, as individuals; it was only, as tribes, that they were supposed to possess it; and granting their title as such to have been good and valid, it was obviously a right which the tribes enjoyed as independent communities – an attribute of sovereignty, which, with the sovereignty naturally and necessarily was transferred to the British Crown. Had the New Zealanders been a civilized people, this would have been the case – if these islands, being inhabited by a civilized people, had been added either by conquest or by voluntary cession to the dominions of the Queen, it is clear that, according to the well-known principles of public law, while the property of individuals would have been respected, all public property, all rights of every description which had appertained to the previous Sovereigns, would have devolved, as a matter of course, to the new Sovereign who succeeded them. It can hardly be contended that these tribes, as such, possessed rights which civilized communities could not have claimed.[17]

Lord Grey's doctrine may not have differed much from that of Lord Stanley, but his application of the doctrine to New Zealand contrasted starkly with the position Lord Stanley took on 13 August 1844 when he conveyed his views to Robert FitzRoy, George Grey's predecessor.

Grey's letter is more important for historians of Vancouver Island than for historians of New Zealand, because, while Lord Grey acknowledged that previous policies had made it impossible to implement these principles in New Zealand at the time:

> Such are the principles upon which, if the colonization of New Zealand were only now about to begin, it would be my duty to instruct you to act; and though I am well aware that in point of fact you are not in a position to do so, and that from past transactions a state of things has arisen in which a strict application of these principles is impracticable, I have thought it right that they should be thus explicitly stated in this Despatch (as they are in the Royal instructions to which it refers), in order that you may clearly understand that, although in many respects you may be compelled to depart from them, still you are to look to them as the foundation of the policy which, so far as it [is] in your power, you are to pursue.
>
> The imperfect information which alone at this distance I can hope to obtain as to the actual state, of affairs in New Zealand, renders it impossible for me to venture to prescribe to you how far you are to go in attempting practically to act upon the principles I have laid down. I should infer from your own Despatches, as well as from those of your predecessors, that the right of the Crown could not now be asserted to large tracts of waste land which particular tribes have been taught to regard as their own. It appears that you have found it expedient to admit these pretensions to a considerable extent; and having done so, no apparent advantage could be suffered to weigh against the evil of acting in a manner either really or even apparently inconsistent with good faith. While, however, you scrupulously fulfil whatever engagements you have contracted, and maintain those rights on the part of the native tribes to land which you have already recognized, you will avoid as much as possible any further surrender of the property of the Crown.
>
> I trust also that the evil which would otherwise arise from the concessions already made, may to a great degree be neutralized by your strictly maintaining the exclusive right of the Crown to purchase land from the native tribes to which it has been assumed that it belongs. This right, resting as it does not only upon what has been called the Treaty of Waitangi, but also upon the general and long-recognized principles of national law, is one so important, that it ought almost at all hazards to be strictly enforced. To suffer it to be set aside would be to acquiesce in the ruin of the

colony, since it would be fatal to the progressive and systematic settlement of the country. It is by the sale of land at more than a nominal price that its appropriation to individuals in allotments proportioned to their power of making use of it can alone be secured. It is the mode by which, with least inconvenience and difficulty, funds can be raised for emigration, and for executing those public works which are necessary for the profitable occupation of the soil; in short, it is the very foundation upon which systematic colonization must be based. But if the native tribes are permitted to sell large tracts of land to individuals for a mere nominal consideration, it is obvious that so much land will be thrown upon the market as entirely to defeat the attempt to sell such lands as the Crown may still retain, at a price sufficient to answer the objects of the policy I have described.[18]

Grey elaborated upon why it was proper for the Crown to offer only token compensation for the surrender of land rights, and why it was reasonable to expect Indigenous people to agree to small compensation:

It has been asserted that the natives of New Zealand will never consent, unless compelled by force of arms, to the adoption of a system by which land bought from them at a nominal, or at all events at a low price, by the servants of the Crown, is to be re-sold at a much higher rate to actual settlers. I fear it may be more difficult than it would have been formerly to reconcile them to this practice, nevertheless the attempt must be made; and I still hope it may not be impossible to convince them that the Crown receives the money so paid for land only as trustee for the public, and that it is applied for their benefit as forming part of the community; that the price obtained for land which is sold to settlers affords the means of constructing roads and bridges, of building churches and schools, and of introducing an additional European population; thus really conducing far more to their advantage than the paltry supply of goods which, if they sold the land for themselves, they would obtain for it.

These remarks apply to lands held by the aboriginal inhabitants as tribes, and by a title not resting upon actual occupation and improvement; as individuals, they should be as free as any of the other inhabitants of New Zealand to acquire and to dispose of property in land.[19]

Earl Grey also reiterated the positions that he and Lord Russell had previously expressed in favour of colonial self-government, but acknowledged that it was "attended with at least one serious danger," that the elected bodies might be "perverted into an instrument for the oppression of the less civilized and less powerful races of men inhabiting the same colony." For that reason, he reminded George Grey that it was the task of the governor to call to the attention of the assemblies "the sacred duty which will be incumbent on them of watching over the interests, protecting the persons, and, as far as may be, cultivating, the minds of the aboriginal race among whom they and their constituents have settled."[20]

Clearly then, at the end of 1846, Earl Grey, the Colonial Secretary for the entire period between 1846 and 1852, adhered to a doctrine that stated that the British government had the right to take possession of all "vacant" or "waste" lands in new colonies unilaterally, that the Crown had the exclusive right to purchase Indigenous title to land occupied by cultivation or settlement, and that it was most appropriate for local executive authorities with knowledge of local circumstances, rather than personnel in the Colonial Office, to be making these complex decisions. At the same time, personnel in the Colonial Office, knowing that elected Legislative Assemblies tended to represent the interests of settlers against those of Indigenous people, believed that appointed governors were obligated to defend those Indigenous people against abuse of settlers and elected assemblies. Earl Grey's insistence that Governor Grey enforce "almost at all hazards" the Crown's exclusive right to purchase Indigenous title was tested immediately upon George Grey's arrival in New Zealand.

On 5 December 1844, Robert FitzRoy, then the Governor of New Zealand, issued a certificate to Charles Hunter McIntosh, waiving the Crown's right of pre-emption over up to 400 acres of land on the island of Taratoroa (Rotoroa), near Auckland. Empowered by that certificate, in January 1845, McIntosh purchased the 200-acre island from Ngatai and Ruinga, and on 22 April 1845, he received his deed of grant from the Crown.[21]

Why did FitzRoy issue such certificates, which violated the principle that the Crown enjoyed the exclusive right to extinguish Indigenous title in its colonies? FitzRoy answered that question in a long letter written on 15 April 1844, in which he described his conundrum. He reported that, during a visit to Wellington following the affray at Wairau in June 1843, he was unsurprised to find that "a bitterness of feeling towards the aborigines should have become very prevalent, and that only a portion of the educated and reflecting members of the community should have escaped the contagious spirit of hostility which showed itself in every conversation, and in every public document."[22] He explained that immigrants were arriving in New Zealand, only to discover that there was no land available to them.[23] He attributed the land shortage to "the absolute inability of the Government to enter into new purchases of land, having neither funds nor articles of trade, nor authority to draw upon the home Government."²⁴ He explained that, while Māori wanted to sell their land, they were demanding prices that were "wholly out of the question." Thus, Māori were insisting that the Treaty of Waitangi gave the Crown nothing more than the right of first refusal for their lands, and that if the government was unwilling to pay the asking price, Māori should have the right to sell to others.²⁵

FitzRoy tried to solve his problem by issuing certificates like the one he granted McIntosh in December 1844. On 10 October 1844, he proclaimed that he would issue certificates waiving the Crown's exclusive right to pre-empt Native land on the condition that the certificate holders agree to pay the Crown "one penny per acre" of land purchased from Māori. FitzRoy justified the proclamation, in part, by asserting that "the Natives of New Zealand have become perfectly aware of the full value of their lands – and are quite alive to their own present interests – however indifferent at times to those of their children."²⁶ Henry Falwasser, the editor of the *Auckland Times* congratulated FitzRoy for "emancipating the lands of the natives of New Zealand from the unjust iron grasp of Downing Street." The editor indicated that the Governor deserved the "thanks and praise of every person – European or Aboriginal – who lives, in any respect, within the influence of his authority."²⁷ In the subsequent months, FitzRoy issued almost two hundred such penny-an-acre certificates that saw private individuals purchase almost 100,000 acres from Māori landowners, but the government received little revenue from the sales.²⁸

FitzRoy may have been heartened by the support he received from settler and Māori interests, and from the local press, but his proclamation had not been approved by Lord Stanley, and it embarrassed the British government in London, because it violated the central principle that the Crown enjoyed the exclusive right to purchase land from Indigenous peoples. Local governors in the British world retained considerable authority to manage Indigenous affairs on their own, but they clearly did not have the power to deviate so dramatically from British policy as FitzRoy had, without approval from London.

Soon after George Grey arrived in New Zealand in November 1845 to replace FitzRoy, settlers pressed Grey to grant them penny-an-acre certificates. He concluded that FitzRoy's 10 October 1844 proclamation, the certificates, and the purchases by third persons that ensued were unlawful. Based on advice from his Attorney General, William Swainson, Grey contrived to test the legality of FitzRoy's certificates. Finding that McIntosh, a government clerk, had in all other respects come to a fair and bona fide agreement with the Māori sellers under complete conformity with FitzRoy's certificate (something that he thought was atypical), he issued a Crown grant to John Jermyn Symonds, his own private secretary and the colony's Aboriginal Protector, of the land claimed by McIntosh, forcing the Supreme Court to determine the legitimate owner. Except for the complicating factor that the governor had waived the Crown's right in this case, it was a replay of the "bitter though erudite debate between ... Sir George Gipps and William Charles Wentworth in 1840."[29]

*R. v. Symonds* may rank as one of the more misunderstood court cases and rulings in the British world.[30] The litigants in this case were both pākehā, and contrary to much of what has been written in Canada and New Zealand about the case, the issue at stake was the Crown's right of pre-emption, not the nature of Indigenous title.[31] During the 4 May 1847 hearing before the Chief Justice William Martin, both lawyers kept their arguments to the specific question: could Indigenous people sell land to anyone other than the Crown? Swainson argued that FitzRoy's certificates were null and void because Governor FitzRoy "had not the power to waive the Right of Pre-emption," because "the sole and absolute right of pre-emption from the aboriginal inhabitants of New Zealand vests in, and can only be exercised by, Her Majesty, Her Heirs and Successors."[32] Thomas Bartley, McIntosh's counsel, responded by arguing that, as British subjects, Māori had the same right to sell land to buyers of their own choice as any other subjects, except that in the Treaty of Waitangi they had agreed "simply to give her [the Queen] the first offer, or the right of pre-emption."[33] Both lawyers assumed that something called "native title" existed, but neither attempted to define what "native title" was, neither attempted to argue how much land was subject to native title, and neither called upon the court to decide such matters.[34] Accordingly, when they explained their ruling in the case, neither judge did so.

The decision, handed down on 9 June 1847, was issued by two judges of different backgrounds. Chief Justice William Martin (1807–1880), before whom the case was argued, had close connections with Anglican missionaries and had already by 1847 done much to defend Māori legal rights and to educate Māori about those rights.[35] Martin consulted with the Justice Henry Samuel Chapman (1803–1881) in Wellington, who was formerly the editor of the *New Zealand Journal*, the unofficial organ of the NZC. Both decided in favour of the Crown. The judges ruled that FitzRoy's certificates were not legal because the Crown "enjoys the exclusive right of acquiring newly found or conquered territory, and of extinguishing the title of any aboriginal inhabitants to be found thereon."[36] Thus, Māori could sell their land to only one buyer: the Crown. Furthermore, "this right of the Crown, as between the Crown and its British subjects, is not derived from the Treaty of Waitangi; nor could that Treaty alter it."[37] Contrary to those who have read the decision out of context, the decision was entirely consistent with the positions of George Gipps in 1840, the Select Committee of 1844, and Earl Grey in 1846. And it was a victory for Governor George Grey.[38] George Grey reported to Earl Grey on 5 July 1847 that the Supreme Court's decision that "the waiver of the Crown's right of pre-emption was illegal and void" had convinced the claimants "that they have acquired no legal rights by such waiver, and that I could not legally issue the grants which they have been so anxious to obtain."[39] When read in context, then, and in its entirety, the oft-quoted words of Chapman take on a different meaning than is often ascribed to them. Both judges were fully aware that, although there was virtual consensus that something called "native title" existed, there was a vociferous debate in both New Zealand and Great Britain on the nature of that title. For that reason, Chapman felt compelled to mention the debate, before *not* ruling on it. In that context, it becomes clear that the sentence that is often quoted as a ruling, was an *obiter dictum* (incidental remark) preamble to the ruling that came in the next two sentences:

> Whatever may be the opinion of jurists as to the strength or weakness of the Native title, whatsoever may have been the past vague notions of the natives of this country, whatever may be their present clearer and still growing conception of their own dominion over land, it cannot be too solemnly asserted that it is entitled to be respected, that it cannot be extinguished (at least in times of peace) otherwise than by the free consent of the Native occupiers. But for their protection, and for the sake of humanity, the Government is bound to maintain, and the Courts to assert, the Queen's exclusive right to extinguish it. It follows, from what has been said, that in solemnly guaranteeing the native title, and in securing what is called the Queen's pre-emptive right, the Treaty of Waitangi, confirmed by the charter of the colony, does not assert, either in doctrine or in practice, anything new and unsettled.[40]

Before this ruling had come down, the New Zealand Legislative Council also passed legislation stipulating fines for the unauthorized purchase or lease of Māori land.[41] As has been noted, on 10 May in London, even as the judges were deliberating on the *Symonds* case in New Zealand, the British government granted to the NZC for three years the Crown's right to pre-empt Indigenous land in New Munster. No one appears to have attempted to resolve the apparent tension.

If the NZC and the members of the 1844 Select Committee had nothing good to say about the Treaty of Waitangi, the same was true of the HBC and the Oregon Treaty of 15 June 1846. In the aftermath of that treaty, the HBC decided to approach the British government with a proposal to establish as a colony under the company's jurisdiction, the British portion of the old Columbia District. The "Oregon Crisis" ended in the final days of Robert Peel's ministry, on 15 June 1846, when the British and American governments finally settled the long-standing uncertainty over the border through the Columbia District (Oregon Territory), although confirmation of "this monstrous treaty," as James Douglas described it, did not reach Fort Victoria until November.[42] The company's directors had hoped that a treaty would give Great Britain the entire territory north of the Columbia River, where the company still dominated, but the treaty established the border well north of that. The treaty's placement of the border along the 49th parallel from the Rocky Mountains to the Pacific Ocean was clear, but the location of the boundary through "the middle of the channel which separates the continent from Vancouver's Island" would be in dispute until 1872.

The status of the HBC's land rights in the territory allocated to Great Britain was also unclear. The third article guaranteed that "the possessory rights of the Hudson's Bay Company, and of all British subjects who may be already in the occupation of land or other property lawfully acquired within the said [United States] territory, shall be respected." But that left the HBC's land rights in the British portion of the territory uncertain. So, in September 1846, Pelly wrote Earl Grey to ask whether the British government would confirm the HBC's possessory rights north of that border in the same way that the treaty recognized them south of the border.[43] Because the HBC occupied trading posts in the Columbia District, including substantial cultivations and pasturage, and because the British Admiralty had already shown interest in the coal lands on Vancouver Island, the question was of some importance to the company.

In a move not unrelated to its uncertain land claims, in early September, J.H. Pelly, the London Governor of the HBC, began discussions with the Colonial Office, both in correspondence and in meetings at Downing Street, regarding the possibility of colonizing the territory. In October 1846, Pelly identified the colonization of Vancouver Island as "an Object of great Importance." He asked "whether that Object, embracing as I trust it will the Conversion to Christianity and Civilization of the native Population, might not be most readily and effectually accomplished through the Instrumentality of the Hudson's Bay Company, either by a Grant of the Island on Terms to be hereafter agreed upon, or in some other Way in which the Influence and Resources of the Company might be made subservient to that End."[44] In March 1847, Pelly wrote Earl Grey to offer that "if Her Majesty's Ministers should be of opinion that the Territory in question would be more conveniently governed and colonized (as far as that may be practicable) through the Hudson's Bay Company, the Company are willing to undertake it, and will be ready to receive a Grant of all the Territories belonging to the Crown which are situated to the North and West of Rupert's Land."[45] The Colonial Office responded by inviting a proposal for a colony comprising Vancouver Island only. The ensuing negotiations were protracted, and by the time they had been completed, the HBC settled for far less than it had proposed, but the British government did decide to create a colony on Vancouver Island.[46]

Officials in the Colonial Office explicitly stated that they were placing the HBC on Vancouver Island in a similar position as they had placed the NZC in New Munster in 1847. Benjamin Hawes, who knew well the 1847 agreement with the NZC, explained that, in vesting the land of Vancouver Island in the HBC, "the same thing or nearly so it will be shewed has been done in the Southern part of New Zealand, where the Crown land and Crown right of pre-emption from natives are vested until 1852 in the NZC, where the right of Government & that of raising revenue is in the Legislative Council."[47] That would imply that, under the arrangement, the HBC could enjoy the proceeds of the sales of Crown lands to settlers on the condition that it also expended money from proceeds of the sale of land to develop infrastructure for the colony, but that ownership of Crown lands would revert to the British Crown when the government ended the agreement. In fact, the HBC sold little land to settlers before the British government ended the arrangement.

Although the British Crown grant of the colony of Vancouver Island to the HBC was dated 13 January 1849,[48] the agreement between the government and the HBC was in place by 31 July 1848, and the HBC's London Committee resolved on 6 September 1848 to accept the grant when it was offered.[49] The London Governor and Committee sent its 1 December 1848 letter to Douglas denying "any outward claims" of Natives knowing that the grant was imminent. The grant of 13 January 1849 mentioned Indigenous people only once, when it stated that "it would conduce greatly to ... the protection and welfare of the native Indians residing within that portion of Our territories in North America, called Vancouver's island, if such island were colonized by settlers from the British dominions, and if the property in the land of such island were vested for the purpose of such colonization in the said Governor and Company of Adventurers of England trading into Hudson's Bay."[50]

When on 23 December 1846, Earl Grey set out for George Grey "the principles upon which, if the colonization of New Zealand were only now about to begin, it would be my duty to instruct you to act," J.H. Pelly had already submitted the HBC's proposal to the Colonial Office to colonize Vancouver Island. The ongoing controversies regarding Indigenous title in New Zealand led Earl Grey to reiterate his opinion thereafter. For example, when George Selwyn, the Anglican Bishop of New Zealand, objected to Earl Grey's 23 December 1846 letter to George Grey, Earl Grey was unrepentant. On 30 November 1847, he restated his opinion that

> if this question were now open for consideration, that is, if we were commencing the colonization of New Zealand at the present time, the doctrine to which the Bishop objects would, in my judgment, be the best foundation of our proceedings, as I conceive it to contain the true principle in regard to property in land. ... All that I advised was this: that the theory of the ownership, by tribes, of unoccupied land, should not be made the foundation of any future transactions; and that, what I conceive to be the rights of the Crown, that is, of the public (where no engagements to the contrary have been made), should be carefully attended to in the disposal of land, wherever no property has yet been recognized.[51]

Clearly then, Earl Grey's position on the proper "doctrine" regarding Indigenous title in new colonies was consistent, before, during, and after the colony of Vancouver Island was established. Notwithstanding this opinion, Earl Grey also consistently stated that local governors, assuming that they could be trusted to defend Indigenous people, should be given authority for developing Indigenous policies appropriate for each colony.

Even in the late 1830s and early 1840s, influential people within the Colonial Office and humanitarians had already concluded that locally appointed officials with superior knowledge of local conditions should be given wide decision-making authority in Indigenous affairs. While colonial legislatures in the 1830s and 1840s were handed increasing powers of self-government, they were not typically given jurisdiction over Indigenous affairs until much later than they were given authority in other spheres. This was a feature of governance in many colonies. For example, while the Colony of Canada acquired responsible government by 1848, it was not given jurisdiction over, and financial responsibility for, Indigenous affairs until 1860. Similarly, the elected assembly in New Zealand was not given jurisdiction over Native affairs when it was created. "Self-government" in terms of Indigenous affairs meant decision making by the most senior appointed governor, not by the elected assemblies. James Stephen, the highly respected and influential Permanent Under-Secretary in the Colonial Office from 1836 to 1847 (his influence was such that he was often referred to as the "Over-Secretary") had concluded that because colonial governors gained indispensable and superior knowledge of local circumstances, London officials should be hesitant to dictate their Indigenous policies.[52]

So, while the Colonial Office maintained that Indigenous peoples everywhere need to be protected from settlers and assisted in the process of "civilization," it also believed that appointed competent and responsible governors needed to be given the freedom to decide how those policies were to be implemented. Decision making in Indigenous affairs could not be entrusted to elected bodies. Even appointed legislative councils, London authorities concluded, were too influenced by settler interests to be trusted with power over Indigenous affairs.

Earl Grey's approach to Vancouver Island in 1849 conformed to the principles he had articulated in the *Report from the Select Committee on New Zealand* in 1844, repeated in his letters to George Grey on 23 December 1846 and 30 November 1847. Believing that the HBC had a wealth of knowledge, experience, and wisdom in dealing with Indigenous peoples, government officials penned a confidential memorandum stating:

> With regard to the Indians it has been thought on the whole the better course to make no stipulations respecting them in the grant. Little is in fact known of the natives of this island, by the Company or by any one else. Whether they are numerous or few, strong or weak; whether or not they use the land for such purposes as would render the reservation of a large portion of it for their use important or not, are questions, which we have not the full materials to answer. Under these circumstances, any provisions that could be made for a people so distant and so imperfectly known, might turn out impediments in the way of colonization, without any real advantage to themselves. And it is thought the more safe to leave this matter to the Company, inasmuch as its dealings with and knowledge of the North American Indians are of course very extensive; and inasmuch as, not withstanding the many accusations of which that Company has been the object, no distinct charges of cruelty or misconduct toward the Indian tribes under its control have been made out by reasonable evidence; while every year brings painful accounts of mutual wrongs and mutual revenge between Indians and whites from the neighbouring regions not under their control. It must however be added that in parting with the land of the island Her Majesty parts only with her own right therein, and

that whatever measures she was bound to take in order to extinguish the Indian title are equally obligatory on the Company.[53]

It would be a mistake to assume that this confidential internal memorandum directed the HBC to conclude land-purchase treaties with Indigenous peoples. Its purpose was to explain why the HBC was being given the freedom to make decisions based on local conditions. This was a crystallization of what had been long-standing practice. If the memorandum was not written by Earl Grey, it conformed to his way of thinking. As far as the British government was concerned at the time, there were many "measures" that could be taken to extinguish Indigenous title. The memorandum anticipated that the HBC might extinguish Indigenous title by establishing reserves (as was then being done in Britain's Australian colonies), and left open the possibility of other measures, but avoided making any stipulations. In the context of what we know about the perspectives of Earl Grey, James Stephen (and even Lord Stanley), and others in the Colonial Office, it would be unreasonable to conclude that these words represented an expectation that the HBC conclude land purchases of "waste" land on Vancouver Island. Indeed, given that the document was an internal Colonial Office memorandum, they did not represent instructions of any kind. The memorandum appears to have been deliberately vague about how the HBC might fulfil its obligation. Humanitarians in the Colonial Office had made stipulations regarding Indigenous policies in New Zealand in the late 1830s and early 1840s and entered into the Treaty of Waitangi in 1840, all of which the officials in the Colonial Office regretted by the late 1840s.

James Douglas was appointed interim Governor of the colony of Vancouver Island on 12 May 1849, but when public and political opposition to the HBC jurisdiction over the new colony of Vancouver Island grew, the Colonial Office decided to ask the company to nominate a man not associated with the company. For reasons unknown, in June 1949, the General Court of the Governor and Committee of the HBC nominated the inexperienced Richard Blanshard.[54] On 9 July 1849, the Colonial Office appointed Blanshard Governor and Commander-in-Chief of the colony of Vancouver Island. Normally, British colonial governors had jurisdiction over Indigenous affairs, but Blanshard's 16 July letter of instructions gave him no written directions regarding the Indians of the colony.[55] The undated 1849 confidential memorandum implied that obligations fell upon the Company, but it is unclear whether that memorandum was written before or after Blanshard was appointed Governor. The instructions given to Douglas do not clarify matters. He was the official agent of the British Crown in charge of Indigenous affairs in the colony as long as he was interim governor. But he had other positions as well. When on 3 August 1849, Archibald Barclay wrote James Douglas to inform him that the Governor and Committee were appointing him as "agent to the Company for all matters relating to the territory of Vancouver's Island conveyed to them by a grant from the Crown," he informed him that Blanshard's duties "will be confined to the administration of the civil government of the Colony and to military affairs, but will not interfere with the duties which will devolve upon you as the representative of the Company and which are quite distinct from those you will have to perform as Chief Factor."[56]

Under the circumstances, it is possible that everyone assumed that Douglas – with decades of experience with Indigenous peoples – not Blanshard – a rank newcomer – should take the lead on Indigenous affairs, but no letter of instructions stipulated it. Traditions of British colonial governance dictated that the appointed governor of the colony would be ex officio in charge of Indigenous affairs. Thus, James Douglas was in charge of Indian affairs while he was interim governor, but should have considered it his duty to consult with the governor after Blanshard arrived in the colony.

Between 1845 and 1849, colonial governors negotiated land-purchase treaties in New Zealand even as officials in the Colonial Office adhered to a narrow interpretation of Indigenous title that did not require such purchases. The practice seems inconsistent, but the policy was consistent: the Crown, which enjoyed the exclusive right to extinguish Indigenous title, was not required to extinguish Indigenous title by negotiating land-purchase agreements but would negotiate them where it was expedient to do so. In sum, chapters 1 to 7 have explained why no one assumed when the British government established the colony of Vancouver Island in January 1849 that it would be necessary to extinguish Indigenous title by land-purchase treaties, but why land-purchase treaties might nevertheless be negotiated there. Chapters 8 to 11 describe how and why historical contingencies determined that treaties were negotiated in New Zealand and Vancouver Island between 1846 and 1854.

# 8 Land Acquisition Policies in New Zealand and Vancouver Island, 1846–1850

George Grey (see figure 16), Governor of New Zealand, was respected within the Colonial Office and by Whigs and Tories. Lord Stanley appointed him governor in June 1845, and the incoming Russell ministry retained him a year later. As governor, he was attentive to the principles of Indigenous title that Earl Grey laid out to him in his long letter of 23 December 1846, but confident enough to seize the authority given him to make his own decisions based on his knowledge of local conditions.[1] Although Earl Grey's 23 December dispatch reached George Grey in April 1847, Grey did not respond directly to it for some time.

Grey enjoyed a significant advantage as Governor of New Zealand not enjoyed by his predecessors, FitzRoy and Hobson. Shortly after he appointed Grey to the governorship in June 1845, Lord Stanley gave Grey access to a fund of £10,000 and secretly authorized him to use it to purchase Māori land.[2] Stanley also resolved to appoint someone "to give his best assistance to the Company [NZC] in their selection of land, to aid in surveying the exterior boundaries of such selections, and to judge of the reasonableness of the terms of any purchase which the company may make from the Natives, with reference to the company's right to reimbursement," a position later given to Major William Anson McCleverty.[3] Freed of the financial constraints that had prevented Hobson and FitzRoy from doing so, and freed of the trouble thereafter of going back to the Colonial Office or to the Legislative Council for funds, George Grey had begun purchasing land by the time Earl Grey's instructions reached him. His first priorities were to acquire the Porirua district of the North Island, near Wellington, and the Wairau district of the South Island, home to the restive and powerful Ngāti Toa. In fact, as early as 20 November 1846, when he instructed McCleverty to negotiate the purchase, he told McCleverty that he was "very anxious that the purchase of the Wairau District should be completed with as little delay as possible."[4] However, he later reported that the Ngāti Toa "unwilling, from feelings of jealousy, to transact with the New Zealand Company's agent any business relating to the districts of land which had previously been in dispute, I found it necessary to take into my own hands the settlement of the most important of these questions."[5] Accordingly, on 18 March 1847, Grey, in the presence of McCleverty and his Native Secretary, Henry Tacy Kemp, treated with three Ngāti Toa signatories for the cession of the Wairau district (approximately 3 million acres) for £3,000 (after Ngāti Toa chiefs backed off their initial demand for £5,000) (see figure 14). A Māori-language version was written on foolscap paper.[6] Then, in April, Grey purchased the Porirua Block, near Wellington, on the North Island.[7] In both cases, Grey departed from the principles articulated by Earl Grey on 23 December 1846 by stipulating in the agreements that the Māori were ceding claims to their entire territories. Ignoring that he had implicitly recognized Indigenous title to their entire territories, Grey explained that "I have no doubt that now the uniform system of purchasing from them such districts in their *bonâ fide* possession as may be required by the Government is adopted, that no further disputes or disturbances on the subject of land will take place throughout the southern portions of New Zealand."[8]

Supposing that George Grey's "uniform system" involved obtaining agreements that stipulated that Māori iwi (tribes) were ceding rights to entire tribal territories, including so-called "waste lands," he was following well-established precedent. Private individuals such as William Wentworth and his ilk, and the NZC, had followed that practice as well. Moreover, that had been the practice in every other place where such cessions had been negotiated, including Upper Canada and the United States of America. Indeed, a Crown negotiator was placed in a difficult position if forced to take the stance that Indigenous communities had rights only to the lands they were going to retain: village sites and fortifications, burial grounds, and cultivated fields. If the Crown denied that the Indigenous people had any rights to the rest of the communities' lands, for what, exactly, was the Crown seeking a cession agreement, and for what was it paying?

The lack of any explicit response from George Grey to Earl Grey's 23 December 1846 letter of instructions became awkward for the Russell government almost a year later in the House of Commons, when Henry Labouchère was forced to admit to William E. Gladstone that no such answer had been received.[9] That forced George Grey on 15 May 1848 to respond directly to the principles Earl Grey had explained in his dispatch of 23 December 1846 (and Earl Grey did not receive that response until 6 October 1848).[10] George Grey obviously expected that the weight of his opinions would be enhanced by his claim that, after considerable conflicts between 1845 and 1847, "New Zealand was never before in so peaceful and prosperous a state as it is now."[11] He warned Earl Grey that "the native population would to the best of their ability, resist the enforcement of the broad principles which were maintained by Dr. Arnold."[12] But George Grey suggested that it was much more expedient to purchase the land from Māori according to the "uniform system" he had described because "they will in nearly all – if not in all – instances dispose, for a merely nominal consideration, of those lands which they do not actually require for their own subsistence." Indeed, he predicted that, if the government required the land "the native chiefs would cheerfully give such land up to the Government without any payment, if the compliment is only paid them of requesting their acquiescence in the occupation of these lands by European settlers."[13] He continued by explaining:

> The only instances in which I have known the natives either to resist the occupation of their lands by the Europeans, or to demand exorbitant prices for them, are those cases in which the lands were not validly purchased before a considerable European population was placed upon them; and the natives thus becoming aware of the value that had been given to their lands, and actuated by motives of self-interest, refused to part with them for a nominal consideration, but insisted upon receiving a price bearing some slight relation to the actual value of the lands at the time the purchase was completed. The obvious means of avoiding this difficulty for the future, is for the Government to keep its purchases of land sufficiently in advance of the spread of the European population.[14]

Grey's description uncannily resembles the experiences of Dutch purchasers in North America in the 1620s. Grey also explained why Māori were so amenable to selling lands for "a trifling consideration." Here, Grey's words resemble William B. Coltman's 1817 characterization of the role that "collateral advantages" played in the negotiations leading towards the Selkirk Treaty:

> the natives are every day becoming more and more aware of the fact, that the real payment which they receive for their waste lands is not the sum given to them by the Government, but the security which is afforded, that themselves and their children shall for ever occupy the reserves assured to them, to which a great value is given by the vicinity of a dense European population. They are also gradually becoming aware that the Government

spend all the money realized by the sale of lands in introducing Europeans into the country, or in the execution of public works, which give employment to the natives, and a value to their property, whilst the payment they receive for their land enables them to purchase stock and agricultural implements.[15]

How did the HBC decide to negotiate treaties on Vancouver Island? If the Vancouver Island treaties must be named after any person, that person ought to be Andrew Colvile, the Deputy Governor of the HBC in London, not James Douglas. The treaties appear to have been Colvile's brainchild. Colvile, the brother-in-law of Lord Selkirk, had joined the Committee of the HBC in 1810 as Andrew Wedderburn (he assumed the name Andrew Colvile in 1814 when he took possession of the Craigflower estate) (see figure 17). He had many years' experience as partner in Wedderburn and Company, which had large plantation holdings in Jamaica. According to E.E. Rich, he "exercised great influence in the administration of their [the HBC Committee's] affairs; he was chiefly instrumental in securing George Simpson for the service and bringing about the amalgamation of the H.B.C. and N.W.C. He was Deputy Governor from 1839 to 1852 and Governor from 1852 until his death." Colvile maintained control of his West Indian business until his death, when the management of those plantations passed to his son, Eden Colvile.[16]

As a leading member of HBC's London Committee, Colvile must have known about the instructions conveyed to Ogden and Douglas on 1 December 1848 that denied the rights of Vancouver Island Natives to any land claim. As a wealthy plantation owner, Colvile had no bona fides as a humanitarian. But he was a practical man. On 6 April 1849, he wrote to George Simpson to say that "it may be of great importance to make safe settlements at these two places [Victoria and at the Coal mines] but it would be best to make some bargain with the Indians in the first instance to prevent disputes – and if the consideration to them be by annual payments it will give some hold over them as it could be stopped if they become troublesome. – The Gov. & I have had a good deal of conversation with Eden on this subject."[17] Colvile's letter reveals that the decision to seek land-purchase agreements originated with the Deputy Governor and Governor (John H. Pelly) of the HBC, and that those two men considered it expedient to negotiate cessions. In the context in which personnel in the Admiralty and elsewhere expressed concern about securing the right of possession to the coalfields, the London Committee's December 1848 message, and Colvile and Pelly's change of heart, are understandable.

George Simpson received Colvile's letter about as quickly as was humanly possible at the time. It was delivered by Eden Colvile, Andrew Colvile's thirty-year-old son.[18] On 3 January 1849, Eden Colvile had been appointed Associate-Governor of Rupert's Land, to assist the company's North American Governor, George Simpson.[19] Eden Colvile was in London on 4 April (the date of his actual commission) immediately after which he departed for North America, where he caught up with George Simpson, who was travelling into the interior.[20]

On 30 June 1849, when he was at Norway House, George Simpson (figure 18) wrote two letters related to Colvile's proposal to purchase the coal lands on Vancouver Island. They are rich with evidence regarding Simpson's opinions and perspectives on the issue. The first was addressed to the Chief Factors in the Columbia District, Peter Skene Ogden, James Douglas, and John Work. Simpson agreed with Colvile's suggestion. After writing in one paragraph that "we shall be anxious until we learn that the establishment at the Coal mine has been formed without any difficulties with the natives, on such a footing as to ensure its security from that source," Simpson latter added:

> If the Indians be well managed, we think they may become very useful in collecting coal and other duties about the mine; and before strangers have an opportunity of tampering with them, with a view to their setting up extravagant claims for the coal lands, we think it highly desirable that a bargain be entered into with the Chiefs, by which a moderate consideration should be given to them for those lands, in the shape of an annual payment. The lands are really of no value to the Indians, nor am I aware that they have any rightful claim to them; it may nevertheless be expedient to satisfy them, if such can be done without material sacrifice. I would suggest that the compensation should be an annual supply of goods to the Chiefs for themselves and their followers, of about £100 per annum, such payment being a charge against the Colony. I shall address the Company's legal adviser at Red River requesting him to send me the form of such a contract or agreement as should be entered into which will be transmitted to you from Lachine by the earliest opportunity after my arrival there.[21]

Simpson's opinion regarding Indigenous title is reminiscent of opinions expressed within the Colonial Office, and by Governor George Grey in New Zealand. Simpson explicitly discussed whether he believed that the Indigenous people enjoyed any rights to the land. He doubted it. But he believed that it was expedient for the company to conclude formal land purchases, and to do so in advance of the arrival of settlers, missionaries, or any others who might "tamper" with them. From his perspective, if the company did not seek an agreement immediately, there was a risk that persons outside the company would cause the Indigenous people to make the kinds of "exorbitant demands"[22] that Robert FitzRoy had complained about, and George Grey had warned about in New Zealand. Again, whether Simpson was aware of what had happened in New Zealand or not, he understood the risk. He anticipated that missionaries or other outsiders might encourage Indigenous people to demand more compensation than they otherwise would. Similarly, he probably feared that competitors for the land, even if their attempts to purchase Indigenous land would eventually be invalidated, would complicate the company's claims. He suggested that "moderate consideration," which might be more than the "nominal" or "trifling" considerations contemplated by Earl Grey or George Grey, might be made in annual payments. The suggestion that the charge should be made "against the Colony" implies that the HBC would purchase the land on behalf of the Crown, and that the Crown would become the eventual owner of the land. The proposal also shrewdly placed the HBC in the same position as Governor George Grey in New Zealand, of having access to the funds to pay for the agreements: the HBC would pay upfront, but the Crown would reimburse the company when the Crown terminated the grant and assumed control of the colony. Simpson's reference to Red River is linked to the fact that the Selkirk Treaty at Red River was the only land-transfer document internal to the company to which he could turn. That explains why Simpson asked the company's legal adviser at Red River, Adam Thom, to send him "the form of such a contract or agreement."

On the same day that Simpson wrote his letter, Eden Colvile embarked from Norway House on his way to the Pacific Coast, with Simpson's letter in hand.[23] Colvile travelled via Fort Chipewyan, New Caledonia, Hope, and Langley to Victoria, where he arrived on 12 October. Clearly, James Douglas became aware around 12 October 1849, that the HBC's directors were considering negotiating land purchases from Indigenous people on Vancouver Island. That was almost exactly five months after Fort Rupert was established.

Simpson's second letter of 30 June 1849 was to the London directors of the company. In words resembling those written by George Grey to Earl Grey, Simpson wrote:

> In order to guard against future difficulty with them arising from extravagant claims for compensation for the coal lands, I have suggested to the Board of Management in my 7th paragraph, that they should be purchased

from them under formal agreement, and at an annual payment in goods to the amount of £100 sterling, at the usual Indian tariff price, and have requested Mr. Recorder Thom to prepare & forward to me in Canada a form of contract or deed to be entered into with the Indians in question, which I shall transmit to the Board of Management via Mexico.[24]

This second letter must have travelled to London via York Factory, on Hudson Bay, on the HBC's annual supply ship, and was read at the 5 September 1849 meeting of the General Court of the London Governor and Committee.[25]

On 26 July 1849, Adam Thom responded to Simpson's instructions by stating that "I have the honor to send annexed a draft of an agreement with respect to the colony of Vancouver's Island between the Hudson's Bay Company and the aboriginal tribes. I have rendered the document as particular and definite as possible making due acknowledgement of course, for the vagueness of my knowledge on the subject."[26] Thom's draft of an agreement – perhaps based upon the Selkirk Treaty – has not been traced, but Simpson enclosed it with a letter he wrote on 13 October 1849 to the London Governor and Committee, but indicated that, in regards to the agreement, he would not "communicate with Chief Factor Douglas until I have your authority for so doing."[27] Simpson had changed his mind, and now thought it best that the Columbia District's Board of Management get its instructions from the London Committee, rather than from him.

By the time the London Governor and Committee received Simpson's letters of 30 June and 13 October, they had already made further decisions about the land-purchase strategy. On 3 August 1849, J.H. Pelly, writing on his own behalf and on behalf of Andrew Colvile and George Simpson, as Agents of the Puget Sound Agricultural Company (a subsidiary of the HBC), wrote to James Douglas to state that "we should hope that by kind treatment & by entering into agreements with the chiefs for the occupation of all lands not actually required by them, all hostile feeling on their part may be removed. The employment of the Natives we should think would be the most likely mode of rendering them subservient to you."[28] While Pelly was ambiguous about the type of "agreements," he was recommending, by the time Douglas received this letter, he had already received Simpson's letter of 30 June that was much more explicit. In the meantime, Douglas and Eden Colvile travelled to Fort Rupert, but did not conclude a treaty, probably because they did not yet get precise instructions, and because they did not apprehend trouble there. That left Blenkinsop to conclude the Garden Treaty in April.

It has already been noted that James Douglas must have learned from Eden Colvile in mid-October 1849 that there were plans afoot to instruct him to conclude treaties in the coal district of Vancouver Island. On 3 September 1849, about six weeks before that, and less than four months after Fort Rupert was established, when he was still unaware of any of the correspondence regarding treaties, James Douglas (figure 19) also recommended purchasing land. His 3 September letter begins by acknowledging Barclay's letter of 1 December 1848, and it is obvious that he was responding to that portion of Barclay's letter that indicated that the HBC would "not admit any outward claims of the wandering natives to lands which were not cultivated or permanently occupied."[29]

Douglas's 3 September 1849 letter made only the most oblique references to Indigenous title, placing emphasis on the pragmatism and justness of ensuring peaceful and friendly relations with the Indigenous peoples by purchasing their lands, and reserving their villages, cultivated fields, and fisheries:

> some arrangements should be made as soon as possible with the native Tribes for the purchase of their lands and I would recommend payment being made in the Shape of an annual allowance instead of the whole sum being given at one time; they will thus derive a permanent benifit [sic] from the sale of their lands and the Colony will have a degree of security from their future good behavior. I would also strongly recommend, equally as a measure of justice, and from a regard to the future peace of the colony, that the Indians Fisheries, Village Sites and cultivated Fields, should be reserved for their benifit [sic] and fully secured to them by law.[30]

Scholars, in assuming that Douglas's letter convinced the London Governor and Committee to negotiate treaties, have exaggerated the significance of this letter. Still, Douglas's letter shows that Douglas had independently concluded that the HBC should arrange purchases. It also reflects the terms and conditions that Douglas regarded as important. Specifically, Douglas recommended annuities, rather than a one-time payment, and recommended that the fisheries, village sites, and cultivated fields should be reserved.

On 17 December 1849, well before the London Governor and Committee received Douglas's letter of 3 September,[31] Archibald Barclay, Secretary to the Governor and Committee of the HBC, wrote James Douglas with the company's instructions. These directives, rich with evidence, were mostly consistent with the principles held by officials in the Colonial Office but with some significant oddities. To begin, the committee directed Douglas that:

> With respect to the rights of the natives you will have to confer with the Chiefs of the tribes on that subject, and in your negocations with them you are to consider the natives as the rightful possessors of such lands only as they occupied by cultivation, or had houses built on at the time when the Island came under the undivided sovereignty of Great Britain in 1846. All other land is to be regarded as waste, and applicable to the purposes of colonization.[32]

The HBC directors' decision to instruct Douglas to recognize rights as of the date when the territory "came under the undivided sovereignty of Great Britain" was unprecedented. Treaty commissioners normally negotiated based on Indigenous groups' use of the land at the time the agreements were concluded.

Had these instructions come from the Colonial Office, as unusual as they were, the most likely rationale for them would have been that they were based on the principles articulated explicitly by Gipps, and implied otherwise, that Indigenous title sprang into being simultaneously with the acquisition of British sovereignty. Because the instructions came from the HBC's Governor and Committee the decision to use the date of the Oregon Treaty was probably rooted in the fact that the third article of the Oregon Treaty recognized the land rights for the HBC and other British subjects in American territory as of the date of the treaty. By stipulating that the date of the Oregon Treaty was to be the basis for determining Indigenous title, the directors were bolstering their argument that British government should also recognize HBC land claims in British territory the same way the Oregon Treaty recognized their rights in American territory.[33] They may also have been attempting to avoid conflicting claims between the HBC and the Indigenous peoples. At any rate, the unusual stipulation was highly significant, given how quickly Indigenous land use was changing at the time.

Thereafter, the Governor and Committee told Douglas to follow the precedents and principles established elsewhere, even to the point of quoting, unwittingly, George Gipps's speech of 9 July 1840, as published in the report of the 1844 Select Committee on New Zealand:

> In other Colonies the scale of compensation has not been uniform, as there are circumstances peculiar to each which prevented them all from being placed on the same footing, but the average rate may be stated £1 per head of the tribe for the interest of the Chiefs, paid on signing the Treaty.
>
> A Committee of the House of Commons, which sat upon some claims of the New Zealand Company reported, in reference to native rights in general, that "the uncivilized inhabitants of any country have but a qualified

dominion over it, or a right of occupancy only, and that until they establish among themselves a settled form of government, and subjugate the ground to their own uses by the cultivation of it, they cannot grant to individuals, not of their own tribe, any portion of it, for the simple reason that they have not themselves any individual property in it."

The principle here laid down is that which the Governor and Committee authorize you to adopt in treating with the Natives of Vancouver's Island, but the extent to which it is to be acted upon must be left to your own discretion and will depend upon the character of the tribes and other circumstances. The natives will be confirmed in the possession of their lands as long as they occupy and cultivate them themselves, but will not be allowed to sell or dispose of them to any private person, the right to the entire soil having been granted to the Company by the Crown. The right of fishing and hunting will be continued to them, and when their lands are registered, and they conform to same conditions with which other settlers are required to comply, they will enjoy the same rights or privileges.[34]

So, although the HBC directors did not define Indigenous title, they stipulated that Douglas was to recognize lands occupied by villages and cultivation, and to protect the usufructuary (hunting and fishing) practices of those communities. It is also noteworthy that the London Governor and Committee referred to the prospective agreement as a "treaty" and process of arriving at the agreements as "treating with the Natives," just as the Treaty of Waitangi had. Douglas himself appears never to have referred to the agreements as "treaties," describing them instead as "purchases," "deeds of conveyance," "arrangements," or "solemn engagements." Although Douglas's letter of 3 September 1849 cannot have influenced the London Governor and Committee's instructions as given on 17 December 1849, Douglas's letter does show that he agreed with this policy at that time. The Governor and Committee appealed to the notion that Indigenous people had rights to lands that they cultivated or upon which they built villages.[35]

Historians of North American treaties might consider the decision on the part of the directors of the HBC to conclude land-purchase treaties with Indigenous people on Vancouver Island as unexceptional, but it was unusual on several levels. The HBC was not in the habit of purchasing land from Indigenous people. There is no evidence that the HBC directors contemplated concluding land purchases with Indigenous people when the company established Fort Vancouver in 1824, Fort Langley in 1827, Fort Nisqually in 1832, or Fort McLoughlin in 1833. Neither did they discuss concluding treaties in 1843 when Fort Victoria was established. Moreover, the development of substantial agricultural operations at Fort Vancouver, Fort Langley, and Fort Victoria did not cause HBC directors in London or the Columbia District to propose purchasing land. Even the development of a substantial salmon trade at Fort Langley did not prompt company officials to consider developing a treaty policy. Although this is not surprising – given that Indigenous people wanted trading posts in their territories and appear not to have demanded payment for the company's use of land – it is noteworthy, because it underscores how unusual the history of treaties on Vancouver Island was. In the period of "joint occupation" of the Columbia District (1818–46), the government of the United States would probably have regarded any attempt by the HBC to conclude land-transfer treaties with Indigenous people as a provocation.[36] After 1846 and before the HBC was given jurisdiction over the colony of Vancouver Island, especially given the recent history of land purchases in New Zealand, British officials likely would have declared null and void any HBC land purchases unless they explicitly conveyed title to the Crown. Thus, the formation of the colony of Vancouver Island and the allocation of jurisdiction of the colony to the HBC made it possible for the HBC to conclude treaties, but it did not make it either probable or necessary.

The London Committee of the HBC decided to negotiate treaties on Vancouver Island because they wished to secure the company's claim to the coalfields along the coast between Beaver Harbour and Port McNeill. The timing of the decision was also related to the formation of the colony of Vancouver Island, which plausibly gave the company the authority to conclude treaties there.

When in August 1849 the HBC Governor and Committee sent Douglas instructions to make agreements with chiefs for occupation of the land, they did so when he was also the interim Governor of the colony of Vancouver Island, although Richard Blanshard had already been appointed to replace him. On 17 December 1849, when they conveyed their more detailed instructions, they had every reason to believe that Douglas would still be the interim Governor when he received the letter. In fact, Douglas had resigned his position on 10 December 1849, immediately upon receiving the letter informing him that Blanshard had been appointed, and he promised to assist Blanshard in dealing with the Indians.[37] Moreover, Blanshard arrived at Fort Victoria on 10 March 1850, and had taken up his position as governor more than a month before Douglas negotiated the first of the Fort Victoria treaties. There can be little doubt that Richard Blanshard, as agent of the Crown in place at Victoria, was the appropriate official either to negotiate or delegate a commissioner to conclude treaties with the Indigenous people of Vancouver Island, although he, like Hobson and FitzRoy in New Zealand, did not have access to the funds to do so.

On Monday, 29 April 1850, James Douglas and leaders of the Songhees concluded the first of the Fort Victoria treaties. We might imagine that the personnel at Fort Victoria thought of this as a red-letter day, but Roderick Finlayson[38] relegated the news to a brief description at the end of the day's entry in the official post journal of Fort Victoria:

> Fine clear weather, with a light breeze from the Eastward, people employed at their several occupations as p[er] labor Book, building, ploughing, discharging Cargo &c. This morning Dr. Tolmie made a final start for Nisqually. In the evening the proprietors of the tract of country lying between the headland [Albert Head] and point McGregor were paid for their land. They are ten in number & got 3 Blkts 2½ pts each at which they appeared well satisfied.[39]

The Vancouver Island treaties are anomalous in many ways. Anyone familiar with treaty negotiations in Canada or the United States would expect to find evidence that the negotiations for the Vancouver Island treaties were accompanied by much gravity, ceremony, and solemnity. On the United States and Canadian plains, thousands of people often attended, including Indigenous people, treaty commissioners, police, militia, or army, traders, journalists, sometimes missionaries and artists, as well as incidental observers who happened to be able to travel to the treaty grounds. Accordingly, some treaty negotiations have several eyewitness and participant accounts written at the time of the negotiations, even if Indigenous participants and eyewitnesses themselves rarely authored such accounts.

By contrast, Finlayson's journal entry suggests that there was little excitement or ceremony over the negotiations at Fort Victoria – nothing to compare with Courtenay's grand military parade of 29 August 1848, or even the ship's salute that greeted Douglas when he was transferred to Fort Victoria in 1849. Moreover, the treaty negotiations on Vancouver Island are poorly documented, thanks in large measure to the fact that Douglas negotiated them before there were many literate exogenous people independent of the company on site, but also, it seems, because they made no effort to have the notables who were at Fort Victoria observe the negotiations.[40]

Finlayson's account even raises the possibility that many of the HBC servants at Fort Victoria were oblivious to the proceedings. Fort Victoria was bustling in late April and early May 1850, and with many HBC men absconding for the California gold fields, the labourers were few. So, although the *Norman Morison* had arrived at Fort Victoria from London on 24 March, more pressing work prevented the men of the fort from beginning to unload its cargo until 25 April.[41] Other ships arriving and departing for other coastal trading posts had to be loaded and unloaded first. And, thanks to an unseasonably cold and wet, even snowy, March and April it seems that the company's farming activities had been delayed until the weather improved.[42] So, in late April and early May, some of the men were also busy planting crops. Even the men of the fort probably did not have the privilege of witnessing the treaty negotiations.

It is difficult to confirm a date upon which James Douglas received the 17 December 1849 letter from the Governor and Committee of the HBC instructing him "to confer with the Chiefs of the tribes" about Indigenous land rights, because his own letters are contradictory. In his 16 May 1850 response to the letter of 17 December, Douglas, perhaps evasively, did not indicate the date of receipt, preferring instead to state that he initiated the treaty negotiations "upon receipt of that letter." Given that Douglas negotiated treaties between 29 April and 10 May, that would imply that the letter arrived shortly before 29 April.[43] A letter written in 1888 by J.W. McKay (to be discussed shortly) indicated that the contents of the 17 December 1849 letter were presented to the Indigenous chiefs at the time of the negotiations.[44] But there is contrary evidence. In a long letter dated 15 May, Douglas indicated that he received three letters on 8 May, the letters of 17 December 1849 and 3 January 1850 by way of Fort Vancouver, and a letter of 16 February 1850 directly from San Francisco.[45] The Fort Victoria journals indicated the arrival of the barque *England* from San Francisco on that day, but do not mention another ship. If Douglas intended to write "8 April" instead of "8 May" (the kind of error that is encountered occasionally) the letter may have arrived aboard the *Sacramento* on 7 April via Nisqually and delivered to Douglas the next day. Given the recent improvements to mail service, it is plausible that the letter of 3 January arrived at Fort Victoria in just over three months if it was delivered directly from San Francisco, but it would have been surprisingly quick if it travelled via Fort Vancouver and Nisqually. Two scholars have concluded that Douglas negotiated the first treaties before he received the letter.[46] The fact that Douglas wrote a letter to James Murray Yale on 7 May that he had been negotiating purchases with the Indians "in consequence of orders to that effect from England," implies that he had received the 17 December letter, but Douglas might have been referring to the letter of 3 August 1849, written the day that he was appointed in charge of all of the HBC's affairs on Vancouver Island, that urged him to enter "into agreements with the chiefs for the occupation of all lands not actually required by them."[47] If Douglas received the 17 December instructions shortly *after* he had completed most of the negotiations, he might have decided to obscure the fact.[48]

Is it plausible, as two scholars recently concluded, that Douglas negotiated the treaties before receiving his 17 December instructions?[49] He had learned in mid-October 1849 that the company had decided to make purchase agreements with the Indigenous people, and that George Simpson would send him a "form of such a contract ... by the earliest opportunity."[50] He had received the letter of 3 August 1849 with instructions. If he had always intended to proceed before receiving the form, he probably would have sought to negotiate with the Kwakiutl in January 1850 when he was at Fort Rupert. The coalfields of Fort Rupert, after all, more than any other location, had driven the company's discussions about treaty policy. Had anything transpired since January 1850 that might have convinced Douglas to proceed with negotiations in late April without the form? Possibly.

The Fort Victoria journal entry for 23 April reports that "Bazil Battineau [Bottineau] with a Hawaiian and a crew of Indians arrived with despatches from Ft. Rupert, explaining that the Miners there 'discontinued work from fear of the Natives &c.'"[51] The reasons behind the miners' job action at Fort Rupert were more complex than this account suggests, but the entry hints at Finlayson's perceptions at Fort Victoria. No doubt Bottineau and his party, which included Wawattie,[52] regarded by the HBC as the head chief at Fort Rupert, also delivered to Fort Victoria the news that, confronted by the Fort Rupert chiefs, George Blenkinsop had negotiated with them for the purchase of the land required "for gardens, mining purposes &c." at Fort Rupert on 15 April. It is possible, then, that the chiefs at Fort Victoria also learned of that transaction on 23 April and began to agitate, or Douglas feared that they would begin to agitate, for a treaty of their own. Perhaps the news that arrived at Fort Victoria from Fort Rupert on 23 April, combined with the unsettled affairs at Fort Rupert and at Fort Victoria (perhaps including the severe shortage of personnel) prompted Douglas to act upon the instructions written on 3 August 1849.

Douglas probably received his instructions shortly before 29 April 1850, but given that we cannot be sure whether Douglas concluded the treaties before or after he received his instructions, both possibilities should be considered, for while our interpretations of the treaties would not change markedly, we would have to adjust our understandings in some interesting ways. If Douglas negotiated the agreements before he received the 17 December instructions, developments on Vancouver

Island in the early months of 1850, not the arrival of instructions, must have determined the timing of the negotiations. Moreover, in that case, we ought to assume that Douglas concluded the negotiations without any knowledge that he was going to be instructed to base the treaty upon the lands occupied by the Indigenous signatories as of 1846, and that he was going to be instructed to acknowledge Indigenous title only to those lands "occupied by cultivation, or had houses built on at the time." In short, it would be easier to understand why the agreements Douglas negotiated with the tribes on Vancouver Island differed so markedly from the instructions written on 17 December.

The early reports of the negotiations of April and May 1850 – the only documentation that the HBC directors ever received – suggest that Douglas made three treaties: one with the "Sangees" (Songhees), one with the "Clallum," and one with the Sooke (see figure 20). On 16 May 1850, James Douglas devoted an entire letter to the topic. It is the most detailed description of the oral terms of the treaties agreed to at the time:

> I have the honor to acknowledge your communication of 17th. December 1849, stating in a more detailed form the views of the Governor and Committee respecting the colonization of this Island, the rights of the Natives, and their instructions as to the extent to which these rights are to be respected.
>
> On the receipt of that letter I summoned to a conference, the chiefs and influential men of the Sangees Tribe, which inhabits and claims the District of Victoria, from Gordon Head on Arro Strait to Point Albert on the Strait of De Fuca as their own particular heritage. After considerable discussion, it was arranged, that the whole of their lands, forming as before stated the District of Victoria, should be sold to the Company, with the exception of Village sites and enclosed fields, for a certain remuneration, to be paid at once to each member of the Tribe. I was in favour of a series of payments to be made annually but the proposal was so generally disliked that I yielded to their wishes and paid the sum at once.
>
> The members of the Tribe on being mustered were found to number 122 men or heads of families, to each of whom was given a quantity of goods equal in value to 17/. Sterling and the total sum disbursed on this purchase was £103..14..0 Sterling at Dept. price.[53] I subsequently made a similar purchase from the Clallum Tribe, of the country lying between Albert Point and Soke Inlet. In consequence of the claimants not being so well known as the Songees, we adopted a different mode of making the payments, by dealing exclusively with the Chiefs, who received and distributed the payments while the sale was confirmed and ratified by

the Tribe collectively. This second purchase cost about £30..0..8.[54] I have since made a purchase from the Soke Tribe of the land between Soke Inlet and Point Sheringham, the arrangement being concluded in this as in the preceeding purchase with the Chiefs or heads of Families who distributed the property among their followers.

The cost of this tract which does not contain much cultivable land was £16..8..8. The Cowichan and other Tribes,[55] have since expressed a wish to dispose of their lands, on the same terms; but I declined their proposals in consequence, of our not being prepared to enter into possession; which ought to be done immediately after the purchase or arrangement may be forgotten, and further compensation claimed by the natives. The lands purchased from the other Tribes embrace the seacoast and interior from Gordon Head on the Arro Strait, to Point Gonzales, and from thence running west along the strait of De Fuca, to Point Sheringham a distance of about 44 miles; which includes the Hudsons Bay and Pugets Sound Company's reserves.

The total cost, as before stated, is £150..3..4.

I informed the natives that they would not be disturbed in the possession of their village sites and enclosed fields, which are of small extent, and that they were at liberty to hunt over the unoccupied lands, and to carry on their fisheries with the same freedom as when they were the sole occupants of the country.

I attached the signature of the native Chiefs and others who subscribed the deed of purchase to a blank sheet, on which will be copied the contract or Deed of conveyance, as soon as we receive a proper form, which I beg may be sent out by return of Post. The other matters referred to in your letter will be duly attended to.

I have the honor to be Sir
Your obedient Servant
James Douglas[56]

It is noteworthy that all reports of the Fort Victoria treaties suggest that only the chiefs and leading men attended the negotiations.

The fact that "headland and point McGregor" of Finlayson's journal entry of 29 April corresponds to Douglas's "Gordon Head on Arro Strait to Point Albert on the Strait of De Fuca," indicates that the first sentence of Finlayson's description of the treaty corresponds to Douglas's "Sangees" treaty, although the second sentence, mentioning only ten chiefs, corresponds better to what later emerged as the Teechamitsa Treaty. Finlayson did not mention purchases again until 4 May when he again ended his entry with treaty-related matters: "Some of the Sanges were repaid paid [sic] for their lands to day, & a party of Tequetsins

[Chewhaytsum] arrived to receive a compensation for their lands about Rocky point."[57] Given that the Chewhaytsum were a Klallam people, Finlayson must have been referring to Douglas's "second purchase." Finally, Finlayson's entry for 10 May reported that "The Sokes were paid for their lands to day."[58] That entry clearly refers to Douglas's "Soke" purchase.

Whether he negotiated the treaties of April and May before or after receiving the 17 December 1849 letter, Douglas's report, written after he received that letter, suggests that the oral agreement he came to with the "chiefs and influential men" of the Fort Victoria district was similar to the terms he recommended in his own letter of 3 September 1849, but differed significantly from the instructions in the letter. Like George Grey in New Zealand, Douglas neither called attention to the ways that he deviated from his instructions, nor offered an apology or defence for doing so. And like Grey, he did not need to be told more than once that the details were left to his own discretion. It is easy to understand why Douglas negotiated for the surrender of "the whole of their lands." He did so for the same reason that George Grey departed from his instructions: he would have been in an unenviable negotiating position if he were to take the stance that Songhees, Klallam, and Sooke had Indigenous title only to the lands that they were to retain. However, J.W. McKay, in 1888 recalled that the Governor and Committee's letter of 17 December 1849 was translated and presented at the treaty negotiations.[59] It is not possible to be certain whether Douglas had received the letter when he conducted the negotiations.

The negotiations appear to have been difficult. At the time, Douglas informed James Murray Yale at Fort Langley that "in consequence of orders to that effect from England, I have been lately engaged in buying out the Indian right to the lands in this neighbourhood and to the westward. It is a rather troublesome business, but we are getting on very well."[60] Douglas's use of the present tense corroborates the evidence in the Fort Victoria journals (but obscured in the eventual written versions of the treaties) that the final treaty was not completed until 10 May. Three years later, Douglas told the Governor and Committee that "the question of Indian rights ... always gives rise to troublesome excitements, and has on every occasion been productive of serious disturbances."[61] Those letters, and Douglas's report to London that the negotiations involved "considerable discussion" are the best indications that the negotiations were difficult, but apart from the fact that Douglas was forced to offer one-time payments rather than annuities, he did not elaborate on any other issues that might have been controversial.

Joseph William McKay (1829–1900) wrote a letter to Dr. James Helmcken thirty-eight years after the Fort Victoria treaties were completed that offers some clues as to what might have made the negotiations difficult. McKay's account must be treated cautiously because its contents (and McKay's interpretation of the treaties) were certainly influenced by the preoccupations of the late 1880s, and by the fact that McKay had an axe to grind when he wrote the letter. However, it must be taken seriously because at the time when the treaties were negotiated, McKay, having been at Fort Victoria for more than three years, was more experienced and more familiar with the local languages than his superior, James Douglas. Moreover, as apprentice clerk and signed witness to eight of the treaties, he was a participant in, not a mere witness to, the proceedings. Moreover, he was only fifty-nine years old when he wrote his letter. Although his letter contains the kinds of errors of fact that can be attributed to mistaken (and perhaps motivated) assumptions and failing memory, it reveals that McKay saw and read Archibald Barclay's letter of 17 December 1849. In 1888, he conveyed to J.S. Helmcken his memory of the treaties:

> The arrangements entered into with the Victoria Sanich and Sooke Districts Indians respecting their claims on lands of those two districts were made at the instance of the Home Government during Governor Blanshard's incumbency. Mr. Douglas was Land Agent for the Crown Lands of Vancouver Island. The then Secretary for the Colonies sent to Mr Douglas through A. Barclay Esqre. HBCo's Secretary instructions as to how he should deal with the so called Indian Title. The instructions were embodied in a somewhat lengthy document which began by reciting the Various general views of the Home Government respecting in regard to the land rights of aborigines in the Countries where they have been might be found sojourning.
>
> Mr. Douglas was very cautious in all his proceedings. The day before the meeting with the Indians, he sent for me and handed me the document above referred to telling me to study it carefully and to commit as much of it to memory as possible in order that I might check the interpreter Thomas should he fail to explain properly to the Indians the substance of Mr. Douglas' address to them.
>
> I remember one clause in the document in question distinctly stated that the Government did not admit that nomad tribes had any property in lands which they had not improved nor occupied for permanently industrial or useful purposes, and over which they had not established any form of government nor system of land tenure, but that where in the course of settlement by immigrants from the mother Country the intruders

interfered materially with the sources of food supply on which the aborigenes had heretofore subsisted, then as a matter of expediency it were well to grant to them such considerations in the way of useful commodities as might allay present irritation and prevent breaches of the peace. It was recommended in a subsequent clause that sufficient land to support them be set apart for the use of the Indians and that the Indians be encouraged to cultivate and improve the same after the manner of the civilized people.[62]

McKay's account offers the valuable information that Douglas retained Thomas Ouamtany, the HBC's interpreter at Fort Victoria and undoubtedly the most appropriate interpreter for the proceedings, for these negotiations.[63] It also reveals that McKay had sufficient facility in Lekwungen to be able to follow the discussions in both languages, but that Douglas did not understand Lekwungen well enough to know whether Ouamtany was interpreting accurately.

McKay's letter also suggests that Douglas took Barclay's letter seriously and instructed Ouamtany to convey the contents of the letter to the chiefs. If so, the contents of the letter may have sparked some considerable discussion. Even though there is no evidence to suggest that the chiefs had demanded or expected payment for the lands that the HBC had occupied, they probably saw the irony in the assertion that they were now being offered payment for land, even as they were being told that they had no rights to any land except for the land that they were to retain. Might the fact that, in the end, Douglas reported that "it was arranged, that the whole of their lands ... should be sold to the Company" be the result of the "considerable discussions" of that day? If Douglas was asked why he was offering payment when he claimed that the Queen already owned the land, might he, as certainly was also true, have answered that the company sought the agreement to secure peace and friendship?

Presumably, the parties also negotiated the size of the compensation, but Douglas provided no account of whether the parties had compromised on their opening demands and offers. The fact that Douglas paid less to the Klallam and Sooke because their territory had less cultivable land implies that haggling over the size of the compensation may have been thorny, and that Douglas bargained hard.[64] Other documents offer further hints. For example, in 1854, Douglas referred to "an Indian Reserve which has been accidentally omitted in Lot no 24 Sec XVIII though reserved to them on the general sale of their lands."[65] That implies that the parties had not only reached a general agreement that the communities would retain their "Village sites and enclosed fields," but had also agreed on specific sites and fields at the time of the negotiations. This impression is reinforced by a document written by British Columbia Indian Superintendent A.W. Vowell in 1893 that he purported was based upon the oral accounts that he had received from Indigenous people who had been present at the negotiations. Vowell reported that the members of the Songhees band who had apparently been present at the treaty negotiations told him "that they had been told by Sir James Douglass [sic] when consenting to the sale of their lands ... that they would for ever be protected in the possession of the land allotted to them and upon which they have since lived, meaning the Songhees Reserve."[66] These two passages raise the possibility that the parties may have negotiated, at the treaty negotiations in 1850 or soon thereafter, the specific plots of land that were to be reserved. If so, any documentary evidence of a catalogue of reserve sites has disappeared. Certainly, if Douglas had made such a list and ensured that it was preserved for posterity, it would be much easier today to determine treaty land entitlements under the treaty.

Douglas's reference to "enclosed" fields was new. In his letter of 3 September 1848, Douglas proposed protecting the "village sites, and cultivated fields" of the Indigenous communities. The difference is probably irrelevant.[67] Douglas probably intended the term to refer to all the fields that were cultivated, as English-speaking people understood the term *cultivation* at the time. While Indigenous languages may not have had a synonym for *cultivated*, given that the Indigenous people already had both potato fields and the places at which they gathered camas or other plant resources, regardless of whether they were tended or not, the concept would not have been difficult to explain.[68] There is little doubt that, as an opening position, Douglas intended to protect only lands that met the contemporary definition of "cultivation," and given prevailing British perceptions of waste versus improved lands, it is implausible that he included camas fields. However, if he had been pressed, he would probably have indicated that the Indigenous people were free to gather resources such as camas from unoccupied lands, just as they remained free to hunt on such lands. The fact that Douglas described the existing enclosed fields as being of small extent reinforces the impression that he promised to protect only the intensively cultivated potato fields, for camas procurement locations would have been considerably more extensive.

We cannot be certain about what Douglas meant when he promised the Indigenous peoples the liberty to "carry on their fisheries with the same freedom as when they were the sole occupants of the country." Douglas, not a lawyer, was not as fluid a writer as many officers in the HBC at the time. He may have intended "occupants" to mean "inhabitants," but dictionaries of the time suggest that people were less apt to use those two words interchangeably than they are now. Dictionaries from the mid-nineteenth century state that *occupants* denoted "possessors," while *inhabitants* meant "residents."[69] He may have intended by "when they were the sole occupants of the country" to mean before they encountered Europeans for the first time (around 1790), but he may also have meant before Europeans began to occupy land in their territory in 1843, or before the British obtained undivided sovereignty over Vancouver Island in 1846.[70] He probably did not consider his word choice deeply. The fact that Douglas did not elaborate on this right indicates that he did not anticipate how important this promise might subsequently be. Douglas lived when many Europeans assumed that Indigenous people throughout the world would either become incorporated into settler societies, or face extinction. It is easy to imagine that Douglas wished to assure the local peoples that they could continue to focus their lives around the fisheries, even as he assumed that the importance of Indigenous fisheries would diminish as Indigenous peoples continued to diversify their economies.

*Fisheries* had multiple meanings in the mid-nineteenth century that could include the occupation and business of fishing, as well as the places where fishing took place. It is difficult to know exactly what the parties understood at the time. It is unlikely, for example, that Douglas was aware of the existence of Indigenous mariculture. The HBC's prospectus for the colony had indicated that "every freeholder will enjoy the right of fishing all sorts of fish in the seas, bays, and inlets thereof, or surrounding said island."[71] Douglas must have intended to protect in his agreements Indigenous rights at least equal to those offered in the prospectus. But neither the prospectus nor the treaty addressed the issue of trade in fish. As has been noted, Indigenous people must have traded fish among themselves for thousands of years and traded with the HBC commercially since 1827. It is simply unknowable whether the parties understood the treaty to enshrine trade in fish as a treaty right. It is possible that Douglas did not think deeply about the question.

Did the parties believe that *fisheries* included places where fishing took place? It is difficult to know. Dictionaries of the time are not definitive. One defines *fisheries* as "the business or place of fishing."[72] Another defined it more narrowly as "the business of catching fish."[73] In August 1851, Anson Dart, the Superintendent of Indian Affairs for the Oregon Territory, concluded a treaty (never ratified by the United States Senate) that reserved for Chinook villagers "the privilege of occupying the grounds they now occupy for the purpose of building, fishing and grazing their stock."[74] Likewise, in 1854 and 1855, treaties negotiated by Isaac I. Stevens (1818–1862), the Governor of Washington Territory, stipulated that the "right of taking fish, at all usual and accustomed grounds and stations is ... secured to said Indians, in common with all citizens of the United States."[75] There is no evidence that the American treaties and Vancouver Island treaties influenced each other, but the American treaties show that it was plausible that the meaning of "fisheries" in the 1850s could include the encampments used for the purpose of catching, processing, and preserving fish. The prospectus for the colony of Vancouver Island stated that freeholders could not be excluded from the waters mentioned, but the evidence presented in earlier chapters suggests that the control of specific locations essential to the procurement and processing of fish had been crucially important to Northwest Coast villagers for thousands of years. The chiefs who negotiated the treaties must have been influenced by their understanding of how their own fisheries were conducted. The wording of Douglas's 3 September 1849 letter, stating that "the Indians Fisheries, Village Sites and cultivated Fields, should be reserved," is amenable to an interpretation that Douglas contemplated "fisheries" as including the land upon which the processing of fish took place, but his report of 15 May 1850, is less amenable to that interpretation. Given what we know of Douglas, it is unlikely that Douglas thought deeply about the question. The fact that many of the fishing encampments were on the mainland and Gulf Islands, outside the boundaries of Vancouver Island, suggests that Douglas could not reserve most of the fishing encampments in the 1850s.

Douglas's reference to "122 men or heads of families" being gathered suggests that the enumeration of the "Songees" in his chart of "Original Indian Population" of Vancouver Island (see Appendix A) dates from the time of the treaty negotiations, for in it the number of "men with beards" matches the number of signatures on each treaty.[76] Given that lower down on the same chart Douglas gave an enumeration of the "Quakeeolth" at Beaver Harbour (to which those tribes relocated only after Fort Rupert was established in 1849), it seems that the Indigenous people and Douglas negotiated these agreements based on the realities at the time of negotiation, not as of 1846 "when the Island came under the undivided sovereignty of Great Britain." The implications of negotiating agreements based on circumstances as of 1846 or 1850 would have been significant. Since long-term population trends at the time were downward, and a measles epidemic had struck in 1848, using 1850 population numbers may have been less costly than using 1846 population numbers. Given that potato cultivation was presumably gradually increasing, basing negotiations on cultivated fields as of

1850 might have worked to the advantage of the Indigenous population. The consolidation of villages prompted by the establishment of Fort Victoria in 1843 was probably largely complete by 1846, but may have continued between 1846 and 1850, with implications for any agreements that the parties may have come to about the specific sites to be reserved. The HBC probably used more land for cultivation and pasturage in 1850 than in 1846, but it is unlikely that the HBC occupied land in 1850 that was occupied by Indigenous cultivation or villages in 1846. At any rate, it seems that, even if he was aware of the instructions to base his negotiations on the status quo as of 1846, Douglas disregarded or abandoned that position in the actual negotiations.

Douglas explained that he obtained the surrenders of the land of the southeastern corner of Vancouver Island for a mere £150. Given the abundant evidence that Indigenous peoples knowingly made such agreements in New Zealand and in North America for "nominal" compensation, it would require significant contrary evidence to conclude otherwise for Vancouver Island. There is no evidence that the Fort Victoria chiefs had demanded or expected any payment at any time between 1843, when Fort Victoria was established, and 1850. It is easier to understand why the leaders might have agreed if we understand that Douglas approached them with a proposal to pay them for something for which they had not previously demanded or expected any payment. After discussing a New Zealand transaction in which Māori received only one kettle for a tract of land, Stuart Banner remarked that "a single kettle was one more kettle than anyone had ever offered for the land before."[77]

The Xes on these treaties are sufficiently uniform to lead one to conclude that the marks were made with one hand and that the "signatories" did not actually make the marks, but merely "touched the pen." This appears to have equally been the practice followed by Kemp in New Zealand, and elsewhere in the United States and Canada.[78]

Douglas's 16 May 1850 report of the oral terms he negotiated with the Indigenous communities in the Fort Victoria district arrived at the HBC London offices on 7 August 1850,[79] and the Governor and Committee's response, together with the long-awaited form, was included as part of a long letter dated 16 August 1850. The Governor and Committee had decided against using the form written by Adam Thom at Red River and opted instead to use the text of the Treaty of Akaroa as the template for subsequent Vancouver Island purchases. The choice was an odd one, for the Governor and Committee should have known that Kemp's purchase had already generated considerable controversy with authorities.

The Fort Victoria treaties must be among the strangest negotiated between the British Crown and Indigenous peoples. The HBC's reliance on the Treaty of Akaroa explains some of the anomalies; Douglas's cavalier approach to treaty making explains others. After 1850, Douglas negotiated further treaties at Fort Rupert, the Saanich Peninsula, and Nanaimo. Each of these treaties has some of the same anomalies as the Fort Victoria treaties, but each has idiosyncrasies of its own. For that reason, we require a contextual history of each treaty.

# 9 The Treaty of Akaroa and Fort Victoria Treaties, 1848–1850

The written versions of the Vancouver Island Treaties are copied directly from the English translation of New Zealand's Treaty of Akaroa (Kemp Deed) made between Ngāi Tahu chiefs and Henry Tacy Kemp (figure 21) at Akaroa on the South Island of New Zealand on 12 June 1848. There is no documentary evidence that the HBC turned to New Zealand for a template treaty on the grounds that they believed that the villagers of the South Island of New Zealand and Vancouver Island used land in similar ways. The Governor and Committee of the HBC may have obtained the document directly from the NZC; the London headquarters of the two companies were not far apart. But it is more likely that the HBC's directors came upon the text of the Treaty of Akaroa by consulting the latest publication of the *British Parliamentary Papers*. After all, the 1849 *Sessional Papers* published the text of the Treaty of Akaroa in a report that appeared immediately before the published copy of the correspondence between the Governor of the HBC and the Colonial Office relating to the colonization of Vancouver Island.[1] The fact that the wording of the template agreement sent to Douglas was drawn, word for word, from the English translation of Kemp's purchase as published in the *Sessional Papers* suggests that personnel in the London office of the HBC drew up the text for Vancouver Island treaties from that volume.

If the Governor and Committee decided upon the text of Kemp's purchase after having read all of the papers published along with it, they should have modified it, for although they could not anticipate that Kemp's unusual purchase was destined to become one of the most contentious in New Zealand, the report would have alerted them to the fact that it had already been controversial.

After purchasing the Wairau District and Porirua block in March and April 1847, George Grey, Governor of New Zealand, turned his mind to the middle third of the South Island. Until the mid-1840s, the South Island had attracted far fewer settlers than the North Island, although since the 1830s, British, French, and American whalers and sealers had established stations there. But, after a visit of several months during 1843–44, Edward Shortland, the Protector of Aborigines, had decided that the "inconsiderable" Indigenous population on the South Island made it an inviting place for exogenous settlement.[2]

Ngāi Tahu of the South Island were not Māori around whom the popular image of the Indigenous New Zealander has been formed. While the Indigenous communities of most of the North Island, particularly the northern part of the North Island, were much larger than those of Vancouver Island, the southern two-thirds of the South Island was far less densely populated than Vancouver Island. Probably no more than 7 per cent of Indigenous New Zealanders lived on the South Island, and most of those lived in the Wairau District near Cook Strait that Grey purchased in March 1847. The population to the south of the Wairau District may have been as small as 2,000 in 1848. The climate of most of the South Island was too cold to permit Māori to cultivate the root crops that supported the large agricultural villages on the North Island. On the South Island, Ngāi Tahu hapū (subtribes) depended primarily on gathering food from "mahinga kai" ("food-gathering places") and processing them at their small seasonal villages (kāinga nohoanga). The abundance of food was, even in some of those locations, capable of supporting socially stratified communities that included slaves.[3]

Most of the crops that early Māori brought to New Zealand from Polynesia, including taro (*Colocasia esculanta*), paper mulberry (*Broussonetia terminalis*), and yams (*Dioscorea* sp.), could not survive on the South Island. Kumara (sweet potatoes) (*Ipomeoa batatas*) may have been cultivated as far south as the Banks Peninsula, but that region had been marginal for that crop, and Shortland reported in 1844 that Ngāi Tahu had abandoned kumara cultivation by 1844, perhaps because they had taken up extensive cultivation of the white potato (*Solanum tuberosum*).[4] He found small villages of about twenty people, reliant mostly on fish, birds, and roots, although they were also employed at whaling stations. Many, perhaps most, had been converted to Wesleyan Methodism or Anglicanism by Indigenous catechists; exogenous missionaries were still few on the South Island.[5] By the mid-1840s, many Ngāi Tahu appear to have been able to read te reo Māori, and some were also conversant in English.[6]

Warfare and disease had taken a heavy toll. Ngāi Tahu, like the villagers of southeastern Vancouver Island, were subject to frequent raids by their more numerous and powerful northern neighbours.[7] Takapūneke, a Ngāi Tahu village near Akaroa, had been the site of the Ngāti Toa attack at the centre of the *Elizabeth* affair of 1830. Beginning in the 1820s, as invasions of northern groups became more dangerous with the introduction of European weaponry, Ngāi Tahu chiefs sought to strengthen the military positions of their communities by convincing European whalers to establish whaling stations in their territories.[8] During the 1830s, warfare, measles, and influenza further decimated Ngāi Tahu.[9] That helps explain why beleaguered Ngāi Tahu, who, according to Harry Evison, were increasingly dependent on Sydney-based whalers for European weaponry, were willing to sell land to men such as William Wentworth and his associates.[10] Even as far south as Otago, Shortland found an old chief who had lost "a great many of his family" to the raids of Te Rauparaha, chief of Ngāti Toa.

Based on a February 1848 visit to the South Island in company with William Wakefield of the NZC, George Grey described Akaroa, on the Banks Peninsula as "a very interesting district, containing a population of about three hundred Europeans and about four hundred natives. ... The harbour is one of the best in this country so celebrated for fine harbours; the soil and climate are excellent, and it would form an admirable site for a large colony."[11] Ngāi Tahu at Banks Peninsula had decades of experience with pākehā by 1848. Whalers from several countries used Akaroa's sheltered harbour before the 1830s. Since whalers left few documents, we are left with Ernest Dieffenbach's rhetorical question regarding their stations: "A fishing place in Europe is not the most civilized part of the community – how then should it be expected to be different in this lone part of the world?"[12]

Europeans had already staked claims to portions of the South Island by 1848. In August 1838, a French whaler, Jean-François Langlois, purchased land on the Banks Peninsula from several Ngāi Tahu chiefs, after which he helped establish the Nanto-Bordelaise Company to control and settle the lands, but Hobson concluded the Treaty of Waitangi on 6 February 1840, and declared British sovereignty over the South Island on 21 May 1840, before any French settlers arrived. A few Ngāi Tahu rangatira signed the Treaty of Waitangi,[13] but the South Island of New Zealand, over which Hobson claimed British sovereignty, arguably was not covered by the Treaty of Waitangi. In July 1840, when a small contingent of French settlers found that the British had asserted sovereignty, a few stayed to settle around Akaroa.[14] By 1848, when George Grey decided to arrange a purchase of a large swathe of the South Island, small Ngāi Tahu villages, a small French settlement, and a few British families and a British government agent dotted the expansive Akaroa harbour.[15]

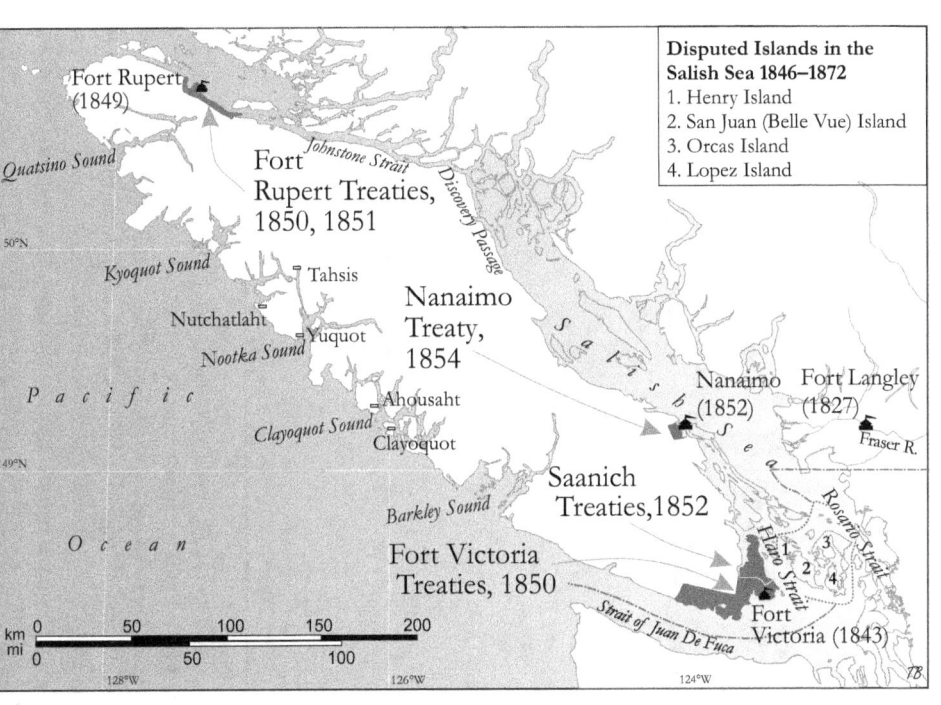

1. **The Kendrick Purchases (1791) and the HBC's Vancouver Island Treaties, 1850–54.**
In July and August 1791, John Kendrick, leader of an American expedition, executed five private deeds of purchase with chiefs of Tahsis, Nutchatlaht, Yuquot, Ahousaht, and Clayoquot. Then, more than fifty years later, after George Blenkinsop purchased a small plot of land around Fort Rupert on 15 April 1850, the HBC concluded fourteen other treaties on Vancouver Island between 1850 and 1854, but those treaties cover only about 3 per cent of the island's area, an enigma explored in the present book. Source: T. Binnema.

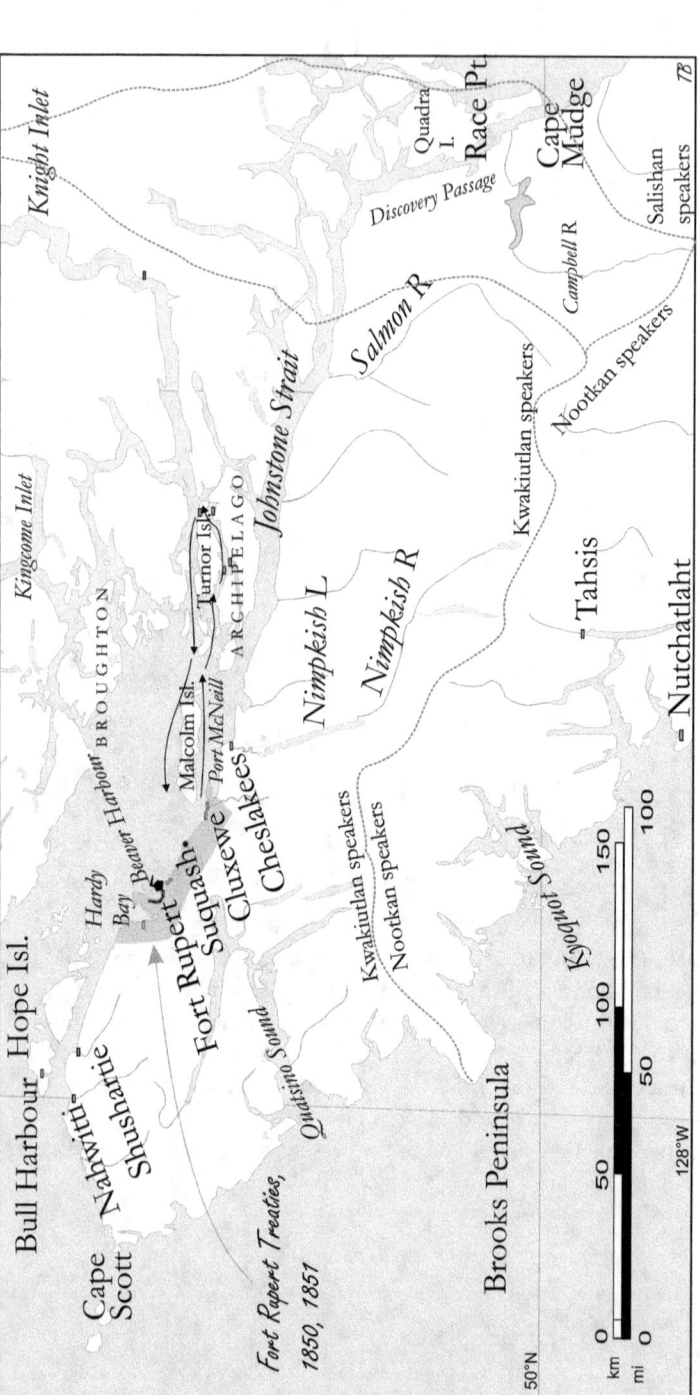

2. **Fort Rupert and Northern Vancouver Island.** The HBC may never have adopted a treaty policy for Vancouver Island had they not learned of coal in northern Vancouver Island. A Kwakiutl party trading at Fort McLoughlin told traders of coalfields in the vicinity of Suquash. Until the HBC established Fort Rupert, the Kwakiutl and Kweeha had summer fisheries along the coast between Hardy Bay and Port McNeill and winter villages on and near Turnor Island in the Broughton Archipelago (arrows show their approximate typical seasonal round). After the HBC established Fort Rupert, the Kwakiutl and Kweeha consolidated their settlements adjacent to the fort allowing other Kwakiutlan peoples to settle on their former village sites. In 1850 the HBC purchased the Fort Rupert garden, and in 1851, purchased the territory shown in grey. The map shows the approximate boundaries of the Kwakiutlan, Nootkan, and Salish speakers, although the Lekwiltok were expanding southward from Salmon River towards Cape Mudge at the expense of Salish

3. **Paul Kane, "Interior of a Clallam Lodge, Vancouver Island,"** 1847, watercolour and pencil on paper, 5 3/8 × 8 15/16 inches (13.7 × 22.7 cm). This field sketch by Paul Kane reveals the substantial and permanent nature of Indigenous homes and winter villages on the Northwest Coast. Source: Stark Museum of Art, Orange, Texas, Bequest of H.J. Lutcher Stark, 1965, 31.78.80.

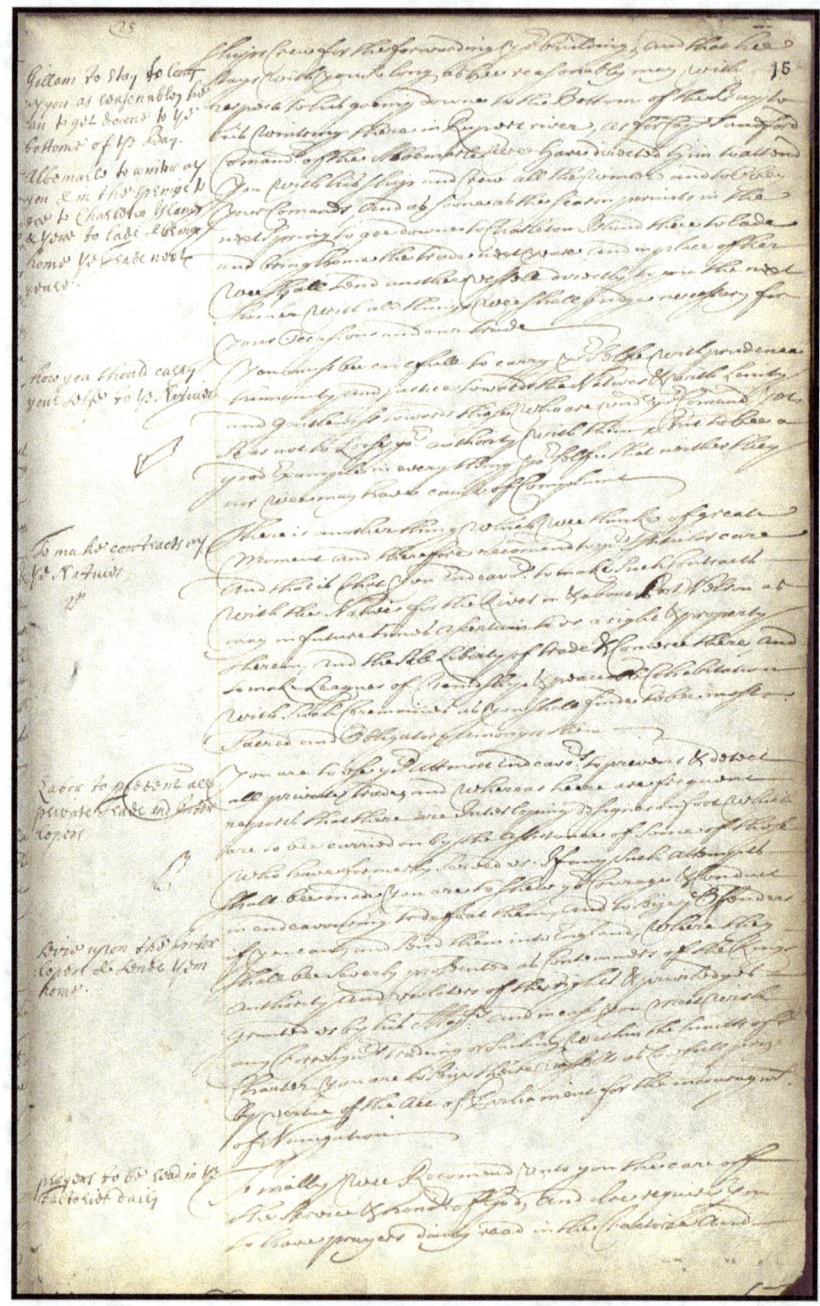

**4. HBC Instructions to "Make Contracts," 1682.** No treaty documents exist to show that HBC traders followed the instructions of the Governor and Committee of the HBC to make "contracts" with local Indigenous leaders. That does not mean that no such agreements were made – many land purchases in New Netherlands and New England in the seventeenth century were not documented – but instructions like that found in the middle paragraph of this page of the 1682 correspondence books of the Governor and Committee of the HBC is the best evidence we have of any such agreements at Hudson Bay. Source: HBCA A.6/1, fo. 15.

**5. The Selkirk Treaty of 1817.** Thomas Douglas, the Fifth Earl of Selkirk, concluded this land-purchase agreement with Saulteaux and Cree leaders of the Red River Valley on 18 July 1817. Copies are held today by Library and Archives Canada in Ottawa and the Hudson's Bay Company Archives in Winnipeg. Selkirk was motivated to seek the agreement to bolster the claims of the HBC and his colony against NWC and Canadian claims, not to acknowledge Indigenous title. Still, by concluding the treaty, Selkirk and the Saulteaux and Cree signatories played a part in the making of Indigenous title. For a short time, company officials pondered using the Selkirk Treaty as the template for the Vancouver Island treaties, but this document appears to have been created with greater formality than the Vancouver Island treaties later were. Source: HBCA E.8/1.

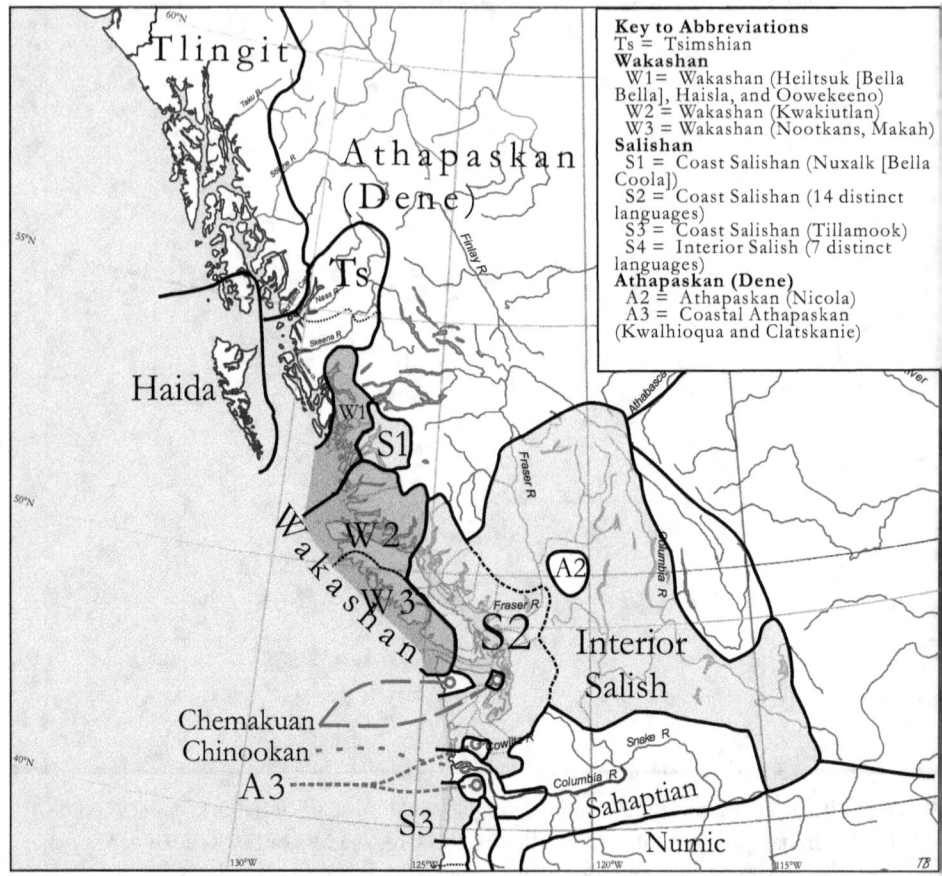

**6. Linguistic Groups along the Northwest Coast in the Area Surrounding Vancouver Island at about 1800.** This linguistic map hints at the complex history of the Northwest Coast. Speakers of two language families inhabited Vancouver Island at the turn of the nineteenth century. Linguists conclude that the fourteen distinct Coast Salish and seven distinct Interior Salish languages probably diverged from a proto-Salish language that developed in the Fraser River delta region thousands of years ago, while the Wakashan speakers probably spread from the vicinity of the Brooks Peninsula. Wakashan speakers expanded down the east coast of Vancouver Island at the expense of Salish speakers in the years before contact with Europeans, but Wakashan and Salish villagers also fought among themselves. Source: T. Binnema.

7. **Paul Kane, "Traveling Lodges."** This field sketch made by Paul Kane in 1846 must be among the earliest depictions of a Northwest Coast summer fishing encampment. The temporary encampments contrasted starkly with the substantial houses of winter villages. It is not known whether either or both of the parties to the Vancouver Island treaties understood such locations were to be protected under the treaties, either as "villages" or "fisheries." Source: Paul Kane (1810–1871), *Clallam Traveling Lodges*, 1847, watercolour and pencil on paper. 5 5/16 × 9 inches (13.5 × 22.9 cm), Stark Museum of Art, Orange, Texas, Bequest of H.J. Lutcher Stark, 1965, 31.78.4.

8. **Paul Kane, "Battle between Clallam and Makah at I-eh-nus."** When Paul Kane arrived at Fort Victoria in 1846, he was told of a Makah attack on a Klallam village on the Olympic Peninsula across the Strait of Juan de Fuca from Victoria a few months earlier. This illustration represents Kane's attempt to imagine that attack, although, as Ian MacLaren has noted, he must have sought to romanticize the portrayal by ignoring the fact that European firearms were widely used by this time (MacLaren, *Paul*, 3: 130–2. Kane must have based his depiction of the village's fortifications on those he saw in the region at the time. Source: Paul Kane (1810–1871), *Battle between Clallam and Makah at I-eh-nus*, 1847, watercolour and pencil on paper, 5 1/4 ×

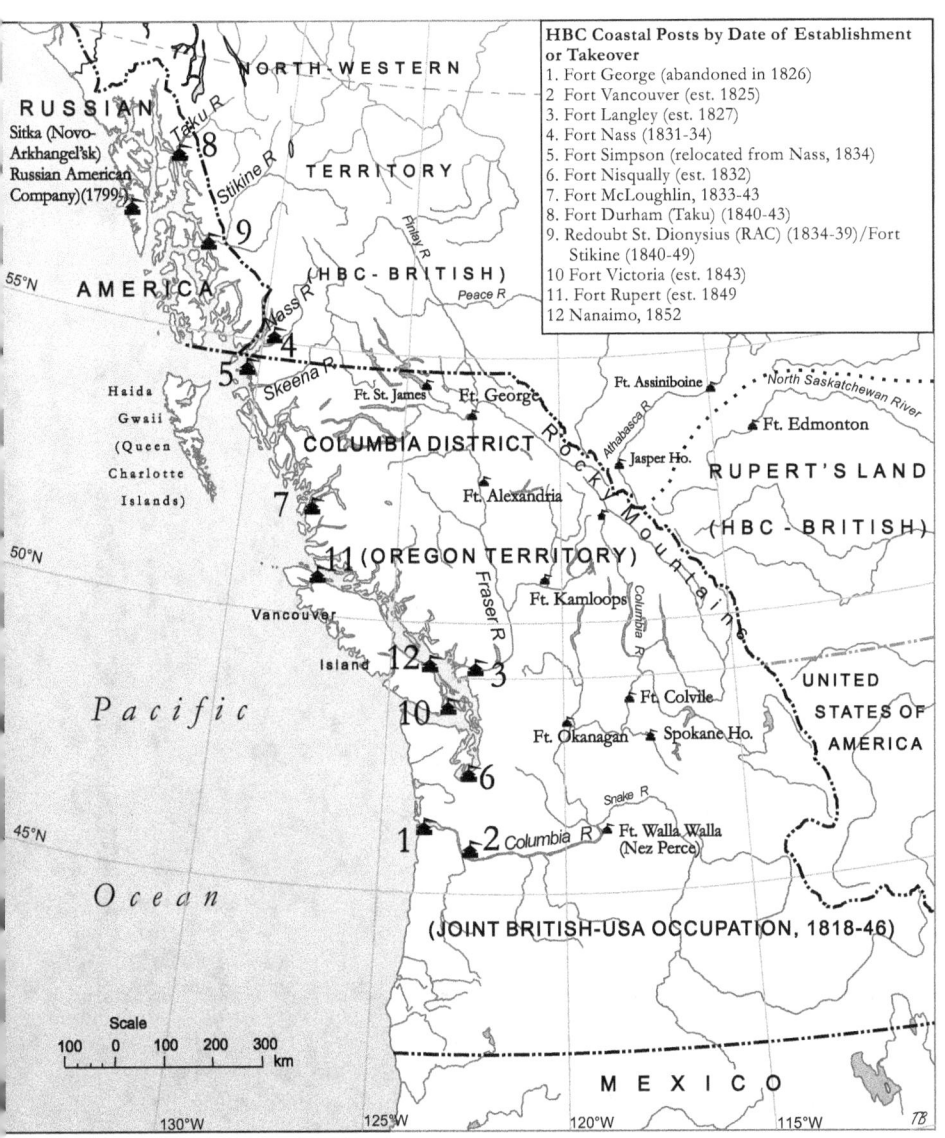

**9. HBC Forts in Western North America, 1821–1850.** The HBC had little presence west of the Rocky Mountains, and none on the Northwest Coast before 1821. Between 1825 and 1840, the company established (or took over from the Russian American Company), posts along the coast from the Columbia River to the Taku River. However, it abandoned Fort McLoughlin and Fort Durham when it established Fort Victoria in 1843, and Fort Stikine when it established Fort Rupert in 1849. Source: Ted Binnema.

> Port Independence, on the Island
> of Keong-King, March 1st 1793.
>
> Sir,
>
> I have the honour of enclosing to you the Copies of several Deeds, by which the tracts of Land therein described, situated on Islands on the North West Coast of America have been conveyed to me, and my heirs forever, by the resident Chiefs of those districts, who, I presume, were the only just proprietors thereof. I know not what measures are necessary to be taken, to secure the property of these purchases to me, and the government thereof to the United States; but it cannot be amiss to transmit them to you, to remain in the Office of the Department of State. My claim to those territories has been allowed by the Spanish Crown: for the purchases I made at Nootka, were expressly excepted in a deed of conveyance, of the Lands adjacent to, and surrounding Nootka Sound, executed in September last, to El Señor Don Juan Francisco de la Bodega, y Quadra, on behalf

**10. John Kendrick letter to Thomas Jefferson, 1793.** In March 1793, John Kendrick wrote this letter to Thomas Jefferson (then United States Secretary of State) along with several "deeds" he had concluded with chiefs along the western coast of Vancouver Island. In his letter, the first page of which is shown here, Kendrick expressed his hope that the United States government would recognize his ownership of the lands and claim sovereignty over the lands. The United States government had banned private land purchases from Indians within the United States, but Kendrick must have hoped that the government would judge this purchase to be legitimate. The letter and deeds are now "Specially Protected Records," at the National Archives and Records Administration in Washington, DC. Source: NARA US RG59, M179, Jan.–June 1793, fo. 148.

11. Paul Kane, "Fort Victoria," Songhees (Central Coast Salish), Hudson's Bay Company." The inhabitants of several villages relocated to a site directly across from Fort Victoria, soon after the HBC established the post. This sketch made by Paul Kane in 1847 shows the palisaded HBC Fort Victoria on the right, and the Songhees village across the harbour. While most Northwest Coast villages were fortified, villagers adjacent to HBC posts appear to have found it unnecessary to fortify their settlements. Source: Royal Ontario Museum, 946.15.212.

**12. John Turnstall Haverfield, "Seamen and Marines of HMS Constance Marching Out of Fort Victoria."** Given how many paintings John Turnstall Haverfield of the Royal Marines made on 29 August 1848, he must have regarded the military exercises conducted by the British Navy near Fort Victoria on that day to have been important. This is one of the paintings of that day. While the exercises may have been intended to intimidate some of the visitors to Victoria, the Songhees and other local visitors may have interpreted it as evidence that the British would protect them from their powerful neighbours. Source: BCA PDP01181.

**13. Sir George Gipps.** Sir George Gipps presented what is probably the clearest summary of British principles of Indigenous title in the mid-nineteenth century. This portrait by British portraitist Henry William Pickersgill, may have been made at the time of his knighting in 1838, shortly before Gipps departed for Australia. With its emphasis on Gipps's head and hands, it seems intended to depict him as a wise man of action. Source: *Portrait of Sir George Gipps by Henry William Pickersgill*. Source: Mitchell Library, State Library of New South Wales, nvg8B051.

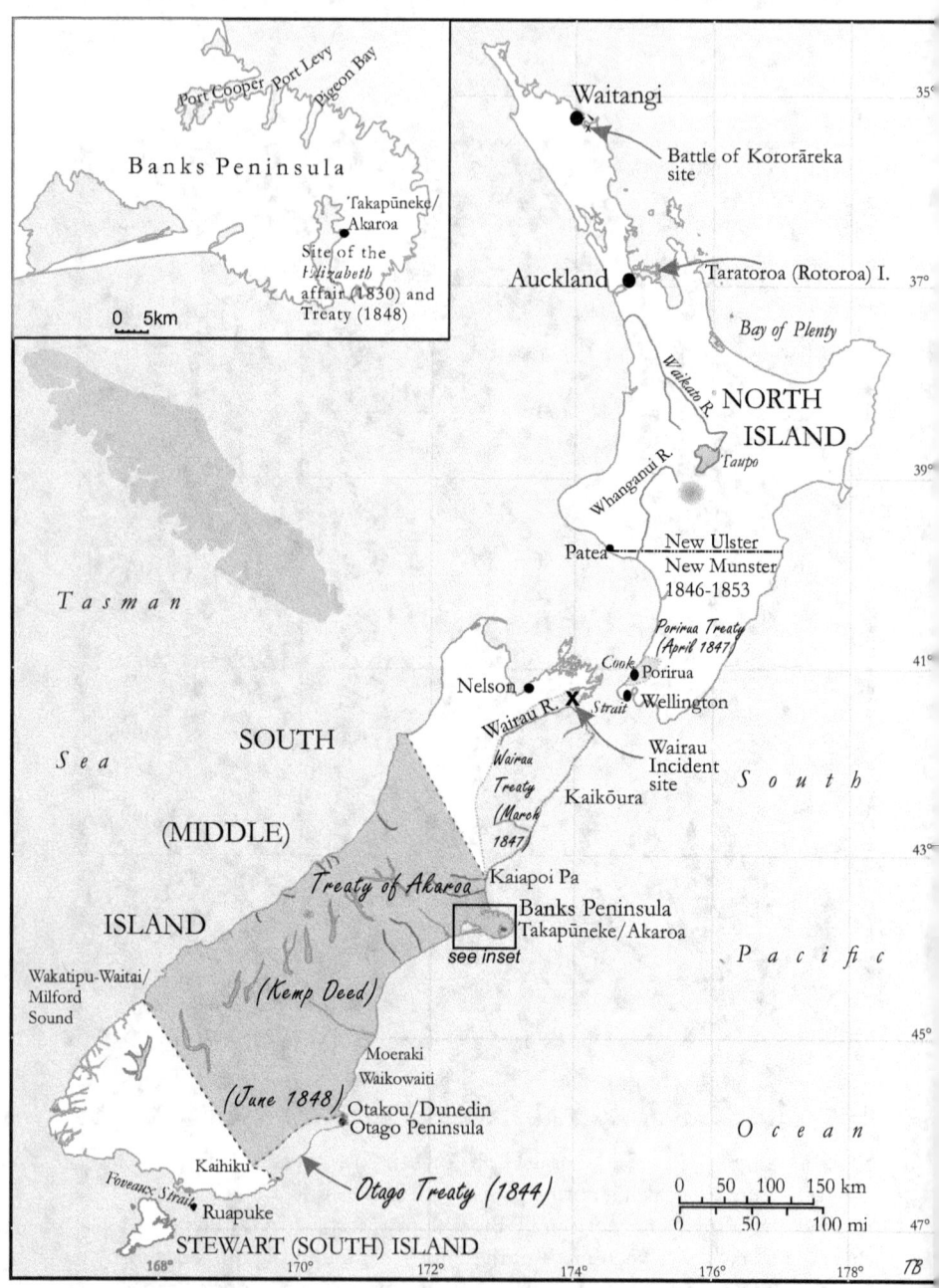

14. **New Zealand (1848).** On 12 June 1848, in the Treaty of Akaroa (Kemp Deed), Ngāi Tahu ceded their rights to approximately 81,000 square kilometres of the South Island of New Zealand in exchange for £2,000 and certain promises, including reserves. By comparison, the area of Vancouver Island (depicted according to the same scale in silhouette just below the inset) is about 31,285 square kilometres, and all of the Vancouver Island treaties combined cover about 1,000 square kilometres. Various locations mentioned in the text are shown on this map. Source: Ted Binnema.

**15. Henry George Grey, 3rd Earl Grey (1861).** Earl Grey was the British Colonial Secretary from 1846 to 1853, years that included the formative time of the Colony of Vancouver Island. He had previously, as Lord Howick, had much experience in, knowledge of, and influence over colonial affairs. Although the Colonial Office under Earl Grey gave local governors considerable authority to determine Indigenous policies, Grey had firm, consistent, and influential ideas about Indigenous title. In this *carte de visite* by photographer Camille Silvy, he appears to have wanted to be portrayed as a learned man. Source: National Portrait Gallery, London, NPG Ax7430.

**16. Sir George Grey.** Sir George Grey was an important governor in the history of Australia, New Zealand, and South Africa, and an influential thinker about British Indigenous policies. During his first term as Governor of New Zealand, he was instrumental in establishing the terms of land surrenders with Māori communities. Similar terms were applied in Vancouver Island. This image of Grey dates from the 1860s. Source Auckland Art Gallery, 2010/5/5. https://www.aucklandartgallery.com/explore-art-and-ideas/artwork/16609.

**17. Andrew Colvile.** The first proposal to conclude treaties on Vancouver Island appears to have originated with Andrew Colvile, the Deputy Governor of the HBC in consultation with John H. Pelly, the HBC Governor. Nothing more evocative than this silhouette portrait exists for Colvile. Source: HBCA P-70.

**18. George Simpson.** George Simpson, the North American governor of the HBC doubted the existence of Indigenous title but supported Colvile and Pelly's proposal to conclude treaties on Vancouver Island as a useful expedient.

**19. James Douglas.** Scholars have exaggerated the role of James Douglas in developing treaty policy for Vancouver Island. Still, he was responsible for negotiating the treaties. This photograph of James Douglas taken in about 1863 from a low camera angle appears to corroborate other evidence that his large physical size was an important part of James Douglas's identity. Douglas did not have the education, training, and experience of a typical British colonial governor (or even of most HBC Chief Factors). This photograph suggests that, although originally reluctant to take on governorships, Douglas was not hesitant to project an authoritarian persona. Source: Victoria City Archives M08650.

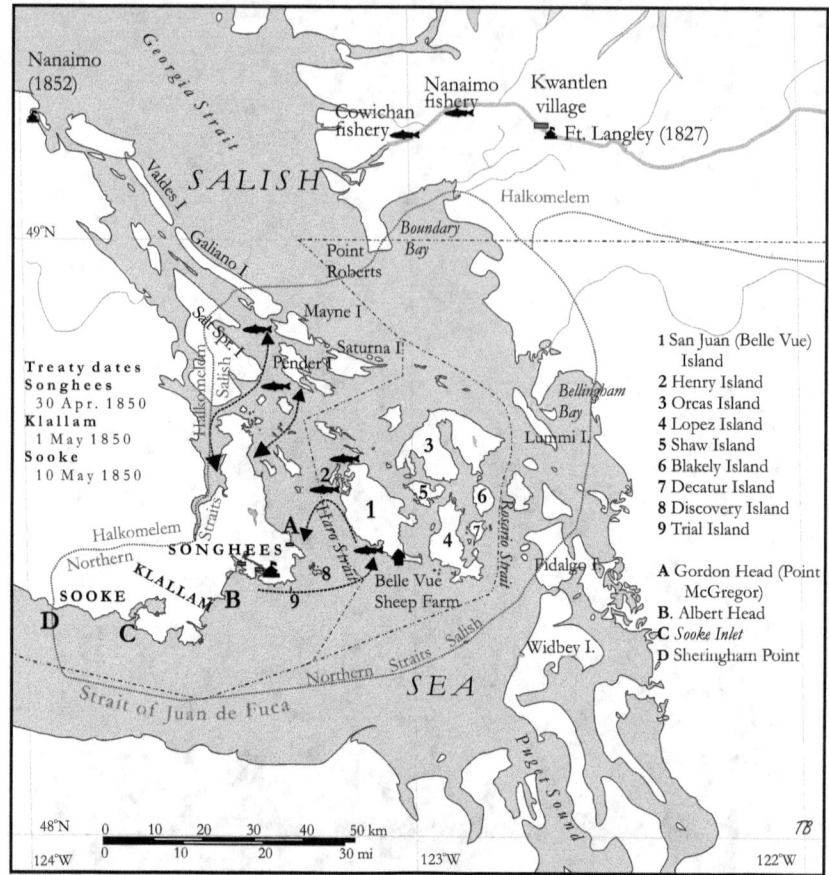

**20. The Fort Victoria Treaties as Reported by James Douglas.** When James Douglas reported on the oral terms of the Fort Victoria treaties on 16 May 1850, he implied only three treaties, one each with the Songhees, Klallam, and Sooke. These covered the "District of Victoria" between Gordon Head and Sheringham Point (A and D on the map). This map also shows in a general way the seasonal rounds of the Songhees and Saanich families. From winter villages on southeastern Vancouver Island, the families travelled to seasonal encampments on islands in the Salish Sea to harvest camas and process fish. There is a remarkable correlation between reef-net fishing technology and the Northern Straits Salish dialects. Halkomelem peoples dominated the fisheries of the Fraser River. The possession of the San Juan Islands was the subject of dispute between Great Britain and the United States from 1846 to 1872, the British claiming the islands west of Rosario Strait, and the United States claiming the islands east of Haro Strait. The HBC officially claimed San Juan Island for Great Britain in 1847 and established the Belle Vue Farm in the 1850s. In 1855, Isaac I. Stevens included the islands within the scope of the Treaty of Point Elliott. In 1872, the boundary dispute was referred to the German Emperor William I for arbitration, and the boundary was set in the Haro Strait. The decision relegated some of the most important resource-gathering sites of the Songhees to American territory. Source: T. Binnema.

**21. Henry Tacy Kemp.** Henry Tacy Kemp, who negotiated the Treaty of Akaroa, was proficient in te reo Māori (the Māori language). The unusual process by which he obtained the agreement has profound implications for Vancouver Island, because his treaty became the template for fourteen treaties on the island. Source: Wikimedia Commons.

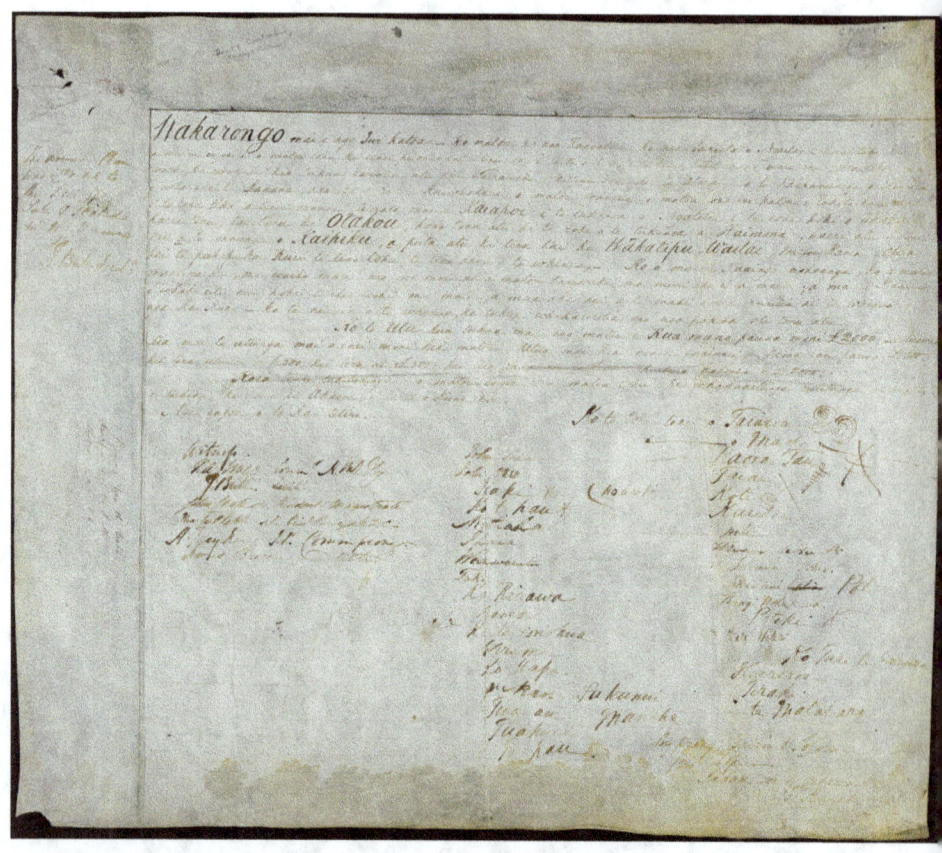

**22. The Treaty of Akaroa (Kemp Deed), 1848.** On 12 June 1848, Henry Tacy Kemp concluded a land-purchase agreement with Ngāi Tahu of the middle third of New Zealand. The original treaty signed by the chiefs was written in te reo Māori and engrossed on parchment. Kemp translated the treaty into English and submitted it to his superiors shortly after the agreement was concluded, and his English translation was published in the *British Parliamentary Papers* in 1849. The Governor and Committee of the HBC used that English translation as the template for the written versions of the Vancouver Island treaties. Source: Canterbury and Otago Archives New Zealand 8102 file 1.

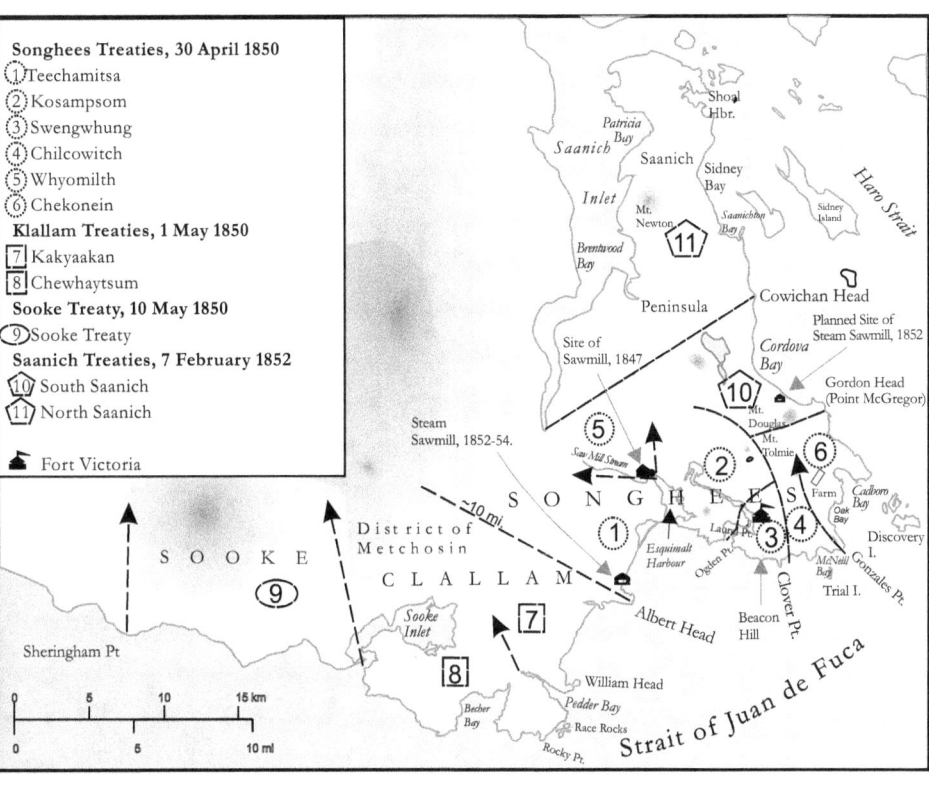

**23. The Fort Victoria and Saanich Treaties.** Despite previously implying that he had negotiated three treaties for the Fort Victoria district and one for the Saanich Peninsula, James Douglas produced nine written Fort Victoria treaties and two Saanich Peninsula treaties. This map presents the boundaries of the written treaties. It would be reasonable to presume that each treaty centred on the winter villages of a particular extended family, but the documentary evidence is too sparse to confirm such an assumption. The map depicts the locations of some of the places (farms and mills) mentioned in the text.
Source: T. Binnema.

> Know all men, We the Chiefs and
> People of the Teechamitsa Tribe who
> have signed our names and made our
> marks to this Deed on the Twenty ninth
> day of April, one thousand eight hundred
> and Fifty, do consent to surrender
> entirely and for ever to James Douglas
> the Agent of the Hudsons Bay
> Company in Vancouvers Island that
> is to say, for the Governor Deputy
> Governor and Committee of the same
> the whole of the lands, situate
> and lying between Esquimalt
> Harbour and Point Albert in-
> cluding the latter, on the Strait
> of Juan de Fuca and extending
> backward from thence to the range
> of mountains on the Sanitch
> Arm about ten miles distant.
> The Condition of or under-
> standing of this Sale is this,

**24. The Teechamitsa Treaty.** These are the first two pages of a notebook entitled "Register of Land purchases from Indians," now held at the British Columbia Archives. It is the text of the treaty with the "Teechamitsa Tribe" of Songhees. Although James Douglas and the Teechamitsa concluded an agreement orally on 29 April 1850, this written version was not created until after 15 November 1850, when Douglas received from London the text of a template treaty based on the Treaty of Akaroa (Kemp Deed). At the top of the second page are words written in pencil on or about 29 April 1850, partially obscured by words overwritten in ink, to the effect that this was a "purchase of land from Teechamitsa Tribe extending from [the?] east side of Esquimalt Harbour to Point McGregor to the range of mountains [?] 10 miles back [?]." Douglas indicated that the names and Xes were inserted

That our village sites and enclosed fields are to be kept for our own use, for the use of our children, and for those who may follow after us; and the land shall be properly surveyed hereafter. It is understood, however, that the land itself, with these small exceptions, becomes the entire property of the White people for ever; it is also understood that we are at liberty to hunt over the unoccupied lands, and to carry on our fisheries as formerly.

We have received as payment Twenty seven pounds Ten Shillings sterling.

In token whereof we have signed our names and made our marks at Fort Victoria 29 April 1850

Done in the presence of
Roderick Finlayson
Joseph William McKay

1 See-sachasis X
2 Key-hay-hene X
3 See-shay-moot X
4 Salsay-nut X
5 Lou-chaps X
6 Thlamie X
7 Chamutston X
8 Tsatsullue X
9 Boquymilt X
10 Jameststelel X
11 Minay-itsu X

on the bottom of the second page at the same time. Note that James Douglas did not sign the treaty document. The text of the treaty was inserted after 15 November 1850 in such a way as to end a few lines above the signatures. That meant that the text of the treaty began part way down the unlined inside cover of the register, and the second page on the first lined page. The colour of ink and the handwriting appear to change after the word "entirely" on the seventh line of the first page. Other treaties concluded at Fort Victoria, the Saanich Peninsula, and Fort Rupert, follow in the same register (the Nanaimo Treaty appears never to have been committed to paper). Douglas does not appear to have submitted a copy of the finalized agreement to his superiors, and the treaties were not published until the 1870s. Source: BCA MS-0772.

**25. Paul Kane, "Chee-a-clah, Head Chief of the Songees."** Chee-a-clah (Jeealthuc, King Freezie, Freezy) (c. 1817–1864), signatory to the Che-ko-nein Treaty, was one of the most famous signatories to the Vancouver Island treaties. This portrait made by Paul Kane in 1847 portrays this chief in traditional dress, although other images, including a photograph, suggest that he normally wore western dress, even a British naval uniform. Some have claimed that his father was a Hawaiian servant of the HBC, evidence that having roots in exogenous communities would not prevent a person from becoming prominent in Northwest Coast societies. For a discussion of this portrait and its subject, see MacLaren, *Paul*, 3: 111–15. Source: Paul Kane (1810–1871), *Chea-clach, Head Chief of the Clallam*, 1847, oil on paper, 12 1/4 × 9 7/8 inches (31.1 × 25.1 cm), Stark Museum of Art, Orange, Texas Bequest of H.J. Lutcher Stark, 1965, 31.78.200 SMA31.78.200.

26. **Paul Kane, "Ska-tel-sun."** Songhees chief, Skatelsun, one of thirty signatories to the Che-ko-nein Treaty, was one of the few Indigenous signatories for whom we have portraits. The notation misidentifying the subject as a "Cowlitz Indian," was made by archivist, John Russell Harper, not Kane. MacLaren, *Paul*, 1: 53; 3: 115–19. Source: Paul Kane (1810–1871), *Ska-tel-sun*, 1847, watercolour and pencil on paper, 5 3/16 × 4 1/4 inches (13.2 × 10.8 cm), Stark Museum of Art, Orange, Texas, Bequest of H.J. Lutcher Stark, 1965, 31.78.104.

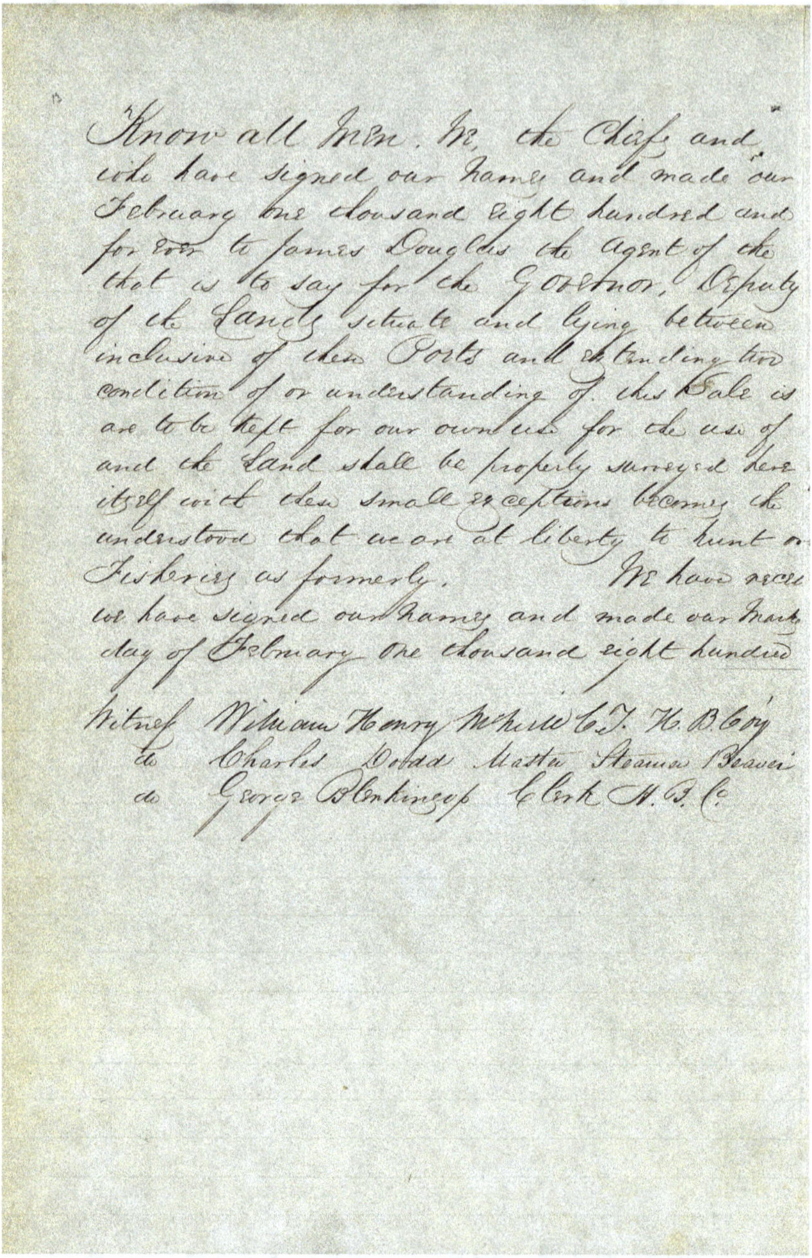

Know all Men. We, the Chiefs and
who have signed our Names and made our
February one thousand eight hundred and
for ever to James Douglas the Agent of the
that is to say for the Governor, Deputy
of the Lands situate and lying between
inclusive of these Ports and extending two
condition of or understanding of this Sale is
are to be kept for our own use for the use of
and the Land shall be properly surveyed here
itself with these small exceptions becomes the
understood that we are at liberty to hunt o
Fisheries as formerly. We have recei
we have signed our Names and made our Mark
day of February One thousand eight hundred

Witness William Henry McNeill C.T. H.B.Coy
do Charles Dodd Master Steamer Beaver
do George Blenkinsop Clerk H.B.Co

**27. The Quakeolth Treaty, 8 February 1851.** The layout of the two Fort Rupert treaties differs from the others in that each line of text of the treaties straddles two loose pages that were evidently later attached to pages of the register, suggesting that Douglas may not have taken the register to Fort

Rupert. There is no evidence to suggest that the Chiefs made their marks before the text was written. Douglas did not sign the treaty, although three witnesses did. Note that the Indigenous signatories marked the treaty with Os rather than Xes. Source: BCA MS MS-0772.

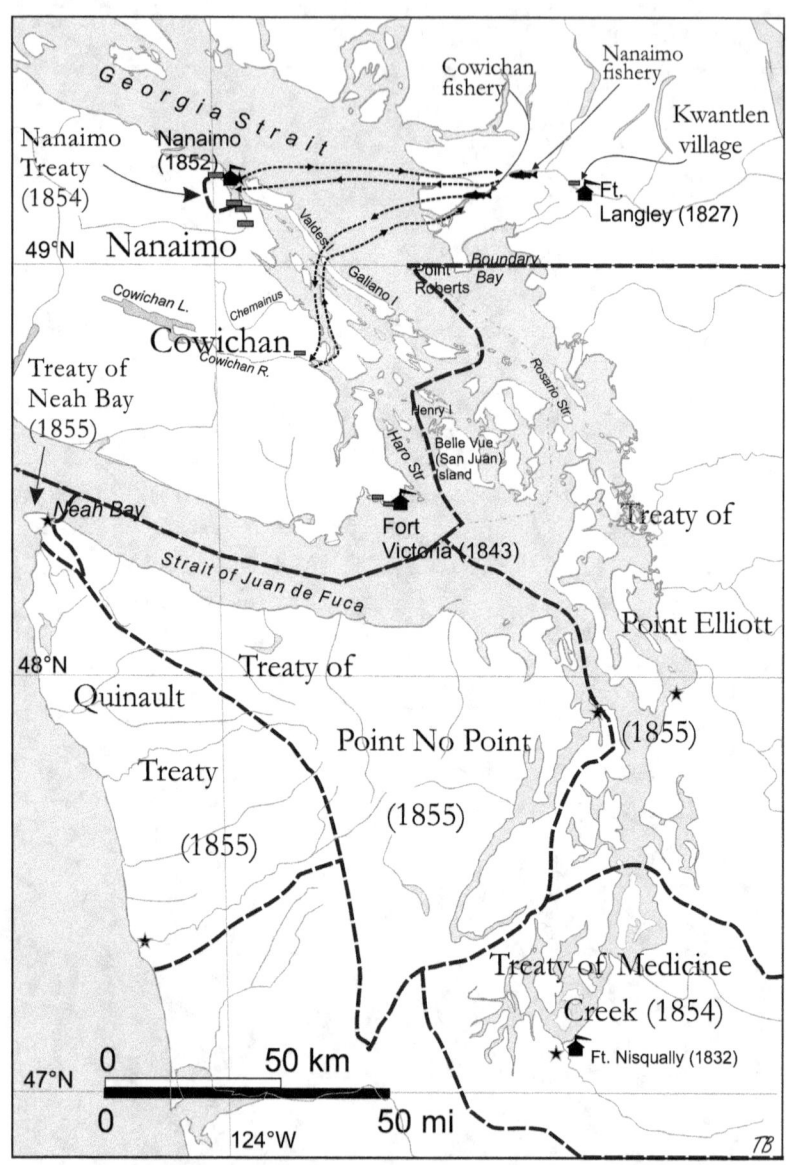

28. **The Nanaimo Treaty (1854) and the Stevens Treaties (1854–55).** In the mid-nineteenth century, the Nanaimo and Cowichan had important summer fisheries on the lower Fraser River (arrows show the typical seasonal rounds), outside the jurisdiction of the colony of Vancouver Island. James Douglas and the Nanaimo concluded a treaty on 24 December 1854 (apparently not written out), shortly before Isaac I. Stevens began negotiating treaties with villagers around Puget Sound and the Olympic Peninsula. Apparently, no treaty was ever reached with the Cowichan. Heavy dashed lines show the approximate boundaries of the treaty areas in the United States, and stars show the location of the negotiations for those treaties. Source: T. Binnema.

29. **Nanaimo in 1855.** The HBC post at Nanaimo was located near several populous Nanaimo villages. James Douglas instructed J.W. McKay to claim possession of the location at the same time that he ordered McKay to establish Nanaimo, but Douglas did not negotiate the Nanaimo Treaty until more than two years after the post was established. Source: BCA NA-40446.

"Know all men that we the Chiefs and people of the Sanitch Tribe who have signed our names and made our marks to this deed, on the 6th day of February 1852 do consent to surrender entirely and forever, to James Douglas the Agent of the Hudsons Bay Company, in Vancouvers Island that is to say for the Governor Deputy Governor and Committee of the same, the whole of the lands situate and lying between Mount Douglas and Cowitchen Head on the Canal de Arro and extending thence to the line running through the centre of Vancouvers Island north and south. The condition of, or understanding of this sale, is this, that our village sites and inclosed fields, are to be kept for our own use, for the use of our children, and for those who may follow after us, and the lands shall be properly surveyed hereafter; it is understood however, that the land itself, with these small exceptions, becomes the entire property of the white people for ever, it is also understood that we are at liberty to hunt over the unoccupied lands, and to carry on our fisheries as formerly. We have received as payment Forty one pounds thirteen shillings and four pence. In token whereof we have signed our names, and made our marks at Fort Victoria, on the seventh day of February. One thousand eight hundred and fifty two."

**30. The South Saanich Treaty, 7 February 1852.** The Saanich treaties resemble the Fort Victoria treaties in the manner in which they were inserted into the colony's land purchase register. Note that Governor James Douglas did not sign the treaty. Source: BCA MS-0772.

Cedar Will
to Neil Turnmoil
Cumber &c

Fort Victoria

| | | |
|---|---|---|
| Whut say mullet | his X mark | chief |
| Com ey uks | X | |
| Kwull Kolatchil | X | |
| Hav Yalunsil | X | |
| Till Kay mut | X | |
| Whey-chee ay | X | |
| Kul quey-tum | X | paid 50 Blankets |
| Ach chev mult | X | |
| Sty ytak | X | |
| Per l'au lus | X | |

Fort Victoria                Witness to signatures
7th Febr 1852                Joseph William MacKay
                             Clerk HB Co Service
                             Richd Golledge Clerk

**31. David Latasse.** David Latasse's 1934 account of the Vancouver Island treaties is the best known of all accounts, although Latasse was almost certainly not born when the treaties were concluded. This photograph was published in the *Victoria Daily Times* alongside his 1934 account of the treaties. Source: British Columbia Royal Museum PN11778.

The status of Ngāi Tahu lands was unsettled in 1848. Some settlers paid rent or tribute to local villagers and compensated them when their livestock destroyed unfenced potato fields, but others were less conciliatory. Thus, relationships between Ngāi Tahu and settlers varied, but Ngāi Tahu at Akaroa had already experienced some the advantages and disadvantages of the pākehā presence, and Shortland acknowledged that the Indigenous villagers were divided on the issue of selling their land. Shortland later claimed to have told some of those opposed that "the land they had not sold was still their own; and, if they did not choose to allow the Europeans to remain on it for the present, they might, of course, tell them so. There was plenty of land to be found in other parts of the country. But if the Pakeha left the place, whence would they procure clothes and tobacco?"[16] In his diary, Shortland wrote that Tiarora, a Ngāi Tahu leader at Akaroa, delivered a long speech about the "low Europeans" who were squatting in the district and "telling the natives that all the land belonged to the Queen and refusing to pay the natives for allowing them to land with their cows &c, or for cutting timber for shipbuilding &c." Shortland wrote that these Ngāi Tahu "were very anxious to know when the Gov$^r$ w$^d$ arrive to settle these matters – & were much dissatisfied at my saying perhaps 4 months – This business must be speedily arranged or else the tranquility of the place will be disturbed."[17]

While Shortland's account conveys the impression that the Ngāi Tahu's eagerness to see the governor was rooted in dissatisfaction, when Governor George Grey visited in February 1848, he accentuated the positive. He later reported that during his conversations, Ngāi Tahu at Akaroa "all acquiesced in the propriety of an immediate settlement of their claims" on the understanding that they would receive reserves and four annual payments. Grey estimated that based on the number of Ngāi Tahu (not the extent of the territory), £2,000 in four annual instalments "would be as large an amount as they could profitably spend, or as was likely to be of any real benefit to them." Accordingly, when he returned to Wellington, he orally informed the recently arrived Lieutenant Governor of New Munster, Edward John Eyre (1815–1901), of the terms under which a treaty should be made and promised to send the Surveyor-General, Charles W. Ligar, to negotiate the treaty.[18]

So, in a development that had rough parallels with what would happen at Vancouver Island a year later, when George Grey penned his letter of 15 May 1848 to Earl Grey that the Natives of New Zealand would "dispose, for a merely nominal consideration, of those lands which they do not actually require for their own subsistence," he did not tell the Colonial Secretary that he had already arranged for the largest land-cession treaty in New Zealand's history. Governor George Grey had decided to arrange a purchase of the entire territory, including "waste lands," not because he disagreed in principle with Earl Grey's instructions of 23 December 1846, but because he preferred a more pragmatic approach.

When he returned to Auckland, Grey discovered that Ligar could not be spared to negotiate the treaty, so he instructed Eyre to arrange the purchase, recommending Henry Tacy Kemp as either the commissioner or interpreter. Kemp was the editor of a recently published elementary introduction to te reo Māori.[19] Grey explained that the agreement should set aside reserves of "ample portions for their present and prospective wants; and then after the boundaries of these reserves have been marked, to purchase from the natives their right to the whole of the remainder of their claims to land in the Middle Island." He indicated that this provision, plus the promise of annual payments for four or five years "will remove all possibility of the occurrence of any future disputes or difficulties regarding native claims to land in that part of the Middle Island," but conveyed in the conclusion to his letter his sense of urgency: "It only remains for me to press upon you the necessity of having the service executed with as little delay as possible."[20]

On 25 April, Eyre, having retained Kemp's services, and having received a letter from William Wakefield regarding the territory that the NZC wished to acquire, and the amount it was willing to pay,[21] informed Kemp that "it will be your duty to reserve to the Natives ample portions of land for their present and prospective wants, and then, *after the boundaries of these reserves have been marked*, to purchase from the Natives their right to the whole of the remainder of their claims to land in the Middle Island. The payment to be made to the Natives must be an annual one, and be spread over a period of four or five years, as the only means of removing all possibility of the occurrence of any further disputes or difficulties regarding Native claims to land in that part of the Middle Island."[22] That Eyre sent Kemp to negotiate a land cession treaty with Ngāi Tahu in late autumn shows that Eyre took seriously Grey's instructions to complete the transaction as soon as possible.

May and June are normally cool and wet on the "cloud-collecting" Banks Peninsula, and the weather of June 1848 was not unusual.[23] Kemp left Wellington aboard HMS *Fly* on 29 April, perhaps hoping to complete his treaty before winter. However, beset with late autumn heavy weather, the *Fly* sought shelter, together with several other ships, at Akaroa for seventeen days in May. Departing again around 18 May, the *Fly* encountered further severe weather, even losing a man overboard, on the way to Otakou.[24] Once there the *Fly* transported sixteen chiefs from Otakou to Akaroa for the negotiations.[25]

After a stormy spell, the weather turned pleasant between 10 and 12 June and Kemp quickly negotiated with approximately 500 Ngāi Tahu at Akaroa for the purchase of an immense tract of land on the South Island. The negotiations were apparently difficult – at times it seemed they might fail – but by the morning of the twelfth, the parties had agreed. According to a newspaper report, the chiefs initially demanded £10,000, but settled for £2,000.[26] Oddly, the newspaper also reported that Ngāi Tahu also agreed that "there are no aboriginal inhabitants on the west coast of the island."[27] And the weather was dry enough on the morning of 12 June 1848 that Kemp could formally present the treaty to the chiefs outdoors, on the deck of the British man-of-war *Fly*. The treaty was engrossed on a large parchment (70 by 60 centimetres) (see figure 22). The text of the agreement, neatly written in sepia ink in te reo Māori, took up less than half of the parchment, leaving ample room below for the names of the signatories. Although Kemp signed the parchment in his capacity as "J.P. Commissioner," his name appears as the fifth of six witnesses, not as a party to the treaty.[28]

In subsequent years, there would be multiple conflicting accounts of what happened that morning, and the fact that Kemp himself left no formal report of the negotiations or signing ceremony leaves much in doubt, but it does appear that Kemp read the words of the treaty aloud in te reo Māori before the treaty was signed. Of the Ngāi Tahu adherents, sixteen apparently signed their names; the rest of the names – to a total of thirty-eight to forty – were probably written by the same hand as wrote the words of the treaty.[29] At least two of the signatories (Karetai and Te Whaikai Pōkene) were among the South Island leaders who had met with George Gipps and arranged purchases with William Wentworth in January 1840.[30] Thus was completed the largest single Crown-sanctioned land sale in the history of New Zealand. According to the treaty, Ngāi Tahu had ceded 20 million acres of land for £2,000 and several promises. Despite the vastness of the sale – over a hundred times the area ceded in the Fort Victoria treaties of 1850 – the Ngāi Tahu adherents to the treaty numbered well under 1,000, perhaps as low as 637, most of them concentrated in and near the Banks Peninsula.

Kemp was probably relieved to arrive in Wellington on Friday, 16 June 1848 after an absence of more than seven weeks.[31] Beginning on the Monday after he returned, he wrote letters to Eyre on three successive days. Eyre probably read them with growing unease, for they revealed the degree to which Kemp had deviated from Eyre's expectations. Historians of the Vancouver Island treaties should find Kemp's letters significant because they, and Eyre's responses to them, were published in the *Sessional Papers* from which the Governor and Committee of the HBC probably derived their copy of the deed. In his first letter, Kemp reported that he had concluded an agreement, but that the treaty's terms were not exactly as he had been instructed, "having thought it desirable in my dealings with the native sellers, to meet their wishes, without, I think, deviating from the general tenor of my instructions."[32] He promised to elaborate in a separate letter.

Kemp's first letter already hinted at aspects of this conduct that might have troubled Eyre, but his letter of the next day must have been alarming. On 20 June, Kemp made it clear that no surveys were conducted before the agreement was struck because Kemp "thought it better to leave the subject to be considered and decided upon between the Government and the Company, so soon as the survey of the district shall take place." Instead, "in obedience to the Lieutenant-Governor's instructions their pahs[33] and cultivations[34] have been guaranteed to them as expressed in the deed of sale; they are, generally speaking, of comparatively small extent."[35]

Although Kemp's second letter may have troubled Eyre far more than the first had, the third letter raised more red flags. On 21 June, Kemp explained that the Ngāi Tahu negotiators had convinced him to promise semi-annual payments instead of annual payments of £500. He explained that the "arrangement was proposed in the first instance by the chiefs themselves, in the presence and with the consent of their people, and one which, I believe, would give general satisfaction."[36]

Enclosed with the letter of 19 June, Kemp submitted the actual treaty parchment, written in te reo Māori, and the following English translation of the treaty, which will look familiar to anyone conversant with the written Vancouver Island treaties:

> Know all men. We the Chiefs and people of the tribe called the "Ngaitahu," who have signed our names & made our marks to this Deed on this 12th day of June 1848, do consent to surrender entirely & for ever to William Wakefield the Agent of the New Zealand Company in London, that is to say to the Directors of the same the whole of the lands situate on the line of Coast commencing at Kaiapoi recently sold by the Ngatitoa and the boundary of the Nelson Block, continuing from thence until it reaches Otakou, joining and following up the boundary line of the land sold to Mr. Symonds, striking inland from this (the east coast) until it reaches the

range of mountains called Kaihiku, and from thence in a straight line until it terminates in a point in the West Coast called Wakatipu-Waitai, or Milford Haven; the boundaries and size of the land sold are more particularly described in the map which has been made of the same. The condition of, or understanding of this sale is this, that our places of residence & plantations are to be kept for our own use, for the use of our Children, and to those who may follow after us, and when the land shall be properly surveyed hereafter, we leave to the Government the power and discretion of making us additional Reserves of land; it is understood, however, that the land itself, with these small exceptions, becomes the entire property of the white people for ever.

We receive as payment two thousand pounds (2000*l.*), to be paid to us in four instalments, that is to say, we have this day received 500*l.*, and we are to receive three other Instalments of 500*l.* each, making a total of 2000*l.*

In token whereof we have signed our names and made our marks at Akaroa on the 12th day of June 1848.

        (Signed)        (Here follow 40 Signatures)
                              *Witnesses*
        (Signed)        R.A. OLIVER, Commander H.M.S. "Fly,"
                              T. BULL, Lieutenant.
                              JOHN WATSON, Resident Magistrate.
                              CHARLES H. KETTLE, J.P., Principal Surveyor,
                              New Zealand Company.
                              H. TACY KEMP, J.P., Commissioner.
                              JAMES BRUCE, Settler
(True Translation)
        (Signed)        H. TACY KEMP.[37]

The map accompanying Kemp's documents identifies sixteen small Ngāi Tahu villages along the east coast of the South Island, and none along the west coast. Most of the villages apparently consisted of extended families of only ten to thirty people each, although a few settlements at Port Levy (260), Moeraki (185), Waikowaiti (135), and Otakou (100) reached a hundred people.

The total population, according to Kemp's map, was about 920 people, uncannily close to the 936 adherents to the Fort Victoria treaties of 1850.[38]

On 21 June, Edward Eyre, appalled by Kemp's conduct, had his secretary William Gisborne write Kemp to say that "His Excellency desires me to state that, upon perusing these documents, he has learnt with surprise and very great regret that you have altogether deviated from the instructions which were given you for your guidance, and have left unsettled the very points you were sent to adjust."[39] Eyre identified no fewer than five ways in which Kemp had departed from his instructions. In the first place, "it was never contemplated by Her Majesty's Government that the very few individuals within the limits referred to should be considered the owners or occupiers of that immense district." The letter explained that in a personal meeting before Kemp departed for the negotiations, Eyre had warned Kemp of "the error of acknowledging validity of title in the few resident Natives to vast tracts, the larger portion of which had probably never even been seen, and certainly never been made use of by them."[40] The Fort Victoria district was much smaller and more densely populated than the territory of the Kemp Deed, but Douglas deviated from the 17 December 1849 instructions given him in the same way that Kemp had deviated from Eyre's instructions.

Kemp's second deviation will also be of interest to the historians of Vancouver Island. Eyre reminded Kemp of his duty to have reserves surveyed before he executed his purchase, "yet, in referring to the map, or to the deed of sale, His Excellency cannot see a single Native reserve indicated or defined." The terms of the treaty, were, in Eyre's opinion, "as indefinite and unsatisfactory as could well have been proposed."[41] The Vancouver Island context was very different than it was at Akaroa. There were few settlers on Vancouver Island, and there was no surveyor there. However, the time lapse between the conclusion of the treaties and the surveys has left uncertainty in both cases about whether the government reserved the lands that the Indigenous signatories expected.

Eyre's third complaint was that Kemp, not having marked the reserves before the sale, also neglected to mark the reserves afterward. The fourth objection was that despite Eyre's instructions to arrange for payment to be made in annual instalments spread over four or five years "as the only means of removing the possibility of the occurrence of any further disputes or difficulties regarding Native claims to land in that part of the Middle Island," Kemp had arranged for the entire payment to be completed in semi-annual instalments over only two years.[42]

Eyre appears to have regarded the fifth deviation as the gravest. Eyre regarded as "a further still more extraordinary and not unimportant error" the fact Kemp's treaty stipulated that the land was conveyed to William Wakefield and the NZC, rather than to the Crown, mimicking the NZC deeds made out in 1839.[43] Considering the ruling in the Symonds's case, Kemp's error is odd, and Eyre's letter suggests that this fifth error "may probably entail upon the Government the necessity of sending down a Commissioner to have another deed of sale executed in a proper form."⁴⁴ Eyre also complained that "you have not defined the extents, so neither have you specified even the number of reserves which are to be set apart for the Natives."⁴⁵ Gisborne's letter concluded by stating that, because Kemp had "completely disregarded both the letter and spirit of the instructions given you for your guidance," the treaty "may hereafter prove the source of much difficulty, anxiety, and expense to the Government, to the New Zealand Company, and to the future settlers whom that body, on the faith of the late purchase, may be induced to send out."⁴⁶

While the Governor and Committee of the HBC did not have access to Eyre's 21 June 1848 letter to Kemp, Gisborne's subsequent report to George Grey was published in the *Sessional Papers* in 1849, and thus should have alerted the directors of the HBC to potential problems with Kemp's purchase document. In that report of 5 July 1848 Kemp's purported errors are described this way:

1st. The recognising native rights over the whole of the country lying between the given circuits.
2nd. The making a purchase without making a single reserve or in any way indicating the number, extent, or situation of the lands to be set apart as reserves.
3rd. The arrangement that the purchase money should be paid half-yearly instead of annually.
4th. The drawing of the deed of sale in a form which is not legally valid.⁴⁷

Admittedly, Eyre articulated Kemp's fourth "mistake" vaguely enough that the HBC directors might not have understood it, but they should not have missed how grave Eyre believed Kemp's errors were, for in this report published in the *British Parliamentary Papers*, Eyre proposed "to send down a new Commissioner, accompanied by a surveyor, for the purpose of defining and determining all the native reserves; and after the due completion of which, I propose that another and more formal deed should be executed by the natives, and the second instalment (which by that time would become due) be paid to them."⁴⁸

Expecting that Grey would be as upset as he was at Kemp's conduct, Eyre did not wait to receive Grey's response. On 2 August 1848, he commissioned Walter Mantell "to complete the negotiations connected with the purchase of certain districts of land in the Middle Island which were partially entered upon by Mr. Kemp in June last."⁴⁹ In a long letter, Eyre instructed Mantell to travel the entire ceded territory "seeing all the Natives or, at least, the principal men of each tribe between the limits mentioned; deciding upon and seeing marked distinctly on the ground the various reserves which you may consider necessary to be set apart for the use of the Natives."[50] He explained that it would be "necessary to have a new deed executed by the Natives conveying the lands to Her Majesty and her successors, instead of Colonel Wakefield or the directors of the New Zealand Company (which was the form adopted by Mr. Kemp), and the Natives should be informed of this, and an explanation given of the reason of the change."[51] Mantell departed aboard the *Fly* on Monday, 7 August 1848.[52]

If the Governor and Committee of the HBC did read the *Sessional Papers*, they may have been reassured by the fact that George Grey was far less worried about the validity of the Treaty of Akaroa than Eyre was. On 25 August 1848, George Grey wrote to Earl Grey that "although I regret Mr. Kemp should have departed from his instructions, I still do not view his proceedings in so unfavourable a light as the Lieutenant-Governor does, and I entertain no doubt that the transaction has been fairly and properly completed." In fact, he concluded by stating that he thought that "Her Majesty's Government may for all practical purposes regard all native claims to land in the Middle Island as now conclusively set at rest, with the exception of the portion of that island in the immediate neighbourhood of Foveaux Straits."[53]

George Grey was apparently so unconcerned about the Treaty of Akaroa that he sent Mantell revised instructions that reached him in October. Grey apparently believed that, notwithstanding the words on the page, Ngāi Tahu rights had been transferred to the Crown. His thinking must have been influenced by the strange May 1847 agreement by which the British government had granted the NZC a temporary right to pre-empt land in New Munster.[54]

The HBC Governor and Committee cannot have known in 1849 about what Mantell accomplished during his mission, but some of the evidence regarding his discussions and negotiations with Ngāi Tahu is nonetheless pertinent. Mantell's expedition was considerably longer than Kemp's of less than eight weeks. Between mid-August 1848 and late January 1849, Walter Mantell travelled through the eastern portions of the ceded territory and set out the reserves for each community, a process complicated by the fact that in some places "Europeans' houses and gardens" were interspersed with those of Ngāi Tahu. He made an extended journey through the ceded territory, conversing with the leaders of the various communities. He heard many complaints. At the pā of Kaiapoi, Ngāi Tahu complained that the Ngatitoa had been paid for lands that Ngāi Tahu claimed as theirs. Others complained that they had not received their first payments.[55]

Mantell found far fewer Ngāi Tahu than Kemp had estimated. He set aside reserves totalling about 6,359 acres for a population of about 637 Ngāi Tahu, conforming almost exactly to George Grey's instructions that he set aside 10 acres per person.[56] Several years after he concluded the agreements with Ngāi Tahu, Mantell claimed that he had made, on behalf of the Crown, additional oral promises not included in the written treaty. Mantell claimed that Eyre "impressed upon me the propriety of placing before the Natives the prospect of the great future advantages which the cession of their lands would bring them in schools, hospitals, and the paternal care of Her Majesty's Government; and, as I have before said, I found these promises of great use in my endeavours to break down their strong and most justifiable opposition to my first commission, and in facilitating the acquisition of my later purchases, adding to the Crown lands an area nearly as large as England."[57]

Many years later, in 1888, Mantell testified that "the Law officers of the Crown" had determined the deed "to be not worth the parchment it was written on,"[58] probably because it had stipulated that the land was conveyed to William Wakefield and the NZC, rather than the Crown. Mantell testified that a new deed was given to him (which he retained in his possession in 1888), written in English, but that, "before I got down as far as Waikouaiti contrary instructions were given that the old deed was to be adhered to."[59] Given that Mantell arrived at Waikouaiti around the end of October, the contrary instructions must have been contained in revised instructions George Grey sent to Mantell, for after Mantell returned without a new deed, Eyre nevertheless praised "the very careful and zealous manner in which Mr. Mantell has discharged the difficult and laborious task assigned to him."[60]

While Walter Mantell was apparently instructed not to replace the 1848 treaty with another stipulating that the land was conveyed to the Crown, not to William Wakefield and the NZC, all the subsequent treaties on the South Island stipulated that the land was surrendered to "Her Majesty the Queen of Great Britain."[61]

In 1888, Mantell was asked "was it not the case that he [Kemp] was sent down, not to buy that [Canterbury] block, the title of the Natives to which the Government did not recognize, seeing that the land had never been traversed and much of it had not even been seen by the Natives – was it not the case that he was instructed simply to buy the Native claims within that block?" Mantell's response is revealing: "That ... was the theory of the Native land purchase in the Middle Island at that time. ... Practically, however, the Government recognised the Native title as extending over the whole block."[62]

On 10 February 1849, George Grey reported to Earl Grey regarding the "extinction of the native title to the tract of land in the Middle Island lying between the block of land purchased for the Nelson settlement and the block purchased for the Otago settlement" that "I think it will be a source of great satisfaction to your Lordship to find that so large a tract of country of the most fertile description is thus unrestrictedly open to British enterprise, without any possibility of any of those embarrassing questions arising in relation to it between the European and native population in reference to titles to land, which have been a source of such loss and embarrassment to the settlers in the Northern Island."[63]

Grey was too optimistic (and Eyre prescient) about the chances of future disputes. In later years, Ngāi Tahu complained that their treaty had been illegitimate. In 1874, some of their leaders submitted a petition stating that "when Kemp landed at Akaroa and demanded the cession of the land from Kaiapoi to Otago the Natives held out for a fair return for that vast extent of territory. When Kemp got tired of the delay he said, 'If you do not consent to this £2,000 I shall hand over the money to Ngatitoa (Rauparaha's tribe); and if you still delay to consent, then soldiers will be sent to clear the land for the pakehas.'"[64] Anticipating that they would be criticized for not raising the complaints earlier, they responded "when these land-transactions took place our chiefs were scarcely able to read written language; they were often too ready to consent their names to be signed under writings the contents of which were either in part or totally absent from their minds. Judge yourselves, the honourable members of Parliament, who listen to our complaints in this petition: Had the eyes of these our chiefs been open in those days, would they have consented to part with all the heritage that God has given them and their future offspring and descendants – all this vast territory – for the crumbs that fell from the whiteman's table – for this £2,000 odd?"[65] In 1876, H.K. Taiaroa submitted a statement that Kemp had not intimidated their leaders, but plied them with alcohol, and deceived them about the amount to be paid and the extent of the territory to be ceded.[66]

In 1868 the Native Land Court accepted Ngāi Tahu's claim that the translation of "mahinga kai" as "plantations," or "cultivations" was too narrow. Thus, the court added "pipi grounds,[67] eel-weirs, and fisheries," but rejected the claim that the term also included "the right of fishing, catching birds and rats, procuring berries and fern-root over any portion of the lands within the block."[68]

Thus, the text of the Treaty of Akaroa was not the most promising or auspicious choice for the Governor and Committee of the HBC to select as the basis for the Vancouver Island treaties. Given the evidence available to the Governor and Committee of the controversy around the treaty, the HBC should have consulted with the Colonial Office before using the document. Had the Colonial Office been involved in drafting template language for the Vancouver Island treaties, the treaties certainly would have looked different than they did. Because they did not, some of the idiosyncrasies of the Treaty of Akaroa influenced the contents of the written versions of the Vancouver Island Treaties.

Douglas's 16 May 1850 report of the oral terms negotiated at Fort Victoria arrived at the HBC London offices in early August.[69] The Governor and Committee responded in a long letter of 16 August 1850. The committee's response to Douglas was much more positive than Eyre's response to Kemp:

> The Governor and Committee very much approve of the measures you have taken in respect of the lands claimed by the Natives. You will receive herewith the form of a Contract or Deed of Conveyance to be used on future occasions when lands are to be surrendered to the Company by the Native Tribes. It is a Copy with hardly any alteration of the Agreement adopted by the New Zealand Company in their transactions of a similar Kind with the natives there.[70]

The template agreement enclosed with the letter of 16 August, entitled "Form of Agreement for Purchases of Land from Natives of Vancouver's Island" was, as Barclay indicated, only slightly different than Kemp's English translation of the Treaty of Akaroa as published in the *Sessional Papers* of 1849, stripped of its specific tribal name, date, geographical description, and payment amount:

> Know all Men, We, the Chiefs and People of the Tribe called _____ who have signed our names and made our marks to this Deed on the _____ day of _____ one Thousand Eight hundred and _____ do consent to surrender Entirely and for Ever to James Douglas the Agent of the Hudson's Bay Company in Vancouver's Island, that is to say, for the Governor Deputy Governor and Committee of the same the whole of the lands situate and lying between _____
> 
> The condition of our understanding of this sale is this that our village sites and Enclosed Fields are to be Kept for our own use, for the use of our Children, and for those who may follow after us; and the lands shall be properly surveyed hereafter; it is understood however that the land itself, with these small Exceptions becomes the entire property of the White

people for Ever; it is also understood that we are at liberty to hunt over the unoccupied lands, and carry on our fisheries as formerly.

We have received as payment _____ In token whereof we have signed our names and made our marks at _____on the _____ day of One thousand Eight hundred and _____

(here follow the Indian Signatures)

Witnesses   )
                )[71]

Given that the wording of the template document is at odds with the position that the Indigenous people owned only the lands that they occupied, it appears to represent the Governor and Committee's explicit endorsement of Douglas's decision to purchase "the whole of their lands." The Governor and Committee also described the document as a deed of conveyance, not a treaty.

That the Governor and Committee replaced the stipulation that Ngāi Tahu were surrendering their land to William Wakefield and the NZC with a parallel stipulation that the Indigenous peoples of Vancouver Island were surrendering their rights to James Douglas and the HBC, rather than "Her Majesty the Queen of Great Britain," suggests either that the Governor and Committee were unaware of the controversy over the Treaty of Akaroa, or judged, even after reading the documents, that Kemp had acted appropriately. That was an error on the part of the HBC that has caused some confusion in Canada.[72]

In a second change, the HBC abbreviated "& when the lands shall be properly surveyed hereafter, we leave to the Government the power & discretion of making us additional Reserves of land," to something shorter and more ambiguous: "and the lands shall be properly surveyed hereafter." This change is also noteworthy because the directors of the HBC could have known that Eyre objected to the provision in the Treaty of Akaroa and criticized Kemp for neglecting to survey the reserves at the time of the negotiations. The directors did not explain the change, but the fact that Vancouver Island in 1850 had virtually no settlers and extremely little capacity to carry out surveys probably explains it.[73]

The directors made another change to a provision in the Treaty of Akaroa that had dismayed Eyre. Eyre disapproved of Kemp's yielding to Ngāi Tahu's demand to complete the payments for the lands in two years. Simpson and Douglas had both preferred annual payments on Vancouver Island, but the directors appear not only to have accepted Douglas's assertion that he had had to concede in favour of a one-time payment, but also to have assumed that he would do so in subsequent treaties.

Another change in the document, replacing "places of residence & plantations" with "our village sites and Enclosed Fields," is easy to explain. The Governor and Committee decided to quote from Douglas's 16 May 1850 description of the oral terms of the treaties. The addition of the clause that "it is also understood that we are at liberty to hunt over the unoccupied lands, and carry on our fisheries as formerly," absent in the Treaty of Akaroa, is in keeping with the intentions expressed in the correspondence between Douglas and the Governor and Committee, although, interestingly, the Governor and Committee chose in this instance to condense "when they were the sole occupants of the country" from Douglas's report, to "as formerly." The directors did not explain why they decided to deviate somewhat from Douglas's report of the oral terms of the agreement with vaguer language on the right of fisheries. Given that the directors of the company had quoted Douglas's language on village sites and enclosed fields, we must conclude that they preferred their language (perhaps for its brevity) over Douglas's in this case.

The HBC directors may have felt free to alter the language on fishing rights because they did not anticipate that Douglas would simply use the unaltered template for the treaties he had already concluded. They had, after all, instructed him that the template was "to be used on future occasions," and correspondence sent to Douglas at the same time makes it clear that the directors were anxious to have an agreement concluded at the coalfields as well.

Kemp had signed the Treaty of Akaroa as the fifth of six witnesses, a fact of which Douglas was unaware. Drawing upon the treaty as template, the HBC's directors did not indicate that they wanted Douglas to sign the treaty. Neither did they ever inform him in what capacity he was authorized either to sign or conclude the treaties. Had they originally thought that he might conclude the treaties before Richard Blanshard took on the official duties as Governor, or had the directors thought of him as a special treaty commissioner, specially empowered by the company to negotiate the treaties? They did not say.

Douglas subsequently noted that he received the letter of 16 August 1850 (with the template treaty) on 15 November 1850.[74] Douglas then used that template, unchanged, for the written version of the agreements he had concluded orally in the previous April and May. That fact leads to the inescapable conclusion that Douglas's written report of the oral treaties and written treaties were different. The fact that the Governor and Committee had modified portions of the treaty suggests that the written provisions relating to the "village sites and enclosed fields" were brought into line with those of Douglas's report of the oral agreements. However, the wording of the provisions relating to the fishing rights was different in ways that could be important. Douglas had the option, at least for the treaties already concluded, to replace the Governor and Committee's wording with that of his own report. He did not explain why he did not do so. That he did not do so reinforces the impression that Douglas did not consider the treaty process to be as significant as later generations would. Perhaps he was untroubled by the new wording because he considered the words supplied by the Governor and Committee to be reconcilable with or broader than the oral agreement.

From Douglas's report of 16 May, the Governor and Committee must have assumed that Douglas concluded three treaties or, based on the wording of the last paragraph of Douglas's report, perhaps only one. But Douglas produced nine written treaties (figure 23). From the negotiations with the Songhees he produced six written treaties, with the Klallam two, and with the Sooke one (see figure 24). In fact, the nine written treaties probably accurately reflect the number of agreements Douglas concluded in April and May. The Fort Victoria journal entry of 29 April that indicated that ten "proprietors" were paid for their land on that day fits approximately with the number of eleven signatories to the Teechamitsa treaty, the only one dated 29 April.[75]

One of the treaties with the Tlallum (Ka-Ky-ookan) notes that they were "ancient possessors of this District, and their only surviving heirs – about 26 in number." That suggests that, contrary to the scholarly literature, the Klallam presence in the district, rather than being new in 1850, was old but waning.[76]

Especially since the "tribes" identified in the treaties do not conform to any known historical tribes or extended families among these communities, they have generated some scholarly discussion. In 1969, Wilson Duff argued that the treaties were based on "ethnographic absurdities." He argued that households, not "tribes," owned houses and fishing sites, and the Songhees generally, not extended families, owned territories.[77] It is unlikely, however, that the proposal to treat separately with the leaders of nine extended families, rather than with larger groups, originated with Douglas. The fact that nine written treaties were produced must, notwithstanding the "ethnographic absurdities," reflect socio-political realities among the signatory communities, even if those are no deeper than the possibility that each of the extended families and their leaders wanted to ensure that Douglas distributed the payment directly to each extended family's leadership (see figure 25, and figure 26). Perhaps disputes in New Zealand offer a hint. When Walter Mantell visited the Canterbury block in 1848–49, he heard complaints from more remote Ngāi Tahu villagers that they had not received from Ngāi Tahu chiefs any portion of the first payment. Given that the Vancouver

Island treaty documents specifically mention the amount to be paid to each extended family, and that the leaders apparently came in separately to be paid, leaders' concerns about getting their share may have led them to demand their own allotments. The straight-line boundaries between family territories must have been fictions, but they were probably agreed-upon fictions.[78] The nine treaties may reflect features of social and political organization among the Coast Salish when that organization was changing significantly and rapidly. Although depopulation and consolidation of communities were already under way well before 1850 among the Coast Salish, the written treaties suggest that the extended families of Songhees, Klallam, and Sooke may still have been more separate and autonomous than they were in the late nineteenth and early twentieth centuries, when the social structure of these communities was recorded systematically for the first time.[79] In addition, Douglas may have preferred negotiating agreements with extended families to avoid any arrangement that might have unified the villagers of the region.[80] Two years after concluding the Fort Victoria treaties, and shortly after concluding the Saanich Peninsula treaties, Douglas advised Earl Grey that:

> It is obviously the interest and should be the constant study of this Government, to avoid every course that may directly or indirectly lead to dissension with the powerful Indian Tribes inhabiting Vancouver's Island, whose numbers are estimated at 20,000 including women and children.
> They fortunately do not all speak the same language, and have their sectional interests and disputes, which keep them, divided, and in a measure hostile to each other; but notwithstanding those intestine [internecine] discords, their friendship is valuable and their opposition would prove a formidable obstacle to the progress of an infant Colony.[81]

Consistent with long-standing Colonial Office policies, Herman Merivale wrote a note on this letter stating that "to give orders from hence as to the conduct to be observed towards Indians in Vancouver's Island seems rather unlikely to be of much service. If the colony is to maintain itself, as was the condition of its foundation, the local government must needs be left very much to its discretion as to dealings with the natives in the immediate neighborhood of the settled parts."[82]

The multiple Vancouver Island treaties, concluded with extended families rather than larger groupings, may have respected the political realities then prevailing among the Salish of southeastern Vancouver Island. They also did nothing towards the formation of larger alliances that Douglas had no interest in encouraging.

The unusual way in which Douglas obtained marks on "a blank sheet" with the expressed intent to copy the text afterwards, combined with the fact that the provisions in the written text, particularly in connection with the provision relating to fishing rights, differ from the provision as explained in Douglas's report, raises the question whether Douglas ever explained the written treaty language to the signatories. We can probably never know the answer. The evidence, however, suggests that in late April 1850, Douglas took a new, plain, foolscap-sized, bound volume, typical of those used for other purposes in the HBC, entitled it "Register of Land purchases from Indians," and used it over the next days to record a brief summary of the agreements and the names and marks of the signatories.[83] The "blank sheet" to which Douglas referred in his report probably corresponds to the pages of the bound book that is preserved today. Apparently on the top of the unnumbered pages 6, 9, 12, 15, 18, 22, 24, and 27, he wrote a description of the territories that each "tribe" (except for the Teechamitsa) agreed to surrender, and towards the bottom of the unnumbered pages 4, 7, 11, 14, 17, 20–21, 23, 26, and 28, he had the chiefs of the respective communities make their marks.[84] He thus typically left two or three intervening pages into which he intended to copy the eventual treaty text. It appears that when the template treaty arrived in November, Douglas had the treaty text inserted into the book in such a way as to leave relatively little room (between zero and six empty lines) between the end of the treaty text and the names of the signatories and witnesses, even though that meant that the treaty text sometimes began in the bottom third of a page.[85]

The near certainty that Douglas had the leaders make their marks in the register in April and May 1850, combined with the fact that the terms of each treaty were identical, except for the immediate compensation offered to the different families, suggests that the six written treaties with the Songhees families could be thought of as one Songhees treaty, as Douglas implied in his report. At any rate, there is no evidence that Douglas ever informed anyone in London that he negotiated more than three treaties in 1850. The marks on these treaties are sufficiently uniform to suggest that the marks were made with one hand and that the Indigenous "signatories" did not actually make the marks, but merely "touched the pen." Although some scholars have found the practice suspicious, treaty commissioners (and notaries) followed that practice – without hiding it – in other contexts in the United States, Canada, and New Zealand, including in the Treaty of Akaroa. It was a long-standing practice also followed by notaries who assisted people unable to provide a signature.[86]

A feature of the template treaty (and thus of the written versions of the Fort Victoria treaties) typical of New Zealand agreements, but atypical of North American treaties, is the absence of any stipulation that persons representing both parties to the transaction should sign as adherents to the treaty. For example, in the Selkirk Treaty, Lord Selkirk's signature appears first, after which the marks of five Indigenous leaders appear. Six witnesses and the interpreter signed separately. In the Robinson-Huron and Robinson-Superior Treaties concluded in Upper Canada in September 1850, W.B. Robinson's signature appears before the marks of the Indigenous signatories and separate from the signatures of the witnesses. In the Numbered Treaties (and adhesions to those treaties) concluded in the 1870s, the Crown's representatives would also indicate the capacities in which they functioned, whether as Indian Commissioner, Lieutenant Governor, or Indian Agent. Kemp signed the Treaty of Akaroa as the fifth of six witnesses, although he did identify his position as "J.P. Commissioner." The Governor and Committee did not instruct Douglas to sign the document, and it either did not occur to Douglas to sign the document, or Douglas decided not to sign it, either as a party to the agreement or as a witness. We would have a much better insight into Douglas's mind if he had signed the document as a party to the document, and had indicated in what capacity he functioned when he made the agreement. Given that Douglas had resigned his position as interim Governor of Vancouver Island and that Richard Blanshard had already assumed the governorship of the colony, Margaret Ormsby's conclusion must be correct: Douglas negotiated the Fort Victoria treaties in his capacity as Agent of the HBC.[87]

In contrast to the strategy of Lord Selkirk in 1817, Douglas appears to have made no effort to add weight to the Fort Victoria treaties by having an agent of the Crown witness them. Roderick Finlayson and Joseph William McKay signed as witnesses to the first treaty, and McKay and "Alfred Robson Benson, M.R.C.S.L. [Member Royal College of Surgeons, London]" witnessed the next six. All witnesses were employees of the HBC. The last two treaties were not witnessed by any persons. No person independent of the HBC signed, even as a witness, even though Governor Richard Blanshard was then at Fort Victoria, and the Reverend Robert John Staines, Anglican priest, had arrived in the colony in March 1849.[88]

The Colonial Office had no role in the treaty-making process on Vancouver Island in April and May of 1850. Indeed, personnel in the Colonial Office did not know about the treaties at all until well into 1851 and were then informed only incidentally by Blanshard. Moreover, when those in the Colonial Office learned about the treaties in 1851, they showed no interest in learning the contents of those treaties.

Blanshard arrived at Fort Victoria on 10 March 1850 aboard the *Driver*.[89] No home being yet ready for him in Fort Victoria, Blanshard then immediately visited Fort Rupert, but returned to Fort Victoria in early April.[90] Blanshard's commission and instructions from the Colonial Office did not mention Indigenous affairs. Moreover, like Hobson and FitzRoy in New Zealand, having no funds to pay for any treaties, Blanshard could not have used his own discretion to negotiate treaties. James Douglas, by contrast, had access to the funds of the HBC.

In his letters to London before and after the Fort Victoria treaties were concluded, Blanshard did not address the issue of Indigenous title. In his first letter to Earl Grey, he noted only that William McNeill, "who is considered to be better acquainted with the Indian population than any other person," estimated that the Indigenous population of Vancouver Island at ten thousand, and steadily diminishing. He also explained that a prohibition on the sale of alcohol to Indians was strictly enforced.[91] When Blanshard sent his next letter to Earl Grey, on 15 June, he indicated that, from his perspective, "nothing of importance has since [since 8 April, that is] occurred in the colony."[92] He was either unaware that Douglas had negotiated treaties, or he did not consider them important. The fact that he did not sign as a witness to any of the treaties – a function he was ideally suited for – raises the distinct possibility that he was not aware of the negotiations. He did note that the HBC had begun to survey lands in the Fort Victoria District, which they claimed for the company and "for the Puget Sound Agricultural Association, the Hudson Bay company under another name, for the Association has no real existence."[93] On 10 July 1850, having visited Fort Rupert and observed circumstances at Fort Victoria, Blanshard reported on his first impressions of the HBC. He informed Earl Grey that the rumours of the HBC's "barbarous treatment of the Indian population" were "entirely without foundation." As far as he could tell, "they are always treated with the greatest consideration, far greater than the white labourers and in many instances are allowed liberties and impunities in the Hudson's bay company's establishments that I regard as extremely unsafe. No liquor is given them by the Company on any pretense but it is impossible to prevent their obtaining it from the merchant vessels that visit the coast."[94]

Blanshard finally mentioned the Fort Victoria treaties to the Colonial Secretary in April 1851 when he complained to Earl Grey about the way the HBC was invoicing the colony. In late January or early February, Douglas submitted to Governor Richard Blanshard a voucher listing the expenditures of the HBC on behalf of the colony of Vancouver Island. These expenditures included "Payments to Indians for purchase of Lands" amounting to $2,130.00 (about £450).[95] Douglas explained that those expenditures were "valued at our Cash Tariff, which is over 200 per Cent on the London cost, if valued at the District Transfer price 33⅓ per Cent on the London Cost, these charges would be … 150.3.4."[96] In other words, Douglas was proposing that the government reimburse the HBC at the rate that reflected what the company could charge non-Indigenous people during the inflationary times of the California gold rush rather than the rate it charged Indigenous people or its own servants. Understandably, Blanshard balked at what he considered to be an inflated claim for reimbursement.

It was probably in connection with Douglas's voucher that personnel in the Colonial Office first learned that the HBC was negotiating purchases from the Indigenous people of Vancouver Island. In November 1850, Blanshard had submitted his resignation as Governor of the colony, citing his failing health and the high prices the HBC charged him for his purchases.[97] Then, on 12 February 1851, Blanshard wrote to Earl Grey to explain that Douglas had presented him with a voucher "for goods paid to Indians to extinguish their title to the land about Victoria and Soke harbours, the remainder also for goods paid also [sic] to Indians for work done for the colony, provisions, and ammunition for the same Indians."[98] In Blanshard's opinion, Douglas badly inflated the cost of the treaties. That was relevant to the Colonial Office because the charter of the colony of Vancouver Island stipulated that the British Government would reimburse the HBC for legitimate colonial expenses when the British Government revoked the HBC's jurisdiction over the colony, something that HBC anticipated would happen at the fifth anniversary of the charter in January 1854. When he forwarded the voucher, Blanshard appended a note protesting that "the balance shall not be considered a true one."[99]

When Blanshard's report arrived in London in late spring, the Colonial Office submitted extracts of Blanshard's letter to the HBC, and asked Pelly to comment. Pelly may, in fact, have been in the dark at the time. Pelly chose to stonewall the Colonial Secretary by replying that "as Mr Blanshard has resigned the Office of Governor of Vancouver's Island, the Hudson's Bay Company do not consider it necessary to make any remarks on the Extracts referred to, nor indeed do they think it fully within the province of the Governor to inquire into the transactions between the Company and the Natives with respect to the extinction of the Titles of the latter to their lands."[100]

Pelly's high-handed and evasive response to Earl Grey's reasonable query raised red flags in the Colonial Office. Herman Merivale wrote a memorandum to Hawes on the letter, stating that "Govr Blanshard therefore seems to have been quite right, & I do not understand the tone adopted by the Co. in the present letter. … It is plain that his vouchers of sums expended by the Company cannot be taken by Government as authentic & binding."[101] However, the correspondence highlighted a difficulty that he admitted had not occurred to him earlier: that appointing an employee of the HBC as Governor of the colony had been a mistake.

Benjamin Hawes amplified Merivale's point by adding: "We are now apparently in the hands of the H.B.C. entirely." It may seem odd today that personnel in the Colonial Office did not instantly perceive that the conflict of interest into which James Douglas had already been placed would be exacerbated if he were appointed Governor of the colony of Vancouver Island, but by June 1851, it was too late; Douglas's commission had been on its way to Douglas on Vancouver Island since 19 May. Had this exchange occurred before Douglas's appointment, the Colonial Office might have understood that it was imprudent that the HBC's agent at Vancouver Island should be appointed Governor of the colony of Vancouver Island.

The unsatisfactory response prompted Benjamin Hawes, at Herman Merivale's suggestion and Earl Grey's direction, to write an indignant letter in return, stating that, in light of the fact that the government would be obligated to repay legitimate expenses, "an account of this description could not be properly vouched by the Governor's Signature unless he had ascertained that the sums specified in it were actually expended, as his signature might be hereafter referred to as authenticating it." The same letter, however, concluded by reassuring the company that Earl Grey "is far from wishing that any unnecessary interference should take place with the proceedings of the Company in the acquisition of land from the natives."[102]

In the context of the immediate controversy over billing rates, the significance of the last sentence might be lost. Earl Grey did not criticize the HBC for failing to inform him of the purchase, and did not demand to see the treaties. Had Grey done no more than examine them, he should have recognized them as based on H.T. Kemp's controversial purchase on the South Island of New Zealand. He might not have been troubled by the Vancouver Island treaties, but he almost certainly would have suggested that future treaties stipulate that the land was being conveyed to "Her Majesty the Queen of Great Britain."

Earl Grey's indifference to the Vancouver Island treaties might seem consistent with the memorandum of 1849 that it was "more safe to leave this matter to the company," but given Earl Grey's own knowledge that injudicious proceedings might come to haunt the government in London, it is extraordinary that he signalled a preference to reside in wilful ignorance about the company's treaty making. It appears that everyone in the HBC was happy to oblige.

# 10 The Fort Rupert Treaties of 1850 and 1851

Unlike at Fort Vancouver, Fort Langley, Nisqually, and Fort Victoria, the HBC occupied little land at Fort Rupert. The climate and land were not conducive to agriculture or pastoralism. It has been noted that the Kwakiutl at Nahwitti and elsewhere had been asking the HBC to establish a post in their territories since the 1830s, and that Sebassa had directed his attacks on northern Vancouver Island after Fort McLoughlin was established. However, the HBC established Fort Rupert only in 1849, to exploit the coal resources in the vicinity.[1] And the Kwakiutl welcomed the establishment of the post as much as the Nahwitti probably regretted it. In early September 1849, James Douglas reported that the defences of the fort had been completed and "most friendly relations have been established with the natives who without being made acquainted with our future plans are exceedingly useful in getting out coal, of which there was 750 tons ready for shipment, in the beginning of last month, so that no disappointment is apprehended in providing the thousand tons we agreed to furnish Captain Stout, Agent of the Mail Steam Company, for the Current year."[2] In November 1850, Douglas reported to London that a small garden of about three acres provided potatoes, cabbages, and greens to the fort's denizens, although he did not then mention Blenkinsop's Garden Treaty.[3]

Some of the dynamics of village consolidation at Fort Rupert are known.[4] In 1862 George Henry Richards, who was employed to survey the coast of Vancouver Island, noted that "there are 4 tribes at Rupert. They used formerly to live at separate villages, but have been attracted here by the nearness of the fort, and the village is the most extensive one I have seen."[5] The village consolidation and forces related to the fur trade appear to have unleashed significant changes in Kwakiutl society. Philip Drucker, who carried out fieldwork in the early 1930s, argued that the consolidation of villages sparked rivalries among chiefs because "the chiefs of the newly organized Fort Rupert Confederacy had no precedents on which to base the relative rankings of the chiefs of the several tribes. This fact led them to initiate a series of potlatches in which certain of them asserted their claims to particular places – first, second, third, or fourth, and so on – in the consolidated precedence list."[6] According to Drucker, the "nouveau riche" that emerged from the fur trade economy also led to the creation of a new titled institution of "Eagle." During gift-giving rituals, Eagles received their gifts, even before the highest-ranking chief did. He explained that "most of these Eagles were not chiefs at all, but were men of intermediate or even common status who through industry or clever trading amassed great quantities of material wealth. Some of them, in addition, were backed by certain chiefs who recognized them as potential tools to assist in the downfall of some high-ranking rival."[7]

The ability of commoners to pursue new avenues of wealth accumulation undermined the advantages that hereditary titleholders enjoyed.[8] On the other hand, the fur trade also allowed traditional elites to amass greater wealth and power, and the hereditary titleholders did not immediately lose control over the food procurement sites. In sum, Fort Rupert apparently significantly destabilized long-standing class relations in the region, but documents do not describe the dynamics in detail.

The Fort Rupert villagers acted as traders, labourers, and suppliers of coal. They did not mine during the cold winter months (the winter of 1849–50 being exceptionally cold and snowy), but they supplied almost all of the coal gathered at Fort Rupert between 1849 and 1854, most of that coal coming from surface deposits at Suquash, located about 15 kilometres southeast of Fort Rupert.[9] Fear of enemy attack also deterred the Kwakiutl. The Fort Rupert journal entry for 23 April 1850 states that the Kwakiutl "appear to be in no hurry to start for coals probably in the course of 20 days or so they may go – the fear of being attacked by their enemies however may keep them at home which will be a bad job for us."[10]

Ironically, opportunities to provide paid labour may have discouraged the villagers from mining. The traders began hiring villagers as day labourers almost immediately after they arrived.[11] Thereafter traders often engaged Indigenous people – sometimes hundreds of them at a time – to perform a range of tasks, including cutting pickets, hauling timber, clearing stumps and burning waste wood, sawing lumber, levelling ground, and hauling stones and clay.[12] In fact, on 23 November 1849 the journal states that "the Indians do two thirds of our work. Unless it rains we have usually from 50 to 100 Indians employed daily at the above jobs."[13] The amount of paid labour available to the villagers appears to have discouraged them even from bringing in fur or provisions. George Blenkinsop, the writer of the journal remarked on 10 October: "We neither get furs or provisions the immense quantity of property paid them for labor &c will always prove an obstacle to getting either of these Articles. Indian hauling home the wood squared for the Store."[14]

Extracting coal grew increasingly toilsome as the most accessible beds of coal were exhausted. After the Scottish miners left Fort Rupert in the summer of 1850, the HBC's reliance on the villagers increased. In August 1850, Douglas expressed his doubts that, with labour costs ballooning because of the California gold rush, coal could be profitably mined by Europeans at Fort Rupert.[15] In early 1851, Blenkinsop reported that the Kwakiutl at Fort Rupert "are a tractable industrious race, and I have strong hopes of getting them, this spring to cultivate the ground, and grow Potatoes for the use of the Establishment, which will tend, to lessen our Expences, at present so very heavy."[16]

Fort Rupert offered protection. Before 1849, the Kwakiutl were relatively at a disadvantage compared with enemies on the outer coast. Because of their inferior access to the trade, they were economically and militarily weaker than some of their rivals. Duncan Finlayson's warning about the coal sources – that without the establishment of an HBC fort anyone sent to work the coal "would be exposed to the attacks of other tribes who frequent this spot"– appears to be rooted in that understanding. Under such conditions, militarily vulnerable groups tended to suffer depopulation caused by deaths and enslavement in warfare.[17] The wealth and security the Kwakiutl obtained by having Fort Rupert established nearby, and their response to their privileged position, appear to have made them a target of their neighbours. In early 1851, Blenkinsop noted that "the large quantity of Property thrown into their hands have made the Quakeolths impudent to their neighbours, who, on their side, feel envious, and so disturbances soon arise and often end in bloodshed. Several serious ones occurred last summer which put a stop to their working the Coals, and procuring either Furs or Provisions."[18]

After James Douglas concluded the Fort Victoria treaties in April and May 1850, the Governor and Committee of the HBC remained preoccupied with the Fort Rupert coalfields. In their long letter of 16 August

1850, they did not indicate until the twelfth paragraph that they approved of the Fort Victoria treaties. The three paragraphs preceding their approval all pertained to the coalfields in the vicinity of Fort Rupert.[19] Moreover, in another letter, written on 23 August 1850 but sent in the same packet as the letter of 16 August 1850, Barclay wrote that "the Governor & Committee consider it highly desirable that no time should be lost in purchasing from the Natives the land in the neighbourhood of Fort Rupert."[20]

George Simpson was also thinking about Fort Rupert, not Fort Victoria. On 26 May 1850, unaware that Douglas had recently concluded treaties at Fort Victoria, he wrote to the London Committee from Norway House reminding them that on 30 June 1849 he had recommended that "an arrangement should be made with the natives, by an annuity of not exceeding £100, for the purpose of extinguishing their claim to the coal lands, on a sale or transfer of the same to the Company, as a means of excluding strangers therefrom." He also reminded the Committee that they had submitted to legal counsel a "form of an agreement" drafted by Adam Thom and forwarded to them in October 1849. He concluded by recommending "that if the form of deed to be entered into has not been forwarded at the time this reaches you, it be transmitted via Panama with the least possible delay, accompanied by the necessary instructions to Chief Factor Douglas."[21]

Douglas may have appreciated the Governor and Committee's approbation of his purchase at Fort Victoria, but he did not miss the urgency they placed upon his concluding a treaty at Fort Rupert. He noted that he received the letters of 16 and 23 August 1850 (with the template treaty) on 15 November 1850, and, without mentioning George Blenkinsop's Garden Treaty, assured the directors that he would "as soon as possible enter into arrangements with the natives of Fort Rupert, for the purchase of the land in the neighbourhood of that Establishment."[22] He arranged to travel to Fort Rupert early in the new year.

Fort Rupert was unusual among HBC trading posts in several respects. For one, it is the first HBC post for which there is evidence that Indigenous people confronted HBC traders demanding that the HBC compensate them for the land the company was occupying there.[23] That is remarkable, because the traders at Fort Rupert occupied only the site of the fort and a small adjacent garden. By contrast, by the late 1840s, the HBC had far more extensive cultivations around many of their other posts. The HBC at Fort Vancouver, Fort Langley, and Fort Victoria occupied considerably more ground. It also did so at posts such as Fort St. James and Fraser Lake in the company's New Caledonia District. At posts on the northern prairies, such as Fort Edmonton and Fort Carlton, the HBC began gardening in the late 1700s without being confronted with demands for payment. By the 1850s, those posts were surrounded by considerable gardens, hayfields, and pastures.[24]

Fort Rupert was also unusual in that there were miners working for the HBC there who were not under the direct supervision of the HBC officers.[25] As early as June 1848, the HBC London Committee, believing that the Kwakiutl could not be relied upon to bring in enough coal to satisfy their contract with the Pacific Mail Steamship Company (PMSC), began recruiting Scottish miners.[26] The miners agreed to come for £50 per annum, with a bonus of 2s/6d for every ton of coal produced over 30 tons per month, "else but for that inducement we should never have left Scotland."[27] By contrast, the Kwakiutl miners were paid in goods at the flat rate of 3s/6d per ton.[28] When the Scottish miners were already on their way, Simpson warned the Columbia District's Board of Management that they were accustomed to more comfortable dwellings and better fare than HBC servants got, and that they therefore had to be "well treated in every point of view." He warned the board that "the officer under whom they are to act ought, therefore, to be instructed to treat them with civility, both in his language & deportment."[29]

The presence of Scottish miners, the fact that people at Fort Rupert had already been told about the HBC's intention to conclude a treaty, and the tumultuous circumstances at the post in 1849–50 explain why chiefs there confronted George Blenkinsop. It is not implausible that when Simpson raised the issue in June 1849 of "strangers" who might have the opportunity of "tampering" with the villagers "with a view to their setting up extravagant claims for the coal lands," he might have included these Scottish miners. If he did not think of them, he should have.

The miners arrived at Fort Rupert on 24 September 1849 aboard the *Mary Dare*.[30] They included several members of the Muir family led by John Muir Sr., the "Oversman," and his wife, Anne; four sons, Andrew (c. 1828–1859), Robert, John Jr., and Michael; and cousins Archibald Muir, John McGregor, and John Smith.[31] The miners injected a dynamic that influenced Indigenous–newcomer relations significantly. For almost the entire time the Scottish miners were at Fort Rupert, they and the HBC officers were at odds. At times, the conflict was acute. Meanwhile, although relationships between the miners and the Kwakiutl were complex and varying, at least several of the Kwakiutl worked alongside the miners. The timing of some of the disputes suggests that they were shaped in part by the complex and unsettled circumstances that prevailed at Fort Rupert between September 1849 and the time of the conclusion of the treaty in 1851.

The Fort Rupert journals and Andrew Muir's reminiscences indicate that from 26 to 28 September, John Work and John Muir headed a party that included five Indians to survey the coalfields.[32] Andrew Muir, who was part of this group, indicated that Kwakiutl who were then mining the surface coal had traced the coal seam to the edge of the forest, which they could not clear.[33] Some Kwakiutl assisted this party in examining the coalfields even as others were mining the surface coal. The Fort Rupert post journals show that the Scottish miners and Kwakiutl regularly worked alongside one another over the ensuing months.[34]

The miners were initially intimidated by the Kwakiutl. According to Michael Muir, "on the day after the arrival of the Muirs at Rupert, sixteen war canoes were in the harbour. They had sixteen poles arranged on the beach, with each an indian's head upon it. They were at war with another tribe and this was a trophy of their revenge. As Mrs Muir was the first white woman who had ever been upon the island, they showed their respects, by offering her a choice of any two of the sixteen heads, to them the most highly prized of presents."[35] The Fort Rupert journal seems to show that the events occurred on 6 October, but it otherwise corroborates Muir's account: "This morning the war party returned, started about a fortnight since, having fallen in with the party who attempted to kill their chief and made sad havoc amongst them. They brought back 14 skulls and about 30 prisoners."[36] It is not difficult to imagine that this event made a significant impression on the newcomers. That was not the only time that the Kwakiutl displayed severed heads at the village. J.S. Helmcken later reminisced that when he arrived at Fort Rupert in July 1850, Beardmore told him "you should have arrived yesterday and you would have seen half a dozen heads on the rocks. ... you will get accustomed to it, for after all it is much the same as civilized men do in war against their enemies."[37]

Although documents present different perspectives on the subsequent disputes that arose between the miners and the HBC officers at Fort Rupert, they show that disagreements occurred soon after the miners arrived. The Fort Rupert journals show that on 10 October, "Mr Muir and party made a demand today for the whole of the 80 ft House which was originally intended for the Servants. This of course was refused him when he plainly said that neither of his party would commence mining operations until they could get it."[38] The 16 October entry notes that "miners go ahead but slowly. as I said before Smith and Macgregor are the only two who work as they ought the rest play half the day. So far we have had no control over them. Mr Muir is their captain. To day they refused the Beef we gave them pork instead. It certainly is any thing but good."[39] By 17 November George Blenkinsop registered frustration: "I must say as I have before remarked in these papers and it is the opinion of Capt McNeill and Mr Beardmore themselves as well as myself that the proceedings of these Miners are shameful and that they do not appear to have the slightest wish to further or promote the interests of the Company who have been so highly liberal to them. A day of reckoning will come at last."[40] Things came to a head on 21 November when McNeill threatened to place some of the men in irons. The entry for 28 November indicates that the threat had its desired effect: "Things now go on much better since the 'turn up' of 21st Novr. these men all appear to do their best at present and they now do double the quantity of work they did formerly."[41]

Given that the miners had sustained contact with the Kwakiutl, and that there was considerable mutual dissatisfaction between the miners and the HBC officers, it is not difficult to understand how the miners might have incited the Kwakiutl. The journals first mention that Indigenous people worked alongside the miners in late October.[42] Then, on 29 October, the journals report that "Indians to day refused to work till more pay is given."[43] The Fort Rupert journals indicate that on 31 October, a disturbance occurred after an "Indian" stole four axes. That issue was settled, but then the miners were informed that "the Indians were coming down to cut all their heads off as they had done to some of their enemies a short time before this it seems frightened them and in the evening they came and requested powder and ball to defend themselves with in case of a row."[44]

As this passage implies, the miners and Kwakiutl did not form an alliance against the company. There were frequent disputes between the miners and the Kwakiutl, although the miners blamed the HBC for failing to protect them from the villagers. A retrospective account written by Andrew Muir shows that their complaints included the lack of quality coal, which prevented them from mining enough coal to earn their bonus, but also included the lack of HBC protection from the Kwakiutl. Muir accused the HBC traders of having several "rows with the Indians and us working at a distance from the Fort without any protection whatsoever the Indians has come down and threatened to shoot us." He complained that the miners asked for protection, "that we might work without molestation but no assistance could we get."[45]

James Douglas and Eden Colvile visited Fort Rupert on 22 January 1850. They must have told Blenkinsop of the HBC's plan to negotiate treaties, but Douglas and Colvile did not negotiate a treaty at the time, perhaps because they were waiting for the specific instructions from London that were then in transit, and did not think it urgent. During that visit, Douglas and Colvile were oblivious to the deteriorating relations between the HBC officers and the miners. Colvile wrote that everything was going well at the new post. The stockades, bastions, and several buildings had been finished, several more were under construction, and "a portion of land cleared for planting potatoes." As for the Kwakiutl, he found that they, "about one thousand in number, who live around the fort have been all along well disposed, and industrious." They had, he estimated, brought about 1,100 tons of coal to the fort. And the miners, he believed, "appear to be well satisfied with all that has been done for them but will be more contented when we shall be in a condition to supply them with fresh provisions occasionally."[46]

Still, relations at Fort Rupert must have remained tense until matters came to a head between mid-March and mid-April. In March 1850, the newly arrived Governor Richard Blanshard visited Fort Rupert, and found the miners "in a very discontented state. ... Before leaving home, they expected to find a good workable seam of coal on reaching the Island; but now find they have to dig to an unascertained depth to obtain that object."[47] While they did not complain to Blanshard about McNeill, they did protest that they had accepted the opportunity to mine coal on Vancouver Island expecting to find a readily worked seam of coal. On that basis, they surely expected to earn the productivity bonus. Having found no workable seam, "nor turned out a single Bushel of coal since their arrival," they demanded 2/6 per day (retroactive to their arrival); "they otherwise decline working as miners."[48] Douglas admitted "all the coal we have hitherto sold being the produce of Indian labour."[49]

In his reminiscences, Michael Muir recalled that the Scottish miners eventually began searching for a workable seam "six miles from Saquash, and a half a mile from the Fort," but "on account of trouble with the Indians, the work had to be abandoned there for there was not a large enough force for protection. The Indians surrounded the mouth of the shaft, protesting that they would kill all below unless compensation was given them for their land rights."[50] The Fort Rupert journals shed further light on these events. On 15 April, George Blenkinsop wrote:

> This afternoon we were stopped by all the Chiefs from working in the Garden on the lower part of the Fort they told us we should inclose no more of their lands as we had not paid them for it and that it blocked up their roads to the forest for wood &c. Knowing it to be had in contemplation by the authorities that the land was to be purchased of them I thought it advisable to make each of them payment for the land necessary for garden purposes &c. They willingly sold me all right to the land in the neighbourhood of the Fort for a Blanket and shirt each. I made them all put their marks to an agreement drawn on it to that effect so we may now consider

ourselves the sole owners of the land or at best appropriate to our own use as much as we may require for gardens, mining purposes &c. They seemed highly pleased with the arrangement and said in putting their marks to the document "Loweelaa Seesaanee" which being interpreted means We have no more to say and no further demands to make on you for our lands.[51]

Combined, the two accounts seem to suggest that the Kwakiutl demanded (or, at least, received) payment for the land used for gardening and mining, although not for land occupied by the fort. The 15 April 1850 journal entry is the oldest document that mentions Indigenous leaders' demands that HBC traders pay for land that the HBC occupied in any of its territories. The entry thus also offers early evidence that those Fort Rupert chiefs could then conceptualize the purchase and sale of land. That is not surprising. People accustomed to purchasing, selling, and trading any other item – and the Northwest Coast peoples were familiar with the sale of everything from fish and furs to slaves – could probably conceptualize purchasing and selling land, even if they had never done so before. The actual document, with the chiefs' marks, has not survived, but a good argument could be made based on this entry that the agreement of 15 April 1850 was the first treaty concluded by the HBC on Vancouver Island.

The entry for 16 April reveals that the events of the prior day occurred as conflicts between the HBC officers and the miners were deepening. By early April, matters there had become serious enough that James Douglas at Fort Victoria reported the miners' discontent to the company directors in London.[52] On the morning of 16 April, less than a day after Blenkinsop's land purchase, things came to a head. Andrew Muir later wrote that "we wrought away and did every thing ourselves until the 16th of April 1850 when we were compelled to stop work."[53] According to the Fort Rupert journals, the day started with news that "the Indians had broken into the Tool House" and taken some of the miners' goods. Blenkinsop, claiming that the HBC traders had been unaware that the Kwakiutl had been "molesting" the miners, blamed the miners, stating that "the place was not so well secured as it might have been especially after the Indians having once before broken in and plundered the house of almost everything it contained." He added that "I think it a downright falsehood saying the Indians have been a hindrance to them although if such has been the case it is entirely owing to themselves by allowing the Indians to take so great liberties with them and not even attempting to keep them outside the fence which was put up for the express purpose."[54] Douglas accepted Blenkinsop's statement that the miners' argument that they could not work on account of the lack of protection from the Indians was "mere pretext," arguing that the Indians "were not badly disposed," and the miners had not hesitated to go hunting during leisure time.[55]

Richard Blanshard, however, believed that Fort Rupert was descending into crisis. In July 1850, he appointed J.S. Helmcken to serve as resident magistrate at Fort Rupert, because "the miners and labourers there have shewn a disposition to riot which if not checked may lead to serious consequences. The Indian population being numerous savage and treacherous, and the distance from Victoria and total want of means of communication between the two places, increases the inconvenience."[56]

Blenkinsop's purchase of 15 April 1850 was clearly made during an extraordinarily tense period. Documents do not reveal all of the factors that influenced the decision to negotiate the purchase, but the Garden Treaty was probably part of Blenkinsop's efforts to defuse the tension. The fact that the treaty document has not been preserved suggests that HBC officials later assumed that subsequent treaties superseded the Garden Treaty of 1850.

While the Garden Treaty may have placated the villagers, the dispute between the HBC and the miners only intensified. On 3 May 1850, a day after the *Beaver* arrived, according to Andrew Muir, "We were all called over to the hall in which were Capt. McNeil, Blinkinsip & Bredmore, on going over Capt. McNeil commenced like a madman swearing and threatening and ordered us to our work. we said not till we were farrly [sic] tried by English Law for what was charged against us. we were ordered to be put in Irons and fed on bread and water during the time they were putting the Irons on McGregor and I were treated in the most shocking manner possible called everything we could be called and threatened to be shot like dogs and we dared not open our Mouths ... thus we remained in Irons 6 Days."[57] Andrew Muir wrote that "on the Seventh Day that was Thursday the 9$^{th}$ [May 1850], after breakfast our Irons were taken off and we were ordered down to the hall where was assembled McNeil, Blinkinsop, Bredmore, Cap$^t$ Dodd D. and My Father with the rest of our men we were ordered to state our mind freely which we did a great change from last day we were there when we durst not open our mouth."[58] On 11 May, the imprisoned miners were released and permitted to stay in their houses.[59] Between 18 June and 3 July 1850, the miners deserted Fort Rupert.[60]

In this tumultuous atmosphere matters became even more chaotic. In early July 1850, three HBC sailors deserted the *Norman Morison* in Victoria and stowed away on the *England*, hoping that the ship would take them to the California gold fields. But it went to Fort Rupert, where the three men apparently stole a canoe and fled north to evade an HBC search party. Shortly thereafter the Kwakiutl reported that the men had been killed. On 16 July 1850, Helmcken reported that the Kwakiutl "declared most positively that the Newitty's committed the murder, but they cannot know excepting from report. Our Indians look upon them as dogs and I think are jealous of them, so that little dependence can be placed upon their evidence."[61] Helmcken later added that the Kwakiutl "ask daily whether they shall go and fight the Newittys for us, ... but we always have told them not ... because we are far from certain who did it, and $2^{ly}$ it appears imprudent to allow Indians to revenge the quarrels of whites."[62] In August, Blanshard reported to Earl Grey that Fort Rupert was in crisis. He claimed that the men of the fort, having accused the officers of inciting the killings, were defying the orders of HBC officers and Helmcken and were demanding that the HBC abandon Fort Rupert, a move that, according to Blanshard, would incite the Kwakiutl, "one of the most warlike tribes on the coast, three thousand in number and well armed," to destroy them all.[63]

In October, after Helmcken confirmed that three Nahwitti men had killed the sailors, Blanshard ordered the British Navy to act. After two punitive raids in October 1850 and March 1851, in which two Nahwitti settlements were destroyed, the Nahwitti produced three bodies, claiming that they were those of the killers. Despite the controversies surrounding the appropriateness of the raids, the response did much to pacify the region surrounding Fort Rupert, but in the shorter term, the Kwakiutl's associations with the HBC and the British Navy made them fear Nahwitti retribution, and thus to value the protection of Fort Rupert.[64]

Earl Grey rejected Blanshard's reasons for launching the punitive raids. He advised Blanshard that "Her Majesty's Government cannot undertake to protect, or attempt to punish injuries committed upon, British subjects, who, voluntarily expose themselves to the violence or treachery of the Native Tribes at a distance from the Settlements. I have no reason to suppose from the accounts which have reached me, both from yourself and from other quarters, that the Settlements themselves are in actual danger."[65] Grey's response was quite different than Douglas's. Not surprisingly, given that the HBC typically preferred quick and decisive action as a deterrent, Douglas welcomed Blanshard's response, although the HBC did not want a permanent British military presence in the colony.

In early February 1851, Douglas arrived at Fort Rupert, and on 8 February he completed the negotiations with the leaders of the Fort Rupert village. Unfortunately, the documentary record of the Fort Rupert negotiations is even scantier than that of the Fort Victoria treaties. On 24 February 1851, after having returned to Victoria, Douglas offhandedly, in the thirtieth paragraph of a long letter, reported to Barclay that "We have concluded an arrangement with the Chiefs of the Quakeolth Tribe, for the purchase of the land about Ft. Rupert, extending from McNeills harbour to Hardy Sound, which the purchase also includes – The agreement was formally executed by all the chiefs, in consideration of a payment of Goods, Amounting at Inventory prices to £64. Stg."[66] The brevity of the report makes it difficult to know what was agreed upon in 1851.

Consistent with his simplification of the Fort Victoria treaties, Douglas implied that he had concluded one treaty at Fort Rupert, but he produced two written treaties (with a total cost of £150), one with the "Quakeolths" and another with the "Queackars," both for exactly the same territory, but at different compensation amounts (£86 and £64) (see figure 27).[67] That two communities, apparently occupying precisely the same territory, concluded two identical treaties hints at some of the complex reality of villages on the Northwest Coast in 1851, and the effects of village consolidation that had occurred since Fort Rupert had been established. An uninformed observer might assume that there was one "Indian village" at Fort Rupert, but it was normal that multiple autonomous extended families occupied houses at one location. In fact, members of four autonomous "tribes" occupied houses at Fort Rupert at some points. In 1857, John Keast Lord described the village at Fort Rupert as

> a long row of huts, each hut nearly square, the exterior fantastically frescoed in hieroglyphic patterns, in white, red, and blue, having, however, a symbolic meaning or heraldic value, like the *totum* of the Indians east of the Rocky Mountains; for immense trees, barked and worked smooth, support each corner, the tops, like pediments to a column, carved to resemble some horrible monster; the huts constructed of cedar plank chipped from the solid tree with chisels and hatchets made of stone: many hands combine to accomplish this, hence a hut becomes the joint property of several families. Five tribes live at this village:–

| | | | |
|---|---|---|---|
| Quq-Kars | [Kweeha] | (numbering about) | 800 warriors |
| Qual-quilths | [Kwakiutl] | " | 100 warriors |
| Kum-cutes | [Komkiutis] | " | 70 warriors |
| Wan-lish | [Walas Kwakiutl] | " | 50 warriors |
| Lock-qua-lillas | [Lakwilala] | " | 80 warriors[68] |

Scholars have concluded that between 1850 and 1890, these groups were merging into one community commonly known as the Kwakiutl.[69]

Douglas certainly had received both the 17 December 1849 instructions and template treaty from the HBC by the time he negotiated the Fort Rupert treaties. That means that Douglas must have been aware that his instructions were to negotiate based on the status of Indigenous occupation as of June 1846, "when the Island came under the undivided sovereignty of Great Britain." If Douglas had attempted to negotiate on that basis, the Fort Rupert villagers would have objected. There may have been no substantial Indigenous settlement at all at Beaver Harbour in June 1846. The winter villages of the Kwakiutl and Kweeha were on islands in the Broughton Archipelago – outside the jurisdiction of the colony of Vancouver Island until 1849. The fact that the HBC later claimed the land upon which Fort Rupert was built – also well after June 1846 – suggests that the actual negotiations at Fort Rupert (and the HBC's later claims) were based on the circumstances as of February 1851.

Douglas apparently left the "Register of Land purchases from Indians" at Fort Victoria, for he had the two agreements written on separate folios that were later attached to the Register. While there may be doubt about the other treaties, in the case of the Fort Rupert treaties, there is no reason to doubt that the treaty text was written before the names were added. To illustrate how similar the Fort Rupert treaties were to the template sent to Douglas, the wording of the Fort Rupert treaties is compared with the written conveyance below (except where "blanks" are filled in, additions are in bold and deletions are struck out):

Know all Men, We, the Chiefs and People of the Tribe, called **Quakeolths/ Queackars** who have signed our names and made our marks to this Deed on the **eighth** day of **February** one Thousand Eight hundred and **fifty-one** do consent to surrender, Entirely and for Ever to James Douglas the Agent of the Hudsons Bay Company in Vancouvers Island, that is to say, for the Governor, Deputy Governor, and Committee of the same, the whole of the lands situate and lying between **McNeill's Harbour and Hardy Bay, inclusive of these ports, and extending two miles into the interior of the Island.**

The condition of our understanding of this sale is this that our village sites and Enclosed Fields are to be Kept for our own use, for the use of our Children, and for those who may follow after us; and the lands shall be properly surveyed hereafter; it is understood however that the land itself, with these small Exceptions becomes the Entire property of the White people for Ever; it is also understood that we are at liberty to hunt over the unoccupied lands, and carry on our fisheries as formerly. We have received as payment £ 86/64 sterling.

In token whereof we have signed our names and made our marks at **Fort Rupert, Beaver Harbour** on the **eight day of February, one thousand eight hundred and fifty-one.**
**Wawattie/Wale his o mark,**
**and 15/11 others.**
**Witnesses**
  William Henry McNeill, C.T., H.B.Co.
  Charles Dodd, Master, Steamer Beaver.
  George Blenkinsop, Clerk, H.B. Co.

In both Fort Rupert treaties, the "mark" of each Indigenous signatory was made with a small circle, not an X. Given the almost universal use of Xes at the time, including in the other Vancouver Island treaties, the Indigenous signatories must have insisted on using small circles instead of Xes, but we can only speculate on the reasons. The first Indigenous signatory in the Quakeolth treaty was Wawattie, who had been present at Fort Victoria a few days before the Fort Victoria treaties were negotiated. He had also been a party to the Garden Treaty of April 1850. However, there is no indication as to whether the parties discussed the previous treaty, concluded less than a year earlier, "for gardens, mining purposes &c."

As had been the case with the Fort Victoria treaties, Douglas did not sign, either as a party to the agreement, or as a witness. Thus, we are deprived again of any indication of the authority by which Douglas believed he made these agreements. In contrast to the earlier Fort Victoria treaties, each of the witnesses to the treaty indicated a credential: Chief Trader of the HBC, Master of the *Beaver*,[70] Clerk of the HBC.

Douglas's estimate of the population of the "Quakeeolth" (Appendix A) indicates the number of "men with beards" and women, but not of children. The compensation given to each community seems to have been determined by the number of "men with beards" who signed each treaty, not by the population of each community, and not by the area of the land surrendered.[71] In his estimates of the populations of other groups (Songhees, Klallam, Sooke, Saanich, and Nanaimo), the adult populations ranged between about 34.6 and 36.9 per cent of the total population, with the overall average falling at 35.9 per cent. If the adult population of the Kwakiutl was at that same proportion, the sub-adult population was about 736 and the total population about 1,148. So, the total number of Indigenous adherents to the Fort Rupert treaties was roughly equal to the number in the Fort Victoria treaties of 1850. That is consistent with other evidence that villages on the northern coasts of Vancouver Island were considerably larger than those in the southeastern parts of the island. Depending on whether one considers the payment in terms of an amount per person, or based upon an amount per square mile, the payments were either roughly equal to or considerably higher for the Fort Rupert villagers than for their counterparts in southeastern Vancouver Island.

It might be argued that the Fort Rupert treaties were less the result of negotiation than the original Fort Victoria treaties, for, while Douglas presumably had the written treaty with him at Fort Rupert, as he had not at Fort Victoria, we can at least conclude that aspects of James Douglas's report of the Fort Victoria oral agreements made it into the written text of those treaties. However, except for the provision relating to size of compensation, Douglas simply used the text of the Fort Victoria treaties at Fort Rupert. He did not even remove the reference to cultivated fields, even though the Fort Rupert villagers apparently did not cultivate potatoes before the treaty was concluded. If the Fort Rupert peoples sought revisions to any of those written terms, they were unsuccessful.

The lack of Fort Rupert post journals for the period after 27 April 1850 makes it impossible to know whether the pattern revealed in the extant journals persisted in 1850 and 1851, but it appears that the Kwakiutl ceased mining altogether in 1851 when the most accessible surface deposits at Suquash were exhausted and fears of attack by enemies such as the Nahwitti deterred them. Douglas reported in August 1851 that "I mentioned in my last letter that the Indians had not collected any Coal from the surface beds this season in consequence of the Neweeti war."[72] On 11 July 1852, James Douglas reported that "the Indians have not procured any coal this season as the labour of getting them out at the depth of ten feet below the surface is greater than Indians are willing or able to encounter."[73] While the Kwakiutl stopped gathering coal by the time the treaty was concluded, the HBC clung for another year to hopes that a valuable seam of coal might still be discovered, and the company appears to have proceeded as if it believed its rights to the coal had been secured, even at Suquash, where the Kwakiutl had mined most of the coal.

To replace the Muirs, in late 1850 the company hired a party led by Edinburgh mining engineer Boyd Gilmour to resume the search for workable coal seams.[74] Gilmour's party was on its way to Vancouver Island when the Fort Rupert treaties were concluded.[75] Gilmour and his party of four miners arrived at Fort Rupert on 9 August 1851.[76] From a base at Suquash, they (together with other men) searched for substantial seams of coal. In early September 1851, James Douglas reported to the Governor and Committee that "no Coal of any consequence had been found."[77] And in October, based on updated information, Douglas wrote that "The boring operations were going on vigorously at Saaquash and Mr Gilmour was daily expecting to meet with a 'coal' in the bore, then 8 fathoms deep. ... Two substantial buildings are erected at Saaquash and a party of men were employed surrounding the place with a strong fence to keep the Indians from encroaching."[78]

Gilmour's party worked at Suquash for about a year – probably from 19 August 1851 to September 1852 – while boring several exploratory holes.[79] Soon after he arrived at Fort Rupert, Boyd Gilmour suspected that there were no workable seams of coal in the vicinity of Fort Rupert, and his investigations gradually bore him out. On 18 March 1852, James Douglas informed Archibald Barclay that Gilmour had not found any coal.[80] And in September 1852, Gilmour wrote that "I am sorry we have not been more fortunate but am convinced there are no coals to be found at least of a workable nature. I could never forgive myself were I to hold wantonly out hopes that would never be realized."[81] Gilmour's failure to find workable coal (and the discovery of a richer source of coal at Nanaimo) convinced the HBC to give up on Fort Rupert coal.

The end of coal mining on northern Vancouver Island led the HBC to consider abandoning Fort Rupert altogether. On 21 March 1853, Douglas wrote to London to say that "it will I presume soon become a question with the Committee, whether Fort Rupert should be maintained much longer, since the coal works have been abandoned, as the mere Fur Trade of the place can be attended to by the Steam vessel."[82] Later that year, Douglas noted that the London Governor and Committee had given him permission to abandon Fort Rupert, although the post was actually maintained until the early 1880s as a fur trade post.[83] The HBC may have decided to maintain the post because of stabilized relations between the HBC and the Kwakiutl. In March 1852, Douglas reported that the Kwakiutl had nearly exhausted the coal at Suquash, but had "given no molestation whatever to our people, they are clearing land and making extensive preparations for planting potatoes for their own use evincing in that and other things a laudable desire to improve their social condition."[84] The Kwakiutl had cast their lot with the HBC. Relations with their neighbours appear to have deteriorated. In November 1853, Blenkinsop wrote that "The Quakeolths have now made so many enemies that they are afraid to stir from their own doors, and what is still worse for us, they are at variance with our best Fur customers, the Bellcoolas."[85]

Apparently, at the end of 1851, 1,200 tons of coal remained unsold at Fort Rupert, "as no purchasers have called since last year and no sales of Coal have been effected with the exception of a few tons for the use of Her Majestys Ships, which have visited this Coast."[86] In 1853, Douglas consigned the stockpiled coal to Thomas Lowe, who believed that he could sell the coal in San Francisco for $8 per ton.[87] But even in 1853 and 1854, Douglas still reported that 700 tons of unsold coal remained at Fort Rupert.[88] Had the HBC known at the beginning of 1851 what it knew at the end of 1852, the company may not have pursued treaty making at Fort Rupert. These events also probably explain why the Kwakiutl reserves in the treaty territory were not surveyed until much later, when permanent exogenous settlement began there.

## 11 Governor James Douglas and the Saanich and Nanaimo Treaties, 1851–1854

George Blenkinsop concluded the Fort Rupert Garden treaty of 1850 in response to a demand of the Fort Rupert chiefs. At Fort Victoria and Fort Rupert, James Douglas subsequently negotiated treaties at the behest of the Governor and Committee of the HBC, and, since he held no other positions at the time, in his capacity as agent of the HBC. But Douglas signed none of those treaties. After he became Governor of the colony of Vancouver Island, Douglas negotiated three more treaties on Vancouver Island, two in 1852 to obtain a cession of Indigenous title to the Saanich Peninsula (figure 30), and one in 1854 to obtain a cession of the coalfields of Nanaimo (figure 28). These three treaties were more typical of British treaties with Indigenous people in that they were completed by the official agent of the British Crown, but they were nonetheless as unusual as their predecessors in many other respects.

Richard Blanshard submitted his resignation as Governor of the colony of Vancouver Island on 18 November 1850 and left the colony on 1 September 1851.[1] Before leaving, he named a governing council, with James Douglas as its senior member and John Tod and James Cooper as members.[2] Shortly after accepting Blanshard's resignation (but before receiving Blanshard's 12 February 1851 letter complaining of Douglas's voucher for the cost of the Fort Victoria treaties), Earl Grey invited the HBC's Governor and Committee to recommend a replacement. J.H. Pelly responded by advising that "the Governor should possess some experience in conducting the requisite intercourse with the Indians and for this and other reasons they have requested me to recommend James Douglas Esq$^{re}$ Chief Factor of the Hudson's Bay Company and Manager of their affairs in the Island as well qualified to fill the Office."[3] Douglas did not want the job. He was dismayed when he learned from the Governor and Committee that the appointment was imminent: "my appointment to the office of Governor of Vancouver's Island, affords me anything but pleasure. I accept it entirely from a sense of duty to the Company, though I greatly fear that it will be out of my power to discharge the responsible duties of the office, either with satisfaction to myself, or advantage to the Colony."[4] Douglas's governorship began officially on 31 October 1851, several months after he concluded the Fort Rupert treaties.[5]

Earl Grey gave Douglas no instructions analogous to the letter he sent to George Grey in New Zealand. Indeed, he did not communicate with Douglas at all regarding Indigenous title on Vancouver Island. His voluminous writings show that Grey's position was consistent with the instructions that the HBC Governor and Committee had given Douglas on 17 December 1849, that Indigenous people had rights to lands they occupied by villages and cultivation but did not have rights to "waste lands." Earl Grey may have agreed that the HBC owned land that the company occupied by posts and cultivation at the time of the Oregon Treaty, but assumed that waste lands belonged to the Crown, and that if the HBC wished to obtain land on Vancouver Island beyond that which it occupied in 1846, it would have to pay the going rate for it.[6] Although Earl Grey was unaware of the wording of the Vancouver Island treaties, he certainly would have considered that land purchased from the Indigenous people became Crown land, not the possession of the HBC, regardless of what the treaties said. And the HBC directors apparently assumed likewise. Given that the Governor and Committee had sent the template treaty to Douglas in August 1850, J.H. Pelly must have known how the treaties were worded, but he reassured Earl Grey that he understood that, should the HBC require any more land than they had occupied in 1846, "the Company will pay for it as other Settlers do."[7]

When Earl Grey asked Pelly to clarify the company's position on its own claims to land, Pelly elaborated, but made no mention of the treaties that Douglas had concluded:

> During the period that elapsed between the original connection of the Hudson's Bay Company with the Country west of the Rocky Mountains and the division of the Territory by the Boundary Treaty of June 1846, while in fact the sovereignty was in abeyance, the Company reclaimed from the Wilderness and occupied portions of land wherever their trading Establishments were planted. These lands they claim as theirs without purchase and the possessory rights thus acquired in that portion of the Territory which is situated to the south of the 49th parallel of North Latitude have been guaranteed to them by the Boundary Treaty. Among the lands occupied by the Company North of the 49th parallel is that situated at Fort

Victoria in Vancouver's Island where they formed an Establishment in the year 1843 ... Its exact extent has not yet been ascertained by the Company's Surveyor, but whatever that may be the Company consider they have a right to hold that land without paying for it, while for any additional quantity that may be required to be taken by the "Fur Trade" (which is merely a subordinate branch of the Hudson's Bay Company) the same price will be paid as is paid by other purchasers of land.[8]

Pelly's thus acknowledged that the HBC should pay the colony of Vancouver Island for any land it wished to acquire that it did not already occupy at the time of the Oregon Treaty in 1846, but that it claimed the exclusive ownership of all lands that it had occupied before the treaty.

Douglas was no more eager to mention the Vancouver Island treaties to the Colonial Secretary than Pelly was. On his first day as Governor of the colony, in his inaugural letter to his new supervisor, Douglas dealt in some depth with Indigenous affairs, but made no mention of Indigenous title or the treaties. He reported that the "war" with the Nahwitti had ended and that the operations of the *Daphne* "have been attended with the happiest effects, and so filled their mind with terror, that they made no attempt at reprisals." He explained that the "Natives generally are turning their attention to the cultivation of the Potatoe, and to other useful arts, such as the manufacture of Shingles and Laths which are becoming popular among them."[9] He also wrote:

I shall probably take the liberty of calling your Lordship's attention hereafter to the best means of improving the condition of the aborigines of this Island, who are in many respects a highly interesting people, and I conceive worthy of attention.

They will become under proper management of service to the Colony and form a valuable auxiliary force, in the event of war with any foreign power. – From my long experience of Indian character and of the tribes on this coast in particular, I am led to regret that the Missionary Societies of Britain, who are sending Teachers to so many other parts of the world have not turned their attention to the natives of Vancouver's Island; as, by the aid of those Societies, schools might be established for the moral training and instruction of the Aborigines, to the manifest and advantage of this Colony.[10]

In a subsequent letter of 16 December, Douglas again dealt in considerable detail with Indigenous affairs without mentioning Indigenous title or treaties. He described an incident in which a white settler, Thomas Hall, duped Tanasman, a Sooke chief (a signatory to the Sooke Treaty of 10 May 1850), into trading a double-barrelled gun for an inferior gun. The dispute raised for Douglas the question of "How far the testimony of Indians is to be admitted as evidence in the Law Courts of this Colony?"[11] He emphasized "how very important it is, to the peace and security of the settlements, that instant attention should be paid to the complaints of Indians, and their wrongs receive speedy redress, as nothing will tend more to inspire confidence in the governing power, and to teach them that justice may be obtained by a less dangerous and more certain method than their own hasty and precipitite [sic] acts of private revenge."[12] Paradoxically, only shortly after Douglas wrote that letter, J.H. Pelly attempted to reassure Earl Grey that it was unnecessary for the government to send a military force to Vancouver Island, because "it has been the uniform policy of the Hudson's Bay Company never to suffer the blood of a white man to be shed by a savage with impunity. This policy is well understood by the tribes who inhabit the regions under the control of the Company, and it is not too much to say that it has saved many a life that would otherwise have been sacrificed."[13] The tension between adherence to British notions of justice and due process, and the HBC's policy of swift retribution must have been obvious to Earl Grey.

Douglas communicated with Earl Grey again on 29 January 1852, without mentioning any intention to conclude a treaty. Douglas even addressed a letter to Earl Grey on 11 February 1852, the very date upon which he negotiated the second Saanich treaty, without mentioning the treaty at all.[14] So, although Douglas concluded three treaties as Governor of Vancouver Island, he did so without instructions or the knowledge of the Colonial Office. He apparently considered them relevant only to his superiors in the HBC. It is impossible to know how much officials in the Colonial Office wished to know. Consistent with earlier documentation, in August 1852, John S. Pakington, the new Colonial Secretary, reassured Douglas that "the mode of dealing with the native Tribes is a point which I must leave to your own discretion, trusting to your disposition to cultivate friendly relations with them as far as may be possible."[15]

The documentary evidence relating to the Saanich Peninsula treaties is contained in the HBC's documents. There had been friction between the HBC and the Saanich in the years after the Fort Victoria treaties of 1850. Douglas reported in late 1850 that Governor Blanshard had seized a runaway Nahwitti slave at Victoria who was suspected of having been involved in the killing of the three seamen on northern Vancouver Island earlier that year. Blanshard had the prisoner sent to Fort Rupert for identification. Complicating matters, the runaway slave was Cowichan by birth, but also related to one of the most prominent Saanich chiefs. According to Douglas, the Saanich chief was seeking, unsuccessfully to that date, the assistance of the Cowichan in harassing the HBC men tending the dairy herds north of Fort Victoria.[16]

In late 1850 and early 1851, Douglas alerted the London Committee to difficulties at Fort Victoria itself. In December 1850, Douglas disputed Blanshard's opinion that it would take only twenty armed men to deal with any hostilities at Fort Victoria. Pointing to the Cayuse War (1847–55) in the adjacent portions of American territory, Douglas argued that the HBC was far more vulnerable than Blanshard suggested.[17] In March 1851, Douglas reported that, under warrant from Governor Blanshard, several Indians at Fort Victoria had been whipped and imprisoned for killing two head of cattle.[18] Douglas did not assume that peaceful relations on southeastern Vancouver Island would continue as settlers arrived in the region.

The villagers of the Saanich Peninsula, like many other villagers on the Northwest Coast, responded to escalating warfare by consolidating their villages in less vulnerable places. The village relocations at Fort Langley, Fort Simpson, Fort Victoria, and Fort Rupert were responses to the establishment of those posts, but the intensification of warfare and depopulation caused by disease spurred relocations even where there were no trading posts. For example, in 1862, Spencer Palmer attributed consolidation of villages in the Bella Coola region to attacks by Haida.[19] It appears that in many places in the mid-nineteenth century, communities with villages along coastlines more exposed to their enemies sometimes relocated their entire villages to safer locations. Diamond Jenness wrote that out of fear of the Comox and Kwakiutl "the Saanich sent their women and children to secluded spots during May and June, the usual seasons for raids, while the men maintained a nightly watch on housetops. During the nineteenth century, indeed, the Saanich abandoned one of their villages near Sidney, on the east side of the peninsula, and moved to Patricia Bay, on the west side where they were less exposed to attack."[20]

The broader context must have influenced the parties to the Saanich treaties, but the immediate impetus for the treaties was a plan to build a sawmill in which James Douglas had an important stake, and in which many other people closely involved in the Vancouver Island treaty process were also interested. The Vancouver Island Steam Saw Mill Company was established on 28 December 1851, "under the Patronage of His Excellency The Governor & Commander in Chief of Vancouvers Island and its Dependencies." James Douglas was the Chair of its Managing Committee, and one of its principal shareholders. Roderick

Finlayson was the Vice Chair, and the Managing Committee included prominent men associated with the HBC, including Charles Dodd, William F. Tolmie, James Sangster, John Sebastian Helmcken, Joseph W. McKay, David D. Wishart, William Henry McNeill, George Simpson, and John Work, and newly arrived surveyor, Joseph Pemberton.[21] The HBC acted as its banker. At the time of its founding, the company investors anticipated establishing their mill at Cordova Bay, on the southeastern part of Saanich Peninsula, because "the anchorage is good and sheltered, and readily approachable during every change of wind or tide, the Supply of Fresh water is ample; & the locality is likely to be, before long the Centre of a flourishing and thickly populated District."[22] The company's records make no mention of a land purchase. Moreover, the company's records do not indicate that it began any activity on Cordova Bay before the Saanich Treaties were concluded, although a meeting of the shareholders in March 1852 resolved that Finlayson be empowered to arrange for the erection of two small houses and other improvements at Cordova Bay, and Governor James Douglas be petitioned to construct roads between Cordova Bay and Victoria and Esquimalt.[23] By 19 January 1853, before the machinery arrived, the shareholders had decided to locate the mill at Albert Head, well within the territory covered by the treaties of 1850.[24] The company did not acquire machinery until late 1852. It was plagued by problems with both machinery and personnel, although it does appear to have operated for at least a short time.[25]

On 18 March 1852, Douglas wrote a long letter to Archibald Barclay. He referred to a map of "Sanitch Inlet," and the mouth of Cowichan River which "though in great part a mere eye sketch and therefore not absolutely correct, gives a good idea of both places and particularly of the extraordinary direction of the Sanitch Inlet which extends to within five miles of Esquimalt nearly insolating the south east angle of Vancouver's Island."[26] Not until the seventh page of the letter (in the seventeenth paragraph), did Douglas explain that, although some Saanich leaders had demanded that he pay for a plot of land required for a sawmill, he ended up purchasing the entire Saanich Peninsula:

> the Steam Saw Mill Company having selected as the site of their operations the section of land, marked upon the accompanying map north of Mount Douglas, which being within the lands of Sanitch Country, those Indians came forward with a demand for payment, and finding it impossible to discover among the numerous claimants the real owners of the land in question, and there being much difficulty in adjusting such claims, I thought it advisable to purchase the whole of the Sanitch country, as a

measure that would save much future trouble and expense. I succeeded in effecting that purchase in a general convention of the Tribe, who individually subscribed the Deed of Sale, reserving for their use only the village sites and potatoe patches, and I caused them to be paid the sum of £109..7..6 in woolen goods, which they preferred to money. That purchase includes all the land north of a line extending from Mount Douglas to the south end of the Sanitch Inlet, bounded by that Inlet and the Canal de Arro, as traced on the map, and contains nearly 50 square miles or 32,000 statute acres of land.[27]

Given that the company had not begun operations on Saanich Peninsula, beyond perhaps marking out the land, when the treaties were negotiated in February 1852, it is not clear how the Saanich learned of the company's plans. Douglas may have informed them. However, his account recalls his letter to James Murray Yale on 7 May 1850, that he had been negotiating land purchases, and adding that "I mention this circumstance as your Indians will no doubt be claiming payment for their lands also; but that can be settled by and bye."[28] Douglas clearly anticipated that, although the villagers near Fort Langley had not demanded payment since the establishment of Fort Langley in 1827, they would do so once they learned of the purchase at Victoria. This letter also recalls the repeated references already mentioned in other contexts, of Indigenous people being "taught" to claim payment for land. Unless Douglas deceived the HBC and approached the Saanich villagers to offer a treaty, this land purchase can be attributed to the demands of the villagers of the Saanich Peninsula, not to the instructions from London. However, the context also seems to imply that Douglas anticipated that he would continue making such treaties in the future.

Unfortunately, the brief account in Douglas's letter of 18 March 1852, written more than a month after the negotiations, is the only written description of the treaty negotiations. He stated that it was difficult to identify the "the real owners of the land in question" without elaboration. However, in 1862, Richard Mayne offered some insight probably gained from his conversations with Douglas. He agreed that "Indians should be duly paid for their land," but that "this is not so simple as it may seem." He explained that difficulty

> would be found in the conflicting claims of the various tribes, arising from their habits of polygamy and inheritance from the female side, together with the absence of any documentary or satisfactory evidence of title.
>
> If, therefore, any one chief or tribe were paid for a piece of land without the acknowledgement on the part of adjacent tribes of the vendor's right

to the land sold, five or six other claimants would in all probability come forward asserting the land to be theirs, and founding their title to it upon some intermarriage of its former possessors.[29]

Douglas's report may allude to conflicting claims of the kind that Mayne was describing.

In his account, Douglas implied that one purchase had been made, but the treaty register includes two treaties, one with 10 signatories, and the other with 118 (see figure 30). However, Douglas apparently did not send a copy of the treaty to London, not even to the HBC's headquarters. The HBC directors almost certainly thought Douglas had concluded one treaty with the Saanich.

Because Douglas concluded the Saanich treaties long after he received the template treaty text, there was no reason for him to ask the Saanich leaders to sign blank pages to which the text of the treaties might be added later.[30] However, the physical layout of the text and "signatures" on the Saanich treaties suggest that he might have. The text of the South Saanich treaty, concluded on 7 February, unlike the previous treaties, begins at the top of the left-hand page and ends six lines before the end of the page. In large handwriting across nine lines of the top half of the right-hand page, someone wrote "Cedar Hill to North Saanich Cowichan Hd South Saanich." The names appear (in different handwriting) beginning on the nineteenth line of this page, with only one empty line at the bottom. More than for any other treaty, this is the kind of layout that one might expect if the names were entered at the bottom of a "blank" (although actually with the brief territorial description) sheet, and the treaty text added later. The text of the North Saanich treaty, signed on 11 February, begins on the eighth line of the page, with two lines spilling onto the second page. Someone wrote "Cowichan Hd North Saanich" across the top of the first page. The 117 North Saanich names begin after eight empty lines and are spread across three pages. The three lists appear to correspond to three villages headed by "Hotutstun," "Is-hamtun," and "Huyla che."[31] The marks in these treaties, as in the Fort Victoria and Fort Rupert treaties, are sufficiently uniform to indicate that the marks were made with one hand and that the "signatories" did not actually make the marks, but merely "touched the pen."

The text of the North Saanich treaty ends abruptly in mid-sentence, ending with "we have received as payment" without indicating what was paid, and does not end, as the others do, with the place and date, or an attestation indicating that the signatures are "in token" of the payments. (This information would have taken up five of the eight blank lines if it had been included.) This deficiency in the North Saanich treaty is further evidence that Douglas did not treat these agreements with the same gravity with which Kemp treated his, or with the solemnity that treaty commissioners normally did. Both treaties were witnessed by HBC clerks Joseph William McKay and R. Golledge. Although Douglas had now become an agent of the British Crown, with authority to appoint treaty commissioners or negotiate treaties himself on behalf of the Crown, he did not sign the documents. He only had the Saanich mark the treaties and some HBC men sign as witnesses.

Given that he did not negotiate the Saanich treaties in response to instructions from London, it is unclear whether Douglas paid any attention to his earlier instructions to negotiate purchases based on Indigenous land use as of 1846. As has already been noted, Indigenous land use on the Saanich Peninsula changed significantly between 1846 and the date upon which the treaties were concluded. The HBC did not have a trading post on the Saanich Peninsula, but the establishment of Fort Victoria had encouraged much greater travel along the east coast of Vancouver Island, including by northern villagers who had raided Saanich villages. The escalating danger of raids had caused Saanich to relocate villages to the west side of the peninsula.

The Saanich peoples today consist of five First Nations, the Tsawout, Tsartlip, Pauquachin, Malahat, and Tseycum, but James Douglas completed two treaties with divisions that are not recognizable today.[32] According to Duff and Frogner, the Saanich had three main winter villages at the time of treaty, at Brentwood Bay, Union Bay (Patricia Bay), and Saanichton Bay.[33] However, Diamond Jenness's informants in 1935 told him that either the Comox or Kwakiutl destroyed the Saanich village at Brentwood Bay in about 1850.[34] James Douglas's enumeration of the "original Indian Population" of Vancouver Island (Appendix A) reveals that the number of signatories on the treaties corresponds with the number of "men with beards" in Douglas's 1853 census.[35] The payment per chief appears to have been the same as for the chiefs of the Fort Victoria treaties – 17 shillings per chief. The list cost was £41.13.4, although the Department Cost was given as £109.7.6. The total population of the North and South Saanich, 739, was roughly equal to that of the Songhees (700).

According to Wilson Duff, the South Saanich, as a group, did not pre-date the establishment of Fort Victoria and did not continue to exist after 1852.[36] On the other hand, according to H.G. Barnett, who did fieldwork with the Saanich in 1935, the West and East Saanich had been distinct and autonomous divisions of the Saanich.[37] Given the evidence that many Saanich villagers along the east side of the peninsula relocated to locations on the west side of the peninsula during the early 1850s in the face of relentless raids from northern groups, Douglas's treaties may in fact have been with actual divisions of the Saanich, and that in the tumultuous 1850s, they appeared to him to be more divided by north and south than east and west. However, unlike the two Fort Rupert treaties, which covered identical territories, the written Saanich Treaties, like the Fort Victoria treaties, identified distinct territories.

As had been the case with the Fort Victoria and Fort Rupert villages, the villagers of the Saanich Peninsula also spent part of each year on the mainland or on Gulf Islands. None of the treaties, however, mentioned the Gulf Islands or mainland.

The final Vancouver Island treaty, like the first, was connected with coal. Personnel in the HBC learned of coal at Nanaimo in much the same way as they learned of the Suquash coalfield. Joseph William McKay later recalled a December 1849 day while he was in his office in Victoria that the foreman of the blacksmiths' shop informed him that a Nanaimo man "named Che-wech-i-kan, later known as Coal Tyee, from the vicinity of Protection Island had been in the shop to have his gun repaired and while waiting and watching operations he picked up some lumps of coal which he observed very closely. Subsequently, when he saw the men use some coal to replenish the fire, he said that there was plenty of such stone where he lived."[38] McKay investigated the site and reported on the coal in 1850, but as long the HBC still hoped that paying coal could be found in northern Vancouver Island, the company did little to pursue this new information. Then, after being reminded of it in 1852, James Douglas visited "Wentuhysen Inlet" (Nanaimo harbour) at the head of a party that included Joseph Pemberton, John Muir (the erstwhile oversman at Fort Rupert with whom the company had reconciled), Richard Golledge, and "a few Indians." On 18 August 1852, James Douglas excitedly reported to the HBC's directors that "the mineral wealth of Vancouver's Island has not been overrated." Accordingly, he decided "to take possession of the Coal District for the Company," to send miners to the site, erect a few buildings, and to "purchase coal from the natives."[39] While Douglas did not explain in this letter how he intended to "take possession" of the district, he instructed Joseph William McKay six days later to take possession in much the same way as he instructed Finlayson to take possession of San Juan Island in 1847:

> proceed with all possible diligence to Wentuhysen Inlet commonly known as Nanymo Bay and formally take possession of the Coal beds lately discovered there for and in behalf of the Hudson's Bay Company.

You will give due notice of that proceeding, to the Masters of all ships arriving there, and you will forbid all persons to work the coal, either directly by means of their own labour or indirectly through Indians or other parties employed for that purpose, except under the authority of a License from the Hudson's Bay Company.[40]

Douglas later explained to the Governor and Committee that he had hurriedly sent McKay and some servants to take possession of the coalfield "in consequence of a report that other parties were going thither to dig and purchase Coal from the Indians a plan which I thought it necessary to anticipate by unequivocally establishing the Company's right to the coal District through actual possession."[41]

These actions shed light on James Douglas's perception of Indigenous title. He saw no contradiction between taking formal possession of land on behalf of the HBC and concluding land-purchase agreements with Indigenous people. Between 1847, when he had instructed Roderick Finlayson to perform the rite of possession on San Juan Island, and 1852, when he instructed J.W. McKay to do so at Nanaimo, Douglas had, on 3 September 1849, recommended to the HBC that "some arrangements should be made as soon as possible with the native Tribes for the purchase of their lands." In August 1852, he acted quickly to take possession of the land on behalf of the HBC (not, evidently, the Crown) but awaited the London Committee's direction regarding any arrangements with the Indigenous people. Douglas clearly believed that the HBC had the right to possess and exploit the coal resources and survey the land around Nanaimo before making a purchase agreement with the local villagers. Joseph Pemberton and B.W. Pearse surveyed the immediate vicinity of Nanaimo in September 1852.[42] On 6 October 1852, Douglas reported to Archibald Barclay that "I have sent an express by Indian conveyance to Fort Rupert directing that Mr Gilmour, and party be sent to Nanaimo by the Steam vessel ... as he can be employed there to much more advantage than at Fort Rupert where he appears to be doing little good."[43] On 14 March 1853, Douglas reported to the company's Northern Council that "we have suspended mining operations altogether at Fort Rupert, in consequence of the failure of every trial made to strike a remunerative seam of Coal in that District, and the Miners, are now much more advantageously employed, on a valuable seam of Coal, discovered last summer at Nanaimo Bay."[44] During 1853, officials in Victoria proceeded to identify lands in the Nanaimo area that the company would want. After receiving a map drawn by Joseph Pemberton and showing the land that was selected for purchase by the HBC, Barclay wrote that "the boundaries of the land to be taken by the Company in the Nanaimo district ... appears to have been well selected. The 6000 acres will be taken, and the sum of £6000, less 10 per cent, will be transferred to the credit of the Trust account as soon as the title is completed."[45]

Between 1852 and 1854, the HBC purchased coal mined by Nanaimo villagers – up to 50 tons per day, but typically 20 tons per day – even as they also employed Scottish miners there. The HBC also developed a salt spring nearby and built a sawmill in 1853.[46] There is no evidence that the Nanaimo protested any of the HBC's activities or demanded payment for the lands. Apart from willingly mining coal, they traded building supplies and salmon.[47]

The Nanaimo villagers had traded with the HBC since the HBC established Fort Langley. In July 1827, as his party was ascending the Fraser River on its way to establish Fort Langley, clerk George Barnston described a Nanaimo fishing village of about 400 people on the south side of the Fraser River near the present-day New Westminster.[48] In July 1829, Archibald McDonald described the Nanaimo as "a numerous tribe and live mostly on the Island – during the Salmon Season they occupy a large Village they have about 3 miles below this [Fort Langley] on Same Side the river."[49] There is little doubt that James Douglas knew well before 1854 that the Nanaimo had winter villages on Vancouver Island and a large summer fishery on the mainland.

HBC traders at Fort Langley had already introduced the Nanaimo to the HBC's trading principles. In August 1827, the traders successfully demanded the return of an axe taken from the HBC by a Nanaimo person.[50] While Nanaimo chiefs facilitated the peaceful outcome of that minor incident, one of their chiefs instigated a more dangerous confrontation on 10 July 1828. James McMillan reported:

> The Nanaimans paid us a visit headed by the two principal Chiefs, Pinnis and Squatches. The former began by offering two Land Otter tails and Said he wanted a knife each for them. After that he would bring his other Skins to trade – They then asked to be allowed to go all in the Fort to see how it was arranged. They were told that every one who had Beaver to trade should be allowed to go inside with his Skins, but them who brought nothing must remain on the bank. At this Monssr. Savage got upon his high horse – Said he had plenty Skins, but as we did not allow the Indians out and in as they pleased he would not allow his tribe to trade any – As this was a thing I would not agree to, on any Condition, but especially as a threat followed – they were immediately told to be off the ground as fast as they Could and never to Shew their faces about the Fort. This prompt behaviour Soon took down Mr. Chief to his level – and Said he would

trade quietly the next time he Came. Nothing would now do with us but they must be off, So they went away very quietly."[51]

J.W. McKay, in charge at Nanaimo, attempted to reinforce these principles at Nanaimo, which was a particularly volatile location. Only a few days after he arrived to establish Nanaimo (see figure 29), McKay learned that on 29 August 1852, a Quamichan (Cowichan) man had killed a Nanaimo man to avenge the death of a Cowichan man at the hands of the Lekwiltok.[52] The Cowichan believed that Nanaimo chief Wun Wun Shin had instigated the killing – an allegation that the Nanaimo denied.[53] Worried that the HBC would become embroiled in this conflict even before they had a chance to build their post, McKay convinced the Nanaimo to send emissaries to the Cowichan valley "to treat with the Cowechins concerning yesterdays murder and to settle affairs if possible by demanding payment on behalf of the victims family."[54] The outreach failed to make peace. On 17 September, a party of forty Cowichan in four canoes attacked and killed a Nanaimo man and enslaved his wife and child while they were away from the post.[55] At the same time, J.W. McKay reported that "A Sku who-mish [Squamish] Indian was murdered at this place eight days ago by a Nanaimo in revenge for three Nanaimoes who were killed by the Skuwhomish the last Winter."[56]

Less than three months after Nanaimo was established, James Douglas seized an occasion upon which to demonstrate to the Cowichan and Nanaimo how the company would respond when any of their members killed an HBC servant. On 5 November 1852, Peter Brown, an Orcadian servant of the HBC at the sheep farm at Christmas Hill about five miles north of Fort Victoria was killed, apparently by two men, a Cowichan and a Nanaimo.[57] James Douglas immediately sent a message to the chiefs demanding that they give up the suspect.[58] The accused Nanaimo man visited Nanaimo "for the purpose of exculpating himself," but was told to present himself to authorities in Victoria.[59] After getting no response at Victoria by 23 December, Douglas, acting as the Governor of the colony of Vancouver Island yet interested as an HBC officer, seized upon the fact that the Royal Navy's *Thetis* was at Esquimalt Harbour at the time, and requisitioned Captain Augustus Kuper, in command of the vessel, to accompany him on a mission that would demonstrate to the Cowichan and Nanaimo that the killing would not be overlooked. Kuper judged that the expedition could be contemplated only with the assistance of the HBC's *Beaver*, which was then away. Once the *Beaver* returned and the weather improved, the HBC's *Beaver* and *Recovery* proceeded with HMS *Thetis* and its launch, barge, and pinnace in tow, together with a very large force – 130 naval seamen, marines and officers, and eleven Voltigeurs from Victoria – "in order to awe the Indians and prevent further murders and aggressions, which I fear may take place if the Indians are emboldened by present impunity."[60]

On 7 January 1853, the expedition landed "on a pretty rising oak-ground" near the mouth of the Cowichan River proposed by Saseiah (Saw-se-a), the Cowichan chief, and lit a fire.[61] They then did something that might hint at what they might have done when negotiating the Vancouver Island treaties: they erected a small tent in the rain under which Douglas stood beside gifts to be presented to the Cowichan.[62] Douglas explained that two large Cowichan canoes then arrived,

> crowded with the friends and relatives of the murderer, hideously painted and evidently prepared to defend the wretched man, who was himself among the number, to the last extremity. On landing they made a furious rush towards the spot where I stood, a little in advance of the force, and their deportment was altogether so hostile, that the marines were with difficulty restrained, by their officers, from opening a fire upon them. When the first excitement had a little abated, the felon, fully armed, was brought into my presence, and I succeeded after a great deal of trouble, in taking him quietly into custody; and sent him a close prisoner on board the Steam vessel.[63]

Rear Admiral Moresby explained that the surrender of the prisoner after two hours of debate occurred "in somewhat striking fashion, for the warriors all sank to the ground, the culprit and his old father alone remaining standing and abashed."[64] According to James Douglas, after the Cowichan surrendered the accused, he then seized the opportunity to address the Cowichan

> on the subject of their relations with the Colony and the Crown. I informed them that the whole country was a possession of the British Crown, and that Her Majesty the Queen had given me a special charge, to treat them with justice and humanity and to protect them against the violence of all foreign nations which might attempt to molest them, so long as they remained at peace with the settlement. I told them to apply to me for redress, if they met with any injury or injustice at the hand of the colonists and not to retaliate, and above all things, I undertook to impress upon the minds of the chiefs, that they must respect Her Majesty's warrant, and surrender any criminal belonging to their respective tribes, on demand of the Court Magistrat and that resistance to the civil power, would expose

them to be considered as enemies. I also told them that being satisfied with their conduct in the present conference, peace was restored and they might resume their trade with Fort Victoria. The distribution of a little tobacco and some speechifying on the part of the Indians, expressions of their regard and friendship for the whites closed the proceedings and the conference broke up.[65]

Douglas then proceeded north with the prisoner to Nanaimo, where he arrived on 10 January 1853 to open "negotiations with the Nanaimoes for the delivering into the hands of justice of Siam-a-tuna son of Tche-hetum. Said Siamaton being accused of having participated in the murder of Peter Brown at Victoria."[66] However, Douglas found it more difficult to take custody of the accused Nanaimo man. The Nanaimo were divided. Some, primarily young men, refused to hand over the accused, and secreted him away, while the older men claimed to wish to hand him over.[67] According to Douglas, on the morning of 12 January, instead of surrendering the accused, the Nanaimo "brought a quantity of furs, which they offered as a ransom from the criminal, this was of course rejected and they were made to understand that no compromise could be made, and that the criminal himself must be delivered into our hands."[68] Lieutenant Arthur Sansum then seized and occupied one of the Nanaimo villages, held in custody two of the Nanaimo's leading men including the accused's father, and threatened to destroy the villagers' winter food stores, until the standoff was resolved by the capture of the fugitive on 15 January.[69] On Monday, 18 January 1853, "Squeis and Siam-a-sit were tried for the murder of Peter Brown. They were found Guilty, condemned and executed at Tide-staff point."[70]

Douglas was pleased with the results of his gambit. He informed the Duke of Newcastle, the Colonial Secretary:

> I found both the Cowegin and Nanaimo Tribes more amenable to reason than was supposed; the objects of the Expedition having, under Providence, been satisfactorily attained, as much through the influence of the Hudson's Bay Company's name, as by the effect of intimidation. The surrender of a criminal, as in the case of the Cowegin murderer, without bloodshed, by the most numerous and warlike of the Native Tribes on Vancouver's Island, at the demand of the Civil power may be considered, as an epoch, in the history of our Indian relations, which augurs well for the future peace and prosperity of the Colony. That object however could not have been effected without the exhibition of a powerful force.[71]

Newcastle responded by writing:

> I have to acknowledge the receipt of your Despatch of the 21$^{st}$ of January last reporting the measures which you had taken for effecting the surrender of the murderers of the late Peter Brown, and to acquaint you that Her Majesty's Government regard the conduct of you[r]self, the Naval Officers, and Seamen, and others engaged in the two expeditions against the Native Tribes, as highly creditable to all the parties concerned, and deserving of their entire approbation.[72]

As pleased as Douglas might have been, the incident surrounding Peter Brown did not pacify the Nanaimo district. In fact, HBC traders found it increasingly difficult to maintain peace at Nanaimo after 1852. In May 1853, two young Nanaimo men fired at a Cowichan man, apparently within sight of the HBC fort. McKay reported that the Cowichan escaped with two flesh wounds but that the attack "occurred so near the premises that I was under the necessity of reprimanding the Nanaimoes very severely for carrying their murderous practices so near our peaceful homes."[73] Douglas commended McKay by stating that "you did right to warn them off the precincts of the Fort, as such barbarous act must not be allowed near our premises."[74]

Nanaimo attracted Suquamish, Sechelt, Chemainus, Sliammon, Bella Bella (Heiltsuk), and other villagers who were often at odds with one another.[75] In 1853, parties of aggressive northern visitors of Tongass Tlingit, Kwakiutl, Tsimshian, and Haida also began travelling to Fort Victoria for trade and employment. The Indian wars in the United States added to the uncertainty. The Nanaimo post journals show that circumstances at Nanaimo were fraught after early 1853.[76] For example, a skirmish on 26 May 1854 involved people from several different rival groups:

> 10 Bilballa [Bella Bella, Heiltsuk] Canoes came alongside on their way north from Victoria. 6 Tongas [a division of the Tlingit] Canoes passed the Harbour a number of Tatakas [Cowichan] who arrived here yesterday with Thomas Ouamtany hearing a report that their Village had been sacked by the Bilballas on their way up. opened fire on the Bilballas which the latter promptly returned, in less than five minutes Commercial Inlet was Covered with war Canoes the Firing continued until the Bilballas were well Clear of the harbour two of them were shot by the first volley from the Cowechins They were afterwards Chased by the latter without any important result.[77]

HBC employees were not targets of these conflicts, but the incidents that occurred within sight of the fort were apparently minor compared with those that occurred between Nanaimo and Cape Mudge, a part of the coast that was not pacified until the early 1860s when the British Navy gunboat HMS *Forward* launched a punitive raid against the Lekwiltok at Cape Mudge in 1860, and another against a Haida encampment in the same vicinity in 1861.[78]

While Douglas apparently negotiated the Saanich Peninsula treaties in response to Indigenous claims without direction from London, the Nanaimo context casts doubt on whether Douglas intended to negotiate a treaty at Nanaimo. At any rate, he negotiated for the Nanaimo coalfields in a belated response to instructions written in London on 14 January 1853 – as the Peter Brown incident was reaching its conclusion. On that date Archibald Barclay wrote Douglas that "the Governor and Committee think you should take an early opportunity of extinguishing the Indian claim in the Coal district. When this is done, and more correct and full surveys made of the Coalfield, as well as the surface of the country, the Governor and Committee will purchase a portion of the Coalfield and of the Harbour, so as to have access to a good shipping place, but by no means to monopolise the Coalfield."[79] Douglas's response shows that he had become considerably less enthusiastic about concluding land purchases, although the wording of his response did not imply a connection with events surrounding Peter Brown. He promised to follow their instructions "as soon as I think it safe, and prudent to renew the question of Indian rights, which always gives rise to troublesome excitements, and has on every occasion been productive of serious disturbances. Any delay in that matter will not interfere with the survey of the District, as the Indians are manageable enough when not exposed to the impulses of violent excitement."[80] Douglas did not explain why he did not consider "it safe, and prudent" to do so in May 1853. Neither did he elaborate on the "troublesome excitements" that always arose when the issue of Indigenous title was raised, but he believed that it was safer at that moment not to arrange a treaty even though the HBC's presence had increased significantly. His wording seems to suggest that issues surrounding Indigenous title sparked conflict among Indigenous leaders or among Indigenous communities, rather than between the company and the Indigenous communities. He may have feared triggering the kinds of descent-based internal conflicts that Richard Mayne described in 1862 (see pages 224–5).

The Governor and Committee were not interested solely in a treaty. They emphasized that they were deeply interested in Indigenous affairs "and consider it their duty to do all in their power to ameliorate the condition of the natives." They commended Douglas for employing Indigenous miners. They hoped such employment might teach "to

Governor James Douglas and the Saanich and Nanaimo Treaties    235

some degree of regular industry, and to the observance of decency in their habits and mode of life." They had higher hopes "that a judicious and zealous religious instructor, who can communicate with them in their own language, may be able to bring them within the pale of Christianity. Much indeed on the way of conversion can hardly be expected from the adult natives, but such influence may be gained over them as to induce them to allow their children to be instructed both in religious and secular knowledge, and in due time an Indian school may be established." To that end, the company was recruiting a Free Church minister who, aside from attending to the exogenous miners and their families, would serve as a missionary to the Nanaimo villagers.[81]

When Douglas did finally complete the land-purchase agreement at Nanaimo, he forgot, at first, to mention it.[82] Even when he did explain his purchase, he provided little detail. On 26 December 1854, Douglas added a postscript to a letter dated Christmas day, to say:

In my letter of yesterday's date I neglected to mention that I concluded a negotiation, on the 23rd Inst. with the Nanaimo Indians for the purchase of the District, claimed as their hereditary possession by that Tribe.

This has been a long pending matter, and of difficult settlement, in consequence of the mineral character of the District purchased.

There was, on that account a strong disposition on the part of the Indians to make a good bargain, and I was of course obliged to allow them better terms, than was given on the occasion of former purchases. The district thus acquired extends from Dodd's narrows in the Canal de Arro, to a headland eight miles north of Colvile Town, which is included, with all the Islands on the coast, in the purchase.

The coast line may on a rough estimate, be given as 20 miles in length, by 10 miles in breadth, forming about 200 square miles of country, less a small reserve for village sites and cultivated fields which remain for the use of the Indians. The outlay made on that purchase was 668 Blankets valued at about £270. The Indian Title being thus extinguished I have instructed Mr Pemberton to prepare the Title Deeds for the 6000 acres of land purchased at Colvile Town by the Company, at his earliest convenience.

The Deed of Sale was signed by every male adult member of the Tribe, Chiefs as well as the common class of people, and they all appeared perfectly satisfied with the arrangement.[83]

The fact that Douglas forgot to mention the treaty in his 25 December letter again shows that he attached little significance to the agreement and did not conduct it with the gravity and pageantry typical of treaty negotiations.[84] The outlay suggests that each signatory received goods worth about 34 shilling at the Departmental cost, considerably more than those of previous treaties. Although Douglas indicated that each adult male member of the community signed the "deed," he enclosed no copy of the treaty. In fact, it is possible that he never produced a written copy of the treaty. The treaty book containing the written version of the other Vancouver Island treaties includes two copies of a document that simply reads: "A Similar conveyance of country extending from Commercial Inlet, 12 miles up the Nanaimo River made by the Sarlequiun Tribe signed Squoniston & others." Following these pages are six pages of blue foolscap with 159 names, followed by:

> Done at Fort Nanaimo Colvile Town this 23$^{rd}$ day of December in the year of our Lord 1854 in presence of us, who in the presence of each other, have hereunder affixed our names
> Signed Charles Edward Stuart H.B.Co. in charge of Fort Nanaimo
> Richard Golledge Hudsons Bay Cos. Service
> George Robinson – Manager of the Nanaimo Coll$^y$
> James Douglas Governor Vancouvers Island[85]

Thus, although the text of the treaty was not written out, this treaty document is the only one that James Douglas signed. He also indicated in what capacity – Governor – he signed it. These pages referring to the Nanaimo treaty were apparently, at one time, pinned or tied into the book, although they no longer are.[86] Douglas's 1856 estimate of the Indigenous population of Vancouver Island (Appendix A) showed four family groups of Nanaimo, with 159 "men with beards." That exactly matches the number of signatures collected.

Thus ended the nineteenth-century history of treaty making on Vancouver Island. Douglas estimated the total Indigenous population of Vancouver Island to be about 25,873. If his estimates are correct, he had concluded treaties with under 17 per cent of the Indigenous population of the island. Meanwhile, the exogenous population did not yet exceed 1,000 by 1856.[87] Douglas may not have been convinced that there was any legal obligation to conclude treaties, and, although he recommended them on 3 September 1849, he appears to have disliked negotiating them by 1854, at least in part because of the "troublesome excitements" they engendered. Still, he considered that the treaties imposed obligations on the government, even if he also believed that the treaty promises only codified the kinds of protective policies that were obligatory on government.

Douglas could not have been aware that on 26 December 1854, the very day that he penned his report of the Nanaimo Treaty, 250 kilometres away near the HBC's Fort Nisqually Isaac I. Stevens, Governor (and ex officio Superintendent of Indian Affairs) of Washington Territory, concluded the Treaty of Medicine Creek with the "Nisqually, Puyallup, Steilacoom Squawskin, S'Homamish, Stehchass, T'Peeksin, Squi-aitl, and Sa-heh-wamish," all of whom were "for the purpose of this treaty, ... to be regarded as one nation."[88] After two days of difficult negotiations, these villagers ceded over 9,000 square kilometres (2.24 million acres) of territory surrounding southern Puget Sound. In one treaty, Stevens obtained a surrender of about nine times as much land as the HBC obtained in all of its Vancouver Island treaties combined! Then, in little more than a month, Stevens negotiated the Treaty of Point Elliott with the leaders of Duwamish, Suquamish, Snoqualmie, Snohomish, Lummi, Skagit, Swinomish, and other villagers for a much larger territory (perhaps 30,000 square kilometres) between Puget Sound and the Cascade Mountains (22 January 1855), the Treaty of Point No Point for lands of the Klallam and the "Sko-ko-mish, To-an-hooch, and Chem-a-kum" on the Olympic Peninsula south of the Strait of Juan de Fuca (26 January 1855), and the Treaty of Neah Bay with the Makah and others (31 January 1855). The Quinault Treaty followed on 1 July 1855 (see figure 28).[89] By January 1856, Stevens, and the Governor of Oregon Territory, Joel Palmer, negotiated treaties for most of the land in Washington and Oregon Territories west of the Cascade Mountains.

The written Stevens treaties, concluded in the context of increasing conflict between settlers and Indigenous people, were far lengthier than the Vancouver Island treaties – each was more than 1,5000 words long. The Indigenous signatories made various commitments, to cede Indian title, to free their slaves, and "not to trade at Vancouver's Island or elsewhere out of the dominions of the United States." In exchange the Indigenous communities were promised monetary compensation (in the form of beneficial goods), reservations, the "right of taking fish, at all usual and accustomed grounds and stations," and education. Douglas must have become aware of these treaties soon after they were concluded but appears not to have been influenced by them in any way. On one hand, negotiating for vast swathes of territory with multiple communities might have seemed to be an attractive alternative to the approach Douglas had taken, but the Stevens treaties were made possible by large treaty commissions with substantial funds backed up by significant military power. Anson Dart, the inaugural Superintendent of Indian Affairs for Oregon Territory, had concluded nineteen poorly documented treaties with much smaller Indigenous groups between June and November 1851, but the United States Congress did not ratify those treaties.[90] No admirer of American Indian policy, Douglas would have been disinclined to emulate either the Stevens or Dart treaties, and his hesitancy would have been deepened by the fact that Congress's failure to ratify the Dart treaties contributed to the outbreak of military conflict in 1853 and 1854, and discontent over the Stevens treaties was one of the causes of the so-called Puget Sound War of 1855–56 and the Yakima War (1855–58).[91]

After 1854, people with knowledge of the Vancouver Island treaties, including Douglas, Blanshard, and Simpson, did not mention them even in contexts in which one might expect they would. For example, there is no evidence that George Simpson or Richard Blanshard mentioned the treaties when testifying before the British Select Committee on the HBC in 1857.[92] In fact, when George Simpson was asked in connection with the Red River colony whether the company "recognise their [Indians] holding their possession of land?," he responded by saying, "No; the land was purchased of them, I think, in the time of Lord Selkirk by a regular purchase; a certain quantity of ammunition and tobacco, and various other supplies being given for it."[93] If Simpson had wanted the committee to know about the Vancouver Island treaties, that would have been the perfect time to mention them. The degree to which Simpson and Blanshard neglected opportunities to mention the treaties attaches more importance to the fact that – as will be discussed in chapter 12 – Douglas himself stopped negotiating them.

# 12 Indigenous Title on Vancouver Island and British Columbia, 1854–1875

Scholars have been puzzled that James Douglas did not negotiate treaties after 1854, but aspects of the history already presented here make his apparent volte-face less surprising. Douglas figured less prominently in the development of treaty policy than scholars have assumed. He also grew less keen to negotiate treaties over time, probably because of the "troublesome excitements" that negotiations stirred up. Moreover, Indigenous people received but nominal compensation for surrendering what British officials considered to be a limited burden on the Crown's ownership. Even if treaty promises were more significant than the payments, many would have thought that those promises merely articulated rights that could otherwise be recognized in policy. In short, few people in Douglas's day – humanitarians or not – considered land-purchase treaties to be essential to just and fair Indigenous policies, and there is no reason to believe that Douglas believed that his abandonment of treaty making was an about-face.

Scholars have agreed that James Douglas's policy in the colonies of British Columbia and Vancouver Island between 1858 and 1864 was to establish Indian reserves according to the wishes of the Indians themselves instead of negotiating treaties with them.[1] Political scientist Paul Tennant and geographer Cole Harris have been critical of Douglas's haphazard and informal policies that appeared to deny Indigenous title, but they did not challenge the argument that Douglas instructed surveyors to set aside as much land for Indigenous people as they requested.[2]

If Douglas had continued concluding treaties, he undoubtedly would have negotiated with the Cowichan next. The Cowichan began trading at Fort Langley, Fort Victoria, and Nanaimo soon after each of those posts was established, but they never had an HBC post in their territory. The Fort Victoria post journals reported that on 1 May 1850 – even as the Fort Victoria treaties were being negotiated – a Cowichan party traded furs and provisions there, and on 16 May 1850, Douglas wrote to London to state that immediately after he concluded the treaties at Victoria, the Cowichan and others (probably including Nanaimo) "expressed a wish to dispose of their lands, on the same terms; but I declined their proposals in consequence, of our not being prepared to enter into possession; which ought to be done immediately after the purchase or arrangement may be forgotten, and further compensation claimed by the natives."[3] This letter is the clearest indication that Douglas believed that it was imprudent to negotiate treaties until non-Indigenous settlement was imminent.

In 1850, Douglas already had reason to believe that the Cowichan Valley, located about 50 kilometres north of Victoria, would be attractive to settlers. On 3 September 1849, he had informed the HBC's directors that the Cowichan had told him that the Cowichan Valley had more good agricultural land than the Victoria district did, and that Cowichan River and a large lake (Cowichan Lake) offered an easy route across the island to a good harbour on the west coast.[4] Despite this information, the Governor and Committee did not encourage Douglas to negotiate a treaty with the Cowichan.

Douglas became more familiar with the valley in the early 1850s. In 1851, Joseph McKay and an interpreter, "under the protection of 'Hosua' chief of the 'Cowetchin' Tribe," visited the valley in response to Cowichan reports that there were coal and salt beds there.[5] Then, in 1851 and 1852 Honoré-Thimotheée Lempfrit (1803–1862), a French Roman Catholic Oblate missionary, launched a solo mission in the Cowichan Valley, but was forced to leave the mission after coming into conflict with the Cowichan. Douglas regarded such missions established away from HBC posts to be dangerous and futile.[6] Douglas visited the valley himself in August 1852 when he also reconnoitred the Nanaimo coalfields. He then explained that the "exceedingly friendly and hospitable" Cowichan kept "large and well kept fields of potatoes in a very flourishing state" at the mouth of the Cowichan River. He also repeated the information that the Cowichan River and Lake were navigable by canoe almost to the west coast of the island.[7]

Douglas continued to show interest in the Cowichan Valley after the Peter Brown incident in 1853. After visiting the valley again in August 1853, Douglas reported that the Cowichan "gave a very flattering account of the beauty and fertility of the country they inhabit, with the view of prevailing upon us to form a white settlement there, from which they would commercially derive much advantage."[8] In 1854 he reported that a village at Cowichan River had about 500 "fighting-men" and an overall population of about 2,100 people.⁹ In retrospect, Douglas would have been wise to pursue negotiations with the Cowichan in about 1854 or 1855 when he also negotiated for the land at Nanaimo. That he did not do so then can probably be attributed to the lack of coal there, the slow pace of settlement on the island, and his generally flagging enthusiasm for treaties.¹⁰

In 1856, Douglas's ability to rule Vancouver Island unilaterally became more conscribed. On 12 August 1856, the General Assembly (Legislative Council and Legislative Assembly) of Vancouver Island met for the first time. James Douglas used the occasion to describe how Vancouver Island was unique: "Self supporting and defraying all the expenses of its own Government, it presents a striking contrast, to every other Colony in the British Empire; and like the native Pines of its storm beaten promontories, it has acquired a slow but hardy growth."¹¹ Douglas's statement hints how the reality on Vancouver Island differed from the realities in British colonies in previous decades. Before the 1850s, when many of the treaties in New Zealand and in the colony of Canada were signed, the British government had traditionally borne the cost of land-transfer treaties with Indigenous people (that changed in the colony of Canada in 1860). Such was not the case on Vancouver Island, where the HBC put forward the money before 1859 (although it intended to charge these costs to the account of the colony), and the Imperial Government expected the colony to pay thereafter.

Douglas was undoubtedly aware that legislative assemblies in British colonies normally represented settler interests and rarely defended those of Indigenous communities, but Douglas and the settlers of Vancouver Island were also aware of the Indian Wars then wracking Washington and Oregon Territories.¹² Douglas's speech to the first General Assembly of the colony of Vancouver Island makes sense in that context. After discussing the arrival each year since 1853 of large parties of northern Indians (which chagrined settlers), Douglas reassured the assembly that the British government was sending a frigate to Vancouver Island.¹³ He urged the assembly, for "reasons of humanity and sound policy," to support his efforts "to conciliate the good will of the native Indian tribes by treating them with justice and forbearance and by rigidly protecting their civil and agrarian rights," reminding them that "the friendship of the natives is at all times useful, while it is not less certain that their enmity may become more disastrous than any other calamity to which the Colony is directly exposed."¹⁴ Douglas's allusion to the potentially disastrous consequences of Indian wars would not have been lost upon his audience. It was also in the context of ongoing conflict in Washington and Oregon Territories that Douglas wrote to

Colonial Secretary Henry Labouchère on 20 October 1856 to say that "as the safety and prosperity of the Colony depends more than upon any other cause, on our maintaining a good understanding with the native Tribes, I have used every possible means to command their respect and conciliate their friendship by protecting their rights and giving them redress, in all cases where they have suffered wrong, and with equal handed justice severely, punishing their own delinquencies."[15]

The Victoria district was further transformed in the spring of 1858 when thousands of migrants arrived in connection with the Fraser River gold rush. With the arrival of so many settlers came also the island's first newspaper, the *Victoria Gazette*, in June 1858. Douglas had never previously had to deal with newspapers and their influential and opinionated editors. He legitimately feared that the new migrants would stir up trouble with the Indigenous communities, and that the press would represent the interests of those migrants. Even after the Indian Wars in the northwestern United States had ended, Douglas was still alive to the importance of maintaining good relations with Indigenous people. In 1859, Douglas wrote to the Colonial Secretary, Sir Edward Bulwer Lytton (1803–1873), that "as friends and allies the Native races are capable of rendering the most valuable assistance to the Colony, while their enmity would entail on the settlers a greater amount of wretchedness and physical suffering, and more seriously retard the growth and material development of the Colony."[16]

Soon after the Indian Wars of Washington Territory died down, members of the assembly sought the removal of the Songhees from their reserve at Victoria. On 25 January 1859, the assembly unanimously passed a resolution moved by local taverner James Yates, a confirmed enemy of James Douglas and the HBC, asking "has the Government of this island the power to remove the Indians (by purchase) from that piece of land inside Victoria Harbour known as the Indian Reservation?"[17] Yates spearheaded a move to dispossess the Songhees of their reserve without the Songhees's enjoying any of the benefits of the sale. He proposed to sell the land and apply the proceeds of the sale of the reserve to settler priorities.

Douglas penned his reply on 5 February 1859, and the Speaker read that letter to the assembly three days later. Douglas considered his letter to be very important. It was published in the *Victoria Gazette* on 12 February 1859 and in the *Journals of the First House of Assembly* later in the year.[18] Furthermore, on 9 February – the day after it was read to the members of the Legislative Assembly – Douglas transmitted copies of his correspondence with the assembly to the Secretary of State for the Colonies, with a covering letter that indicated that "the subjects referred to in that correspondence are not of an important nature with the exception of that marked letter, dated 5th February, 1859, which touches on the subject of land reserved near the town of Victoria for the benefit of the native Indian population." After summarizing the letter, he wrote that "I have but little doubt that the proposed measure will be in accordance with the views of Her Majesty's Government, and I trust it may meet with their approval, as it will confer a great benefit on the Indian population, will protect them from being despoiled of their property, and will render them self-supporting, instead of being thrown as outcasts and burdens upon the Colony."[19] For all these reasons, the introductory portion of that letter can reasonably be interpreted to represent Douglas's intention to articulate publicly a clear and explicit statement of his Indian policy for the colony. It is significant, however, that his important letter referred only obliquely to the Fort Victoria treaties:

> I have to observe that previously to the grant of Vancouver's Island to the Hudson's Bay Company the whole island was vested in the Crown as part of its domains. When the Settlement at Victoria was formed certain reservations were made in favour of the native Indian Tribes.
> First. They were to be protected in their original right of fishing on the Coasts and in the Bays of the Colony, and of hunting over all unoccupied Crown Lands; and they were also to be secured in the enjoyment of their village sites and cultivated fields. These rights they have since enjoyed in full and the Reserves of land covering their Village sites and cultivated fields have all been distinctly marked on the maps and surveys of the Colony, and the faith of the Government is pledged, that the occupation shall not be disturbed.
> For that reason the Government will not cause them to be removed, because it is bound by the faith of a solemn engagement to protect them in the enjoyment of those Agrarian rights.[20]

Not willing to let the matter rest, James Yates pursued his agenda further on 15 February 1859 by moving that the Songhees reserve be sold. The minutes of the meeting are revealing for they show that Yates's motion failed to find a seconder but elicited a cutting response from Joseph D. Pemberton, the colony's surveyor (again, without mentioning treaties):

> Mr. Yates moved That the Indian reserve be sold and the proceeds taken after paying the Indians for the improvement of Victoria Harbour and other improvements. (see notice of motion Febr. 8th)

The motion not seconded but a discussion arose.

Mr. Yates declared the Indians a nuisance often insulting to the modesty of females or families and ought to be removed. That his Excellency the Governors proposition was absurd, because whilst the Indians remained in a position where spirits could so easily be had, nothing could be done in the way of civilizing them; besides the income derived from the sale of part of the reserve as proposed by his Excellency would bring in an enormous income, which would only be wasted or give room for gross speculation; if the proceeds were applied to the purpose intended by the Governor, the Indians would have such an idea of the value of land that hereafter their title could not be extinguished by this means.

Mr. Pemberton Thought that in common justice the land reserved for the Indians ought to be used for their benefit; it was only now that these lands had become valuable, that the Indians were found to be a nuisance; if bad spirits were the cause of preventing the improvement of Indians let the grog shops be removed. He thought if the Indians enquired how we had acquired their lands that we should stand in much worse light than they would with their reserve.

After some further discussion, the motion was lost, not having been seconded.[21]

So, as of 1859 Pemberton and almost all of the members of the Vancouver Island Legislative Assembly opposed Yates's motion to sell the Songhees reserve, although there is no indication that anyone referenced the treaties.[22] (Even if the motion had passed, it would have had no real effect, because the Legislative Assembly was not able to execute such a decision.)

Even as the assembly was debating the Songhees reserve, Douglas had his hands full. Until 1858, the mainland portion of what is now British Columbia, which the HBC referred to as the Columbia District, was an unorganized British territory to which the British Parliament had renewed the HBC's twenty-one-year revokable exclusive licence of trade in 1838. Except for HBC traders, a few missionaries, and some prospectors, there were few non-Indigenous people in the district. Historians have assumed that the there were no land purchases on the mainland, but intriguing evidence suggests that HBC officers may have negotiated some purchases before 1859. On 12 March 1860, Donald McLean, the HBC's Chief Trader at Kamloops, informed the Assistant Gold Commissioner at Lytton that he had been "authorized by A.G. Dallas, Esquire, to claim and take possession of Ten Miles square of land for and on behalf of the Hudson's Bay Company, the same having been granted to the said Company by the Government for the pre-emptive right of Trade in this District."[23] He wrote that "the said land was purchased originally from the Chief of the Aborigines by the Hudson's Bay Company's agent in this District."[24]

Circumstances on the mainland changed suddenly and dramatically in 1858 when at least 20,000 gold seekers, many of them citizens of the United States, travelled up the Fraser River to reach the gold fields of the Fraser Canyon.[25] Douglas feared that, unless he asserted greater British authority over the territory, the Columbia District might be lost to the United States. Although he did not have legal authority to do so, Douglas began administering the lower Fraser River region and gold fields as if they were in a formally established colony, issuing proclamations and licences, appointing officials, organizing a police force, and contracting for steamship services. He did so to protect British claims to the region, maintain law and order, and protect Indigenous people from abuse.[26]

Upon learning of the gold rush, the British government acted quickly to establish a formal colony there. On 1 July 1858, the British Colonial Secretary, E.B. Lytton, instructed Douglas, in light of the gold discoveries on the Fraser River, that "all claims and interests must be subordinated to that policy which is to be found in the peopling and opening up of the new country, with the intention of consolidating it as an integral and important part of the British Empire."[27] Fifteen days later Lytton wrote Douglas to inform him that the government planned to terminate the HBC's licence to the Columbia District, to establish a colony, and to appoint a Governor. Lytton asked Douglas to be the Governor, but on the condition that he sever his connection with the HBC.[28] Then, on 2 August 1858, the British government formally established the colony of British Columbia, and appointed James Douglas as its Governor. From 1858 to 1864 Douglas was Governor of the colonies of Vancouver Island and British Columbia but had ended his affiliation with the HBC.

Three days before the colony was officially created, Lytton wrote a long letter containing information and instructions. He told Douglas that he would be sending to the new colony a detachment of Royal Engineers, elite British soldiers, to survey the land in preparation for settlement.[29] Aside from his primary objective, of preserving British possession of British Columbia and ensuring the settlement of British subjects in the colony, Lytton also wanted to ensure the protection of the new colony's Indigenous peoples. In his 31 July 1858 letter Lytton transmitted to Douglas instructions regarding Indians that gave Douglas an opening to recommend the conclusion of treaties:

I have to enjoin upon you to consider the best and most humane means of dealing with the Native Indians. The feeling of this country would be strongly opposed to the adoption of any arbitrary or oppressive measures towards them. At this distance, and with the imperfect means of knowledge which I possess, I am reluctant to offer, as yet, any suggestion as to the prevention of affrays between the Indians and the immigrants. This question is of so local a character that it must be solved by your knowledge and experience, and I commit you, in the full persuasion that you will pay every regard to the interests of the Natives which an enlightened humanity can suggest. Let me not omit to observe, that it should be an invariable condition, in all bargains or treaties with the Natives for the cession of lands possessed by them, that subsistence should be supplied to them in some other shape, and above all, that it is the earnest desire of Her Majesty's Government that your early attention should be given to the best means of diffusing the blessings of the Christian Religion and of Civilization among the Natives.[30]

These are fascinating instructions. Lytton mentioned land-purchase "bargains or treaties" without instructing Douglas to negotiate them. Why was he so ambiguous? Was he keeping with long-standing policy of leaving that decision to Douglas's discretion? His first sentences suggest that he was, but it would have been prudent to say so explicitly about treaties. Lytton also failed to explain what he meant by lands "possessed" by the Indigenous people. Did he like Earl Grey and the HBC's Governor and Committee in 1849 believe that only land occupied by villages and cultivation needed to be purchased, or had he concluded like George Grey, James Douglas, and presumably the HBC's Governor and Committee since 1850, that treaties might as well encompass all of the territory claimed by an Indigenous community? His instructions would be easier to interpret if we knew whether Lytton was aware of the treaties Douglas had previously concluded on Vancouver Island. If he did know about them, he did not let on. Lytton's direction that "subsistence should be supplied to them [Natives] in some other shape" was a novel provision although he did not elaborate upon how it might be implemented. That part of his instructions, however, betrays that he believed that the lives of Indigenous people in the lower Fraser River region were about to change dramatically.

Lytton's position was similarly ambiguous when on 2 September 1858 he forwarded to Douglas correspondence he had received from F.W. Chesson, the Secretary of the London-based Aborigines Protection Society, warning Lytton of warfare with the Indigenous people of the newly formed colony of British Columbia unless wise policy was adopted promptly. Chesson's recommendations were wide-ranging but included land-purchase treaties, which had not previously figured prominently in the society's advocacy. After noting that "the recognition of native rights has latterly been a prominent feature in the aboriginal policy of both England and the United States," Chesson presented a distorted history by arguing that wherever Indigenous title had been recognized, "peace and amity have characterized the relations of the two races, but wherever a contrary policy has been carried out, wars of extermination have taken place." Rather than referring to the Vancouver Island treaties – of which he must not have been aware – or any other treaties concluded between 1682 and 1858, Chesson argued that "a Treaty should be promptly made between the delegates of British authority and the chiefs and their people, as loyal, just, and pacific as that between William Penn and the Indians of Pennsylvania."[31] When passing on Chesson's letter to Douglas, Lytton emphasized that, while he was very concerned that Indigenous communities must be protected, "I must not be understood as adopting the views of the Society as to the means by which this may be best accomplished."[32] Lytton clearly wanted to avoid being seen as rejecting or endorsing treaties.

The lives of Indigenous people in the lower Fraser River region changed quickly in 1858. Before the end of 1858, steamboats connected Victoria, Fort Langley, Hope, and Yale.[33] On 23 August 1858, Richard Clement Moody (1813–1887) of the Royal Engineers, was appointed Chief Commissioner of Lands and Works and Lieutenant Governor of British Columbia.[34] The promised detachment of 220 Royal Engineers under Moody's leadership arrived between November 1858 and April 1859 to maintain order in the new colony, and to begin to establish the basic infrastructure and foundations of the colony. On 19 November 1858, Douglas formally proclaimed the colony of British Columbia.[35] These developments had profound implications for the Indigenous inhabitants of the region; over a few months in 1858, the autonomy of the Indigenous people of the lower Fraser River region ended.[36]

Lytton and Douglas continued to correspond about Indigenous affairs, but Douglas did not seize upon the fact that Lytton had mentioned and the Aborigines Protection Society had urged the negotiation of treaties. On 30 December 1858, Lytton wrote to Douglas to state that "the success that has attended your transactions with these tribes induces me to inquire if you think it might be feasible to settle them permanently in villages; with such settlement civilization at once begins."[37] Douglas replied with a long letter stating that he considered a policy of settling the Indians in villages as being "the only plan which promises to result in the moral elevation of the native Indian races, in rescuing them from degradation; and protecting them from oppression and rapid decay."[38] He then reiterated his oft-repeated warning that "as friends and allies the native races are capable of rendering the most valuable assistance to the Colony, while their enmity would entail on the settlers a greater amount of wretchedness and physical suffering, and more serious retard the growth and material development of the Colony, than any other calamity to which, in the ordinary course of events, it would be exposed." If he had thought then that treaties were essential to maintaining the friendship of the Indigenous people of British Columbia, this was the time to recommend them. Instead, he noted: "Anticipatory reserves of land for the benefit and support of the Indian races will be made for that purpose in all the districts of British Columbia inhabited by native tribes. Those reserves should in all cases include their cultivated fields and village sites, for which from habit and association they invariably conceive a strong attachment, and prize more, for that reason, than for the extent or value of the land."[39] In Lytton's absence, it fell to Lord Carnarvon to reply to Douglas's letter. He, in words that recall Lytton's instructions of 31 July 1858, endorsed Douglas's proposed Indian reserve policy, "but whilst making ample provision, under the arrangements proposed, for the future sustenance and improvement of the Indian Tribes, you will I am persuaded bear in mind the importance of exercising due care in laying out and defining the several reserves so as to avoid checking at a future day the progress of the White Colonists."[40]

James Douglas was on the same page as Lytton and Newcastle. In May 1860 he reported to the Duke of Newcastle, who had succeeded Lytton as Colonial Secretary in June 1859, about a trip he made up the Fraser River towards Hope. After he described the "wealth and luxuriance of nature" in the region surrounding the Brunette, Coquitlam, and Pitt Rivers, and the lush forests along the Fraser River, the career fur trader admitted that he "could not repress the wish that those gorgeous forests might soon be swept away by the efforts of human industry, and give place to cultivated fields and the other accessories of civilization."[41]

If the slowness of settlement deterred Douglas from negotiating treaties between 1854 and 1858, the speed of immigration must have overwhelmed him after that. By the autumn of 1859, Douglas was concerned that the time it would take the government to complete surveys could seriously hinder the settlement of British migrants in the colony. On 1 October 1859, Douglas wrote a circular to the gold commissioners and magistrates of British Columbia, indicating that to deal with the lack of surveys "I have decided on introducing a Preemption Law, for the purpose of enabling such persons to settle at once on any unoccupied Crown Land, which may suit their purpose, on condition of immediate improvement."[42] When he explained his intentions to Newcastle, Douglas wrote that "there is no doubt that ... the pre-emptive law and other enactments, might enable thousands of the destitute poor of Britain, by a few years of steady industry, to secure for themselves, happy homes and a comfortable independence for life."[43] In his circular, however, Douglas also stipulated that "you will also cause to be reserved, the sites of all Indian villages, and the Land they have been accustomed to cultivate, to the extent of several hundred acres round each village for their especial use and benefit."[44] On 7 October he repeated these instructions to R.C. Moody.[45]

On 4 January 1860, Douglas issued the first of his pre-emption proclamations, which enabled British subjects and others willing to swear allegiance to the Crown to "acquire unoccupied and unreserved, and unsurveyed Crown land in British Columbia (not being the site of ... an Indian Reserve or settlement)."[46] The proclamation and Douglas's explanation of it show that Douglas hoped to facilitate the rapid settlement of a loyal British agrarian population on the land, but was also determined to protect the lands and interests of Indigenous people. In 1861, Douglas issued a similar proclamation for southeastern portions of Vancouver Island,[47] and on 6 September 1862, he expanded it to the entire colony of Vancouver Island: "British Subjects, and aliens who shall take the oath of allegiance to Her Majesty and Her successors, above the age of eighteen, may acquire the right to hold and purchase in fee simple, unsold, unoccupied and unreserved Crown Lands in Vancouver Island and its Dependencies, not being the site of an existent or proposed town, or auriferous land available for mining purposes, or an Indian Reserve or Settlement."[48] Given that the documentary records show that most of the "Indian reserves" were then nothing more than notional reserves, not marked on the ground, and perhaps not even on maps, the land reserved in the proclamations may be the "anticipatory reserves" Douglas had mentioned to the Colonial Secretary on 14 March 1859.

Curiously, although Douglas did not follow up on Lytton's 31 July 1858 suggestion that treaties might be concluded in British Columbia, he did urge the Colonial Secretary to approve them for Vancouver Island. He probably did so because of the Vancouver Island's legislative assembly. On an early spring day in Victoria in 1861, James Douglas, having been for almost ten years the Governor of the colony of Vancouver Island, sat down to pen a letter on behalf of the assembly to the Duke of Newcastle (1811–1864), the Colonial Secretary in Lord Palmerston's

Liberal ministry (1859–65), "praying for the aid of Her Majesty's Government in extinguishing the Indian title to the public lands in this Colony." He enclosed a petition of the assembly "setting forth, with much force and truth, the evils that may arise from the neglect of that very necessary precaution."[49] Douglas, who had already negotiated fourteen such agreements with Indigenous communities on Vancouver Island between 1850 and 1854, who had thorough knowledge of Indigenous societies throughout the HBC territories, and whose wife had roots in a Cree band in present-day northern Ontario, implied that the government needed to be attentive to the land rights of Indigenous communities on Vancouver Island. It probably did not help his case that in the previous decade he had not communicated with the Colonial Office at all about Indigenous title, or about the fact that he had concluded land purchases. For that reason, he was in the awkward position of having to provide background of which the Colonial Secretary must have been completely ignorant:

> [1.] I have the honour of transmitting a petition from the House of Assembly of Vancouver Island to your Grace, praying for the aid of Her Majesty's Government in extinguishing the Indian title to the public lands in this Colony; and setting forth, with much force and truth, the evils that may arise from the neglect of that very necessary precaution.
>
> 2. As the native Indian population of Vancouver Island have distinct ideas of property in land, and mutually recognize their several exclusive possessory rights in certain districts, they would not fail to regard the occupation of such portions of the Colony by white settlers, unless with the full consent of the proprietary tribes, as national wrongs; and the sense of injury might produce a feeling of irritation against the settlers, and perhaps disaffection to the Government that would endanger the peace of the country.
>
> 3. Knowing their feelings on that subject, I made it a practice up to the year 1859, to purchase the native rights in the land, in every case, prior to the settlement of any district; but since that time in consequence of the termination of the Hudson's Bay Company's Charter, and the want of funds, it has not been in my power to continue it. Your Grace must, indeed, be well aware that I have, since then, had the utmost difficulty in raising money enough to defray the most indispensable wants of Government.[50]

When citing purchases made as late as 1859, Douglas must have been thinking of two purchases conducted by William Eddy Banfield of small patches of ground in Alberni Canal in late 1859 and early 1860, and preserved as loose pages in the same "Register of Land purchases from Indians" as the other treaties.⁵¹ Douglas was putting his finger on the main issue; having been in the same position as George Grey in New Zealand until 1859 – having access to funds to pay for land purchases – he had been, since the end of the HBC's jurisdiction over the colony and his separation from the HBC, in the same position as Governors Hobson and FitzRoy, without the funds to pay for land purchases. Moreover, since Douglas now had to work with the Legislative Assembly, his ability to allocate funds unilaterally was circumscribed.

The second paragraph of Douglas's letter indicates that the land purchases were crucial for maintaining peace in the colony. He did not indicate that the company had initiated the treaty policy, and that Indigenous communities appear to have become alive to the importance of compensation for their claims only after the company had decided to negotiate the transactions.

Douglas then attempted to persuade the Colonial Secretary of the importance of concluding the purchases, pointing out that settlement had begun in three districts not yet purchased, that the cost of the purchases was small but escalating, but that the colony was unable to take on the expense, implying that the colony's position was made more difficult because the British government had not yet fully compensated the HBC for the expenses of running the colony until 1859:

> 4. All the settled districts of the Colony, with the exception of Cowichan, Chemainus, and Barclay Sound, have been already bought from the Indians, at a cost in no case exceeding £2.10/ Sterling for each family. As the land has, since then increased in value, the expense would be relatively somewhat greater now, but I think that their claims might be satisfied with a payment of £3 to each family: so that taking the native population of those districts at 1000 families, the sum of £3000. would meet the whole charge.
> 
> 5. It would be improper to conceal from your Grace the importance of carrying that vital measure into effect without delay.
> 
> 6. I will not occupy Your Grace's time by any attempt to investigate the opinion expressed by the House of Assembly, as to the liability of the Imperial Government for all expenses connected with the purchase of the claims of the aborigines to the public land, which simply amounts to this, that the expense would in the first instance, be paid by the Imperial Government, and charged to the account of proceeds arising from the sales of public land. The land itself would therefore be ultimately made to bear the charge.
> 
> 7. It is the practical question as to the means of raising the money, that at this moment more seriously engages my attention. The Colony being

already severely taxed for the support of its own Government, could not afford to pay that additional Sum; but the difficulty may be surmounted by means of an advance from the Imperial Government to the Extent of £3000., to be eventually repaid out of the Colonial Land Fund.

8. I would in fact strongly recommend that course to Your Grace's attention, as specially calculated to extricate the Colony from existing difficulties, without putting the Mother Country to serious expense; and I shall carefully attend to the repayment of the sum advanced, in full, <u>as soon as the Land Fund recovers in some measure</u> from the depression, caused by the delay Her Majesty's Government has experienced in effecting a final arrangement with the Hudsons Bay Company for the reconveyance of the Colony; as there is little doubt <u>when our new system of finance comes fully into operation</u>, that the revenue will be fully adequate to the expenditure of the Colony.[52]

Douglas evaded the question of who would ultimately pay for the treaties – whether the British government or the government of the colony of Vancouver Island. It would have been risky for him to follow the lead of the assembly and argue that the British government was obligated to bear the costs. The British government had covered the costs of such land purchases in the colonies of Canada and New Zealand, but the tide had turned quickly. For example, in 1860, the British government had transferred jurisdiction, and all financial responsibility, for Indian Affairs in the colony of Canada from London to the colonial government. Douglas might legitimately have argued that the British government could expect larger and more established colonies to assume the costs of managing Indigenous affairs after the government had subsidized those costs for decades while those colonies were in their infancy, but that it was unjust and unrealistic for it to assume that the tiny young colony of Vancouver Island could do so. He decided instead to skirt the question.

The House of Assembly of Vancouver Island passed a motion approving the following petition on 6 February 1861 to Newcastle, the Colonial Secretary:

> We, Her Majesty's faithful and loyal subjects, the Members of the House of Assembly of Vancouver Island in Parliament assembled, would earnestly request the attention of your Grace to the following considerations:
>
> 1. That many Colonists have purchased land, at the rate of one pound sterling per acre, in districts to which the Indian title has not yet been extinguished.
>
> 2. That, in consequence of the non-extinction of this title, these persons, though most desirous to occupy and improve, have been unable to take

possession of their lands – purchased, in most cases, nearly three years ago; and of this, they loudly and justly complain.

3. That the Indians, well aware of the compensation heretofore given for lands, appropriated for colonization, in the earlier settled districts of Vancouver Island, as well as in the neighbouring territory of Washington, strenuously oppose the occupation by settlers of lands still deemed their own. No attempts of the kind could be persisted in, without endangering the peace of the Country, for these Indians, though otherwise well disposed and friendly, would become hostile if their supposed rights as regards land were systematically violated; and they are still much more numerous and warlike, than the petty remnants of tribes, who in 1855 and 1856, in the western part of the adjacent United States territory of Washington, kept up for nearly a year, a desultory and destructive warfare, which compelled the whole agricultural population of the Country, to desert their homes, and congregate in blockhouses.

4. That, within the last three years, this Island has been visited by many intending settlers, from various parts of the world. Comparatively few of these have remained, the others having, as we believe, been in a great measure, deterred from buying land as they could not rely on having peaceable possession; seeing that the Indian Title was still unextinguished to several of the most eligible agricultural districts of the Island.

5. That the House of Assembly respectfully considers, that the extinction of the aboriginal title is obligatory on the Imperial Government.

6. That the House of Assembly, bearing in mind, that from the dawn of modern colonization until the present day, wars with aborigines, have mainly arisen from disputes about land, which by timely and moderate concession on the part of the more powerful and enlightened of the disputants concerned, might have been peaceably and economically adjusted; now earnestly pray, that Her Majesty's Government would direct such steps to be taken, as may seem best, for the speedy settlement of the matter at issue, and the removal of a most serious obstacle to the well being of this Colony.[53]

The petition of the House of Assembly and Douglas's letter sparked considerable discussion within the Colonial Office. Arthur Johnstone Blackwood, senior clerk in the Colonial Office wrote a memo to Thomas Frederick Elliot, Assistant Under-Secretary of State (the second-ranked civil servant in the Colonial Office), stating that:

> The early settlement of this matter is of much importance. I frequently am called upon to see at this office persons of all classes, desirous of settling in V.C. Isl$^d$ or B. Columbia and one of the questions proposed to me is usually how the claims of the Natives to Land are arranged; To which I have had

to ans$^r$ that I concluded they w$^d$ have to be bought up. But this has not been quite satisfactory to an enquiring settler, who, before he leaves these shores naturally desires to know exactly & positively what he may expect in the acquisition of Land in the Colony he has selected as his residence. Therefore if these Indian claims c$^d$ be fairly extinguished the arrangement w$^d$ facilitate immigration. But buying them by means of a Loan from the British Exchequer is probably questionable. I do not see why a loan sh. not be raised in the Colony, the amount wanted being only £3000. It is, however, to be observed that the Colony has lately borrowed £10,000 for harbor improvements.[54]

Internal correspondence within the Colonial Office reveals that personnel were worried about setting a precedent by lending the colony £3,000 to purchase Indian title. Elliot mused that the colony's prospects must have been dire if it needed to borrow a sum as small as £3,000.[55] Newcastle, one of the British Parliament's most vocal critics of the HBC, decided to apply to the Treasury for the money on behalf of the colony, but anticipated a refusal.[56] Accordingly, in June, Elliot submitted a letter to George A. Hamilton, Secretary of the Treasury, requesting the loan.[57]

Newcastle's hunch was correct. In late September, the Treasury refused the application, in the first place because the petition of the Vancouver Island Assembly argued that the Home Government should pay for the purchases, but also because they argued that the colony could continue making small, manageable purchases as necessary, paying for the purchases out of their own funds.[58] The refusal appears to have inspired those within the Colonial Office to share their true feelings with their colleagues. Sir Frederic Rogers, the permanent Under-Secretary of State for the colonies, wrote that, since the colony would get the profit of the eventual land sales to settlers, the duty of "buying up the Indian title" rested with the local legislature.[59] Elliot and Blackwood agreed. Blackwood wrote: "The reason why the Governor finds it difficult to get money for the service of the Govt of Van C. Island is simply because the Legislature is unwilling to tax the Community sufficiently for the purpose."[60] Newcastle concluded with "I quite agree. It is miserable work to see the Colony objecting to pay so small a sum for an object at once essential to their interests and purely Colonial in its character."[61]

Those exchanges explain Newcastle's 19 October 1861 response to Douglas's request:

> I am fully sensible of the great importance of purchasing without loss of time the Native title to the soil of Vancouver Island: but the acquisition of the title is a purely Colonial Interest and the Legislature must not entertain

any expectation that the British Taxpayer will be burthened to supply the funds or British Credit pledged for the purpose. I would earnestly recommend therefore to the House of Assembly that they should enable you to procure the requisite means; but if they should not think proper to do so, Her Majesty's Government cannot undertake to supply the money requisite for an object which, whilst it is essential to the interests of the people of Vancouver Island, is at the same time purely Colonial in its character, and trifling in the charge that it would entail.[62]

The British government's response was in keeping with trends within the British world. It was the British Crown that promised to purchase the Indian title in the Royal Proclamation of 1763, that continued to supervise Indian affairs in the Canadas, and that paid for treaties in Canada until 1860. But in keeping with the trend towards handing over powers and responsibilities to British colonies, the British government had transferred jurisdiction over Indian affairs in Canada to the local government in 1860, together with the responsibility for the cost of treaty annuities. After paying the price for extinguishing Indigenous title for many years in older colonies, the Colonial Office insisted that small colonies like Vancouver Island and the new colony of British Columbia would have to assume the costs themselves.

It cannot have helped, however, that the HBC and James Douglas had not informed anyone in the Colonial Office until 1861 that the purchases had ever been made. Far from being made at the Colonial Office's behest, treaties were in fact made without the Colonial Office's knowledge. An English translation of the treaty of Akaroa of New Zealand arrived in the Colonial Office within months, and was published in the *British Parliamentary Papers* within a year. By contrast, there was only ever one copy of the Vancouver Island treaties, and that copy stayed in Victoria, never acknowledged or endorsed by the British government. The assembly's promotion of treaties appears to have been predicated upon the assumption that treaties would bring an infusion of British money into the colonial economy, but their enthusiasm for treaties dissipated after it became clear that the British government would not pay.

However, by the mid-1860s, there were "strangers" of the kind that George Simpson in June 1849 feared might eventually "tamper" with the Indians and advocate on their behalf. In 1865, the Reverend Alexander C. Garrett of the Anglican Church Missionary Society wrote to Pearse to remind him that Douglas had personally in August 1862 made "definite promises" to the Cowichan, telling "them in the presence of the settlers, that in the ensuing Autumn he would return to Cowichan, have a gathering of all their tribes and make them suitable presents."[63]

Garrett must have been referring to a meeting of 18 August 1862, in the presence of settlers, in which Douglas appears to have offered the Cowichan terms much like those of the written treaties:

> The few natives at present in the district (the major portion of the tribes being absent fishing) agreed without hesitation to the surrender of their lands to the Government, with the exception of their village-sites and potato patches, being informed that when the absent members of the tribes had returned to their homes in the autumn, compensation for the lands taken up by the settlers would be made at the same rate as that previously established – amounting in the aggregate to the value of a pair of blankets to each Indian – the chiefs of course coming in for the lion's share of the *potlatch*. The Indians, one and all, expressed themselves as perfectly content with the proposed arrangement, and even appeared anxious that settlers should come among them.[64]

Garrett assumed that Douglas had not kept his promise because "the Lamalchas unhappily became troublesome, three of their number were hanged, and the Governor did not think it would be expedient then to carry out his original intention." However, he warned that "the matter is fast becoming complicated and made difficult of management. ... I now feel a strong and settled apprehension that, if something be not done by competent authority to adjust matters in a more satisfactory manner, some grievous disturbance may ensue, and the action of the Government be rendered vastly more difficult."[65] Garrett explained that the perception that Douglas never intended to keep his promise, the destruction of the Cowichan's potato crops by settlers' cattle and swine, and the threats of the Cowichan to take matters into their own hands convinced Garrett that the valley could soon face a serious crisis. Garrett did not recommend a land purchase, but advised that 100 acres around each of the five Cowichan villages and burial grounds, including the fifty acres that they cultivated in potatoes, be enclosed in strong fences.[66]

In March 1869, the Anglican catechist William Henry Lomas wrote a letter at the behest of a delegation of Cowichan leaders asking for a visit from the governor. He explained that "today they came to me to the number of about 200 men and named the chiefs chosen.–one of their principal grievances is, –'That a large portion of the country has been taken from them, and given to the white men; the Government at that time promising to pay the natives for it, which promise, they say has not yet been performed.'"[67] Nine years later, in 1878, Gilbert Malcolm Sproat noted that the Cowichan then complained to him that "Governor Douglas had paid Indians both North and South of them, for their lands, namely the Sooke, Metchosin, Esquimalt, Victoria, Saanich, Nanaimo, Fort Rupert Indians, but that the Cowichan Indians had not been paid."[68] He also indicated that "there is some evidence in Land Office records that Governor Douglas, not long before he left office in 1864, was still of opinion that the Indian title at Cowichan especially, should be extinguished, and it appears further from the Land Office correspondence that the Indians at Chemainus & Cowichan have constantly had the subject in their minds, in fact the mission to pay them for their lands, has always been, and now is at the bottom of their complaints."[69]

As the members of the assembly indicated, the fact that the colony was granting land in districts that had not been purchased made it difficult for settlers to occupy the lands they had been granted. Surveys of the Cowichan valley began in 1859 without any land-purchase agreement, but the work had to be repeated in 1863, "owing mainly to the removal of the posts of the original survey by Indians, and to the obliteration of lines by fires, &c."[70] In 1868, Gilbert Malcolm Sproat published an account describing the days in August 1860 when he took possession of land near the head of Alberni Inlet. He explained that, with two armed vessels, and about fifty men, he approached a summer camp of "Seshahts" on a beach near the head of the inlet, and:

> sent for the chief, and explained to him that his tribe must move their encampment, as we had bought all the surrounding land from the Queen of England, and wished to occupy the site of the village for a particular purpose. He replied that the land belonged to themselves, but that they were willing to sell it. The price not being excessive, I paid him what was asked – about twenty pounds' worth of goods – for the sake of peace, on condition that the whole people and buildings should be removed the next day.[71]

If Sproat's account is accurate, these villagers understood the concept of selling their land. Sproat reported that he and his men then debated around their campfire by what right strangers settled on the land of Indigenous people. His lengthy account of the conversation paralleled familiar debates held among far more powerful people in more influential forums.[72]

Despite evidence that Douglas was unenthusiastic about negotiating treaties, and even though he appears to have approached the transactions with less gravity than most treaty commissioners, even in 1861, he advocated for treaties on behalf of the Legislative Assembly of the colony of Vancouver Island. The end of treaty making was tied to the financial constraints acting upon the governor. That was the impression that Richard Mayne had gained during his time there. In 1862, referring to Salt Spring Island, he wrote that, while it might be desirable that the land be purchased, "Vancouver Island, however, has no revenue available or sufficient for such a purpose, and of course the revenue of British Columbia cannot, while the two colonies are distinct, be applied to it."[73] In 1878, Gilbert Malcolm Sproat guessed that "the purchase of the lands from the Cowichan, Chemainus, and other Indians was probably postponed as the public funds were small, and nobody was then going to settle at these places."[74]

In 1863, James Trimble, a member of the third Vancouver Island House of Assembly, responded to the news that the British government intended to hand over control of Crown lands on Vancouver Island to the legislature by spearheading the creation of a seven-person Select Committee on Crown Lands.[75] On 26 October 1863, this committee passed a motion "to find the extent, locality, value, and character of the Public Reserves of the Colony."[76] Public reserves could include government, military, mining, navigational (lighthouse), church, school, hospital, park, and Indian reserves. The committee met several times between then and 15 June 1864.[77] On 2 December 1863, the committee asked B.W. Pearse, the Acting Chief Surveyor, to describe the government reserves already set aside as shown on a map entitled in print "General Map Showing Reserves," and in handwriting, "Indian & Government Reserves – Tracing lodged with Select Comm$^{ee}$ of House on Crown Lands, 2$^{nd}$ Dec$^{r}$. 1863. B.W. Pearse, Act$^{g}$. Surveyor Gen$^{l}$."[78] A second map was subsequently provided to the committee: "Map No 1: Reserves May 1, 1864 supplied to Crown Lands Committee by BW Pearse Acting Surveyor General."[79]

Probably because the map lacked labels, the members of the committee asked Pearse about the purpose of each reserve. The meeting minutes suggest that, pointing in turn to each reserve on the map, Pearse explained whether they had been set aside for the purposes of government, military, navigation, clergy, or Indians.[80] That some of these reserves might appropriately have been described as anticipatory reserves is evident from Pearse's explanation of a reserve on the southwest corner of Salt Spring Island. The reserve's large size and proximity to Victoria apparently prompted the committee to inquire about it. Pearse responded that it was "Reserved for Indians, in case there should be any there."[81] Obviously, the reserve had been marked on the map without knowledge of the Indigenous population there.

In April 1864, James Douglas retired as Governor of Vancouver Island and British Columbia. The unsystematic and informal nature of his approach meant that his influence on Indigenous policy did not long outlast his governorship. Roughly coincident with Douglas's retirement surveyor, William McColl reported on some Indian reserves he had surveyed in British Columbia by stating that "in addition to the written instructions, I had further verbal orders given to me by Sir James Douglas, to the effect that all lands claimed by the Indians were to be included in the reserve; the Indians were to have as much land as they wished, and in no case to lay off a reserve under 100 acres. The reserves have been laid off accordingly."[82]

On 11 January 1864, Frederick Seymour was appointed to replace Douglas as Governor of British Columbia, and Arthur Edward Kennedy replaced Douglas as Governor of Vancouver Island. Neither took much personal interest in Indigenous affairs. In British Columbia, Seymour left that portfolio to a friend of James Douglas, Joseph W. Trutch, the Commissioner of Lands and Works. Historians have characterized Trutch as unsympathetic to Indigenous people. He was probably more sympathetic than the average British Columbian at the time, but he was convinced that Indian reserves set aside under Douglas had been far too large.[83] In August 1867, Trutch advised Governor Seymour that it was important to survey and mark the Indian reserves along the Lower Fraser River "so that the uncertainty now existing as to what lands are to be permanently held by the Indians may be terminated, and the risk of disputes and collisions between the white settlers and the Indians as to their respective land rights be as far as practicable removed."[84] He was not far off the mark when he explained:

> The subject of reserving lands for the use of the Indian tribes does not appear to have been dealt with on any established system during Sir James Douglas' administration.
> The rights of Indians to hold lands were totally undefined, and the whole matter seems to have been kept in abeyance, although the Land Proclamations specially withheld from pre-emption all Indian reserves or settlements.[85]

Trutch was motivated to convince Governor Seymour that Douglas's administration really had no policy at all, and seizing upon Douglas's lack of formality, Trutch advocated a very different policy than that which Douglas had pursued:

> The Indians have really no right to the lands they claim, nor are they of any actual value or utility to them; and I cannot see why they should either retain these lands to the prejudice of the general interests of the Colony, or be allowed to make a market of them either to Government *or to individuals*.

It seems to me, therefore, both just and politic that they should be confirmed in the possession of such extents of lands only as are sufficient for their probable requirements for purposes of cultivation and pasturage, and that the remainder of the land now shut up in these reserves should be thrown open to pre-emption.[86]

Seymour did not interfere with Trutch's policy.

The colonies of Vancouver Island and British Columbia merged in 1866, the merged colony retaining the name of the Colony of British Columbia. Then, in 1871, the colony joined Canada as the new province of British Columbia, with British Columbia retaining control of Crown lands within the new province. Clause 13 of the terms of union between British Columba and Canada, negotiated by Trutch, John Sebastian Helmcken, and Robert William Weir Carrall, stipulated the following:

> The charge of the Indians, and the trusteeship and management of the lands reserved for their use and benefit, shall be assumed by the Dominion Government and a policy as liberal as that hitherto pursued by the British Columbia Government shall be continued by the Dominion Government after the Union.
>
> ... To carry out such policy, tracts of land of such extent as it has hitherto been the practice of the British Columbia Government to appropriate for that purpose, shall from time to time be conveyed by the Local Government to the Dominion Government in trust for the use and benefit of the Indians on application of the Dominion Government; and in case of disagreement between the two Governments respecting the quantity of such tracts of land to be so granted, the matter shall be referred for the decision of the Secretary of State for the Colonies.[87]

The transfer of jurisdiction over Indian affairs from British Columbia to the Canadian government led Canadian government officials to inquire with the government of British Columbia about the state of Indian affairs. On 16 October 1871, B.W. Pearse informed the Canadian Secretary of State for the Provinces (then in charge of Indian Affairs) about Indian affairs in the province without mentioning treaties:

> SIR, I have the honour to acknowledge the receipt of your Instructions under date of 5th September, to prepare tracings of the Indian Reserves existing in this Province, together with statistics of the Natives generally.
>
> I have now to transmit herewith a series of tracings lettered A to Q inclusive, showing all the Indian Reserves which have been surveyed, together with a Schedule showing the locality, number of section, general description, acreage, name of tribe in whose favour each reserve has been made,

...
I have no statistics as to the number of Indians in each tribe, and have no means of obtaining them. It would cost a great deal of time and money, and would involve a visit to each Indian Village throughout the Province. There are, especially in Vancouver Island, a great many tribes which have no Reserves marked out either on plan or on the ground.

The "Land Ordinance, 1870," under which alone lands can be acquired by intending settlers, especially exempts all Indian lands and settlements from its operation. It has generally been the practice to lay out on the ground the Indian Reserves synchronously with the settlement of the district by the whites. This system has been found effectual and far less costly than that of surveying the reserve all together, as they are naturally scattered and often at great distances apart. In the latter case the posts and marks on the ground might become obliterated before the white men advanced, as the Indians, though tenacious of their rights in the lands when once surveyed, will not take the trouble to perpetuate these posts and marks, or to preserve them in any way.

...

Other reserves can be made from time to time as may be found necessary. No titles to lands held by the Indians have been issued.

The Executive has always exercised a general control and supervision over the Indians and their lands, and has always prevented them from alienating in any way any portion of their reserves.

No Indian Reserves have been laid out on Vancouver Island on the west side, and none beyond Comox on the east side. No Indian Reserves have been laid out on the coast of the Mainland beyond Burrard Inlet.

The total area of land laid out on the ground for the use of the Natives is 28,437 acres.[88]

Pearse's letter offers important evidence about the state of affairs in 1871. It refers to "a series of tracings," and "a Schedule showing the locality, number of section, general description, acreage, name of tribe in whose favour each reserve has been made."[89] But Pearse made it clear that Indian reserves were not normally surveyed and marked on the ground until settlers arrived. Pearse admitted, even in 1870, that he had no precise information about the number of people in each Indigenous community, and no way of getting that information. When Trutch transmitted Pearse's letter to the Secretary of State for the Provinces, he elaborated somewhat on the status of the reserves, but also made no mention of treaties:

As to the title by which the various Indian Reservations in this Province are held, I may add to Mr. Pearse's letter that all these lands have been severally set apart at various times for the use and benefit of the Indians resident thereon, or who, being members of the particular tribe for which any such reservation was created are entitled to participate therein, by order of the Governor, publicly notified in the Government *Gazette*, or in such manner as was held to be sufficient advertisement of such notice previous to the establishment of the Government *Gazette*.[90]

On 7 October 1872, Pearse resigned his position as surveyor to take up a position with the federal government's Department of Public Works.[91] In the same month, the Canadian government appointed Victoria resident Israel Wood Powell to be the federal government's Indian Commissioner for British Columbia. In that role, Powell became embroiled in the controversies over Indian lands in British Columbia. Obviously sceptical of Trutch's characterizations of James Douglas's Indian policies, Powell decided to write a letter directly to the retired Douglas. On 9 October 1874, Powell asked Douglas:

Would you be good enough to inform me, if, during the period of your Governorship in British Columbia, there was any particular basis of acreage used in setting apart Indian Reserves. I am unable to find anything referring to the subject among any Archives to which I have had access, except that contained in a speech delivered by you to the first Legislature of V. I. in 1856. A circumstance which compels me to ask you upon matters which of course, must only indirectly concern you now.[92]

It is odd that Powell in this instance inquired about Douglas's policy in British Columbia, and then referred to a speech Douglas delivered in Victoria on 12 August 1856, before the colony of British Columbia was established. However, Powell's query gave Douglas the perfect opportunity to mention and describe the Vancouver Island treaties. In his answer, Douglas did not do so:

The question presented in your letter of the 9th of October, being limited to one specific point, hardly affords breadth or scope enough to admit of an explicit reply, without going more largely into the matter. ...

In laying out Indian reserves no specific number of acres was insisted on. The principle followed in all cases was to leave <u>the extent and selection of land, entirely optional with the Indians,</u> who were immediately interested in the Reserve. The surveying Officers having instructions to meet their wishes in every particular, and to include in each Reserve the permanent village sites, the fishing stations and burial grounds, cultivated lands and all the favourite resorts of the tribes; and, in short, to include every piece of ground, to which they had acquired an equitable title through continuous occupation, tillage, or other investment of their labor. This was done with the object of securing to each community their natural or acquired rights; of removing all causes for complaint on the ground of unjust deprivation of the land indispensable for their convenience or support, and to provide, as far as possible against the occurrence of agrarian disputes with the white settlers.

Before my retirement from Office several of these Reserves, chiefly in the lower districts of Fraser's River; and Vancouver Island, were regularly surveyed and marked out, with the sanction and approval of the several communities concerned; and, it was found, on a comparison of acreage with population, that the land reserves, in none of these cases, exceeded the proportion of 10 acres per family; – so moderate were the demands of the natives.

It was, however, never intended that they should be limited or restricted to the possession of ten acres of land; on the contrary, we were prepared, if such had been their wish, to have made for their use much more extensive grants.

The Indian Reserves in the pastoral country east of the Cascades, especially in the Lytton and Thompson's River districts, where the natives are wealthy (having in many instances large numbers of horses and cattle) were, on my retirement from Office, only roughly traced out upon the ground by the Gold Commissioners of the day: the regular surveys not having been completed.

These latter Reserves were, necessarily, laid out on a large scale, commensurate with the wants of these Tribes, to allow sufficient space and range for their cattle at all seasons.

Such is an outline of the policy and motives which influenced my Government when determining the principle on which these grants of land should be made.

Moreover, as a safeguard and protection to these Indian Communities, who might, in their primal state of ignorance and natural improvidence, have made away with land, it was provided that these Reserves should be the common property of the Tribes, and that the title should remain vested in the Crown, so as to be inalienable by any of their own acts.

The policy of the Government was carried even a step beyond this point in providing for the future. Contemplating the probable advance of the Aborigines in knowledge and intelligence, and assuming that a time would certainly arrive when they might aspire to a higher rank in the social scale, and feel the essential wants and claims of a better condition, it was determined to remove every obstacle from their path by placing them in the most favorable circumstances for acquiring land, in their private and individual capacity, apart from Tribal Reserves.

They were, therefore, legally authorized to acquire property in land, either by direct purchase at the Government Offices, or through the operation of the pre-emption laws of the Colony, on precisely the same terms and conditions in all respects as other classes of Her Majesty's subjects.

A departure from the practice then adopted with respect to this class of native rights will give rise to unbounded disaffection, and may imperil the vital interests of the Province.

This letter may be regarded and treated as an Official Communication.

I remain, Sir, Your obedient servant, James Douglas. Late Governor British Columbia.[93]

James Douglas was obviously aware of the controversy over Indian land policy in British Columbia when he wrote the above response to Powell, and he was motivated to defend his legacy. He can rightly be accused of oversimplifying his policies, particularly when it came to Vancouver Island, but given the narrow question put to him, and the issues that we must assume he understood were at stake at the time, his answer to Powell's question was a fair summary of his policies. Cole Harris described this letter as "Douglas's clearest statement of his Indian land policies."[94] Perhaps it is. It is telling, however, that Douglas decided not to refer at all to the treaties he had made in the 1850s and did not advocate for the negotiation of treaties. It was apparently the last time Douglas explained his Indigenous policies. He died on 2 August 1877.

In 1909, when A.W. Vowell, then Superintendent of Indian Affairs in British Columbia, submitted to Ottawa lists of Indian Reserves in British Columbia, he remarked as follows:

> In preparing these, great difficulty has been experienced owing to the lack of information as to the extent of the reservations made prior to 1871, or to the date on which they were made.
>
> No records of reserves were kept previous to that year, the only evidence obtainable being a number of plans on which some of the Reserves that had been surveyed are shown, and even these have, with few exceptions, no date attached to them.
>
> In olden times every Stipendiary Magistrate was virtually the Indian Agent in his district. He settled disputes between natives and the settlers, perhaps blazing a tree to show where the dividing line should be, and these decisions were as a rule respected. In very few cases, however, were these allotments surveyed nor as a rule were they reduced to writing.[95]

The historical geographer Cole Harris, who carried out a thorough study of Indian reserve policy in British Columbia, was probably correct when he concluded:

> Overall, the creation of reserves in colonial British Columbia had been a piecemeal work, a composite of different Indian land policies with no systematic geographical application. British Columbia was about the business of becoming a British settler colony, and even for Douglas, and much more for his successors, this dominating agenda had relegated the allocation of reserves to a marginal project to be fitted in around the edges when moments of time and limited funds allowed.[96]

Harris was right. The fact that James Douglas did not develop a settled and formal policy towards Indigenous title in the colonies of Vancouver Island and British Columbia has had significant consequences for the Indigenous and non-Indigenous people of the province. But Douglas's record suggests that he did not attribute much significance to the treaties he negotiated, either when he was concluding them, or in the years between 1858 and 1875.

# 13 The Evolving Memories of the Vancouver Island Treaties to 1934

In July 1934, in what is certainly the best-known and most influential Indigenous account of the negotiations of the Vancouver Island treaties, Chief David Latasse of the Tsartlip First Nation apparently said: "More than eighty years ago I saw James Douglas, at the place now called Beacon Hill, stand before the assembled chiefs of the Saanich Indians with uplifted hand. ... I heard him give his personal word that, if we agreed to let the white man use parts of our land to grow food, all would be to the satisfaction of the Indian peoples. Blankets and trade were to be paid. We, knowing a crop grows each year, looked for gifts each year, what is now called rent. Our chiefs then sold no part of Saanich."[1] Although scholars have known about David Latasse's account, it reached new prominence in a dissertation in which Neil Vallance examined the accounts of the Vancouver Island treaties that were recorded long after the events took place, "to ascertain the likely terms of the treaties."[2] Explaining his approach, Vallance wrote that he made "First Nation accounts the standard against which other accounts are measured."[3] More recently, in a book whose title was clearly inspired by his work, Vallance published his work in a peer-reviewed article.[4] It is important, however, to subject to critical inquiry the various accounts of the treaty negotiations preserved after – often long after – the events in question. Such accounts range from written reminiscences and sworn statements by persons who were present at the negotiations, to accounts committed to paper much later by members of subsequent generations. Although some of them were probably never orally presented, all ought to be subjected to the methods recommended by some of the most prominent oral historiographers. That means that no account, whether produced by James Douglas in the 1850s or by David Latasse in 1934, should be accepted as definitive.

Vallance argued that oral accounts of the Vancouver Island treaties produced by First Nations people after the 1850s "are few, and they are not without serious problems, but to no greater degree than the colonial versions."[5] Vallance is not far off if researchers seek to understand informants' understandings of the Vancouver Island treaties at the time the informants provided their accounts, but historians consider it axiomatic that the amount of time that passes between an event and any record of that event is one of the factors that complicates attempts to use the record to understand what happened at the time.

Scholars typically differentiate between oral history and oral tradition. Jan Vansina, one of the most prominent scholars of oral tradition, explained that "the sources of oral historians are reminiscences, hearsay, or eyewitness accounts about events and situations which are contemporary, that is, which occurred during the lifetime of the informants. This differs from oral traditions in that oral traditions are no longer contemporary. They have passed from mouth to mouth, for a period beyond the lifetime of the informants."[6] None of the accounts of the Vancouver Island treaties was recorded or preserved in a way that conforms to the current scholarly methods of oral historiography, but there are several accounts of the Vancouver Island treaties that appear to shed light on the later understandings of people present at the negotiations. They are reminiscences. Vansina defined reminiscences as "the recollections of past events or situations given by participants long after the events. Reminiscences are bits of life history. Everyone holds such reminiscences. ... Here we see the full power of memory at work. Events and situations are forgotten when irrelevant or inconvenient. Others are retained and reordered, reshaped or correctly remembered according to the part they play in the creation of this mental self-portrait."[7]

Neil Vallance raised "a much broader issue: the reliability of oral history and oral tradition."[8] However, it is naive and simplistic to rank types of historical sources as more or less reliable. To ask whether oral history and oral tradition are reliable is as strange as asking whether automobiles are reliable, and to ask whether written documents are more reliable than oral accounts is like asking whether microscopes are more reliable than telescopes. Historians ought to weigh the reliability of all evidence in every source critically in relation to their research questions. More appropriately, Vallance has noted that the oral accounts of the Vancouver Island treaties "reflect the understanding of the narrators at the time their stories were told, not at the date of the original meetings."[9] In that way, Vallance highlighted the great value of oral accounts; they are the best sources available for exploring the understandings of the Vancouver Island treaties at various times.[10]

Historians ask certain questions of all sources. Is the source authentic? Who authored it? Who was the intended audience? How and why was the source created, and what is the significance of the format of the source? What connection did the author have with the events of relevance to the researcher, and how might that connection have shaped the author's account? These are questions asked of almost all sources. But historical critical analysis is art and science. Not only the weight of a source, but every aspect of a source needs to be considered. Accounts of the same event are more likely to differ when the authors are addressing contentious topics in which they have a clear stake. When sources contradict one another, historians carefully consider why certain ones are more likely to be accurate representations of events, and which author might be more likely to misrepresent or misunderstand the events. On the other hand, evidence that is presented aside from the author's central purpose and that the author did not anticipate would be significant to an audience (we may call this "unwitting evidence") is more likely to reflect an honest and sincerely held belief. For example, a historian of gender would interpret a statement made by David Latasse about women ("there were lots of women to do the work and provide wives for all") differently if the source was created to advocate for a particular role for women in society, rather than to defend a certain interpretation of the Vancouver Island treaties.

Historians are also inevitably influenced, at least in part, by assumptions – informed by their training and experience – about human nature. For example, scholars who assume that people are more likely to distort the past or to have highly subjective and selective memories of the past when their own interests are at stake than if they are detached will interpret sources through that lens. Persons who assume that human nature does not differ significantly among people of different races, genders, and cultures, will tend to interpret sources differently than people who believe that there are fundamental differences among different groups of humans. Scholars wary of confirmation bias are better able to arrive at new insights than those who are oblivious to it.

Prominent oral historians have argued that critical source analysis of oral accounts is inherently more complex than the analysis of written documents. William Warner Moss, former president of the Oral History Association, noted:

> Documents may decay with time, but they do not very often change before your very eyes. Interviewees, on the other hand, are capable of rapid

and startling changes. Memory is not merely a passive reservoir of data, the contents of which can be pored over and scrutinized at leisure. It is engaged and integrated with the present – with continuously changing attitudes, perspectives and understandings – working and reworking the data of experience into new formulations, opinions and perhaps even new creations.[11]

Ruth Finnegan, another eminent scholar of oral tradition, agreed:

> The notion that when using "oral tradition" one can suspend many of the normal critical canons of historical research is, despite the caution of more experienced historians, surprisingly prevalent. Perhaps this is because the various assumptions about oral tradition coming down word for word, about its unitary nature, or about its supposed freedom from individual originality or artistry seem to add up to the conclusion that oral tradition is somehow impervious to the kinds of factors of which historians are so aware with other sources – the effects of, say, prejudice or propaganda, personal interests or fantasies, aesthetic forms, or just the variations between different types of sources.
>
> I would suggest that the opposite of this assumption is in fact true. Oral sources are in many ways even more open to such factors than written ones. A written document is certainly liable to many influences as it is written down, but once written it can be taken as permanent. Oral forms, on the other hand, are open to all these influences, not only on the occasion of the first formulation and delivery, but on every single occasion of delivery afterward. Because they are oral, and thus can exist only as and when they are rendered by word of mouth, obviously they are closely affected by a number of additional factors that do not apply to documentary sources.[12]

More recently, the prominent Canadian scholar Julie Cruikshank has cautioned that

> even though both oral and written accounts refer to the *past*, they are usually told in order to make a statement about the *present*. In other words, their purpose is to provide some background for explaining events that are happening *now*. They do this by emphasizing some events and by leaving out others. Both oral and written accounts about the past are *interpretations* which may change as circumstances change.[13]

Another Canadian scholar, Brian Calliou, has also argued that oral histories, "like written documents, must be cross-checked for validity and accuracy."[14]

Whenever any source created after the events being researched purports to convey first-hand or even second-hand knowledge of events, researchers should be alert to what oral historiographers have come to label "feedback."[15] David Henige, an eminent oral historiographer, has noted that "a great deal of testimony obtained from informants is really feedback; that is, it originated as information that entered the society and was absorbed into traditions because it proved useful or entertaining. In many cases informants themselves fail to realise this because it happened long enough ago and in subtle enough ways that it quickly became indistinguishable from oral tradition."[16] Jan Vansina warned scholars that

> When the content of writings comes to be known, people who hear them adopt them. .... When writing came to be practiced in a society, oral traditions did not die out as long as literacy was not general. Rather, people incorporated them into their traditions just as some literate persons incorporated traditions into writings. The transmission became mixed and could remain so for centuries. ... Historians should be aware of possible mixed transmissions and loans from written sources, and it behooves them to carefully examine all the writings that were available to the communities studied and especially those that concerned them.[17]

The presence of feedback does not automatically invalidate all of the evidence contained in a source, but Henige cautioned researchers that

> Recognition that feedback materials may be co-opted into traditional accounts is essential when working with materials that may claim to be undiluted oral traditions. In turn the investigator must understand the whole range of problems that the process of feedback implies for his assessment of "oral" data. For instance, it cannot be assumed that accounts are mutually supportive because they are consistent with each other. In his scepticism the investigator must *a priori* assume that any consistency is the result of recourse to printed, written, or para-literate sources or because of deference to "official" accounts.[18]

In short, researchers should always be alert to evidence of feedback, particularly when there is reason to believe that informants concealed the fact that they incorporated knowledge gained through other means into their accounts, implying that their memories of the past were clearer than they were.

After 1864, and particularly after British Columbia joined the Canadian federation in 1871, the issue of Indigenous title became controversial in

British Columbia. The government of the Dominion of Canada, formed in 1867, adopted the policies that had prevailed in Upper Canada, rooted in the Royal Proclamation of 1763, that guaranteed that the Crown would purchase the Indian title when the government sought to use the land for settlement or development purposes. The government of Canada pursued the policy of extinguishing Indigenous title by way of purchase on the Canadian prairies between 1871 and 1877 and sought also to apply that policy in British Columbia. Because the government of British Columbia had denied the existence of Indigenous title since 1864, and because the province retained jurisdiction over Crown lands, the question of the extinguishment of Indian title became a thorny one, especially when British Columbia's Indigenous communities, working with missionaries and other allies, advocated for such treaties. In that political climate, the existence of the Vancouver Island treaties seemed to undermine the British Columbia government's argument that Indigenous title did not exist – or, if it did exist, could be extinguished without purchase. When the Songhees faced pressure to surrender their reserve in downtown Victoria, they appealed to their treaties to defend their land rights.

The very charged context appears to have shaped people's memories. Dr. John S. Helmcken, a very influential British Columbian, became one of the assertive supporters of British Columbia's position that Indian title did not exist. Helmcken had come to Vancouver Island in 1850 as a surgeon with the HBC, but was posted to Fort Rupert in March of that year, thus was not present when the Fort Victoria treaties were concluded. In 1852, he married James Douglas's daughter Cecilia. He rose eventually to the position of Chief Trader in the HBC. In 1856 he was elected to the inaugural Legislative Assembly of the colony of Vancouver Island, and he was speaker of the assembly through the merger of the colony of Vancouver Island and British Columbia in 1866 until British Columbia's federation with Canada in 1871. He, with Joseph W. Trutch, was influential in negotiating clause 13 in the 1871 terms of union between British Columbia and Canada.[19] In 1861, while he was Speaker of the Legislative Assembly of Vancouver Island, the assembly had submitted a petition to the Duke of Newcastle, the Colonial Secretary, stating in part that "the House of Assembly respectfully considers, that the extinction of the aboriginal title is obligatory on the Imperial Government."[20] Helmcken's opinion about Indigenous title, like that of his colleagues in the assembly, must have changed with the prospect that the British taxpayers would not foot the bill to extinguish Indigenous title.

The political controversy surrounding Indigenous title appears to have influenced Helmcken's memories of the Vancouver Island treaties. After British Columbia joined Canada in 1871 and Canadian government officials sought to extend Canada's treaty-making policies to British Columbia, Indigenous communities and some of their allies called for the British Columbia government to pursue land-purchase treaties. The 1880s were watershed years in the history of Canadian thinking about Indian title as a legal concept. In the second half of that decade the *St. Catherine's Milling* case (often referred to as the *Indian Title Case*) made its way through the courts. The trial opened on 18 May 1885 (during the North-West Uprising) and was decided later that year. The Supreme Court of Canada ruled on 20 June 1887, and the Privy Council in 1888. Each court ruled that Indian title was a moral burden upon the Crown. The Supreme Court cited many of the same examples and commentaries as George Gipps had in Sydney, NSW, on 9 July 1840, including Kent's *Commentaries*, and the Marshall cases in the United States, but it also considered the history of purchases as far back as the purchases of the Dutch in the 1620s, and the *Symonds* case in New Zealand. However, as in *Symonds*, Indigenous people were not among the litigants in the *St. Catherine's Milling* case.[21]

As the case was making its way through the courts, in October 1886, the Anglican missionary William Duncan wrote a letter to the Victoria *Daily British Colonist* defending the land claims of the Metlakatlans by pointing to the treaties negotiated by Douglas on Vancouver Island.[22] Helmcken responded with letters of his own. Douglas, he wrote, knew that buying the land was unnecessary because "the Indians were not averse to the settlement of white people among them." Thus, he had negotiated treaties of "amity and friendship."[23] He argued that "misleaders," by encouraging Indians to press "mythical Indian title," were neglecting the greater and more expensive duty of the government to civilize the Indian.[24] His position was that "'Indian title' and the question of the duty of the government to civilize the aborigines of the country are two separate and distinct questions, and must be kept apart."[25] When challenged by the Methodist missionary Ebenezer Robson, who quoted Douglas's 25 March 1861 letter indicating that Indians had distinct ideas of property,[26] Helmcken doubled down:

> In a former letter the fact was mentioned that the judges both in England and Canada had decided that Indians had no legal title. Further, that whatever was given them by governments was given not on account of title but for moral reasons, policy politics and peace sake. ... Now observe: Sir James does *not state that the Indians have a title to the land*, but that the native Indians have distinct ideas of property in land, that is to say *Indian ideas*, not legal ones, and *so to prevent any feeling of irritation against*

*the settlers* I made it a practice to purchase the native rights in the land. Can anything be more plain than that in this way Sir James made treaties of amity and friendship and paid for them as a matter of policy?

It matters not how the papers were made out; the Indians not having any legal right in the land could not give any conveyance of land. What they could give goodness only knows; but nothing more than some mysterious, undefined, perhaps non-existing rights for something or other, worth £2 10s. per head – evidently in this case peace and friendship – something to prevent a feeling of irritation against the settlers and endanger the peace of the country, the Indians probably supposing their distinct ideas of property had been bought.

Now, what are the rights of the Indians? A conundrum! The fact is, "Indian title" to land is a misnomer. There is legally no such thing. Yet people by using the term and seeing it used frequently have come, more or less, to believe in its existence! – in the same manner that people begin to believe a fiction after having heard it often repeated – hence the dispute – a heap of trouble not yet ended.[27]

Notwithstanding his rejoinder, it cannot have escaped Helmcken that the fact that his father-in-law had negotiated treaties in the 1850s undermined his argument.[28] In a personal letter written in November 1888, Helmcken asked his former HBC colleague J.W. McKay, who he knew had been present at the treaty negotiations, for information:

According to the best of my recollection, Mr. Douglas called the neighbouring Indians together at Fort Victoria and gave them blankets and so forth ostensibly for the purchase of (which was unnecessary as the Company held the land by "grant from H.M.") land. As to purchase, this was all moonshine – they had to take or leave it alone. My feeling is, the blankets &c were given to appease or make friends with the Indians, in order that no trouble might arise in case settlers arrived upon the land. Why Douglas should have given such a document as he did is a conundrum. I suppose he had no legal adviser! My impression is, the whole thing had a twofold object 1$^{st}$ to gain the good will of the Indians. 2$^{nd}$ to give a quasi title for the Fur trade – for their claims of the ten mile belt around Victoria – not traded them in the charter of grant.

I know Douglas was altogether averse to making any treaty with Indians similar to those of the Americans.

Why did the Company always refuse to buy out the Cowichans – I do not know the reason, save that they disapproved for some reason or other.

I wish you would give me some notes of your recollection of these matters to refresh my memory – I will not make any bad use of them.[29]

McKay had signed eight of the Fort Victoria treaties as a witness and understood the Lekwungen language well. In 1888, he conveyed to Helmcken an account that illustrates both the strength and frailty of human memory:

> The arrangements entered into with the Victoria Sanich and Sooke Districts Indians respecting their claims on lands of those two districts were made at the instance of the Home Government during Governor Blanshard's incumbency. Mr. Douglas was Land Agent for the Crown Lands of Vancouver Island. The then Secretary for the Colonies sent to Mr Douglas through A. Barclay Esqre. HBCo's Secretary instructions as to how he should deal with the so called Indian Title. The instructions were embodied in a somewhat lengthy document which began by reciting the Various general views of the Home Government respecting in regard to the land rights of aborigines in the Countries where they have been might be found sojourning.
>
> Mr. Douglas was very cautious in all his proceedings. The day before the meeting with the Indians, he sent for me and handed me the document above referred to telling me to study it carefully and to commit as much of it to memory as possible in order that I might check the interpreter Thomas [Thomas Ouamtany, also known as Tomo Antoine and Tomo Ouamtany] should he fail to explain properly to the Indians the substance of Mr. Douglas' address to them.
>
> I remember one clause in the document in question distinctly stated that the Government did not admit that nomad tribes had any property in lands which they had not improved nor occupied for permanently industrial or useful purposes, and over which they had not established any form of government nor system of land tenure, but that where in the course of settlement by immigrants from the mother Country the intruders interfered materially with the sources of food supply on which the aborigenes had heretofore subsisted, then as a matter of expediency it were well to grant to them such considerations in the way of useful commodities as might allay present irritation and prevent breaches of the peace. It was recommended in a subsequent clause that sufficient land to support them be set apart for the use of the Indians and that the Indians be encouraged to cultivate and improve the same after the manner of the civilized people.
>
> Mr Douglas made no purchase of the country from the Indians. They were told that only such places as they had occupied and improved properly belonged to them, that in addition to their garden patches and village sites some of the lands contiguous to their Villages would be reserved to them and the rest of the country would be open for sale to white settlers.

You will remember that the Districts for which Indians received payments in blankets were the main producers of the kamas root for the whole surrounding country. The destruction of this plant by cattle and sheep caused a great loss to the Songhees Saanich and Sooke Indians as it was the most important article of trade which they had to offer in dealing with the neighbouring tribes. Hence the expediency of giving the above named Indians a valuable consideration for the loss sustained in their kamas trade. The Cowichans did not suffer in any way by the settlement of whites in their country and there never has been any reason which [sic] they should have had any payments made to them in respect to their country. The payments made to the Fort Rupert Indians were entirely out of order. The Nanaimos had to surrender their principal village sites to make room for the mining operations carried on there.[30]

McKay's first paragraph obviously represents his recollection of the 17 December 1849 letter sent to Douglas and which, contrary to McKay's flawed memory, had its origins in the Governor and Committee of the HBC, not in the Colonial Secretary.[31] However, the description of the document in McKay's third paragraph, penned thirty-eight years after he saw it, is sufficiently accurate that it is apparent that McKay did read the document, and that Douglas likely did instruct him to commit it to memory.

McKay's attempt to summarize Barclay's letter is interesting because it illustrates what commonly happens to memories over time: they are altered by hindsight. In the 1860s, the British Columbia government began to assert that Indian title in British Columbia could be extinguished without land-surrender treaties. That view was consistent with views in the Colonial Office and in many other British colonies at the time. By 1888, the British Columbia government's position on treaties had been in place for several decades. In 1888, McKay's memory of the "one clause in the document" is generally correct, but McKay appears to have incorrectly also remembered that the document contained words that it did not contain. For example, Barclay's 1849 instructions did not mention the formation of Indian reserves – McKay appears to have projected backwards in time an Indian reserve policy that developed later.

McKay may not have been dishonest in his depiction of Barclay's letter, but his memory of the letter appears to have been altered as a result of the debates over Indian title, particularly by disagreements that had developed between Canada and British Columbia after British Columbia joined Canada in 1871. His account of the treaties in this letter was probably also influenced by Helmcken's query, and by McKay's friendship with Helmcken. In other words, the letter can only be properly understood if we consider the passage of time, the identity of the author and his connection with the addressee, and the purpose of the letter. McKay's own flawed memory, or his purpose in writing Helmcken, caused him to write the third paragraph the way he did.

But the most significant new evidence in McKay's account is in his second paragraph. It contains evidence neither contradicted nor corroborated by any other documents. However, documents related to other treaties show that interpreters were enjoined to translate properly, or even made to swear an oath to translate faithfully.[32] McKay's account is strong evidence that Thomas Ouamtany was instructed to translate all speeches accurately, and that McKay was instructed to check his interpretations for accuracy.

If James Douglas truly did have Thomas Ouamtany present the content of Archibald Barclay's letter at the negotiations, he placed himself in an awkward position. According to the letter, the Crown regarded the Indigenous people to be possessors only of village sites and cultivations, the very lands they were to retain; the Crown already claimed possession of the rest of the land. If Ouamtany accurately conveyed that principle to the Indigenous attendees in a way that they could understand, as McKay implied he did, it would be no leap for any person attending the negotiations to conclude that no land transaction was taking place – each party was retaining the land to which they had rights, and Douglas was making certain promises and presenting gifts. Now, Douglas's report on the negotiations, and the Fort Victoria journals, suggest that he obtained a cession for all of the territory in exchange for the payment, in which case he must have modified his position and told the Indigenous people that he was acknowledging, and purchasing, their title to the entire territories eventually identified in the written treaties. It is impossible to know whether McKay had come to the same conclusion as Helmcken had before Helmcken elicited McKay's views, but the fourth and fifth paragraphs nicely illustrate an ambiguity; McKay explicitly agreed with Helmcken in the fourth paragraph, but appeared to qualify his position in the last paragraph.[33] Nevertheless, Helmcken's published letter ensured that already in 1888, the British Columbia public (including its Indigenous public) had access to an opinion written by a prominent man who was on Vancouver Island in 1850, that, notwithstanding the existence of the Vancouver Island Treaties, those treaties were not land purchases, and that Indigenous title did not exist. McKay's letter suggests that one of the interpreters and witnesses to the treaties seems to have agreed with that interpretation.

Neil Vallance indicated that he was aware of five "first-person First Nations accounts," only one of which was obviously first-hand, "and all were reduced to writing long after the events described."³⁴ The accounts he consulted were committed to paper between 1913 and 1934. Vallance included in this list documents that were written by non-Indigenous people, purporting to be reports on what was said to them. There are more accounts. Some are older than any analysed by Vallance, and one is a sworn statement of Songhees men who were at the 1850 negotiations.

The oldest known account was an 1885 affidavit sworn by Chief Comiak (c. 1797–1892) and others who claimed to be signatories to the 1850 Swengwhung treaty. The treaty documents appear to corroborate the claim. Swengwhung treaty signatories include "Comayits," Kuskaynum," and "Snâw nuck." "Chee-althluc" was signatory to the Che-ko-nein treaty of the same date.³⁵ That affidavit was signed in connection with a suit launched by the Songhees to prevent the Canadian Public Works Department from constructing temporary immigration sheds on their reserve. The affidavit reads as follows:

1 I Comiak Chief of the Swengwhung Tribe of the Songhees nation of Indians residing on the Songhees Indian Reserve, Victoria Harbour make oath and say as follows
2 That I am one of the persons who signed the paper writing dated the thirtieth day of April 1850 consenting to surrender and sell to James Douglas the agent of the Hudson Bay Co. ... the whole of the land situate and lying between the Island of the Dead, in the Arm or Inlet of Comosun, where the Kosampsom lands terminate on the Straits of de Fuca in the Bay immediately East of Clover point including all the country between that line and the Inlet of Comoson subject to the conditions and reservations therein contained.
3 The Plaintiff Kuskaynum also signed the said document.
4 The Plaintiff Chees Snawnuck is the son of Snawnuch who signed the said paper writing.
5 Charles Fraser and Louis Fraser otherwise Freezie are the sons of old Freezie otherwise See Alsh Luck who signed the said paper writing he was the former chief of the said Swengwhung tribe and died more than 20 years ago.
6 I and other Indians of the said Swengwhung tribe have lived and occupied and been in possession for some 40 years and more of a portion of that piece of land sold and surrendered to James Douglas as aforesaid and known as the Indian village site situate in Victoria Harbor.³⁶

This affidavit was written with the assistance of lawyers in the case in which the use of the Songhees reserve, not whether the treaties represented land sales, was at issue. Indeed, given that the chiefs were appealing to the promises contained in the written document, it is understandable that they would be disinclined to cast doubt on the validity of other provisions of the document. Nevertheless, it explicitly shows that the leaders of the Songhees band in 1885 who claimed to be either signatories to the treaty or sons of signatories, did not object to presenting a sworn statement that they had "sold and surrendered" the territory in 1850.

Similarly, in 1893, several years after Helmcken published his letter asserting that land was not purchased in the Vancouver Island treaties, and at a time when government officials were pressuring the Songhees to sell their reserve in central Victoria and relocate elsewhere, A.W. Vowell, the Superintendent of Indian Affairs for British Columbia, reported that the members of the Songhees band who apparently had been present at the treaty negotiations told him "that they had been told by Sir James Douglass [sic] when consenting to the sale of their lands ... that they would for ever be protected in the possession of the land allotted to them and upon which they have since lived, meaning the Songhees Reserve."[37] Although Vowell's second-hand account requires cautious reading, it suggests that the Songhees in 1893 stated that their 1850 treaty included a "sale of their lands." Thus, two brief statements from the 1880s and 1890s, one of them sworn by Indigenous chiefs, and another attributed to Indigenous people signatory to the Vancouver Island treaties, appear to assume that those people believed, at the time, that they had engaged in a land sale or surrender in 1850.

The value of accounts preserved after the turn of the twentieth century diminishes significantly for scholars aiming to reconstruct the events at treaty negotiations, although they are essential for those seeking to understand how recollections changed over time. During the early twentieth century, many Indigenous groups in British Columbia, having become familiar with Canada's treaty policies, were pressing land claims. In 1906, a delegation of British Columbia chiefs, including Cowichan chief Charley Isipaymilt brought a petition to London that stated that "in other parts of Canada the Indian title has been extinguished reserving sufficient land for the use of the Indians, but in British Columbia the Indian title has never been extinguished, nor has significant land been allotted to our people for their maintenance."[38] By 1910 three Indigenous organizations in British Columbia were pressing the issue of Indigenous title, and on 3 March 1911 a delegation of leaders met British Columbia Premier Richard McBride in a failed attempt to convince McBride to refer the question of Indigenous title to the Canadian courts.[39]

It was in that state of impasse that in 1912 British Columbia and Canada established a Royal Commission on Indian Affairs for British Columbia (McKenna-McBride Commission) "to settle all differences between the Governments of the Dominion and the Province respecting Indian lands and Indian Affairs generally in the Province of British Columbia," although at British Columbia's insistence, the commission was not to consider issues of Indigenous title. That mandate may explain why few Indigenous witnesses who testified before this commission mentioned the Vancouver Island treaties. However, in May 1913, Dick Whoakum, an octogenarian Nanaimo leader and signatory to the Nanaimo treaty, testified that:

> I was amongst the first people who found coal in Nanaimo. We took a trip up to Victoria to sell some furs, and we took the coal in the basket to show it to Sir James Douglas. After we had sold all the furs, one of them went down to the canoe and brought up the basket of coal, to show it to one of the store-keepers there, who sent word to Sir James Douglas. ... Next day Mr. McKay came along with us in another canoe. When he saw the coal he said it was very good coal. Mr. McKay started dancing on top of the coal for joy. He asked if there was any more of this coal, and we told him "Yes," just a little way off. ... About a week later a crowd of white people came here and when they came they started working on it. Two months later, Sir James Douglas himself came over to see where the coal was. Sir James Douglas said "I will buy this coal" but he said "I will not buy anything but the coal." "All the wood and the land is yours." "The land where the coal is, is yours, and the land up the River is yours." When the fishing season came we used all to go up the River to live. The Indians that used to live here, their main home was at Departure Bay, at other times they lived on the Island, and on Nanaimo River. The Indians of this band have three homes. They draw the salmon from Nanaimo River, and they go to Departure Bay for curing the herrings. I told Sir James Douglas that these three places were our land. Sir James Douglas said "I don't take any land away from you at all. All these three places where you live at different times are yours."[40]

Whoakum's description of this meeting as having taken place two months after the HBC had learned about the coal, and when "there was no white man here"[41] does not fit the treaty date of 23 December 1854, by which time the fort at Nanaimo had been established for more than two years. Whoakum was either describing an earlier meeting, or he had forgotten the context in which the treaty negotiations occurred. The formality of commission hearings presses upon witnesses the importance of telling the truth, but as Helmcken and McKay's accounts illustrate, a person's memory of controversial events can be significantly shaped.[42]

Chief David Latasse, of the Tsartlip Saanich band, was the most prolific and influential communicator of Indigenous perspectives of the Vancouver Island treaties, although he was a problematic informant (see figure 31). His involvement in Indigenous land issues began by 1913. In June of that year, Jimmy Jim, John Samson, and David Latasse submitted a letter (each of them signing with an X) to the Royal Commission on Indian Affairs for the Province of British Columbia (the McKenna-McBride Commission) on behalf of the Saanich people. Latasse's letter made no mention of a treaty.[43] Two other letters submitted by other Saanich men the same day similarly did not mention a treaty, although one of them indicated that "We want to be in full possession of our land which Sir James Douglas has made or Surveyed for us, for we have kept what Sir James Douglas said, when he told us the line he had made for the Saanich Indians. The land is great benefit to us, and will be still greater benefit for our children & their children, as we chiefly depend upon the land from time now on."[44]

In the early 1920s, even as the Canadian and British Columbia governments were still seeking to agree between themselves and with the Indigenous communities of British Columbia on the Indian land question in the province, officials in the Department of Indian Affairs sought to complete treaties in regions of Canada not yet covered by treaty. In 1923 Duncan Campbell Scott, the Deputy Superintendent General of Indian Affairs (DSGIA), misleadingly characterized the conclusion of Treaty No. 11 in 1921 as "bringing under the supervision of the Dominion Government practically the only Indians in Canada with whom treaty had not been made."[45] In 1924, Scott reported that the government had dealt with seventy-year-old claims of Chippewa and Mississauga bands in southern Ontario.[46]

The situation in British Columbia was more difficult, but Scott reported that on 19 July 1924 the government of Canada had ratified an agreement with the province of British Columbia based on the McKenna-McBride Commission, as revised by an inquiry led by W.E. Ditchburn and J.W. Clark.[47] During that process, officials in the Canadian government attempted to obtain the agreement of the Indigenous people, in part by assuring them that the government of Canada would still be willing to negotiate treaties in British Columbia after the commission's recommendations were ratified. In fact, as early as 1922 and 1923, Duncan Campbell Scott and W.E. Ditchburn spearheaded an effort to conclude treaties in British Columbia. In August 1922, Scott wrote Ditchburn about how they could arrange a treaty in British

Columbia that both government and Indigenous communities would consider "valid and binding."[48] Ditchburn's inquiries were hampered by the death of James Teit, whose opinion the Department of Indian Affairs valued, and the realization that there was no Indian organization that represented all of the Indians of the province. Eventually though, Ditchburn responded by recommending that "each treaty should cover an Agency as at present constituted, as it would then mean that when the treaties are signed the Aboriginal Title will have been extinguished over the whole of the Province."[49]

Significantly for those relatively few Indigenous communities that had concluded treaties, Ditchburn added that "the Peace River section has already been dealt with under Treaty No. 8. The Indians of the southern portion of Vancouver Island, Nanaimo and Fort Rupert, signed treaties with the Hudson's Bay Company in the early days and so possibly the tribes in these sections need not necessarily have signatories to the treaties."[50] In the spring of 1923, Charles Stewart, the Superintendent General of Indian Affairs, informed the Reverend P.R. Kelly, the head of the Allied Tribes of British Columbia, that, rather than ask the courts to decide the question, the government of Canada had decided "to acknowledge that the aboriginal title in the lands of B.C. had not been ceded."[51]

Upon learning of a planned meeting to discuss the treaty process, Chief Edward Jim of the Tseycum band, a signatory to one of the Saanich treaties, requested permission to attend the meeting with Charles Stewart and D.C. Scott.[52] Ditchburn replied that he did not object to Chief Jim's attending the meeting (scheduled for 25 July 1923), but that because "the Indians of the Saanich tribe made treaty with the Hudson's Bay Company about the year 1850 and extinguished the Indian title these Indians would not appear to have any interest in the business to be dealt with at the meeting."[53] Thus, from July 1923 onward, the signatories to the Vancouver Island treaties had reason to be worried that they would be excluded from any land-purchase treaties negotiated in British Columbia on the grounds that the Canadian government had concluded that their title had already been extinguished. The British Columbia government effectively halted the treaty process shortly after that meeting when it indicated that Duff Patullo, the premier of British Columbia, had concluded that "it is not necessary or advisable that the Province should be represented at any conference between the Indians and the Government of Canada."[54] Officials in the Department of Indian Affairs and Indigenous communities in British Columbia continued to ponder the possibility of treaties, but the communities covered by the Vancouver Island treaties understandably worried that they would not be included in any future benefits.

On 5 April 1932, a delegation of fifteen members of the Saanich bands, including David Latasse, met with Ditchburn, "the subject to be discussed being the treaties made between the Saanich Indians and the Hudson's Bay Company in 1851."[55] At that meeting, the interpreter, Simon Pierre, read out two statements, one by Latasse, and another by the chiefs and councillors of the bands. Latasse's statement was signed with an X and witnessed by Simon Pierre. The Saanich chiefs argued that they had never been compensated for their land:

> I Chief David Latasse, Tsarlip Reserve, Saanich tribe of Indians, been [sic] an old man, been of good sound mind, solemnly deny any knowledge of the so call Saanich treaty, as shown on Exhibit No. 6. Filed by P.R. Kelly, Chairman of the Allied Indian Tribes of British Columbia, as set forth in their Petition, submitted to Parliament [sic] in June 1926. Said treaty was signed by What-say-Mullet and nine others of the South Saanich, and Hotutstun and 119 others, of North Saanich. As we have never been told by our old peoples, if there was any we would of [sic] been told.
>
> 2nd. That the Sum of Fourty [sic] one Pounds, Thirteen Shillings, four Pence, as shown on same exhibit, I flatly ignor [sic] and deny.
>
> 3rd. The only Knowledge we Know as in regards to a dispute between the whites and Indians at the time of James Douglas – that there was a settlement of that dispute (been regards to timber matter,) that James Douglas gaved [sic] four bundle of Blankets, one Bundle to Tseycum, one Bundle to Tsarlip, 2 Bundle to Tseaut, none to Paquachin. It was not to sell land or surrender any Territory rights.
>
> 4th. We fully know that the parties mentioned on said treaty, What-say-mullets and Hotutstun were not members of the Saanichs. Said What-say-mullet comes from Cowichan head, outside of the Sch Territory. Hotutstun comes from the Ganges Harbour.[56]

The second statement, signed by Latasse and four other Saanich Chiefs and four Councillors, read:

> We the undersigned been the Chiefs and Councillors of the Saanich Tribe, Hereby declare that the statement of Chief David Latasse is true and nothing but the truth
>
> We base our ground as follows,
>
> 1st. There were some of our men from the Saanich Indians were employed by the late James Douglas, and have stated to us same as stated by Chief David Latasse and they were present at the time, and they were the ones was hueing [sic] the timber for James Douglas

The four Bundles of Blankets was merely for peace purpose there names are Thowhiz, father of Edward Tla-ma-hus, and Ko-la-thil-too, they state to us that

2nd. Said Blankets was not to buy land or Surrender any territory rights.

3rd. The Indian fully understood what was said As it was Interpreted by Mr. McKay, who spoke the Saanich language very well as well as we speake [sic] our language, so our old peoples fully understood what took place. Mr. McKay, Interpretering [sic] for James Douglas, saying these blankets is not to buy your lands, but to shake hands the Indian in good Harmony and good tumtums (hearts) When I get enough of your timber I shall leave the place and it was carried, When James Douglas knew he had enough of our timber he left the place[57]

The same men also presented a petition that clarified their position. They were not asking that they be included in a treaty process:

We the Saanich Band of Indians humbly pray that we want the so called treaty deleted on the following

1st. That the said treaty was made in the dark. We fully deny any knowledge of same. As we are fully aware what Sir James Douglas gaved to our peoples, was not for no land transaction whatever.

2nd. We want to be recognized by the Authority simlaral [sic] as other Indian tribes in the Province of British Columbia.

3rd. We do not mean to say, that we want the land back. No! – as it is settled by the settlers.

4th. We want the Authority to be lenient to us – and favor us compensation as saw fit.[58]

In his report of the meeting at which these documents were presented, Ditchburn stated that "I explained to the Indians that these treaties were made with the Hudson's Bay Company about 81 years ago and it was doubtful if any of the present generation had any knowledge of what had taken place so long ago." He did not indicate that any of the Saanich leaders claimed to have been present at the treaty negotiations. He continued by writing that "upon their being asked just what was on their mind," they responded that:

they wished to know that if the [Saanich] treaties were held to be good and at some later date the Government of Canada decided to pay treaty annuities to British Columbia Indians for the surrender of the Indian title as in other Provinces, whether the Indians of Saanich would be treated the same as other Indians in the Province. They were informed that some years ago Duncan C. Scott, the late Deputy Superintendent General, had told Messrs. Kelly and Paull, representing the Allied Tribes, that the fact of the Saanich and other Indians having made treaties with the Hudson's Bay Company in the early days would not militate against them should it transpire that the Canadian Government decided to pay treaty annuities to the Indians of British Columbia at some future date.[59]

The context in which the 1932 statements were made certainly influenced the content of those statements, and the anxiety among the Saanich between 1923 and 1932 that they might be excluded from a treaty process must have played a role in reshaping the understandings that these Saanich leaders had of the 1852 agreements. It would be contrary to the standards of oral historiography simply to accept the men's statements as reflecting the understandings of the Indigenous men who put their mark on the 1852 treaties. Moreover, we should be most cautious with the witting evidence – the content of the statements that are most likely to have been influenced by the context in 1932 – whether there was a land purchase in 1852. The fact that Douglas's assertion that it was the Saanich themselves who demanded the land transaction was not contradicted until 1932 when the Saanich leaders feared the implications of the treaty for their involvement in a treaty process, combined with the evidence that the men had only fragmentary knowledge of the treaties, suggests that it is reasonable to assume that the parties in 1852 did regard the agreement as a purchase agreement.

On the other hand, aspects of the statements – aspects relating to the internal dynamics of Indigenous societies – have the ring of truth. The 1932 chiefs and councillors disputed the right of two of the signatories to have been party to the treaties. That statement seems to corroborate James Douglas's statement that he had found it impossible to determine who were the true owners of the land, and Richard Mayne's 1862 statement regarding rival claims to land.[60]

The chiefs' assertions about the legitimacy of What-say-mullet and Hotutstun to be party to a treaty relating to Saanich territory may be rooted in disputes known to have taken place in 1852. While not impossible given that Mayne's book had been published since 1862, it is unlikely that the chief's assertions about What-say-mullet and Hotutstun is evidence of feedback.

The best-known oral account of the Vancouver Island treaties, David Latasse's 1934 account, is also the most problematic. Because Latasse's account has gained such prominence, and because the article has never been republished in its entirety, it is reproduced in full in Appendix B.

There is no evidence that Latasse's account has ever been subjected to the kind of critical source analysis that oral historiographers recommend. For that reason, its contents have been accorded weight that it cannot bear. Any researcher must acknowledge the complex authorship of the article. It is no surprise that David Latasse's account was not recorded and preserved according to today's standards of oral historiography (in which audio recordings of the words of the interviewer and informant should be preserved), but given that this is a newspaper article published under Frank Pagett's name, Pagett, a journalist who had recently been forced by ill health to retire, should be considered the author of the article.[61] Still Pagett placed words purported to be Latasse's in quotation marks, so it is reasonable to assume that Pagett believed that he was recording the words of Latasse as translated for him. Still, the fact that Latasse's grand-nephew actually translated the words, with some interventions at unidentified times by Latasse's wife, and that Frank Pagett (who presumably did not understand the original words) wrote the words, does complicate our efforts to interpret the account. It would be simplistic to say that David Latasse is the author of this document. Had the document actually been written by Latasse – rather than written by Pagett after listening to Baptiste Paull's translation of Latasse – the uncertainties about whether Latasse's story was preserved properly would be far less significant. David Latasse, his wife, and Baptiste Paull understood the probable audience of this account: the readers of the *Victoria Daily Times*. What were the aims of Frank Pagett, and Baptiste Paull and David Latasse? The context of the 1920s and early 1930s already discussed and the document itself make that clear: to defend an argument that the Saanich treaties were not land purchases. The first four paragraphs make it clear that Frank Pagett understood that as Latasse's main purpose. Those paragraphs also show that Pagett did not question Latasse's claim to have been 105 years old in 1934.[62]

David Latasse (d. 1937) was born between 1856 and 1868. In 1903, Latasse indicated that he had been born on the Songhees Reserve and lived there for about five years before moving to the Tsartlip reserve, where he claimed to have lived for twenty-five to thirty years (implying that he was born in the 1860s).[63] Other official documents appear to corroborate that statement. According to the Canadian government's census of 1891, "David Letess" was then thirty-five years old.[64] The census of 1901 records "David lee tees" a "Salish" from Tsartlip as forty-two years, living in the same house with a forty-three-year-old wife (Madeline), a thirty-two-year-old sister, a twenty-four-year-old brother, an eighteen-year-old son, a twelve-year-old daughter, and a sixty-four-year-old widowed mother.[65] According to the 1921 census, "David Latess" was then sixty-five years old, and his wife (Genevieve) was sixty-three.[66] Even giving some room for error (typical of census records), that would suggest that Latasse was no more than fifty-five years old in 1903, and eighty-five years old in 1934.[67]

It is only in the 1930s that Latasse began to assert that he had been an adult in 1850. In the *Victoria Daily Times* article, he (or Baptiste Paull or Frank Pagett) told a different story. The conclusion seems unavoidable: Latasse's adamant 1934 statements about his age were not true. Latasse, Latasse's wife, Baptiste Paull, and/or others deliberately misled Pagett about Latasse's age. Vallance downplayed this misrepresentation by stating that "a possible attempt by Latass to bolster the legitimacy and authority of his account has had the opposite effect."[68] This deception is not trivial. Interpretations of this document should be influenced by assessments of the likelihood that the informant's account was first-hand. Latasse was almost certainly not at the treaty negotiations as he claimed to have been, and it is impossible to ascertain the source of his information. It would be injudicious to downplay the evidence that Latasse, Latasse's wife, and/or Baptiste Paull were willing to lie to bolster his account.

The weight of Latasse's account of the treaty negotiations should also be gauged by reference to the plausibility of other parts of his account. The sections of the article entitled "First White Men," "Potent Fire-Water," and "People Not Warlike" are clearly inaccurate. The Songhees were fully familiar with Europeans well before 1843. The Spanish officer Manuel Quimper entered Esquimalt Harbour on 19 July 1790 (naming it Puerto de Córdova). Indeed, the journals of Quimper's expedition that indicated that the bay "was inhabited by Indians who called to him, manifesting their joy," suggest that the Indigenous inhabitants had had previous positive relations with Europeans.[69] In 1792, Galiano's expedition spent 9–10 June at Esquimalt Bay.[70] Furthermore, Vancouver Island peoples had been visiting Fort Langley since that fort was established in 1827. So, the entire section of Latasse's account entitled "First White Men" is inaccurate. Still, Latasse claimed to have witnessed the events first-hand. Either Latasse was confused, or his account is fiction. In either case, the obvious inaccuracies of these sections of the account give ample reason to doubt the accuracies of the entire account.

Similarly, the section subtitled "People Not Warlike" is contradicted by abundant evidence about Northwest Coast warfare. Latasse may have been influenced by concepts of "noble savages" that circulated in society in the 1930s. Thus, scholars can extract valuable information from Latasse's account about how Indigenous people imagined their own pasts in the 1930s, but it would be unscholarly to assume that Latasse's account would be a reliable account of Indigenous understandings of events in the 1850s. Latasse's account clearly does not outweigh the abundant evidence of warfare in the region in the forty years before the Vancouver Island treaties were concluded.

Some of the contents of Latasse's account that Latasse claimed to be recalling from memory are clear examples of feedback. For example, the account notes that "The vessel was the brigantine Cadboro." It is implausible that Latasse (or any other person) in 1934 knew the name and type of ship from first-hand experience or through purely orally transmitted memories. It is possible that Frank Pagett added this line. Or it is possible that Latasse knew this because his well-educated wife had told him the name of the ship after reading this information. Similarly, in various places, this account mentions specific years and even specific dates ("1843," "about March 1843," "May 24, 1850," "1852"). It is implausible that, in 1934, David Latasse would have remembered such specific dates. The dates he gave (or Pagett inserted) offer evidence that his account has been informed by historical documents. The feedback would be less problematic if he had acknowledged that some of his information originated in the documentary record, but in this instance he (or perhaps his wife) appears to have included the information hoping that the audience would interpret congruence between this account and historical documents as corroboration.

In fact, some of the descriptions of the treaty negotiations, including the date, are contradicted by the documents. Latasse's assertion that a "Beacon-Hill Party" occurred on 24 May 1850 is contradicted by the historical documents. The archival documents (Fort Victoria journals and correspondence) show that all of the Fort Victoria treaties had been concluded before 24 May. The Fort Victoria journals of 24 May mention no large gathering near Fort Victoria. Latasse's description of the treaty negotiations – that word of the negotiations went out weeks beforehand and that "natives were seated in big circles" – are clearly drawn from descriptions, including illustrations, of other treaty negotiations in Canada and the United States. The documentary record shows that the treaty proceedings were convened hurriedly, were conducted on separate days with different chiefs, and may have passed without significant fanfare or ceremony.

No historian could avoid being tantalized by the thought that a genuine, detailed first-person Indigenous account of the Vancouver Island treaties might exist, but as intriguing as the prospect is, the evidence that David Latasse was dishonest about his age in 1934, that his status as eyewitness is almost certainly false, and that many parts of the account are certainly inaccurate – perhaps even deliberately falsified – means that dispassionate scholars can place little weight on David Latasse as a reliable informant on the understandings of Aboriginal signatories in 1850.[71]

Accounts preserved later by actual participants in and witnesses to the treaty negotiations add to our understanding of what happened in the 1850s. However, as oral historiographers have explained, as the time between an event and the recollection of the event grows, the recollection becomes less reliable as a source about the event itself, and more important as a source about changing understandings of the events. In the case of the Vancouver Island treaties recollections by Indigenous and non-Indigenous people preserved between 1877 and 1934 appear to illustrate the oral historiographers' maxim.

# Conclusion

If, as many scholars seem to have assumed, the fact that only part of Vancouver Island is covered by land-purchase treaties makes Vancouver Island exceptional, that fact might be interesting only to historians of Vancouver Island or Canada. However, that the history of treaties on Vancouver Island reflects the paradoxical history of treaties throughout former British colonies makes the Vancouver Island treaties globally significant. Treaties were negotiated in some parts of the British world, but not in others. Moreover, just as no pattern of Indigenous land use can explain why treaties were negotiated with some Vancouver Island villagers but not with others, nothing can explain why treaties were concluded with some of the most sparsely populated hunting and gathering peoples along the shores of Hudson Bay, but not among similarly sparsely populated communities in Australia ... except expediency. A contextual history of the Vancouver Island treaties allows us to understand better the strange history of those treaties, and the history of Indigenous title.

The history of the Vancouver Island treaties, understood in the broad context of treaties in the HBC and the British world generally, shows that scholarly interpretations require revision. When the Dutch in the New Netherlands and their neighbours in the New England colonies began negotiating land-purchase treaties with Indigenous peoples on the eastern seaboard of North America in the 1620s, they did not do so to conform to any legal principles regarding Indigenous title. They did so hoping that such agreements might bolster their claims against other Dutch and English rivals. The circumstances on the eastern seaboard at the time were unique. Rival claims based on discovery, government charters, or actual occupation were open to dispute. Conquest was no option, the Dutch and English were at peace, and other rival colonies were all English. Dutch and English colonial officials (and plausibly individuals as well) enjoyed the authority to make compacts with Indigenous people. Under those circumstances, rivals discovered that land-purchase treaties were inexpensive and expedient ways to strengthen claims to land, especially after both Dutch and English entities started using them. Precisely because they attached weight to the agreements (although some people almost immediately denied Indigenous land rights), the English and Dutch colonists began the process of creating principles of Indigenous title that others would reject, modify, and elaborate upon in different situations.

Evidently, the New Englander Zachariah Gillam and his employer, the HBC, adopted a short-lived land-purchase strategy beginning in 1668 for lands around Hudson Bay. However, when the HBC, without any evident support of the Crown, added evidence of those purchases to the list of other evidence (discovery, mapping, naming of geographical features, occupation) to support its claims to land around Hudson Bay, the French did not take the bait. Then, after the French and English crowns went to war, such purchases would have carried no weight with the French. Accordingly, the HBC made no further purchases until 1817. When Lord Selkirk negotiated for lands around Red River in 1817, he did so to support the HBC's claims to Rupert's Land and to demonstrate Indigenous support for the company.

Similarly, the first treaties had little or nothing to do with satisfying the demands of Indigenous peoples, who apparently had no traditions of purchasing land from each other in North America, Australia, or New Zealand. But Indigenous communities who learned of the possibility of obtaining compensation for surrendering land rights to exogenous people learned to request or demand it. Over time, therefore, officials (and individuals) in the British world embraced the utility of land-purchase agreements with Indigenous communities, not only when they might support claims against rival colonists, but also when those agreements could obtain the consent of Indigenous people for the peaceful transfer of the control of land. So, Indigenous communities also participated in the process by which principles of Indigenous title were created and elaborated. In this process, the expediency of such agreements, more than any other consideration, determined whether land-purchase agreements were sought.

Many scholars, particularly those interested in British–Indigenous relations in the antipodes, have theorized that by the time Australia and New Zealand were colonized, the British were guided by legal principles regarding Indigenous title, including the concept of *terra nullius*, and the related principle that Indigenous communities that used land intensively (by agriculture and settlement) enjoyed Indigenous title, whereas nomadic hunting and gathering peoples did not. That theory appeared plausible because the British authorities sought land purchases in places such as New Zealand (where Māori lived in villages and practised agriculture) but not in sparsely populated Australian colonies where most Indigenous communities were nomadic hunters and gatherers. The theory is less plausible for North America, especially the northern half of North America. There, authorities negotiated the surrender of Indigenous title from some of the most sparsely populated nomadic hunting and gathering peoples on the continent but did not do so from some of the most populous villagers on the Northwest Coast who had adopted potato cultivation before British settlers arrived. The fact that the theory has been challenged and arguably refuted, even for the antipodes, forces historians to re-examine the evidence. Practical considerations, not legal considerations, were most important in determining whether the British arranged land purchases in any location. Considerations of the likelihood that land purchases would bolster claims against rivals, and related questions about whether treaties would facilitate the peaceful settlement of exogenous people, were paramount. Theorists may have subsequently defended (or attacked) decisions to negotiate treaties or not based on Indigenous land use, but Indigenous land use was a minor consideration among those who made the decisions. Still, if the practice was to carry weight either within the British (or American) world, or internationally, legal principles should be developed to explain and justify it. Treaty policy did not initially emerge from legal principles; legal principles emerged from practice, before beginning to influence policy.

By the early 1840s, the process by which historical practice had begun to create legal and moral concepts of Indigenous title had developed in both the United States and the British world. Jurists, particularly in the United States, had done much to draw upon historical practice and concepts of stadial history to codify legal principles of Indigenous title. Although the existence of Indigenous title was widely but not universally accepted, it was still largely undefined. In the British world, events in New Zealand in the 1840s forced rivals to articulate systematic and consistent principles of Indigenous title – often drawing upon historical practice and jurisprudence from the United States. It was in response to the many private individuals who claimed land in New Zealand by right of purchase from Māori – threatening the interests of the state and threatening the peace – that George Gipps, William Wentworth, James Busby, Earl Grey, the New Zealand judges in the *Symonds* case, and others, competed to establish legal principles. Representatives of the British Crown (and the Supreme Court of the United States) had long asserted the principle that only representatives of the state could purchase Indigenous title, but companies and private individuals continued to defy the claims of the state in both the British world and the United States – boldly in New Zealand. British proponents of rival theories turned to American jurisprudence on the question, although it was precisely in the years that they did so that the interpretations of Indigenous title in the British world diverged from those in the United States, because the contexts in which purchases were made differed so significantly. In the British world, for example, land-purchase agreements with Indigenous communities – even when labelled "treaties," were not treaties like international treaties (or were not treaties at all), but were unique agreements contracted between the state and communities of its own subjects. That principle differed starkly from the idiosyncratic ruling by the United States Supreme Court that Indian tribes were "domestic dependent nations," and that American treaties with those nations were analogous to international treaties. By the end of the 1840s, the theorists had also developed the principle that Indigenous title was not ownership, but a burden (whether legal or moral) upon the state – the owner – which could be extinguished in any number of ways. The state might purchase the title by way of formal treaties, but it might also terminate the right by providing reserves, police and military protection, education, medical and emergency assistance, and religious instruction.

While some principles of Indigenous title were fairly well established by the end of the 1840s, others were still being shaped by practice. Although officials at the Colonial Office and in the periphery asserted that Indigenous communities had title only to lands that they actually occupied, whether by settlement or cultivation, those who actually negotiated land purchases consistently generated written agreements that stipulated that Indigenous communities, or their leaders, were surrendering Indigenous title to their entire territories, including "waste" lands. Negotiators on the ground found it expedient to do so. And so again, principles evolved to explain practice. Neither was it clear in the 1840s that Indigenous title was legally enforceable by Indigenous communities. No Indigenous claimant had asserted in a court of law any rights based on Indigenous title. The early jurisprudence developed from litigation – such as *Symonds* and *St. Catherine's Milling* – to which Indigenous communities were not parties. As a *legal* doctrine, Indigenous title was still in its infancy even after 1850. But the metropole and periphery, state and non-state actors, Indigenous and exogenous people, all contributed to the development of its principles.

Abundant evidence from many locations shows that Indigenous people knew that they were selling their land rights in land-transfer treaties. Representatives of the state believed that it was essential that Indigenous people understand the terms and conditions of the treaties as best they could. Indigenous communities accepted nominal payments for lands because, in many cases they had not anticipated payment at all, because they did not know the exchange value of the land, because they had experienced and anticipated the collateral benefits that they believed had, and would, ensue from exogenous settlement and treaties, and because they valued the promises contained in the treaties. Indigenous leaders must also have been influenced by how treaty making might have enhanced their status within their communities. For their part, representatives of governments believed that the trifling monetary compensation that they offered was fair and just because they believed Indigenous title was a limited right far short of ownership, and because they believed that the monetary compensation was only a small part of the benefits that the Indigenous signatories would enjoy. Although it may seem implausible today that Indigenous people would part with their land rights for paltry compensation, the documentary evidence from the New Netherlands, Red River, New Zealand, and Vancouver Island confirms it. Indeed, the evidence that many (certainly not all) Indigenous communities continued to value their treaties long after they learned of the monetary value of real estate seems to corroborate it.

In the context of the long historical process just described, much of the history of the Vancouver Island treaties makes sense. Neither the 3 per cent of the land covered by treaties, nor the 97 per cent that was not (figure 1), seems any longer to be an exception to any rule or legal principles established in the 1850s. Neither need we be puzzled by the fact that some parts of Canada and some parts of the British world are covered by treaties, but others are not. Expediency, rather than law or morality, was the key consideration at the time. Only after the principles of Indigenous title became legally defined by the courts did that change.

The Vancouver Island treaties were not the brainchild of James Douglas or the Colonial Office. The London Governor and Committee of the HBC and the HBC's North American governor deemed it expedient to conclude them. They were not guided by any perceived legal obligation – certainly not by humanitarian concern – but by a desire to strengthen the HBC's claims to Vancouver Island coal lands (and subsequently other lands), against any potential rival claimants and to gain greater influence over Indigenous leaders. Company officials were also probably motivated by the benefits and profits the company could enjoy by concluding the treaties (in the shape of the immediate goodwill of the

Indigenous leaders, and the eventual reimbursement from the British government). James Douglas was not the first to propose the treaties and was not a particularly ardent proponent of land-transfer treaties. Less than three years before he negotiated the first Fort Victoria treaty, he had ordered Roderick Finlayson to take possession of San Juan Island using a centuries-old rite of possession. Even in 1852, he instructed J.W. McKay to do so at Nanaimo. When instructed to negotiate treaties, he executed his instructions in an extraordinarily casual and perfunctory way. While financial constraints prevented him from concluding treaties on Vancouver Island after the colony became a Crown colony in 1859, his enthusiasm for treaties appears to have diminished because, in his experience, treaty negotiations always roused "troublesome excitements ... productive of serious disturbances." After 1861, Douglas was never a strong proponent of treaties. Still, between 1850 and 1854, including when he diverged from his instructions in ways that other treaty negotiators elsewhere also had, he and the Indigenous people with whom he treated participated in the formulation of principles of Indigenous title.

The HBC pursued the Vancouver Island treaties even though the company never acknowledged Indigenous title. Nothing about the way Douglas and the HBC conducted the negotiations, or created and preserved the treaties, suggests that James Douglas or other personnel in the HBC anticipated the importance that the treaties would later take on. Nevertheless, in purporting to conclude land purchases on Hudson Bay in the 1680s, concluding the Selkirk Treaty in 1817, and concluding the Vancouver Island treaties in the 1850s, the HBC participated unwittingly in the process by which the concept of Indigenous title would be defined.

Documents contain little direct evidence about why the Indigenous leaders at Fort Rupert, Fort Victoria, and the Saanich Peninsula agreed to the Vancouver Island treaties, although the history of Indigenous peoples on the Northwest Coast, the history of Indigenous–exogenous relations on Vancouver Island, and evidence from other contexts are suggestive. Indigenous leaders and communities must have placed great value on their control of specific rich resource-procurement sites for thousands of years before encountering Europeans. Elite members of societies possessed much wealth – even in the form of human chattel – since time immemorial. Property, including slaves, could be traded or exchanged in other ways. Wealth, amassed in any number of ways, often in warfare, was key to attaining and maintaining status and prestige, particularly when it was dispensed. Humans and resource-procurement sites had also been seized in warfare. But there is no evidence that the peoples of the Northwest Coast had compensated one another for land before Europeans arrived. Evidence suggests the

Conclusion 295

contrary. At Fort Victoria, the HBC's proposal to negotiate payments for land came after the Indigenous people were already aware that the HBC had occupied extensive acreage in buildings, cultivation, and pasturage at Fort Victoria, Fort Langley, Fort Nisqually, and elsewhere, without ever offering compensation, and without facing Indigenous protest. The Kwakiutl chiefs who demanded payment for the garden at Fort Rupert in April 1850 – where the company occupied little land – almost certainly did so after learning that the company planned on concluding treaties. The treaty process on Vancouver Island in the 1850s was initiated and driven by the interests of the HBC. That fact is somewhat obscured by the demands made by the Kwakiutl chiefs on 15 April 1850. Under the circumstances, the chiefs probably considered any payment a windfall, especially when accompanied by certain promises.

Indigenous people at Fort Rupert, Fort Victoria, the Saanich Peninsula, and elsewhere knew of the collateral benefits (military and economic) of having HBC posts adjacent to their villages. The elite, commoners, and even slaves, had experienced them. In the fluid socio-economic circumstances of these villages, the monetary payments and the prestige of being recognized as a prominent chief elevated the status of the leaders whose marks were made in the HBC's treaty register. At the same time, such agreements were likely to excite and inflame rivalries within those societies.

Did the Indigenous people understand the implications of the treaties? Certainly not. Did they assume that the newcomers would always be able to assert the permanence and finality stipulated in the treaties? Perhaps not. But it was contrary to the interest of the HBC to mislead the Indigenous leaders about the terms and conditions of the treaties. Indigenous signatories to the Vancouver Island treaties continued to value their treaties well after the blankets handed out at their conclusion had worn out.

Reminiscences and accounts of the Vancouver Island treaties recorded at various times between the 1880s and the 1930s shed much light on the evolution of the memory of the treaties. As the legal interpretations of Indigenous title and the importance of treaties evolved, memories of the treaties have also changed. While some of the more recent accounts of the Vancouver Island treaties may shed little light on what was actually said and understood by the parties in the 1850s, they highlight the fact that the relationship between Indigenous polities and the Canadian government, and between Indigenous and non-Indigenous Canadians can, and must, continue to adapt to meet new circumstances. As important as it is to understand the past, it is also crucial that we not be imprisoned by it.

# Appendix A: "Original Indian Population Vancouver Island"

| Tribe | Family | Place of habitation | Men with beards | Women | Boys | Girls | Totals | Payment £.s.d[a] |
|---|---|---|---|---|---|---|---|---|
| Songees | Teechamit | | 11 | 10 | 16 | 14 | 51 | 27.10.0 |
| | Kosampsom | | 21 | 23 | 35 | 26 | 105 | 52.10.0 |
| | Swengwhung | | 30 | 33 | 57 | 63 | 183 | 75.0.0 |
| | Chilcowitch | Victoria District | 12 | 13 | 17 | 16 | 58 | 30.0.0 |
| | Whyomilth | | 18 | 20 | 36 | 39 | 113 | 45.0.0 |
| | Chekonein | | 30 | 35 | 60 | 65 | 190 | 79.10.0 |
| | [Total] | | **122** | **134** | **221** | **223** | **700** | **103.14.0** |
| Tlallum | Kakyaakun | Metchosin | 10 | 12 | 20 | 17 | 59 | 43.0.0 |
| | Chewhaytsun | Rocky Point | 30 | 35 | 54 | 58 | 177 | 45.10.0 |
| | [Total] | | **40** | **47** | **74** | **75** | **236** | **30.0.8** |
| Soke | Soke | Soke Inlet | **34** | **40** | **65** | **71** | **210** | 48.6.8/ 16.8.8 |
| [Total Signatories to the Fort Victoria Treaties, April and May 1850] | | | **196** | **221** | **360** | **369** | **1,146** | **150.3.4** |
| Quakeeolth | Quakeeolth | | 130[b] | 140 | | | | £1.18.0 per chief |
| | Queehaw | Beaver Harbor | 70 | 72 | | | | £1.18.0 per chief |
| [Total Signatories to the Fort Rupert Treaties] | | | **200** | **212** | **[~736]** | | **[~1,148]** | **[380.0.0?]** |
| Sanitch | Sanitch | Mount Douglas | 10 | 12 | 16 | 18 | 56 | |
| | Sanitch | Sanitch Arm | 118 | 130 | 210 | 225 | 683 | |
| [Total Signatories to Saanich Treaties] | | | **128** | **142** | **226** | **243** | **739** | £109.7.6 |
| Nanaimo | Saalequun | Nanaimo District | 159 | 160 | 300 | 306 | 923 | ~£270.0.0 |
| Grand Total | | | **649** | **695** | | | **3,010 +~1,148 =4,158** | |

Sources: "Original Indian Population Vancouver Island," BCA B/20/1853, Private Papers of Sir James Douglas, 1853 and the original treaties.

[a] The cost per treaty is that given in the treaty. The actual costs (in bold) represent the total actual Dept prices, thus is not a sum of the cost of each treaty.

[b] The number of signatories to the Fort Rupert Treaties (15 Quakeeolth and 11 Queehaw) does not match the number of signatories to the treaties. Douglas's estimate did not include boys and girls. The estimate of boys and girls is extrapolated from the data given for other Indigenous communities at the time.

Appendix A: "Original Indian Population Vancouver Island"

| Tribe | Family | Place of habitation | Men with beards | Women | Youths and children Boys | Youths and children Girls | Totals |
|---|---|---|---|---|---|---|---|
| Songees | Teechamitsa | | 11 | 10 | 16 | 14 | 51 |
| | Kosampsom | | 21 | 23 | 35 | 26 | 105 |
| | Swengwhung | | 30 | 33 | 57 | 63 | 183 |
| | Chilcowitch | Victoria District | 12 | 13 | 17 | 16 | 58 |
| | Whyomilth | | 18 | 20 | 36 | 39 | 113 |
| | Chekonein | | 30 | 35 | 60 | 65 | 190 |
| | [Total] | | **122** | **134** | **221** | **223** | **700** |
| Tlallum | Kakyaakan | Metchosin | 10 | 12 | 20 | 17 | 59 |
| | Chewhaytsun | Rocky Point | 30 | 35 | 54 | 58 | 177 |
| | [Total] | | **40** | **47** | **74** | **75** | **236** |
| Soke | Soke | Soke Inlet | 34 | 40 | 65 | 71 | 210 |
| Sanitch | Sanitch | Mount Douglas | 10 | 12 | 16 | 18 | 56 |
| | Sanitch | Sanitch Arm | 118 | 130 | 210 | 225 | 683 |
| | | | **128** | **142** | **226** | **243** | **739** |
| Cowegin | Komiakun | | 100 | 120 | 87 | 113 | |
| | Thimthimelitz | Cowegin Valley | 160 | 165 | 158 | 162 | |
| | Quamichen | | 430 | 450 | 400 | 450 | |
| | Tataka | Cowegin Gap | 160 | 162 | 160 | 165 | |
| | Penalahats | Cowegin Gap | 200 | 219 | 205 | 195 | |
| | Saumina | Cowegin Valley | 80 | 75 | 63 | 80 | |
| | Chemanis | Cowegin Valley | 200 | 203 | 264 | 283 | |
| | Sumlumalcha | | 20 | 22 | 36 | 44 | |
| | Whe-whulla | Cowigin Gap | 25 | 28 | 35 | 43 | |
| | Akmanis | | 20 | 18 | 38 | 41 | |
| [Total Cowegin] | | | 1,395 | 1,462 | 1,446 | 1,576 | **587** |
| | | | | Carried Forward | | | **7,764** |
| Nanaimo | Souleequun | Nanaimo District | 159 | 160 | 300 | 306 | 923 |
| | Nono-oss | Nono-oss Bay | 20 | 23 | 28 | 32 | |
| | Saathlum [Qualicum] | Valdez Inlet [at Qualicum River] | 12 | 15 | 17 | 19 | |
| | Comox | Point Holmes | 80 | 93 | 150 | 165 | |
| | Puntlach [Pentlatch] | Puntlach River | 10 | 13 | 14 | 16 | |
| [Total Nanaimo] | | | 281 | 294 [304] | 509 | 556 | **1,640** [1,650] |
| Laycooltach [Lekwiltok] | Huck-ha-mateese | Point Mudge | 330 | 340 | | | |
| | Wee-waa-Rum | and other | 200 | 210 | | | |
| | Wee-waa-Kay | parts of | 300 | 313 | | | |
| | Que-hao | Johnstone's | 100 | 106 | | | |
| | Thaloo-eese | Straits | 63 | 63 | | | |
| [Total Laycooltach] | | | 990 | 1,032 | 990 Estimate | 990 Estimate | **4,002** |

(*continued on next page*)

Appendix A: "Original Indian Population Vancouver Island" 299

| Tribe | Family | Place of habitation | Men with beards | Women | Youths and children Boys | Girls | Totals |
|---|---|---|---|---|---|---|---|
| Quakeeolth [Kwakiulth] | Quakeeolth | | 200 | 206 | | | |
| | Nimkeese | Cheslakeese | 130 | 143 | | | |
| | Queehaw | Beaver Harbor | 70 | 72 | | | |
| | Lackwalla | Cheslakeese | 80 | 95 | | | |
| | Kumkootis | McNeils Harbour | 93 | 91 | | | |
| | Thlowitsis | Johnstones Straits | 85 | 93 | | | |
| | Mameeleeleekala | | 700 | 756 | | | |
| | Chowatty | | 110 | 114 | | | |
| | Tanuctaw | | 56 | 60 | | | |
| [Total Quakeeoolth] | | | 1,524 | 1,630 | 1,300 Estimate | | **4,454** |
| Carried Forward | | | | | | | **17,860** |
| | | | | | Indian Statements | | |
| | Nitinat | Port San Juan | 250 | 258 | 292 | | |
| | O.J. apa | Barclay Sound | 180 | 200 | 120 | | |
| | Shata | and vicinity | 50 | 60 | 90 | | |
| | Toqua-ata | | 10 | 12 | 18 | | |
| | Youcluetyet | Barclay Sound | 100 | 100 | 150 | | |
| | Clayo-quot | Port Cox | 175 | 180 | 195 | | |
| | Ahouset | --ditto-- | doubtful 80 | 90 | 160 | | |
| | | | **845** | **900** | **1,025** | | **2,770** |
| | Moachet | Nootka Sound | 180 | 143 | 203 | | |
| | Muchelat | and neighbour- | 45 | 50 | 65 | | |
| | Chatesit | ing coast | 75 | 81 | 101 | | |
| | Newchatlet | | 45 | 43 | 59 | | |
| | Kiyoucut | | 1,000 | 1,091 | 1,025 | | |
| | Cheakleset | | 20 | 23 | 24 | | |
| | | | **1,365** | **1,481** | **1,477** | | **4,323** |
| | Koskeema | 30 miles south of Cape Scott | 90 | 82 | 150 | | |
| | Classet | Cape Scott | 75 | 78 | 95 | | |
| | Ko-up-at | near Cape Scott | 63 | 67 | 80 | | |
| | Katseno | Scott's Island | 44 | 48 | 48 | | |
| | | | **272** | **275** | **373** | | **920** |
| | | Total population | | | | | 25,873 |

Source: Chart 3. "Original Indian Population, Vancouver Island." This transcription is based primarily upon the version in NA CO 305/7, fos. 108–109, but is also influenced by the version found at BCA B/20/1853.

# Appendix B: A 1934 Account of a Fort Victoria Treaty Attributed to David Latasse

Frank Pagett, "105 Years in Victoria and Saanich! Chief David Recalls White Man's Coming; 80 Years Rent Unpaid," *Victoria Daily Times* 14 July 1934, Features Section

Tribal groups of Saanich have claims against the Hudson's Bay Company and the British Columbia Government, for a capital sum to make good an agreed rental of Saanich now unpaid for eighty years, according to Chief David Latass, famous orator of the Brentwood division of the Saanich tribe.

Chief David is now in his 105th year and is still mentally keen, although extremely fragile. He lives on a reserve named Tsartlip (Land of Maples), Brentwood, one of the most beautiful areas overlooking the waters of Saanich Arm. His tidy little cottage is modernly furnished and is looked after by a well-educated wife, half his age, who aided in interpreting the ancient's vigorous statements.

The principal interpreter of Chief David's reminiscences was his grand-nephew, Baptiste Paull, professionally known as Baptiste Thomas, a boxer and wrestler, whose prowess has won fame throughout the Pacific Coast.

### Chief Tells His Story

"More than eighty years ago I saw James Douglas, at the place now called Beacon Hill, stand before the assembled chiefs of the Saanich Indians with uplifted hand" the old chief said. "I heard him give his personal word that, if we agreed to let the white man use parts of our land to grow food, all would be to the satisfaction of the Indian peoples. Blankets and trade were to be paid. We, knowing a crop grows each year, looked for gifts each year, what is now called rent. Our chiefs then sold no part of Saanich.

"White people doubt my age can be 105 years. They see my bright eyes, they saw me move quickly until a few years ago, they heard me speak in council and address the tribes when long past ninety years old, and they said it was impossible for me to have known James Douglas. But I was a man grown when the big powwow was held in Beacon Hill. I was fourteen when the first white men came to Victoria Harbor in 1849.

"I was born a member of the Songhees tribe, who then lived in small bands along the waterfront from Beacon Hill to Cadboro Bay and Cordova Bay. The tribe also had a central camp site on Mud Bay in Victoria Harbor, where now stands the Empress Hotel and the Union Club.

**First White Men**

When I was seven years of age I went to Brentwood to live, joining aunts who had become wives of members of the Saanich tribe. It was six years later that the first reports of white men spread around the land, and by some chance there was a prophetic warning in the episode.

"Songhees used to visit Cordova Bay to collect camas and wild carrot as vegetables. Such a party in 1843 saw a sailing ship round the point. The Indians made a fire on the beach and the vessel anchored. She lay there two days, the object of much interest to the tribesmen and some recalled seeing many years earlier such a ship far off-shore. The vessel was the brigantine Cadboro.

"On the second day young men manned canoes and went out to inspect the vessel. Bearded faces looked over the side of the ship, a ladder was thrown overboard and the natives invited on deck where they were offered a drink. When the natives hesitated the white leader board a drink into a tumbler and tossed it off.

**Potent Fire-Water**

A young buck named Gietluck, who later became chief, took the bottle, poured the tumbler full and tossed the drink down his throat. He strangled, gasped for breath and fell to the deck. His frightened fellows threw him overside into a canoe and fled to shore. By the time the canoe was beached Gietluck was insensible. He was carried ashore amid cries of wrath and grief. Women started wailing and messengers were sent to all the tribal groups for medicine men. One doctor lived with the Brentwood colony of the Saanich Indians and when an exhausted messenger arrived all we boys started running to Cordova Bay to see the horrid sight. When we got there we found the vessel gone. Instead there were five tribal doctors making incantations over the paralyzed Gietluck, amid an alarmed circle of old folk. After prayers the medicine men took turns in rubbing the sleeper's face and hands, they slapped him, poured water on him and then rubbed him warm again. Gietluck slept through it all until the evening of the next day. He was the first island Indian to taste the white man's fire-water. He later became a confirmed drunkard and was slain in a brawl at Esquimalt.

**Cattle Cause Fear**

It was not until the next year, in the spring months, that would be about March 1843, we had another word of the white men. Then messengers came to Brentwood from Mud Bay, now Victoria, advising all to hasten southward to see the big vessel. So we ran. I was a big boy of fourteen years at the time, and was one of the first to arrive.

"Off Laurel Point stood a tall ship, there were sails bralled up and she was anchored. For two days nothing happened that I know of, though the whites may have been having talks with tribal leaders. Then there was action which terrified we youths though I believe the elders knew what was coming. The ship changed her position, wide runways were let down from one side to the water and huge animals, armed with horns charged down into the sea and swam for shore. Men in four boats came around the other side of the ship and drove the monsters to Mud Bay, where they came ashore, close to the Songhees village. We youngsters were terribly frightened when those great beasts came snorting through the water, to be the first cattle on Vancouver Island.

**People Not Warlike**

Right here is a good time to explode a long-standing myth of the warlike habits of the Songhees and Saanich tribesmen. For forty years prior to the coming of James Douglas there had been profound peace in all parts of Saanich. In fact, modern ideas would class the people as a lot of cowards. There had been warrior chiefs in past generations, our traditions tell of them, but they went out and slaughtered each other or fell under the spears of raiders from the north. Murder was almost unknown throughout all the land now known as Saanich. There was plenty of food for everyone, there were lots of women to do the work and provide wives for all. This country was a land of beauty, inhabited by people who knew not the meaning of slaughter.

"True, we had big dug-outs which the white men termed war canoes, but no raids were ever made and no battles had been fought for nearly half a century. Therefore, there cannot be truth in stories that the early settlers shivered in their beds at night, while vigilant guards around stockade walls kept howling Songhees at bay.

"The truth is, at the time of the gold rush to the Fraser River, the Indians were profiting largely from taking eager miners in their canoes from Victoria to the mainland. There were many potlatch parties and much noise was made at the celebrations. There was also much gunfire, weapons being discharged in the air just for pleasure. The whites were glad to supply the Indians with liquor and the Indians, with their usual lack of foresight, spent everything they made as fast as they got it.

**Tzouhalem, the Brave**

There was one wild warrior in those days, however, but he was not a Songhee or Saanich Indian. His name was Tzouhalem, a war chief of the Cowichan Indians, who came to Victoria when James Douglas dared him to come to the fort. Tzouhalem had his gun and his knife. Many Songhees and Saanich Indians knew of the challenge and were present to see what would happen. I was one of the spectators and it was a great sight. Tzouhalem appeared from some bush, crouching, and bounded swiftly towards the fort. Guns were fired at him, but he could see the big bullets rolling through the air and he leaped from side to side as he advanced. Arriving at the gate he knocked and cried loudly.

"Joseph William Mackay, the right-hand man and interpreter of Douglas, flung the gate open and with peace signs greeted Tzouhalem, calling him brother and praising him as a brave man. As a reward for his courage MacKay gave the war chief pipes, twist tobacco, guns and powder. He also made a great feast in his honour at which MacKay told Tzouhalem, in a long speech, that he was the greatest and bravest man of the Indians and the white men were proud to call him brother.

"That alliance of the whites and the Cowichan chief, arranged by MacKay on behalf of Douglas, was a mistake. Tzouhalem got wilder and at last became too made for his Cowichans. More and more all the tribes of the Indians feared him and his furies. He would pop out of the bush and slay travelers. He met his end when about sixty years old. He went to Valdez Island and in a tribal guesthouse reached for his gun to slay men whom his arguments had provoked. But while he had been feasting the bullet had been shaken from his gun. Tzouhalem died under many knives. But that was long after the whites were well settled.

Appendix B: A 1934 Account of a Fort Victoria Treaty    305

**Fort Is Built**

When the first white men had put their cattle ashore they set about building themselves shelters and store buildings. Indians brought logs and James Douglas paid the chiefs for much work. I forget how long it took to build the fort and the other structures, but Douglas went away for a while. I am not sure whether it was at his first visit that he arranged for the withdrawal of the Songhees to the other side of Victoria Harbor, but I think not. At the time I was resident at Brentwood with the Saanich Indians. I do well remember hearing that Douglas called a meeting of the four sub-chiefs of the Songhees, heads of the groups living at Clover Point, at Cadboro Bay, at Cordova Bay and at Mud Bay. I remember the sense of wealth shared by the Mud Bay group when, after they had agreed to abandon Mud Bay and remove to the old Songhees reserve on the Inner Harbor, Douglas gave the sub-chief a bale of fifty blankets for distribution among the families of the group. He also gave the other groups presents for waiving their rights of assembly at Mud Bay.

A few years later, when the gold rush was on, practically all the colonies of Songhees removed to the Inner Harbor reserve, to share in the wealth to be earned by transporting the miners and their supplies to the Fraser River fields.

For some time after the whites commenced building their settlement they ferried their supplies ashore. Then they desired to build a dock, where ships could be tied up close to shore. Explorers found suitable timbers could be obtained at Cordova Bay, and a gang of whites, Frenchmen and Kanakas [Hawaiians] were sent there to cut piles. The first thing they did was set a fire which nearly got out of hand, making such smoke as to attract attention of the Indians for forty miles around.

Chief Hotutstun of Salt Spring sent messengers to chief Whutsaymullet of the Saanich tribes, telling him that the white men were destroying his heritage and would frighten away fur and game animals. They met and jointly manned two big canoes and came down the coast to see what damage was being done and to demand pay from Douglas. Hututstun was interested by the prospect of sharing in any gifts made to Whutsaymullet but also, indirectly, as the Chief Paramount of all the Indians of Saanich.

**Groundless Panic**

As the two canoes rounded the point and paddled into Cordova Bay they were seen by camp cooks of the logging party, who became panic stricken. Rushing into the woods they yelled the alarm of Indians on the warpath. Every Frenchman and Kanaka dropped his tool and took to his heels, fleeing through the woods to Victoria. As they ran they spread the cry that the Indians were on the warpath.

Douglas hastened to meet the two chieftains and found that the party, with scarcely a weapon other than a few fish spears, were camping in harmony with the white members of the logging detachment. All that was asked was pay for trees cut and damage wrought, which Douglas promptly agreed was right and proper. He ordered two bales of blankets brought from the fort and gave each chief one of them. There was no suggestion that the compensation was for anything other than the timber, no suggestion of title to any land was involved in that matter. That fact is important in view of claims made later, that other big talks for use of land, in which similar small payments of goods and trade were made to Indians to pay for title to land given by the Indian chieftains.

In the years around 1850 the Indians considered that there was lots of land and had no thought of or fear of extensive settlement by white men. The whites were welcomed, they provided a fine market for the large amount of fur which the tribesmen annually collected. The trade goods the whites gave in return for the furs were highly regarded. The whites at that time also had no idea of asking the Indians to give up their lands. Areas proposed to be used by whites were limited and the gifts of blankets and trade goods were nominal annual dues.

**Beacon Hill Party**

I was twenty-one when Governor Douglas gave a big party to the Indians of southern Vancouver Island. The entertainment took place at Beacon Hill on May 24, 1850,[1] and was to celebrate the birthday of Queen Victoria. For weeks in advance of the party was the talk of all encampments within eighty miles of Victoria. Invitations were sent to the Songhees, Saanich, Cowichan and other tribes and the gathering included men, women and children.

The natives were seated in big circles, the chiefs forming the innermost line, the lesser braves being further to the rear, according to their relative importance or youth. The women and children hung around the outskirts of the circles of men grouping themselves in eager clusters.

Hudson's Bay men distributed hard biscuits smeared with molasses and also other foodstuffs. After all had eaten Governor Douglas addressed the crowd. He was dressed in a coat of blue with gold shoulder pieces and trimmings. He preceded his speech with a salute to the

Great White Queen given with upraised hand. He stressed the desire of the white men to be friends with the tribes. He assured the chiefs that trade in furs, with peaceful use of enough land to grow food, were the only reasons for establishment of the settlement.

His statement was welcomed by the peace-loving tribes, whose view of white settlement, had it been voiced at all, would have been that there was lots of land and no harm could come from letting the whites have some of it. It must be remembered that the Indians were great bargainers and they would not have had any idea of letting the whites use their land from year to year unless some equivalent trade or gifts be made each year.

### No Hidden Payments

It has been suggested that the tribal chiefs received payments not known to the members of their tribal groups. That was not possible under the Indian system of living. As each sub-chief received a share of such community profits as gifts of blankets or food he was under the eyes of his group of men and women, among whom he was required to distribute his award.

### Simple Treaty Terms

It is in this matter that the Indians claim they have been unjustly treated. When Douglas met with Chief Hotutston in 1852, and discussed with him and his sub-chiefs the allotment of lands to the Hudson's Bay Company, it was arranged that lands not needed by the natives might be occupied by the whites. The Indians were to have reserved to their use some choice camping sites, were to have hunting rights everywhere and fishing privileges in all waters, with certain water areas exclusively reserved to the use of the tribes.

In return for the use of meadow lands and open prairie tracts of Saanich, the white people would pay to the tribal chieftains a fee in blankets and goods. That was understood by us all to be payable each year. It was so explained to us by Joseph MacKay, the interpreter for Governor Douglas. The governor himself solemnly assured us that all asked to be ratified would be entirely to the satisfaction of the Indians. He also stated that the only object of the writing was to assure the Hudson's Bay Company peaceful and continued use of land tracts suitable for cultivation. That was accompanied by [a] gift of a few blankets. We all understood that similar gifts would be made each year, what is now called rent.

I was unmarried and therefore considered too young to take part in those proceedings as a tribal representative, but I was present, in attendance upon my uncles, who were among the tribal elders. At the time I thought as did the other Indians that the proceedings were just a powwow for the purpose of receiving a few trade gifts. I say truly that I have no knowledge of payments of money, as mentioned in papers supposed to have been signed by Chief Hotutston and Whutsaymullet and their sub-chiefs. I know of no act of signing such papers and believe that no such signatures were in fact made by those tribesmen. There was no payment in goods, instead of money. If there had been, custom would have required immediate public distribution of the trade goods to the tribesmen and the women folk. Then all members of each sub-tribe would have known of the payment and the reason why it had been made by the white men."

**Rights Forgotten**

Speaking in broken English at the conclusion of his long address the ancient chieftain summed up the Indians' complaint as follows:

"Ha! Japanese here old time? No!

"Germans? Nah!

"Any white peoples here only few days.

"Indians here hundreds of years. First peoples here. Some say we belong Chinamens.

"But it hurts, hurts for people to forget we aboriginals and have rights.

"Our generations go back to the big flood, when only Mount Newton's top was above the waters. In those days our people saved themselves by tying themselves to the mountaintop trees with rope of cedar fibres.

"Today," (reverting to the Chinook language) "why should the white people treat us so? We never fought them, yet they took away our property. This land is ours It was as I knew it when a boy and it should be ours to-day. Never, never did the Indians sign away title to their land just for a few blankets."[2]

# Notes

## Introduction

1 The HBC ship captain, David Durham Wishart, described Fort Rupert that way four months later. D.D. Wishart, Victoria, to J.S. Helmcken, Fort Rupert, 17 August 1850, Helmcken Family Papers, J.S. Helmcken, correspondence inward, D.D. Wishart, British Columbia Archives (hereafter BCA), A/E/H37/W75, box 1, folder 2, p. 26. John Sebastian Helmcken had travelled from London to Vancouver Island aboard the HBC's *Norman Morison*, captained by Wishart, between October 1849 and March 1850. Hudson's Bay Company Archives (hereafter HBCA) C.1/613 *Norman Morison*, 1849–51.
2 For a biography of Blenkinsop, see Richard Mackie, "George Blenkinsop, *DCB* http://www.biographi.ca/en/bio/blenkinsop_george_13E.html.
3 Shortly after James Douglas concluded treaties with the chiefs at Fort Rupert in 1851, he wrote that "I cannot help regretting that McNeill was allowed a furlough last year as we have had nothing but trouble and expense with Fort Rupert since he left it. The responsibility of that charge was too much for Blenkinsop, and it was an injustice to the young man to leave him there, with that madman [Charles] Beardmore, who has thank God left the service." James Douglas to George Simpson, 24 February 1851, HBCA D.5/30, fo. 309.
4 Fort Rupert Post Journals, HBCA B.185/a/1, 15 April 1850.
5 HBCA B.185/a/1, 15 April 1850.
6 Duff, "Fort," 3–57. The *White and Bob* case revolved around the Nanaimo Treaty.
7 Fisher, *Contact*, 66; Tennant, *Aboriginal*, 19; Harris, *Making*, 19; Cook, *To Share*, 5, 56, 213. The neglect of the Fort Rupert treaties is particularly problematic for Brazier, "Land," 187–219. In an otherwise important paper, James Hendrickson did not mention the Fort Rupert treaties. James E.

Hendrickson, "The Aboriginal Land Policy of Governor James Douglas, 1849–1864," unpublished paper presented at the BC Studies Conference, 4–6 Nov. 1988, UBC Library, Rare Books and Special Collections Library.
8 See the works by Cole Harris, Paul Tennant, Raymond Frogner, James Hendrickson, and Hamar Foster.
9 Cook, *To Share*.
10 Miller, *Skyscrapers*, 3rd ed.,187. Miller's summary was apparently based on his reading of Robin Fisher and Paul Tennant (the two sources he cited). By the time he published the fourth edition of *Skyscrapers*, Miller must have understood one of his mistakes, but still wrote "Interestingly, as Europeans began to encroach on Aboriginal lands in British Columbia and Governor Douglas asked the Colonial Office for advice and models on which to base treaties, London referred him, not to the Royal Proclamation of 1763, but to New Zealand's land agreements." *Skyscrapers*, 4th ed., 154. Also see Miller, *Compact*, 147. Some scholars continue to state that the Treaty of Waitangi was the template for the Vancouver Island treaties. See Frogner, "Innocent," 65, 72. A recently published collection of essays does little to clarify the issues; Cook, *To Share*. Stuart Banner deals with the Vancouver Island treaties in *Possessing*, 195–230.
11 Wardhaugh, et al., *Origins*, 462.
12 Lutz, *Makúk*, 67. Many scholars have erroneously concluded that the Colonial Office was behind the treaties. See Foster, "Saanichton," 630; Foster and Grove, "Trespassers," 53; Harring, *White*, 191; Makmillen, "Colonial," 88, 92; Storey, *Settler*, 104–5.
13 Lutz, *Makúk*, 78. In 1988, James Hendrickson wrote that "in the colonies of Vancouver Island and British Columbia, Douglas was the pivotal figure in formulating aboriginal land policies." Hendrickson, "Aboriginal Land Policy," UBC Library, Rare Books and Special Collections Library, 2. Also see Harris, *Making*, 18; Frogner, "Innocent," 74; Banner, *Possessing*, 204–21, 319. The belief that James Douglas is key to understanding the Vancouver Island treaties persists. Douglas is the only person to garner any biographical attention in the articles in Cook, et al., *To Share*.
14 Attwood, *Empire*, 6. Emphasis in the original.
15 Attwood, *Empire*, 3. Emphasis in the original.
16 Attwood, *Empire*, 35–7; Attwood, *Possession*.
17 Tennant, *Aboriginal*, 19.
18 J.R. Miller's book-length study of the history of Aboriginal treaties in Canada devotes less than a page to the Vancouver Island treaties. See Miller, *Compact*, 147. A longer treatment is found in Madill, *British Columbia*. By devoting, in *Possessing*, an entire chapter to Vancouver Island and British Columbia, Stuart Banner recognized the significance of the Vancouver Island treaties.

19 I use *exogenous* to refer in general to people who came to parts of North America to which they were not indigenous. "Settlers" is unsatisfactory because before the 1860s most newcomers to Vancouver Island did not intend to settle. Given that many arrivals and many migrants were not from Europe, "Europeans" is also an unsatisfactory term. As early as the eighteenth century, the crews of trading ships included Chinese artisans, native Hawaiians, Filipinos, and Africans, and some representatives of each of these groups apparently stayed on the Northwest Coast and were integrated into Indigenous communities. See Quimby, "Culture," 247–55. Moreover, a considerable portion of arrivals to Vancouver Island in the first half of the nineteenth century were Indigenous North Americans (Iroquois, Cree, Metis) who came as employees of the HBC or spouses of those employees.

20 My emphasis on expediency is greater than that of previous scholars, but Attwood does at times mention the importance of expediency See Attwood, *Empire*, 2–3, 61, 95.

21 Harris, *Making*, 21; Brazier, "Land," 187–219.

22 This historiographical literature has been synthesized in Ned Blackhawk's *The Rediscovery of America*. The neglect of the role of Indigenous people in the making of Indigenous title is the most significant weakness of Attwood's *Empire*.

23 A superficial examination is provided in Brazier, "Land," 187–219. Although scholars have used the HBC records held by the British Columbia Archives, they have largely neglected those held by the Hudson's Bay Company Archives and the Nanaimo Community Archives.

24 The Kemp Deed is analogous to Indigenous treaties in Canada, and perhaps ought to be considered a treaty in New Zealand. Understandings and definitions of Indigenous treaties differ significantly in Canada, the United States, New Zealand, and Australia. In Canada, *treaty* was long used informally and legally, including in Canada's *Indian Act*, to refer to agreements between governments and the leaders of Indigenous communities, even though they were not ratified the way that international treaties were. Whether or not the Vancouver Island treaties were "treaties" or merely "deeds of conveyance" was the subject of legal dispute as early as the 1960s. In 1964, the Justices of the British Columbia Court of Appeal were split on the question. *R. v. White and Bob*, (1964), *Dominion Law Reports* (*DLR*) 50 2nd 613–66. Justice H.W. Davey ruled that although the Vancouver Island agreements were not "executive act[s] establishing relationships between what are recognized as two or more independent states acting in sovereign capacities," they were "treaties" under Section 87 of the 1952 *Indian Act*. Justice Norris depended not only on the unusual wording of the agreements, but also

on the instructions given to Douglas and concluded that "in the light of the history and circumstances it is difficult to conceive of a term which would be more appropriate to describe the engagement entered into" (651) and that "notwithstanding the informality of the transaction on the part of the Hudson's Bay Company, it was just as much an act of state as if it had been entered into by the Sovereign herself" (655). F.A. Sheppard dissented, arguing that the document was "a deed of surrender" (623). Justice Arthur Lord similarly argued that the treaties were "simply an agreement for the sale of land between Indians and the Hudson's Bay Co. to provide for the acquisition of lands required by that company for the purposes of its own business." (665). In 1965, the Supreme Court dismissed the Crown's appeal, indicating that "we are all of the opinion that the majority in the Court of Appeal were right in their conclusion that the document, Exhibit 8, was a 'treaty' within the meaning of that term as used in s. 87 of the *Indian Act* [R.S.C. 1952, c.149]." 52 *DLR* (2d) 481. In 1985, in relation to an agreement concluded by Mi'kmaq in 1725, the Supreme Court ruled that "while it may be helpful in some instances to analogize the principles of international treaty law to Indian treaties, these principles are not determinative. An Indian treaty is unique; it is an agreement *sui generis* which is neither created nor terminated according to the rules of international law." *Simon v. The Queen* (1985) 2 S.C.R. 387. For an account of the White and Bob case from the perspective of Thomas Berger, counsel for the defendants, see Berger, *One*, 87–106. By American definitions of "Indian treaties," Canada (and perhaps New Zealand) does not have any Indigenous treaties, because they have not been treated as international treaties. As early as 1832, Chief Justice John Marshall, of the United States Supreme Court, ruled that "The words 'treaty' and 'nation' are words of our own language, selected in our diplomatic and legislative proceedings, by ourselves, having each a definite and well understood meaning. We have applied them to Indians as we have applied them to the other nations of the earth. They are applied to all in the same sense." *Worcester v. Georgia*, 31 U.S. (6 Pet.) 515 (1832). Accordingly, treaties between the American government and American Indian nations were ratified by Congress in the same way as international treaties, and Indian tribes have been regarded as "domestic dependent nations." When that practice ended in 1871, the agreements in the United States were no longer called "treaties," but were called "agreements." Those "agreements" are more like Canadian "treaties" than American "treaties" are. New Zealanders normally think of the Treaty of Waitangi as *the* treaty. Presumably, the Kemp Deed and other deeds in New Zealand would be deemed "treaties" by Canadian standards, while the Vancouver Island treaties might be regarded as "deeds" by New Zealanders. However, there is growing realization in

New Zealand that agreements commonly called "deeds" in New Zealand are analogous to treaties in Canada. For example, the Waitangi Tribunal expressed a clear opinion about the early deeds, particularly the pre-1865 deeds in New Zealand. It argued that "the circumstances surrounding the early New Zealand land conveyances are sufficiently the same as those for the treaties with North American Indians for the principles of treaty interpretation developed in North America to be applied to them." Waitangi Tribunal, *Muriwhenua*, 387–8. Also see O'Malley, "Treaty," 137–54; Boast, "Treaties," 653–70; and Belich, *Making*, 202.

## 1. The Hudson's Bay Company and Vancouver Island Land Policy to 1849

1 William Fraser Tolmie Diary, 5 August 1835, William Fraser Tolmie Records, BCA MS-0557, Vol. 3, fo. 275. The HBC had hired Tolmie, an especially intelligent and curious surgeon-naturalist, in 1832. See W. Kaye Lamb, "William Fraser Tolmie," *DCB*.
2 "Memo re Coal on Vancouver Island," BCA MS-0557, Vol. 1, f. 15. Tolmie mentioned the arrival of two parties of "Quaghcuills" all summer. Given that Tolmie had a sample of coal in hand before the end of summer, the first party must have informed him of the coal, and the second delivered the sample.
3 Dunn, *History*, 240–1.
4 Roberts, *Geology*, 2.
5 Tolmie noted the arrival at Fort McLoughlin of "a large band of Quaghcuils" on 14 August. The fact that he did not mention the coal in his diary suggests that he did not yet consider it significant. William Fraser Tolmie Diary, 1830–1842, BCA MS-0557, Vol. 3, fo. 275.
6 "Memo re Coal on Vancouver Island," BCA MS-0557, Vol. 1, fo. 15.
7 Gerald Friesen, "Duncan Finlayson," *DCB*.
8 Dunn, *History*, 240–1. For Finlayson's report, see Duncan Finlayson, Fort McLoughlin, to John McLoughlin, Fort Vancouver, 29 September 1836, HBCA B.223/b/12, fos. 24–24d.
9 Duncan Finlayson, Fort McLoughlin, to John McLoughlin, Fort Vancouver, 29 September 1836, HBCA B.223/b/12, fo. 24d. The "very populous village" referred to in this letter is a reference to the Kweeha and Kwakiutl villages at the mouth of the Cluxewe [Klickseewy] River. See Galois, *Kwakwaka'wakw*, 201, 211.
10 John McLoughlin to George Simpson, 20 March 1837, HBCA B.223/b/15, fo. 147.
11 William R. Sampson, "John Work," *DCB*.
12 John Work to James Douglas, 20 October 1838, HBCA B.223/c/1, fos. 126–126d. HBCA B.201/a/4, 2 May & 1 August 1838.

13 See Galois, *Kwakwaka'wakw*, 201, 211.
14 Kendrick, *Voyage*, 185; Jane, trans., *Spanish*, 83.
15 See Vancouver, *Voyage*, 2: 268–73. Also see Galois, *Kwakwaka'wakw*, 317–18
16 James Douglas, Fort Vancouver, to Governor and Committee, 14 October 1839, Rich, *Letters, 1839–44*, 215.
17 James Douglas, Fort Vancouver, to Governor and Committee, 14 October 1839, Rich, *Letters, 1839–44*, 228.
18 HBC traders at Fort Vancouver appear to have been aware of coal along the Cowlitz River by 1833. See Roberts, *Geology*, 2.
19 Governor and Committee to John McLoughlin, 31 December 1839, HBCA A.6/25, fo. 55d.
20 Governor and Committee to John McLoughlin, 31 December 1839, HBCA A.6/25, fo. 55d.
21 John McLoughlin, Fort Vancouver, to Governor and Committee, London, 20 November 1840, HBCA B.223/b/28, fos. 58–65. This letter is published in Rich, *Letters, 1839–44*, 22–3.
22 George Simpson, Honolulu, Woahoo, to the Governor and Committee, 1 March 1842, para. 7, HBCA D.4/11, fos. 42–67d. This letter is published in Williams, *London*, 109.
23 George Simpson, Honolulu, Woahoo, to the Governor and Committee, 1 March 1842, para. 53, HBCA D.4/11, fos. 42–67d. This letter is published in Williams, *London*, 132–3. George Simpson had just visited the Russian American Company post at Sitka (Novo-Arkhangelsk) as part of his round-the-world trip of 1841–2.
24 John McLoughlin to Governor and Committee, 31 October 1842, Rich, *Letters, 1839–44*, 94–5.
25 Governor and Committee to John McLoughlin, 21 December 1842, in Rich, *Letters, 1839–44*, 302.
26 Gough, *Royal*.
27 Raeside, "Journals," 88.
28 John McLoughlin, Fort Vancouver, to Robert C. Wyllie, 6 January 1845, in Rich, *Letters, 1844–46*, 258.
29 Longstaff and Lamb, "Royal," 115; HBCA B.226/a/1, 26 June 1846.
30 HBCA B.226/a/1, 9 March 1850 (fo. 169d); Longstaff and Lamb, "Royal," 126.
31 Seymour to Duntze, 14 January 1846, as quoted in Longstaff and Lamb, "Royal," 114.
32 Peter Keen [sic] Ogden and James Douglas to J.A. Duntze, 7 September 1846, *BPP* 1849 (103), 5–6.
33 Ogden and Douglas to Duntze, 7 September 1846, *BPP* 1849 (103), 6.
34 Ogden and Douglas to Duntze, 7 September 1846, *BPP* 1849 (103), 6.

35 Longstaff and Lamb, "Royal," 115.
36 James Douglas and John Work, Victoria, to Governor and Committee, 7 December 1846, HBCA A.11/72, fo. 15. A typescript of the logs of the *Cormorant*, can be found at BCA O/A/C811, "The Doings of H.M.S. Cormorant," 24 September–1 October 1846.
37 G.T. Gordon to John A. Duntze, 7 October 1846, *BPP* 1849 (103), 4–5.
38 James Douglas and John Work, Victoria, to Governor and Committee, 7 December 1846, HBCA A.11/72, fos. 15d–16.
39 "The Doings of H.M.S. Cormorant," BCA O/A/C811, 3 December 1847; "Coal at Vancouver's Island," *Hampshire Telegraph*, 29 January 1848, p. 5, col. 2.
40 "The Discovery of Coal at Vancouver's Island," *Times* (London), Saturday, 29 January 1848, p. 6, col. 2. The *Times* (London) issue of Thursday, 27 January 1848 appears to be missing, but the article cited appears to have been republished in many other newspapers including "Coal at Vancouver's Island," *Hampshire Telegraph*, 29 January 1848, p. 5, col. 2.
41 S. Cunard, London to H.G. Ward, Secretary, the Admiralty, 3 January 1848, HBCA B.223/b/37, fo. 32. A version of this letter was published in *BPP* 1849 (103), 11. Cunard had close connections with people in the Admiralty. See Phillis R. Blakeley, "Samuel Cunard," *DCB*.
42 James Edward Fitzgerald to Herman Merivale, 21 February 1848, with enclosed "A Proposal to Form a Company for the Purpose of Working the Coal, and Establishing a Colony in Vancouver's Island." CO 305/1, no. 386,517. For context, see Gough, "Crown," esp. 39–43; and Mouat, "Situating," esp. 19–21.
43 J.L. Folsom, San Francisco, to James Douglas, 22 December 1847, HBCA B.223/b/37, 29–29d. In early 1849, the US Navy's USS *Edith*, a screw-propeller steamer, arrived at San Francisco. It was grounded and lost along the California coast before the end of the year.
44 James Douglas to J.L. Folsom, San Francisco, 9 March 1848, HBCA B.223/b/37, fo. 29d.
45 James Douglas to J.L. Folsom, San Francisco, 9 March 1848, HBCA B.223/b/37, fo. 30.
46 Peter Skeen Ogden and James Douglas to George Simpson, 16 March 1848, HBCA B.223/b/38, fo. 45.
47 Kemble, "Coal," 123.
48 See Wm. H. Aspinwall, New York, to Sir George Simpson, 10 March 1848, HBCA D.5/21, fos. 409–10; George Simpson to William H. Aspinwall, 17 March 1848, and George Simpson to the Governor and Committee, 17 March 1848, HBCA D.4/69, pp. 504–10.
49 George Simpson to Board of Management, 6 May 1848, HBCA D.4/69, pp. 621–2.

50 George Simpson, Norway House, to Chief Factors P.S. Ogden, J. Douglas, & J. Work, Board of Management, Fort Vancouver, 24 June 1848, HBCA D.4/69, p. 772. In November 1850, Archibald Barclay wrote to Douglas regarding reports of coal found on the mainland: "there has appeared in the Newspapers an account of the visit of the Massachusets [sic] to Vancouver Island, which gives a florid description of the coal districts there – namely at Beaver Harbour and Quatsenah. It is also stated that there is coal on the mainland obliquely opposite to Beaver Harbour. Should this be true I am to instruct you to take such steps as you may consider necessary for taking possession of the coalfield lest it should be pre-occupied by other parties – the exclusive licence not extending beyond the trade with the natives." Archibald Barclay, London to James Douglas, Victoria, 1 November 1850, HBCA A.6/28, fo. 174d. Clearly the HBC considered establishing a right to that coal, even though it was outside the established colony of Vancouver Island.

51 G.W.C. Courtenay to Finlayson, 25 July 1848, HBCA B.223/b/37, 32d.

52 G.W.C. Courtenay to Finlayson, 29 July 1848, HBCA B.223/b/37, 33d.

53 G.W.C. Courtenay to Finlayson, 30 July 1848, HBCA B.223/b/37, 31d. James Douglas was not at Fort Victoria, but Finlayson indicated in the Fort Victoria post journal entry of 30 July 1848 that Courtenay had handed him a copy of Cunard's letter on that day. See HBCA B.226/a/1, 30 July 1848, and Longstaff and Lamb, "Royal," 122.

54 G.W.C. Courtenay to Finlayson, 17 August 1848, HBCA B.223/b/37, fo. 37-37d. The Fort Victoria Post Journal indicates that the letter was received on that day; HBCA B.226/a/1, 17 August 1848.

55 G.W.C. Courtenay to Finlayson, 17 August 1848, HBCA B.223/b/37, fo. 38. Finlayson wrote in the Fort Victoria post journals of the same date that "Captain Courtenay brought a printed notice on shore, shewing his having taken possession of the coal district on this Island for the British Crown which he is to leave here for the Company to erect as early as possible in order to keep away all foreign intruders." HBCA B.226/a/1, 17 August 1848.

56 James Douglas and John Work, to Governor and Committee, 5 December 1848, HBCA A.11/72, fo. 42d.

57 Kemble, "Coal," 123-4. Also see Kemble, "Genesis," 251; James Douglas to Archibald Barclay, 23 November 1848, HBCA A.11/72, fos. 31-32. Simpson had been under the impression that the coal would be sold for 50 shillings per ton.

58 George Simpson to the Board of Management, Fort Vancouver, 13 October 1848, HBCA D.4/70, fos. 61-62. Also see Kemble, "Coal," 126-7.

59 Archibald Barclay, Secretary HBC, London to Peter Skene Ogden and James Douglas, Fort Victoria, 1 December 1848, HBCA A.6/27, fo. 176.

## 2. The Hudson's Bay Company and Indigenous Title, 1668-1849

1 Miller, *Compact*, 11–14; Ray, Miller, and Tough, *Bounty*, 5, 24; Brown, "Rupert's," 32; Storey, *Settler*, 13.
2 Tennant, *Aboriginal*, 20.
3 Onesiphorus Albin, Secretary, HBC, to King Charles II, ca. 20 January 1682, HBCA A.6/1, 26d. Also see Rich and Johnson, *Copy-book*, 70; and Rich, *History*, 1: 62–3; Moriarty, "Zachariah Gillam," *DCB* 1: 337; Brown, "Rupert's," 31–2. Hayes asserted that Gillam had "made a league of Friendship" – a typical French rite of possession at the time – before mentioning the purchase, a practice that the French did not recognize. See Seed, *Ceremonies*, 63–8.
4 Gillam's instructions for this voyage are published in Nute, "Radisson," 419–23. The facts that no treaty documents exist and that the earliest record of the purchase dates from thirteen years after it was purportedly completed cast doubt on whether Gillam actually completed the purchase. But, for present purposes, the *claim* that a purchase was made is important. No Indigenous community or government today places any weight on this purported transaction.
5 Rich, *Minutes, 1671–1674*, 226.
6 It may seem odd therefore, that the origins of land-transfer treaties in the British world are not well known. Perhaps because the United States repudiated British Indian policy when the thirteen colonies declared independence, American historians have shown little interest in the history of colonial treaties. Canadian historians tend to ignore that same history because those treaties were concluded outside the boundaries of present-day Canada. Nevertheless, the history of the dealings of the British Crown with Indigenous peoples throughout the British world can only be understood appropriately in the context of the history of land-transfer treaties along the eastern seaboard before 1763.
7 Mark Meuwese has aptly argued that historians have underestimated the historical significance of the New Netherlands, probably because it was only a small, short-lived colony. Meuwese, *Brothers*, 8. In fact, the historical context strongly suggests that the English colonists would not have adopted land-purchase treaties if the Dutch had not set the precedent. Oddly, Patricia Seed did not consider the importance of Dutch (or English) land-purchase agreements in her *Ceremonies of Possession*.
8 See Seed, *Ceremonies*, although the evidence presented here suggests that Seed's arguments require elaboration.
9 Brown, *Genesis*, 1:52–3. The charter can also be found in the Yale Law School's Avalon Project website: http://avalon.law.yale.edu/17th_century/va01.asp.

10 Brown, *Genesis*, 1:53. http://avalon.law.yale.edu/17th_century/va01.asp.
11 Jennings, *Invasion*, 230.
12 *The Royal Charter for Incorporating the Hudson's Bay Company*, 9.
13 Brown, "Rupert's Land," 27–8.
14 Scholars have argued that the Dutch were more likely than other Europeans to contemplate that "sovereignty" might be divided and shared by Europeans and Indigenous people. The Dutch republic was a confederation in which the provinces and cities had significant autonomy while the powers of the States General were circumscribed. Merwick, *Shame*, 70–6; Meuwese, *Brothers*, 11.
15 Brodhead, *Address*, 24.
16 The WIC was preceded by the New Netherlands Company, whose charter expired in 1618. The New Netherlands, of course, was only a small part of the WIC's operations. Meuwese, *Brothers*, 231.
17 "A Charter given by the High and Mighty Lords, the States General, to the West India Company, dated the 3d of June, 1621." O'Callaghan, *History*, 399–407.
18 Meuwese, *Brothers*, 230–1, 235.
19 Brodhead, *History*, 164. Brodhead, *Address*, 26. Brodhead implied that the idea for the purchase originated in New Netherlands, but a century and a half later, Mark Meuwese understood that the initiative came from the Amsterdam directors, not from Minuit.
20 Meuwese, *Brothers*, 235.
21 For examinations of Dutch treaties see Merwick, *Shame*; Bassi, "Dutch-Indian"; and van Ittersum, "Empire," 153–77. The WIC also attempted to bolster its claims by bringing permanent settlers to the New Netherlands, which until 1624 had consisted of only a few seasonally occupied trading posts. Meuwese, *Brothers*, 230–1.
22 Bassi, "Dutch-Indian," 108–10. Bassi argued that the Indigenous people did understand that the agreements represented land transfers, and that the WIC considered it crucial that the Indigenous people understand that the treaties were land-transfer agreements. At least some of the Indigenous people, however, sold land again if the Dutch did not settle the land shortly after treaties were signed. Bassi, "Dutch-Indian," 23, 108–16.
23 Glover, *Paper*, 164.
24 Young, *Chronicles*, 159. Also quoted in Salisbury, *Manitou*, 180–1.
25 Young, *Chronicles*, 176.
26 Salisbury, *Manitou*, 195.
27 Brodhead *History*, 213–14. For recent scholarly literature on the *Eendracht* affair, see Merwick, *Shame*, 76–85, and Glover, *Paper*, 158–68.
28 Brodhead, *History*, 216.

29 Brodhead, *History*, 216.
30 Brodhead, *History*, 232.
31 Brodhead, *History*, 234.
32 Brodhead, *History*, 240. Van Twiller was director of the colony from 1632 to 1638.
33 The Dutch, instrumental in creating the "Black Legend" of Spanish conquest, often compared themselves favourably to the Spanish. See Meuwese, *Brothers*, 12; Glover, *Paper*, 166.
34 Salisbury, *Manitou*, 195–6, Glover, *Paper*, 194. Glover's study includes treaties of amity and alliance that predated this land-transfer treaty.
35 Salisbury, *Manitou*, 199–200.
36 Salisbury, *Manitou*, 200.
37 Salisbury, *Manitou*, 198. Banner, *How*, 10–84; Glover, *Paper*, 168–215.
38 Winthrop, quoted in Salisbury, *Manitou*, 176–7.
39 It may be appropriate for scholars employing a juridical approach to explore the legal roots of Indigenous title as far back as the time of the Roman Empire, looking to Latin legal principles such as *terra nullius* and *res nullius*. These are not considered in this contextual history because I have encountered no evidence that the historical actors between the 1620s and the 1850s were influenced by legal principles antedating the 1620s.
40 Glover, *Paper*, 187–215. Daniel Richter has argued convincingly that William Penn's decision to purchase lands from Indians in the 1680s, and to appeal to precedent set by the Dutch in purchasing lands from Indians, served to bolster Penn's claims over those of Lord Baltimore. See Richter, *Trade*, 135–54. Penn's approach to land purchases was important because it asserted the land rights of Indigenous people while simultaneously asserting the King's right to grant land to his subjects. Richter, "To," 47. For more histories of Indian policies and treaties in this period see the following articles in Washburn, *History of Indian-White Relations*: Wilbur R. Jacobs, "British Indian Policies to 1783," (5–12), Francis Jennings, "Dutch and Swedish Policies," (13–19), and Dorothy V. Jones, "British Colonial Indian Treaties," (185–94).
41 Williams, *American*; Green, "Claims to Territory in Colonial America," in Green and Dickason, *Law*, 1–140; Seed, *American*, 12–44.
42 Glover, *Paper*, 168–79, esp. 178.
43 Thorpe, *Federal*, 6:3210. Still, the inclusion of the statement must have been intended to place some weight upon the practice.
44 Rich, *History*, 1: 62–3.
45 HBCA A.6/1, fos. 107, 111d; and Rich and Johnson, *Copy-book*, 277, 287. For a discussion of French rites of possession, see Seed, *Ceremonies*, 41–8.
46 Edward H. Borins argued that Couture never reached James Bay. See Borins, "Compagnie," 9.

47 Brown, "Rupert's," 33; Borins, "Compagnie," 12–13; Rich and Johnson, *Copy-book*, 288, 350.
48 Rich, *History*, 1: 120.
49 Rich, *History*, 1:128; Borins, "Compagnie," 19–33.
50 "Extrait d'une Leter de Mr. De Labarre," HBCA A.6/1, fo. 26; Rich and Johnson, *Copy-book*, 68–9; Rich, *History*, 1: 128–9.
51 Onesiphorus Albin, Secretary, HBC, to King Charles II, ca. 20 January 1682, HBCA A.6/1, fos. 26–26d.
52 Onesiphorus Albin, Secretary, HBC, to King Charles II, ca. 20 January 1682, HBCA A.6/1, fo. 26d. Although the letter is signed by Albin, and is undated, marginalia and Minutes of the HBC state that it was written by Hayes, and read and approved at the Governor and Committee's meeting of 20 January 1863. Rich, *Minutes, 1682–84*, 67. These rites of possession were typical of English ceremonies of possession at this time. See Seed, *Ceremonies*, 16–40.
53 Glover explained that no one at the time considered land purchases alone to be sufficient to establish a right of possession. Glover, *Paper*, 12.
54 Onesiphorus Albin, Secretary, HBC, to King Charles II, ca. 20 January 1682, HBCA A.6/1, fos. 26d–27. The wording of Hayes's letter suggests that Gillam and Bayly were making annual agreements and annual payments.
55 Rich, *Minutes, 1671–1674*, 211.
56 Rich and Johnson, *Copy-book*, 345–6.
57 HBCA A.6/1, fos. 36–36d.
58 Governor and Committee to John Nixon, 22 May 1680, HBCA A.6/1, fos. 5d, 6, 6d.
59 Governor and Committee to John Nixon, 22 May 1680, HBCA A.6/1, fo. 6d.
60 Glover, *Paper*, 5.
61 Governor and Committee to John Bridgar, Governor of Port Nelson, 15 May 1682, HBCA A.6/1, fo. 15. The same instructions were conveyed to John Nixon in a letter written on the same day; HBCA A.6/1, fo. 17d.
62 Rich, *History*, 1: 138.
63 Borins, "Compagnie," 72–3; Rich, *History*, 1: 138, 161.
64 Onesiphorus Albin to Henry Sergeant, 27 April 1683, HBCA A.6/1, fo. 28.
65 Onesiphorus Albin to Henry Sergeant, 27 April 1683, HBCA A.6/1, fo. 28d.
66 Onesiphorus Albin to Henry Sergeant, 27 April 1683, HBCA A.6/1, fo. 28.
67 Onesiphorus Albin to Henry Sergeant, 27 April 1683, HBCA A.6/1, fo. 30d.
68 The *CBH* acquired a charter from the French Crown in May 1685, giving it the authority to defend its interests militarily. Borins, "Compagnie," 92–106.
69 "A True State of the Case," HBCA A.6/1, fo. 100d.

Notes to pages 42–4    321

70 While the French did not even bother with the HBC's assertion Gillam had purchased land from the Cree, they made much of the fact that Henry Hudson had apparently never officially taken possession of the lands he explored: "Henry Hudson might have sailed into the Streights of the Bay on the north of Canada as diverse others have done but it is certain that hee tooke not possession thereof, there being noe act that makes mention of it." HBCA A.6/1, fo. 105d. Notice that the French assertion cleverly avoids mentioning the strait or bay by name.
71 Rich and Johnson, *Copy-book*, 363.
72 Epp, *Three*, 219. I have deviated from Epp's transcription based on my belief that although the runic thorn þ appears similar to a "y," it was pronounced and should be transcribed as "th."
73 Moses Norton, instructions to Samuel Hearne, 6 November 1769, HBCA A.11/14, fo. 131.
74 Hearne, *Journey*, 163–4. It is uncertain that Hearne actually went through this ritual. Hearne's original journals no longer exist, and the two known surviving manuscript versions of his journal (one dated as late as 1791) make no reference to any rite of possession. MacLaren, "Notes," 25. The circumstances surrounding the publication of those journals leave open many possibilities for how the passage was inserted into the published version. Hearne revised the manuscript for publication, so it is possible that he added it. But Hearne died in 1792, well before the journals were published, so it is also possible that John Douglas, the editor, added it. Given that journals could be published only with the cooperation of the HBC, it is possible that officials at the HBC influenced the decision to add the passage. In any case, the fact that the published journals of 1795 include the passage left out in older copies of the journal suggests that people in the late eighteenth century continued to believe that such rites of possession added weight to the rights gained by "discovery" not accompanied by acts of possession.
75 Dease and Simpson, "Account of the Recent Arctic Discoveries," 221.
76 Thomas Simpson, Fort Confidence to Hargrave, 17 January 1838, Library and Archives Canada (hereafter LAC) M19, A21 Hargrave Papers.
77 Dease and Simpson, "Account of Arctic Discovery," 330.
78 Rae, *Narrative*, 118.
79 Rae, *Narrative*, 156.
80 HBCA B.226/a/1, fo. 57, 3 August 1847. The 4 August entry reveals that while at Belle Vue, Finlayson also left a keg of salt with the Songhees at their fishing station. Clearly, he intended to perform this rite of possession with Songhees witnesses present. Also see Finlayson, *Biography*, 17.
81 For the Selkirk Treaty, see HBCA E.8/1, and LAC RG10, Vol. 1846, box IT257. The reverse side of the copy of the Selkirk Treaty housed at the

HBCA has the following memorandum: "I the Right Hon.[ble] Dunbar James Earl of Selkirk do hereby Admit and Acknowledge and Declare that whatever right title a state or interest I derive or am now entitled to either under the within written Indenture or otherwise in the lands and Hereditaments within mentioned or so much thereof as lie not within the Territories of the United States of North America is hereby conveyed and Transferred by me unto the Governor and Company of Adventurers of England trading into Hudsons Bay and their Successors for ever. In Witness whereof I have hereunto set my hand this fourth day of May one thousand eight hundred and thirty six." Dunbar Douglas, the 6th Earl of Selkirk, was the son of Thomas Douglas, the 5th Earl of Selkirk. The memorandum suggests that both men contemplated that the agreement gave them a title that they could convey to others. Documents accompanying the copy at the LAC indicated that that copy was conveyed to the Canadian government from the HBC (by Donald A. Smith) in April 1875.

82 Friesen, *Canadian*, 72.
83 Morris, *Treaties*, 300. Historians have long argued that Selkirk's very notion of establishing a colony at Red River "was intended to vindicate the Hudson's Bay Company's Charter." Martin, "Introduction," in Rich, *Journal*, xxii; Martin, *Lord*, 47–9.
84 Oliver, *Canadian North-West*, 173.
85 And in 1817, Samuel Gale, Selkirk's lawyer, published *Notices on the Claims of the Hudson's Bay Company and the Conduct of its Adversaries*, which argued that the HBC owned the land granted to it in the HBC Charter. Gale's discussion of the Royal Proclamation of 1763 (48–53) shows that Gale was aware of the proclamation but knew that it excluded Rupert's Land from the territory reserved for the Indians.
86 HBCA B.235/a/3, 18 October 1814 (fo. 12d). Readers seeking more details about the private war can turn to Binnema and Ens, *Edmonton: 1806–1821*, 51–65; and Friesen, *Canadian*, 66–84.
87 In collaboration with Roy C. Dalton, "William Bacheler Coltman," in *DCB*.
88 Selkirk to Coltman, 17 July 1817, Selkirk Papers, LAC MG19, E 1, 3807. Samuel Gale, Selkirk's lawyer, probably had a role in developing the notion of concluding a treaty. Gale published in 1817 his assertion that "the Indians have shewn every disposition to favour and encourage the settlers." Gale, *Notices*, 64. For Gale's defence of colonization, see 62–5.
89 Selkirk to Coltman, 17 July 1817, LAC MG19, E 1, 3809–3810. Context for this battle for legitimacy can be found in Bradford and Connors, "Making," 188–193; and Hughes, "Within," 519–40, esp. 527.
90 Selkirk to Coltman, 17 July 1817, LAC MG19, E 1, 3810.
91 Selkirk to Coltman, 17 July 1817, LAC MG19, E 1, 3811.

92 Coltman to Selkirk, 17 July 1817, LAC MG19, E 1, 3812.
93 Coltman to Selkirk, 17 July 1817, LAC MG19, E 1, 3813.
94 Peguis ("William Prince") to the Aborigines Protection Society, approx. 1857, quoted in *BPP* (1857)(224.260): 445.
95 Coltman to Selkirk, 17 July 1817, LAC MG19, E 1, 3813.
96 Selkirk to Coltman, 17 July 1817, LAC MG19, E 1, 3807.
97 The treaty text is given in Morris, *Treaties*, 299.
98 This practice dates to treaties of the mid-1600s. Glover, *Paper*, 198–9, 214. This practice was also often used on land-purchase treaties with the Ojibwa of Upper Canada before and after 1817.
99 HBCA B.22/a/20, 18 July 1817.
100 Coltman to Sherbrooke, 20 May 1818, "Papers Relative to the Red River Settlement," *BPP* 548 (1819), 244. The evidence presented here undermines Adam Gaudry's interesting argument that Selkirk was guided by a combination of Métis hostility evinced by the Battle of Seven Oaks, and by principles of Indigenous title. See Gaudry, "Fantasies," 52–6.
101 Morris, *Treaties*, 300.
102 Boxberger, "Comparison," 36.

## 3. The History of the Northwest Coast to 1774

1 James Douglas to Archibald Barclay, 18 March 1852, HBCA A.11/73, fo. 401.
2 Mayne, *Four*, 165.
3 Rogers, "Glacial," 130–7; Rogers, "Wisconsin," 105–13; Gruhn, "Linguistic," 77–100.
4 Beck, "Grammatical," 147–213.
5 This conclusion is reached by "upstreaming" backwards in time from the period for which we have documentary evidence and using oral traditions. See Inglis and Haggarty, *Pacific*; McMillan and St. Claire, *Huu7ii*, 11–25.
6 Kinkade, "Prehistory of Salishan Languages," https://lingpapers.sites.olt.ubc.ca/icsnl-volumes/.
7 Thompson and Kinkade, "Languages," in Suttles, *Northwest Coast*, 45; Kinkade, "Prehistory."
8 McMillan, "Reviewing," 248–9.
9 Fortescue, "Drift," 295–324. The growing evidence of glacial refugia around northern Vancouver Island makes it possible that that region (including areas that may now be submerged) was the proto-Wakashan homeland. Hebda, et al., "Late."
10 Fortescue, "Drift," 295–6; McMillan, "Reviewing," 256; Donald and Mitchell, "Nature," 105.

11 Ames, "Northwest Coast," in *Evolutionary Anthropology*, 26–8. For book-length surveys of the history of the Northwest Coast before 1778, see Matson and Coupland, *Prehistory*; Ames and Maschner, *Peoples*; and Moss, *Northwest Coast*. For a discussion of some of the earliest evidence of humans on the Northwest Coast, see McLaren, et al., "Terminal."
12 Fladmark, *British Columbia*, 53; Fladmark, Ames, and Sutherland, "Prehistory," in Suttles, *Northwest Coast*, 229–39.
13 Matson, "Intensification," 125–48; Matson, "Evolution," 367–428.
14 Donald, *Aboriginal*, 134.
15 Matson and Coupland, *Prehistory*, 145; Carlson, "Trade,", 345–7. Also see Matson, "Evolution," 367–428; Sneed, "Of," 229–42.
16 Erlandson, "Archaeology," 296–7; Wadewitz, *Nature*, 16–17.
17 Matson and Coupland, *Prehistory*, 6, 25.
18 Among the Salish these villagers were not slaves (skʷaýəθ) but "low people" (st'éxəm). Jenness, *Faith*, 86; Carlson, "Toward," 159–61.
19 Archaeological evidence appears to confirm that social stratification was a fact of life on the Northwest Coast for at least 3,000 years. Grier, "Temporality," 97–119; Ames, "Slaves," 2.
20 Ames and Maschner, *Peoples*, 177.
21 Matson and Coupland, *Prehistory*, 6; Ames and Maschner, *Peoples*, 177.
22 Matson and Coupland, *Prehistory*, 29.
23 Donald and Mitchell, "Nature," 114, 116–17.
24 Donald, *Aboriginal*, esp. 134–7; Ames, "Chiefly," 155–87; Donald, "Was," 108–19; Todd-Bresnick, "Prevalence," 81–93; Ames, "Slaves," 1–17.
25 Matson and Coupland, *Prehistory*, 27; Ames and Maschner, *Peoples*, 180.
26 Ames, "Chiefly," 172.
27 Kane, *Wanderings*, 214–15. Also see an account of the ritual killing of slaves at 216. For a detailed discussion see MacLaren, *Paul*, 3: 56–7.
28 George Simpson noted the fact in 1840. See Simpson, *Narrative*, 1: 183. Also see Barnett, "Coast," 122; Richling, *W̱SÁNEĆ*, 7, 8; and Duff, "Fort," 5.
29 James Douglas, Observations recorded after entry for 14 May 1840 (but the trade took place on 9 May), "James Douglas Diary from 22 April–2 October 1840," BCA A/B/40/D75.2, p. 14, This diary is published in Leader, "Douglas Expeditions, 1840–41"; and in Gibson, *Opposition*, 219–53.
30 Williams, *Clam Gardens*, 60–1; Lepofsky, et al., "Ancient," 236–59; Deur, Dick, Recalma-Clutesi, and, Turner, "Kwakwaka'wakw," 201–12; Grier, Angelbeck, and McLay, "Terraforming," 118–20; Moss, *Northwest Coast*, 43; Groesbeck, "Ancient."
31 For an introduction to the literature, see Turner, Deur, and Lepofsky, "Plant," 107–33; and Deur and Turner, *Keeping*.

32 HBCA B.226/b/8, fo. 10.
33 Grant, "Description," 301.
34 Grant, "Description," 301.
35 Sproat, *Scenes*, 38.
36 Sproat, *Scenes*, 38, 50.
37 Meares, *Voyages*, 125–6. In the 1860s, Richard Mayne wrote that "this habit among the Indians of changing their places of residence, not at any particularly season, but as the fish and game shift their quarters, appears to have misled Vancouver, who, in passing, concluded all villages which he found uninhabited to have been deserted altogether by their people." Mayne, *Four*, 208. While Vancouver may have been mistaken on occasion, the context of his journals suggests that many of the villages that he observed had been abandoned after a devastating smallpox epidemic. Also see Banner, *Possessing*, 202. Barnett described "permanent villages and temporary summer encampments," in Barnett, "Coast," 119.
38 Dunn, *History*, 251–2; Sproat, *Scenes*, 39. For a scholarly discussion, see Drucker, *Indians*, 7.
39 James Douglas to Henry Labouchere, 20 October 1856, NA CO 305/7, fos. 103d–104.
40 Cook, *Voyage*, 2: 281.
41 Sproat, *Scenes*, 37–8, 40.
42 Northwest Coast communities sought red meat to avoid hypervitaminosis D, a potentially fatal condition that can accompany long-term dependence on salmon. Chisholm, Nelson, and Schwarez, "Marine," 396–8; Lazenby and McCormack, "Salmon," 379–84; Folan, "On the Diet," 123–4.
43 The concept of prey switching can explain how and why populations of terrestrial mammals were suppressed. See Bergerud, "Prey," 130–6, 140–1. By the time of the treaties in the 1850, the pressure on land mammal populations may have been reduced by depopulation caused by disease, the fact that Indigenous people were able to acquire blankets acquired by trade, and by the cultivation of potatoes. This phenomenon is discussed in more detail in Ted Binnema, "When Salmon Ate Moose: Exploring the Reasons for the Absence of Moose (and Bison) in North-Western North America, 1793–1900." Second World Congress of Environmental History, Guimarães, Portugal, 11 July 2014.
44 Bears were considerably more common in the Alexander Archipelago between 15,000 and 9,000 years ago than afterward, probably because of competition with the growing human population. Lesnek, et al., "Deglaciation," p. 4 of 8; Heaton and Grady, "Late," 39. Also see Grayson, "Archaeological," 1–68; McLaren, "Bear Hunting," 3–29.
45 HBCA B.226/b/8, fo. 9

46 Mackenzie, *Voyages*, 2: 297 (15 July 1793); Richling, *The W̱SÁNEĆ and Their Neighbours*, 37.
47 MacLaren, *Paul*, 3: 38–51; Kane, *Wanderings*, 210; Simpson, *Narrative*, 1: 198; and Barnett, "Coast," 123.
48 Melville Jacobs argued that linguistic evidence suggests that there were long-standing trading relationships between the coast and interior in Oregon and Washington. Jacobs, "Historic," 55–74.
49 Donald, *Aboriginal*, 17.
50 Ruyle, "Slavery," 605, 610.
51 Suttles, "Variations," 522–37; Suttles, "Coping," 56–68; Donald and Mitchell, "Nature," 95–117; Matson, "Introduction: The Northwest Coast in Perspective," in Matson, Coupland, and Mackie, *Emerging*, 1–11.
52 See Orchard and Szpak, "Zooarchaeological," 87–127; Orchard, "Otters."
53 Grier, "Affluence," 132; Szpak, et al., "Historical," 1–19; Hay and McCarter, *Status*, 57.
54 Donald and Mitchell, "Nature," 105; Ames, "Northwest Coast," in *Evolutionary Anthropology*, 20; Finney, "Impacts," 795–802; Beamish and Bouillon, "Pacific," 1002–16.
55 Clark, *Rewriting*, 7.
56 Ricker, "Cycle Dominance," 6–26; Ward and Larkin, *Cyclic*, 4–10; Levy and Wood, "Review," 241–61; Cass and Wood, "Evaluation," 1839–54; Ricker, "Cycles of Abundance," 950–68; Killick and Clemens, *Age*, 3–5. Noteworthy dominant years included 1793 (the year of Alexander Mackenzie's trip to the Pacific), 1829, 1833, 1837, 1841, 1845, and 1849.
57 James Douglas to James Hargrave, 5 February 1843, in Glazbrook, *Hargrave*, 420.
58 Richling, *W̱SÁNEĆ*, 18.
59 Wadewitz, *Nature*, 18; Matson and Coupland, *Prehistory*, 8, 34; Kew, "Salmon," 198; Hewes, "Aboriginal," 140. For an extended description of reef nets, see Suttles, "Economic,"155–61.
60 Richling, *W̱SÁNEĆ*, 7, 9. In 1875, the botanist John Macoun found that camas "covered at times many square rods of meadow land" in the Victoria region. Macoun, "Report," 112.
61 Trade in camas is mentioned in Sproat, *Scenes*, 55.
62 Wagner, *Spanish*, 151.
63 Angelbeck, "They," 261.
64 Suttles, *Coast*, 198; Carlson, "Toward," 138–81; Carlson, "From," 79–112.
65 Angelbeck and Cameron, "Faustian," 98; Angelbeck, "They," 289–96.
66 Yesner, "Maritime," 731–2.
67 Grier, "Affluence," 127.
68 Hewes, "Aboriginal," 34.
69 Hill, "Language," 16.

70 Donald, *Aboriginal*, 26; Angelbeck and Cameron, "Faustian," 94; Ames, "Chiefly," 155–87.
71 Angelbeck, "Balance," 52; Angelbeck, "They," passim. Also see Ames, "Northwest Coast," in *Annual Review of Anthropology*, 223. In some contexts, over 30 per cent of male burials exhibited signs of violent trauma, and, after AD 500, more than 27 per cent of burials throughout the Northwest Coast did. See Cybulski, "Conflict," 415–53; Cybulski, "Culture," 75–85; Fladmark, "Introduction," 116; Moss and Erlandson, "Forts," 73–90; Angelbeck, "They," 1; Richling, W̱SÁNEĆ, 34; Lovisek, "Aboriginal," 58–73; Maschner, "Evolution," 269–70. Also see Maschner and Reedy-Maschner, "Raid," 19–51; Ferguson, "Warfare," 134.
72 Ferguson, "Warfare," 134; Angelbeck, "They," 2.
73 Warriors on the Northwest Coast were often buried with their war clubs or other war implements. The documentary evidence of warrior societies, and of a class of "warrior shaman," also hint at the social and cultural significance of war in the more aggressive Northwest Coast societies. Angelbeck, "They," 91, 109–13.
74 Lovisek, "Human," 45–64; Maschner and Reedy-Maschner, "Heads," 34; Cybulski, "Modified," 15–31.
75 Angelbeck, "They," 137; Angelbeck and Cameron, "Faustian," 94. The atlatl (95) had come to dominate over spears in the period between 9000 and 5000 BP; Angelbeck, "They," 159–61; Maschner and Mason, "Bow and Arrow," 137; Maschner. "Evolution," 286; Angelbeck, "Balance," 52.
76 Maschner, "Evolution," 286.
77 Moss and Erlandson, "Forts," 75; Mitchell, "Excavations," 29–46; Maschner, "Evolution," 267; Angelbeck, "They," esp. 108–9, 159, 168–221.
78 Moss and Erlandson, "Forts," 77; Keddie, "Fortified," 7.
79 Wagner, *Spanish*, 131
80 Wagner, *Spanish*, 110, 131, 189–90.
81 Cook, *Voyage*, 2: 302–3.
82 Mitchell, "Changing Patterns," 245–90. An alternate theory, that the ancestors of the Salish-speaking Nuxalk (Bella Coola) moved into the coast from the Interior, also suggests a dynamic history of the region.
83 Moss and Erlandson, "Forts," 74.
84 Ferguson, "Warfare," 133.
85 Ruyle, "Slavery," 614–15. For an example, see Sproat, *Scenes*, 59–60. The influence of a leader was tied not only to that person's wealth, but also his generosity. Ames, "Chiefly," 172.
86 Ferguson, "Warfare," 137–8.
87 Donald, *Aboriginal*, 31–2 (quoted passage), and 5. Also see Carlson, "Trade," 308. Kane, *Wanderings*, 221–2; Richling, W̱SÁNEĆ, 47.
88 Ferguson, "Warfare," 133–47.

89 Galm, "Prehistoric," 275; Donald, *Aboriginal*, 26.
90 Gibson, *Otter*, 8.
91 MacLaren, *Paul*, 3: 209–10; Simpson, *Narrative*, 1: 193. Also see Kane, *Wanderings*, 248–9; Sproat, *Scenes*, 79; and Goddard, *Indians*, 26.

## 4. Indigenous and Exogenous Peoples on Vancouver Island, 1774–1821

1 Some long-standing traditions did end during this period. Simpson indicated that the labret was dying out in the 1840s at Fort McLoughlin (although not farther north), "having been found to be disagreeable to the whites, to whose opinions and feelings the native ladies pay the highest possible respect." Simpson, *Narrative*, 1: 205.
2 Acheson, "Thin Edge," 215–18. Also see John McLoughlin to the Governor and Committee, 18 November 1834, in Rich, *Letters, 1825–38*, 128–9; Anderson, "Notes," 80; Anderson, "Indians," 220; Keddie, "Japanese."
3 For the range of goods offered by traders and the primary importance of blankets and firearms, see Gibson, *Opposition*, 34–7.
4 LaPier, *Invisible*, 25.
5 Richling, W̱SÁNEĆ, 89–106, 111–12; Guilmet, et al., "Legacy," 5.
6 The HBC offered vaccination at posts along the Northwest Coast in 1837. Guilmet et al., "Legacy," 14. Northwest Coast people assumed that any human might have the ability and desire to employ "black magic" to bring death to others, and exogenous traders may have threatened to spread smallpox to Indigenous people, although that would have been a very risky gambit. See Lutz and Carlson, "Smallpox," esp. 92. There is no evidence, however, that exogenous negotiators threatened Indigenous signatories on Vancouver Island with harm if they did not agree to the Vancouver Island treaties.
7 John Work noted this explicitly in HBCA B.201/a/4, 23 January 1839.
8 Fisher, *Contact*, 1–48 (quoted passage on 1). For the older view, see Howay, "Outline," 5–14.
9 Carlson, "Toward," 139.
10 Drucker, *Indians*, 31.
11 Angelbeck, "They," 261; Angelbeck, "Conceptions"; Fisher, *Contact*, 1–23.
12 Marshall, "Dangerous," 160–75; Fisher, *Contact*, 18.
13 Cook, *Voyage*, 2: 274–5.
14 Meares, *Voyages*, 142.
15 Gibson, *Opposition*, 39–40, Begg, *History*, 20.
16 Clayton, *Islands*, 108–9.
17 Gormly, "Early," 7–8, 25; Cook, *Voyage*, 2: 277, 298–9 and 319–20, 399–400. See Vancouver, *Voyage*, 2: 234, 254, 262, 266–7, 284.
18 Miller and Boxberger, "Creating," 272.

19 Suttles, *Coast*, 197.
20 Vancouver, *Voyage*, 2: 91. Guilmet et al., "Legacy," 7, 276-7. Scholars have debated whether the smallpox epidemic of the early 1780s reached the peoples of northern Vancouver Island. See Harris, "Voices," 591-626. For a more speculative argument, see Boyd, "Smallpox," 5-40; Boyd, "Demographic," 135-48; Boyd, *Coming*, 21-39. Also see Harris, "Social Power." The Kwakiutl may have escaped smallpox again in the 1830s. In the early 1840s, George Simpson wrote of the Kwakiutl of the Johnstone Strait region that "they have been exempted from the smallpox, though their brethren, both to the south of the Columbia and in Russian America, have suffered severely from that terrible scourge." Simpson, *Narrative*, 1: 189. The origin of this epidemic can probably never be ascertained definitively, but the evidence that smallpox may have affected groups with relatively little contact with ship-borne traders while sparing those with greater contact opens the possibility that smallpox reached the Northwest Coast from the Interior. Simpson went on to suggest why the HBC did not vaccinate Indigenous people more consistently than they did: "to secure to them a continuance of this happy immunity, we begged permission from the chiefs of the Quakeolths to vaccinate the children of the tribe; but, as they neither did nor could appreciate the unknown blessing, we preferred leaving things as they were, knowing well, from our experience of the native character, that our medicine would get the credit of any epidemic that might follow, or perhaps of any failure of the hunt or the fishery." Simpson, *Narrative*, 1: 189. Still, when smallpox raged on the Olympic Peninsula in 1853, Douglas reported that "the Indians residing within the Colony, have been generally vaccinated." James Douglas to Archibald Barclay, 16 May 1853, BCA A/C/20/Vi2. On this epidemic, see Boyd, *Coming*, 160-71.
21 Carlson, "From," 79-112.
22 Miller, *Problem*, 75-7; Guilmet, et al., "Legacy," 1-32. Evidence of the destabilization of societies is discussed in Angelbeck, "They," 278-80, 283-9.
23 Carlson, "Toward," 157; Carlson, *Power*, especially 140-1.
24 Carlson, "Toward," 140-1; Carlson, *Power*, especially 140-1; Suttles, *Coast*, 197.
25 Carlson, "Toward," 164; Carlson, *Power*, 141. Also see Guilmet, et al., "Legacy," 9-11.
26 Archaeologists have found that the kinds of skeletal trauma found in burial sites, from the Alaskan panhandle to northern Vancouver Island, were relatively more likely to have been caused by offensive than defensive action, while the reverse is true of burials farther south. See Cybulski, "Conflict," 416-18.
27 Angelbeck, "Balance," 52; Angelbeck, "Conceptions," 269-72; Clayton, *Islands*, 145-8.

28 Duff, *Indian*, 1: 59. For the effects of warfare on the west coast of Vancouver Island, see Inglis and Haggarty, *Pacific*, 6, 88, 90–1, 279, 305–20.
29 Angelbeck, "They," 99.
30 Vancouver, *Voyage*, 2: 264.
31 Vancouver, *Voyage*, 2: 272–3.
32 Howay, "Indian Attacks," 287–309; Howay, "Loss," 83–92; Howay, "Attempt"; Howay, "Early," 280–8; Jewitt, *Journal*; Jewitt, *Narrative*. Jewitt explained that the twenty-five crew members were decapitated, and their heads displayed. Jewitt, *Narrative*, 32–3.
33 Howay, "Trading," 5–10. An account was published in "Barbarous Massacre of the Crew of the Ship Atahualpa, by the Indians," *Naval Chronicle for 1806* (London: Joyce Gold, 1806), 382–5.
34 Archer, "Seduction," 127–59.
35 Vancouver, *Voyage*, 2: 235.
36 Angelbeck, "They," 261–75.
37 Angelbeck, "They," 271–2.
38 Vancouver, *Voyage*, 2: 77. Paul Kane described the same custom on the Olympic Peninsula in *Wanderings*, 232.
39 Vancouver, *Voyage*, 2: 69.
40 Beaglehole, *Journals*, vol. 3, part I, ccxxiii.
41 Cook, *Voyage*, 2: 284; For a discussion of this incident, see Clayton, *Islands*, 47–8.
42 Cook, *Voyage*, 2: 331.
43 See Frost, "Nootka," 104–26.
44 Frost, "Nootka," 109–10; McDowell, *José Narváez*, 37.
45 [Evan Nepean] "To the Captain of the Frigate [William Cornwallis] to be dispatched from the East Indies to Owhyhee, March 1790," The National Archives (Kew) (hereafter TNA), Home Office, Admiralty, Supplementary Correspondence HO 28/61, fos. 275–275d.
46 [Evan Nepean] "To the Captain of the Frigate [William Cornwallis] to be dispatched from the East Indies to Owhyhee, March 1790," TNA HO 28/61, fos. 275d–76.
47 John Meares, "Copy of the Memorial Presented to the House of Commons, May 13, 1790:–Containing every Particular Respecting the Capture of the Vessels in Nootka Sound," in Meares, *Voyages*, n.p; Begg, *History*, 29–40; Frost, "Nootka," 117. Meares may not have been the first British man to purchase land on Vancouver Island. That distinction may go to James Strange, who claimed to have bought a house at Yuquot in the summer of 1786 "for about the Value of a Shilling," to take care of sick members of his expedition. He abandoned the house within days. Venkatarama Ayyar, ed., *James Strange's Journal*, 20–1; Gough, *Northwest*, 79.

48 Meares, "Copy of the Memorial," in Meares, *Voyages*, n.p.; Begg, *History*, 34. For a biography, see Robin A. Fisher, "Wikinanish," in *DCB*.
49 Meares, *Voyages*, 110–12. For a biography of Maquinna see Robin A. Fisher, "Muquinna," *DCB*.
50 Meares, *Voyages*, 114. Meares referred to this "treaty" again on page 131. In September 1792, Robert Duffin, first officer on the *Felice* signed a sworn statement that Meares had purchased an island in Friendly Cove "for eight or ten sheets of copper and several other trifling articles. The natives were fully satisfied with their agreement." Begg, *History*, 56.
51 Meares, *Voyages*, 216–17.
52 Meares, *Voyages*, 146. Also see 149.
53 Meares, *Voyages*, 173.
54 Frost, "Nootka," 117.
55 Frost, "Nootka," 117.
56 See Wellcome Library WMS Amer. 42. Relación de los Méritos y Servicios de D. Martín de Sessé, Director de la Expedición Botánica de Nueva España. Aranjuez, 1804. I am indebted to Jacqueline Holler for calling my attention to this document. Meares's claims are discussed in Manning, *Nootka*, 290–2; Pethick, *Nootka*, 18–23; Barry M. Gough, "John Meares," *DCB*; and King, "George Vancouver," 6–34.
57 United States, Congress, Senate Document, 32d Congress, 1st Session, *Reports of Committees*, Vol. 2, Report of Committee, No. 335 (1852), 16. John Kendrick, the leader of the expedition commanded the *Columbia Rediviva*, while Robert Gray commanded the sloop *Lady Washington*. For more on Kendrick, see Richard A. Pierce, "John Kendrick," *DCB*.
58 NARA USA RG59 (Department of State, 1763–2002), M179 (Miscellaneous Letters of the Department of State, 1789–1906), January–June 1793, fos. 150–8. Quanteno, one of the signatories to the Tarassom treaty was apparently a woman, although the published version of the treaty replaced "her mark" with "his mark." Some deeds obtained by Kendrick were lost. Subsequently, Kendrick's heirs indicated that they believed that in total, the deeds "are believed to be entirely of lands on the island of Quadra or Vancouver, and cover nearly its entire extent." Senate Document, 32d Congress, 1st Session, Report of Committee, No. 335 (1852), 7. These transactions are also discussed in Bancroft, *History*, 1: 253–4; and Begg, *History*, 59.
59 National Archives and Records Administration of the United States (NARA USA) RG59 (Department of State, 1763–2002), M179 (Miscellaneous Letters of the Department of State, 1789–1906), January–June 1793, fos. 155–6. United States, Congress, Senate Document, 32d Congress, 1st Session, *Reports of Committees*, Vol. 2, Report of Committee, No. 335 (1852), 20.

60 United States, Congress, Senate Document, 32d Congress, 1st Session, *Reports of Committees*, Vol. 2, Report of Committee, No. 335 (1852), 20–5.
61 Senate Document, 32d Congress, 1st Session, Report of Committee, No. 335 (1852), 5.
62 Senate Document, 32d Congress, 1st Session, Report of Committee, No. 335 (1852), 5–6. The fact that Kendrick had endeared himself to the Spanish at Nootka Sound influenced the demeanour of the Spanish towards him.
63 John Kendrick, Hong Kong to Thomas Jefferson, 1 March 1793, NARA USA RG59 (Department of State, 1763–2002), M179 (Miscellaneous Letters of the Department of State, 1789–1906), fos. 148–9. The letter is published in United States, Congress, Senate Document, 32d Congress, 1st Session, *Reports of Committees*, Vol. 2, Report of Committee, No. 335 (1852), 19–20. Also see Cook, *Flood*, 323.
64 Simpson, *Narrative*, 1: 242.
65 Kane, *Wanderings*, 247. For a discussion, see MacLaren, *Paul*, 3: 209.
66 British Library Ms. 32641, 2 June 1792 (fos. 136).
67 Fisher, *Contact*, 12; Galois, *Kwakwa̱ka'wakw*, 28; Gibson, *Otter*, 206–7.
68 Gibson, *Otter*, 11,17–18; Fisher, *Contact*, 30–2,46–7.
69 Wagner, *Spanish*, 3.
70 Wagner, *Spanish*, 118; Blumenthal, *Early*, 32.
71 Wagner, *Spanish*, 48; Kendrick, *Voyage*, 100–2.
72 Kendrick, *Voyage*, 155, 169, 190; Wagner, *Spanish*, 113.
73 Carlson, "Toward," 138–81.
74 Whitehead, "Tribes," 128; Angelbeck and McLay, "Battle," 363–4.
75 Angelbeck, "They," 241–3.
76 Angelbeck, "They," 229–41; Angelbeck and McLay, "Battle," esp. 386; Angelbeck, "Conceptions," 269–72; Miller and Boxberger, "Creating," 267–93.
77 For the most recent description of this period as stable see Brazier, "Land," 191.

## 5. Indigenous Peoples of Vancouver Island and the Hudson's Bay Company, 1821–1849

1 For a survey that explores the breadth of the trade in the region see Mackie, *Trading*.
2 See Binnema, *Common*.
3 Gibson, *Opposition*, 29–31.
4 See Gibson, *Opposition*, 1–23.
5 The threat of the Russians was reduced in 1824 and 1825 by agreements between the Russian government and the American and British governments. Gibson, *Opposition*, 4–6.

6 See Fisher, *Contact*, 26; Gibson, *Opposition*, 21, 40–55.
7 For a time, scholars had argued that the Tsilhqot'in (Chilcotin) were an exception to this rule, but Bill Turkel convincingly argued that "far from 'opting out' of the fur trade, the Tsilhqot'in did everything in their power to be part of it." Turkel, *Archive*, 146–62 (quoted passage on 160).
8 Fisher, *Contact*, 12. In 1851, James Douglas reported that "a weak tribe [from Haida Gwaii] oppressed by all their neighbours" arrived at Fort Simpson and "made an offer of their lands to the Company at a price to be agreed upon hereafter and begged hard that people might be sent immediately to form an establishment there." James Douglas, Victoria, to Archibald Barclay, London, 24 February 1851, HBCA A.11/73, fo. 75d, 76.
9 Fisher, *Contact*, passim, but see especially 1, 24.
10 Kobrinsky, "Dynamics," 38, 43.
11 To avoid this, HBC officials would have had to have adopted a policy of refusing to hire any person known to be a slave, but it may not always have been successful. Charles Wilson, who had four years of experience as secretary with the British Boundary Commission between 1858 and 1862, wrote that: "prisoners of war, when not decapitated, become the property of the victor, and are held in a state of bondage. The slaves are harshly treated by their masters, and in time of scarcity fare but badly; their hair is cut short, and their children are not allowed to undergo the process of flattening the head, except when adopted into the tribe, which occasionally takes place. Some of the Indians make a good deal of money by sending their slaves to work for the whites, and appropriating their wages. A Chilukweyuk Indian, whose slave was employed for several months by the Commission, pocketed a large sum in this way; the money was of course paid to the slave, but his master was always near at hand on pay-day to look after the dollars. Slaves are bought and sold amongst the Indians, and not unfrequently form the stake of the gambler; those who are good hunters, or fishermen, are the most highly valued." Wilson, "Report," 290. For insight into the complexity of HBC's attempt to suppress slavery see Merk, *Fur Trade*, 352–6; and Governor and Committee, London, to John McLoughlin, Fort Vancouver, 14 September 1839, HBCA B.201/c/1, fo. 130d.
12 Rich, *History*, 2: 634–5. Also see Gibson, *Opposition*, 27–8.
13 Simpson, *Narrative*, 1: 194.
14 Simpson, *Narrative*, 1: 241. While the quoted words were written for publication and thus may have been embellished to suit the popular audience, they reflect Simpson's sentiments conveyed in private business correspondence. See George Simpson to the Governor and Committee, 15 November 1841, HBCA D.4/110, fos. 16d–17.
15 Simpson, *Narrative*, 1: 236.

16 Chittenden, *American*, 1: 340.
17 HBCA B.185/a/1, 30 March 1850.
18 Fisher, *Contact*, 26, 33; Mackie, *Trading*, 269–70.
19 Binnema, *Common*, 178, 199.
20 HBCA B.201/a/3, 23 May 1837. Also see HBCA B.201/a/4, 25 April 1839.
21 Fisher *Contact*, 42–3; also see 56. And see Cole and Darling, "History," 127.
22 I borrow the concept of "emporialists" from Donna Merwick, who wrote, after explaining that the Dutch East India Company was not interested in acquiring territory or in interfering in Indian politics, that "they were 'emporialists' rather than imperialists." Merwick, *Shame*, 89.
23 Reid, *Patterns*, passim, but esp. 118–49.
24 George Simpson to Governor and Committee, 1 September 1825, HBCA D.4/88, fo.77. Also see George Simpson to John Clarke, 10 July 1825, HBCA D.4/10, fo. 17d; and Minutes of the Northern Council, 2 July 1825, Fleming, *Minutes*, 104. For scholarly literature on this incident, see Krech, "Banditti," 36–31; Krech, "Beaver Indians," 35–45; Burley, Hamilton, and Fladmark, *Prophecy*, 126–36; Binnema and Ens, *Edmonton: 1821–1826*, lvii–lxi.
25 See Rich, *Letters, 1844–46*, 311–12. For a contextual discussion, see Reid, *Patterns*; this incident is discussed on 90–1 and 129–30.
26 Rich, *Letters, 1825–38*, 57.
27 Fleming, *Minutes*, 447; Rich, *Letters, 1825–38*, 57, 63–5; George Simpson, Norway House, to Governor and Committee of the HBC, 30 June 1829, HBCA D.4/96, fos. 7d–8. For a journal of the expedition see Francis Ermatinger, "Journal of Clallum Expedition," BCA A/B/20/V5.
28 John McLoughlin, Fort Vancouver, to Governor and Committee of the HBC, 7 August 1828, in *Letters, 1825–38*, 65.
29 George Simpson, Norway House, to Governor and Committee of the HBC, HBCA D.4/96, 30 June 1929, fo. 8. In relation to this same incident, Simpson had previously told the Governor and Committee that "the rule of retaliation is the only standard of equity which the tribes on this coast are capable of appreciating." Simpson, *Narrative*, 1: 194.
30 J.H. Pelly to Lord Glenelg, 10 February 1837, in "Copies or Extracts of Correspondence Relating to the Charter of the Hudson's Bay Company," in Great Britain, Parliament, *North American Boundary*, 12. It is noteworthy that, in writing of "peace, order, and tranquility," Pelly offered a rare instance in which a representative of the HBC seemed to be implying that the company was acting as a quasi-government.
31 George Simpson to J.H. Pelly, 1 February 1837, in "Copies or Extracts of Correspondence Relating to the Charter of the Hudson's Bay Company," in Great Britain, Parliament, *North American Boundary*, 16–17. Also see *BPP* 1857 (224.260), 42; Rae, "On," 139; and Binnema and Ens, *Edmonton: 1821–1826*, xxxiii–xli.

32 Parker, *Journal*, 173.
33 Cavanagh, "Company," 28.
34 Cavanagh, "Company," 28.
35 Smith, "Hudson's Bay," 75. Also see Bradford and Connors, who argue that the company evolved into "a corporation with a political role and identity similar to a colonial administration though not that of a sovereign state." Bradford and Connors, "Making," 177–8.
36 For the NWC, see Harmon, *Journal*, 181 (21 July 1808), and for the AFC see Point, *Wilderness*, 212.
37 Sproat, *Scenes*, 41; Kane, *Wanderings*, 227, 229; Angelbeck, "They," 72; and Richling, W̱SÁNEĆ, 4.
38 Wilkes, *Narrative*, 4: 511; E.G. Fenshawe, Victoria to Commander in Chief, CO 305/3, no. 9092, fos. 209d–210.
39 Quoted in Angelbeck, "They," 76. Also see Angelbeck, "They," 170–4; and Moss and Erlandson, "Forts," 75, 84–5.
40 Fisher, *Contact*, 29–30. Also see Lutz, *Makúk*, 73; Drucker, *Indians*, 118; Duff, *Indian*, 18; Fisher, *Contact*, 27–8.
41 Drucker, *Indians*, 118
42 For a summary history of Fort Langley, see Gibson, *Opposition*, 40–5. For a more detailed history, see Maclachlan, *Fort*; and Cullen, *History*. For a history of the HBC's search for an appropriate depot, see Lamb, "Founding," 71–92.
43 George Simpson to the Governor and Committee, 1 March 1829, in Rich, *Simpson's*, 41.
44 Harris, "Lower," 47; James Douglas, Fort Vancouver, to HBC Governor and Committee, London, 14 October 1839, Rich, *Letters, 1839–44*, 216. Original is HBCA A.11/50, para. 16.
45 On 14 September 1827, James McMillan reported that "the Cowichan and the Indians of point Roberts," who he indicated spent winters on Vancouver Island, were both then above Fort Langley "making their Winter stock of Salmon." James McMillan to John McLoughlin, 14 September 1827, HBCA D.4/121, fo. 15d. That McMillan so indicated only a few months after Fort Langley was established shows that the Cowichan and Songhees were accustomed to doing so before the fort was established.
46 Archibald McDonald assembled a remarkably detailed "general abstract" of Indigenous communities dated February 1830. See HBCA D.4/123, fos. 67d–72.
47 James McMillan to John McLoughlin, 14 September 1827, HBCA D.4/121, fo. 15d.
48 James McMillan to John McLoughlin, 14 September 1827, HBCA D.4/121, fo. 15.

49 Maclachlan, *Fort*, 56–7. Also see 11 August 1827 (p. 32), 56 (13 March 1828), 8 May 1828 (pp. 61–2), 12 June 1828 (65), 71 (11 August 1828), 21 July 1830 (152).
50 Maclachlan, *Fort*, 101 (13 March 1829).
51 Dee, "Journal, Part 5," 139.
52 Dee, "Journal, Part 5," 139.
53 For a time following the Anglo-Russian Convention of 1825, which forbade the trade in firearms, the HBC had a policy forbidding its men from trading arms, but the policy proved impossible to implement. See Gibson, *Opposition*, 37.
54 Maclachlan, *Fort*, 11 (24 April 1829), 111.
55 Maclachlan, *Fort*, 11 (24 April 1829), 111.
56 George Simpson explained that "matrimonial connections are a heavy tax on a post, in consequence of the increased demand for provisions, but form, at the same time, a useful link between the traders and the savages." Simpson, *Narrative*, 1: 231.
57 Galois, *Kwakwaka'wakw*, 233–5; and Taylor and Duff, "Post-Contact," 56–66. James Douglas, 14 May 1840, BCA A/B/40/D75.2, p. 13.
58 McMillan, "Reviewing," 257–8; Kennedy and Bouchard, "Northern Coast Salish," in Suttles, *Northwest Coast*, 441–3; Arima and Dewhirst, "Nootkans of Vancouver Island," in Suttles, *Northwest Coast*, 393.
59 Angelbeck, "Conceptions"; Harris, "Voices"; Carlson, "Toward"; Miller and Boxberger, "Creating"; Thom, "Coast"; Angelbeck, "They," 94.
60 Many recorded oral histories point to a battle at Maple Bay (between Salt Spring Island and Vancouver Island), probably between 1830 and 1855, as pivotal in this history. Angelbeck, "They," 229–41; Angelbeck and McLay, "Battle." The fact that the Lekwiltok destroyed the Comox village at Cape Mudge between 1841 and 1853 suggests that the tide turned against the Lekwiltok closer to 1855 than 1830.
61 James Douglas to Newcastle, 24 October 1853, CO 305/4, no. 12345, fo. 90.
62 Anderson, "Notes," 74.
63 Elmendorf, "Chemakum," 438–40.
64 Dee, "Journal, Part 5," 136.
65 John McLoughlin, Fort Vancouver, to George Simpson, 3 March 1835, as published in Reid, "Fort," 188.
66 James Douglas, Fort Vancouver, to James Murray Yale, 21 November 1838, HBCA B.223/b/22, fos. 38, 38d.
67 Wadewitz, *Nature*, 37; Mackie, *Trading*, 218–30. In the late 1840s, salmon had become a more valuable item at Fort Langley than furs. Cullen, *History*, 35. http://parkscanadahistory.com/series/chs/20/chs20-1a.htm; Wadewitz, *Nature*, 38–9.

68 Maclachlan, *Fort*, 22 September 1828 (p. 75). For the "Nanimoos," see 30 July 1829 (p. 122). During the nineteenth century variants of the term "Cowichan" were often used generally to refer to Halkomelem-speaking Salish people. Thus, not all references to the "Cowichan" in nineteenth-century documents were to people ancestral to those who refer to themselves as "Cowichan" today. Dee, "Journal, Part 5," 135.
69 Maclachlan, *Fort*, 20 July 1829 (121).
70 Maclachlan, *Fort*, 14 August 1829 (123–4).
71 Maclachlan, *Fort*, 226.
72 Bowsfield, *Fort Victoria Letters* (hereafter *FVL*), xxx, 45, 63; Grant, "Description," 282; Cullen, *History* (no pagination). Each barrel weighed about 180 pounds (80 kilograms).
73 James Douglas and John Work to the Governor and Committee, 7 December 1846, HBCA A.11/72, fo. 17.
74 Dee, "Journal, Part 5," 137.
75 Reid, "Early," 83; Mackie, *Trading*, 230.
76 See Gibson, *Farming*, passim, but especially 179–84; Suttles, "Early," 137–51; Wenstob, "Profusion," 133–60. Also see Dee, "Journal," passim.
77 Scouler, "Journal," 191. Also see Scouler, "Observations," 219–20.
78 Dee, "Journal, Part 5," 137.
79 James Douglas, Fort Vancouver, to HBC Governor and Committee, London, 14 October 1839, HBCA B.223/b/23, fo. 8. Here Douglas used the term "Cowegins" to refer to Halkomelem speakers generally.
80 Suttles, *Coast*, 145.
81 Suttles, *Coast*, 144.
82 Wayne Suttles found that, at least in later years, potato fields were owned by families. Suttles, *Coast*, 147.
83 Dee, "Journal, Part 5," 136.
84 Dee, "Journal, Part 5," 136; Gibson, *Opposition*, 58–63.
85 Simpson, *Narrative*, 1: 202.
86 Alexander Caulfield Anderson, Fort McLoughlin District Report, 15 March 1834, HBCA B.120/e/1, fo. 1d.
87 Simpson, *Narrative*, 1: 202–3. Also see Alexander Caulfield Anderson, Fort McLoughlin District Report, 15 March 1834, HBCA B.120/e/1, fos. 1d–2.
88 George Simpson to the Governor and Committee," 15 November 1841, HBCA D.4/110, fo. 9d.
89 Taylor and Duff, "Post-Contact," 56–66.
90 HBCA B.201/a/3, 11 August 1837 (fos. 130d–131).
91 HBCA B.201/a/3, 16 & 24 August 1837 (fos. 130d–131).
92 Galois, *Kwakwaka'wakw*, 56–7.

93 James Douglas to Sir George Simpson, 16 November 1843, HBCA D.5/9, fos. 231–231d.
94 Charles Ross, Fort Victoria to George Simpson, 10 January 1844, as published in Lamb, "Five Letters," 114; Gibson, *Opposition*, 50–2; James Douglas to Sir George Simpson, 16 November 1843, HBCA D.5/9, fos. 231–231d.
95 John McLoughlin, Fort Vancouver, to John Work, Fort Simpson, 8 December 1836, HBCA B.223/b/15 (fo. 62). Simpson reiterated the importance of all of these factors in 1841, when the final decisions about the future depot were made. See Lamb, "Founding," 81.
96 Fort Simpson (Nass) post journal, 10 August 1837, HBCA B.201/a/3, fo. 130; Lamb, "Founding," 75–6. After visiting the location on 12 December 1839, John McLoughlin was less positive: "It is a very fine harbour, accessible at all seasons, but not a place suitable to our purpose." John McLoughlin, Fort Vancouver to George Simpson, 20 March 1840, HBCA B.223/b/26, fo. 2.
97 Report of James Douglas, 12 July 1842, *BPP* 1848 (619), 5.
98 James Douglas to James Hargrave, 5 February 1843, in Glazebrook, *Hargrave*, 421.
99 J.B.Z. Bolduc, Cowlitz, to Mr. Cayenne, 15 February 1844, as published in Thwaites, *Early*, 29: 149.
100 Thwaites, *Early*, 29: 149–50. Thwaites concluded that the reference to Toungletats was to the "Cowichan Indians, named for their chieftain Tsoughilam (Toungletats). The Cowichan are a large subdivision of the Coast Salishan tribe, occupying the east coast of Vancouver Island, and up the Fraser River as far as Yale." The editor cited Boas, "The Indian Tribes of the Lower Fraser River," 454–63. "Tsoughelum" is indeed mentioned several times in the Fort Victoria post journals as a particular enemy of the Songhees. See HBCA B.226/a/1, 21 & 27 September 1848, 17 April, 17 May, 4 June1849. Grant Keddie has interpreted "the powerful and warlike tribe" to be the Yougletas [Lekwiltok]. Keddie, *Songhees*, 21. While that is a plausible interpretation, it renders as problematic Bolduc's description of the territory of those people. On balance, Thwaites's interpretation is the more likely. Also see Grant Keddie, "The 1843 Observations of the Lekwungen People by Jean Baptiste Zacharie Bolduc," Royal BC Museum, Research Articles by Staff, Grant Keddie, 22 June 2020, https://royalbcmuseum.bc.ca/collections/research/research-articles.
101 Thwaites, *Early*, 29: 151. This mass was probably held at Cadboro Bay. Duff, "Fort," 39. Bolduc was clearly using the term *Kawitskins* to refer to Halkomelem speakers imprecisely, although his previous reference to the Cowichan as the "Toungletats" suggests that he was excluding the people now known as Cowichan from his "Kawitskins." The other people mentioned were the Klallam, and Saanich (W̱SÁNEĆ).

102 "Letter of Mr. Bolduc, Apostolical Missionary," 15 February 1844, in Thwaites, *Early*, 29: 146 (letter, 145–55).
103 In 1951, Wayne Suttles, who would later become one of the most respected anthropologists of the Northwest Coast, wrote, based on fieldwork conducted with elderly Indigenous people in the late 1940s, that "my informants have indicated that Songish from Cadboro Bay, Oak Bay and elsewhere did collect at Victoria to be near the fort and near the church." Suttles, "Economic," 18. In an article published in the highly respected *Handbook of North American Indians* in 1990, Suttles went into no more detail than to write that Fort Victoria "became an even greater magnet [than Fort Langley] for Indian trade, at first drawing people throughout the Strait of Juan de Fuca, Puget Sound, and the strait of Georgia but by the 1850s drawing people from as far north as Alaska." Suttles, "Central," 471. Given that the *Handbook* is much more oriented towards anthropology than history, the superficial discussions of historical change are not surprising.
104 Duff, "Fort," 39.
105 Simpson to the London Committee, 21 June 1844, *BPP* 1848 (619), 7.
106 Charles Ross to George Simpson, 10 January 1844, as published in Lamb, "Five," 114–15.
107 *Weekly Victoria Gazette*, 28 August 1858; Memorandum of Joseph Trutch to the Colonial Secretary, 30 December 1869, published in British Columbia, *Papers Connected with the Indian Land Question* (hereafter *PCILQ*), 65–6, and found in LAC RG10, Vol. 3608, f. 3102; Hill-Tout, "Report," 307.
108 Finlayson, *Biography*, 10–11. For a description of the relocation process by the prominent British Columbia anthropologist Wilson Duff, see Duff, "Fort," 5.
109 Keddie, "Salvage."
110 Charles Ross, Victoria to W.F. Tolmie, Nisqually, 11 January 1844 as published in Lamb, "Five," 112; Lamb, "Founding," 90.
111 George Simpson to the London Committee, 18 June 1846, *BPP* 1848 (619), 8.
112 HBCA B.226/a/1, 30 October 1846, 5 May 1847. The potato harvests at Fort Victoria were 2,774 bushels in 1846, 3,028 bushels in 1847, 2,774 bushels in 1848, and 996 bushels in the droughty 1849. See HBCA B.226/a/1, 14 October 1846, 9 October 1847, 29 September 1848, and 10 October 1849.
113 HBCA B.226/a/1, passim. For the sale of garden produce, see 28 August 1846.
114 Douglas and Work to the Governor and Committee, 7 December 1846, HBCA A.11/72, fo. 16d.
115 HBCA B.226/a/1, 29 July 1846. For a hay sale, see 12 October 1846.

116 George Simpson to the London Committee, 18 June 1846, *BPP* 1848 (619), 8.
117 HBCA B.226/a/1, 30 October & 8 December 1846, 5 & 26 November 1847, 26 January and 23 March 1850.
118 For cattle, see HBCA B.226/a/1, 13 November 1847. For sheep, see HBCA B.226/a/1, 23 March 1850
119 HBCB.226/a/1, 3 April 1848.
120 HBCA B.226/a/1, 23 March 1850 (fo. 171d).
121 HBCA B.226/a/1, April 1850 (fo. 170).
122 Barry Gough, "Walter Colquhoun Grant," *DCB*.
123 HBCA B.226/a/1, fo. 57, 3 August 1847.
124 The journals of the farm from 1854 to 1862 can be found at HBCA B.15/a/1–2.
125 Lutz, *Makúk*, 73.
126 Mackie, *Trading*, 280.
127 HBCA B.226/a/1, passim. Surprisingly, the journals do not mention a single instance of trade in elk hides, although the HBC traders did occasionally kill elk.
128 James Douglas to Sir George Simpson, 16 November 1843, HBCA D.5/9, 232.
129 HBCA B.226/a/1, 16 September 1846.
130 HBCA B.226/a/1, 4 & 5 August 1847.
131 James Douglas to R. Finlayson, 11 April 1849, HBCA B.226/b/2.
132 HBCA B.226/a/1, 13 August 1849.
133 See for example, HBCA B.226/a/1, 17 November 1849, and 1 April 1850 for herring; 11 February, 28 April and 1 October 1847, 7 February & 12 June 1848, 12 June 1848 for cod; and 19 and 21 July 1846, 8 July 1847, 14 November 1847, 11 January and 1 March 1848 for other fish.
134 HBCA B.226/a/1, see 10 August 1849. Based on his time in the area in the early 1860s, John Keast Lord indicted that salmon was "a very important article both of food and commerce" at Victoria. Lord, *The Naturalist*, 1: 61.
135 James Douglas to the Governor and Committee of the HBC, 27 October 1849, Bowsfield, *FVL*, 63.
136 HBCA B.226/a/1, 26 & 27 September & 10 October 1949. Also see 9 May 1846, 26 April 1847, 2 September 1848.
137 For some examples, see HBCA B.226/a/1, 28 May 1846, 13 June 1846, 16 & 21 November 1846.
138 References to trade in whale oil and whale bone are abundant, but for references to trade by the villagers named, see HBCA B.226/a/1, 1 June 1846, 18 August and 5 October 1847, 9 February 1849.
139 HBCA B.226/a/1, 8, 26, 27 January 1847. For dentalium ("hayquois"), which was shipped to the Columbia River, see 3 June and 22 August

1846. See Galois and Mackie, "Curious," 1-3; Mackie and Galois, "Curious," 6-9.
140 Report of James Douglas, 12 July 1842, *BPP* 1848 (619), 5.
141 James Douglas to R. Finlayson, 11 April 1849, HBCA B.226/b/2.
142 James Douglas to the Governor and Committee, 3 September 1849, HBCA A.11/72, fo. 120.
143 James Douglas to the Governor and Committee, 27 October 1849, in Bowsfield, *FVL*, 63.
144 Lamb, "Founding," 87; James Douglas, "Diary of a Trip to Victoria, 1-21 March 1843," BCA A/B/40/D75.4A, 16 March 1843.
145 For examples, see HBCA B.226/a/1, 22 August 1846, 17 November 1846, 21 December 1846, 4 June 1846, 12 March 1847.
146 For example, see HBCA B.226/a/1, 27 June 1846, 1 August 1846, 4 February 1848.
147 Finlayson, "Autobiography," 32.
148 For example, see HBCA B.226/a/1, 16 July 1846.
149 HBCA B.226/a/1, 4 July 1846, 18 January 1847.
150 HBCA B.226/a/1, 11 June 1846.
151 HBCA B.226/a/1, 28 July 1846
152 HBCA B.226/a/1, 1 April 1849.
153 HBCA B.226/a/1, 12 May 1847.
154 HBCA B.226/a/1, 3 August 1846, 7 May 1848.
155 HBCA B.226/a/1, 18 September 1847.
156 HBCA B.226/a/1, 23 December 1846.
157 For example, see HBCA B.226/a/1, 9 & 14 July 1846, 16 & 18 January 1847, 25 March 1847, 24 July 1847.
158 HBCA B.226/a/1, 18 January 1847.
159 Simpson, *Narrative*, 1: 242.
160 See for example, HBCA B.226/a/1, 2 June 1846, 26 February 1847, 14 February 1848, 14 February 1848, 20 & 22 February 1848. Paul Kane noted that "the gentlemen in charge of the various posts have frequent occasion to send letters, sometimes for a considerable distance, when it is either inconvenient or impossible for them to fit out a canoe with their own men to carry it. In such cases the letter is given to an Indian, who carries it as far as suits his convenience and safety. He then sells the letter to another, who carries it until he finds an opportunity of selling it to advantage; it is thus passed on and sold until it arrives at its destination, gradually increasing in value according to the distance, and the last possessor receiving the reward for its safe delivery. In this manner letters are frequently sent with perfect security, and with much greater rapidity than could be done otherwise." Kane, *Wanderings*, 247-8.
161 HBCA B.226/a/1, 16 February & 22 March 1847.

162 HBCA B.226/a/1, 12 August 1846, 30 January & 4 March 1847, 13 May 1847.
163 HBCA B.226/a/1, 4 August 1847, 27 October 1847, 27 January–1 February 1848.
164 James Douglas and John Work to Governor and Committee of the HBC, HBCA A.11/72, fos. 28d–29.
165 James Douglas to the Governor and Committee, 3 September 1849, HBCA A.11/72, fo. 118d–119.
166 When the Songhees surrendered their reserve in 1910, the band members' activities reflected those of the 1840s in many ways. For example, they typically had gardens (some with orchard trees), and they worked as stevedores, fishermen, domestic servants, boat builders, sawmillers, cannery workers, bakers, and tree pruners. For example, Willie Jack had a garden with "over 70 fruit trees, all bearing," and Tommy George was a stevedore who had a garden with 50 fruit trees. Some of the band still lived in "rancherie" style houses, but many lived in frame houses more typical of the settlers. See "Census of the Songhees Band," 21–25 November 1910, LAC RG10, Vol. 3690, f. 13,886-4.
167 Finlayson, "Autobiography," 32–3.
168 Finlayson, "Autobiography," 33.
169 Finlayson, "Autobiography," 33.
170 HBCA B.226/a/1, 7 June 1846. It is possible, of course, that the incident described in Finlayson's autobiography was this same incident, and that Finlayson's autobiography got the date wrong.
171 HBCA B.226/a/1, 30 October 1848.
172 HBCA B.226/a/1, 6 March 1850.
173 HBCA B.226/a/1, 6 July 1846.
174 HBCA B.226/a/1, 27 September 1846. The Makah were housed within the stockades again on 4 July 1847.
175 HBCA B.226/a/1, 27 June 1847.
176 HBCA B.226/a/1, 20 July 1847.
177 James Douglas and John Work to Governor and Committee of the HBC, HBCA A.11/72, fos. 28d–29.
178 HBCA B.226/a/1, 24 August 1848.
179 HBCA B.226/a/1, 25 August 1848.
180 Fort Victoria post journal, 29 August 1848 (fo. 104), HBCA B.226/a/1; Finlayson, *Biography*, 17–18.
181 Lutz, "Taking."
182 HBCA B.26/a/1, 28 September 1849
183 HBCA B.26/a/1, 25 April 1849, 14–15 May 1849.
184 HBCA B.226/a/1, 21 September 1848.
185 An HBC map from 1842 depicts an "Indian Fort" at Cadboro Bay. See "Ground Plan of Portion of Vancouver's Island selected for New

Establishment," HBCA G.2/25. In 1969, Wilson Duff reported what some of his Indigenous informants had told him that "the point south of the Yacht Club [on Cadboro Bay], they said, was used as a fort and lookout for raiding parties of Yukwilthtaq (...)(Euclataw Kwakiutl [Lekwiltok])." Duff, "Fort," 48.
186 R.J. Staines to the Rev. Edward Cridge, 10 October 1949, BCA quoted in Slater, "Rev. Robert," 237–8.
187 Eden Colvile to J.H. Pelly, 15 October 1849, in Rich, *London*, 5.
188 Galois, "Measles,," 31–43; Boyd, "Pacific," 6–47; Boyd, *Coming*, 145–60; and Galois, *Kwakwaka'wakw*, 43.
189 HBCA B.226/a/1, 5 February 1848.
190 HBCA B.226/a/1, 14 April 1848; Boyd, "Pacific," 36–7.
191 Boyd, "Pacific," 22; Galois, "Measles," 34–6.
192 HBCA B.226/a/1, 13 March–2 June 1848; Boyd, *Coming*, 157.
193 HBCA B.226/a/1, 16 March 1848.
194 HBCA B.226/a/1, 17 March, 9, 15 April 1848. Yale also dispatched letters to Victoria while measles was prevalent at Fort Langley, HBCA B.226/a/1, 13 April 1848, and letters arrived from Vancouver on 16 April. The disease also appears to have been spread by the HBC's steamship, *Beaver*. See Boyd, "Pacific," 31–4; Galois, "Measles," 36–7.
195 HBCA B.226/a/1, 3 April 1848.
196 HBCA B.226/a/1, 7 April 1848.
197 HBCA B.226/a/1, 8 April 1848.
198 HBCA B.226/a/1, 30 June and 4 July 1848; and 5 January 1849; Galois, "Measles," 40.
199 Galois, "Measles," 37–8.
200 Boyd, "Pacific," 41.
201 Galois states that this was the case farther north. See Galois, "Measles," 41.

## 6. Articulating Principles of Indigenous Title, 1835–1846

1 Samuel Clyde McCulloch, "Gipps, Sir George (1791–1847)," *ADB*, http://adb.anu.edu.au/biography/gipps-sir-george-2098/text2645, published first in hardcopy 1966, accessed online 5 May 2020; Gipps, *Every*, 29. See Buick, *Treaty*.
2 *An Act to empower the Governor of New South Wales to appoint Commissioners, with certain powers to examine and report on Claims to Grants of Land in New Zealand*, 4 Victoria No. 7 (August 1840), *Public General Statutes of New South Wales: From 1 Victoriæ to 10 Victoriæ, inclusive (1838–1846)* (Sydney: Thomas Richards, 1861), 1042–47. The legislation can also be found in Tonk, "First," 327–33.

3 Recent contrasting interpretations can be found in Attwood, *Empire*, 174–86, and Fletcher, *English*, 398–417. Also see Tonk, "First"; and Sweetman, *Unsigned*.
4 A long, almost verbatim transcript of the proceedings can be found in "Legislative Council," *Sydney Herald*, 6 July 1840, 2–4. Also see "Domestic Intelligence: Legislative Council," *The Colonist* (Sydney), 1 July 1840, 2; "Legislative Council," *Australasian Chronicle*, 2 July 1840, 1.
5 "Legislative Council," *Sydney Herald*, 6 July 1840, 2–3. The summary of Busby's presentation is almost 14,000 words long.
6 "New Zealand Commissioner's Bill," *Australasian Chronicle*, 2 July 1840, 3. Also see "Legislative Council," *Sydney Herald*, 2 July 1840, 2.
7 "Legislative Council," *Australasian Chronicle*, 2 July 1840, 1; "Domestic Intelligence: Legislative Council," *The Colonist* (Sydney), 1 July 1840, 2.
8 Michael Persse, "Wentworth, William Charles (1790–1872)," *ADB*, http://adb.anu.edu.au/biography/wentworth-william-charles-2782/text3961, published first in hardcopy 1967, accessed online 23 May 2020; Tink, *William Charles Wentworth*. For another view, see Evison, "Wentworth-Jones," 43–60.
9 Macintyre, *Concise*, 72.
10 Liston, "William Charles Wentworth," 20–3.
11 Fifer, "Man," 147–48; Persse, "Wentworth," *ADB*.
12 "Legislative Council," *Sydney Herald*, 6 July 1840, 4.
13 "Legislative Council," *Australasian Chronicle*, 2 July 1840, 1.
14 "Legislative Council," *Australasian Chronicle*, 2 July 1840, 1.
15 E.G. Coppel, "à Beckett, Sir William (1806–1869)," *ADB*, http://adb.anu.edu.au/biography/a-beckett-sir-william-2862/text4079, published first in hardcopy 1969, accessed online 23 May 2020. William à Beckett had served in November 1838 as counsel for the eleven men accused in the Myall Creek massacre.
16 "Legislative Council," *Sydney Herald*, 6 July 1840, 4.
17 *Sydney Herald*, 30 June 1840
18 For the weather in Sydney, see "The Crops," and "The Streets," *Sydney Commercial Journal and Advertiser* 11 July 1840, 2. My estimate of the time taken to deliver the speech is based on the fact that the published versions of the speech show that it was over 15,000 words long.
19 "Colonial Politics: The New Zealand Question," *The Colonist* (Sydney) 11 July 1840, 2.
20 A transcript of what must have been Gipps's written speech appears in "Domestic Intelligence: Legislative Council," *The Colonist* (Sydney), 11 July 1840, 4, 2–3. A shorter description of the speech delivered orally, and which explains that, on at least one occasion, Gipps held "up in ridicule a deed of grant given in by Mr Wentworth," can be found in

"Legislative Council," *The Australian*, 11 July 1840, Supplement, p. 1, col. 5–6. A transcript of the debates of 10 July can be found in "Domestic Intelligence: Legislative Council," *The Colonist* (Sydney), 14 July 1840, 2–3.

21 Edward Sweetman has noted that the published version was less vitriolic than what was delivered. Sweetman, *Unsigned*, 63, 65–6, 75.

22 "Speech of His Excellency Sir George Gipps, in Council, on Thursday, 9th July 1840, on the second reading of the Bill for appointing Commissioners to inquire into Claims to Grants of Land in New Zealand," *BPP* 1841 (311), 63–4. The speech continues to page 78. This speech was quoted in multiple places before the HBC Governor and Committee quoted it in their letter to Douglas. See, for example, W., "Epitome," 196; Anonymous, "New Zealand Question," 257. The HBC Governor and Committee, however, cited the Report of the British Select Committee on New Zealand, 1844.

23 "Speech of His Excellency Sir George Gipps," *BPP* 1841 (311), 63–4.

24 Kent's *Commentaries* had been published in a third edition in 1836. Kent's *Commentaries*: "It is a fundamental principle in the English law, derived from the maxims of the feudal tenures, that the king was the original proprietor of all the land in the kingdom, and the true and only source of title. ... The natives were admitted to be the rightful occupants of the soil, with a legal as well as just claim to retain possession of it, and to use it according to their own discretion, though not to dispose of the soil at their own will, except to government claiming the right of pre-emption." Lecture 51, "Of the Law Concerning Real Property."

25 Story, *Commentaries*, 6–7: "The principle ... that discovery gave title to the government ... being once established, it followed almost as a matter of course, that every government ... excluded all other persons from any right to acquire the soil by any grant whatsoever from the natives. No nation would suffer either its own subjects, or those of any other nation, to set up or vindicate any such title. ... It may be asked, what was the effect of this principle of discovery in respect to the rights of the natives themselves. ... They were admitted to be the rightful occupants of the soil, with a legal, as well as a just claim to retain possession of it; and to use it according to their own discretion. ... But notwithstanding this occupancy, the European discoverers claimed and exercised the right to grant the soil, while yet in possession of the natives, subject, however, to their right of occupancy; and the title so granted was universally admitted to convey a sufficient title in the soil to the granters in perfect dominion, or, as it is sometimes expressed in treaties of public law, it was a transfer of *plenum et utile dominimum*."

26 In the Batman Treaty of 1835, the Port Phillip Association, represented by John Batman, claimed to have purchased 600,000 acres of land from

eight chiefs of the Kulin people. The most significant difference between that purchase and the purchases in New Zealand was that the land covered by Batman's Treaty was within the boundaries of the colony of New South Wales at the time. See Attwood, *Possession*; Attwood, *Empire*, 43–64.
27 "Speech of His Excellency Sir George Gipps," *BPP* 1841 (311), 78.
28 Gipps quoted from Julius Caesar's Commentaries on the Gallic Wars: "*ego certe meum rei publicæ atque imperatori officium præstitero.*" The words mean "I, for my part, shall have done my duty to my country and my commander."
29 "Speech of His Excellency Sir George Gipps," *BPP* 1841 (311), 78. Perceptive readers will wonder if Gipps here was also intentionally alluding to the dying words of Christ.
30 Tonk, "First," 25; Sweetman, *Unsigned*, 73.
31 "Domestic Intelligence: Legislative Council," *The Colonist*, 6 August 1840, 2. The legislation, officially disallowed on ground of form, was superseded by legislation in New Zealand in 1840. See Sweetman, *Unsigned*, 74; Tonk, "First," 47–8.
32 McCulloch, "Sir," 261–69; Gipps, *Every*.
33 Samuel Clyde McCulloch, "Gipps," *ADB*.
34 McCulloch, "Sir," 264.
35 Sweetman, *Unsigned*, 75. James Stephen did have credentials as a humanitarian. He had given up a £3,000 salary in private practice to take a position in the Colonial Office and Board of Trade – at half the salary – to help further the cause of slavery abolition. Burns, *Fatal*, 32. Stephen understood the cynical side of Chief Justice Marshall's decisions regarding Indigenous title. In 1840, when asked about Marshall, Stephen wrote that "British Law in Canada is far more humane, for there, the Crown purchases of the Indians before it grants to its own subjects. Whatever may be the ground occupied by international jurists, they never forget the policy and interests of their own Country. Their business is to give rapacity and injustice the most decorous veil which legal ingenuity can weave." Attwood, *Empire*, 169.
36 Lord John Russell to Sir George Gipps, 16 January 1841, *BPP* 1841 (311), 78; also published in *Historical Records of Australia* (hereafter *HRA*) (Sydney: Alfred James Kent, Government Printer, 1924), series 1, vol. 21, p. 187; Tonk, "First," 28.
37 "Speech of His Excellency Sir George Gipps," *BPP* 1841 (311), 63–4.
38 "Speech of His Excellency Sir George Gipps," *BPP* 1841 (311), 75.
39 Phillip was given a commission "extending from Cape York, lat. 11 deg. 37 min. south; to the South Cape, lat. 43 deg. 30 min. south; and inland to the westward as far as 135 deg. East long., comprehending all the islands

adjacent in the Pacific Ocean within the latitude of the above-named Capes." Anonymous "New Zealand Question," 250–60.
40 Adams, *Fatal*, 52. Gipps argued that the British government probably left New Zealand out of Thomas Brisbane's commission by accident. "Speech of His Excellency Sir George Gipps," *BPP* 1841 (311), 75.
41 W., "Epitome," 205–7.
42 New Zealand, *Fac-Similes*, 3. Busby himself had much to gain personally from the independence of the United Tribes of New Zealand. Ross, "Busby," 83–9. Busby admitted that the 1835 declaration of independence to which he referred had been "drawn up by himself, and agreed to by the chiefs at his request; and … the chiefs who met were selected by himself; and that they were such men as *would do whatever he desired them*." "New Zealand Commissioner's Bill," *Australasian Chronicle*, 2 July 1840, 3. Also see "Speech of His Excellency Sir George Gipps," *BPP* 1841 (311), 75.
43 *BPP* 1837/38 (680), p. 159; New Zealand, *Fac-Similes*, 5.
44 *An Act for the more effectual Punishment of Murders and Manslaughters committed in Places not within His Majesty's Dominions* (57 Geo III c.53 Adams), *Statutes of the United Kingdom or Great Britain and Ireland, 57 George III. 1817* (London: J. Butterworth and Son, 1817), 183. Adams, *Fatal*, 52. As Attwood has explained, by legislating in respect to such places, the British government was placing them in a different category than obviously sovereign countries not listed in the legislation. Attwood, *Empire*, 106.
45 Adams, *Fatal*, 53.
46 *BPP* 1837/38 (680), 107; Buick, *Treaty*, 72. Attwood, *Empire*, 132–3.
47 For an excellent discussion of the ambiguity of British recognition/non-recognition of Māori sovereignty between 1814 and 1839, see Attwood, *Empire*, 102–30.
48 Attwood, *Empire*, 107.
49 Mein Smith, *Concise*, 35–9.
50 Burns, *Fatal*, 78.
51 Sweetman, *Unsigned*, 25–7.
52 Sweetman, *Unsigned*, 26, 28; Tonk, "First," 42; Attwood, *Empire*, 104.
53 Sir Richard Bourke to James Busby, 13 April 1833, *BPP* 1840 (283), 4; Mein Smith, *Concise*, 36–7.
54 Adams, *Fatal*, 26.
55 Adams, *Fatal*, 20–1.
56 Adams, *Fatal*, 24.
57 Adams, *Fatal*, 27.
58 Captain William Hobson to Richard Bourke, 8 August 1837, *BPP* 1840 (283), 10–11; James Busby to the Colonial Secretary, New South Wales, 16 June 1837, *BPP* 1840 (283), 12–18.

59 Adams, *Fatal*, 13, 19, 56–8, 64; Mein Smith, *Concise*, 41–2.
60 W., "Epitome," 198 (emphasis in original), quoting Par. Papers, 3 August 1840, p. 48.
61 Tonk, "First," 3.
62 Tonk, "First," 14; Evison, "Wentworth-Jones." https://paperspast.natlib.govt.nz/periodicals/TLR19950101.2.7. Not including purchases made by the New Zealand Company, the approximately 300 transactions that took place in 1839, and 110 in 1838 exceeded the approximately 280 land transactions that had occurred between 1823 and 1837. Attwood, *Empire*, 126.
63 Sweetman, *Unsigned*, 48.
64 Adams, *Fatal*, 14, 148, 155; Burns, *Fatal*, 92.
65 Burns, *Fatal*, 94.
66 Mein Smith, *Concise*, 43.
67 The land claims of the New Zealand Company were eventually dealt with through a separate process.
68 Sweetman, *Unsigned*, 56.
69 The letters patent were issued in London on 15 June 1839. William Hobson was appointed lieutenant governor on 30 July 1839, *BPP* 1840 (560), 3, 7.
70 *BPP* 1840 (560), 3; Sweetman, *Unsigned*, 57–8; Tonk, "First," 13, Ward, "Interpreting," 89.
71 *BPP* 1840 (560), 8.
72 George Gipps to John Russell, *HRA*, series 1, vol. 20, p. 492.
73 "New Zealand," Sydney *Herald*, 21 February 1840, 2.
74 *The Colonist* [Sydney] 1 February 1840, 2; Evison, "Wentworth-Jones"; Attwood, *Empire*, 172.
75 Sir George Gipps to Lord John Russell, 16 August 1840, *BPP* 1841 (311), 63.
76 Sweetman, *Unsigned*, 64.
77 Sweetman, *Unsigned*, 64.
78 Sir George Gipps to Lord John Russell, 16 August 1840, *BPP* 1841 (311), 63.
79 Sir George Gipps to Lord John Russell, 16 August 1840, *BPP* 1841 (311), 63. In fact, it appears that the chiefs were promised £100 per year for life. The deeds have survived. See Evison, "Wentworth-Jones." Also see Evison, *Ngai Tahu*, 44–5.
80 Sir George Gipps to Lord John Russell, 16 August 1840, *BPP* 1841 (311), 63. For a discussion, see Persse, "Wentworth," *ADB*; McCulloch, "Gipps," *ADB*; Tonk, "First," 17; Sweetman, *Unsigned*, 65. One researcher has concluded that Wentworth and his associates deliberately negotiated this agreement to challenge Gipps's proclamation of 14 January; Sweetman, *Unsigned*, 67.
81 *The Colonist*, 25 March 1840, 2; *Australasian Chronicle* [Sydney] 3 April 1840, 2.

82 Tonk, "First," 19.
83 *Hansard Parliamentary Debates* 3rd ser., vol. 81 (18 June 1845), col. 766; Sweetman, *Unsigned*, 49, 68.
84 George Gipps to John Russell, 19 February 1841, *HRA*, series 1, vol. 20, p. 515. The scholarly literature on the Treaty of Waitangi is large. The most recent interpretations, with ample references to the previous literature, can be found in Attwood, *Empire*, esp. 140–61, and Fletcher, *English*.
85 Given that the British Crown did not claim land on the Pacific slope in 1763, it cannot have intended the proclamation to have applied there. Given that it excluded Rupert's Land from its promises, it is implausible that it was articulating a general principle of Indigenous title.
86 *BPP* 1840 (560), 10. See Adams, *Fatal*; Burns, *Fatal*.
87 Of course, the Royal Proclamation, unlike the Treaty of Waitangi, was issued before stadial history emerged as an influential theoretical construct.
88 Mackay, *Compendium*, Section 1: "Public Documents," 26–7; Evison, *Ngai Tahu*, 35–6; Attwood, *Empire*, 158–9.
89 Belich, *Victorian*, 21; Belich, *Making*, 205; Anderson, Binney, and Harris, *Tangata Whenua*, 235–6, Mein Smith, *Concise*, 63–5; Evison, *Ngai Tahu*, 45.
90 *BPP* 1840 (556), ii. The members of the Committee were Henry A. Aglionby (a Director in the New Zealand Company, Whig), Lord Francis Egerton (Tory), Viscount Howick (Whig), George William Hope (Tory) (as Under-Secretary of State for War and the Colonies, 1841–46, was appointed to represent the Colonial Office), Robert Clive (Tory), Benjamin Hawes (Whig), Sir Robert H. Inglis (Tory), Viscount Ebrington (Whig), Francis Charteris (Whig), Sir John Hanmer, Monckton Milnes (Tory), Viscount Robert Jocelyn (Tory), John A. Roebuck, and John Wilson-Patten.
91 "House of Commons Committee," (Auckland) *New Zealander*, 9 August 1845, 4.
92 *BPP* 1840 (556), iii.
93 *BPP* 1840 (556), iv.
94 *BPP* 1840 (556), iv.
95 *BPP* 1840 (556), v. Neither the Select Committee on Aborigines (1837), nor the Aborigines Protection Society, made any recommendations about land-cession treaties or the extinguishment of Indigenous title. The Select Committee also discouraged diplomatic treaties with Indigenous people. *BPP* 1837 (238): 80. The Aborigines Protection Society, however, saw value in them. *Report of the Parliamentary Select Committee on Aboriginal Tribes (British Settlements): Reprinted with Comments by the "Aborigines Protection Society,"* (London: William Ball, Aldine Chambers, 1837), 122–3.
96 *BPP* 1840 (556), xii.
97 *BPP* 1840 (556), xiii.

98  *BPP* 1840 (556), v–vi.
99  *BPP* 1840 (556), vii.
100  *BPP* 1840 (556), ix. For a detailed analysis of the Select Committee, its report, and the responses to the report, see Attwood, *Empire*, 256–81.
101  Lord Stanley to Governor FitzRoy, 13 August 1844, *BPP* 1845 (1), 3. Evidence of the influence of this letter can be found in the fact that the letter was republished in several places, including Knight, *Political*, 1: 518, and the *Nelson Examiner and New Zealand Chronicle*, 5 April 1845.
102  Lord Stanley to Governor FitzRoy, 13 August 1844, *BPP* 1845 (1), 3.
103  Lord Stanley to Governor FitzRoy, 13 August 1844, *BPP* 1845 (1), 3–4. Stuart Banner has discussed at some length the fact that in the middle of the nineteenth century many of those who believed in Indigenous title believed that such title could be extinguished simply by setting aside reserves and civilizing the Indigenous communities. See Banner, "Why," 126–9.
104  Lord Stanley to Governor FitzRoy, 13 August 1844, *BPP* 1845 (1), 3–4. The government of New Zealand started publishing *Ko te Karere o Nui Tireni* in 1842.
105  Indeed, in light of the degree to which the Royal Proclamation of 1763 created the expectation among Indigenous people in the reserved territory (most of which was in what became in 1783 part of the United States of America), it is likely that, had King George III not issued the Proclamation, the United States would not have offered its guarantees in the Northwest Ordinance of 1787.
106  See W., "Epitome," 194; *Times* (London), 11 December 1844, 6; 25 December 1844, 6; Wellington *New Zealand Spectator and Cook's Straits Guardian*, 11 January 1845, Supplement, 1.
107  *Hansard Parliamentary Debates* 3rd ser., vol. 81 (1845), cols. 725–6. For a detailed analysis, see Attwood, *Empire*, 305–29. Charles Buller (1806–1848) will be known to historians of Canada familiar with the Durham Report. For a biography, see Heather Lysons-Balcon, "Charles Buller," *DCB*.
108  Attwood, *Empire*, 320.
109  See *Times* (London), 13 June 1845, 5. In fact, warfare had already broken out on the North Island in March 1845 and would continue until January 1846. See Belich, *Victorian*, 29–70.
110  W., "Epitome," 194. Emphasis in the original. Evison, *Ngai Tahu*, 47. The debates over New Zealand can be found in *Hansard Parliamentary Debates* 3rd ser., vol. 81 (1845), cols. 665–756, 761–846, 853–971 (17, 18, 19 June 1845). The debates were also published separately as *A Corrected Report of the Debate in the House of Commons, on the 17th, 18th and 18th of June, on the State of New Zealand and the Case of the New Zealand Company* (London: John Murray, 1846).

111 *Hansard Parliamentary Debates* 3rd ser., vol. 81 (1845), cols. 815–46 (18 June 1845).
112 *Hansard Parliamentary Debates* 3rd ser., vol. 81 (1845), cols. 816, 817 (18 June 1845).
113 *Hansard Parliamentary Debates* 3rd ser., vol. 81 (1845), col. 823 (18 June 1845).
114 *Hansard Parliamentary Debates* 3rd ser., vol. 81 (1845), col. 825 (18 June 1845).
115 *Hansard Parliamentary Debates* 3rd ser., vol. 81 (1845), cols. 844–5 (18 June 1845).
116 *Hansard Parliamentary Debates* 3rd ser., vol. 81 (19 June 1845), col. 857.
117 *Hansard Parliamentary Debates* 3rd ser., vol. 81 (19 June 1845), col. 863.
118 *Hansard Parliamentary Debates* 3rd ser., vol. 81 (1845), col. 968 (19 June 1845).
119 Unless *Hansard* is inaccurate, Ebrington here apparently omitted the following words in Arnold's article: "– that is, there is either some one person, or family, or tribe, or nation, who have a greater right to it than any one else has; it does not and cannot belong to everybody."
120 *Hansard Parliamentary Debates* 3rd ser., vol. 82 (30 July 1845), cols. 1247–8. Thomas Arnold originally published those words in "Labourers of England" in June 1831, but they had recently been republished in Arnold, *Miscellaneous*, 156–7. The *Englishman's Register* was a weekly paper created by Thomas Arnold (1795–1842) during debates over the Reform Bill.
121 Mr. Hume, *Hansard Parliamentary Debates* 3rd ser., vol. 82 (30 July 1845), col. 1240.

### 7. The Colonial Office, Local Authorities, and Indigenous Title, 1846–1849

1 Foster, "Saanichton," 634–5.
2 Upon his father's death in 1845, Howick became Henry Grey, 3rd Earl Grey. He served as Colonial Secretary during the entire span of Lord John Russell's first ministry, from July 1846 until 21 February 1852. Russell's Whig government was replaced in 1852 by a short-lived minority government of Edward George Geoffrey Smith-Stanley, 14th Earl of Derby, who, as Lord Stanley, had served as Colonial Secretary from 3 September 1841 to 23 December 1845 in Robert Peel's government.
3 Sir George Grey, 2nd Baronet.
4 Attwood, *Empire*, 359.
5 *Hansard Parliamentary Debates* 3rd ser., vol. 81 (1845), cols. 968–9.
6 Ellice Senior was behind the scenes by the 1840s, but Junior was a member of the London Governor and Committee of the HBC from 1837 to 1858.
7 *An Act to make further Provision for the Government of the New Zealand Islands* (9 & 10 Vict. c. 103) 1846; "New Zealand Charter," *BPP* 1847 (763), 73. Edward John Eyre was made Lieutenant-Governor of this province.

8 Memorandum enclosed with B. Hawes to T.C. Harington, [10 May 1847], *BPP* 1847 (837), 112; *An Act to promote Colonization in New Zealand, and to authorize a Loan to the New Zealand Company*, 10 & 11 Vict. c. 112, (1847), sec. 2, *Statutes of the United Kingdom* (London: Her Majesty's Printers, 1847), 667; Burns, *Fatal*, 292–3.
9 "An Act to Authorize a Loan from the Consolidated Fund to the New Zealand Company," 9 & 10 Vict. c. 42 (1846); and *Act to Amend an Act of the present Session for Authorizing a Loan from the Consolidated Fund to the New Zealand Company*, 9 & 10 Vict. c. 82 (1846).
10 George Grey, Governor of South Australia from 1841 to 1845, had replaced Robert FitzRoy on 14 November 1845. He was no relation to either Earl Grey or Sir George Grey, 2nd Baronet. George Grey himself would be knighted in 1848.
11 Earl Grey to Governor George Grey, 23 December 1846, *BPP* 1847 (763), 67, 84.
12 See Attwood, *Empire*, 358–63.
13 "New Zealand," *Times* (London), 29 December 1846, 6.
14 Earl Grey to Governor George Grey, 23 December 1846, *BPP* 1847 (763), 67–8.
15 Earl Grey to Governor George Grey, 23 December 1846, *BPP* 1847 (763), 68.
16 Earl Grey to Governor George Grey, 23 December 1846, *BPP* 1847 (763), 68. The quoted passage is from Arnold, "Labourers of England." Earl Grey was wrong, of course, that the passage "was written not with reference to passing events, or to any controversy which was at that time going on." It was written to defend the cause of reform during debates over the Reform Bill. Perhaps Earl Grey meant to make the odd claim that greater weight should be placed upon Arnold's discussion of Indigenous title because the issue of Indigenous rights was not the occasion for the writing of those words. Viscount Ebrington quoted this passage in the House of Commons on 30 July, *Hansard Parliamentary Debates* 3rd ser., vol. 82 (30 July 1845), cols. 1247–8.
17 Earl Grey to Governor George Grey, 23 December 1846, *BPP* 1847 (763), 68–9. Paragraph breaks added.
18 Earl Grey to Governor George Grey, 23 December 1846, *BPP* 1847 (763), 69–70.
19 Earl Grey to Governor George Grey, 23 December 1846, *BPP* 1847 (763), 70.
20 Earl Grey to Governor George Grey, 23 December 1846, *BPP* 1847 (763), 71.
21 "Supreme Court, Auckland," *Wellington Independent*, 7 July 1847, 3.
22 Governor FitzRoy, Auckland, to Lord Stanley, 15 April 1844, *BPP* 1845 (131), 18.
23 Governor FitzRoy, Auckland, to Lord Stanley, 15 April 1844, *BPP* 1845 (131), 21. As a result, immigrants were illegally squatting on Māori land,

or entering contracts with Māori to buy or occupy Māori land. See "An Ordinance to Provide for the Prevention, by Summary Proceedings, of Unauthorized Purchases and Leases of Land," 1846 (10 Victoriæ 1846, No. 19); and Banner, "Conquest," 59.

24 He added that, even if he had the money, he did not have the personnel to negotiate the necessary purchases. Governor FitzRoy, Auckland, to Lord Stanley, 15 April 1844, *BPP* 1845 (131), 21–2.
25 Governor FitzRoy, Auckland, to Lord Stanley, 15 April 1844, *BPP* 1845 (131), 24.
26 "Proclamation," *Auckland Times*, 15 October 1844, 2–3.
27 "Free Trade in Land," *Auckland Times*, 15 October 1844, 2.
28 The penny-an-acre certificates were issued after ten-shilling-per-acre certificates, issued since 26 March, failed to produce many sales. Fitz-Roy was responding to pressure from both settlers and Māori to permit private sales of land. George Grey to Earl Grey, 19 April 1847, *BPP* 1847 (892), 30; Mackay, *Compendium*, 1: pt.1, p. 8; Adams, *Fatal*, 203; Anderson, Binney, and Harris, *Tangata Whenua*, 246. For a discussion of the penny-an-acre certificates, see Attwood, *Empire*, 293–8.
29 Williams, "Queen," 391; Attwood, *Empire*, 352–8. The issue at stake in Symonds parallels that of the *Johnson v. M'Intosh* in the United States. Oddly, that case was also contrived. In the case of *Johnson v. M'Intosh*, Robert Goodloe Harper contrived to pit Thomas Johnson Jr., a revered octogenarian with strong ties to George Washington and the Federalists (and with whom Chief Justice Marshall would instinctively sympathize), against William M'Intosh, even though the two men did not actually claim the same land. As Eric Kades has noted, the case of *Johnson v. M'Intosh* "appears to have been a sham." Marshall ruled for M'Intosh. Kades, "Dark," 1092; Robertson, *Conquest*, 47–51.
30 Those interested in the case should turn to Hickford, "Vague," 175–206; Williams, "Queen."
31 Of course, the people whose interests were then at stake understood the case. See "Auckland," *Nelson Examiner and New Zealand Chronicle* 10 July 1847, 1; "Fieri non debuit, factum valere debet," (Auckland) *New Zealander*, 12 June 1847, 2. For a mistaken interpretation of the case in relation to the Vancouver Island treaties, see Foster, "Saanichton," 635–6.
32 "Supreme Court, Auckland," *Wellington Independent*, 7 July 1847, 3.
33 "Supreme Court, Auckland," *Wellington Independent*, 7 July 1847, 3.
34 The most complete report of the trial can be found at "Supreme Court, Auckland," *Wellington Independent*, 7 July 1847, 3. I find no evidence in the documents that Grey negotiated a land-cession agreement with Māori before issuing the grant to Symonds.

35  D.G. Edwards, "Henry Samuel Chapman," *Dictionary of New Zealand Biography online (DNZBo)*, first published in 1990. Te Ara – the Encyclopedia of New Zealand, https://teara.govt.nz/en/biographies/1c14/chapman-henry-samuel (accessed 29 September 2020); G.P. Barton, "William Martin," *DNZBo*, https://teara.govt.nz/en/biographies/1m21/martin-william (accessed 29 September 2020).
36  "Supreme Court," (Auckland) *New Zealander*, 12 June 1847, 3.
37  *BPP* 1847 (892), 69. The entire ruling was also published in "Supreme Court," (Auckland) *New Zealander*, 12 June 1847, 3.
38  It also has, in *Johnson v. M'Intosh* (1823), a remarkable parallel in American jurisprudence. In that case, the Marshall court did not define Indigenous title, beyond assuming its existence, and ruled that Indigenous people could convey native title only to the government. The same principle has prevailed throughout the British world. Curiously, Chapman later asserted that his ruling in *Symonds* was entirely consistent with the principles Earl Grey laid out in his dispatch of 23 December 1846; Attwood, *Empire*, 375.
39  George Grey to Earl Grey, 5 July 1847, *BPP* 1847 (892), 64.
40  *R. v. Symonds* (1847) NZPCC 388; *BPP* 1847 (892), 65–71; Foster, "Saanichton," 635; Evison, *Ngai Tahu*, 33. The reference elsewhere in the ruling to the Charter of New Zealand, which claimed waste lands for the Crown, makes it difficult to sustain the argument that Chapman intended to state that native title extended to all waste lands in New Zealand.
41  "An Ordinance to Provide for the Prevention, by Summary Proceedings, of Unauthorized Purchases and Leases of Land," (16 November 1846) (10 Victoriæ 1846, No. 19).
42  James Douglas, Fort Victoria, to Governor and Committee, London, 7 December 1846, HBCA A/11/72, fo. 13d.
43  J.P. Pelly, London, to Earl Grey, 7 September 1846, *BPP* 1848 (619), 3.
44  Pelly to B. Hawes, 24 October 1846, *BPP* 1848 (619), 5.
45  Pelly to Earl Grey, 5 March 1847, *BPP* 1848 (619): 9
46  For the historical context, see Gough, "Crown"; Mouat, "Situating"; Mackie, "Colonization," 3–40; and Knaplund, "James Stephen," 259–71.
47  Benjamin Hawes, Permanent Undersecretary, "Colonization of Vancouver's Island," Minute, 1849, CO 305/2, pp. 7–8, at The Colonial Despatches Team, The Colonial Despatches of Vancouver Island and British Columbia 1846–1871: Home page. *The Colonial Despatches of Vancouver Island and British Columbia 1846–1871*, Edition 2.1, ed. James Hendrickson and the Colonial Despatches project. Victoria, BC: University of Victoria. https://bcgenesis.uvic.ca/index.html. https://bcgenesis.uvic.ca/V49000A.html (accessed 30 September 2020). Hawes was referring to the agreement of May 1847, and *An Act to promote Colonization in New*

*Zealand, and to authorize a Loan to the New Zealand Company*, 10 & 11 Vict. c. 112 (1847).
48 CO 381/77m 23–74, as published in Hendrickson, *JCL*, 1: 379. The grant, and correspondence between the HBC and the Colonial Office relating to the negotiations, can be found in *BPP* 1849 (103)
49 HBCA A.1/65, pp. 190–1. These minutes show (p. 189) that J.H. Pelly, and Edward Ellice (Jr.) were present at that meeting. Edward Ellice did not attend another Committee meeting that year. Meanwhile, Andrew Colvile was not present at a Committee meeting until 4 October (p. 201). In fact, both Pelly and Colvile were not present at the same Committee meeting again until 22 November (HBCA A.1/65, p. 221), after which they were both present at almost all of the Committee meetings before April 1849. Ellice was only an occasional attender of Committee meetings, although he did attend some of the March 1849 meetings.
50 *BPP* 1848 (619),15. Also see Harris, *Making*, 16.
51 Earl Grey to George Grey, 30 November 1847, *BPP*, 1847 (892): 83–4.
52 J.E. Egerton, "Sir James Stephen, (1789–1859)," *ADB*. Heartfield, *Aborigines*, 7.
53 Confidential Memorandum, British Foreign Office, 1849, National Archives of the UK, CO 305/1. The Colonial Despatches of Vancouver Island and British Columbia 1846–1871. Ed. James Hendrickson and the Colonial Despatches project. Victoria: University of Victoria. http://bcgenesis.uvic.ca/getDoc.htm?id=V495PA03.scx. Consulted 10 March 2019. This memorandum is discussed in Harris, *Making*, 16. It is also discussed in Banner, *Possessing*, 198, and Foster, "Saanichton," 630.
54 Minutes of the General Court of the London Committee, 13 June 1849, HBCA A.1/66, p. 67. Blanshard later wrote that he returned to England from India after a relative informed him that "Vancouvers Island was to be colonized on a large scale and that it had been intimated to him that he could procure the appointment of Governor for me." Blanshard to Earl Grey, January 1852, CO 305/3, no. 957, fo. 44d.
55 CO 381/77m 23–74, as published in Hendrickson, *JCL*, 1: 379–91.
56 Barclay to Douglas, 3 August 1849m and 4 August 1849, HBCA B.226/c/1, fo3, 9d–10. Also see Barclay to Douglas, 3 August 1849, BCA M-430 (A/C/20/Vi7).

**8. Land Acquisition Policies in New Zealand and Vancouver Island, 1846–1850**

1 Lord Russell, of course, was already familiar with George Grey. In June 1840, in his capacity as commander of an exploring expedition in Western Australia, George Grey had submitted to Lord Russell – then the Colonial Secretary – a "Report upon the Best Means of Promoting the

Civilization of the Aboriginal Inhabitants of Australia," which described Australian Indigenous peoples "as apt and intelligent as any other race of men I am acquainted with," but which also emphasized the necessity of their becoming civilized. See Grey, *Journals*, 2: 373–88. That report, very well received in the Colonial Office, was sent to the governors in Australia and New Zealand. Grey, *Journals* 2: 372. George Grey may also be the person who introduced to Herman Merivale and the Colonial Office, in 1841, the concept of the *amalgamation* of Indigenous and European societies. The complex meaning of that term, used well before the term *assimilation* took hold and not necessarily a synonym, has never been fully explored, but Grey identified only two possibilities for "the future destiny of the Australian races," aside from "their amalgamation with Europeans." He argued that "either they must disappear before advancing civilization, successively dying off ere the truths of christianity, [sic] or the benefits of civilization have produced any effect on them, – or they must exist in the midst of a superior numerical population, a despised and inferior race; and none but those who have visited a country in which such a race exists, can duly appreciate the evils both moral and physical, which such a degraded position entails upon them." Grey, *Journals* 2: 366–7. Grey served as governor of South Australia from 1841 to 1845. Merivale quoted Grey in his *Lectures on Colonization* (1842), although he did not discuss the concept of "amalgamation" in the first edition of *Lectures*. The 1861 edition defined "amalgamation" as "the union of natives with settlers in the same community, as master and servant, as fellow-labourers, as fellow-citizens, and, if possible, as connected by intermarriage." Merivale, *Lectures*, 511.

2 Evison, *Ngai Tahu*, 62; and Attwood, *Empire*, 344, both quoting or citing Stanley to George Grey, 28 June 1845.
3 G.W. Hope to Lord Ingestre, 7 August 1845, *BPP* 1845 (661), 5; Evison, *Ngai Tahu*, 64.
4 Grey to McCleverty, 20 November 1846, as quoted in Evison, *Ngai Tahu*,
5 George Grey to Earl Grey, 26 March 1847, *BPP* 1847 (892), 7.
6 Evison, *Ngai Tahu*, 71–4.
7 Evison, *Ngai Tahu*, 66–7; Attwood, *Empire*, 363–4.
8 George Grey to Earl Grey, 26 March 1847, *BPP* 1847 (892), 9.
9 *Hansard Parliamentary Debates* 3rd ser., vol. 95 (13 December 1847), cols. 1011–12, 1028.
10 For an analysis of George Grey's response, see Attwood, *Empire*, 389–93.
11 Governor Grey to Earl Grey, 15 May 1848, *BPP*, 1849 (1120), 23. New Zealand did enjoy a period of peace from 1847 to 1860.
12 Governor Grey to Earl Grey, 15 May 1848, *BPP*, 1849 (1120), 23.
13 Governor Grey to Earl Grey, 15 May 1848, *BPP*, 1849 (1120), 23.

14 Governor Grey to Earl Grey, 15 May 1848, *BPP*, 1849 (1120), 24.
15 Governor Grey to Earl Grey, 15 May 1848, *BPP*, 1849 (1120), 25.
16 Rich, *Journal*, 435; Wedderburn, *Wedderburn Book*, 1: 308, 310–11.
17 Andrew Colvile, London, to George Simpson, 6 April 1849, HBCA D.5/25, fos. 76–77. The adjournment of the meeting of the General Court of the London Committee on Wednesday, 4 April 1849 (HBCA A.1/66, p36), which Colvile and Pelly had attended, may well have provided the men the opportunity to have the conversation mentioned, although the context implies that the conversations had begun earlier than that, and may have been inspired by Colvile's concerns about the Committee's position taken in its letter sent to the Columbia District in December 1848.
18 Eden Colvile was scheduled to depart London for Liverpool on 6 April, and sail for New York, after which he was to attempt to catch up to George Simpson as both of the men headed to the Interior. Archibald Barclay to George Simpson, 5 April 1849, HBCA D.5/25, fo. 74d.
19 Minutes of the General Court of the London Committee, 3 January 1849, HBCA A.1/66, p. 3; Rich, *History*, 2: 553; Rich, *London*, xiv.
20 Rich, *History*, 2: 553–4. He appears to have departed Montreal on 6 May. HBCA B.26/a/1, 12 October 1849.
21 George Simpson, Norway House, to P.S. Ogden, J. Douglas and J. Work, Fort Vancouver, 30 June 1849, HBCA A.11/70, paragraph 5 & 7 (fos. 373, 374–374d).
22 Governor FitzRoy, Auckland, to Lord Stanley, 15 April 1844, *BPP* 1845 (131), 24.
23 Rich, *London*, xiv.
24 George Simpson to the HBC London Governors and Committee, 30 June 1849, HBCA A.12/4, fos. 527d.
25 Minutes of the General Court of the London Committee, 5 September 1849, HBCA A.1/66, p. 85.
26 Adam Thom, Recorder of Rupert's Land, to George Simpson, 26 July 1849, HBCA D.5/25 fo. 413.
27 George Simpson, Lachine, to Governor and Committee, London, 13 October 1849, HBCA A.12/4, fo. 593. This letter and Thom's draft agreement were read at the General Court of the London Governor and Committee, on 31 October 1849. Minutes of the General Court of the London Governor and Committee, 31 October 1849, HBCA A.1/66, p. 107.
28 J.H. Pelly, for self, A. Colvile & George Simpson, Agents to the Puget's Sound Company to James Douglas, 3 August 1849, HBCA B.226/c/1, fos. 13d.
29 HBCA A.11/72, fo. 117.
30 James Douglas, Chief Factor, Fort Victoria to Archibald Barclay, Secretary, Hudson's Bay Company, 3 September 1849 (24th head), HBCA A.11/72, fo. 121d. There are four copies of this letter in HBCA A.11/72. The one

published in Bowsfield (with apparently idiosyncratic spelling) is the first one (at fos. 87–96d). See Bowsfield, *FVL*, 43. The other versions are more neatly written. I quote the neatest version at fos. 117–125.

31 Cole Harris has written that "it is usually assumed that Barclay had not received Douglas's letter of 3 September when he wrote from London in mid-December. However, as the US government had just opened a thirty-five-day postal service from New York to San Francisco via Panama, it had recently become possible to reach London from Victoria in three months." Harris, *Making*, 339n3. The first arrival of the *California*, the first Pacific Mail Steamship Company ship to arrive at San Francisco, was on 28 February 1849. It departed on its first mail run to Panama on 1 May 1849. According to John Haskell Kemble, "from that time forward, the steamers sailed with remarkable regularity, and carried out the service in an effective manner." Kemble, "Genesis," 396, 403. It is implausible, however that Barclay's letter of 17 December 1849 was written in response to Douglas's letter of 3 September. Barclay's letter did not mention Douglas's suggestion and did not acknowledge receipt of Douglas's letter of 3 September. Furthermore, Barclay did not acknowledge the receipt of Douglas's letter of 3 September 1849 and did not respond to the contents of heads 18 and 28 of Douglas's 3 September 1849 letter until 8 February 1850. On 8 February he noted the receipt of copies of the letters of 3 and 24 September via China, on 26 January 1850, with the originals sent together with a letter of 18 October, arriving via Panama and New York, on 5 February. See Archibald Barclay, London, to James Douglas, 8 February 1850, HBCA A.6/28, fo. 96. The minutes of the General Court of the London Committee indicate that Douglas's letter was read at the Meeting of the Committee of 30 January 1850. Minutes of the General Court of the London Committee, 30 January 1850, HBCA A.1/66, p. 147. A perusal of the correspondence suggests that it was usual for correspondence to travel back and forth on the HBC's ships – a voyage of between five and seven months, until 1850, when correspondence routed through San Francisco appears to have made the trip in about 90 days. The last meeting of the General Court of the London Committee before 17 December, was held on 12 December. The minutes of that meeting indicate that a draft of a letter to Douglas "was approved and ordered to be sent by next mail." HBCA A.1/66, p. 130. That was probably the draft of the letter sent on 17 December 1849.

32 Archibald Barclay, London, to James Douglas, Fort Victoria, 17 December 1849, HBCA A.6/28, fo. 91d. A copy of this letter can be found at BCA A/C/20/Vi7.

33 The Governor and Committee ordered that "no time should be lost" in documenting the boundaries of the land occupied by the HBC at the time

of the Oregon Treaty. Governor and Committee, London, to Board of Management, 16 November 1848, HBCA B.201/c/1, fo. 315d.
34 Archibald Barclay, London, to James Douglas, Fort Victoria, 17 December 1849, HBCA A.6/28, fo. 92. It is noteworthy that Douglas appears to have been instructed to pay by population, not by acreage.
35 The internal quote beginning with "the uncivilized inhabitants of any country have but a qualified Dominion over it," originates, of course, with Sir George Gipps's speech of 9 July 1840. It should be remembered that this statement was the focus of some controversy in Great Britain at the time.
36 The term "joint occupation" is a mischaracterization of the treaty terms, which stipulated that the territory would be "free and open ... to the vessels, citizens and subjects, of the two powers." The term "joint occupation," appears to have been coined in 1844.
37 Bowsfield, *FVL*, lxvi–lxvii.
38 Roderick Finlayson had overseen Fort Victoria from 1844 to 1849 but became the fort's accountant when Douglas was transferred to Victoria in 1849. Begg, *History*, 179–80.
39 HBCA B.226/a/1, 29 April 1850 (fo. 175d). William Tolmie was returning to Nisqually after having arrived on 24 April with the news that American customs officials had seized the HBC's *Cadboro* and all of the goods in store at Fort Nisqually for alleged violations of American law. HBCA B.226/a/1, 24 April 1850 (fo. 175); Bowsfield, *FVL*, 96–8. That may have caused more of a stir at Victoria than the treaties did.
40 It appears that James Douglas made no effort to have the newly arrived Governor Richard Blanshard, or the newly arrived Anglican clergyman, Reverend Robert J. Staines, or the settler/surveyor Walter Colquhoun Grant attend the negotiations.
41 HBCA B.226/a/1, 24 March 1850 (fo. 171d), and 25 April 1850 (fo. 175).
42 There had been several snowfalls in March, including a heavy snowfall on 20 March.
43 Mail could have arrived aboard the brig *Sacramento* on 7 April, the steamer *Massachusetts* on 18 April, or by William Tolmie on 24 April.
44 Joseph McKay, Kamloops, to Dr. James S. Helmcken, 3 December 1888, Joseph William McKay Fonds BCA PR-0560, MS-1917, file 27.
45 James Douglas, Victoria, to Archibald Barclay, 15 May 1850, in Bowsfield, *FVL*, 89; HBCA B.226/a/1, 8 May 1850 (fo. 177).
46 Brazier, "Land," 205, and Lutz, "Rutter's," 222.
47 For the letter to Yale, see James Douglas to James Murray Yale, 7 May 1850, James Murray Yale, Correspondence Inward, 1850–59, BCA MS-0105.1. For his appointment, see Archibald Barclay to James Douglas, 3 August 1849, fo. 10d, HBCA B.226/c/1. For his 3 August 1849

360  Notes to pages 167–70

instructions, see J.H. Pelly, for self, A. Colvile & George Simpson, Agents to the Puget Sound Company to James Douglas, 3 August 1849, HBCA B.226/c/1, fo. 13d. When Douglas negotiated the treaties of April and May 1850, he did so as an agent of the HBC. The governor of the colony of Vancouver Island at the time was Richard Blanshard, whose commission was read before "all of the British residents who were at hand," on 10 March 1850. HBCA B.226/a/1, 10 March 1850.

48 Or, given that, as will be shown, the last of those treaties was not concluded until 10 May, he may have felt that he was concealing nothing, since he did meet with at least some chiefs again after receipt of the letter.
49 Graham Brazier, "Land," 205–6; Lutz, "Rutter's," 222.
50 George Simpson, Norway House, to P.S. Ogden, J. Douglas and J. Work, Fort Vancouver, 30 June 1849, HBCA A.11/70, paragraph 5 & 7 (fos. 373, 374–374d).
51 HBCA B.226/a/1, 23 April 1850 (fo. 175).
52 The Fort Rupert journals indicate that Bottineau's party included two miners and eight Indians, including Wawattie. HBCA B.185/a/1, 17 & 18 April 1850 (fo. 53d).
53 Given the sum disbursed, Douglas appears to be referring here to the agreements reached with the Teechamitsa and Swengwhung leaders. On the other hand, Douglas's later estimation of the number of men in the first six signatory communities (Songhees), 122 men, matches his estimate of the number of men in this letter. The published version records the sum incorrectly as £103.4..0.
54 This amount matches the amount expended on the Chilcowitch treaty.
55 The Fort Victoria post journals of 1 May reported that "some furs & provisions were traded today from Kawitichins and others." HBCA B.226/a/1, 1 May 1850 (fo. 176). A party of "Nanaimaults" traded on 3 May.
56 This letter can be found in James Douglas to Archibald Barclay, 16 May 1850, BCA A/C/20/Vi2, 1–3, and in HBCA A.11/72, fos. 246–47. The transcription here is derived from a comparison of those documents. The second version is transcribed in Bowsfield, *FVL*, 94–6. The letter was received in London on 7 August 1850.
57 HBCA B.226/a/1, 4 May 1850 (fo. 176d). The word "repaid" may be struck in the original.
58 HBCA B.226/a/1, 10 May 1850 (fo. 177).
59 Joseph McKay to Dr. James S. Helmcken, 3 December 1888, Joseph William McKay Fonds BCA PR-0560, MS-1917, file 27.
60 James Douglas, Victoria to James Murray Yale, Langley, 7 May 1850, BCA MS-0105.1.
61 James Douglas to Archibald Barclay, 16 May 1853, BCA A/C/20/Vi2.

62 Joseph McKay to Dr. James S. Helmcken, 3 December 1888, Joseph William McKay Fonds BCA PR-0560, MS-1917, file 27.
63 For a brief biography of Thomas Ouamtany, see Watson, *Lives*, 746–7. I agree with those who have concluded that the negotiations were carried out in Lekwungen, not in Chinook jargon. Vallance, "Sharing," 92–4; Vallance, STOLȻEŁ John Elliott, Sr., and George, "SENĆOTEN," 155–6.
64 On this point, see Duff, "Fort," 55.
65 Douglas to Barclay, 26 August 1854, HBCA A.11/75, fo. 281.
66 A.W. Vowell to Deputy Superintendent General of Indian Affairs, 10 April 1893, LAC RG10, Vol. 3688, f. 13866-1.
67 Douglas almost certainly thought of "enclosed" fields as those that had been, by cultivation, converted from "waste" lands. A legal dictionary of the nineteenth century defined "inclosure" as "The extinction of commonable rights in fields and waste lands." Mozley and Whiteley, *Concise*, 203. Especially in the North American context, one need not assume that "enclosed" necessarily meant "fenced": "In every case where one man has a right to exclude another from his real immovable property, the law encircles his estate, if it is not already enclosed, with an imaginary fence." Bouvier, *Law*, 1: 269.
68 Gilbert Malcolm Sproat wrote in 1868 that the Coast Salish of Vancouver Island "have never attempted to increase the production of camas by any kind of cultivation." Suttles, "Coast Salish Resource," 188.
69 Dictionaries of the time define *occupant* as "one who takes or has possession," and "inhabitant" as "one who resides in a place." Reid, *Dictionary*, 282, 221; Walker, *Johnson's*, 376, 293; Webster, *American*, 687, 542.
70 This last possibility seems the least likely, but if Douglas was influenced by the instructions of 17 December 1849, he may have meant that. However, in that case, one might have expected him to use the language of the 17 December letter, either referring to the date or using the word *sovereignty*.
71 Begg, *History*, 187.
72 Reid, *Dictionary*, 164. Others show that a fishery could be an occupation and a place. For example, see "the business or employment of catching fish; a place where fishing is practiced." Worcester, *Universal and Critical Dictionary*, 280, and Webster, *American*, 497.
73 Walker, *Johnson's*, 213.
74 Coan, "First," 76
75 Kappler, *Indian*, 2: 662, 670, 674, 682.
76 The fact that the nine eventual written versions of the treaties correspond to the nine "families" listed in the enumeration, confirms that Douglas must have depended upon these numbers when he negotiated the purchases.

77 Banner, *Possessing*, 75.
78 A few examples will suffice. A newspaper account of the 1865 (unratified) treaty between the government of the United States and the Blackfeet and Gros Ventre noted that "in conclusion, the treaty was signed, each chief touching the pen in turn as a token of his assent." M. "The Treaty with the Blackfeet," *The Montana Post* (Virginia City), 9 December 1865, 1. In 1879, Constantine Scollen recalled that when Treaty No. 7 was concluded in 1877, because the Indigenous signatories "could not write they were made to touch the pen which was equivalent to signing their names." Scollen family fonds, Glenbow Archives M4343, Constantine Scollen, Fort Macleod to Major A.G. Irvine, Asst Comm. NWMP (Fort Walsh), 13 April 1879. See DeMaillie, "Touching," 171–83.
79 See the note to that effect in BCA A/C/20/Vi2, 1.

## 9. The Treaty of Akaroa and Fort Victoria Treaties, 1848–1850

1 See "Copy of the Correspondence between the Chairman of the Hudson's Bay Company and the Secretary of State for the Colonies Relative to the Colonization of Vancouver's Island," in Great Britain. Parliament. House of Lords. *Sessional Papers*, Vol. 9 *Accounts and Papers*, 501–18, and *BPP* 1849 (1120), 365–500.
2 Shortland, *Southern*, vii.
3 Evison, *Ngai Tahu*, 19.
4 Edward Shortland, "Copy of a Report from E. Shortland, Exq., Sub-Protector of Aborigines to the Chief Protector," 18 March 1844, in Mackay, *Compendium*, 2: 125. Successful cultivation of kumara on the South Island required planting and storage techniques not used by Māori or Polynesians elsewhere. See Bassett, Gordon, Nobes, and Jacomb, "Gardening," 185–218. For potato cultivation see Challis, *Ka Pakihi*, 57.
5 Shortland, *Southern*, 136, 221.
6 When a party led by the sub-protector of Aborigines, Edward Shortland, left their tent in 1843–4 at Otakou, at the Otago Peninsula, they felt comfortable "merely taking the precaution to leave a written notice in 'maori,' saying to whom they belonged; we thus felt confident that, although they must remain for several days with no other protector than this paper sentinel, none of the natives – the only persons likely to come this way – would meddle with our property." Shortland, *Southern*, 166.
7 Evison, *Ngai Tahu*, 18–19.
8 Evison, *Ngai Tahu*, 20.
9 Evison, *Ngai Tahu*, 26.
10 Evison, "Wentworth-Jones."
11 George Grey to Earl Grey, 17 March 1848, *BPP* 1848 (1002), 105.

Notes to pages 180–3 363

12 Dieffenbach, *New Zealand*, 16.
13 Evison, *Ngai Tahu*, 35. Tuhawaiki ("Bloody Jack") was a Ngāi Tahu signatory to the Treaty of Waitangi. His son, Kihau (Tuhawaiki having drowned in 1844) was a signatory by proxy to the Kemp Deed.
14 Earl Grey to George Grey, 30 November 1848, and two enclosures, *BPP* 1849 (1120), 109–11; Foster, "Akaroa, French Settlement," https://teara.govt.nz/en/1966/akaroa-french-settlement-at (accessed 1 October 2020). Edward Shortland later told Ngāi Tahu that the French purchase was void because it had come after Hobson's declaration of British sovereignty. Shortland, *Southern*, 252.
15 Selwyn, *Journal*, 119–20.
16 Shortland, *Southern*, 252–3.
17 Edward Shortland Journal, 11 February 1844, "Edward Shortland Journal, Middle Island of New Zealand, 16 January to 6 March 1844," Hocken Library, University of Otago, PC-0023.
18 George Grey, Wellington to Earl Grey, 25 August 1848, "Further Papers Relative," *BPP* 1849 (1120), 40–1. Eyre, like Grey, was convinced that Ngāi Tahu were willing, even eager, to sell their land. E. Eyre to George Grey, 5 July 1848, *BPP* 1849 (1120), 46. Eyre was appointed Lieutenant-Governor of New Munster in 1846 but arrived there only in July 1847. He is generally regarded as having been sympathetic with Māori, but his relations with Grey were always bad. He resigned in 1853. Geoffrey Dutton, "Edward John Eyre (1815–1901)," *ADB*; Handford, "Edward John Eyre," 829.
19 *Wellington Independent*, 12 January 1848, 1.
20 George Grey, Auckland to Eyre, 8 April 1848, *BPP* 1849 (1120), 41–2. Also published in *Appendix to the Journals of the House of Representatives of New Zealand* (hereafter *AJHRNZ*), 1888, I.—8, pp. 7–8. For a discussion of the Otago purchase, see Evison, *Ngai Tahu*, 44–61.
21 Eyre to Wakefield, 25 April 1848, *AJHRNZ*, 1888, I.—8, pp. 8–9.
22 William Gisborne, Wellington, Secretary to Edward Eyre, to H.T. Kemp, 25 April 1848, in *AJHRNZ*, 1888, I.—8, p. 8. Emphasis in the original.
23 Selwyn, *Journal*, 119.
24 *Wellington Independent*, 21 June 1848, 3.
25 *Wellington Independent*, 21 June 1848, 3
26 *New Zealand Spectator and Cook's Strait Guardian*, 21 June 1848, 2.
27 *New Zealand Spectator and Cook's Strait Guardian*, 21 June 1848, 2. A cession of the west coast of the island was negotiated in the Arahura Treaty of 21 May 1860.
28 Evison, *Ngai Tahu*, 90.
29 Evison, *Ngai Tahu*, 89–95. Readers should understand that this treaty has been the subject of considerable dispute since 1848. I do not intend here to take a position among the conflicting interpretations of the agreement,

but to present the essential details for those who are interested primarily in understanding the Vancouver Island treaties.
30. Attwood, *Empire*, 172; Evison, "Wentworth-Jones."
31. *Wellington Independent*, 29 April 1848, 2; 21 June 1848, 3.
32. H. Tacy Kemp, Commissioner, Wellington, to William Gisborne, Private Secretary, 19 June 1848, *BPP* 1849 (1120), 42. Also published in *AJHRNZ*, 1888, I.—8, p. 9.
33. Kemp appears to be using the Māori word *pa* in a general sense to mean "village," although the term *pā* (*pah*) is particularly associated with fortified villages. The term *kāinga nohoanga* is used in the treaty.
34. In his English translation of the treaty, Kemp used *plantations* as a translation of *mahinga kai* (food-gathering places.)
35. H. Tacy Kemp, Commissioner, Wellington, to William Gisborne, Private Secretary, 20 June 1848, *BPP* 1849 (1120), 42. Also published in *AJHRNZ*, 1888, I.—8, pp. 9–10.
36. H. Tacy Kemp, Commissioner, Wellington, to William Gisborne, Private Secretary, 21 June 1848, *BPP* 1849 (1120), 43. Also published in *AJHRNZ*, 1888, I.—8, p. 10.
37. "Further Papers Relative to the Affairs of New Zealand," 413. The same report was also published in a stand-alone volume, in which the treaty appears on page 43. The fact that other published versions of the treaty differ slightly seems to suggest that the HBC obtained its version of the treaty from that report or from the New Zealand Company. New Zealand, Parliament, House of Representatives, "Deeds of Purchase of Land in the Middle Island," (18 June 1858) *AJHRNZ*, 1858, C.—4, p. 2; New Zealand, Parliament, House of Representatives, "Middle Island Native Claims," *AJHRNZ*, 1888, I.—8, p. 10. The Māori and English versions were published in *AJHRNZ*, 1871, F.—7, pp. 3–4. For more of the controversy, see *AJHRNZ*, 1921, G.—5, pp. 27–40. Ten land deeds dated between 1844 and 1864 cover the South Island of New Zealand. The wording of these ten deeds differs sufficiently to allow a firm conclusion that the Kemp Deed of 12 June 1848 served as the template for the Vancouver Island Treaties. Subsequently, slightly different translations of the Kemp Deed were published. See *AJHRNZ*, 1858, C.—4, p. 2, which includes the names of the forty Māori signatories. For the Kemp Deed, see Evison, *Ngai Tahu*, especially chapter 5 ("Kemp's Deed") 81–98.
38. The number must be regarded as an estimate only, since Kemp recorded population numbers ending in zero or five only.
39. William Gisborne to Kemp, 21 June 1848, *AJHRNZ*, 1888, I.—8, p. 10.
40. William Gisborne to Kemp, 21 June 1848, *AJHRNZ*, 1888, I.—8, pp. 10–11.
41. William Gisborne to Kemp, 21 June 1848, *AJHRNZ*, 1888, I.—8, p. 11.
42. William Gisborne to Kemp, 21 June 1848, *AJHRNZ*, 1888, I.—8, p. 11.

43 William Gisborne to Kemp, 21 June 1848, *AJHRNZ*, 1888, I.—8, p. 11. For deeds made out in 1839, see *AJHRNZ*, 1888, I.—8, pp. 57–60.
44 William Gisborne to Kemp, 21 June 1848, *AJHRNZ*, 1888, I.—8, p. 11. The documentary record implies that Eyre subsequently discovered that the Crown Solicitor was responsible for this error.
45 William Gisborne to Kemp, 21 June 1848, *AJHRNZ*, 1888, I.—8, pp. 11–12.
46 William Gisborne to Kemp, 21 June 1848, *AJHRNZ*, 1888, I.—8, p. 12.
47 William Gisborne to George Grey, 5 July 1848, *BPP* 1849 (1120), 44. Also published in William Gisborne to Kemp, 21 June 1848, *AJHRNZ*, 1888, I.—8, pp. 12–13.
48 William Gisborne to George Grey, 5 July 1848, *BPP* 1849 (1120), 44–5. Also published in William Gisborne to Kemp, 21 June 1848, *AJHRNZ*, 1888, I.—8, p. 13.
49 William Gisborne, Private Secretary, Wellington to Walter Mantell, 2 August 1848, *AJHRNZ*, 1888, I.—8, p. 14. Walter Mantell, was, according to his biographer, a man of high ethical standards, who argued relentlessly that the promises to Māori should be kept. M.P.K. Sorrenson. "Mantell, Walter Baldock Durrant," *DNZB* online. He was the son of the celebrated geologist Gideon Algernon Mantell. He went to New Zealand in 1839. Mantell published "The Geology of the Middle Island of New Zealand," *New Zealand Magazine* (1850).
50 William Gisborne, Private Secretary, Wellington to Walter Mantell, 2 August 1848, *AJHRNZ*, 1888, I.—8, p. 14.
51 William Gisborne, Private Secretary, Wellington to Walter Mantell, 2 August 1848, *AJHRNZ*, 1888, I.—8, p. 15.
52 *Wellington Independent*, 9 August 1848, 3.
53 George Grey, Wellington to Earl Grey, 25 August 1848, "Further Papers Relative," *BPP* 1849 (1120), 41.
54 Burns, *Fatal*, 292–5.
55 Walter Mantell, Commissioner for Extinguishing Native Claims, Wellington, to Alfred Domett, Colonial Secretary of New Munster, 30 January 1849, *AJHRNZ, 1858*, C.—3, pp. 3–7. Matiahha Tiramorehu's complaint about the purchase, as early as 7 February 1849, appeared in newspapers. Mackay, *Compendium*, 2: 77. Also see the letter from Matiaha Tiramorehu, to Eyre in *AJHRNZ, 1858*, C.—3, pp. 9–10. The report is also published in *AJHRNZ*, 1888, I.—8, pp. 16–19. Mantell returned to Wellington on 27 January 1849.
56 *AJHRNZ, 1858*, C.—3, p. 8, Sorrenson, "Mantell, Walter Baldock Durrant," *DNZB* online. Mantell's enumeration of Ngāi Tahu is substantially smaller than Kemp's estimate of 920, but Mantell's detailed enumeration, based on a visit to each community, should be regarded as more reliable than Kemp's. For Mantell's enumeration, see *AJHRNZ, 1858*, C.—3,

p. 8. Mantell later testified that he knew that Lieutenant-Governor Eyre would have approved larger reserves, but that "Governor Grey would have taken a directly contrary view of it; and the Governor-in-Chief was a more important person for an unfortunate Government officer to look to." Testimony of Walter Mantell, 24 July 1888, *AJHRNZ*, 1888, I.—8, p. 92.

57 Walter Mantell, London, to Herman Merivale, Under-Secretary, 31 July 1856, *AJHRNZ*, 1888, I.—8, p., 22.
58 Testimony of W. Mantell, 24 July 1888, *AJHRNZ*, 1888, I.—8, p. 88.
59 Testimony of W. Mantell, 24 July 1888, *AJHRNZ*, 1888, I.—8, p. 88.
60 Eyre to William Fox, 26 February 1849, *AJHRNZ*, 1888, I.—8, p. 20.
61 See *AJHRNZ*, 1858, C.—4, 4–6.
62 Testimony of W. Mantell, 24 July 1888, *AJHRNZ*, 1888, I.—8, p. 90.
63 George Grey, Auckland, to Earl Grey, London, 10 February 1849, *BPP* 1849 (1120), 71. Also published *AJHRNZ*, 1888, I.—8, p. 16.
64 F.D. Fenton, Native Land Court, "Report on the Petition ..." *AJHRNZ*, 1888, I.—8, p. 30. In 1876, Kemp submitted a memorandum in response to these assertions that stated that "I am not aware that I made use of any threat or intimidation whatever on the occasion of the cession of the land comprised within what is commonly known as Kemp's Deed." *AJHRNZ*, 1888, I.—8, p. 40. Fenton responded by stating that he doubted that Kemp had threatened Ngāi Tahu, but that Kemp had probably told Ngāi Tahu that selling the land would increase their security from their northern neighbours. *AJHRNZ*, 1888, I.—8, p. 32. It is likely that Ngāi Tahu were intimidated by the very fact that the Ngāti Toa chiefs had already sold, in the Wairau Purchase, lands that Ngāi Tahu claimed as theirs.
65 F.D. Fenton, Native Land Court, "Report on the Petition ..." *AJHRNZ*, 1888, I.—8, p. 30.
66 H.K. Taiaroa, "Statement of Tairoa ...," 26 October 1876, Wellington, *AJHRNZ*, 1888, I.—8, pp. 40–5.
67 Pipi (*Paphies australis*) are mollusks common in sandy and silty beaches and estuaries.
68 Fenton, *AJHRNZ*, 1888, I.—8, p. 32; *AJHRNZ*, 1888, I.—8, p. 68.
69 A note in the letter book indicates that it was received on 7 August. BCA A/C/20/Vi2, 1.
70 Barclay, London, to Douglas, Victoria, 16 August 1850, HBCA A.6/28, fo. 159d.
71 Barclay, London, to Douglas, Victoria, 16 August 1850, HBCA A.6/28, fo. 161d.
72 Many still assume that the ownership of the land was actually conveyed to the HBC by the treaty. In fact, despite the language, the land became Crown land.

73 Walter Colquhoun Grant, who was unreliable and apparently incompetent, had resigned as surveyor on 25 March 1850. The colony did not get a reliable surveyor until Joseph Despard Pemberton arrived on 25 June 1851. See Richard Mackie, "Joseph Despard Pemberton," in *DCB*.
74 Douglas to Barclay, 16 November 1850, HBCA A.11/72, fo. 354.
75 HBCA B.226/a/1, 29 April 1850 (fo. 175d).
76 See Gunther, "Klallam," 171–314; Eells, "Twana," 605–81; Suttles, "Central," 454, 456.
77 Duff, "Fort," 52.
78 Duff articulated the same point; Duff, "Fort," 54–5.
79 Duff also appears to have considered this possibility. Duff, "Fort," 53–4.
80 Boxberger, "Comparison"; Miller and Boxberger, "Creating," 275–6; Boxberger and Taylor, "Treaty," 40–5.
81 James Douglas to Earl Grey, 15 April 1852, CO 305/3, no. 6485, fos. 104–104d.
82 Minute by "HM, Jy 19," on James Douglas to Earl Grey, 15 April 1852, CO 305/3, no. 6485, fo. 108d.
83 The treaty register is found at BCA MS-0772.
84 BCA MS-0772. In this numbering, the inside of the cover is considered page 1. These pages do not correspond to the pages in the digital version of this book available online at the time of writing because the pages left blank in the original volume are not included in the digital version.
85 Considering that scenarios other than the one presented here might suggest considerably different interpretations of the significance of the written treaties, much effort was expended to try to confirm and falsify all scenarios. Scholars have too confidently come to the same conclusion as that presented here, and discounted the possibility, how ever remote, that, although a "blank sheet" was produced in April and May 1850, the chiefs and others were summoned again in November 1850 to confirm their agreement to the written version by signing the treaties in the book that exists today. Unfortunately, rather than clinching any particular interpretation, the handwriting in the treaties only adds a new mystery. Wilson Duff's conclusion that much of the handwriting in the treaty books is James Douglas's (Duff, "Fort," 8–9) is problematic. The handwriting in Douglas's private papers seems distinctly different from all of the handwriting in the treaties. But the handwriting in these nine treaties is puzzling. In each of the nine treaties, the handwriting changes abruptly in mid-sentence at approximately the same place. In each of them the first part of the treaty is written in one hand, and the rest of the treaty text is in a different hand. (In seven of the treaties, "surrender" is the last word written in the first hand. In the first treaty one more word, "entirely," and in the second treaty, one fewer word, is written in this hand.) Then, the handwriting changes again at the bottom of each treaty

when the place, date, and the names of the signatories and witnesses are recorded. Wilson Duff implied that the words in the first writer's hand were written before Douglas received the template treaty, and the words in the second writer's hand were written afterwards. (Duff, "Fort," 11, 19, and especially 21.) But it is inconceivable that Douglas knew, or could have guessed, the first twenty-five unique words of the template treaty before November 1850. There can be no doubt that, although they were written in two hands, all of the main treaty text in all nine cases was written after 16 November 1850. However, above the main treaty text of all but one of the treaties are words almost certainly written in April and May of 1850. Why each of the treaties was copied in two different hands is a mystery. Unfortunately, if the Fort Victoria official post journal ever mentioned what actions Douglas took after receiving the template treaties we will never know, because all Fort Victoria journals after the first volume (ending on 28 May 1850) have almost certainly been destroyed. For discussions, see see Simmons, *Keepers*, 140–2; and Binnema and Ens, *Edmonton: 1826–1834*, xiii–xvii.

86 In 1838, an expert on conveyancing advised notaries on how to ensure compliance with statutes passed in 1579 and 1681 when they served people who were unable to write. It suggested including a note stating: "We A.B. and C.D., notaries-public and co-notaries in the premises, at the desire of the before named and designed E.F., who declares he cannot write by reason of, (state the cause,) and he having, in token of his warrant and authority to us, touched each of our pens respectively, in presence of the witnesses before named and designed, do subscribe for him, before and in presence of the said witnesses." Duff, *Treatise*, 14–15. Also see Menzies, *Conveyancing*, 106–7, 113; and Bell, *Lectures*, 1: 32, 38, 40.

87 Margaret A. Ormsby, "Introduction," in Bowsfield, *FVL*, lvi.

88 In "Reminiscences of 1850," someone who arrived on the *Norman Morison* in March 1850, very likely J.S. Helmcken, provided a detailed description of his experiences and impressions upon arrival at Victoria, but did not mention the treaties. See Begg, *History*, 213–19.

89 HBCA B.226/a/1, 10 March 1850; Richard Blanshard, Victoria to Earl Grey, 8 April 1850, CO 305/2, no. 5505, p 49; HBCA A.11/72, fos. 205–205d, James Douglas to Archibald Barclay, 3 April 1850.

90 Richard Blanshard, Victoria to Earl Grey, 8 April 1850, CO 305/2, no. 5505, p 49.

91 Richard Blanshard, Victoria to Earl Grey, 8 April 1850, CO 305/2, no. 5505, p. 50.

92 Richard Blanshard, Victoria to Earl Grey, 15 June 1850, CO 305/2, no. 7378, p. 57.

93 Richard Blanshard, Victoria to Earl Grey, 15 June 1850, CO 305/2, no. 7378, p. 57–8.
94 Blanshard to Earl Grey, 10 July 1850, CO 305/2, No. 9152, p. 69.
95 James Douglas, Victoria, to Archibald Barclay, 29 January 1851, HBCA A.11/73, fo. 38. On 16 April 1851, Archibald Barclay had indicated that the wages and other expenses of Fort Rupert were to be billed to the colony, "at the invoice prices with the advance of 33.⅓ p cent." Archibald Barclay to James Douglas, 16 April 1851, HBCA A.6/29, fos. 66d–67. On 29 January 1851, Douglas asked Barclay whether he should bill the colony "our Cash Tariff, which is over 200 per Cent on the London cost," or "at the District Transfer price 33⅓ p cent." James Douglas to Archibald Barclay, 29 January 1851, HBCA A.11/73, fos. 36–40d (paragraph 11). The fact that he already used the inflated expenditures in the written versions of the treaties suggests that Douglas had intended to use the higher tariffs. Obviously, that is what he did, before receiving any instructions from London.
96 James Douglas to Archibald Barclay, 29 January 1851, HBCA A.11/73, fo. 38d.
97 Blanshard to Earl Grey, 18 November, CO 305/2,
98 Blanshard to Earl Grey, 12 February 1851, CO 305/2, no. 4441, p. 6.
99 Blanshard to Earl Grey, 12 February 1851, CO 305/2, no. 4441, pp. 7–8. The HBC had two tariffs. Indigenous People and the company's own employees paid a 33⅓ per cent markup on what the company paid for the goods in London. To all others the company charged what the market could bear. Given the inflated prices prevailing along the entire west coast of North America brought on by the California gold rush, the HBC was charging about three times the London prices. Blanshard was arguing that the colony of Vancouver Island should not be required to pay the higher prices.
100 J.H. Pelly to Earl Grey, 12 June 1851, CO 305/3, no. 5122, fos. 378–78d.
101 Herman Merivale, memorandum written on J.H. Pelly to Earl Grey, 12 June 1851, CO 305/3, no. 5122, fos. 378–79.
102 Benjamin Hawes to J.H. Pelly, 26 June 1851, CO 305/3, no. 5122, fos. 380d–383. The HBC did eventually include the "Amount paid to Indians in liquidation of claims in Land held by them," in its statements of the accounts of the colony, and, although the government challenged the legitimacy of some of their expenditures, it appears to have paid the cost of the treaties. See "The Statement of Accounts, Vancouver's Island Colony" 31 January 1858" CO 305/15, fo. 380d; John Shepherd, Governor of HBC to Henry Labouchere, 24 February 1858, CO 305/9, no. 1987, fos. 440–440d.

## 10. The Fort Rupert Treaties of 1850 and 1851

1 Bowsfield, *FVL*, xxxviii.
2 James Douglas to Governor and Committee, 3 September 1849, HBCA A.11/72, fo. 124.
3 James Douglas to Archibald Barclay, 16 November 1850, HBCA A.11/72, fo. 355.
4 See Galois, *Kwakwaka'wakw*, 196–7, 214; Boas, *Ethnology*, 973, 976–7; Gough, *Gunboat*, 38; Wilson Duff's notes also indicate that "When HBC established Ft. Rupert, these 4 tribes amalgamated and moved there." (1966). For a discussion of how the sites of villages were fluid, see Boas, *Kwakiutl*, 44–6.
5 Excerpt from Captain George Henry Richard's Journal, 1860 to 1862, HMS *Plumper* & HMS *Hecate*, 11 April 1862, as quoted in Dorricott and Cullon, *Private*, 160.
6 Drucker, *Indians*, 138. Unfortunately, Drucker's *Indians* does not include citations, but an unpaginated page in the frontmatter of the book indicates that Drucker did fieldwork on Vancouver Island in the early 1930s.
7 Drucker, *Indians*, 139. Drucker pointed to a similar development at Fort Simpson but indicated that it did not seem to occur at other places on Vancouver Island.
8 Kobrinsky, "Dynamics," 38.
9 HBCA B.185/a/1. 11, 23, 28, 31 May 1849; 1, 4, 15, 30 June; 8, 17, 18, 21, 22, 27 July; 3, 6, 30 August; 2, 5, 6 8, 9, 16, 17, 19, 22 September; 10, 28, 30 October; and 2, 3, 4, 6, 10, 11, 18 November 1849; 9 April 1850; HBCA A.11/72, fos. 193d–195, James Douglas to Archibald Barclay, 7 February 1850.
10 HBCA B.185/a/1, 23 April 1850.
11 HBCA B.185/a/1, 12 May 1849.
12 An incomplete list includes HBCA B.185/a/1, 12, 18, 22 May; 1, 6 June; 6, 7, 9, July; 19 September; 19, 20, 23, 27, 28, 30 November 1849.
13 HBCA B.185/a/1, 23 November 1849.
14 HBCA B.185/a/1, 10 October 1849.
15 James Douglas, Victoria to Archibald Barclay, 17 August 1850, HBCA A.11/72, fo. 292d–293.
16 George Blenkinsop to James Douglas, 24 January 1851, HBCA D.5/30.
17 Helen Codere suggested that Kwakiutl themselves told her that the establishment of Fort Rupert led to a reduction in warfare. Codere, *Fighting*, 11–25.
18 George Blenkinsop to James Douglas, 24 January 1851, HBCA D.5/30.
19 Barclay to Douglas, London, 16 August 1850, HBCA A.6/28, fos. 159–159d. Douglas subsequently informed the Committee that reports of

coal at Quatsino were incorrect. Douglas to Barclay, 16 November 1850, HBCA A.11/72, fo. 357d.
20 Barclay to Douglas, London, 23 August 1850, HBCA A.6/28, fo. 163.
21 George Simpson, Norway House to Governor and Committee, London, 26 June 1850, HBCA A.12/5, para. 11 (fos. 140–140d).
22 James Douglas to Governor and Committee, 16 November 1850, HBCA A.11/72, fo. 359. It is unlikely that Douglas forgot about Blenkinsop's purchase, since, in the very same letter, he mentioned that the HBC had cleared and cultivated about three acres of land at Fort Rupert.
23 Fort Rupert Post Journals, HBCA B.185/a/1, 15 April 1850.
24 Moodie, "Agriculture and the Fur Trade," 39–58. For the beginnings of gardening on the prairies see Binnema and Ens, *Edmonton, 1806–1821*, 71–3. As early as 1833, the HBC cultivated about 35 acres of crops, and pastured hundreds of horses and cattle at Fort Edmonton. See HBCA B.60/a/27, 30 April 1833. The company also introduced cattle at Fort Carlton and Fort Edmonton in 1830. HBCA D.4/125, fo. 87.
25 On 25 August 1849, James Douglas instructed William McNeill that "it is however understood that the conduct and management of these men, while employed at their trade, is to be left to the Oversman, a practical man who understands the business and can work them to the greatest advantage. Douglas to McNeill, 25 August 1849, HBCA A.11/72, fos. 85–85d.
26 George Simpson, Norway House, to Chief Factors P.S. Ogden, J. Douglas, & J. Work, Board of Management, Fort Vancouver, 24 June 1848, HBCA D.4/69, p. 772.
27 John Muir Jr., Archibald Muir, John McGregor, John Smith, Robert Muir, Andrew Muir, and Michael Muir, Beaver Harbour, to James Douglas, Fort Victoria, 27 March 1850, HBCA A.11/72, fo. 233.
28 James Douglas, Victoria to Archibald Barclay, 16 April 1851, HBCA A.11/73, fo. 106d.
29 George Simpson, Norway House, to Board of Management, Fort Vancouver, 30 June 1849, HBCA D.4/70, fo. 254–254d.
30 Andrew Muir, Diary, Andrew Muir fonds, BCA PR-1553 (E/B/M91), 44d; HBCA B.185/a/1, 23–4 September 1849. A comparison of the documents written by the miners, most of which were evidently written retrospectively, and the Fort Rupert journals, which were updated each day, shows that in many respects, the documents corroborate each other, although the HBC journals and correspondence, because they were recorded at the time, provide a more reliable record of the timing of events and developments. Still, the miners' records provide some evidence not contained in the journals.
31 Daniel T. Gallacher, "Andrew Muir," *DCB*, http://www.biographi.ca/en/bio/muir_andrew_8E.html; Nesbitt, "Diary," 101.

32  HBCA B.185/a/1, 26 & 28 September 1849; Andrew Muir, Diary, BCA PR-1553 (E/B/M91), fo. 45.
33  Andrew Muir, Diary, BCA PR-1553 (E/B/M91), fos. 45d–46.
34  An incomplete list includes HBCA B.185/a/1, 25, 26, 27, 29 October, 2, 3, 12, 13, 16, 24 November, 8 December 1849, and 10 February, 22 April 1850. The employment of Indigenous people with the miners appears to have begun just as the deliveries of coal were ending.
35  Reminiscences of Michael Muir, BCA E/B/M91,2, p. 15.
36  HBCA B.185/a/1, 6 October 1849.
37  J.S. Helmcken, "Fort Rupert in 1850," *Victoria Daily Colonist*, 1 January 1890, 4. Also found in Blakey-Smith, *Reminiscences*, 299.
38  HBCA B.185/a/1, 10 October 1849.
39  HBCA B.185/a/1, 16 October 1849.
40  HBCA B.185/a/1, 17 November 1849.
41  HBCA B.185/a/1, 21, 28 November 1849.
42  HBCA B.185/a/1, 25 October 1849.
43  HBCA B.185/a/1, 29 October 1849.
44  HBCA B.185/a/1, 31 October 1849. The words in angled brackets are inserted above the line in the journal.
45  Andrew Muir, Diary, BCA PR-1553 (E/B/M91), 46d–47d.
46  Eden Colvile, Victoria, to J.H. Pelly, London, 6 February 1850, HBCA A.12/13, fos. 13–13d.
47  James Douglas, Fort Victoria to Archibald Barclay, 8 April 1850, HBCA A.11/72, fo. 231.
48  Douglas to Barclay, 3 July 1850, HBCA A.11/72, fo. 272 (first quote); and James Douglas, Fort Victoria to Archibald Barclay, 8 April 1850, HBCA A.11/72, fo. 231(second quote).
49  Douglas to Barclay, 3 July 1850, HBCA A.11/72, fo. 272.
50  Reminiscences of Michael Muir, BCA E/B/M91,2, pp. 13–14.
51  HBCA B.185/a/1, 15 April 1850. A "Quakeeolth" word list made by James Douglas a decade before this purchase indicated that "Laweela" meant "Done, no longer expended," and "Susanay" meant "speak." James Douglas Diary, 13 September 1840, BCA A/B/40/D75.2, (p. 58).
52  James Douglas to Archibald Barclay, 8 April 1850, HBCA A.6/28, fo. 146.
53  Andrew Muir, Diary, BCA PR-1553 (E/B/M91), fo. 47d.
54  HBCA B.185/a/1, 16 April 1850.
55  James Douglas to Archibald Barclay, 24 February 1851, HBCA A.11/73, fos. 72–72d.
56  Blanshard to Earl Grey, 10 July 1850, CO 305/2, no. 9152, p. 68.
57  Andrew Muir, Diary, BCA PR-1553 (E/B/M91) fos. 53–53d, 54.
58  Andrew Muir, Diary, BCA PR-1553 (E/B/M91), fo. 54d.
59  Andrew Muir, Diary, BCA PR-1553 (E/B/M91), fo. 55d.

Notes to pages 210–14   373

60  Andrew Muir, Diary, BCA PR-1553 (E/B/M91), fos. 61–61d; James Douglas to Archibald Barclay, 3 July 1850, HBCA A.11/72, fos. 271–272. For a history of the miners' strike see Sellers, "Negotiations," 14–23.
61  J.S. Helmcken, "Vancouver Island – Courts, Magistrate's Court, Fort Rupert – Diary, June 27–August 20, 1850, "Fort Rupert Reports to Governor Blanshard, July 2 and 17, 1850, Vancouver Island Magistrates Court," BCA C/AA/40.3/R3, 16 July 1850 (p. 26).
62  Helmcken, "Vancouver Island," BCA C/AA/40.3/R3, p. 28.
63  Blanshard to Earl Grey, 18 August 1850, CO 305/2, no. 9564, pp. 77–8.
64  See Gough, *Gunboat*, 41–9; Galois, *Kwakwaka'wakw*, 423–6.
65  Earl Grey to Richard Blanshard, 20 March 1851, LAC RG7-G-8-C/1, pp 16–18. Grey appears here to acknowledge that the ability of the British to exercise authority over Vancouver Island was limited. Jane Samson has shown that British authority was constrained even into the 1860s. Samson, "British," 39–63.
66  James Douglas to Archibald Barclay, 24 February 1851, HBCA A.11/73, fos. 77–77d. As is the case with Fort Victoria, only one post journal has survived at Fort Rupert. However, the journals for the period of the treaty negotiations do not exist. The *Beaver* was anchored at Fort Rupert from 6 to 13 February 1851, and Charles Dodd, the master of the *Beaver*, served as witness to the treaty, but the ship's logs do not mention the treaty. HBCA C.1/208, fos. 54–55. It would have been out of character, however, for a ship's log to record information not directly related to the operations of the ship. Douglas must have initially left the treaty document at Fort Rupert for he acknowledged receiving it from Blenkinsop on 7 March. James Douglas, Victoria, to George Blenkinsop, Fort Rupert, 7 March 1851, HBCA B.226/b/3, fo. 64d.
67  Most scholarly maps of the Fort Rupert treaties misleadingly suggest that they covered overlapping areas. See Cook, *To Share*, 11.
68  Lord, "How," 21.
69  Codere, "Kwakiutl," 361. Robert Galois grouped the Kweeha, Kwakiutl, Komkiutis, and Walas Kwakiutl together as the "Kwakiutl," and grouped the Walas Kwakiutl and Lakwilala together. See Galois, *Kwakwaka'wakw*, 188–222.
70  The *Beaver*'s log makes no mention of the treaty.
71  According to Douglas's list, the "Quakeeolth" men with beards were 65 per cent of the total male population (130/200), and the "Quakeeoth" adults were about 65.5 per cent of the total adult population (270/412). However, the "Quakeeolth" signatories were about 57 per cent of the signatories (15/26). They received about 57 per cent of the compensation (86/150). So, blankets were evidently distributed in equal numbers to each chief, not to each family or individual. They were paid £1.18.00 per chief at the Department price.

72 James Douglas, Victoria to Archibald Barclay, London, 18 August 1851, HBCA A.11/73, fo. 158d.
73 James Douglas to Archibald Barclay, 11 July 1852, HBCA A.11/73, fo. 503.
74 Archibald Barclay to P.S. Ogden, 13 December 1850 and Archibald Barclay to James Douglas, 6 December 1850, HBCA A.11/69, fo. 20d and 23d.
75 Rich, *London*, 145n.
76 Bowsfield, *FVL*, lxxix.
77 James Douglas to Archibald Barclay, 3 September 1851, HBCA A.11/73, fo. 174, (with copy at 173). In 1852, Douglas wrote that "Suquash 7 miles south of Fort Rupert ... furnished all the coal sold by the Indians at Fort Rupert." James Douglas to Archibald Barclay, 18 March 1852, HBCA A.11/73, fo. 398.
78 James Douglas to Archibald Barclay, 6 October 1851, HBCA A.11/73, fo.186.
79 James Douglas to Archibald Barclay, 24 November 1851, HBCA A.11/73, fos. 214–214d; Boyd Gilmour, Fort Rupert, to D. Landale, Edinburgh, 2 March 1852, HBCA A.11/73, fo. 31; James Douglas to Archibald Barclay, 11 July 1852, HBCA A.11/73, fos. 502–503; Boyd Gilmour, Fort Rupert to Board of Management, 27 September 1852, HBCA A.11/73, fo. 587–587d. In Douglas's 11 July 1852 letter to Barclay, Douglas indicates that Gilmour began his third bore at Suquash on 8 March 1852.
80 James Douglas to Archibald Barclay,18 March 1852, HBCA A.11/73, fo. 398.
81 Boyd Gilmour, Fort Rupert to Board of Management, 27 September 1852, HBCA A.11/73, fo. 587–587d.
82 James Douglas, Victoria, to Archibald Barclay, 21 March 1853, HBCA A.11/74, fo. 93–93d.
83 James Douglas, Victoria to Archibald Barclay, 21 September 1853, HBCA A.11/74, fo. 336.
84 James Douglas to Archibald Barclay, 18 March 1852, HBCA A.11/73, fo. 400d, and BCA A/C/20/Vi2, 43–4 (paras. 13 and 14).
85 HBCA B.5/35, fo. 265, George Blenkinsop to George Simpson, 23 November 1853.
86 James Douglas, Victoria to Archibald Barclay, London, 18 August 1851, HBCA A.11/73, fo. 158d.
87 James Douglas, Victoria to Archibald Barclay, London, 15 June 1853, HBCA A.11/74, fo. 205–205d.
88 James Douglas, Victoria to Archibald Barclay, 21 November 1853, HBCA A.11/74, fo. 423d; James Douglas, Victoria to Archibald Barclay, 3 April 1854, HBCA A.11/75, fo. 113d.

## 11. Governor James Douglas and the Saanich and Nanaimo Treaties, 1851–1854

1. Bowsfield, *FVL*, lxxvii, lxxx, 213.
2. Bowsfield, *FVL*, 213; Ormsby, *British Columbia*, 105.
3. J.H. Pelly to Earl Grey, 16 April 1851, CO 305/3, no. 3118, pp. 368–9.
4. James Douglas to Archibald Barclay, 7 August 1851, in Bowsfield, *FVL*, 206–7.
5. Upon Richard Blanshard's departure from Vancouver Island on 1 September, James Douglas (senior member), James Cooper, and John Tod served as provisional councillors for the colony. Richard Blanshard to Earl Grey, 30 August 1851, CO 305/3, no. 9339, 38. Earl Grey's letter and commission appointing Douglas as Governor was written on 19 May 1851. Earl Grey, London to James Douglas, Victoria, 19 May 1851, CO 410/1, p. 9 (as found in Colonial Despatches).
6. Earl Grey, memorandum attached to J.H. Pelly to Earl Grey, 10 September 1851, CO 305/3, no. 7742, fo. 398. It should be mentioned that the company did attempt to claim land in the Fort Victoria region considerably in excess of what they actually did occupy in 1846, but they did not do so based on the treaties.
7. J.H. Pelly, London, to Earl Grey, London, 7 November 1851, CO 305/3, no. 9281, fo. 405d. Also see Pelly to Earl Grey, 14 January 1852, CO 305/3, no. 409, fo. 411,
8. J.H. Pelly to Earl Grey, 4 February 1852, CO 305/3, no. 1128, fos. 429–30.
9. James Douglas to Earl Grey, 31 October 1851, in CO 305/3, no. 484, fos. 65d–66d. The version of this letter sent to the Governor and Committee is published in Bowsfield, *FVL*, 226–9.
10. James Douglas to Earl Grey, 31 October 1851, CO 305/3, no. 484, fos. 66d–67; and Bowsfield, *FVL*, 228–9. The Colonial Office responded to Douglas's suggestion by approaching missionary societies. See Carleton, "Colonialism," 113, 121–2.
11. James Douglas to Earl Grey, 16 December 1851, CO 305/3, no 1865, fo. 75d, and printed in Bowsfield, *FVL*, 248.
12. James Douglas to Earl Grey, 16 December 1851, CO 305/3, no 1865, fo. 76, James Douglas to Earl Grey, 16 December 1851, in Bowsfield, *FVL*, 248.
13. J.H. Pelly, London to Earl Grey, 14 January 1852, CO 305/3, no. 409, fo. 414d.
14. James Douglas to Earl Grey, 11 February 1852, CO 305/3, no. 3778, fos. 91–91d.
15. J.S. Pakington to James Douglas, 2 August 1852, LAC RG7-G-8-C/1, pp. 67–8.
16. James Douglas to Earl Grey, 22 December 1850, CO 305/3, no. 3558, fo. 370; and Bowsfield, *FVL*, 142.

17 James Douglas to Archibald Barclay, 22 December 1850, in Bowsfield, *FVL*, 142–3.
18 James Douglas to Archibald Barclay, 27 March 1851, in Bowsfield, *FVL*, 164.
19 Palmer, *Report*, 7, 11. It is noteworthy that Alexander Mackenzie did not note the existence of fortifications in the Bella Coola region in 1793, but villages were subsequently fortified. See Baker, "Linguistic," 43.
20 Richling, *W̱SÁNEĆ*, 2. Richling (2n5) added that "The Sidney village was known as Sai'klam, 'Clay,' and Patricia Bay was called Klangan, 'Salty Place'; but when the Sidney inhabitants moved over to Patricia Bay, they transferred the name 'Clay' to their new home." In 1840, James Douglas wrote that the "Comoks" (Comox) had three villages, one of them "fortified with a stockade." He described them as a tribe of 300 adult males, whose interactions with the HBC had been limited until then to "a few visits" to Fort Langley. He indicated "that they are still in a state of unmitigated barbarism and decidedly the most dare-devil, forward and saucy Indians that ever came under my observation." James Douglas, 14 May 1840, BCA A/B/40/D75.2, p. 13.
21 HBCA F.32/1, pp. 5, 11. James Douglas reported the plans to establish the company in a letter written on 9 December 1850. See Bowsfield, *FVL*, 241–2; Lamb, "Early," 42–6.
22 HBCA F.32/1, p. 6.
23 HBCA F.32/1, p. 13.
24 HBCA F.32/1, p. 35.
25 The logs of the HBC's steamship *Otter* show that the ship "supplied the Steam Saw mill Company with 6 Bushels of Coal" on 6 June 1854, and "anchored off the saw mill about ½ mile to the northward of Albert head" on 28 July 1854, and took on 11,000 feet of lumber on 29 July, and delivered it to Bellevue on 29 and 30 July. See HBCA C.1/625,
26 James Douglas to Archibald Barclay, 18 March 1852, HBCA A.11/73, fos. 400d–401.
27 James Douglas to Archibald Barclay, 18 March 1852, HBCA A.11/73, fo. 401.
28 James Douglas, Victoria, to James Murray Yale, Langley, 7 May 1850, BCA MS-0105.1.
29 Mayne, *Four*, 164–5.
30 Duff appears to have concluded that Douglas had the treaty text written before obtaining the signatures. Duff, "Fort," 20–1. Frogner assumed that he continued the practice of having the chiefs sign blank pages, although he did not explain his conclusion. Frogner, "Innocent," 66–7.
31 Duff, "Fort," 22. The three known villages at the time were at Saanichton Bay, Patricia Bay, and Brentwood Bay.
32 Frogner, "Innocent," 56.

Notes to pages 226-30   377

33  Frogner, "Innocent," 56; Duff, "Fort," 22.
34  Richling, WSÁNEĆ, 2.
35  The treaty actually has 117, not 118, signatories.
36  Duff, "Fort," 53.
37  Barnett, "Coast," 140.
38  J.W. McKay, "Recollections of a Chief Trader in the Hudson's Bay Company Fort Simpson, 1878," MS, Bancroft Library BANC MSS P-C 24 (Photocopy, BCA). Also see James Douglas to Archibald Barclay, 23 June 1852, BCA A/C/20/Vi2. For a history of early Nanaimo, see McKelvie, "Founding," 169-188.
39  HBCA A.11/73, fos. 526-28, James Douglas, Victoria, to Archibald Barclay, London, 18 August 1852.
40  James Douglas to J.W. McKay, 24 August 1852, HBCA B.226/b/7, fo. 1. Also found at NCA HBC Letterbook
41  James Douglas to Archibald Barclay, 26 August 1852, BCA A/C/20/Vi2, p 83.
42  NCA, E-02-04, Box 1 (HBC Fonds), Folder 5, Joseph William McKay, Nanaimo, to James Douglas, Victoria, 9 & 16 September 1852.
43  HBCA A.11/73, fo. 590d, James Douglas to Archibald Barclay, 6 October 1852.
44  HBCA A.11/74, fo. 79d, James Douglas, Victoria, to Governor and Council, Northern Department, 14 March 1853.
45  Barclay to Douglas, 18 November 1853, HBCA A.6/30, fo. 158d.
46  McKelvie, "Founding," 177-82, 186
47  Vaughan, "Co-operation," 19-22; McKelvie, "Founding," 183, 186.
48  HBCA B.113/a/1, 25 July 1827 (fos. 5-5d).
49  HBCA B.113/a/3, 30 July 1829 (fo. 18), and Maclachlan, *Fort*, 30 July 1829 (p. 122).
50  HBCA B.113/a/1, 1 August 1827 (fo. 6d).
51  HBCA B.113/a/2, 10 July 1828 (fo. 10). Also see Maclachlan, *Fort*, 10 July 1828 (p. 68).
52  Journals for the HBC's fort at Nanaimo have survived only for the period from its founding (24 August 1852) to 27 September 1854 and from 1 August 1855 to 31 March 1857. A letterbook containing correspondence dated 1852 and 1853 has also survived. These are all held by the Nanaimo Community Archives (NCA).
53  NCA, E-02-04, Box 1 (HBC Fonds), Folder 4, 29 August 1852. McKay was probably in no position to know the truth of the matter, but two years later he did remark that "Wunwunshim the Nanaimo Chief" was "well acquainted with the Ucultas." NCA, E-02-04, Box 1 (HBC Fonds), Folder 5, Joseph William McKay to James Douglas, 22 October 1854.
54  NCA, Hudson's Bay Co Fonds Daybook, 1852-1854, 30 August 1852.

55 NCA, E-02-04, Box 1 (HBC Fonds), Folder 4, 17 and 20 September 1852; NCA, E-02-04, Box 1 (HBC Fonds), Folder 5, Joseph William McKay to James Douglas, 18 September 1854.
56 NCA, E-02-04, Box 1 (HBC Fonds), Folder 5, Joseph William McKay to James Douglas, 30 September 1854.
57 James Douglas, Victoria to Pakington, 11 November 1852, CO 305/3, no. 933, p. 147; NCA, HBC Fonds, Joseph McKay's Journal, 24 August 1852–27 September 1854, 12 & 17 November 1852.
58 Captain Augustus Kuper to Rear-Admiral Moresby, 9 December 1852, in Lamb, "Four," 199.
59 NCA, HBC Fonds, Joseph McKay's Journal, 24 August 1852 – 27 September 1854, 6 December 1852.
60 Captain Augustus Kuper to Rear-Admiral Moresby, 9 December 1852, in Lamb, "Four," 201. Quoted words from BCA B/20/1853 James Douglas, Private Papers, 3 January 1853, (p 34).
61 BCA B/20/1853, 7 January 1853 (p. 37). For more on Saw-se-a, see MacLaren, *Paul*, 3: 71–3.
62 Morseby, *Two*, 129.
63 James Douglas, Victoria, to Pakington, 21 January 1853, CO 305/4, no. 3852, p. 1. Douglas wrote a similar letter to the HBC. See James Douglas, Victoria, to Archibald Barclay, 20 January 1853, in Lamb, "Four," 203. A similar scene is presented in John Moresby, *Two Admirals*, 130–1, and BCA B/20/1853, pp. 38–9.
64 Moresby, *Two*, 131.
65 James Douglas Private Journal, 7 January 1853 (pp. 39–40). For more detail, see McKelvie, "Founding," 185; and Begg, *History*, 237.
66 NCA, HBC Fonds, Joseph McKay's Journal, 24 August 1852–27 September 1854, 10 January 1853.
67 Morseby, *Two Admirals*, 133.
68 James Douglas Private Papers, 12 January 1853, BCA B/20/1853, 44. Also see James Douglas, Victoria, to Archibald Barclay, 20 January 1853, in Lamb, "Four," 204.
69 NCA, HBC Fonds, Joseph McKay's Journal, 24 August 1852–27 September 1854, 11–15 January 1853; James Douglas, Victoria, to Pakington, 21 January 1853, CO 305/4, no. 3852, p. 1; James Douglas, Victoria, to Archibald Barclay, 20 January 1853, in Lamb, "Four," 204.
70 NCA, HBC Fonds, Joseph McKay's Journal, 24 August 1852–27 September 1854, 15 January 1853.
71 James Douglas, Victoria, to Pakington, 21 January 1853, CO 305/4, no. 3852, p. 1; James Douglas, Victoria, to Archibald Barclay, 20 January 1853, in Lamb, "Four," 205–6. Douglas conveyed similar sentiments in James Douglas to John Todd, Senior Member of Counsel of Vancouver Island,

7 January 1853, BCA B/2/0/1853 (p 42–4). Also see Captain Augustus Kuper to Rear-Admiral Moresby, 9 December 1852, in Lamb, "Four," 201.
72  Newcastle to Douglas, 12 April 1853, LAC, RG7-G-8-C/1, p. 117. For scholarly discussions of the Peter Brown incident see Fisher, *Contact*, 54–5; Marshall, *Those*, 99–100; Foster, "Queen's Law," 65–6; Harris, *Resettlement*, 65–6.
73  NCA, E-02-04, Box 1 (HBC Fonds), Folder 4, 12 May 1853. Also see NCA, E-02-04, Box 1 (HBC Fonds), Folder 5, J.W. McKay to Douglas, 18 May 1853.
74  NCA, E-02-04, Box 1 (HBC Fonds), Folder 5, Douglas to McKay 20 May 1853.
75  NCA, HBC Fonds, Joseph McKay's Journal, 24 August 1852 – 27 September 1854, 15 September, 8 November 1852, 5, 9, 25 February, 28, 29 March, 26 April, 23 June, 14 August 1853.
76  See NCA, E-02-04, Box 1 (HBC Fonds), Folder 4, 17 June 1853. NCA, E-02-04, Box 1 (HBC Fonds), Folder 5, J.W. McKay to James Douglas, 16 June 1853; NCA, E-02-04, Box 1 (HBC Fonds), Folder 4, 27 July 1853; NCA, E-02-04, Box 1 (HBC Fonds), Folder 5, J.W. McKay to James Douglas, 31 July 1853.
77  NCA, E-02-04, Box 1 (HBC Fonds), Folder 4, 26 May 1854. For more examples, see NCA, E-02-04, Box 1 (HBC Fonds), Folder 4, 29 May 1854, 24 July 1854, and 27 July 1854.
78  Gough, *Gunboat*, 129–37; Mayne, *Four*, 245–6.
79  HBCA A.6/30, fo. 60, Archibald Barclay, London, to James Douglas, Victoria, 14 January 1853.
80  James Douglas to Archibald Barclay, 16 May 1853, BCA A/C/20/Vi2.
81  Barclay to Douglas, 18 November 1853, HBCA A.6/30, fos. 158–158d.
82  An unfortunate gap in the surviving records of the HBC's post at Nanaimo from 27 September 1854 to 1 August 1855 means that there is no other report of the negotiations.
83  HBCA A.11/75, fo. 450, James Douglas, on board the *Beaver*, to Archibald Barclay, London, 26 December 1854.
84  Douglas did not inform the Colonial Secretary of the treaties, but Andrew Colvile did so in May 1855. Andrew Wedderburn Colvile, to John Russell, 9 June 1855, CO 305/6, fo. 257d.
85  BCA MS-0772. Charles Edward Stuart (1817–1863), who joined the HBC in 1842, served most of his career on HBC ships along the Northwest Coast but was a clerk at Nanaimo, probably from late 1854 to 1859. See "Charles Edward Stuart," HBCA Biographical Sheets, Bowsfield, *FVL*, 29n. George Robinson (c. 1825–1895) had arrived on Vancouver Island in November 1854 to take up his position as superintendent of the colliery at Nanaimo. Vickers, "George Robinson," 44–50. Richard Golledge had

arrived on Vancouver Island on 9 May 1851 as an apprentice clerk. He became Douglas's private secretary. See Bowsfield, *FVL*, 182n5.
86 Lindsay, "Archives," 42, 46, 48; Duff, "Fort," 8.
87 Ormsby, *British Columbia*, 127.
88 Kappler, *Indian*, 2: 662.
89 Kappler, *Indian*, 2: 669–77, 682–5; Marino, "History," 169–72; Coan, "Adoption," 1–38; Reddick and Collins, "Medicine Creek to Fox Island," 374–97; Reddick and Collins, "Medicine Creek Remediated," 80–98; Richards, "Stevens," 342–50.
90 Coan, "First," 54–63. Senators found some of the provisions "objectionable," but more specific grounds for their failure to ratify the agreements appear not to have been recorded. See *Congressional Globe*, 33d Cong. 1st sess., p. 744 (24 March 1854).
91 Marino, "History," 171–2.
92 For Blanshard's testimony, see *BPP* 1857 (197), 285–97.
93 *BPP* 1857 (197), 63. This testimony was dated 26 February 1857.

## 12. Indigenous Title on Vancouver Island and British Columbia, 1854–1875

1 Duff, *Indian*, 61; Fisher, *Contact*, 154–6; Cail, *Land*, 179.
2 Tennant, *Aboriginal*, 26–38. For Robin Fisher's response to Tennant, see Fisher, *Contact*, xviii–xix. In his highly respected study of reserve formation in British Columbia, Harris agreed with Duff, Fisher, and Cail, although he, like Tennant, was critical of aspects of Douglas's administration. Harris, *Making*, 30–44; Harris, "Native," 101–22 (see especially 116–17).
3 HBCA B.226/a/1, 1 May 1850 (fo. 176). James Douglas to Archibald Barclay, 16 May 1850, BCA A/C/20/Vi2, 1–3, and in HBCA A.11/72, fos. 246–7. The transcription here is derived from a comparison of those documents. The second version is transcribed in Bowsfield, *FVL*, 94–6. The letter was received in London on 7 August 1850. A party of "Nanaimaults" traded on 3 May, so they may have been among the "others."
4 James Douglas, Chief Factor, Fort Victoria to Archibald Barclay, Secretary, Hudson's Bay Company, 3 September 1849 (21st head), HBCA A.11/72, fos. 120d–121. Also see Eden Colvile to J.H. Pelly, 15 October 1849, in Rich, *London*, 5.
5 James Douglas to Archibald Barclay, 7 May 1851, in Bowsfield, *FVL*, 180–1.
6 James Douglas to Archibald Barclay, 8 October 1851, in Bowsfield, *FVL*, 222, James Douglas to Earl Grey, 28 May 1852, CO 305/3, no. 7372, fo. 115–116. See Carleton, "Colonialism," 118–19.

7 James Douglas, Victoria, to Archibald Barclay, London, 18 August 1852, HBCA A.11/73, fo. 526d. Elsewhere, Douglas reported that "these Indians partially cultivate the alluvial islands near the mouth of the river, where we saw many large and well-kept fields of potatoes in a very flourishing state, and a number of fine cucumbers, which had been raised in the open air without any particular care." Douglas, "Report," 246.
8 James Douglas to Newcastle, Colonial Secretary, 24 October 1853, CO 305/4, fo. 89d.
9 Douglas, "Report," 246.
10 In 1878, Gilbert Malcolm Sproat guessed that the slow pace of settlement deterred Douglas. Gilbert Malcolm Sproat to the Hon Attorney General, Canada, "Memorandum on Cowichan Reserve," LAC RG10, Vol. 3662, file 9756, Pt. 1.
11 Scholefield, *Minutes*, 13.
12 These included the Cayuse War (1847–55), the Rogue River War (c. 1855–7) and the Yakima War (1856–8). Douglas and the members of the assembly monitored the events of these wars closely. See Carleton, "Colonialism," 123–31.
13 In late winter 1856, the members of the Assembly had petitioned Douglas calling his attention to "the Indian war that is now raging on the American shores within a few miles of our own homes. From the most recent accounts the attacks of the Indians have been most frightful and daring atrocities have been committed on the persons of women and children." Carleton, "Colonialism," 129.
14 Scholefield, *Minutes*, 15 (12 August 1856); and James Douglas to Labouchere, 20 August 1856, CO 305/7, 89–90.
15 James Douglas to Henry Labouchere, 20 October 1856, CO 305/7.
16 Douglas to Lytton, 14 March 1859, *PCILQ*, 16.
17 *Journals of the First House of Assembly of the Colony of Vancouver Island*, 12 August 1856 to 7 December 1859, 71; *Weekly Victoria Gazette*, 27 January 1859. For Yates's enmity with Douglas, see Ormsby, *British Columbia*, 122.
18 *Weekly Victoria Gazette*, 28 August 1858; *Journals of the First House of Assembly of the Colony of Vancouver Island*, 12 August 1856 to 7 December 1859, 71.
19 Douglas to Secretary of State, 9 February 1859, in *PCILQ*, 15.
20 James Douglas to the Speaker of the House of Assembly, 5 February 1859, CO 305/10. The letter was published (with insubstantial differences in capitalization, and paragraph structure) in *Journals of the First House of Assembly of the Colony of Vancouver Island*, 12 August 1856 to 7 December 1859, 71–2. The importance of this statement was recognized even in 1906. The Deputy Superintendent General of Indian Affairs, Frank Pedley, quoted it in a report on the Songhees Reserve. See Frank Pedley,

"Report on the Songhees Reserve Question," 17 December 1906, RG10, Vol. 3689, f. 13,886-3.

21 *Journals of the First House of Assembly of the Colony of Vancouver Island*, 12 August 1856 to 7 December 1859, 15 February 1859, 74–5. Those present were Thomas J. Skinner, Dr. John F. Kennedy, J. Yates, J.W. McKay, Joseph D. Pemberton, and the Speaker. Herman Merivale in the Colonial Office appears to have agreed that the reserve should be sold, although he also argued that proceeds of the sale of the reserve should be used for the benefit of the Indians. Memorandum written by Herman Merivale on letter by James Douglas to Edward Lytton, 9 February 1859, CO 60/10, 17.
22 Pemberton's defence of the Songhees was not unqualified. In 1859, with apparent frustration, he remarked that "as to satisfying the Indians that was impossible – you might go on settling with and paying them till the last day, and yet they would not be satisfied. An Indian always asked for and expected more than was given him." *Weekly Victoria Gazette*, 26 February 1859.
23 Laing, "Hudson's Bay," 328.
24 Laing, "Hudson's Bay," 328.
25 Most of the gold was brought in by Indigenous people until April 1858. Begg, *History*, 264.
26 Gibbard, "Early," 119–31. See Barman, *West*, 63–71.
27 E.B. Lytton to James Douglas, 1 July 1858, *BPP* 2476 (240), 41.
28 Edward Lytton to James Douglas, 16 July 1858, as published in Begg, *History*, 221–2.
29 E.B. Lytton to James Douglas, 31 July 1858, in *BPP* 2476 (240), 45.
30 E.B. Lytton to James Douglas, 31 July 1858, in *BPP* 2476 (240), 45–6.
31 F.W. Chesson to E.B. Lytton (undated), *PCILQ*, 12–14.
32 E.B. Lytton to James Douglas, 2 September 1858, *PCILQ*, 12.
33 Gibbard, "Early," 123.
34 See Margaret A. Ormsby, "Richard Clement Moody," *DCB*.
35 "Proclamation By His Excellency James Douglas, Governor and Commander-in-Chief of Her Majesty's Colony of British Columbia and its Dependences," 19 November 1858, https://open.library.ubc.ca/collections/bchistoricaldocuments/bcdocs/items/1.0370688 (accessed 23 June 2021); Barman, *West*, 70.
36 Harris, "Lower," 38.
37 Lytton to Douglas, 30 December 1858, in British Columbia, *PCILQ*, 15.
38 James Douglas, Victoria to the Colonial Secretary, 14 March 1859, in British Columbia, *PCILQ*, 16.
39 James Douglas, Victoria to the Colonial Secretary, 14 March 1859, in British Columbia, *PCILQ*, 16.

40 Lord Carnarvon, Colonial Office, London, despatch to Governor James Douglas, 20 May 1859, British Columbia, *PCILQ*, 18.
41 James Douglas to Newcastle, 31 May 1860, CO 60/7, no. 7721, fo. 293d. Despatches to the Colonial Secretary, Provincial Archives of British Columbia, https://bcgenesis.uvic.ca/B60053SQ.html?hi=derby_city.
42 James Douglas, "Copy of a Circular to the Gold Commissioners and Magistrates of British Columbia," 1 October 1859, BCA GR1372, Reel B1325, File 485/8f.
43 James Douglas to Newcastle, 31 May 1860, CO 60/7, no. 7721, fo. 293d. Despatches to the Colonial Secretary, Provincial Archives of British Columbia, https://bcgenesis.uvic.ca/B60053SQ.html?hi=derby_city. Also see James Douglas to Duke of Newcastle, 12 January 1860 as published in *BPP 1860* (2724), 90–2; and Governor James Douglas to Colonel R.C. Moody, Chief Commissioner of Lands and Works, New Westminster, 7 October 1859, BCA GR1372, Reel B1325, file 485/8f.
44 Douglas, "Copy of a Circular," 1 October 1859, BCA GR1372, Reel B1325, File 485/8f.
45 Governor James Douglas, to Colonel R.C. Moody, Chief Commissioner of Lands and Works, New Westminster, 7 October 1859, "Memorandum to Moody," BCA GR1372, Reel B1325, file 485/8f.
46 British Columbia: Proclamation, 4 January 1860 James Douglas (Governor) BCA GR 1372, File 1715.
47 The Land Proclamation, Colony of Vancouver Island, 1861, c. 27.
48 Vancouver Island Proclamation, 1862 S.B.C., 1862, c. 9.
49 James Douglas to the Secretary of State for the Colonies, 25 March 1861, CO 305/17, no. 4779, fo. 126d. The entire original letter is found from fo. 126 to 131d. It is published in *PCILQ*, 19.
50 James Douglas to the Secretary of State for the Colonies, 25 March 1861, CO 305/17, no. 4779, fos. 126–127d; published in *PCILQ*, 19
51 BCA MS-0772.
52 James Douglas to the Secretary of State for the Colonies, 25 March 1861, CO 305/17, no. 4779, fos. 127d–130. Also published in *PCILQ*, 19. The underlining, which appears in the original, was most likely made by personnel in the Colonial Office.
53 J.S. Helmcken Speaker, February 6th 1861, Petition of the House of Assembly of Vancouver Island, Enclosed in James Douglas to Pelham-Clinton, 25 March 1861, CO 305/17, no. 4779, fos. 133–134d.
54 CO 305/17, no. 4779, fo. 130d.
55 TFE memorandum, 14 June 1861, CO 305/18, no. 5329, fo. 172d.
56 N memorandum, CO 305/18, no. 5329, fo. 172d. In 1849, the Earl of Lincoln (as Newcastle was then titled) had delivered in the British House

of Commons a four-and-a-half-hour diatribe against the HBC that ended only when the House lost quorum. Rich, *History*, 2: 791.
57 T.R. Elliot to George A. Hamilton, 22 June 1861, CO 305/17, no. 4779, fos. 135d–36.
58 Frederick Peel to Frederic Rogers, 25 September 1861, CO 305/18, no. 8612, fos. 336–37.
59 FR memorandum, 26 September 1861, CO 305/18, no. 8612, fo. 337d.
60 ABd memorandum, 5 October 1861, CO 305/18, no. 8941, fo. 211d, accompanying Stephen Walcott to Frederic Rogers, 4 October 1861. For Elliot's opinion, see TFE memorandum, 11 October 1861, CO 305/18, no. 8941, fo. 211d–12.
61 N memorandum, 12 October 1861, CO 305/18, no. 8941, fo. 212.
62 Newcastle to Douglas, 19 October 1861, LAC RG7-G-8-C/2, pp. 573–4 (Colonial Despatches); and in British Columbia, *PCILQ*, 20.
63 Alex C. Garrett, Victoria to B.W. Pearse, Acting Surveyor General, 10 March 1865, BCA GR1372, File 911/9. For more on Garrett, see Carleton, "Colonialism," 135–40.
64 "The Cowichan Expedition," *British Colonist*, 22 August 1962, 3. Italics in original.
65 Alex C. Garrett, Victoria to B.W. Pearse, Acting Surveyor General, 10 March 1865, BCA GR1372, File 911/9.
66 Alex C. Garrett, Victoria to B.W. Pearse, Acting Surveyor General, 10 March 1865, BCA GR1372, File 911/9.
67 William H. Lomas to the Hon. Colonial Secretary, Victoria, 3 March 1869, BCA B1347, File 1171.
68 G.M. Sproat, c. January–February 1878 "Memorandum on Cowichan Reserve," LAC RG10, Vol. 3662, f. 9756, Pt. 1. These two documents show that non-signatory villagers on Vancouver Island in the 1860s and 1870s were aware that the previous treaties were land purchases and sought to sell their land rights on similar terms.
69 G.M. Sproat, c. January–February 1878 "Memorandum on Cowichan Reserve," LAC RG10, Vol. 3662, f. 9756, Pt. 1.
70 B.W. Pearse to the Colonial Secretary, 16 October 1863, BCA C/AA/30.J/3, (PR-0410), p. 195.
71 Sproat, *Scenes*, 2–3.
72 Sproat, *Scenes*, 7–9.
73 Mayne, *Four*, 164.
74 Gilbert Malcolm Sproat to the Hon Attorney General, Canada, "Memorandum on Cowichan Reserve," LAC RG10, Vol. 3662, file 9756, Pt. 1. Sproat must not have realized that the funds for the Vancouver Island treaties had been from the HBC's coffers, not from public funds.

Notes to pages 258–61   385

75   Vancouver Island, House of Assembly, *Minutes of Proceedings*, 1. Minutes show that the committee comprised Amor De Cosmos, Robert Burnaby, Joseph Charles Ridge, James Duncan, James Trimble, William Fraser Tolmie, and Colonel George F. Foster. *Minutes of the Third House of Assembly of Vancouver Island-First Session*, 13.
76   *Minutes of Proceedings*, 1.
77   Vancouver Island, House of Assembly, *Minutes of Proceedings*.
78   "Indian and Government Reserves – Tracing Lodged with Select Committee of House on Crown Lands, 2nd Dec. 1863 B.W. Pearse, Act. Surveyor General Crown Lands, Surveyor General's Branch, Map # 6T1 Land Reserves." A high-resolution electronic version of this map can be found at https://vault.library.uvic.ca/concern/generic_works/bb9a6776-4f04-4a5b-9052-8b8c0058c6f3?locale=en.
79   Reserves May 1, 1864 supplied to Crown Lands Committee by B.W. Pearse Acting Surveyor General, Indian and Government Reserves Tracing and Map No. 1, Reserves Surveyor General Branch, Land Reserves, maps #6T1 and #6AT1. A high-resolution electronic image of this map can be found at https://vault.library.uvic.ca/images/c89ee4bf-96b8-40d7-8767-173973cfc6ca%252Ffiles%252F368cce8b-8c5e-4249-bb50-abcb87a101d4/full/7392,/0/default.jpg.
80   Vancouver Island, House of Assembly, *Minutes of Proceedings*, 19–20.
81   Vancouver Island, House of Assembly, *Minutes of Proceedings*, 1.
82   William McColl, New Westminster, 16 May 1864, in British Columbia, *PCILQ*, 43.
83   Robin Fisher, "Joseph William Trutch," *DCB*.
84   Joseph W. Trutch, "Lower Fraser River Indian Reserves," in British Columbia, *PCILQ*, 41.
85   Joseph W. Trutch, "Lower Fraser River Indian Reserves," in British Columbia, *PCILQ*, 41.
86   Joseph W. Trutch, "Lower Fraser River Indian Reserves," in British Columbia, *PCILQ*, 42. Emphasis in the original.
87   Terms of Union, 20 July 1871.
88   B.W. Pearse to the Colonial Secretary, 16 October 1871, in *PCILQ*, 102–3. Although addressed to the "Colonial Secretary" (in London), it is clear from subsequent correspondence that the letter was intended for and actually sent to Canada's Secretary of State for the Provinces in Ottawa.
89   "Schedule of all Indian Reserves (surveyed) in the Province of British Columbia," *PCILQ*, 104. The historical geographer Cole Harris found the schedule problematic. He wrote that the schedule did not clearly distinguish between government and Indian reserves, "moreover, the government may have considered that it had withdrawn some reserves, but had not left records of its decisions." Harris, *Making*, 65–6.

90  James W. Trutch to the Secretary of State for the Provinces, 3 November 1871, *PCILQ*, 101–2.
91  Richard Mackie, "Benjamin William Pearse," *DCB*, http://www.biographi.ca/en/bio/pearse_benjamin_william_13E.html.
92  Irsael Wood Powell (Indian Commissioner) to James Douglas, 9 October 1874, LAC RG10, Vol. 3611, f. 3756-1.
93  James Douglas, James Bay to Israel Wood Powell, 14 October 1874, LAC RG10, Vol. 3611, f. 3756-1. The underlining in this passage was probably added by Powell, or some other person other than Douglas. Historians have noted that, in fact, some reserves did exceed 10 acres per family. See Fisher, *Contact*, xviii–xix; Harris, "Native," 116.
94  Harris, *Making*, 43; Fisher, *Contact*, 146–74.
95  LAC RG10-A, Vol. 1283, A.W. Vowell, SIABC to J.D. McLean, Secretary, DIA, 19 February 1909, Indian Reserve Commission, Letterbooks,
96  Harris, *Making*, 66–8.

## 13. The Evolving Memories of the Vancouver Island Treaties to 1934

1  Frank Pagett, "105 Years in Victoria and Saanich! Chief David Recalls White Man's Coming; 80 Years Rent Unpaid," *Victoria Daily Times* 14 July 1934, Features Section, 1.
2  Vallance, "Sharing," iii.
3  Vallance, "Sharing," 15. John Lutz had previously presented parts of the Latasse account in *Makúk*, 70, 79.
4  Vallance, "Earliest," 123–54.
5  Vallance, "Earliest," 127.
6  Vansina, *Oral*, 12–13.
7  Vansina, *Oral*, 8.
8  Vallance, "Earliest," 137.
9  Vallance, "Earliest," 127.
10 Despite this acknowledgment, Vallance then relied on the oral accounts to present an argument about the Indigenous understandings of the treaty at the time they were concluded.
11 Moss, *Oral History*, 9.
12 Finnegan, "Note," 200.
13 Cruikshank, *Reading*, 59. Emphasis in the original.
14 Calliou, "Methodology," 79.
15 "The principal mechanism by which the contents of oral traditional accounts were adapted to form new coalesced traditions may be called 'feedback.' Feedback may be defined as the co-opting of extraneous printed or written information into previously oral accounts. This process occurred very widely, if not obviously." Henige, *Chronology*, 96.

16 David Henige, *Chronology*, 81.
17 Vansina, *Oral*, 156–7. Elsewhere, he wrote that "Historians should ... examine oral traditions for feedback from earlier writings." Vansina, *Oral*, 31.
18 Henige, *Chronology*, 118. Elsewhere, Henige wrote that "it is rare to find any really substantial similarity between an oral testimony and a written account since the two sources generally evoke different time-scales and points of view. Should the historian encounter high consistency, he should carefully consider the possibility that one of the sources has directly influenced the other." Henige, *Oral*, 71.
19 Daniel P. Marshall, "John Sebastian Helmcken," in *DCB*.
20 J.S. Helmcken Speaker, 6 February 1861, Petition of the House of Assembly of Vancouver Island, Enclosed in James Douglas to Pelham-Clinton, 25 March 1861, CO 305/17, no. 4779
21 *St. Catherines Milling and Lumber Co. v. R.* (1885), 10 O.R. 196 (Ch.); (1887) 13 SCR 577; (1888), 14 App. Cas. 46 (J.C.P.C.). For the scholarly literature on the case, see Cottam, "Indian," 249–65; Hall, "St. Catherine's," 267–86; Harring, *White*, 125–47; and McNeil, *Flawed*.
22 W. Duncan, "The Indian Question," *Daily British Colonist*, 10 November 1886, 2
23 E. Robson, "Dr. Helmcken's Letters," *Daily British Colonist*, 25 November 1886, 2.
24 J.S. Helmcken, "Indian Title," *Daily British Colonist*, 5 November 1886, 2.
25 J.S. Helmcken, "Indian Title," *Daily British Colonist*, 5 November 1886, 3.
26 E. Robson, "Dr. Helmcken's Letters," *Daily British Colonist*, 25 November 1886, 2. According to C.M. Tate, Ebenezer Robson (1836–1911) established "the first Methodist mission work among Indians in British Columbia." Tate, *Our*, 2. As a Canadian Wesleyan Methodist missionary who arrived in the colony in February 1859, having been acquainted with many missionaries to Indigenous people in the Colony of Canada, including those who were Indigenous themselves, he was familiar with the land-purchase treaties concluded there. He later remarked that, upon his arrival on the west coast, he "observed with grief the ignorance and degradation of the Indians in these vicinities, rendered all the deeper by their contact with white adventurers. The moral tide rip produced by the meeting of different races, in the swirling waters of which so many have gone down, is one of the saddest features of national expansion, whether in India, Africa or America." He, together with HBC personnel, quickly vaccinated Indigenous people at Nanaimo during the 1862 smallpox epidemic. Robson, *How*, 19; Begg, *History*, 484–5; Fawcett, *Some*, 293; Madge Wolfenden, "Edward White (1822–72)" *DCB*.
27 J.S. Helmcken "The Indian Title," *Daily British Colonist*, 28 November 1886, 3. Emphasis in the original.

28 In August 1888, a member of the Kincolith band explicitly mentioned the Vancouver Island treaties when presenting his claim for Indigenous title to representatives of the British Columbia and Canadian governments. See "Kincolith Indians, Echo Bay, Naas River, 31 August 1888," LAC RG10, Vol. 3699, f. 16,680.
29 J.S. Helmcken, Victoria, to J.W. McKay, Victoria, 30 November 1888. BCA PR-0560, MS-1917, Box 1, File 15. Joseph William McKay Papers, Correspondence Inwards, John S. Helmcken.
30 Joseph McKay to Dr. James S. Helmcken, 3 December 1888, Joseph William McKay Fonds, BCA PR-0560, MS-1917, file 27.
31 Archibald Barclay, London, to James Douglas, Fort Victoria, 17 December 1849, HBCA A.6/28, fo. 91d.
32 For example, interpreters at a treaty negotiation in Montana in the 1850s were made to swear as follows: "I solemnly swear that I will faithfully discharge my duties of Interpreter at this Council, and that I will truly and to the best of my ability interpret the speeches of the Commissioner on the one side, and of the Indians on the other. So help me God." Partoll, "Blackfoot," 200.
33 It appears that, although McKay worked for the Canadian government in 1888, he, like J.S. Helmcken, believed that Indians did not enjoy land rights. It is possible that McKay's long involvement in resource development in British Columbia may have, by the late 1880s, convinced him that the recognition of Indian land rights threatened the economic development of the province. See Richard Mackie, "Joseph William McKay," *DCB*.
34 Vallance, "Earliest," 126.
35 BCA MS-0772. A person identified as "Comey-uks" was signatory to the South Saanich Treaty. It is possible that Comiak was signatory to two treaties since he had been a leader of the Saanich and Songhees during the decades before and after 1850.
36 Affidavit of Chief Comiak, 27 October 1885, in *Comiak et al. v. W.J. Findlay & R. McLellan*, Supreme Court of BC, Joseph Algernon Pearce Collection, 1854–1920, BCA PR-2153, Container 949498-0003, File 2. The dispute is the subject of the following file: LAC RG10, Vol. 3718, f 22560-2. That folder includes several instances in which the Songhees Chiefs referred to the treaty, although the documents do not state explicitly whether the chiefs regarded the treaty as a land surrender. The Swengwhung treaty lists "Comayits," "Snâw nuck," and Kuskaynum, as signatories. "Freezy" (Chee-al-thluc, Jeelathuc) was a signatory to the Che-ko-nein treaty. BCA MS-0772. See Kennedy, "Aboriginal," 80–1, https://docs2.cer-rec.gc.ca/ll-eng/llisapi.dll/fetch/2000/90464/90552/548311/956726/2392873/2449925/2450020

/2785351/C123%2D3%2D3_%2D_Appendix_B_%2D_James_Bay_Litigation_Report_%2D_A4L5L6.pdf?nodeid=2784907&vernum=-2.
37 A.W. Vowell to DSGIA, 10 April 1893, LAC RG10, Vol 3688, f. 13866-1 "Correspondence, reports, memorandum, Orders in Council and Council Meeting regarding the Songhees Indians on the Reserve within the City of Victoria & the Proposed move of their Reserve to another Location."
38 Galois, "Indian," 7.
39 Galois, "Indian," 14–17.
40 Testimony of Dick Whoakum, 28 May 1913, "Royal Commission on Indian Affairs for the Province of British Columbia," 51–2, as found on Union of British Columbia Indian Chiefs, "Our Homes Are Bleeding," https://ourhomesarebleeding.ubcic.bc.ca/; Allooloo, et al., "Treaty," 58.
41 Testimony of Dick Whoakum, 28 May 1913, "Royal Commission on Indian Affairs for the Province of British Columbia," 52.
42 For another account of the Nanaimo treaty that poses interpretive challenges, see the account of Joe Wyse in Cryer, *Two*, 189–90.
43 Jimmy Jim, John Samson, and David Latass, Tsarlip Reserve, to The Royal Commissioners of Indian Affairs in BC, 13 June 1913, LAC RG10, Vol. 11023, f. 637A.
44 The quoted letter is from Willie H. Squelum, Louie Whitsemult, and Kelly Clatoah, to The Royal Commissioners of Indian Affairs in BC, 13 June 1913; and the other is Johnston B. Koeloino, Jim Klaniston, and Henry Sealaquesit, to The Royal Commissioners of Indian Affairs in BC, 13 June 1913. Both are in LAC RG10, Vol. 11023, f. 637A. The similarity in the names of Louie Whitsemult, signatory to this letter, and "What-say-mullet," signatory to one of the Saanich treaties is intriguing. In his 1932 statement, Latasse denied that "What-say-mullet" was a Saanich person; Louie Whitsemult might have been descended from What-say-mullet. That would not mean that Latasse was incorrect, but it would suggest that "What-say-mullet" may have had a plausible claim in 1852.
45 Duncan Campbell Scott, DSGIA, to Charles Stewart, SGIA, 1 November 1923, "Summary of Indian Affairs in the various provinces based on the report of the department's agents, and the inspectors for the fiscal year ended March 31, 1923," *Annual Report of the Department of Indian Affairs (ARDIA)*, 1923, 21.
46 Duncan Campbell Scott, DSGIA, to Charles Stewart, SGIA, 6 November 1924, "Report of the Deputy Superintendent General," *ARDIA*, 1924, 9.
47 Duncan Campbell Scott, DSGIA, to Charles Stewart, SGIA, 6 November 1924, "Report of the Deputy Superintendent General," *ARDIA*, 1924, 8. See Harris, *Making*, 248–59. I thank Adrian Clark for alerting me to the documents pertaining to the Canadian government's attempt to negotiate treaties in British Columbia in the 1920s.

48 Duncan Campbell Scott, Ottawa to W.E. Ditchburn, Chief Inspector of Indian Agencies, Victoria, 12 August 1922, LAC RG10, C-II-2, Vol. 11302.
49 Ditchburn, Victoria, to D.C. Scott, Ottawa, 28 November 1922, LAC RG10, C-II-2, Vol. 11302. In 1920, Duncan Campbell Scott invited James Teit to assist the Chief Inspector W.E. Ditchburn in securing the assent of Indians to the recommendations of the Royal Commission. Duncan Campbell Scott, Ottawa, to James Teit, Spences Bridge, 6 October 1920, LAC RG10, C-II-2, vol 11302. Teit did work with the commissioners until shortly before he died in October 1922.
50 Ditchburn, Victoria, to D.C. Scott, Ottawa, 28 November 1922, LAC RG10, C-II-2, Vol. 11302.
51 Charles, Stewart, DGIA to the Rev. P.R. Kelly, 14 May 1923, LAC RG10, C-II-2, Vol. 11046, f. 33/General pt 3.
52 The request was conveyed by Simon C. Pierre, a member of the Katzie band, who had been a translator during the earlier Royal Commission to D.H. Macdowall, who had also served that commission. Simon C. Pierre, Katsey Indian Reserve to D.H. Macdowall, 9 July 1923, LAC RG10, C-II-2, Vol. 11046, f. 33/General pt 3. Macdowall informed Ditchburn of the request on 14 July. See D.H. Macdowall, Sidney, BC to W.E. Ditchburn, Victoria, LAC RG10, C-II-2, Vol. 11046, f. 33/General pt 3.
53 W.E. Ditchburn, Victoria, to D.H. Macdowall, 19 July 1923, LAC RG10, C-II-2, Vol. 11046, f. 33/General pt 3.
54 J. Morton, Secretary to the premier, Victoria, to W.E. Ditchburn, Victoria, 31 July 1923, LAC RG10, C-II-2, Vol. 11046, f. 33/General pt 3.
55 W.E. Ditchburn, Victoria, Memorandum, 5 April 1932, LAC RG10, C-II-2, Vol. 11303, f. 974/1-9.
56 Statement of David Latasse to W.E. Ditchburn, Indian Commissioner for BC, 4 April 1932, LAC RG10, C-II-2, Vol. 11303, f. 974/1-9.
57 Statement of Chiefs Edward Jim (Tseycum), Louie Pekley (Tseaut), David Latasse (Tsarlip), Jim Tlawesten (Poquachin), and Alex Peter (Malahat), and Councillors Joseph Kelly (Tseaut), Johnny Samson (Tsarlip), Tommy Paul (Tsarlip), Jimmy Jim (Tsarlip) to W.E. Ditchburn, Indian Commissioner for BC, 4 April 1932, LAC RG10, C-II-2, Vol. 11303, f. 974/1-9.
58 Petition of Chiefs Edward Jim (Tseycum), Louie Pekley (Tseaut), David Latasse (Tsarlip), Jim Tlawesten (Poquachin), and Alex Peter (Malahat), and Councillors Joseph Kelly (Tseaut), Johnny Samson (Tsarlip), Tommy Paul (Tsarlip), Jimmy Jim (Tsarlip) to W.E. Ditchburn, Indian Commissioner for BC, 4 April 1932, LAC RG10, C-II-2, Vol. 11303, f. 974/1-9.
59 W.E. Ditchburn memorandum, 5 April 1932, LAC RG10 C-II-2, Vol. 11303, f. 974/1-9. After reassuring the delegation that the treaty would not disadvantage them in the future if other British Columbia Indians were given annuities (which had been the focus of the delegation's concern),

Ditchburn noted that "This statement appeared to perfectly satisfy them and they left the office after expressing thanks to myself as Commissioner for the manner in which I had explained the situation to them." Ditchburn appears to have misjudged how satisfied David Latasse was.

60 James Douglas to Archibald Barclay, 18 March 1852, HBCA A.11/73, fo. 401; Mayne, *Four*, 164–5.

61 Frank Pagett (c. 1882–1944) was a journalist and magazine salesperson. He had been a member of the *Victoria Daily Times* editorial staff and the Victoria Press Club for many years. For some years, he reported on the Saanich Municipal Council meetings. See "Frank Pagett," *Victoria Daily Colonist*, 19 March 1944, 4.

62 Latasse appears to have claimed to be a centenarian as early as 1932. See N. de Bertrand Lugrin, "Indian Saga: Heroic Tales from the Golden Age of the Indian's Supremacy on the West Coast," *Maclean's Magazine*, 15 December 1932, 38.

63 D. Latasse to W. Robertson, LAC RG10-A, Vol. 1343.

64 The census indicates that his wife at the time, Christine, was 36, and that the couple had an uncle and aunt, both 65 years old, living with them. Canada, Census of Canada, 1891, https://central.bac-lac.gc.ca/.item/?app=Census1891&op=img&id=30953_148093-00385.

65 Canada, Census of Canada, 1901, British Columbia, Cowichan Agency, https://central.bac-lac.gc.ca/.item/?app=Census1901&op=&img&id=z000183401.

66 Canada, Census of Canada, 1921, British Columbia, District 19 (Nanaimo), New Castle Indian Reserve, https://central.bac-lac.gc.ca/.item/?app=Census1921&op=img&id=e002873076.

67 In 1934, anthropologist, Diamond Jenness estimated that "David Latess" was 85, and his wife at 60 years old, although Latasse then told Jenness that he was 105. See "Coast Salish Mythology," Diamond Jenness Collection, Canadian Museum of History VII-G-9M; and Richling, *W̱SÁNEĆ*, 18. Likewise, Bouchard and Kennedy asserted that Latasse was born in the 1850s. Kennedy and Bouchard, "Traditional," 16."

68 Vallance, "Earliest," 129. Similarly, after uncritically identifying Latasse as a "centurion" [centenarian?] in the main text of his discussion of Latasse's account, John Lutz admitted in a footnote that "Later censuses suggest that Latasse may not have been old enough to witness the event himself and that this may be a secondhand account." Lutz, *Makúk*, 336n70.

69 Wagner, *Spanish*, 118; Blumenthal, *Early*, 32.

70 Wagner, *Spanish*, 48; Kendrick, *Voyage*, 100–2.

71 The assertion that the Vancouver Island treaties were not land purchases had ebbed and flowed. It appears that during the 1960s, when there

appeared to be no prospect of treaty negotiations in British Columbia, no one put forward the assertion in the White and Bob case in the 1960s that the Nanaimo Treaty was not a land surrender. Berger, *One*, 87–106. Indeed, Wilson Duff, who was an expert witness for the plaintiffs in that case, presciently predicted in 1969, that if Canada and British Columbia ever agreed to negotiate treaties in British Columbia, the signatories to the Vancouver Island treaties "will rue the day" when their ancestors ceded their lands for a nominal compensation. Duff, "Fort," 55.

**Appendix B: A 1934 Account of a Fort Victoria Treaty Attributed to David Latasse**

1 This date is problematic. The treaties in question were concluded on 30 April and 1 May. Douglas had written his report before 24 May 1850.
2 Pagett, "105 Years in Victoria and Saanich!" 7–8.

# Bibliography

## Abbreviations

| | |
|---|---|
| ADB | *Australian Dictionary of Biography*, online |
| AJHRNZ | *Appendix to the Journals of the House of Representatives of New Zealand* |
| ARDIA | *Annual Report of the Department of Indian Affairs* (Canada) |
| BCA | British Columbia Archives |
| BCHQ | *British Columbia Historical Quarterly* |
| BPP | *British Parliamentary Papers* |
| CO | Colonial Office |
| DCB | *Dictionary of Canadian Biography*, online |
| HBCA | Hudson's Bay Company Archives |
| HRA | *Historical Records of Australia* |
| JCL | *Journals of the Colonial Legislatures of the Colonies of Vancouver Island and British Columbia, 1851–1871. Vol. 4: Journals of the Executive Council, 1864–71, and of the Legislative Council, 1864–66* |
| LAC | Library and Archives Canada |
| NARA USA | National Archives and Records Administration, Washington, DC, USA |
| NCA | Nanaimo Community Archives |
| PCILQ | *Papers Connected with the Indian Land Question* |
| TNA | The National Archives (UK) |

## Archival Sources

British Columbia Archives, Victoria, British Columbia, Canada (BCA)
    A/B/20/V5    Francis Ermatinger fonds, Journal of Clallum Expedition from Fort Vancouver, 1828

A/B/40/D75.2	James Douglas Diary of a Trip to the Northwest Coast Ap. 22–Oct. 2, 1840
A/C/20	Fort Victoria Correspondence Inbound
A/C/20/Vi2	Fort Victoria Correspondence Book Outward to HBC on affairs of V.I. Colony, 16 May 1850–6, November 1855
A/E/H37/W75	Helmcken Family Papers, J.S. Helmcken, correspondence inward, D.D. Wishart
B/20/1853	Private Papers of Sir James Douglas, Second Series (Census 1853)
E/B/M91	Andrew Muir Fonds
MS-0557	William Fraser Tolmie Records
MS-0772	Vancouver Island Treaties, 1850–1854
MS-1917	Joseph William McKay Papers
O/A/C811	The Doings of H.M.S. Cormorant
PR-2153	Joseph Algernon Pearce Collection, 1854–1920

British Library, London, United Kingdom
Ms. 32641	Journal of Archibald Menzies, Surgeon and Botanist on Board the *Discovery* under Captain George Vancouver, 1790–1794. (Empire online. Section I, Cultural contacts, 1492–1969)

Canadian Museum of History, Ottawa, Ontario, Canada (CMH)
VII-G-9M	"Coast Salish Mythology," Diamond Jenness Collection

Glenbow Archives, Calgary, Alberta, Canada
M4343	Scollen family fonds

Hocken Library, University of Otago, Dunedin, New Zealand
PC-0023	Edward Shortland Journal, Middle Island of New Zealand, 16 January–6 March 1844

Hudson's Bay Company Archives, Winnipeg, Manitoba, Canada (HBCA)
A. London Headquarters Records
A.1	Governor and Committee Minutes
A.6	Governor and Committee Official General Outward Correspondence
A.11	Governor and Committee Correspondence Inward from Posts
B. Official Post Records
B.120	Fort McLoughlin Records
B.185	Fort Rupert Records

B.201 Fort Simpson Records
B.223 Fort Vancouver Records
B.226 Fort Victoria Records
B.239 York Factory Records
Minutes of Northern Council
C. Ships' Records
D. Governor George Simpson's Records
F. Private Records
F.32/1 Vancouver Island Steam Sawing Mill Company Records
G. Maps

Library and Archives Canada, Ottawa, Ontario, Canada (LAC)
M19 A21 Hargrave Papers
MG19 E 1 Selkirk Papers
RG7-G-8-C Records of the Governor of Vancouver Island, 1849–1872 as found at "Colonial Despatches: The Colonial Despatches of Vancouver Island and British Columbia 1846–1871," Edition 2.2, ed. James Hendrickson and the Colonial Despatches project. Victoria, B.C.: University of Victoria, 2020. https://bcgenesis.uvic.ca/
RG10 Canada, Department of Indian Affairs
  Vol. 1846 Treaties, Surrenders, and Agreements
  Vol. 3608, Cowichan Agency–John Ashe's claim for compensation in a
    f. 3102 cancelled lease to a lot on the Songhees Reserve, 1874–1884
  Vol. 3611, Reports concerning the work of a committee of the
    f. 3756 Executive Council dealing with land questions in B.C., 1878
  Vol. 3662, Cowichan Agency–Correspondence regarding a BC
    f. 9756-1 Government Crown grant of land allotted to the Cowichan Indians, 1878–1880
  Vol. 3688, Cowichan Agency–Correspondence, reports,
    f. 13866-1 memorandum, Orders in Council & council minutes regarding the Songhees Indians on the reserve within the City of Victoria & the Proposed move of their Reserve to another Location (Detailed Maps of South Eastern Vancouver Island, Victoria & the Reserve; Copies of the Surrender of Reserve), 1879–1894
  Vol. 3689, Cowichan Agency–Correspondence, Reports &
    f. 13,886-3 memoranda regarding the removal of the Songhees Indians from their Reserve in the City of Victoria to a Location outside the City (Lists of Songhees Indians & their families, sketch of Reserve showing name & location of each family, maps, publications, including the Songhees Indian Question & Clippings, 1899–1909

Vol. 3690, f. 13,886-4     Cowichan Agency–Correspondence, Reports, Memoranda, Orders in Council, Terms of Agreement regarding the Surrender of the land of the Songhees Indian band & their removal to a new Reserve at Esquimalt Harbour (Petitions, Maps, Plans, Clippings, a Census of the Songhees Reserve 1910 Listing all members of family, occupations, education & lists of Payments made for the land to each family, 1909–1913

Vol. 3699, f. 16,682     Northwest Coast Agency–Correspondence, memoranda and reports regarding the land at Fort Simpson

Vol. 3718, f. 22,560-2     Cowichan Agency–Correspondence regarding a proposed site for an immigrant shed on the Songhees Reserve, Victoria District, B.C., 1885–1886

Vol. 11023, f. 637A     Cowichan Agency–Exhibits A1 to A51. Statistics on different Bands, 1913

RG10-A

Vol. 1343     Cowichan Agency–Incoming Correspondence, 1902–04

RG10-C-II-4 (Indian Commissioner for British Columbia) (microfilm indicates C-II-2)

Vol. 11046     Chief Inspector of Indian Agencies/Indian Commissioner for BC–General correspondence re land in various agencies including: disposition of reserve lands; federal–provincial negotiations towards settling BC Indian land disputes; visit of Chas. Stewart (SGIA) to BC, 1922

Vol. 11302     Land – General – Correspondence re Royal Commission and Ditchburn-Clark review of Commission's findings, 1916–1928

Vol. 11303     Cowichan Agency – Correspondence re 1851 treaty between Saanich Indians and Hudson's Bay Co. – Including petition re validity of treaty, 1932

Nanaimo Community Archives, Nanaimo, British Columbia, Canada (NCA)
E-02-04 Box 1 (HBC Fonds)
Folder 2, Letter Douglas to McKay, 24 August 1852
Folder 4, Nanaimo Daybook, 1852–1854
Folder 5, Nanaimo Correspondence 1852–1853
Folder 6, Nanaimo Memoranda: 1855–57

The National Archives, London (Kew), United Kingdon (TNA)
HO 28/61     Home Office, Admiralty, Supplementary Correspondence

CO    Colonial Office, Original Correspondence-Secretary of State, as found at "Colonial Despatches: The Colonial Despatches of Vancouver Island and British Columbia 1846–1871," Edition 2.2, ed. James Hendrickson and the Colonial Despatches project. Victoria, B.C.: University of Victoria, 2020. https://bcgenesis.uvic.ca/
CO 60 British Columbia, 1858–
CO 305 Vancouver Island, 1849–
CO 410 Entry Books, Letters from Secretary of State; Despatches, 1849–1864

National Archives and Records Administration, Washington, DC, USA (NARA USA)
RG59 M179    Department of State, 1763–2002, Miscellaneous Letters of the Department of State, 1789–1906

University of British Columbia, Rare Books and Special Collections Library
Hendrickson, James E. "The Aboriginal Land Policy of Governor James Douglas, 1849–1864." unpublished paper presented at the BC. Studies Conference, Simon Fraser University, November 1988.
Finlayson, Roderick. "History of Vancouver Island and the Northwest Coast." Volume 1, Issue 1 of Studies, series B. Social sciences, St. Louis University Press, 1945.

Wellcome Library, London, UK
WMS/Amer. 42. Relación de los Méritos y Servicios de D. Martín de Sessé, Director de la Expedición Botánica de Nueva España. Aranjuez, 1804.

**Published Sources**

*Government Publications*

Great Britain. Parliament. House of Commons. *British Parliamentary Papers*
BPP 1819 (584)    Papers Relative to the Red River Settlement.
BPP 1837 (238)    Report of the Select Committee on Aborigines (British Settlements).
BPP 1837–38 (443)    New Zealand. A Bill for the Provisional Government of the British Settlements in the Islands of New Zealand.
BPP 1837–38 (680)    New Zealand. Report from the Select Committee of the House of Lords, Appointed to Inquire into the Present State of the Islands of New Zealand, and the Expediency of Regulating the Settlement of British Subjects Therein.

*BPP* 1838 (122)     New Zealand. Copy of a Despatch from Governor Sir R. Bourke to Lord Glenelg.

*BPP* 1840 (283)     New Zealand. Correspondence with the Secretary of State Relative to New Zealand.

*BPP* 1840 (560)     New Zealand: Despatches from the Governor of New South Wales Relative to New Zealand: Ordered to be Printed 29 July 1840.

*BPP* 1840 (582)     New Zealand. Report from the Select Committee on New Zealand.

*BPP* 1841 (311)     New Zealand: Copies or Extracts of Correspondence Relative to New Zealand.

*BPP* 1842 (547)     Hudson's Bay Company: Copy of the Existing Charter or Grant by the Crown to the Hudson's Bay Company; together with Copies or Extracts of the Correspondence which took place at the last Renewal of the Charter between the Government and the Company, or of Individuals on behalf of the Company; also, the Dates of all former Charters or Grants to that Company.

*BPP* 1842 (569)     New Zealand. Copies of Papers and Despatches Relative to New Zealand.

*BPP* 1844 (556)     New Zealand. Report from the Select Committee on New Zealand, 29 July 1844.

*BPP* 1844 (641)     New Zealand. Copy of letter from the Secretary of the Church Missionary Society to Lord Stanley Relative to the Affairs of New Zealand.

*BPP* 1845 (1)     New Zealand. Papers Relative to the Affairs of New Zealand.

*BPP* 1845 (108)     Copies of Letters from Mr. Shortland and Mr. Busby to Lord Stanley and Mr. G.W. Hope.

*BPP* 1845 (130)     Copies or Extracts from any Recent Despatches from the Governor of New South Wales Respecting Outrages by the Natives in the Bay of Islands in New Zealand.

*BPP* 1845 (131)     New Zealand. Papers Relative to the Affairs of New Zealand.

*BPP* 1845 (246)     Return to Two Addresses of the Honourable The House of Commons, dated 18 and 20 March 1845.

*BPP* 1845 (247)     Copies or Extracts of Despatches from the Governor of New Zealand.

*BPP* 1845 (357)     Return to an Address of the Honourable the House of Commons, dated 30 May 1845.

*BPP* 1845 (369)     Copies or Extracts of Despatches from the Governor of New Zealand.

## Bibliography 399

| | |
|---|---|
| *BPP* 1845 (378) | Returns of All Claims to Land in New Zealand. |
| *BPP* 1845 (571–I) | Copy of All Correspondence that Passed between Her Majesty's Government and the New Zealand Company between 19 June and 6 July 1845. |
| *BPP* 1845 (571–II) | Copies or Extracts of Correspondence Relative to an Attack on the British Establishment at the Bay of Islands of New Zealand. |
| *BPP* 1845 (661) | Return to an Address of the Honourable the House of Commons, dated 8 August 1845. |
| *BPP* 1846 (203) | Copies of Despatches from the Governor of New Zealand. |
| *BPP* 1846 (337) | Copies or Extracts of Further Correspondence between Lord Stanley and Governor FitzRoy and Lieutenant-Governor Grey Relative to New Zealand. |
| *BPP* 1846 (712) | Papers Relative to the Affairs of New Zealand: Correspondence with Lieutenant Governor Grey. |
| *BPP* 1847 (763) | New Zealand. Papers Relative to the Affairs of New Zealand. Correspondence with Governor Grey, January 1847. |
| *BPP* 1847 (837) | Further Papers Relative to the Affairs of New Zealand. Correspondence with Governor Grey, June 1847. |
| *BPP* 1847 (892) | New Zealand. Papers Relative to the Affairs of New Zealand. Correspondence with Governor Grey, December 1847. |
| BPP 1847 (899) | New Zealand. Further Papers Relative to the Affairs of New Zealand: Correspondence with Governor Grey. Also in Great Britain, Parliament, House of Lords, Accounts and Papers, Vol. 8, (1847–48). |
| *BPP* 1848 (619) | Vancouver Island. Copy of the Correspondence between the Chairman of the Hudson's Bay Company and the Secretary of State for the Colonies Relative to the Colonization of Vancouver's Island. |
| *BPP* 1848 (1002) | New Zealand. Further Papers Relative to the Affairs of New Zealand: Correspondence with Governor Grey." Also in Great Britain, Parliament, House of Lords, Accounts and Papers, Vol. 8 (1847–48), p. 521. 105. |
| *BPP* 1849 (103) | Vancouver's Island. Copies and Extracts of Despatches and Other Papers Relating to Vancouver's Island ... Ordered, by the House of Commons, to be Printed, 7 March 1849. |
| *BPP* 1849 (1120) | New Zealand. Further Papers Relative to the Affairs of New Zealand. Correspondence with Governor Grey. |

BPP 1850 (1136)     Further Papers Relative to the Affairs of New Zealand.
BPP 1852 (83)     Vancouver Island. Return Made since 1849 by the Hudson's Bay Company to the Secretary of State for the Colonies, Relating to Vancouver Island.
BPP 1857 (224.260)     Report from the Select Committee on the Hudson's Bay Company; Together with the Proceedings of the Committee, Minutes of Evidence, Appendix and Index.
BPP 1859 (2476)     Papers Relative to the Affairs of British Columbia, 11 February 1859.
BPP 1860 (2724)     Further Papers Relative to the Affairs of British Columbia, Part III, 1860.

*Newspapers and Magazines*

*Auckland Times*
*Australasian Chronicle* (Sydney)
*Australian* (Sydney)
*Colonist* (Sydney)
*Hampshire Telegraph* (Portsmouth, England)
*Nelson Examiner and New Zealand Chronicle*
*New Monthly Magazine*
*New Zealand Spectator and Cook's Strait Guardian* (Wellington)
*New Zealander* (Auckland)
*Sydney Commercial Journal and Advertiser*
*Sydney Herald*
*Times* (London)
*Victoria Daily Colonist/British Colonist*
*Victoria Daily Times*
*Wellington Independent*

*Secondary Sources*

Abel, Kerry, and Jean Friesen, eds. *Aboriginal Resource Use in Canada: Historical and Legal Aspects*. Winnipeg: University of Manitoba Press, 1991.

Acheson, Steven. "The Thin Edge: Evidence for Precontact Use and Working of Metal on the Northwest Coast." In *Emerging from the Mist: Studies in Northwest Coast Culture History*, ed. R.G. Matson, Gary Coupland, and Quentin Mackie, 213–29. Vancouver: UBC Press, 2003.

Adams, Peter. *Fatal Necessity: British Intervention in New Zealand 1830–1847*. Auckland: Auckland University Press, 1977.

Allooloo, Siku, Michael Asch, Aimée Craft, Rob Hancock, Marc Pinkoski, Neil Vallance, Allyshia West, and Kelsey Wrightson. "Treaty Relations as a

Method of Resolving IP and Cultural Heritage Issues." Victoria: University of Victoria, 2014.
Ames, Kenneth M. "Chiefly Power and Household Production on the Northwest Coast." In *Foundations of Social Inequality*, ed. T. Douglas Price and Gary M. Feinman, 155–87. New York: Plenum Press, 1995.
– "The Northwest Coast: Complex Hunter-Gatherers, Ecology, and Social Evolution." *Annual Review of Anthropology* 23 (1994): 209–29.
– "The Northwest Coast." *Evolutionary Anthropology* 12 (2003): 19–33.
– "Slaves, Chiefs and Labour on the Northern Northwest Coast." *World Archaeology* 33, no. 1 (2001): 1–17.
Ames, Kenneth M., and Herbert D.G. Maschner. *Peoples of the Northwest Coast: Their Archaeology and Prehistory*. London: Thames and Hudson, 1999.
Anderson, Alexander Caulfield. "Indians." In *Guide to the Province of British Columbia for 1877–8*. Victoria: T.N. Hibben, 1877, 214–21.
– "Notes on the Indian Tribes of British North America, and the Northwest Coast." *Historical Magazine* 7, no. 3 (March 1863): 73–81.
Anderson, Atholl J. "The Chronology of Colonization in New Zealand." *Antiquity* 65, no. 249 (1991): 767–95.
– "Towards an Explanation of Protohistoric Social Organisation and Settlement Patterns amongst the Southern Ngai Tahu." *New Zealand Journal of Archaeology* 2 (1980): 3–23.
– *The Welcome of Strangers: An Ethnohistory of Southern Maori A.D.1650–1850*. Dunedin, NZ: University of Otago Press, 1998.
Anderson, Atholl J., Judith Binney, and Aroha Harris. *Tangata Whenua: An Illustrated History*. Wellington: Bridget Williams Books, 2014.
Angelbeck, William O. (Bill). "The Balance of Autonomy and Alliance in Anarchic Societies: The Organization of Defences in the Coast Salish Past." *World Archaeology* 48, no. 1 (2016): 51–69.
– "Conceptions of Coast Salish Warfare, or Coast Salish Pacificism) Reconsidered: Archaeology, Ethnohistory, and Ethnography." In *Be of Good Mind: Essays on the Coast Salish*, ed. B.G. Miller, 260–83. Vancouver: UBC Press, 2007.
– "'They Recognize No Superior Chief': Power, Practice, Anarchism and Warfare in the Coast Salish Past." PhD Diss., University of British Columbia, 2009.
Angelbeck, Bill, and Eric McLay. "The Battle at Maple Bay: The Dynamics of Coast Salish Political Organization through Oral Histories." *Ethnohistory* 58, no. 3 (Summer 2011): 359–92.
Angelbeck, Bill, and Ian Cameron. "The Faustian Bargain of Technological Change: Evaluating the Socioeconomic Effects of the Bow and Arrow Transition in the Coast Salish Past." *Journal of Anthropological Archaeology* 36 (2014): 93–109.

Angelbeck, Bill, and Colin Grier. "Anarchism and the Archaeology of Anarchic Societies: Resistance to Centralization in the Coast Salish Region of the Pacific Northwest Coast." *Current Anthropology* 53, no. 5 (2012): 547–87.

Anonymous. "The New Zealand Question." *New Monthly Magazine* 84, no. 3 (October 1848): 250–60.

Archer, Christon I. "Seduction before Sovereignty: Spanish Efforts to Manipulate the Natives in Their Claims to the Northwest Coast." In *From Maps to Metaphors: The Pacific World of George Vancouver*, ed. Robin Fisher and Hugh Johnston, 127–59. Vancouver: UBC Press, 1993.

Arnett, Chris. *The Terror of the Coast: Land Alienation and Colonial War on Vancouver Island and the Gulf Islands, 1849–1863*. Vancouver: Talonbooks, BC, 1999.

Arnold, Thomas. "The Labourers of England." *Englishman's Register* 6 (11 June 1831): 155–9.

– *Miscellaneous Works of Thomas Arnold, D.D.* London: George Woodfall and Son, 1845.

Attwood, Bain. *Empire and the Making of Native Title: Sovereignty, Property and Indigenous People*. Cambridge: Cambridge University Press, 2020.

– *Possession: Batman's Treaty and the Matter of History*. Carlton, Victoria, Australia: Miegunyah Press, 2009.

Baker, James W.E. "A Linguistic and Ethnohistoric Approach to Bella Coola Prehistory." MA Thesis, Simon Fraser University, 1969.

Bancroft, Hubert Howe. *History of the Northwest Coast*. 2 vols. San Fransisco: A.L. Bancroft, 1884.

Banner, Stuart. "Conquest by Contract: Wealth Transfer and Land Market Structure in Colonial New Zealand." *Law & Society Review* 34, no. 1 (2000): 47–96.

– *How the Indians Lost Their Land: Law and Power on the Frontier*. Cambridge, MA: Belknap Press of Harvard University Press, 2005.

– *Possessing the Pacific: Land, Settlers, and Indigenous People from Australia to Alaska*. Cambridge, MA: Harvard University Press, 2007.

– "Why Terra Nullius? Anthropology and Property Law in Early Australia." *Law and History Review* 23, no. 1 (Spring 2005): 95–131.

Barman, Jean. *The West beyond the West: A History of British Columbia*. Toronto: University of Toronto Press, 199.

Barnett, H.G. "The Coast Salish of Canada." *American Anthropologist* 40, no. 1 (1938): 118–41.

Bassett, Kari N., Hamish W. Gordon, David C. Nobes, and Chris Jacomb. "Gardening at the Edge: Documenting the Limits of Tropical Polynesian Kumara Horticulture in Southern New Zealand." *Geoarchaeology: An International Journal* 19, no. 3 (2004): 185–218.

Bassi, Daniella F. "Dutch-Indian Land Transactions, 1630–1664: A Legal Middle Ground of Land Tenures." MA Thesis: University of Vermont, 2017.
Beaglehole, J.C., ed. *The Journals of Captain James Cook on his Voyages of Discovery*. Volume 3, Part I: *The Voyage of the Resolution and Discovery 1776–1780*. Cambridge: Cambridge University Press, 1967.
Beamish, R.J., and D.R. Bouillon. "Pacific Salmon Production Trends in Relation to Climate." *Canadian Journal of Fisheries and Aquatic Sciences* 50, no. 5 (May 1993): 1002–16.
Beck, David. "Grammatical Convergence and the Genesis of Diversity in the Northwest Coast Sprachbund." *Anthropological Linguistics* 42, no. 2 (Summer 2000): 147–213.
Begg, Alexander. *History of British Columbia from Its Earliest Discovery to the Present Time*. Toronto: William Briggs, 1894.
Belich, James. "Hobson's Choice." *New Zealand Journal of History* 24, no. 2 (1990): 200–7.
– *Making Peoples: A History of the New Zealanders*. Honolulu: University of Hawai'i Press, 1996.
– *The Victorian Interpretation of Racial Conflict: The Maori, the British, and the New Zealand Wars*. Montreal and Kingston: McGill-Queen's University Press, 1986.
Bell, Alexander Montgomerie. *Lectures on Conveyancing*. 2 vols. Edinburgh: Bell & Bradfute, 1867.
Berger, Thomas R. *One Man's Justice: A Life in the Law*. Vancouver: Douglas & McIntyre, 2002.
Bergerud, A.T. "Prey Switching in a Simple Ecosystem." *Scientific American* 249 (1983): 130–41.
Binnema, Ted (Theodore). *Common and Contested Ground: A Human and Environmental History of the Northwestern Plains*. Norman: University of Oklahoma Press, 2001.
Binnema, Ted, and Gerhard J. Ens, eds. *The Hudson's Bay Company Edmonton House Journals, Correspondence, and Reports: 1806–1821*. Calgary: Historical Society of Alberta, 2012.
– eds. *The Hudson's Bay Company Edmonton House Journals: Reports from the Saskatchewan District Including the Bow River Expedition, 1821–1826*. Calgary: Historical Society of Alberta, 2016.
– eds. *The Hudson's Bay Company Edmonton House Journals, Including the Peigan Post, 1826–1834*. Calgary: Historical Society of Alberta, 2020.
Blackhawk, Ned. *The Rediscovery of America: Native Peoples and the Unmaking of U.S. History*. New Haven: Yale University Press, 2023.
Blakey-Smith, Dorothy. *The Reminiscences of Doctor John Sebastian Helmcken*. Vancouver: UBC Press, 2011.

Blumenthal, Richard. *Early Exploration of Inland Washington Waters: Journals and Logs from Six Expeditions, 1786–1792*. Jefferson, NC: McFarland, 2004.

Boas, Franz. *Ethnology of the Kwakiutl, Based on Data Collected by George Hunt. Bureau of Ethnology, 25th Annual Report*, Parts 1 and 2. Washington: Government Printing Office, 1921.

– *Kwakiutl Ethnography*. Edited by Helen Codere. Chicago: University of Chicago Press, 1966.

Boast, Richard P. "Treaties Nobody Counted On." *Victoria University of Wellington Law Review* 42, no. 4 (March 2011): 653–70.

Borden, Charles E. "Notes on the Pre-History of the Southern North-West Coast." *BCHQ* 14, no. 4 (October 1950): 241–6.

Borins, Edward H. "La Compagnie du Nord, 1682–1700." MA Thesis, McGill University, 1968.

Bouvier, John. *A Law Dictionary, Adapted to the Constitution and Laws of the United States of America*. 2nd ed. 2 vols. Philadelphia: T. & J.W. Johnson, 1843.

Bowsfield, Hartwell, ed. *Fort Victoria Letters: 1846–1851*. Winnipeg: Hudson's Bay Record Society, 1979.

Boxberger, Daniel L. "A Comparison of British and American Treaties with the Klallam." MA Thesis, Western Washington University, 1977.

Boxberger, Daniel L., and Herbert Taylor. "Treaty or Non-Treaty Status?" *Columbia* 5, no. 3 (1991): 40–5.

Boyd, Robert T. *Coming of the Spirit of Pestilence: Introduced Infectious Diseases and Population Decline among Northwest Coast Indians, 1774–1874*. Vancouver: UBC Press, 1999.

– "Demographic History, 1774–1874." In *Northwest Coast*. Volume editor, Wayne Suttles. Volume 7 of *Handbook of North American Indians*. General editor William Sturtevant. Washington, DC: Smithsonian Institution Press, 1990.

– "The Pacific Northwest Measles Epidemic of 1847–1848." *Oregon Historical Quarterly* 95, no. 1 (1994): 6–47.

– "Smallpox on the Northwest Coast: The First Epidemics." *BC Studies* 101 (1994): 5–40.

Bradford, Tolly, and Rich Connors. "The Making of a Company Colony: The Fur Trade War, the Colonial Office, and the Metamorphosis of the Hudson's Bay Company." *Canadian Journal of History* 55, no. 3 (2020): 171–96.

Brazier, Graham. "Land, First Nations, James Douglas, and the Background to Treaty Making on Vancouver Island." In *To Share, Not Surrender: Indigenous and Settler Visions of Treaty Making in the Colonies of Vancouver Island and British Columbia*, ed. Peter Cook, et al., 187–219. Vancouver: UBC Press, 2021.

British Columbia. *Papers Connected with the Indian Land Question (PCILQ)*. Victoria: Wolfenden, 1875.

Brodhead, John Romeyn. *An Address, Delivered before the New York Historical Society*. New York: Press of the New York Historical Society, 1844.
– *History of the State of New York*. New York: Harper and Brothers, 1853.
Brown, Alexander, ed. *The Genesis of the United States*. Boston: Houghton, Mifflin, 1890.
Brown, Jennifer S.H. "Rupert's Land, Nituskeenan, Our Land: Cree and English Naming and Claiming around the Dirty Sea." In *New Histories for Old: Changing Perspectives on Canada's Native Pasts*, ed. Ted Binnema and Susan Neylan, 18–40. Vancouver: UBC Press 2007.
Buick, T. Lindsay. *The Treaty of Waitangi: How New Zealand Became a British Colony*. Cambridge: Cambridge University Press, 2011.
Burley, David V., J. Scott Hamilton, and Knut Fladmark. *Prophecy of the Swan: The Upper Peace River Fur Trade of 1794–1823*. Vancouver: UBC Press, 1996.
Burns, Patricia. *Fatal Success: A History of the New Zealand Company*. Auckland, NZ: Heinemann Reed, 1989.
Cail, Robert E. *Land, Man, and the Law: The Disposal of Crown Lands in British Columbia, 1871–1913*. Vancouver: UBC Press, 1974.
Calliou, Brian. "Methodology for Recording Oral Histories in the Aboriginal Community." *Native Studies Review* 15, no. 1 (2004): 73–105.
Carleton, Sean. "Colonialism, Capitalism, and the Rise of State Schooling in British Columbia, 1849–1900." PhD Dissertation, Trent University, 2016.
Carlson, Keith Thor. "From the Great Flood to Smallpox." In *The Power of Place, the Problem of Time: Aboriginal Identity and Historical Consciousness in the Cauldron of Colonialism* by Keith Thor Carlson, 79–112. Toronto: University of Toronto Press, 2010.
– "'The Last Potlatch' and James Douglas's Vision of an Alternative Settler Colonialism." In *To Share, Not Surrender: Indigenous and Settler Visions of Treaty Making in the Colonies of Vancouver Island and British Columbia*, ed. Peter Cook, et al., 288–328. Vancouver: UBC Press, 2021.
– gen. ed. *A Stó:lō-Coast Salish Historical Atlas*. Vancouver: Douglas & McIntyre, 2001.
– "Toward an Indigenous Historiography: Events, Migrations, and the Formation of 'Post-Contact' Coast Salish Collective Identities." In *Be of Good Mind: Essays on the Coast Salish*, ed. B.G. Miller, 138–81. Vancouver: UBC Press, 2007.
Carlson, Roy L. "Trade and Exchange in Prehistoric British Columbia." In *Prehistoric Exchange Systems in North America*, ed. Timothy G. Baugh and Jonathan E. Ericson, 307–61. New York: Plenum Press, 1994.
Cass, A.J., and C.C. Wood. "Evaluation of the Depensatory Fishing Hypothesis as an Explanation for Population Cycles in Fraser River Sockeye Salmon (*Oncorhynchus nerka*)." *Canadian Journal of Fisheries and Aquatic Sciences* 51, no. 8 (1994): 1839–54.

Cavanagh, Edward. "A Company with Sovereignty and Subjects of Its Own?: The Case of the Hudson's Bay Company, 1670–1763." *Canadian Journal of Law and Society* 26, no. 1 (2011): 25–50.
Challis, Aidan J. *Ka Pakihi Whakatekateka o Waitaha: The Archaeology of Canterbury in Maori Times*. Science and Research Series No. 89. Wellington, New Zealand: New Zealand Department of Conservation, 1995.
Chisholm, Brian S., E. Erle Nelson, and Henry P. Schwarez. "Marine and Terrestrial Protein in Prehistoric Diets on the British Columbia Coast." *Current Anthropology* 24, no. 3 (June 1983): 396–8.
Chittenden, Hiram M. *The American Fur Trade of the Far West*. 2 vols. Lincoln: University of Nebraska Press, [1935] 1986.
Clark, Terence N. *Rewriting Marpole: The Path to Cultural Complexity in the Gulf of Georgia*. Archaeology Paper 172. Ottawa: Canadian Museum of Civilization, 2013.
Clayton, Daniel Wright. *Islands of Truth: The Imperial Fashioning of Vancouver Island*. Vancouver: UBC Press, 2000.
Coan, C.F. "The Adoption of the Reservation Policy in Pacific Northwest, 1853–1855." *Oregon Historical Quarterly* 23, no. 1 (March 1922): 1–38.
– "The First Stage of the Federal Indian Policy in the Pacific Northwest, 1849–1852." *Oregon Historical Quarterly* 22, no. 1 (March 1921): 46–89.
Codere, Helen. *Fighting with Property: A Study of Kwakiutl Potlatching and Warfare, 1792–1930*. Seattle: University of Washington Press, 1950.
– "Kwakiutl: Traditional Culture." In *Handbook of North American Indians*, vol. 7: *Northwest Coast*, ed. Wayne Suttles, 359–77. Washington, DC: Smithsonian Institution Press, 1990.
Cole, Douglas, and David Darling. "History of the Early Period." In *Handbook of North American Indians*, vol. 7: *Northwest Coast*, ed. Wayne Suttles, 119–34. Washington, DC: Smithsonian Institution Press, 1990.
Cook, James. *A Voyage to the Pacific Ocean Undertaken, by the Command of His Majesty, for Making Discoveries in the Northern Hemisphere*, Volume 2. London: W. and A. Strahan, 1784.
Cook, Peter, et al., eds. *To Share, Not Surrender: Indigenous and Settler Visions of Treaty Making in the Colonies of Vancouver Island and British Columbia*. Vancouver: UBC Press, 2021.
Cook, Warren L. *Flood Tide of Empire: Spain and the Pacific Northwest, 1543–1819*. New Haven: Yale University Press, 1973.
Cottam, S. Barry. "Indian Title as 'Celestial Institution': David Mills and the *St. Catherine's Milling Case*." In *Aboriginal Resource Use in Canada*, ed. Kerry Abel and Jean Friesen, 249–65. Winnipeg: University of Winnipeg Press, 1991.
Coupland, Gary. "Warfare and Social Complexity on the Northwest Coast." In *Cultures in Conflict: Current Archaeological Perspectives: Proceedings of the*

Bibliography    407

*Twentieth Annual Conference of the Archaeological Association of the University of Calgary*, ed. Diane Claire Tkaczuk and Brian C. Vivian, 205–14. Calgary: University of Calgary Press, 1989.

Coupland, G., T.N. Clark, and A. Palmer. "Hierarchy, Communalism and the Spatial Order of Northwest Coast Plank Houses: A Comparative Study." *American Antiquity* 74 (2009): 77–106.

Cruikshank, Julie. *Reading Voices: Dan Dha Ts'edenintth'e: Oral and Written Interpretations of the Yukon's Past*. Vancouver: Douglas and McIntyre, 1991.

Cryer, Beryl Mildred. *Two Houses Half-Buried in Sand: Oral Traditions of the Hulq'umi'num Coast Salish of Kuper Island and Vancouver Island*. Vancouver: Talonbooks, 2007.

Cullen, Mary K. *The History of Fort Langley, 1827–96*. Canadian Historic Sites: Occasional Papers in Archaeology and History No. 20. Ottawa: Parks Canada 1979.

Cybulski, Jerome S. "Conflict on the Northern Northwest Coast: 2,000 Years Plus of Bioarchaeological Evidence." In *The Routledge Handbook of the Bioarchaeology of Human Conflict*, ed. Christopher Knüsel and Martin J. Smith, 415–53. London: Routledge, 2014.

– "Culture Change, Demographic History, and Health and Disease on the Northwest Coast." In *In the Wake of Contact, Biological Responses to Conquest*, ed. C.S. Larsen and G.R. Milner, 75–85. New York: Wiley-Liss, 1994.

– "Modified Human Bones and Skulls from Prince Rupert Harbour, British Columbia." *Canadian Journal of Archaeology* 2 (1978): 15–31.

Dease, Peter Warren, and T. Simpson. "An Account of the Recent Arctic Discoveries by Messrs. Dease and T. Simpson. Communicated by J.H. Pelly, Esq., Governor of the Hudson's Bay Company." *Journal of the Royal Geographical Society of London* 8 (1838): 213–25.

– "An Account of Arctic Discovery on the Northern Shore of America in the Summer of 1838." *Journal of the Royal Geographical Society of London* 9 (1839): 325–30.

Dee, Henry Drummond, ed. "The Journal of John Work, 1835: Being an Account of his Voyage Northward from the Columbia River to Fort Simpson and Return in the Brig Lama, January–October, 1835." *BCHQ* Part 1: 8, no. 2 (April 1944): 129–46; Part 2: 8, no 3 (1944): 227–44; Part 3: 8, no. 4 (October 1944): 307–18; Part 4: 9, no. 1 (January 1945): 49–69; Part 5: 9, no. 2 (April 1944): 129–46.

DeMaillie, Raymond J. "Touching the Pen: Plains Indian Treaty Councils in Ethnohistorical Perspective." In *American Indian: Past and Present*, 6th ed., ed. Roger L. Nichols, 171–83. Norman: University of Oklahoma Press, 2008.

Deur, Douglas, and Nancy J. Turner, eds. *Keeping It Living: Traditions of Plant Use and Cultivation on the Northwest Coast of North America*. Vancouver: UBC Press, 2005.

Deur, Douglas, Adam Dick, Kim Recalma-Clutesi, and Nancy J. Turner. "Kwakwaka'wakw 'Clam Gardens': Motive and Agency in Traditional Northwest Coast Mariculture." *Human Ecology* 43, no. 2 (2015): 201–12.

Dieffenbach, Ernest. *New Zealand, and Its Native Population*. London: Smith, Elder, 1841.

Donald, Leland. *Aboriginal Slavery on the Northwest Coast of North America*. Berkeley: University of California Press, 1997.

– "Was Nuu-chu-nulth-aht (Nootka) Society Based on Slave Labour?" In *The Development of Political Organization in Native North America*, ed. Elisabeth Tooker, 108–19. Washington, DC: American Ethnological Society, 1983.

Donald, Leland, and Donald H. Mitchell. "Nature and Culture on the Northwest Coast of North America: The Case of Wakashan Salmon Resources." In *Key Issues in Hunter-Gatherer Research*, ed. Ernest S. Burch, Jr., and Linda J. Ellanna, 95–117. Oxford: Berg Publishers, 1994.

Dorricott, Linda, and Deirdre Cullon, eds. *The Private Journal of Captain G.H. Richards: The Vancouver Island Survey (1860–1862)*. Vancouver: Ronsdale Press, 2012.

Douglas, James. "Report of a Canoe Expedition along the East Coast of Vancouver Island." *Journal of the Royal Geographical Society of London* 24 (1854): 245–9.

Drucker, Philip. *Indians of the Northwest Coast*. Garden City, NY: Natural History Press, 1955.

Duff, Alexander. *Treatise on the Deeds and Forms Used in the Constitution, Transmission, and Extinction of Feudal Rights*. Edinburgh: Bell & Bradfute, 1838.

Duff, Wilson. "The Fort Victoria Treaties." *BC Studies* 3 (Autumn 1969): 3–57.

– *The Indian History of British Columbia*, vol. 1: *The Impact of the White Man*. 2nd ed. Victoria: British Columbia Provincial Museum, 1969.

Dunn, John. *History of the Oregon Territory and British North-American Fur Trade*. London: Edwards and Hughes, 1844.

Eells, Myron. "The Twana, Chemakum, and Klallum Indians of Washington Territory." *Annual Report of the Smithsonian Institution for 1887* (1889): 605–81.

Elmendorf, William W. "Chemakum." In *Handbook of North American Indians*, vol. 7: *Northwest Coast*, ed. Wayne Suttles, 438–40. Washington, DC: Smithsonian Institution Press, 1990.

Epp, Henry, ed. *Three Hundred Prairie Years: Henry Kelsey's "Inland Country of Good Report."* Regina: Canadian Plains Research Center, 1993.

Erlandson, Jon M. "The Archaeology of Aquatic Adaptations: Paradigms for a New Millennium." *Journal of Archaeological Research* 9, no. 4 (2001): 287–350.

Evison, Harry C. *The Ngai Tahu Deeds: A Window on New Zealand History.* Christchurch: Canterbury University Press, 2006.
– "The Wentworth-Jones Deeds of 15 February 1840." *Turnbull Library Record* 28, no. 1 (January 1995): 43–60.
Fawcett, Edgar. *Some Reminiscences of Old Victoria.* Toronto: William Biggs, 1912.
Ferguson, R. Brian. "A Re-Examination of the Causes of Northwest Coast Warfare." In *Warfare, Culture, and Environment,* ed. R. Brian Ferguson, 267–328. Orlando, FL: Academic Press, 1984.
– "Warfare and Redistributive Exchange on the Northwest Coast." In *The Development of Political Organization in Native North America,* ed. Elisabeth Tooker, 133–47. Washington, DC: American Ethnological Society, 1983.
Fifer, D.E. "Man of Two Worlds; The Early Career of William Charles Wentworth." *Journal of the Australian Historical Society* 70, no. 3 (August 1984): 147–70.
Finlayson, Roderick. "An Autobiography of Roderick Finlayson." *Washington Historian* 2, no. 1 (October 1900): 29–33.
– *Biography of Roderick Finlayson.* Victoria: ?, 1891.
Finnegan, Ruth. "A Note on Oral Tradition and Historical Evidence." *History and Theory* 9, no. 2 (1970): 195–201.
Finney, Bruce P., et al. "Impacts of Climate Change and Fishing on Pacific Salmon Abundance over the Past 300 Years." *Science* 290, no. 5492 (2000): 795–802.
Fisher, Robin. *Contact and Conflict: Indian European Relations in British Columbia, 1774–1890,* 2nd ed. Vancouver: UBC Press, 1992.
Fitzgerald, James Edward. *An Examination of the Charter and Proceedings of the Hudson's Bay Company, with Reference to the Grant of Vancouver's Island.* London: Trelawney Saunder, 1849.
– *Vancouver's Island, the Hudson's Bay Company, and the Government.* London: Simmonds & Co. 1848.
Fladmark, Knut R. *British Columbia Prehistory.* Ottawa: National Museum of Man, Archaeological Survey of Canada, 1986.
– "An Introduction to the Prehistory of British Columbia." *Canadian Journal of Archaeology* 6 (1982): 95–156.
– "Routes: Alternate Migration Corridors for Early Man in North America." *American Antiquity* 44, no. 1 (January 1979): 55–69.
Fladmark, Knut R., K.M. Ames, and P.D. Sutherland. "Prehistory of the North Coast of British Columbia." In *Handbook of North American Indians,* vol. 7: *Northwest Coast,* ed. Wayne Suttles, 229–39. Washington, DC: Smithsonian Institution Press, 1990.
Fleming, R. Harvey, ed. *Minutes of Council Northern Department of Rupert* [sic] *Land, 1821–31.* Toronto: Champlain Society, 1940.
Fletcher, Ned. *The English Text of the Treaty of Waitangi.* Wellington, NZ: Bridget Williams Books, 2022.

Folan, William J. "On the Diet of Early Northwest Coast Peoples." *Current Anthropology* 25, no. 1 (February 1984): 123–4.

Fortescue, Michael. "Drift and the Grammaticalization Divide between Northern and Southern Wakashan." *International Journal of American Linguistics* 72, no. 3 (July 2006): 295–324.

Foster, Hamar. "The Imperial Law of Aboriginal Title at the Time of the Douglas Treaties." In *To Share, Not Surrender: Indigenous and Settler Visions of Treaty Making in the Colonies of Vancouver Island and British Columbia*, ed. Peter Cook, et al., 92–120. Vancouver: UBC Press, 2021.

– "'Queen's Law Is Better Than Yours': International Homicide in Early British Columbia." *Essays in the History of Canadian Law* 5 (1994): 41–111.

– "The Saanichton Bay Marina Case: Imperial Law, Colonial History and Competing Theories of Aboriginal Title." *UBC Law Review* 23 (1989): 629–50.

Foster, Hamar, and Alan Grove. "Trespassers on the Soil: *United States v. Tom* and a New Perspective on the Short History of Treaty Making in Nineteenth-Century British Columbia." *BC Studies* 138/139 (2003): 51–84.

Friesen, Gerald. *The Canadian Prairies: A History*. Toronto: University of Toronto Press, 1984.

Frogner, Raymond. "'Innocent Legal Fictions': Archival Convention and the North Saanich Treaty of 1852." *Archivaria* 70 (Fall 2010): 45–94.

Frost, Alan. "Nootka Sound and the Beginnings of Britain's Imperialism of Free Trade." In *From Maps to Metaphors: The Pacific World of George Vancouver*, ed. Robin Fisher and Hugh Johnston, 104–26. Vancouver: UBC Press, 1993.

Galbraith, John S. "Fitzgerald versus the Hudson's Bay Company: The Founding of Vancouver Island." *BCHQ* 16 (July–October 1952): 191–207.

Gale, Samuel. *Notices on the Claims of the Hudson's Bay Company and the Conduct of Its Adversaries*. Montreal: William Gray, 1817.

Galm, Jerry R. "Prehistoric Trade and Exchange in the Interior Plateau of Northwestern North America." In *Prehistoric Exchange Systems in North America*, ed. Timothy G. Baugh and Jonathan E. Ericson, 275–305. New York: Plenum Press, 1994.

Galois, Robert M. "The Indian Rights Association, Native Protest Activity and the 'Land Question' in British Columbia, 1903–1916." *Native Studies Review* 8, no. 2 (1992): 1–34.

– *Kwakwaka'wakw Settlements, 1775–1920: A Geographical Analysis and Gazetteer*. Vancouver: UBC Press, 1994.

– "Measles, 1847–1850: The First Modern Epidemic in British Columbia." *BC Studies* 109 (1996): 31–43.

Galois, Robert M., and Richard Mackie. "A Curious Currency: Part 1: Haiqua Shells on the Northwest Coast in the 19th Century." *The Midden* 22, no. 4 (October 1990): 1–3.

Gaudry, Adam. "Fantasies of Sovereignty: Deconstructing British and Canadian Claims to Ownership of the Historic North-West." *Native American and Indigenous Studies* 3, no. 1 (2016): 46–74.
Gibbard, John Edgar. "Early History of the Fraser Valley." MA Thesis, UBC, 1937.
Gibson, James R. *Farming the Frontier: The Agricultural Opening of the Oregon Country, 1786–1846*. Vancouver: UBC Press, 1985.
– *Opposition on the Coast: The Hudson's Bay Company, American Coasters, the Russian American Company, and the Native Traders on the Northwest Coast, 1825–1846*. Toronto: Champlain Society, 2019.
– *Otter Skins, Boston Ships, and China Goods: The Maritime Fur Trade of the Northwest Coast, 1785–1841*. Montreal and Kingston: McGill-Queen's University Press, 1992.
Gipps, John. *Every Inch a Governor: Sir George Gipps, Governor of New South Wales, 1838–46*. Port Melbourne, Vic.: Hobson's Bay Publishing, 1996.
Glazebrook, G.P.T. ed. *The Hargrave Correspondence, 1821–1843*. Toronto: Champlain Society, 1938.
Glover, Jeffrey. *Paper Sovereigns: Anglo-Native Treaties and the Law of Nations, 1604–1664*. Philadelphia: University of Pennsylvania Press, 2014.
Goddard, Pliny Earle. *Indians of the Northwest Coast*. New York: American Museum of Natural History, 1924.
Gormly, Mary. "Early Culture Contact on the Northwest Coast, 1774–1795: Analysis of Spanish Source Material." *Northwest Anthropological Research Notes* 11, no. 1 (Spring 1977): 1–80.
Gough, Barry M. "Crown, Company, and Charter: Founding of Vancouver Island Colony – A Chapter in Victorian Empire Making." *BC Studies* 176 (Winter 2012–13): 9–54.
– *Gunboat Frontier: British Maritime Authority and Northwest Coast Indians, 1846–90*. Vancouver: UBC Press, 1984.
– *The Northwest Coast: British Navigation, Trade, and Discoveries to 1812*. Vancouver: UBC Press, 1992.
– *The Royal Navy and the Northwest Coast of North America 1820–1914: A Study of Maritime Ascendancy*. Vancouver: UBC Press, 1971.
– "Send a Gunboat! Checking Slavery and Controlling Liquor Traffic among Coast Indians of British Columbia in the 1860s." *Pacific Northwest Quarterly* 69, no. 4 (October 1978): 159–68.
Grant, Walter Colquhoun. "Description of Vancouver Island by Its First Colonist, W. Colquhoun Grant F.R.G.S., of the 2nd Dragoon Guards, and late Lieut.-Col. Of the Cavalry of the Turkish Contingent." *Journal of the Royal Geographical Society* 27 (1857): 268–320.
– "Remarks on Vancouver Island, Principally Concerning Townsites and Native Population." *Journal of the Royal Geographical Society* 31 (1861): 208–13.

Grayson, Donald K. "The Archaeological Record of Human Impacts on Animal Populations." *Journal of World Prehistory* 15, no. 1 (2001): 1–68.

Great Britain. Parliament. *North American Boundary: Supplementary Reports Relating to the Boundary between the British Possessions in North America and the United States of America under the Treaty of 1783*. London: T.R. Harrison, 1842.

Great Britain. Parliament. House of Lords. *Sessional Papers, Printed by Order of the House of Lords 1849*, vol. 9: *Accounts and Papers*. London: William Clowes and Sons, 1849.

Green, L.C., and Olive P. Dickason. *The Law of Nations and the New World*. Edmonton: University of Alberta Press, 1989.

Grey, George. *Journals of Two Expeditions of Discovery in North-West and Western Australia*. 2 vols. London: T. and W. Boone, 1841.

Grey, Henry George. *The Colonial Policy of Lord John Russell's Administration*. 2 vols. London: Richard Bentley, 1853.

Grier, Colin. "Affluence on the Prehistoric Northwest Coast of North America." In *Beyond Affluent Foragers: Rethinking Hunter-Gatherer Complexity*, ed. Colin Grier, Jangsuk Kim, and Junzo Uchiyama, 126–35. Oxford, UK: Oxbow Books, 2006.

– "Temporality in Northwest Coast Households." In *Household Archaeology on the Northwest Coast*, ed. Elizabeth A. Sobel, D. Ann Trieu Gahr, and Kenneth M. Ames, 97–119. Ann Arbor, MI: International Monographs in Prehistory 16, 2006.

Grier, Colin, Bill Angelbeck, and Eric McLay. "Terraforming and Monumentality as Long-Term Social Practice in the Salish Sea Region of the Northwest Coast of North America." *Hunter Gatherer Research* 3, no. 1 (2017): 107–32.

Groesbeck, Amy S., Kirsten Rowell, Dana Lepofsky, and Anne K. Salomon. "Ancient Clam Gardens Increased Shellfish Production: Adaptive Strategies from the Past Can Inform Food Security Today." *PLoS One* 9, no. 3 (2014).

Gruhn, Ruth. "Linguistic Evidence in Support of the Coastal Route of Earliest Entry into the New World." *Man* 23 (1987): 77–100.

Guilmet, George M., Robert T. Boyd, David L. Whited, and Nile Thompson. "The Legacy of Introduced Disease: The Southern Coast Salish." *American Indian Culture and Research Journal* 15, no. 4 (1991): 1–32.

Gunther, Erna. "Klallam Ethnography." *University of Washington Publications in Anthropology* 1, no. 5 (1927): 171–314.

Hall, Anthony J. "*The St. Catherine's Milling and Lumber Company versus the Queen*: Indian Land Rights as a Factor in Federal-Provincial Relations in Nineteenth-Century Canada." In *Aboriginal Resource Use in Canada: Historical and Legal Aspects*, ed. Kerry Abel and Jean Friesen, 267–86. Winnipeg: University of Manitoba Press, 1991.

Handford, Peter. "Edward John Eyre and the Conflict of Laws." *Melbourne University Law Review* 32, no. 3 (2008): 822–60.
Harmon, Daniel Williams. *A Journal of Voyages and Travels in the Interiour of North America.* Andover: Flagg and Gould, 1820.
Harring, Sidney L. *White Man's Law: Native People in Nineteenth-Century Canadian Jurisprudence.* Toronto: Osgood Society for Canadian Legal History, 1998.
Harris, Cole. "The Lower Mainland, 1820–81." In *Vancouver and Its Region,* ed. Graeme Wynn and Timothy Oke, 38–68. Vancouver: UBC Press, 1992.
– *Making Native Space: Colonialism, Resistance, and Reserves in British Columbia.* Vancouver: UBC Press, 2002.
– "The Native Land Policies of Governor James Douglas." *BC Studies,* 174 (Summer 2012): 101–22.
– *Resettlement of British Columbia: Essays on Colonialism and Geographical Change.* Vancouver: UBC Press, 1997.
– "Social Power and Cultural Change in Pre-Colonial British Columbia." *BC Studies* 115/116 (Autumn/Winter 1997–98): 45–82.
– "Voices of Disaster: Smallpox around the Strait of Georgia in 1782." *Ethnohistory* 41, no. 4 (Autumn 1994): 591–626.
Hay, Douglas, and P.B. McCarter. *Status of the Eulachon Thaleichthys pacificus in Canada.* Ottawa: Fisheries and Oceans Canada, 2000.
Hearne, Samuel. *A Journey from Prince of Wales's Fort, in Hudson's Bay, to the Northern Ocean: Undertaken by Order of the Hudson's Bay Company for the Discovery of Copper Mines, a North West Passage, & c. in the Years 1769, 1770, 1771 & 1772.* London: Printed for A. Strahan and T. Cadell, 1795.
Heartfield, James. *The Aborigines' Protection Society: Humanitarian Imperialism in Australia, New Zealand, Fiji, Canada, South Africa, and the Congo, 1836–1909.* New York: Columbia University Press, 2011.
Heaton Timothy H., and Frederick Grady. "The Late Wisconsin Vertebrate History of Prince of Wales Island, Southeast Alaska." In *Ice Age Cave Faunas of North America,* ed. Blaine W. Schubert, Jim I. Mead, and Russell William Graham, 17–53. Bloomington: Indiana University Press, 2003.
Hebda, Christopher F.G., Duncan McLaren, Quentin Mackie, Daryl Fedje, Mikkel Winther Pedersen, Eske Willerslev, Kendrick J. Brown, and Richard J. Hebda. "Late Pleistocene Palaeoenvironments and a Possible Glacial Refugium on Northern Vancouver Island, Canada: Evidence for the Viability of Early Human Settlement on the Northwest Coast of North America," *Quaternary Science Reviews* 279 (March 2022).
Hendrickson, James E. "The Aboriginal Land Policy of Governor James Douglas, 1849–1864." *BC Studies Conference,* 4 November 1988, 1–27.
– ed. *Journals of the Colonial Legislatures of the Colonies of Vancouver Island and British Columbia, 1851–1871,* vol. 4: *Journals of the Executive Council, 1864–71,*

and *of the Legislative Council, 1864–66.* (JCL) Victoria: Provincial Archives of British Columbia, 1980.

Henige, David. *The Chronology of Oral Tradition: Quest for a Chimera.* Oxford: Clarendon Press, 1974.

– *Oral Historiography.* London: Longman, 1982.

Hewes, Gordon. "Aboriginal Use of Fishery Resources in Northwestern North America." PhD Dissertation, University of California, 1947.

– "Indian Fisheries Productivity in Pre-Contact Times in the Pacific Salmon Area." *Northwest Anthropological Research Notes* 7, no. 2 (1973): 133–55.

Hickford, Mark. "'Vague Native Rights to Land': British Imperial Policy on Native Title and Custom in New Zealand, 1837–53." *Journal of Imperial and Commonwealth History* 38, no. 2 (2010): 175–206.

Hill, Jane. "Language Contact Systems and Human Adaptations." *Journal of Anthropological Research* 34 (1978): 1–26.

Hill-Tout, Charles. "Report on the Ethnology of the South-Eastern Tribes of Vancouver Island, British Columbia." *Journal of the Royal Anthropological Institute of Great Britain and Ireland* 37 (July–December 1907): 306–74.

*Historical Records of Australia (HRA).* Series 1, vol. 20. Sydney: Alfred James Kent, Government Printer, 1924.

Howay, F.W. "The Attempt to Capture the Brig Otter." *Washington Historical Quarterly* 21, no. 2 (July 1930): 179–88.

– "An Early Account of the Loss of the Boston in 1803." *Washington Historical Quarterly* 17, no. 4 (1926): 280–8.

– "Indian Attacks upon Maritime Traders of the North-West Cost, 1785–1805." *Canadian Historical Review* 6, no. 4 (December 1925): 287–309.

– "The Loss of the Tonquin." *Washington Historical Quarterly* 13, no. 2 (April 1922): 83–92.

– "An Outline Sketch of the Maritime Fur Trade." *Canadian Historical Association Report* 11 (1932): 5–14.

– "The Trading Voyages of the Atahualpa." *Washington Historical Quarterly* 19, no. 1 (January 1928): 3–12.

Hughes, Michael. "Within the Grasp of Company Law: Land, Legitimacy, and the Racialization of the Métis, 1815–1821." *Ethnohistory* 63, no. 3 (July 2016): 519–40.

Inglis, Richard I., and James C. Haggarty. *Pacific Rim National Park: Ethnographic History.* Calgary: Parks Canada, 1986.

Jacobs, Melville. "Historic Perspectives in Indian Languages of Oregon and Washington." *Pacific Northwest Quarterly* 28 (1937): 55–74.

Jane, Cecil, trans. *A Spanish Voyage to Vancouver and the North-West Coast of America.* London: Argonaut Press, 1930.

Jenness, Diamond. *The Faith of a Coast Salish Indian.* Victoria: British Columbia Provincial Museum Anthropology in British Columbia, Memoir 3, 1955.

Jennings, Francis. *The Invasion of America: Indians, Colonialism, and the Cant of Conquest*. New York: W.W. Norton, 1976.
Jewitt, John R. *A Journal Kept at Nootka Sound*. Boston: For the Author, 1807.
– *A Narrative of the Adventures and Sufferings of John R. Jewitt*. Middletown, CT: Seth Richards, 1815.
Kades, Eric. "The Dark Side of Efficiency: *Johnson v. M'Intosh* and the Expropriation of American Indian Lands." *University of Pennsylvania Law Review* 148, no. 1065 (2000): 1065–1190.
Kane, Paul. *Wanderings of an Artist among the Indians of North America*. London: Longman, Brown, Green, Longmans, and Roberts, 1859.
Kappler, Charles J. *Indian Affairs: Laws and Treaties*, vol. 2: *Treaties*. Washington: Government Printing Office, 1904.
Keddie, Grant. "Fortified Defensive Sites and Burial Cairns of the Songhees Indians." *The Midden* 16, no. 4 (1984): 7.
– "Japanese Shipwrecks in British Columbia–Myths and Facts." in Royal BC Museum, Research Articles by Staff, Grant Keddie, 29 August 2013. https://royalbcmuseum.bc.ca/collections/research/research-articles.
– "Salvage Excavations in Northwest Cadboro Bay Archaeological site DcRt9." Unpublished report held by the Resource Information Centre, Heritage Conservation Branch, British Columbia Government, Victoria, British Columbia, 1987.
– *Songhees Pictorial: A History of the Songhees People as Seen by Outsiders, 1790–1912*. Victoria: Royal BC Museum, 2003.
Kemble, John Haskell. "Coal from the Northwest Coast, 1848–1850." *BCHQ* 2 (1938).
– "Genesis of the Pacific Mail Steamship Company." *California Historical Society Quarterly* 13, no. 3 (September 1934): 240–54.
Kendrick, John. *The Men with Wooden Feet: The Spanish Exploration of the Pacific Northwest*. Toronto: NC Press, 1986.
– *The Voyage of Sutil and Mexicana 1792: The Last Spanish Exploration of the Northwest Coast of America*. Spokane, WA: Arthur H. Clark, 1991.
Kennedy, Dorothy. "Aboriginal Affiliation of the James Bay Reserve." Unpublished report dated 17 April 2006.
Kennedy, Dorothy, and Randy Bouchard. "Traditional Territorial Boundaries of the Saanich Indians." Prepared for Treaties and Historical Research Branch, Indian and Northern Affairs, Ottawa, 1991.
Kent, James. *Commentaries on American Law*. 3rd ed. New York: Author, 1836.
Kew, Michael J.E. "Reflections on Anthropology at the University of British Columbia." *BC Studies* 193 (Spring 2017): 163–85.
– "Salmon Availability, Technology, and Cultural Adaptation." In *A Complex Culture of the British Columbia Plateau: Traditional Stl'átl'mx Resource Use*, ed. Brian Hayden, 177–221. Vancouver: UBC Press, 1992.

Killick, S.R., and W.A. Clemens. *The Age, Sex Ratio and Size of Fraser River Sockeye Salmon: 1915–1960*. New Westminster: International Pacific Salmon Fisheries Commission, 1963.

King, Robert J. "George Vancouver and the Contemplated Settlement at Nootka Sound." *The Great Circle* 32, no. 1 (2010): 6–34.

Kinkade, M. Dale. "Prehistory of Salishan Languages." "Papers for the 25th International Conference on Salish and Neighbouring Languages, 1990." https://lingpapers.sites.olt.ubc.ca/icsnl-volumes/.

Knaplund, Paul. "James Stephen on Granting Vancouver Island to the Hudson's Bay Company, 1846–1848." *BCHQ* 9 (October 1945): 259–71.

– *James Stephen and the British Colonial System, 1813–1847*. Madison: University of Wisconsin Press, 1953.

– "Letters from James Edward Fitzgerald to W.E. Gladstone Concerning Vancouver Island and the Hudson's Bay Company, 1848–1850." *BCHQ* 13, no. 1 (January 1949): 1–22.

Knight, Charles. *Political Dictionary: Forming a Work of Universal Reference*. 2 vols. London: Charles Knight, 1845,

Kobrinsky, Vernon. "Dynamics of the Fort Rupert Class Struggle: Fighting with Property Vertically Revisited." In *Papers in Honour of Harry Hawthorn*, ed. Vernon C. Serl and Herbert C. Taylor, Jr., 32–59. Bellingham, WA: Western Washington State College, 1975.

Krech, Shepard, III. "The Banditti of St. John's." *The Beaver* 313, no. 3 (1982): 36–31.

– "The Beaver Indians and the Hostilities at Fort St. John's." *Arctic Anthropology* 20, no. 2 (1983): 35–45.

Laing, F.W. "Hudson's Bay Company Lands and Colonial Farm Settlement on the Mainland of British Columbia 1858–1871." *Pacific Historical Review* 7, no 4 (December 1938): 327–42.

Lamb, W. Kaye "Early Lumbering on Vancouver Island. Part I: 1844–1855." *BCHQ* 2 (1938): 31–55.

– ed. "Five Letters of Charles Ross." *BCHQ* 7, no. 2 (April 1943): 103–18.

– ed. "Four Letters Relating to the Cruise of the 'Thetis,' 1852–53," *BCHQ* 6, no. 3 (July 1942): 189–206.

– "The Founding of Fort Victoria." *BCHQ* 7, no. 2 (April 1943): 71–92.

LaPier, Rosalyn R. *Invisible Reality: Storytellers, Storytakers, and the Supernatural World of the Blackfeet*. Lincoln: University of Nebraska Press, 2017.

Lazenby, Richard A., and Peter McCormack. "Salmon and Malnutrition on the Northwest Coast." *Current Anthropology* 26, no. 3 (June 1985): 379–84.

Leader, Herman A. "Douglas Expeditions, 1840–41." *Oregon Historical Quarterly* Part 1: 32, no. 1 (March 1931): 1–23; Part 2: 32, no. 2 (June 1931): 135–64; Part 3: 32, no. 3 (September 1931): 262–78; Part 4: 32, no. 4 (December 1931): 350–72.

Bibliography 417

Lepofsky, Dana, Nicole F. Smith, Nathan Cardinal, John Harper, Mary Morris, Gitla (Elroy White), Randy Bouchard, Dorothy I.D. Kennedy, Anne K. Salomon, Michelle Puckett, Kirsten Rowell, and Eric McLay. "Ancient Shellish Mariculture on the Northwest Coast of North America." *American Antiquity* 80, no. 2 (2015): 236–59.

Lesnek, Alia J., Jason P. Briner, Charlotte Lindqvist, James F. Baichtal, and Timothy H. Heaton. "Deglaciation of the Pacific Coastal Corridor Directly Preceded the Human Colonization of the Americas." *Science Advances* 4, no. 5 (2018).

Levy, David A., and Chris C. Wood. "Review of Proposed Mechanisms for Sockeye Salmon Population Cycles in the Fraser River." *Bulletin of Mathematical Biology* 54, no. 2 (1992): 241–61.

Lindsay, Anne. "Archives and Justice: Willard Ireland's Contribution to the Changing Legal Framework of Aboriginal Rights in Canada, 1963–1973." *Archivaria* 71 (Spring 2011): 35–62.

Liston, Carol A. "William Charles Wentworth – The Formative Years, 1810–1824." *Journal of the Royal Australian Historical Society* 62, no. 1 (June 1976): 20–34.

Longstaff, F.V., and W. Kaye Lamb. "The Royal Navy on the Northwest Coast, 1813–1850." *BCHQ* 9 (April 1945): 20–4.

Lord, John Keast. "How We Went to Fort Rupert and Made a Strange Purchase." *Once a Week* 13 (24 June 1865): 19–21.

– *The Naturalist in Vancouver Island and British Columbia*. 2 vols. London: R. Bentley, 1866.

Lovisek, Joan. "Aboriginal Warfare on the Northwest Coast: Did the Potlatch Replace Warfare?" In *North American Indigenous Warfare and Ritual Violence*, ed. Richard J. Chacon and Rubén Mendoza, 58–73. Tucson: University of Arizona Press, 2007.

– "Human Trophy Taking on the Northwest Coast." In *The Taking and Displaying of Human Body Parts as Trophies by Amerindians*, ed. Richard J. Chacon and David H. Dye, 45–64. New York: Springer, 2007.

Lutz, John S. *Makúk: A New History of Aboriginal-White Relations*. Vancouver: UBC Press, 2008.

– "The Rutters' Impasse and the End of Treaty Making on Vancouver Island." In *To Share, Not Surrender: Indigenous and Settler Visions of Treaty Making in the Colonies of Vancouver Island and British Columbia*, ed. Peter Cook, et al., 220–43. Vancouver: UBC Press, 2021.

– "Taking Power from the Whites: Coast Salish Grave Markers in the Settlement Era." Paper presented at the BC Studies Conference, 7 May 2021.

Lutz, John S., and Keith Thor Carlson. "The Smallpox Chiefs: Bioterrorism and the Exercise of Power in the Pacific Northwest." *Western Historical Quarterly* 55, no. 2 (Summer 2024): 87–104.

Macintyre, Stuart. *A Concise History of Australia*. 2nd ed. Cambridge: Cambridge University Press, 2004.

Mackay, Alexander. *A Compendium of Official Documents Relative to Native Affairs in the South Island*. 2 vols. Wellington: Government Printer, 1872–73.

Mackenzie, Alexander. *Voyages from Montreal, on the River St. Laurence, through the Continent of North America*. 2 vols. New York: W.B. Gilley, 1814.

Mackie, Richard. "The Colonization of Vancouver Island, 1849–1858." *BC Studies* 96 (1992–93): 3–40.

– *Trading beyond the Mountains: The British Fur Trade on the Pacific, 1793–1843*. Vancouver, UBC Press, 1997.

Mackie, Richard, and Robert M. Galois. "A Curious Currency: Part 2: The Hudson's Bay Company's Trade in Haiqua Shells." *The Midden* 22, no. 5 (December 1990): 6–9.

Maclachlan, Morag. *The Fort Langley Journals, 1827–30*. Vancouver: UBC Press, 1998.

MacLaren, I.S. "Notes on Samuel Hearne's Journey from a Bibliographical Perspective." *Papers of the Bibliographical Society of Canada*, 31, no. 2 (Fall 1993): 21–45.

– *Paul Kane's Travels in Indigenous North America: Writings and Art, Life and Times*. 4 vols. Montreal and Kingston: McGill-Queen's University Press, 2024.

MacLeod, William Christie. "Economic Aspects of Indigenous American Slavery." *American Anthropologist* 30 (1928): 632–50.

Macoun, John. "Report of Professor Macoun Botanist to the Expedition, Addressed to Alfred R.C. Selwyn." *Report of Progress for 1875–76*. Ottawa: Geological Survey of Canada 1877, 110–85.

Madill, Dennis F.K. *British Columbia Indian Treaties in Historical Perspective*. Ottawa: Research Branch, Corporate Policy, Department of Indian and Northern Affairs, 1981.

Makmillen, Shurli "Colonial Texts in Postcolonial Contexts: A Genre in the Contact Zone." *Linguistics and the Human Sciences* 3, no. 1 (2007): 87–103.

Manning, William Ray. *The Nootka Sound Controversy*. Washington: Government Printing Office, 1905.

Marino, Cesare. "History of Western Washington since 1846." In *Northwest Coast*, vol. ed. Wayne Suttles, Vol. 7 of *Handbook of North American Indians*, gen. ed. William Sturtevant, 169–79. Washington: Smithsonian Institution Press, 1990.

Marshall, Daniel P. *Those Who Fell from the Sky: A History of the Cowichan Peoples*. Duncan, BC: Cultural and Education Centre, Cowichan Tribes, 1999.

Marshall, Yvonne. "Dangerous Liaisons: Maquinna, Quadra, and Vancouver in Nootka Sound, 1790–5." In *From Maps to Metaphors: The Pacific World of George Vancouver*, ed. Robin Fisher and Hugh Johnston, 160–75. Vancouver: UBC Press, 1993.

Martin, Chester. *Lord Selkirk's Work in Canada*. London: Oxford University Press, 1916.
Maschner, Herbert D.G. "The Evolution of Northwest Coast Warfare." In *Troubled Times: Violence and Warfare in the Past*, ed. Debra L. Martin and David W. Frayer, 267–302. New York: Gordon and Breach, 1997.
Maschner, H., and Brian Fagan. "An Introduction to Hunter and Gatherer Complexity on the West Coast of North America." *Antiquity* 65, no. 249 (1991): 921–3.
Maschner, H.D.G., and Owen K. Mason. "The Bow and Arrow in Northern North America." *Evolutionary Anthropology* 22, no. 3 (2013): 133–8.
Maschner, Herbert D.G., and Katherine L. Reedy-Maschner. "Heads, Women, and the Baubles of Prestige: Trophies of War in the Arctic and Subarctic." In *The Taking and Displaying of Human Body Parts as Trophies by Amerindians*, ed. Richard J. Chacon and David H. Dye, 32–44. New York: Springer, 2007.
Maschner, Herbert D.G., and Katherine L. Reedy-Maschner. "Raid, Retreat, Defend (Repeat): The Archaeology and Ethnohistory of Warfare on the North Pacific Rim." *Journal of Anthropological Archaeology* 17 (1998): 19–51.
Matson, R.G. "The Evolution of Northwest Coast Subsistence." *Research in Economic Anthropology*, Supplement 6 (1992): 367–428.
– "Intensification and the Development of Cultural Complexity: The Northwest versus the Northeast Coast." In *Evolution of Maritime Culture on the Northeast and the Northwest Coasts of America*, ed. R.J. Nash, 125–48. Burnaby: Simon Fraser University, Department of Archaeology Publication no. 11, 1983.
Matson, R.G., and Gary Coupland. *Prehistory of the Northwest Coast*. San Diego: Academic Press, 1995.
Matson, R.G., G. Coupland, and Q. Mackie, eds. *Emerging from the Mist: Studies in Northwest Coast Culture History*. Vancouver: University of British Columbia Press, 2003.
Mayne, R.C. *Four Years in British Columbia*. London: John Murray, 1862.
McCulloch, Samuel Clyde. "Sir George Gipps and Eastern Australia's Policy toward the Aborigine, 1838–46." *Journal of Modern History* 33, no. 3 (September 1961): 261–9.
McDowell, Jim. *José Narváez: The Forgotten Explorer: Including His Narrative of a Voyage on the Northwest Coast in 1788*. Spokane, WA: Arthur H. Clark, 1998.
McKelvie, B.A. "Coal for the Warships." *Beaver* (June 1951): 8–11.
– "The Founding of Nanaimo." *BCHQ* 8, no. 3 (July 1944): 169–88.
McLaren, Duncan, Daryl Fedje, Angela Dyck, Quentin Mackie, Alisha Gauvreau, and Jenny Cohen. "Terminal Pleistocene Epoch Human Footprints from the Pacific Coast of Canada." *PLoS ONE* 13, no. 3 (March 2018): e0193522.

McLaren, Duncan, Rebecca J. Wigen, Quentin Mackie, and Daryl W. Fedje. "Bear Hunting at the Pleistocene/Holocene Transition on the Northern Northwest Coast of North America." *Canadian Zooarchaeology* 22 (2005): 3–29.

McMillan, Alan D. "Reviewing the Wakashan Migration Hypothesis." In *Emerging from the Mist: Studies in Northwest Coast Culture History*, ed. R.G. Matson, Gary Coupland, and Quentin Mackie, 244–59. Vancouver: UBC Press, 2003.

McMillan, Alan D., and Denis E. St. Claire. *Huu7ii: Household Archaeology at a Nuu-chah-nulth Village Site in Barkley Sound*. Burnaby, BC: Archaeology Press, Simon Fraser University, 2012.

McNeil, Kent. *Flawed Precedent: The St. Catherine's Case and Aboriginal Title.* Vancouver: UBC Press, 2019.

Meares, John. *Voyages Made in 1788 and 1789, from China to the North West Coast of America.* London: J. Walter 1790.

Mein Smith, Philippa. *A Concise History of New Zealand.* Cambridge: Cambridge University Press, 2005.

Menzies, Allan. *Conveyancing According to the Law of Scotland.* Edinburgh: Thomas Constable, 1856.

Merivale, Herman. *Lectures on Colonization and Colonies.* London: Longman, Green, Longman, and Roberts, 1861.

Merk, Frederick. *Fur Trade and Empire.* Cambridge, MA: Belknap Press of Harvard University Press, 1968.

Merwick, Donna. *The Shame and the Sorrow: Dutch-Amerindian Encounters in New Netherland.* Philadelphia: University of Pennsylvania Press, 2006.

Meuwese, Mark. *Brothers in Arms, Partners in Trade: Dutch-Indigenous Alliances in the Atlantic World, 1595–1674.* Leiden: Brill, 2011.

Miller, Bruce G. *The Problem of Justice: Tradition and Law in the Coast Salish World.* Lincoln: University of Nebraska Press, 2001.

– ed. *Be of Good Mind: Essays on the Coast Salish.* Vancouver: UBC Press, 2007.

Miller, Bruce G., and Daniel L. Boxberger. "Creating Chiefdoms: The Puget Sound Case." *Ethnohistory* 41 (1994): 267–93.

Miller, J.R. *Compact, Contract, Covenant: Aboriginal Treaty-Making in Canada.* Toronto: University of Toronto Press, 2009.

– *Skyscrapers Hide the Heavens: A History of Indian-White Relations in Canada*, 3rd ed. Toronto: University of Toronto Press, 2000.

– *Skyscrapers Hide the Heavens: A History of Native-Newcomer Relations in Canada*, 4th ed. Toronto: University of Toronto Press, 2018.

Mitchell, Donald H. "Changing Patterns of Resource Use in the Prehistory of Queen Charlotte Strait, British Columbia." *Research in Economic Anthropology*, Supplement 3 (1988): 245–90.

– "Excavations at Two Trench Embankments in the Gulf of Georgia Region." *Syesis* 1, no. 2 (1968): 29–46.

– "Predatory Warfare, Social Status, and the North Pacific Slave Trade." *Ethnology* 23(1984): 39–48.
Morris, Alexander. *The Treaties of Canada with the Indians of Manitoba and the North-West Territories*. Toronto: Belfords, Clarke, 1880.
Morseby, John. *Two Admirals*. London: John Murray, 1909.
Moss, Madonna. *Northwest Coast: Archaeology as Deep History*. Washington, DC: SAA Press, 2011.
Moss, Madonna L., and Jon M. Erlandson. "Forts, Refuge Rocks, and Defensive Sites: The Antiquity of Warfare along the North Pacific Coast of North America." *Arctic Anthropology* 29, no. 2 (1992): 73–90.
Moss, William W. *Oral History Program Manual*. New York: Praeger Publishers, 1974.
Mouat, Jeremy. "Situating Vancouver Island in the British World, 1846–49." *BC Studies* 145 (Spring 2005): 5–30.
Mozley, Herbert Newman, and George Crispe Whiteley. *A Concise Law Dictionary*. London: Butterworths, 1876.
Nesbitt, James K. "Diary of Martha Cheney Ella." *BCHQ* 13, no. 2 (April 1949): 91–112.
New Zealand. *Fac-Similes of the Declaration of Independence and the Treaty of Waitangi*. Wellington: George Didsbury, 1877.
New Zealand. Parliament. House of Representatives. *Appendix to the Journals of the House of Representatives of New Zealand (AJHRNZ)*, 1858. C.—3. "Reports Relative to Land Purchases and the Condition of the Natives in the Middle Island," and C.—4. "Deeds of Purchase of Land in the Middle Island."
– *Appendix to the Journals of the House of Representatives of New Zealand (AJHRNZ)*, 1888. Volume 3. I.—8. "Middle Island Native Claims."
– *Appendix to the Journals of the House of Representatives of New Zealand (AJHRNZ)*, 1871. Volume 2. F.—7. "Papers Relating to a Purchase of Land from the Natives in the Middle Island of New Zealand."
– *Appendix to the Journals of the House of Representatives of New Zealand (AJHRNZ)* 1921. G.—No.5, "Native-Land Claims Commission."
Nute, Grace Lee. "Radisson and Groseilliers' Contribution to Geography." *Minnesota History* 16 (1935): 414–26.
O'Callaghan, E.B. *History of New Netherland; or, New York under the Dutch*. New York: D. Appleton, 1846.
O'Malley, Vincent. "Treaty Making in Early Colonial New Zealand." *New Zealand Journal of History* 33, no. 2 (1999): 137–54.
Orchard, Trevor J. "Otters and Urchins: Continuity and Change in Haida Economy during the Late Holocene and Maritime Fur Trade Periods." PhD Diss., University of Toronto, 2007.
Orchard, Trevor J., and Paul Szpak. "Zooarchaeological and Isotopic Insights into Locally Variable Subsistence Patterns: A Case Study from

Late Holocene Southern Haida Gwaii, British Columbia." *BC Studies* 187 (Autumn 2015): 87–127.
Ormsby, Margaret A. *British Columbia: A History*. Vancouver: Macmillan, 1958.
Palmer, H. Spencer. *Report of a Journey of a Survey from Victoria to Fort Alexander via North Bentinck Arm*. New Westminster: Royal Engineer Press, 1863.
Parker, Samuel. *Journal of an Exploring Tour beyond the Rocky Mountains*. Ithaca: The Author, 1838.
Partoll, Albert J., ed. "The Blackfoot Indian Peace Council." *Frontier and Midland: A Magazine of the West* 17 (Spring 1937): 199–207.
Pethick, Derek. *The Nootka Connection: Europe and the Northwest Coast 1790–1795*. Vancouver: Douglas & McIntyre, 1980.
Pike, Sarah. "The Colony of British Columbia's Unsurveyed Land System." In *To Share, Not Surrender: Indigenous and Settler Visions of Treaty Making in the Colonies of Vancouver Island and British Columbia*, ed. Peter Cook, et al., 247–87. Vancouver: UBC Press, 2021.
Point, Nicholas. *Wilderness Kingdom: Indian Life in the Rocky Mountains, 1840–1847*. New York: Holt, Rinehart and Winston, 1967.
Quimby, George I. "Culture Contact on the Northwest Coast, 1785–1795." *American Anthropologist* 50 (1948): 247–55.
Rae, John. *Narrative of an Expedition to the Shores of the Arctic Sea in 1846 and 1847*. London: T. & W. Boone, 1850.
– "On the Esquimaux." *Transactions of the Ethnological Society of London* 4 (1865): 138–53.
Raeside, James D. "The Journals and Letter Books of R.C. Wyllie: A Minor Historical Mystery." *Hawaiian Journal of History* 18 (1984): 87–95.
Ray, Arthur J., Jim Miller, and Frank J. Tough. *Bounty and Benevolence: A History of Saskatchewan Treaties*. Montreal and Kingston: McGill-Queen's University Press, 2000.
Reddick, SuAnn M., and Cary C. Collins. "Medicine Creek to Fox Island: Cadastral Scams and Contested Domains." *Oregon Historical Quarterly* 106, no. 3 (October 2005): 374–97.
– "Medicine Creek Remediated: Isaac Stevens and the Puyallup, Nisqually, and Muckleshoot Land Settlement at Fox Island, August 4, 1856." *Pacific Northwest Quarterly* 104, no. 2 (Spring 2013): 80–98.
Reid, Alexander. *Dictionary of the English Language*. Edinburgh: Oliver and Boyd, 1844.
Reid, John Phillip. *Patterns of Vengeance: Crosscultural Homicide in the North American Fur Trade*. Pasadena: Ninth Judicial Circuit Historical Society, 1999.
Reid, Robie L. "Early Days at Old Fort Langley: Economic Beginnings in British Columbia." *BCHQ* 1, no. 2 (April 1937): 71–86.
– "Fort Langley Correspondence: 1831–1858." *BCHQ* 1, no. 3 (July 1937): 187–94.

Rich, E.E. *History of the Hudson's Bay Company*. 2 vols. London: Hudson's Bay Record Society, 1959.
- ed. *Journal of Occurrences in the Athabasca Department by George Simpson, 1820 and 1821, and Report*. London: Hudson's Bay Record Society/Champlain Society, 1938.
- ed. *Letters of John McLoughlin from Fort Vancouver, First Series, 1825–38*. London: Hudson's Bay Record Society, 1941.
- ed. *Letters of John McLoughlin from Fort Vancouver to the Governor and Committee, Second Series, 1839–44*. London: Hudson's Bay Record Society, 1943.
- ed. *Letters of John McLoughlin from Fort Vancouver to the Governor and Committee, Third Series, 1844–46*. London: Hudson's Bay Record Society, 1944.
- ed. *London Correspondence Inward from Eden Colvile: 1849–1852*. London: Hudson's Bay Record Society, 1956.
- ed. *Minutes of the Hudson's Bay Company: 1671–1674*. London: Hudson's Bay Record Society, 1942.
- ed. *Minutes of the Hudson's Bay Company, 1679–1684, Second Part, 1682–84*. London: Hudson's Bay Record Society, 1946.
- ed. *Simpson's 1828 Journey to the Columbia*. London: Hudson's Bay Record Society, 1947.

Rich, E.E., and A.M. Johnson, eds. *Copy-book of Letters Outward &c: 1680–1689*. London: Champlain Society for the Hudson's Bay Record Society, 1948.

Richards, Kent. "The Stevens Treaties of 1854-1855." *Oregon Historical Quarterly* 106, no. 3 (October 2005): 342–50.

Richling, Barnett. *The W̱SÁNEĆ and Their Neighbours: Diamond Jenness on the Coast Salish of Vancouver Island, 1935*. n.p.: Rock's Mills Press, 2016.

Richter, Daniel K. "To 'Clear the King's and Indian Title': Seventeenth-Century Origins of North American Land Cession Treaties." In *Empire by Treaty: Negotiating European Expansion, 1600–1900*, ed. Saliha Belmessous, 45–77. Oxford: Oxford University Press, 2014.
- *Trade, Land, Power: The Struggle for Eastern North America*. Philadelphia: University of Pennsylvania Press, 2013.

Ricker, William E. "Cycle Dominance among the Fraser Sockeye." *Ecology* 31, no. 2 (1950): 6–26.
- "Cycles of Abundance among Fraser River Sockeye Salmon (Oncorhynchus nerka)." *Canadian Journal of Fisheries and Aquatic Sciences* 54, no. 4 (1997): 950–68.

Roberts, Albert E. *Geology and Coal Resources of the Toledo-Castle Rock District Cowlitz and Lewis Counties, Washington*. Geological Survey Bulletin 1062. Washington: Government Printing Office, 1958.

Robertson, Lindsay G. *Conquest by Law: How the Discovery of America Dispossessed Indigenous Peoples of Their Lands*. Oxford: Oxford University Press, 2005.

Robson, Ebenezer. *How Methodism Came to British Columbia.* Toronto: Methodist Young People's Forward Movement for Missions, 1904.

Rogers, Richard A. "Glacial Geography and Native North American Languages." *Quaternary Research* 23 (1985): 130–7.

– "Wisconsin Glaciation and the Dispersal of Native Ethnic Groups in North America." In *Woman, Poet, Scientist: Essays in New World Anthropology Honoring Dr. Emma Lou Davis,* ed. Thomas C. Blackburn, 105–13. Los Altos, CA: Ballena Press, 1985.

Ross, John O. "Busby and the Declaration of Independence." *New Zealand Journal of History* 14 (1980): 83–9.

Rutherford, James. *Sir George Grey, K.C.B., 1812–1898: A Study in Colonial Government.* London: Cassell, 1961.

Ruyle, Eugene E. "Slavery, Surplus, and Stratification on the Northwest Coast: The Ethnoenergetics of Incipient Stratification System." *Current Anthropology* 14, no. 5 (December 1973): 603–31.

Sage, Walter Noble. *Sir James Douglas and British Columbia.* Toronto: University of Toronto Press, 1930.

Salisbury, Neal. *Manitou and Providence.* New York: Oxford University Press, 1982.

Samson, Jane. "British Authority or 'Mere Theory'?: Colonial Law and Native People on Vancouver Island." *Western Legal History* 11, no. 1 (1998): 39–63.

Saw, Reginald. "Sir John H. Pelly, Bart., Governor, Hudson's Bay Company, 1822–1852." *BCHQ* 13, no. 1 (January 1949): 23–32.

Schaepe, David M. "Pre-Colonial Stó:lō-Coast Salish Community Organization: An Archaeological Study." PhD Thesis, University of British Columbia, Vancouver, 2009.

Scholefield, E.O.S. *Minutes of the House of Assembly of Vancouver Island, August 12th, 1856, to September 25th, 1858.* Victoria: William H. Cullin, 1918.

Scouler, John. "Journal of a Voyage to N.W. America, Part II." *Quarterly of the Oregon Historical Society* 6 (1905): 159–205.

– "Observations on the Indigenous Tribes of the N.W. Coast of America." *Journal of the Royal Geographic Society* 11 (1841): 216–50.

Seed, Patricia. *American Pentimento: The Invention of Indians and the Pursuit of Riches.* Minneapolis: University of Minnesota Press, 2001.

– *Ceremonies of Possession in Europe's Conquest of the New World.* Cambridge: Cambridge University Press, 1995.

Sellers, Marki. "Negotiations for Control and Unlikely Partnerships: Fort Rupert, 1849–1851." *British Columbia Historical News* 36, no.1 (Winter 2002–3): 14–23.

Selwyn, George Augustus. *Journal of the Bishop's Visitation Tour.* London: Society for the Propagation of the Gospel, 1849.

Shortland, Edward. *The Southern Districts of New Zealand.* London: Longman, Brown, Green & Longmans, 1851.
Simmons, Deidre. *Keepers of the Record: The History of the Hudson's Bay Company Archives.* Montreal and Kingston: McGill-Queen's University Press, 2007.
Simpson, George. *Narrative of a Journey Round the World, during the Years 1841 and 1842.* 2 vols. London: Henry Colburn, 1847.
Slater, G. Hollis. "Rev. Robert John Staines: Pioneer Priest, Pedagogue, and Political Agitator." *BCHQ* 14, no. 4 (October 1950): 187–240.
Smith, David Chan. "The Hudson's Bay Company, Social Legitimacy, and the Political Economy of Eighteenth-Century Empire." *William and Mary Quarterly* 75, no. 1 (January 2018): 71–108.
Sneed, Paul G. "Of Salmon and Men: An Investigation of Ecological Determinants and Aboriginal Man in the Canadian Plateau." In *Aboriginal Man and Environments on the Plateau of Northwest America*, ed. Arnoud H. Stryd and Rachel A. Smith, 229–42. Calgary: University of Calgary Student's Press, 1971.
Sproat, Gilbert Malcolm. *Scenes and Studies of Savage Life.* London: Smith, Elder, 1868.
Stannard, Barbara, and T.D. Sale. "Joseph William McKay: 1829–1900." *British Columbia Historical News* 19, no. 1 (1985): 6–9.
Storey, Kenton. *Settler Anxiety at the Outpost of Empire: Colonial Relations, Humanitarian Discourses, and the Imperial Press.* Vancouver: UBC Press, 2016.
Story, Joseph. *Commentaries on the Constitution of the United States: With a Preliminary Review of the Constitutional History of the Colonies and States, before the Adoption of the Constitution.* Boston: Hallard, Gray/Brown, Shattuck, 1833.
Suttles, Wayne Prescott. "Affinal Ties, Subsistence, and Prestige among the Coast Salish." *American Anthropologist* 62, no. 2 (April 1960): 296–305.
– "Central Coast Salish." In *Handbook of North American Indians*, vol. 7: *Northwest Coast*, ed. Wayne Suttles, 453–75. Washington, DC: Smithsonian Institution Press, 1990.
– *Coast Salish Essays.* Vancouver: Talonbooks, 1987.
– "Coast Salish Resource Management: Incipient Agriculture?" In *Keeping It Living: Traditions of Plant Use and Cultivation on the Northwest Coast of North America*, ed. Douglas Deur and Nancy J. Turner, 183–91. Vancouver: UBC Press, 2005.
– "Coping with Abundance: Subsistence on the Northwest Coast." In *Man the Hunter*, ed. R.B. Lee and I. DeVore, 56–68. Chicago: Aldine, 1968.
– "The Early Diffusion of the Potato among the Coast Salish." In *Wayne Prescott Suttles, Coast Salish Essays*, 137–51. Vancouver: Talonbooks, 1987.

– "Economic Life of the Coast Salish of Haro and Rosario Straits." PhD. Diss., University of Washington, 1951.
– vol. ed., *Northwest Coast*. Vol. 7: *Handbook of North American Indians*, gen. ed. William Sturtevant. Washington: Smithsonian Institution Press, 1990.
– "The Persistence of Intervillage Ties among the Coast Salish." *Ethnology* 2, no. 4 (1963): 512–25.
– "Private Knowledge, Morality, and Social Classes among the Coast Salish." *American Anthropologist* 60, no. 3 (1958): 497–507.
– "Variations in Habitat and Culture on the Northwest Coast." In *Proceedings of the 34th International Congress of Americanists*, 522–37. Vienna: Verlag Ferdinand Berger, 1962.
Sweetman, Edward. *The Unsigned New Zealand Treaty*. Melbourne: Arrow Printery, 1939.
Szpak, Paul, Trevor J. Orchard, Iain McKechnie, and Darren R. Gröcke. "Historical Ecology of Late Holocene Sea Otters (*Enhydra lutris*) from Northern British Columbia: Isotopic and Zooarchaeological Perspectives." *Journal of Archaeological Science* 30 (2012): 1–19.
Tate, Charles Montgomery. *Our Indian Missions in British Columbia*. Toronto: Methodist Young People's Forward Movement for Missions, [1900?].
Taylor, Herbert C., and Wilson Duff. "A Post-Contact Southward Movement of the Kwakiutl." *Research Studies of the State College of Washington* 24 (1956): 56–66.
Tennant, Paul. *Aboriginal Peoples and Politics: The Indian Land Question in British Columbia, 1849–1989*. Vancouver: UBC Press, 1990.
Thom, Brian. "Coast Salish Senses of Place: Dwelling, Meaning, Power, Property and Territory in the Coast Salish World." PhD Dissertation, Department of Anthropology, McGill University, Montreal, 2005.
Thompson, Laurence C., and M. Dale Kinkade. "Languages." In *Handbook of North American Indians*, vol. 7: *Northwest Coast*, ed. Wayne Suttles, 30–51. Washington, DC: Smithsonian Institution Press, 1990.
Thorpe, Francis Newton, ed. *Federal and State Constitutions, Colonial Charters, and Other Organic Laws*. 7 vols. Washington: Government Printing Office, 1909.
Thwaites, Reuben Gold, ed. *Early Western Travels, 1748–1846*. 29 vols. Cleveland: A.H. Clark, 1904–7.
Tink, Andrew. *William Charles Wentworth: Australia's Greatest Native Son*. Sydney: Allen and Unwin, 2009.
Todd-Bresnick, Lois. "The Prevalence of Slavery on the Northwest Coast of North America during the Pre-Contact Period." In *Western Washington Indian Socio-Economics: Papers in Honor of Angelo Anastasio*, ed. Herbert C.

Taylor, Jr. and Garland F. Grabert, 81–93. Bellingham: Western Washington University, 1984.
Tonk, Rosemarie V. "The First New Zealand Land Commissions, 1840–1845." MA Thesis, University of Canterbury, 1986.
Turkel, Willam J. *The Archive of Place: Unearthing the Pasts of the Chilcotin Plateau*. Vancouver: UBC Press, 2007.
Turner, Nancy J., Douglas Deur, and Dana Lepofsky. "Plant Management Systems of British Columbia's First Peoples." *BC Studies* 179 (Autumn 2013): 107–33.
United States. Congress. Senate Document, 32d Congress, 1st Session, Reports of Committees, Vol. 2, *Report of Committee*, No. 335 (1852).
Vallance, Neil. "The Earliest First Nations Accounts of the Formation of the Vancouver Island (or Douglas) Treaties of 1850–54." In *To Share, Not Surrender: Indigenous and Settler Visions of Treaty Making in the Colonies of Vancouver Island and British Columbia*, ed. Peter Cook, et al., 123–54. Vancouver: UBC Press, 2021.
– "Sharing the Land: The Formation of the Vancouver Island (or 'Douglas') Treaties of 1850–1854 in Historical, Legal and Comparative Context." PhD Diss.: University of Victoria, 2015.
Vallance, Neil, STOLĆEŁ John Elliott, Sr., and Elmer George. "SENĆOŦEN and Lekwungen Texts of the Vancouver Island Treaties." In *To Share, Not Surrender: Indigenous and Settler Visions of Treaty Making in the Colonies of Vancouver Island and British Columbia*, ed. Peter Cook, et al., 155–61. Vancouver: UBC Press, 2021.
van Ittersum, Martine. "Empire by Treaty?: The Role of Written Documents in European Overseas Expansion, 1500–1800." In *The Dutch and English East India Companies: Diplomacy, Trade and Violence in Early Modern Asia*, ed. Adam Clulow and Tristan Mostert, 153–77. Amsterdam: Amsterdam University Press, 2018.
Vancouver, George. *A Voyage of Discovery to the North Pacific Ocean*. 6 vols. London: John Stockdale 1801.
Vancouver Island. House of Assembly. *Minutes of Proceedings of the Select Committee of the House of Assembly*. Victoria: Harries and Company, 1864.
Vansina, Jan. *Oral Tradition as History*. Madison: University of Wisconsin Press, 1985.
Vaughan, Patricia Elizabeth. "Co-operation and Resistance: Indian European Relations on the Mining Frontier in British Columbia, 1835–1858." MA Thesis, University of British Columbia, 1978.
Venkatarama Ayyar, A.V., ed. *James Strange's Journal and Narrative of the Commercial Expedition from Bombay to the Northwest Coast of America*. Madras: Government Press, 1928.

Vickers, Randolph Sydney. "George Robinson: Nanaimo Mine Agent." *Beaver* 315 (2) (Autumn 1984): 44–50.

W. "Epitome of New Zealand Affairs." *Simmonds's Colonial Magazine and Foreign Miscellany* 4 (January–April 1845): 194–217.

Wadewitz, Lissa K. *The Nature of Borders: Salmon, Boundaries, and Bandits on the Salish Sea.* Vancouver: UBC Press, 2012.

Wagner, Henry R. *Spanish Exploration in the Strait of Juan de Fuca.* Santa Ana, CA: Fine Arts Press, 1933.

Waitangi Tribunal. *Muriwhenua Land Report.* Wellington: GP Print, 1997.

Walker, John. *Johnson's Dictionary of the English Language.* London: John Williamson, 1839.

Ward, Alan. "Interpreting the Treaty of Waitangi: The Maori Resurgence and Race Relations in New Zealand." *Contemporary Pacific* 3, no. 1 (Spring 1991): 85–113.

Ward, Frederick James, and P.A. Larkin. *Cyclic Dominance in Adams River Sockeye Salmon.* New Westminster: International Pacific Salmon Fisheries Commission, 1964.

Wardhaugh, Robert, et al. *Origins: Canadian History to Confederation*, 8th ed. Toronto: Nelson, 2017.

Washburn, Wilcomb E., Volume editor. *History of Indian-White Relations*, Volume 4 of *Handbook of North American Indians.* General editor William Sturtevant. Washington, DC:: Smithsonian Institution Press, 1990.

Watson, Bruce McIntyre. *Lives Lived West of the Divide.* Kelowna, BC: Centre for Social, Spatial and Economic Justice, 2010.

Weaver, John C. *The Great Land Rush and the Making of the Modern World, 1650–1900.* Montreal and Kingston: McGill-Queen's University Press, 2003.

Webster, Noah. *An American Dictionary of the English Language.* Philadelphia: J.B. Lippincott, 1857.

Wedderburn, Alexander. *The Wedderburn Book.* 2 vols. n.p.: A.D.O. Wedderburn, 1898.

Wenstob, Stella. "The Profusion of Potatoes in Pre-Colonial British Columbia." *Platforum* 12 (2011): 133–60.

Whitehead, Neil L. "Tribes Make States and States Make Tribes: Warfare and the Creation of Colonial Tribes and States." In *War in the Tribal Zone: Expanding States and Indigenous Warfare*, ed. R. Brian Ferguson and Neil L. Whitehead, 127–50. Sante Fe, NM: School of American Research Press, 1992.

Wilkes, Charles. *Narrative of the U.S. Exploring Expedition during the Years, 1838, 1839, 1840, 1841 & 1842.* 5 vols. Philadelphia, C. Sherman, 1844.

Williams, David. "*The Queen v. Symonds* Reconsidered." *Victoria University of Wellington Law Review* 19, no. 4 (1 November 1989): 385–402.

Williams, Glyndwr, ed. *London Correspondence Inward from Sir George Simpson, 1841–42.* London: Hudson's Bay Record Society, 1973.

Williams, Judith. *Clam Gardens: Aboriginal Mariculture on Canada's West Coast.* Vancouver: New Star Books, 2005.

Williams, Robert A. Jr. *The American Indian in Western Legal Thought: The Discourses of Conquest.* New York: Oxford University Press, 1990.

Wilson, Captain Charles. "Report on the Indian Tribes Inhabiting the Country in the Vicinity of the 49h Parallel of North Latitude." *Transactions of the Ethnological Society of London* 4 (1866): 275–332.

Yesner, David R. "Maritime Hunter-Gatherers: Ecology and Prehistory." *Current Anthropology* 21, no. 5 (1980): 727–50.

Young, Alexander. *Chronicles of the First Planters of the Colony of Massachusetts Bay.* Boston: Charles C. Little and James Brown, 1846.

# Index

à Beckett, William, 117, 121–2, 128, 344n15
Aborigines Protection Society, 46, 246–7, 349n95
*Act to empower the Governor of New South Wales to appoint Commissioners*. *See* New Zealand Land Claims Bill
Aglionby, Henry A., 130–1
agriculture: at HBC posts, 4, 30, 83, 96, 98, 100, 102, 106, 163–4, 166, 201, 295, 371nn22, 24; Indigenous North American, 47, 96–7, 105–6, 129, 157, 161, 173, 215, 220, 256, 260, 262; Indigenous response to settler, 45; and land rights, 28–9, 37, 48, 118–19, 130, 133, 136, 155, 161–3, 168, 175, 219, 243, 246, 248, 290, 292, 307; Māori, 140–1, 179, 291, 362n4; pasturage, 100, 148, 176, 260, 295; settler, 4, 248. *See also* cultivation; enclosed fields; gardening; potatoes
Ahousaht, 77, 299
Akaroa, 124, 178, 180–3, 185–6, 188, 190–1
Albert Head (Point Albert), 165, 168–9, 223, 376n25
alcohol, 65, 190, 244, 286, 302; sale of banned, 198
Alexander VI (Pope), and Papal Bull of 1493, 72
Allied Indian Tribes of British Columbia, 281–2, 284
Amor De Cosmos (William Alexander Smith), 385n75
Anderson, Alexander Caulfield, 94, 98
Angelbeck, William, 69, 71, 81–2
Anglo-American Treaty of Washington (1846). *See* Oregon Treaty (15 June 1846)
Anglo-Russian Convention (1825), 332n5, 336n53
annuities: and Canadian treaties, 255, 283, 390n59; and New Zealand treaties, 182, 187; and Selkirk Treaty, 44, 46, 48; and Vancouver Island treaties, 158, 161, 168, 170, 192, 204, 307
Arnold, Thomas, 136, 138, 140, 156, 351n119
Arteaga y Bazán, Ignacio de, 72
Aspinwall, William Henry, 25, 27
*Atahualpa* (ship), attack on (1805), 70
Attwood, Bain, 6, 124, 134
Auckland (New Zealand), 144, 182

Australia, 6, 7, 117, 121–2, 134, 289–90; Indigenous people of, 6, 133, 311n24, 355n1; and treaties, 8. *See also* New South Wales

Banks Peninsula (New Zealand), 124, 179–83
Banner, Stuart, 176, 310n18, 350n103
Barclay, Archibald, 28, 153, 161, 171, 204, 216, 223, 228, 234, 274–6, 316n50, 369n95
Barkley, Charles, 80–1
Barkley Sound (Port Effingham) (Vancouver Island), 73, 251, 299
Barnett, H.G., 226
Barrell, Joseph, 77
Bartley, Thomas, 146
Batman Treaty (Port Phillip,1835), 7, 120, 345n26
Battle of Kororāreka (1845), 136
Battle of Seven Oaks (1816), 45, 323n100
Bayly, Charles, 39–40, 42, 320n54
Beardmore, Charley, 206–7, 210, 309n3
bears: furs of, 84, 104; history of, 56, 325n44
*Beaver* (HBC steamship), 3, 15, 17, 27, 86–7, 89, 113, 210, 214, 216, 228, 230, 373n66; effect on Indigenous people, 87; spreads measles in 1848, 343n194
Beaver Harbour, 22, 84, 164, 175, 213–14, 297, 299, 316n50
Bella Bella (Heilstuk), 69, 233
Bella Coola (Nuxalk), 3, 80, 98, 222, 376n19
Belle Vue (San Juan) Island, 44, 55; sheep farm at, 104, **fig. 20**
Benson, Alfred Robson, 197
Blackstone, William, commentaries by, 116

Blackwood, Arthur Johnstone, 253–4
blankets: cedar-bark, 57, 84; as currency, 57, 107; as gift item, 62, 74; importance of, 57 328n3; of mountain goat and dog wool, 57; as payment in treaties, 4, 208, 235, 256, 266, 273, 275, 282–3, 301, 306, 308, 373n71; as trade item, 92, 106, 325n43; woollen, 64, 84
Blanshard, Richard, 4, 171, 193, 199, 210–11, 221–2, 238, 274; appointed Governor of Vancouver Island, 152, 164, 355n54; arrival at Victoria, 19, 164, 198, 360n47; complains of the voucher for the Vancouver Island treaties, 199, 218; departs Vancouver Island, 218, 375n5; duties as governor of Vancouver Island, 153, 198; and the Nahwitti affair, 211; opinion of HBC's treatment of Indigenous Peoples, 198; resignation as Governor, 199, 218; and the Vancouver Island treaties, 197–8, 359n40; visit to Fort Rupert, 19, 198, 208
Blenkinsop, George, 3–4, 203, 216, 309n3; and the Garden Treaty, 4, 160, 167, 201, 204–10, 214, 218, 371n22, 373n66
Board of Management (Columbia District). *See under* Columbia District
Bolduc, Jean-Baptiste-Zacharie, 100–1
*Boston* (ship), attack on (1803), 70
Bottineau (Battineau, Bottenau), Bazil, 167, 360n52
Boundary Bay, 54, 59
Bourke, Richard, 120, 123
bow and arrow technology, 59–60
Boxberger, Daniel, 49

Brentwood Bay, 226, 302, 376n31
Bridgar, John, 40–1
Brisbane, Thomas, 347n40
British Columbia (colony): established (1858), 245; joins Canada (1871), 270–2, 275; merged with colony of Vancouver Island (1866), 260; terms of union with Canada, 260, 271
British Columbia (province), 270–2, 275, 280–1
British Parliament, 130, 132, 134–7, 139, 244, 254. *See also* select committees
*British Parliamentary Papers*, 118, 122–3, 178, 187, 255
British Resident (diplomat), New Zealand, 115, 123–5
British Treasury, 254
Brodhead, John Romeyn, 34–5
Brooks Peninsula, 51, **fig. 2**
Broughton Archipelago, 54, 213, **fig. 2**
Brown, Peter, 230–4, 240, 379n72
buffalo, hide of, 61
Buller, Charles, 134–8, 350n107
burial grounds, 155, 256, 262
Busby, James, 115–17, 122–4, 291, 344n5, 347n42
Button, Thomas, 33, 39

Caarshucornook, 77
*Cadboro* (ship), 287, 302; seized by American officials, 359n39
Cadboro Bay, 101–2, 111, 302, 305, 338n101, 339n103, 342n185
California gold rush, 107, 165, 199, 203, 210, 369n99
Callicum (Nootka chief), 74
Calliou, Brian, 269
camas (*Camassia quamash*), 54–5, 58–9, 98, 103, 107, 173, 302; destruction of, 275; near Fort Victoria, 326n60; trade in, 63, 326n61; whether cultivated, 361n68
Camósun (Camosack), 100. *See also* Fort Victoria
Canada (colony), 150, 387n26
Canada (Dominion of), 260, 271, 280–1, 283; Department of Indian Affairs, 280–1; treaties with Indigenous people, 165
Cape Flattery Indians. *See* Makah
Cape Mudge, 68, 70, 94, 234, 336n60, **fig. 2**
Cape Scott, 20, 22, 299
Carleton, Dudley, 33
Carlson, Keith, 68–9
Carnarvon, 4th Earl of (Henry Herbert), 248
Carrall, Robert William Weir, 260
Cavanagh, Edward, 90
Cedar Hill, 225
Chapman, Henry Samuel, 146–7, 354n38
charcoal, 15, 18–19
Charles I (King), 32, 34, 39
Charles II (King), 32, 39
Charles Fort, 42
Chastacktoos, 77
Chees Snawnuck, 277
Chekonein, 297–8. *See also* Songhees
Chemainus (Cowichan division), 233, 257–8, 298
Chemainus district, 251
Chemakum, 94
Cheslakees, 17, 20, 54, 70
Chesnay, Charles Aubert de la, 39
Che-wech-i-kan (Coal Tyee) (Nanaimo man), 227
Chewhaytsun, 169, 297–8. *See also* Klallam
Chilcowitch, 297–8, 360n54. *See also* Songhees

children: labourers, 106–7, 145, 298–9, 306, 329n20, 333n11; and warfare,101, 111, 381n13
Christianity, 32, 127, 133, 148, 235, 246, 356n1
Christmas Hill, 230
civilization and civility, 32, 143, 148, 151, 172, 180, 206, 244, 246–8, 272, 274; degree of, 134; and Indigenous rights, 118–21, 132–4, 136, 140–1, 162–3, 246, 350n103; perceived benefits of, 46, 96–7, 356n1
Claiborne, William, 38
Clark, J.W., 280
Clayoquot Sound (Port Cox), 70, 73
Clive, Robert, 349n90
Clover Point, 109, 277
Cluxewe [Klickseewy], 16, 17, 54, 313n9, **fig. 2**
coal: at Cowlitz River, 314n18; at Nanaimo, 216, 227; on northern Vancouver Island, 17–18, 25–6, 27, 157–8; Pacific Mail Steamship Company contract to buy, 27; quality of Vancouver Island coal, 25; strategic value of, 20
coal miners, 205; desert Fort Rupert, 210; Indigenous, 20, 22–3, 27, 201–2, 208, 215, 229, 234
Coast Salish peoples, 65, 69, 71, 92, 93, 195, 338n100, 361n58, **fig. 6**; displacement of, 61
Colnett, James, 72
Colonial Office (London), 4, 11, 24, 115, 126, 131–40, 144, 150–4, 158, 161–2, 178, 191, 195, 199–200, 253–4, 275, 356n1, 375n10; and Richard Blanshard, 198; and the cost of treaties, 255; and HBC jurisdiction over Vancouver Island, 148, 149, 150, 152; humanitarians in, 125; and Indigenous title, 292; and New Zealand, 131; not informed of treaties, 13, 379n84; perspectives on Indigenous title on Vancouver Island, 200; role in treaty making on Vancouver Island, 5, 114; and the Treaty of Waitangi, 129; and the Vancouver Island treaties, 171, 197, 199, 221, 250, 254–5, 274, 293, 310n12. *See also names of individuals in the Colonial Office*
Colonial Secretary (London), 11–12, 56, 94, 122–3, 127, 132, 136, 138–9, 144, 181, 198–9, 220–1, 232, 242, 245, 248–9, 251–2, 271, 275, 351n2, 355n1. *See also names of individual Colonial Secretaries*
Coltman, William B., 45–7, 156
Columbia District, 15, 17, 48, 90–1, 100, 148, 164, 244, 245, **fig. 9**; Board of Management of, 4, 25, 27, 70, 85–6, 158–60, 205
Columbia River, 15, 24, 66, 84, 91, 101, 148
Colvile, Andrew, 160, 355n49, **fig. 17**; background of, 157; informs Colonial Secretary of treaties, 379n84; proposes treaty making on Vancouver Island, 11–12, 157, 357n17
Colvile, Eden, 112, 157–61, 207, 357n18
Comekela (Nooka chief), 74
Comiak (Scomiak, Comey-uks, Kumayaks, Skomiax, Skomiak, Scomiax Somiax, James Squameyuqs) (Songhees chief), 277, 388nn35–6
commentaries (legal), 116–17, 272, 345n24
Comox, 94, 222, 226, 261, 298, 336n60, 376n20

Compagnie de la Baie d'Hudson, 39, 41, 320n68
*Constance* (RN frigate), 26–7
contextualist history. *See* historical methods and approaches
Cook, James, 56, 61, 67, 71–2
Cooper, James, 218, 375n5
Cordova Bay, 50, 223, 302–3, 305
*Cormorant* (RN steamship), 19, 21, 23–4
Cornwallis, William, 72–3, 76
Coté, François Xavier, 44
Courtenay, George W.C., 26–8, 110–11, 165; military parade of, 111, 165, **fig. 12**
courts, testimony of Indians in, 221
Couture, Guillaume, 38, 319n46
Cowichan, 108, 222, 239, 304, 306, 338n100; agreement of 1862, 256; divisions of, 298; Fraser River fisheries, 54–5, 335n45; populous, 58; potato crops destroyed, 256; promised a treaty, 255; reasons for lack of treaty, 258, 275; request a treaty, 169, 240–1, 256–7, 273, 278; retribution against, 230–1; trade at Fort Langley, 92–5; trade at Fort Victoria, 105; trade with HBC, 112; use of the name, 337n68, 338n100; warfare, 92, 94, 101, 111, 230, 233
Cowichan district, 251
Cowichan Head, 225, 282
Cowichan Valley, 14, 112, 223, 230–1, 240, 257
Cowlitz River coal, 15, 18
Cree, 9, 29, 30, 38–40, 42, 44–6, 321n70
Crown Lands, 171, 231, 243, 249, 258, 274
Cruikshank, Julie, 269
cucumbers, cultivated by Indigenous people, 381n7

cultivation, 28, 48, 97–8, 118–19, 133, 144, 162–3, 235, 361n67; meaning of, 173, 190. *See also* agriculture
Cunard, Samuel, 23–4, 26–7
Cunard Steamship Company, 23

Dallas, A.G., 244
*Daphne* (ship), 220
Dart, Anson, 174, 237
Darvall, John Bayley, 117, 122, 128
Dease, Peter Warren, 43
decapitation: archaeological evidence of, 60; documentary evidence of, 61, 70–1, 92–3, 206, 333n11; threats of, 207. *See also* warfare
deer, 56, 59; trade in, 104, 105
dentalium (hayquois), 105
Detootche (Tatootche) (Nootka chief), 73, 75
diseases, 61, 65, 68–9, 73, 82, 90, 113, 175, 325n37, 329n20, 387n26. *See also* epidemics
Ditchburn-Clark Inquiry, 280–3
Dodd, Charles, 210, 214, 223, 373n66
dogs, 57
Donald, Leland, 62
Douglas, Cecilia, 271
Douglas, James, 12–13, 28, 95–6, 100, 114, 160–1, 165, 171, 173, 191–2, 198, 201, 204, 209, 213, 215–16, 218, 227, 229, 236, 239, 242, 245–6, 248–9, 255–6, 259, 266, 271–80, 282–4, 294, 297, 301–7, 316n53, 333n8, 359n40, 367n85, **fig. 19**; appointed Governor of Vancouver Island, 218; appointed HBC agent on Vancouver Island and instructed to negotiate treaties, 11, 115, 118, 153, 160, 164, 166–7; appointed to the governing council of Vancouver Island, 218,

Douglas, James (*cont.*)
375n5; arrival at Victoria, 165; Chief Factor in charge of HBC on Vancouver Island, 4; and coal, 18, 20, 22, 24, 26, 374n77; and the Colonial Office, 5, 310n10; conflict of interest, 200; and the Cowichan, 112, 231, 240; death of, 14; Indian land policy in British Columbia, 248, 259, 262, 264–5; Indian policy of, 94, 242; and Indigenous agriculture, 96, 105; and Indigenous ideas of property, 250, 272–3; informs J.M. Yale of treaties, 224; instructed to take possession of coalfields, 26, 316n50; interim governor of Colony of Vancouver Island, 152–3; knowledge of Indigenous fisheries, 104; knowledge of Indigenous settlements, 54, 56; learns of HBC's intention to conclude treaties, 159; letter to I.W. Powell (1874), 262, 264; letter to the House of Assembly of Vancouver Island, (1859), 242, 381n20; orders J.W. McKay to take possession of Nanaimo, 227; orders Roderick Finlayson to take possession, 44, 103; and the Oregon Treaty, 148; "Original Indian Population," 175, 226, 297–8; perceptions of Indigenous title, 228; receives letter of 17 December 1849, 166; recommends treaties, 12, 161, 163, 170, 173, 175, 228, 357n30, 358n31; reports on oral terms of Fort Victoria treaties, 166–8, 176, 191–3, 240; resigns interim governorship of Colony of Vancouver Island, 164; retires, 258; and retribution, 88, 230; role in treaty policy development, 11, 310n10, 310n13; and the Saanich treaties, 50, 226; sent to Fort Victoria, 101; and slavery, 86; speech of 12 August 1856, 241, 262; stops making treaties, 8; and treaty policy, 157, 293; and the Vancouver Island Sawmill Company, 222; visits Fort Rupert, 207

*Driver* (Royal Navy steamship), 19, 87, 198

Drucker, Philip, 91, 201

Duff, Wilson, 5, 69, 194, 226, 343n185, 367n85, 376n30, 392n71

Duffin, Robert, 331n50

Duncan, James, 385n75

Duncan, William, 272

Dunn, John, 15–16, 19

Dunne-za (Beaver Indians), 88

Duntze, John Alexander, 20, 21

Ebrington, Viscount (Hugh Fortescue, 2nd Earl Fortescue), 136, 138, 140, 349n90, 352n16

Edmonton House, 30, 204

education and schools, 127, 143, 189, 220, 235, 237, 258, 292

*Eendracht* affair, 35

*Elizabeth* affair (1830), 124, 180

elk (*Cervus canadensis*), 56, 59; hides of, 59, 61, 66, 340n127

Ellice, Edward, Jr., 135, 138, 351n6, 355n49

Ellice, Edward, Sr., 135, 138, 351n6

Elliot, Thomas Frederick, 253, 254

enclosed fields, 168–9, 172–3, 191, 193, 213; meaning of, 361n67

Endicott, John, 34, 35

*England* (barque), 166, 210

epidemics, 10, 61, 68, 71; influenza, 113, 180; measles, 69, 113, 175, 180, 343n194; smallpox, 68–9, 325n37,

Index    437

328n6, 329n20, 387n26. *See also* diseases; vaccination
Esquimalt (Puerto de Córdova), 26–7, 81, 107, 223, 230, 257, 286, 303
eulachon (*Thaleichthys pacificus*), 51, 54, 57, 58, 63; trade in, 63
European goods, 10, 61, 64–5, 67, 69–70, 75, 82, 84, 86, 87, 98–9; tools, 84, 207; weapons, 10, 61–70, 77, 78, 82, 84–5, 87, 92–3, 99, 124, 180, 304, 336n53
exogenous, defined, 311n19
expediency, importance of, 7, 12, 29, 35–6, 48, 256
Eyre, Edward John, 12, 181, 182–92, 351n7, 363n18, 365n44, 366n56

Falwasser, Henry, 145
famine, 57, 88; Irish potato famine, 137
feasts and ceremonies, 53, 62, 74, 101, 107, 165, 202, 256, 287, 304; "potlatch," 256
Fidler, Peter, 44, 47
Finlayson, Duncan, 16–17, 203
Finlayson, Roderick, 43, 101–2, 105, 107–10, 113, 165, 167, 169–70, 197, 222–3, 228, 294, 316n53, 321n80, 359n38
Finnegan, Ruth, 269
*Fisgard* (ship), 20
fish: cod, 105; halibut, 63; herring (*Clupea pallasii*), 54, 58, 63, 105, 107; rockfish (*Sebastes* spp.), 58; trade in, 68, 95, 96, 104–5, 164, 174 *See also* eulachon; fisheries; salmon
Fisher, Robin, 66, 88, 91, 104
fisheries, 17, 23, 51, 54–5, 56, 60, 68, 81, 91–2, 95, 101, 103–4, 107, 174–5, 194, 229, 321n80; meaning of the term, 174, 361n72; to be protected, 161, 169, 174, 190, 192–3, 214, 262, 307
Fitzgerald, James Edward, 24
FitzRoy, Robert, 132, 134, 142, 144–6, 154, 159, 165, 198, 251, 352n10; fired as governor, 137; penny-an-acre certificates, 145, 353n28
Fletcher, John, 45
*Fly* (ship), 183, 188
Folsom, Captain Joseph L., 24–5
Fort Albany, 41
Fort Alexandria, 113
Fort Carlton (Saskatchewan District), 205, 371n24
Fort Charles, 38
Fort Chipewyan, 159
Fort Durham (Taku), 84, 99
fortifications, 60, 70, 84, 90, 93, 111, 155, 208, 364n33, 376n19, **fig. 8**; archaeological evidence for, 61
Fort Langley, 84, 86–98, 101, 104, 107, 111, 159, 163, 170, 201, 204, 222, 224, 229, 239, 247, 286, 295, 335n42, 339n103, 343n194, 376n20, **fig. 1**; farm at, 96
Fort McLoughlin, 15–17, 70, 84, 86–7, 98–9, 112, 163, 201, 313n5, 328n1, **fig. 9**; establishment of, 84, 98; garden at, 98
Fort Nisqually, 21, 79, 84, 86–7, 94, 102, 107, 113, 163, 165–6, 201, 237, 295, 359n39, **fig. 9**
Fort Rupert, 3, 4, 12, 19, 84, 87, 114, 159–61, 167, 175, 177, 198, 201–2, 225, 227–8, 257, 271, 281, 294–7, 309n1, 374n77; coal mining ended at, 228; establishment in 1849, 201; expenses billed to the colony, 369n95; garden at, 371n222; proposal to abandon, 216; Scottish miners at, 27, 203, 205–8, 210, 229,

Fort Rupert (*cont.*)
371n25; villages adjacent to, 201, 212
Fort Rupert official post journals, 3, 87, 202, 206–9, 215, 360n52, 371n30, 373n66
Fort Rupert treaties, 13, 203–15, 219, 225, 227, 309n7, 373n67, 5; of 8 February 1851, 13, 204, 211, 215, 275, **figs. 1, 2, 27**; Garden Treaty at, 3–5, 9, 13, 49, 114, 160, 167, 201, 204, 208, 209–10, 214, 295, 371n22
Fort Simpson/Fort Nass, 17, 84, 88, 91, 99, 113, 222, 333n8, 370n7, **fig. 9**
Fort Stikine (Wrangell), 84, 86–7, 112
Fort St. James, 88, 204
Fort St. John, 88
Fort Vancouver, 15, 18–19, 53, 87, 89–91, 95, 100, 113, 163, 166, 201, 204, 314n18, **fig. 9**
Fort Victoria, **fig. 11**; established in 1843, 100; farm and livestock at, 102; grist mill at, 102; harbour, 100; as a market, 108; measles and influenza at, 69, 113; orchard at, 102; sawmill at, 107; welcomed by Songhees, 306
Fort Victoria official post journals, 101–2, 104, 105, 107, 109, 110, 111, 113, 165, 166, 167, 170, 194, 239, 276, 287; destroyed, 368n85
Fort Victoria treaties (April–May 1850), 5–6, 12–13, 157–77, 183, 185, 191–200, 203, 212–15, 218, 220–1, 226–7, 240, 243, 271, 274, 287, 306, **figs. 1, 23**; Che-ko-nein treaty, 277, 388n35; Chewhaytsum Treaty, 169; Chilcowitch treaty, 360n54; Clallum treaties, 168, 170; committed to paper, 12; handwriting on, 367n85; hunting rights, 163, 169, 192–3, 213, 243; intended to ensure peace and friendship, 172, 273; last concluded on 10 May 1850, 170; number of, 194, 221; oral agreements, 12, 170, 193, 215, **fig. 20**; signed on a blank sheet, 169, 196, 367n85; Songhees treaties, 168, 170, 194; Sooke Treaty, 168, 169–70, 220–1; Swengwhung treaty, 277, 388n35; Teechamitsa Treaty, 169, 194, 196, 360n53, **fig. 24**

*Forward* (Royal Navy gunboat), 234
Foster, George F., 385n75
Foster, Hamar, 5
Foveaux Strait, 188
Foxe, Luke, 33
Fraser Canyon gold rush, 242, 245, 304–5
Fraser Lake (New Caledonia District), 204
Fraser River, 51, 54–5, 58–9, 63, 83–4, 91–5, 104, 113, 229, 242, 245–8, 259, 305, 338n100
Freezie (Freezy, Chee-a-clah, Chee-al-thluc, See Alsh Luck, Jeelathuc, Cheyálheq), 277, 388n35, **fig. 25**
Freezie (Louis Fraser), 277
Friendly Cove, 331n50
Frobisher, Martin, 39
Frogner, Raymond, 376n30
fur-bearing animals, 56–7, 104
furs, 10, 80, 83, 104, 106, 203, 232, 279
fur trade, 39, 57, 61, 63 66, 68–9, 74–5, 85, 92, 98, 108–9, 209, 240, 279, 306–7; mutually beneficial, 83, 113; ship based, 66, 67, 70, 80–1, 84, 86, 91, 93, 98, 99, 329n20; and wealth accumulation, 68

Gale, Samuel, 322n85
Galiano, Dionisio Alcalá, 17, 81, 286
Galiano Island, 90

Galois, Robert, 113
gardens and gardening, 91, 97, 102, 188, 205, 209, 214, 342n166; beets, 102; cabbages, 98, 102, 201, carrots, 98, 102, cucumbers, 381n7; turnips, 98, 102. *See also* agriculture; cultivation
Garrett, Alexander C., 255–6
*Gazette* (Victoria), 242
George III (King), 134, 350n105
George (chief from Cape Flattery), 110
Georgia Strait, 55, 97
Gietluck, 302
Gillam, Benjamin (father of Zachariah Gillam), 31
Gillam, Benjamin (son of Zachariah Gillam), 41
Gillam, Zachariah, 8, 30, 31, 37–9, 42, 48, 71, 290, 317n3, 320n54, 321n70
Gilmour, Boyd, 215–16, 228
Gipps, Sir George, 11–12, 130, 132, 139, 146, 183, **fig. 13**; and New Zealand Land Claims Bill, 115–28; speech of 9 July 1840, 11, 115, 118–23, 131, 137, 147, 162, 272, 291, 346n28, 347n40, 359n35
Gisborne, William, 185, 187
Gladstone, William Ewart, 155
Glenelg, 1st Baron (Charles Grant), 123, 125
goats, mountain (*Oreamnos americanus*), 57
Golledge, Richard, 226–7, 236; arrival at Vancouver Island, 379n85
Gordon, George Thomas, 21
Gordon, William Ebrington, 90
Gordon Head (Point McGregor), 168, 169
Gosford Commission, 115
Grant, Cuthbert, 44
Grant, Walter Colquhoun, 55–7, 102, 108, 359n40, 367n73

Gray, Robert, 78, 331n57
Grey, 2nd Baronet (Charles Grey), 131, 352n10
Grey, 2nd Baronet (George), 138, 352n10
Grey, 3rd Earl (Henry George Grey) (earlier Lord Howick), 11–12, 131, 138–9, 143–4, 147–55, 159, 181, 188, 190, 195, 198–200, 211, 218–19, 221, 246, 291, 351n2, 352n10, 354n38, **fig. 15**; letter of 23 December 1846, 139, 150–1, 154–5, 182; letter of 30 November 1847, 150–1, position on the role of governors, 144. *See also* Howick, Lord
Grey, George, 11, 137, 138–9, 142–5, 147, 150–1, 154–6, 158–9, 170, 178–81, 187, 188–90, 246, 251, 352n10, 355n1, **fig. 16**; on amalgamation of Indigenous peoples, 356n1; appointed governor of New Zealand, 154; approach to land purchases, 156; letter of 15 May 1848, 155–6, 181
Gulf Islands, 43, 59, 175, 227

Haida, 69, 80, 88, 96, 98, 222, 233–4; request treaty, 333n8
Haida Gwaii (Queen Charlotte Islands), 80, 96, 333n8
Hall, Thomas, 220
Hamilton, George A., 254
Hanna (Nootka man), 75
Hardy Bay, 7, 16, 212–13
Haro Straits (Arro Strait, Canal de Arro), 168–9, 224, 235
*Harpooner* (ship), 105
Harris, Cole, 239, 264–5, 358n31, 385n89
Hawaii, 96, 105
Hawaii (Sandwich Islands), 19

440  Index

Hawes, Benjamin, 138, 149, 199–200, 349n90
Hayes, James, 30, 39, 317n3, 320n54
Hearne, Samuel, 43; rite of possession, 321n74
Helmcken, John S., 3, 171, 206, 210–11, 223, 260, 271–6, 278, 280, 368n88, 388n32; arrival on Vancouver Island, 309n1
Henige, David, 270, 387n18
herring, 54, 58, 63, 105, 107
historical methods and approaches: contextualist history, 7, 14, 49; juridical history, 5–6, 9, 319n39; oral historiography, 266–70, 284–5, 288; presentism, 5–6
Hobson, William, 123–4, 126–8, 130, 132, 154, 165, 180, 198, 251, 348n69, 363n14; appointed lieutenant-governor of New Zealand, 1840, 127
Hōne Heke, 136
Hope (HBC post), 159, 247–8
Hope George, William, 349n90
Hornby, Phipps, 26
Hosua, 240
Hotutstun, 225, 282, 284, 305
Howick, Lord, 11, 131, 134, 137–9, 349n90, **fig. 15**; becomes Henry Grey, 3rd Earl Grey, 351n2; position on the role of governors, 135; speech of 18 June 1845, 134, 137. *See also* Grey, 3rd Earl (Henry George Grey)
Hudson, Henry, 39; failure to take possession of land, 321n70
Hudson River, 33–4
Hudson's Bay Company: charter (1670), 32, 46; Columbia District Board of Management, 4, 25, 27, 70, 85–6, 158–60, 205; exclusive licence to the trade of the Columbia District, 21, 244; Governor and Committee, 4, 8, 12–13, 18–19, 23, 27–8, 30, 39, 40–2, 44, 48, 70, 85, 88–9, 95, 100, 115, 118, 135, 137, 149, 152, 157, 160–4, 166, 168, 170, 176, 178, 184, 187–8, 190–4, 197, 203–5, 216, 218–19, 222, 228, 234, 240, 246, 275, 293, 320n52, 351n6, 357n17, 358n33; Governor and Committee's letter of 1 December 1848, 28, 149, 157, 161; Governor and Committee's letter of 16 August 1850, 176, 191, 193, 203, 204; Governor and Committee's letter of 17 December 1849, 115, 118, 161, 163–4, 166, 168, 170–2, 186, 213, 219, 274–5, 358n31, 361n70; land claims at Fort Victoria, 375n6; Northern Council, 25, 99, 228; perspectives on Indigenous title, 11, 28–9, 149, 160–2, 345n25; and Plains peoples, 65, 84; proposal to colonize Vancouver Island, 148; treatment of Indigenous people of Vancouver Island, 198
Hudson's Bay Company Archives, 6, 26, 311n23
humanitarians, 7, 125, 150, 157, 239, 293, 346n35
Hume, Joseph, 137
Huyla che (Saanich chief), 225
hypervitaminosis, 325n42

*Indian Act* (Canada), 311n24
Indian Wars (USA), 238, 241–2, 253, 381n13
Indigenous policies, 14, 150, 151, 152, 239, 264; amalgamation and assimilation, 157, 356n1; civilization, 247; left to the HBC on Vancouver Island, 151; role

of appointed colonial governors in, 135–6, 139, 143–4, 150–4, 195, 221, 246, 254–5; role of elected assemblies in, 144, 151. *See also* Christianity; civilization
Indigenous societies: commoners in, 52–3, 57, 68, 84, 86, 88, 107, 202, 295; depopulation of, 61, 65, 69, 81–2, 114, 124, 195, 203, 222, 325n37; gender roles in, 53, 268; ideas of property in, 72, 250, 272; linguistic diversity of, 50–1; militaristic nature of, 60, 112; military security, 10, 83; nobility in, 52–3, 57, 60, 62, 68, 84, 86, 88, 97, 107, 114; population of, 57, 61, 65, 69, 175, 297; relations among, 84; role of prestige in, 53, 60, 62, 66–8, 84, 112, 114, 294, 295; seasonal rounds of, 54–6, 107; social changes in, 81; social tensions in, 10, 59, 62, 65–8, 83, 86, 114, 202; stratified nature of, 324n19; tribalization among, 81. *See also* slavery; villages
Indigenous title, 4–12, 29, 36–8, 79, 115, 147, 152, 237, 250, 252, 254–5, 257, 271–3, 275, 278, 281, 283; English/British Crown's perspective on, 32–7, 73, 76; extinguished by consent of Indigenous people, 147; extinguished only by the Crown, 36–7, 119, 120, 142, 144, 146, 147, 153; extinguished without treaty, 350n103; HBC perspectives on, 28–9, 48–9, 163; as legal concept, 9, 36–8, 119, 163, 272–3, 290–2, 354n38; Massachusetts Bay Company perspective on, 35; methods of extinguishment, 244; obligations on the Crown, 119, 121, 143; principles of, 9, 11, 29, 115, 118–19, 122, 129, 131, 133–6, 139, 141–2, 150, 154, 158, 163, 171, 186–7, 189, 274, 290–4, 323n100; role of Indigenous people in the development of principles of, 13, 34–5, 103, 155, 168–9, 172, 176, 190, 208–9, 223–4, 256–7, 263, 278, 290–4; John Winthrop on, 37
Ingraham, Joseph, 78
interpreters, 15, 102, 109, 172, 182, 197, 240, 282, 301, 304, 307; made to swear an oath, 388n32
Is-hamtun (Saanich chief), 225
Isipaymilt, Charley, 278

James I (King), 32
James, Thomas, 33
Japanese, 64, 308; castaways and wrecks, 64
Jeelathuc. *See* Freezie
Jefferson, Thomas, 79
Jenness, Diamond, 65, 222, 226, 391n67
Jewitt, John, 70
Jim, Edward, 281, 390nn57–8
Jim, Jimmy, 280–1, 390nn57–8
Joe (Cowichan chief), 93
*Johnson v. M'Intosh* (1823), 353n29, 354n38
Johnstone Strait, 18, 70, 86, 87, 329n20
Jones, John, 128

Kaiapoi, 184, 188, 190
kāinga nohoanga (pā) (seasonal villages), 179, 184, 188, 364n33
Kakyaakun (Ka-Ky-ookan), 194, 297. *See also* Klallam (Clallam, Tlallum)
Kamloops, 244
Kanakas (Indigenous Hawaiians), 91, 95, 167, 306

Kane, Paul, 53, 79, 330n38, 341n160
Karetai, 183
Keddie, Grant, 338n100
Kelly, Joseph, 390nn57–8
Kelly, P.R., 281, 282, 284
Kelsey, Henry, 42, 43
Kemp, Henry Tacy, 12, 155, 178, 182, 185–8, 190
Kendrick, John, 77–80, 331n58, 332n62
Kennedy, Arthur Edward, 259
Kennedy, John F., 382n21
Kent, James, 120
Kettle, Charles H., 185
Kiete (chief), 70
Kingcome Inlet, 51, 54
Klallam (Clallam, Tlallum), 61, 89, 101, 104–5, 110, 168, 170, 172, 194–5, 214, 237, 297–8, 338n101; at Fort Victoria, 194; Treaty, **figs. 20, 23**
Klickseewy. *See* Cluxewe
Knight Inlet, 51, 54
Ko-la-thil-too, 283
Komiakun (Cowichan division), 298
Kosampsom, 277, 297–8. *See also* Songhees
kumara (sweet potatoes) (*Ipomeoa batatas*), 179, 362n4
Kuper, Augustus, 230
Kuskaynum, 277, 388n35
Kwakiutl (Kwagiulth, Quakeeolth), 3, 5, 9, 13, 15–17, 21, 49, 54, 87, 98–9, 114, 167, 175, 201, 202–17, 222, 226, 233, 295, 297, 299, 313nn5–9, 329n20, 343n185, 370n17, 373n69; adopt potato cultivation, 216; Komkiutis, 212, 373n69; Kweeha (Queackars), 13, 17, 54, 212–13, 313n9, 373n69; Lakwilala, 212; Walas Kwakiutl, 212, 373n69; word list, 372n51

Kwakiutlan speakers, 51
Kwantlen, 92–7, 101
Kweeha (Queackars), 13, 212–13, 297, 299

Labouchère, Henry, 138, 155, 242
labour (Indigenous): contract, 85, 107; within Indigenous societies, 52, 57, 60, 62, 97; wage, 3, 16, 20, 85–6, 95–6, 106–8, 113, 202–3, 208, 215. *See also under* coal miners; slaves
labrets, use of abandoned, 328n1
*Lady Washington* (ship), 77, 331n57
Lakwilala. *See under* Kwaikiutl
land claims: by papal grants, 31, 36; by prior occupation, 8, 25, 31, 33–5, 39, 42, 143, 289; by right of discovery, 8, 31, 33–5, 39, 41, 117, 132; by right of government charter, grant, or patent, 9, 33, 35, 39, 41–2, 48, 90, 289; by right of treaties with Indigenous people, 31, 39; rites of possession, 8, 13, 26–7, 31, 33, 38–9, 42–3, 45, 71–2, 74, 76, 80, 102, 121, 130, 136, 140, 144, 227–8, 253, 257, 294, 316n50, 316n55, 317n3, 320n52, 321n74
land purchases: on British Columbia mainland, 245; on eastern seaboard of North America, 31–4, 36; at Hudson Bay, 30; at low cost, 35, 46, 102, 143, 156, 158–9, 181, 255, 293, 331n50; described as deeds or contracts of sale, 44, 46–7, 79, 144, 160, 163, 169, 178, 184–92, 204, 213, 224, 235–6, 311n24; French responses to, 290; instructions to make, 13, 35, 73, 158, 162, 168, 170, 182, 204; Land Titles Validity Proclamation

(New Zealand) (14 January 1840), 126; Manhattan Island (1625), 34; in New Netherlands, 34; by private individuals, 124–8, 143, 180, 257; by James Strange in 1786, 330n47; on Vancouver Island by John Meares, 73–4, 76, 331n50. *See also* treaties
Langlois, Jean-François, 180
Latasse, David, 266, 268, 280, 282, 284–87, 390nn57–8, 391n59, **fig. 31**; 1934 account of Saanich treaties, 284, 301–8
Laurel Point, 111, 303
*Lectures on Colonization* (1842) (Merivale), 356n1
Le Febvre de La Barre, Joseph-Antoine, 39
legislatures (colonial), 14, 144, 149–51; in New South Wales, 115–18, 121–6; in New Zealand, 147, 154; in Vancouver Island, 241–4, 249-55, 257–8, 262, 271
Lekwiltok (Yewkultas), 92–3, 230, 234, 298, 336n60, 338n100, 343n185
Lempfrit, Honoré-Thimotheée, 240
Ligar, Charles W., 181–2
livestock, 30, 102, 112, 181, 275; cattle, 47, 96, 102, 109, 140, 222, 256, 263, 275, 303, 305, 371n24; horses, 102, 263, 371n24; oxen, 96, 102, 106, 108; pigs, 96; sheep, 72, 102, 230
Lomas, William Henry, 256
Lord, Arthur, 312n24
Lord, John Keast, 212, 340n134
Louis XIV, 39
Lowe, Thomas, 217
Lower Canada, 45, 115
Lutz, John, 5, 104, 111, 386n3, 391n68

Lytton, Edward Bulwer, 242, 244–9, 263; letter of instructions to James Douglas 31 July 1858, 245, 248–9

Macarthur, Hannibal, 121
Macdonell, Miles, 44
Mackenzie, Alexander, 57, 80, 326n46, 376n19
Macoun, John, 326n60
mahinga kai (food gathering places), 179, 190, 364n34
mail (postal) service, 23–5, 113, 166, 358n31, 359n43
Majoa, 17
Makah, 105, 109–11, 237, 342n174
Manson, Donald, 15–16
Mantell, Walter, 187–9, 194, 365n56; reputation of, 365n49
Māori, 10, 117, 119, 123–6, 128–36, 145–7, 154–6, 176, 179, 182–4, 291, 347n47, 353n28, 362n4; and squatters, 352n23
*Maori Gazette*, 133
Māori language (te reo Māori), 124, 129, 179, 182–4
Maple Bay (battle), 336n60
Maquinna (Maquilla, Macquinnah), 56, 73–80, 84, 88, 104, 331n48
mariculture, 54, 174
marine mammals, 57
marriages, 93, 336n56
Marsden, Samuel, 124
Marshall, John, 120, 272, 312n24, 346n35, 353n29, 354n38
Martin, William, 146
Martínez, Estéban José, 72, 76
*Mary Dare* (ship), 205
*Massachusetts* (ship), 316n50, 359n43
Massachusetts Bay Colony, 33–7
Mayne, Richard Charles, 50, 224, 234, 258, 284, 325n37
McBride, Richard, 278

444    Index

McCleverty, William Anson, 154
McColl, William, 259
McDonald, Archibald, 92, 95, 229; general abstract of Indians, 1830, 335n46
McGregor, John, 205, 206, 210
McIntosh, Charles Hunter, 144–6
McKay, Joseph William, 113, 166, 170–2, 197, 223, 226–8, 230, 233, 240, 273–6, 279–80, 283, 294, 304, 307, 377n53, 382n21, 388n33; facility in the Saanich language, 283; reminiscence of 1888, 166
McKenzie, Alexander, 89
McLean, Donald, 244
McLoughlin, John, 15, 18–19, 84, 86, 89, 95, 100, 338n96
McMillan, James, 92, 229, 335n45
McNeill, William Henry, 3, 17, 84, 100, 198, 207, 210, 214, 223, 309n3
Meares, John, 55–6, 67, 72–76, 78, 330n47, 331n50
medicine and emergency relief, 65, 79, 89–90, 107, 113, 258, 302, 329n20. *See also* vaccination
Melbourne, William Lamb, 3rd Viscount, 126
Menzies, Archibald, 80
Merivale, Herman, 195, 199–200, 356n1, 382n21
Metchosin, 257, 297–8
Metlakatla, 272
Meuwese, Mark, 34, 317n7, 318n19
Mexican-American War (1846–1848), 27
Middle Island. *See* South Island (New Zealand)
Milbanke Sound, 15, 70, 98–9
Miller, J.R., 5, 310n10, 310n18
mills, grist and saw, 102, 107, 222–3, 229, 376n25, **fig. 23**
Minuit, Peter, 34, 36, 318n19

missionaries, 47, 86, 90, 100, 124–5, 130, 133, 135, 146, 159, 165, 179, 235, 240, 244, 271–2, 375n10; Ebenezer Robson, 387n26
Moeraki, 185
Moody, Richard Clement, 247, 249
moose (*Alces alces*), 56; hides of, 57
Moose Factory, 39, 41
Morseby, Fairfax, 231
Moss, William Warner, 268
Mud Bay, 302, 303, 305
Muir, Andrew, 205–7, 209–10
Muir, Anne, 205–6
Muir, Archibald, 205
Muir, John, Sr., 205, 210
Muir, Michael, 206, 208
Myall Creek Massacre, 121, 344n15

Nahwitti, 87, 99, 201, 211, 215, 220–1
Nahwitti Incident of 1850–51, 211, 215
Nanaimo (HBC post), 13, **fig. 29**; coal at, 228; established, 87, possession of, 227; post journals of, 377n52, 379n82
Nanaimo official post journals, 233
Nanaimo people (Snuneymuxw), 95, 232, 236, 297, 360n55, 389n42
Nanaimo Treaty (1854), 5, 13, 227–36, 275, 279, 392n71, **figs. 1, 28**; and White and Bob case (1965), 309n6
Nanoose (Nono-oss), 94, 298
Nanto-Bordelaise Company, 180
Natawanute, 36
Nelson (New Zealand), 130
Nepean, Evan, 72
*Nereide* (ship), 18
New Caledonia, 88, 96, 98, 159, 204
Newcastle, 5th Duke of (Henry Pelham-Clinton), 232–3, 248–9, 252, 254, 271; opinion on the HBC, 383n56

New England, 8, 11, 31, 33, 38, 48, 117, 289–90
Newitty. *See* Nahwitti
New Munster (New Zealand), 139, 147, 149, 181, 188, 363n18; Colony of Vancouver Island modelled on, 149
New Netherlands, 9, 31, 33–36, 38, 289, 293, 317n7, 318n19
New Netherlands Company, 318n16
New South Wales, 6, 11, 72, 115–17, 120–3, 126–8, 346n26
New Ulster (New Zealand), 139
New Zealand, 6, 11, 115–19, 122–6, 128, 130–1, 133–9, 141–2, 144–5, 147, 150, 152, 153, 158, 164–5, 170, 176, 178, 182, 194, 198, 219, 241, 251, 272, 291, 312n24, 346n26, **fig. 14**; Declaration of Independence of the United Tribes of New Zealand (1835), 116–17, 123–4, 135, 347n42; William Hobson appointed lieutenant-governor of, 127; treaties in, 311n24; wars, 350n109
New Zealand Association, 117, 128
New Zealand Charter (1846), 139, 354n40
New Zealand Company (and New Zealand Land Company), 10, 126, 130–1, 134–6, 138–9, 146, 148–9, 154–5, 162, 178, 180, 182, 184–6, 188–9, 191–2, 348n67, 349n90, 364n37; granted the Crown's exercise of right to pre-empt Indigenous land (1847), 139, 147, 149, 188
New Zealand Land Claims Bill, 115–21, 123, 127–8
New Zealand Legislative Council, 147

Ngāi Tahu, 124, 127, 178–85, 188–92, 194, 363n18, 366n64; population estimates, 365n56
Ngāti Toa, 124, 130, 154–5, 180, 184, 188, 190, 366n64
Nimpkish River, 17, 22, 51, 70
Nitinat Inlet, 299
Nixon, John, 40, 320n61
*Nonsuch* (ship), 30
Nootka Convention (1790), 72
Nootka Sound, 55, 70, 72–4, 76–8, 80, 299, 332n62
Normanby, 1st Marquis of (Constantine Henry Phipps), 120, 124
*Norman Morison* (ship), 3, 102, 166, 210, 309n1, 368n88
Norry Youk, 77
North Island (New Zealand), 117, 122–6, 128, 130–1, 134, 139, 154, 179, 190
North West Company, 21, 44–5, 47, 83, 84, 90
Northwest Ordinance (1787), 37, 77, 350n105
Norton, Moses, 43
Norway House, 158, 159, 204
Novo-Arkhangelsk. *See* Sitka
Nuu-chah-nulth (Nootka), 61, 67, 69, 72
Nuxalk (Bella Coola), 69, 327n82

occupation, meaning of, 173, 174, 361n69
Ogden, Peter Skene, 20, 28, 158
Olympic Peninsula, 71, 89, 237, 329n20, 330n38
Opetchesaht, 94
oral histories, oral traditions, and reminiscences, 69, 267, 269, 336n60
oral historiography. *See under* historical methods and approaches

oral history: critical analysis of, 268; differentiated from oral tradition, 267
oral tradition, 267, 269–70, 323n5, 387n18; feedback, 270, 284, 287, 386n15, 387n17
Oregon Crisis (1846), 19, 148
Oregon Territory/Columbia District, 24, 148, 174, 237, 241
Oregon Treaty (15 June 1846), 21, 43, 103, 148, 162, 174, 219, 220, 359n33; HBC land rights under, 148, 219; joint occupation a mischaracterization, 359n36
Otago (Otakou), 180, 183–5, 190, 362n6
*Otter* (HBC steamship), 376n25
otters: river otters (*Lontra canadensis*), 104; sea otters (*Enhydra lutris*), 10, 58, 67–8, 72, 76–7, 80, 83–4, 104
Ouamtany, Thomas, 44, 102, 171–2, 233, 274, 276, 361n63

pā (pah) (village or fortification), 184, 188, 364n33
Pacific Mail Steamship Company, 25, 27–8, 201, 205
Pagett, Frank, 285–7, 301; identity of, 391n61
Pākehā (exgenous New Zealander), 125, 130, 146, 180–1
Pakington, John S., 221
Palmer, Joel, 237
Palmer, Spencer, 222
Palmerston, Henry John Temple, 3rd Viscount, 249
Panama, 19, 24–5, 204, 358n31
Papal Bull of 1493 (Alexander VI), 72
Paquachin, 282
Parker, Samuel, 90
Parliament. *See* British Parliament
Patricia Bay, 222, 226, 376n31

Patullo, Duff, 281
Paul, Tommy, 390nn57–58
Paull, Baptiste (Baptiste Thomas), 285–6, 301
Peace River, 57, 80, 88, 281
Pearse, B.W., 228, 255, 258, 260–2
Pedley, Frank, 381n20
Peel, Sir Robert, 134, 137–8, 148, 351n2; resignation of, 137
Peguis, 46
Pekley, Louie, 390nn57–8
Pelly, John H., Governor of the HBC, 12, 90, 148, 150, 160, 199, 218–21, 355n49; and the first proposal to make treaties on Vancouver Island, 157, 357n17
Pemberton, Joseph Despard, 223, 227–8, 235, 243–4, 382n22; arrives on Vancouver Island, 367n73
Penalahats (Cowichan division), 298
Penn, William, 37, 247, 319n40
Pentlatch, 94, 298
Pequot, 36
Pérez Hernández, Juan José, 64, 72
Peter, Alex, 390nn57–8
Phillip, Captain Arthur, 122
Pierre, Simon C., 282, 390n52
Pinnis (Nanaimo chief), 229
Pipi (*Paphies australis*), 190, 366n67
plantations. *See* mahinga kai (food-gathering places)
Plunkett, John, 121
Plymouth colony, 33, 35–6
Point Gonzales, 169
Point Roberts, 54, 59, 335n45
Point Sheringham (Thlowuck), 169
Porirua Treaty (1847), 154, 178, **fig. 14**
Port Discovery, 71
Porter, Oliver, 70
Port McNeill (McNeill Harbour), 7, 16, 17, 20, 21, 164
Port Nelson, 40–2

Port Townsend, 94
postal service. *See* mail (postal) service)
potatoes (*Solanum tuberosum*), 3, 84, 86, 96–99, 102, 105–6, 108, 134, 140, 175, 179, 201, 208, 215–16, 224, 240, 256, 325n43; cultivated by Māori, 179; harvests at Fort Victoria, 339n112; Indigenous cultivation of on Northwest Coast, 97, 106, 216, 220, 337n82, 381n7; trade in, 106
potlatch. *See* feasts and ceremonies
Powell, Israel Wood, 262, 264, 386n93
pre-emption proclamations, 249
*Prince Albert* (ship), 18
*Prince Rupert* (ship), 41
property, Indigenous concepts of, 72
Providence (colony), 38
Puerto de Córdova (Esquimalt Harbour), 81, 286
Puget Sound, 80, 84, 89, 93–4, 237, 339n103
Puget Sound Agricultural Company, 160, 198
Puntlach, 298

Quacos, 17
Quadra, Juan Francisco de la Bodega y, 72, 79
Qualicum, 94, 298
Quamichen (Cowichan division), 298
Quanteno, 331n58
Quatsino Sound, reports of coal at, 316n50, 371n19
Queackars. *See* Kweeha (Queackars)
Quebec, 38–9, 45, 100, 128
Quimper, Manuel, 61, 81, 286

Rae, John, 43
*Recovery* (ship), 230

red meat, significance of, 56–7, 63, 325n42
Red River Colony, 44, 47; established (1812), 44; intended to strengthen HBC claims, 322n83
reef nets, 51, 54, 58
refugia, 323n9
reserves, 14, 152, 156, 169, 181–2, 186–9, 192, 217, 239, 248–9, 258–61, 263–5, 275, 292, 350n103, 385n89; anticipatory reserves, 14, 249, 258; Indian reserves, 172, 243, 244, 249, 260–4, 277, 385n89; in New Zealand, 366n56; Songhees reserve, 173, 242, 278, 285, 381n20, 382n21
resource procurement sites, 60–1, 84, 173
retaliatory violence, 3, 89, 98, 211, 221, 230–1, 234; as HBC policy, 221, 334n29
Rich, E.E., 39, 86, 157
Richard, François, 98
Richards, George Henry, 201
Ridge, Joseph Charles, 385n75
rivalries, 13, 59, 65, 68, 75, 201, 295
Robinson, George, 236, 379n85
Robinson, W.B., 197
Robson, Ebenezer, 272, 387n26
Rocky Point, 110, 170
Rogers, Sir Frederic, 254
Ross, Charles, 99, 101
Royal Commission on Indian Affairs for the Province of British Columbia (the McKenna-McBride Commission), 279–80
Royal Engineers, 245, 247
Royal Navy (Britain) (Admiralty), 19–20, 22, 24, 26–8, 50, 71, 148, 157, 230
Royal Proclamation of 1763, 5, 31, 37, 128–30, 134, 255, 271,

Royal Proclamation of 1763 (*cont.*)
310n10, 322n85, 349n87, 350n105;
compared with the Treaty of
Waitangi, 129; and the Pacific
slope, 349n85
Rupert House, 41
Rupert River, 30, 37–9, 41
Russell, Lord John, 122, 127, 137–9,
143, 154–5, 351n2, 355n1; becomes
Prime Minister, 137
Russian America, 96, 329n20, 332n5
Russian American Company, 18, 84,
314n23
*R. v. Symonds*. *See* Symonds case

Saanich Peninsula, 50, 177, 195, 221,
223–4, 226, 234, 294–5
Saanich peoples (W̱SÁNEĆ), 101,
105, 171, 222–4, 226–7, 274, 280,
297–8, 338n101, 390nn57–8; Fraser
River fisheries, 55; Malahat, 226,
390nn57–8; Pauquachin, 226;
Tsartlip, 226, 266, 280, 285, 301;
Tsawout, 226; Tseycum, 226, 281,
282
Saanichton Bay, 226, 376n31
Saanich treaties (1852), 13, 216,
218, 221–7, 281, 282, 285, 388n34,
389n44, **figs. 1, 23, 30**
*Sacramento* (brig), 166, 359n3
Salishan languages: Halkomelem,
51, 337n68, 338n101, **fig. 6**; origins
of, 51
Salish Sea, 9–10, 43, 51, 58, 68–9,
80–3, 86–7, 90–2, 94, 98–9, 103, 114
salmon, 54, 58, 60, 94, 95, 108, 229,
340n134; economic mainstay, 51,
56; four-year cycle of sockeye,
58, 95, 96, 104, 326n56; in the
Fraser River, 58, 95; pink salmon
(*Oncorhynchus gorbuscha*), 58;
sockeye (*Oncorhynchus nerka*),

51, 58, 59, 95–6, 104–5; uneven
availability of, 58, 63. *See also* fish;
fisheries
Salmon River, 94
Salt Spring Island, 258, 336n60
Samson, John, 280, 390nn57–8
San Francisco, 24, 166, 217, 358n31
Sangster, James, 21, 223
San Juan Island, 54–5, 59, 102, 227–8,
294, 299
Sansum, Arthur, 232
Sarlequiun (Nanaimo), 236
Saseiah (Saw-se-a) (Cowichan chief),
231
Saulteaux, 9, 44–6, 48–9
Saumina (Cowichan division), 298
Scheenuck (Songhees chief), 93
Scott, Duncan Campbell, 280–1, 284,
390n49
sea lions, 58
Sebassa. *See* Ts'ibassa (Sebassa)
Sechelt, 233
Secretary of State for the Provinces
(Canada), 385n88
select committees: on Aborigines
(British settlements) (1835–7),
349n95; on the HBC (1857), 238; on
New Zealand (1844), 11–12, 122,
130–2, 134, 137–9, 147–8, 162. *See
also* British Parliament
Selkirk, Dunbar Douglas, 6th Earl of,
322n81
Selkirk, Thomas Douglas, 5th Earl of,
9, 12, 44–5, 48, 157, 197, 238, 290
Selkirk Treaty (18 July 1817), 9, 12,
30, 44–9, 156, 159–60, 197, 294,
321n81, **fig. 5**
Selwyn, George Augustus, 150
Sergeant, Henry, 41
Sessé y Lacasta, Martín, 77
settlers, 14, 151, 192, 241, 250, 256,
257, 274; arrival of in colonies, 44,

102, 108, 113, 158, 180, 222, 242, 253, 261, 273, 291; relations with Indigenous people, 130, 237, 256, 259, 263, 356n1; welcomed by Indigenous people, 46, 256
Seymour, Frederick, 259
Seymour, George F., 20
shellfish, 51–2, 54–7; butter clams, 54
Sheppard, F.A., 312n24
Sherbrooke, John C., 45, 47
Shillinglaw, John, 24
Shortland, Edward, 179–81, 362n6, 363n14
Shushartie Bay, 22
Siam-a-tuna (Siamaton, Siam-a-sit) (Nanaimo man), 232
*Simon v. The Queen* (1985), 312n24
Simpson, George, 12, 16, 18, 25, 27, 63, 79, 86, 88, 90–1, 98, 99, 101, 104, 107, 157, 158, 160, 167, 204, 223, 238, 255, 329n20, 357n18, **fig. 18**; letters of 30 June 1849, 158–9, 204; and retaliatory violence, 334n29; views on Indigenous title, 12; views on intermarriage, 336n56; views on treaties, 158, 159, 160
Simpson, Thomas, 43
Sitka (Novo-Arkhangelsk), 18–9, 84, 314n23
Skagit, 105, 109–11, 237
Ska-tel-sun (Songhees), **fig. 26**
Skeena River, 84
Skinner, Thomas J., 382n21
Sku who-mish (Squamish), 230
slavery, 52–3, 85, 94, 101, 333n11; abolition, 346n35
slaves, 52–3, 57, 62, 64, 66, 69, 84–5, 88, 96–99, 107, 131, 179, 209, 237, 294, 295, 324n18, 333n11; labour of, 85, 95, 97
Sliammon, 94, 233

smallpox: epidemic of 1780s, 69, 329n20; epidemic of 1853, 329n20. *See also* diseases; epidemics
Smith, David Chan, 90
Smith, Donald A., 322n81
Smith, John, 205, 206
Snâw nuck (Snawnuch), 277, 388n35
Snitlum (chief), 110
Snohomish, 92, 109, 113, 237
Songhees, 54–5, 61, 91–3, 101, 103–11, 165, 168–70, 173, 175, 194, 196, 214, 226, 242–4, 271, 275, 277–8, 285–6, 297–8, 302–6, 321n80, 338n100, 339n103, 360n53, 388n35; economy in 1910, 342n166; on the mainland, 335n45; reserve of, 381n20, 382n22
Sooke, 102, 105, 168, 170, 171–2, 194–5, 214, 220, 257, 274–5
Sooke Inlet (Syusung), 168, 297, 298
Sooke Treaty, 168–70, 220–1, **figs. 20, 23**
Soulequun (Nanaimo division), 298
South Island (Middle Island) (New Zealand), 12, 122, 125, 127–30, 154, 178–83, 185– 90, 200, 362n4; British declaration of sovereignty over, 123, 130, 180; Indigenous population of, 179, 189; land deeds in, 364n37
sovereignty, 6, 35, 37, 73, 90, 118–19, 124, 129–32, 134, 137, 141, 162, 174–5, 180, 213, 219, 361n70, 363n14; Dutch perceptions of, 318n14; Indigenous, 6; Māori, 347n47; principles related to, 115
Sproat, Gilbert Malcolm, 55–6, 256–58, 361n68; pays for land, 257
Squatches (Nanaimo chief), 229
Squeis (Cowichan man), 232
Squoniston (Nanaimo chief), 236
Staines, Robert J., 111, 197, 359n40

Stanley, Lord (Edward Smith-Stanley), 132–4, 137, 139–40, 142, 145, 152, 154, 351n2; letter of 13 August 1844 to FitzRoy, 142, 350nn101–4; resignation of, 137
*St. Catherines Milling and Lumber Co. v. R.*, 272
steamships, impact on Indigenous people, 86
Stephen, James, 122, 151–2, 346n35
Stevens, Isaac I., 175, 237
Stewart, Charles, 281
Stewart, John, 124
Stewart Island (Southern Island) (New Zealand), 125
Story, Joseph, 120
Stout, William C., 27, 201
Strait of Juan de Fuca, 61, 73, 81, 237, 339n103
Strange, James, 330n47
Stuart, Charles Edward, 236, 379n85
Sumlumalcha (Cowichan division), 298
Sungayka. *See* Cadboro Bay
supernatural, 65
Suquamish, 94, 233, 237
Suquash, 16, 17, 202, 208, 215–6, 227, 374n77, **fig. 2**
surveyors, 186, 187, 239; Peter Fidler, 44; Walter C. Grant, 359n40; William McColl, 259; B.W. Pearse, 262; Joseph Despard Pemberton, 223, 243; on Vancouver Island, 367n73
surveys of reserves, 185, 191–2, 213
Suttles, Wayne, 68, 97, 101, 337n82, 339n103
Swainson, William, 145–6
Swengwhung, 277, 297–8, 360n53, 388n35. *See also* Songhees
Sydney (NSW), 11, 115–18, 121–2, 126–7, 130, 134, 180, 272

Symonds, John Jermyn, 146
Symonds case (1847), 11, 146–7, 272, 291, 354n38

Tahsis, 77
Taiaroa, H.K., 190
Takapūneke, 124, 179, 180
Tama-i-hara-nui, 124
Tanasman, 220
Tarassom, 77
Tarassom treaty, 331n58
taro (*Colocasia esculanta*), 179
Tataka (Cowichan division), 298
Tche-hetum (Nanaimo chief), 232
technology, 52, 58–61
Teechamitsa, 297, 298. *See also* Songhees
Teit, James, 281, 390n49
Tennant, Paul, 5, 29, 239
Te Rauparaha, 180, 190
*terra nullius*, doctrine of, 37, 290, 319n39
Te Whaikai Pōkene, 183
*Thetis* (Royal Navy ship), 230
Thierry, Charles Philip Hippolytus, Baron de, 123
Thimthimelitz (Cowichan division), 298
Thom, Adam, 159–60, 176, 204
Thowhiz, 283
Thwaites, Reuben Gold, 338n100
Tiarora, 181
*Times* (London), 139
Tiramōrehu, Matiahha, 365n55
Tla-ma-hus, 283
Tlawesten, Jim, 390nn57–58
Tlingit, 69, 84, 88, 99, 233
tobacco, 181, 232, 238, 304
Tod, John, 218, 375n5, 378n71
Tolmie, William Fraser, 15–16, 113, 165, 223, 313nn1–5, 359n39, 385n75
*Tonquin* (ship), attack on (1811), 70

touching the pen. *See under* treaties (Indigenous-exogenous)
*Tory* (ship), 126
Toungletats (Tsoughilam, Tsoughelum, Tzouhalem), 101, 111, 304, 338n100. *See also* Cowichan
trade networks, among Indigenous groups, 63, 66, 76, 88
trading posts: abandoned in retribution, 88; as neutral grounds, 87–9, 92–3, 112; significance of, 83–4, 204; well-defended, 87
treaties (among Indigenous peoples), 63, 67, 75
treaties (Indigenous-exogenous), 66; collateral benefits of, 46, 49, 156, 189, 293, 295; definitions of, 311n24, 312n24, 313n24; diplomatic, 62–3, 349n95; HBC instructions to negotiate, 40–1; at Hudson's Bay, 30, 39, 42; Indigenous perspectives of, 7, 46–7; involving John Kendrick, 77–79, 331n58, **figs. 1, 10**; lack of written documents, 40; as land purchases, 384n68, 391n71; land transfer agreements with Indigenous peoples, 7, 31, 33, 36–7, 134, 164, 241, 292–4; legal definitions of, 312n24; Manhattan Island (1625), 34; in New England, 31; in New Netherlands, 31, 34, 272; Numbered Treaties (Canada), 271; in Oregon Territory, 174, 238; origins of, 317n6; peace, 75; signed with pictographs, 47; Stevens Treaties (USA), 236–7; as *sui generis*, 312n24; touching the pen, 176, 196, 225, 362n78, 368n86; Treaty No. 8, 281; Treaty No. 11, 280; Upper Canadian, 323n98; in Washington Territory, 237, 253, **fig. 28**; witnesses to, 47, 197, 198, 214, 226, 274, 322n81, 373n66. *See also* Treaty of Akaroa; Treaty of Waitangi; and *names of individual treaties on Vancouver Island*

Treaty of Akaroa (Kemp Deed, Canterbury Purchase) (12 June 1848), 12–13, 176–8, 183–93, 196–7, 255, 311n24, 312n24, 363n13, 366n64, **figs. 14, 22**; English translation of, 184, 364n34; oral promises, 189; as template for Vancouver Island treaties, 12, 176, 178, 191–3, 196–7, 204, 213, 219, 225, 364n37; villages and cultivations protected in, 185, 193
Treaty of Guadalupe Hidalgo (1848), 27
Treaty of Paris (10 February 1763), 128
Treaty of Tordesillas (1494), 72
Treaty of Waitangi (6 February 1840), 5, 117, 123, 128–32, 135–7, 142, 145–48, 152, 163, 180, 310n10, 312n24, 349n84, 363n13; compared with Royal Proclamation of 1763, 128, 130; scholarly literature on, 349n84
Trimble, James, 258, 385n75
Trutch, Joseph W., 259, 271
Tseaut, 282, 390nn57–58
Ts'ibassa (Sebassa), 98–9, 201
Tsilhqot'in (Chilcotin), 333n7
Tsimshian, 69, 91, 98, 233
Tuhawaiki (Bloody Jack), 363n13
Turkel, Bill, 333n7

United States Navy, 19, 315n43
United States of America, 8, 23–5, 27, 37, 78–9, 117, 120, 148, 155, 164–5, 174, 176, 196, 233, 237, 242, 245, 247, 253, 272, 287, 291,

United States of America (*cont.*) 312n24, 317n6, 350n105, 353n29; Indigenous treaties in, 165, 237, 311n24, **fig. 28**; Supreme Court of, 78, 291–2. *See also* Marshall, John
Upper Canada, 117, 134, 155, 197, 271

vaccination, 65, 89; fears of, 329n20; in 1837, 328n6; in 1853, 329n20; in 1862, 387n26
Valdés, Cayetano, 17
Valdes Island, 90
Vallance, Neil, 266, 267, 276–7, 386n10
Valparaiso, 20, 23
*Vancouver* (ship), 18
Vancouver, George, 17, 68, 70, 71, 325n37
Vancouver Island: Indigenous population of, 198, 236; regional environmental conditions, 7, 58, 59, 83, 101, 176
Vancouver Island (colony), 4, 11, 21, 28, 54, 94, 115, 135, 138, 140, 149, 152–3, 164, 175, 199– 200, 213, 218, 220, 230, 241, 249, 252, 257, 271, 316n50, 369n99; becomes a Crown colony (1859), 251; created (1849), 11, 153; governing council of, 218; Legislative Assembly of, 14, 241–2, 244, 249–52, 254–5, 257–8, 262, 271; merged with colony of British Columbia (1866), 260; Select Committee on Crown Lands, 258
Vancouver Island Steam Saw Mill Company, 50, 222–3
Vancouver Island treaties: based on Treaty of Akaroa 12, 176, 178, 191–3, 196–7, 204, 213, 219, 225, 364n37; book containing the treaties, 196, 213, 251; Colonial Office role in, 197; cost to be paid by the Crown, 44; described as deeds, and engagements, 163, 169, 191–2, 204, 213, 224, 235–6, 311n24; difficulties in negotiating, 50, 168, 170, 172, 223, 225, 234–6, 239, 253, 294; Douglas signatures on, 226; fishing rights, 163, 169, 173, 174, 192, 193, 214, 243; how paid for, 199; Indigenous signatory marks on, 176, 214, 225; Kincolith knowledge of, 388n28; later interpretations of, 274; oral accounts of, 173, 267, 268, 386n10; as peace treaties, 273, 307; promise of surveys, 192; role of land in, 168, 170, 172, 192; Adam Thom's draft of, 160; written versions of, 170, 178, 191, 193, 197, 361n76, 369n95. *See also* Fort Rupert treaties; Fort Victoria treaties; Kendrick, John; Saanich treaties
Van Diemen's Land (Tasmania), 122
Vansina, Jan, 267–70
Van Twiller, Wouter, 36, 319n32
Vattel, Emmerich de, 120; commentaries by, 116
Verhulst, Willem, 34
Victoria (Queen), 26, 306
*Victoria Daily Times*, 285–6, 301
villages: adjacent to HBC posts, 90–2, 99, 102, 112; consolidation and relocation of, 60, 81, 90–2, 101–2, 114, 176, 195, 201, 212, 222, 226, 339n108; kāinga nohoanga (pā), 179, 184, 188, 364n33; on the South Island of New Zealand, 185; seasonal, 55, 179; summer, 17, 54, 55, **fig.7**; village sites protected in treaties, 155, 161, 169, 173, 191, 193, 213, 224, 235, 243, 248, 256, 262, 274, 275–6; winter (main), 52, 54–6, 81, 91–2, 95, 213, 226, 229, **figs. 3, 11**

Virginia Company, 32
Vowell, A.W., 173, 264, 278

Waikouaiti (Waikowaiti), 185, 189
Wairau incident (1843), 130, 144, **fig. 14**
Wairau Treaty (1847), 154–5, 366n64, **fig. 14**
Waitangi Tribunal, 313n24
Wakashan languages, history of, 51, 61, 69, 94, 323n9, **fig. 6**
Wakefield, William, 180, 182, 184, 186, 188–9, 192
Wale, 214
Walker, Nehemiah, 42
Walla Walla, 113
Ward, Henry George, 24
warfare, 10, 60, 61, 179, 329n26, 370n17; in antiquity, 60, 84; armour, 61; factors leading to escalation, 60, 65, 69–70, 81, 222; Indian Wars (USA), 241–2, 253, 381nn 12–13; trophies taken in, 60, 71; war implements, 60, 327n73
Washington Territory, 175, 237, 241–2, 253
waste lands: concept of, 136, 139, 141–2, 155–6, 173, 182, 219, 361n67; vested in the Crown, 132
Watson, John, 185
Wawattie, 167, 214, 360n52
weaponry. *See* bows and arrows; European goods
Wedderburn, Andrew. *See* Colvile, Andrew
Wellington (New Zealand), 130, 146, 183
Wentuhysen Inlet (Nanaimo Harbour), 227

Wentworth, William Charles, 116–18, 120, 122–3, 126–8, 146, 155, 180, 183, 291
West India Company (Dutch), 31, 33, 35, 40, 48, 318n16
whalers, in New Zealand, 179–80
whales, 58; trade in products of, 105, 340n138
What-say-mullet, 282, 284, 305, 308, 389n44
wheat, 96, 102
Whe-whulla (Cowichan division), 298
White and Bob case (1965), 309n6, 311n24, 392n71
Whitman, Marcus and Narcissa, 113
Whoakum, Dick, 279
Wickaninnish (Wicananish), 67, 73, 75, 77, 84, 88, 104, 331n48
Wilson, Charles, 333n11
Winthrop, John, 37
Wishart, David Durham, 3, 223, 309n1
women, 53, 89, 93, 95, 97, 99, 101, 106, 195, 206, 214, 222, 268, 303, 306–8, 331n58, 381n13
*Worcester v. Georgia* (1832), 312n24
Work, John, 17–18, 22, 92, 94, 96–7, 158, 206, 223
writing, significance of, 79, 107, 341n160
Wun Wun Shin (Wunwunshim) (Nanaimo chief), 230, 377n53
Wyllie, Robert C., 19

Yale (HBC post), 247
Yale, James Murray, 93, 166, 170, 224
yams (*Dioscorea* sp.), 179
Yates, James, 242, 243–4, 382n21
Yewkultas. *See* Lekwiltok

www.ingramcontent.com/pod-product-compliance
Lightning Source LLC
Chambersburg PA
CBHW071144070526
44584CB00019B/2649